The Labor of the Mind

INTELLECTUAL HISTORY
OF THE MODERN AGE

Series Editors
Angus Burgin
Peter E. Gordon
Joel Isaac
Karuna Mantena
Samuel Moyn
Jennifer Ratner-Rosenhagen
Camille Robcis
Sophia Rosenfeld

The
LABOR
of the
MIND

Intellect and Gender
in Enlightenment Cultures

Anthony J. La Vopa

PENN

UNIVERSITY OF PENNSYLVANIA PRESS

PHILADELPHIA

Published by
University of Pennsylvania Press
Philadelphia, Pennsylvania 19104-4112
www.upenn.edu/pennpress

Printed in the United States of America on acid-free paper
1 3 5 7 9 10 8 6 4 2

A Cataloging-in-Publication record is available from the Library of Congress
ISBN 978-0-8122-4928-6

For Gail

Contents

A Note on Translations   ix

Introduction   1

Chapter 1. The Social Aesthetic of Play in Seventeenth-Century France   19
    Aisance and Labor
    The Intelligence of Women

Chapter 2. Poullain de la Barre: Feminism, Radical and Polite   44
    Conversion
    The Mind Has No Sex
    Cartesianism for Ladies

Chapter 3. Malebranche and the *Bel Esprit*   63
    Montaigne's Sin of Style
    The Cartesian Augustinian
    Original Sin and the Labor of Attention
    The *Bel Esprit*
    The Author Despite Himself

Chapter 4. Love, Gallantry, and Friendship   97
    The Loves and Friendships of Saint-Évremond
    The Dissent of Mme de Lambert

Chapter 5. Shaftesbury's Quest for Fraternity   115
    The Turn to Stoicism
    The French Menace
    Friendship
    Critics, Markets, and Labor
    The Moralists

Chapter 6. The Labors of David Hume   162
   Writing the *Treatise*
   The Essayist
   The Vicissitudes of Taste
   The Philosopher and the Countess

Chapter 7. Genius and the Social: Antoine-Léonard Thomas
and Suzanne Curchod Necker   215
   Friends
   Amphibians
   The Labor of Genius
   Gallantry Corrupted

Chapter 8. Minds Not Meeting: Denis Diderot and Louise d'Épinay   257
   Diderot's Paternal Voice
   Diderot's Clinical Voice
   Mme d'Épinay's Feminism

Conclusion   298

Notes   311

Index   337

Acknowledgments   349

A Note on Translations

Depending on the context, I have either rendered in English or, more often, kept in the original the following terms used in the French aristocratic discourse of politeness:

aisance—The rough English equivalent is "ease" or "effortlessness," but those translations do not evoke the emphasis on performance in the French social aesthetic of play.

complaisance—Only indirectly related to what "complacency" has come to mean in the Anglophone world. The French word connotes the art of "pleasing"—of being *agréable*—in rituals of politeness.

délicat—Literally "delicate," with the implication of weakness or fragility, but sometimes implying the strength of a kind of intellectual acuity.

esprit—Connotes "mind," "spirit," "wit," etc., depending on its usage in the text.

honnête (*honnêteté*)—The best translation is probably "polite," but the French word evokes an entire way of life in Parisian elite circles of the seventeenth and eighteenth centuries. In some contexts its older meaning of "honesty" or "integrity" continued through the early modern era.

mondain (*mondanité*)—Of "The World," the elite milieu of Paris. The word suggests a secular worldliness, a certain indifference to religious strictures, but has a much wider range of meaning.

Introduction

In one of his private *pensées*, written sometime in the middle decades of the eighteenth century, Charles-Louis de Secondat, baron de Montesquieu, laments that the French no longer have a taste for the works of Corneille and Racine, two of the most exalted figures in seventeenth-century neoclassicism. Works that require concentrated mental effort (*esprit*) have come to seem "ridiculous." The "problem," he continues, "is more general":

> Nothing that has a specific object is bearable anymore: men of war can no longer stand war: men of politics can no longer stand politics, and so forth. Only general objects are known, and in practice, that amounts to nothing. It is the company of women that has led us there, because it is in their character not to be attached to anything fixed. [Thus we have become like them.] There is only one sex anymore, and in our minds (*par l'esprit*) we are all women in spirit (*esprit*), and if we were to change faces one night, no one would notice that anything else had changed. Even if women were to move into all the employments that society offers, and men were deprived of all those that society can take away, neither would be disoriented.[1]

The entry sounds virtually all the themes pursued in this book. French high culture is in decline, and this cultural change is due to a social innovation, the modern commerce between the sexes. The change has not simply feminized society; it has resulted in a process of effeminization, the emasculation of the male mind. In the world as it should be, and as it once was, there is in fact nothing neuter about the mind's sex or gender: there are manly minds and feminine minds, different by nature. But in the unnatural culture of polite sociability that the word "company" evokes, the manly mind has disappeared. The connection between mind and sexed body has become irrelevant. A manly mind could endure sustained concentration; female minds—and now all minds—flit about in a void of nothingness. Implicit is that the widening commercialization of print culture has combined with the commerce of the sexes to produce this situation. Since the mind is no longer required to labor, a sexual division of labor no longer has any justification. If women began practicing occupations once exclusive to men, no one would notice.

The cultural gloom Montesquieu voices here is now quite familiar to historians and literary scholars, but we are only beginning to plumb the social and cultural logic of conceiving the mind as manly; to interrogate the textual representations of the manly mind; and to understand the ways in which it was subverted or at least obliquely questioned. While this book focuses on texts written by men, it also investigates the ways in which women in their circles challenged their perceptions. The story of the discursive formation of the manly mind in the age of politeness is a crucial chapter in the history of modern gender relations and modern literature. Beneath an overarching narrative of the tenacity of assumed dichotomies between men and women, sanctioned by Nature and hence not to be questioned, we find a lexicon fraught with ambivalence, ambiguity, and argument.

Hence the questions I have posed. How did educated and cultivated men in early modern France and Britain perceive and value their own and women's cognitive capacities, and how did women in their circles challenge those perceptions, if only by revaluing the kinds of intelligence attributed to them? What was thought to distinguish the manly mind from the feminine mind? What dangers to its manliness did it face? How did awareness of these questions, often tinged with ambivalence and anxiety, inform various kinds of published and unpublished texts, including the philosophical treatise, the dialogue, the polite essay, and the essay in literary criticism?

Our story takes a circular path; we begin with seventeenth-century France, when the Enlightenment is emergent, move on to England and Scotland, and return to France in the High Enlightenment of the third quarter of the eighteenth century. Perhaps the best way to provide an initial map of the terrain is to introduce the cast of characters. Guez de Balzac (1597–1654) was a *savant* and man of letters who tried to inform the marquise de Rambouillet's famous Blue Room in Paris, the prototype of the old-regime salon, with what he called the *urbanité* of the ancient Roman patriciate. Madeleine de Scudéry (1607–1701), one of the progenitors of the modern novel, was the central figure in the Parisian circle of society women who were celebrated and ridiculed as the *précieuses*. In 1673 Poullain de la Barre (1647–1724), a theology student at the Sorbonne who had been captivated by Descartes's new paradigm of the human body, published *On the Equality of the Two Sexes*, which arguably made him the first modern feminist. Bernard Le Bovier de Fontenelle (1657–1757), author of the much-loved *Conversations on the Plurality of Worlds*, was an eminent natural philosopher, a master of the "modern taste" in literature, and the unrivaled polite gentleman (*honnête homme*) of his generation. Through his long years of exile in London Charles de Saint-Évremond (1613–1703) remained the epitome of the French epicurean gallant and casual polite essayist. In this group of seventeenth-century French authors Nicolas Malebranche (1638–1715), Oratorian priest, natural philosopher, and moralist, was the odd-one-out, and that is what makes him so relevant; from his clerical residence in Paris he found in the mixed-gender worldliness and polite taste of his contemporaries confirmation of his Augustinian conviction that man was innately sinful. In the next generation Anne-Thérèse de Marguenat de Cour-celles, marquise de Lambert (1647–1733), a worldly but rigorously moral woman, brought together a wide range of scholars and men of letters in her salon and dared become a thoughtful critic in public of the denigration of women's intelligence.

Across the Channel we focus on the English grandee and essayist Anthony Ashley Cooper, third earl of Shaftesbury (1671–1713), and David Hume (1711–1776), whose call for a "science of man" in 1740 did so much to shape the Scottish Enlightenment. We return, via Hume's initially exhilarating but in the end crest-fallen visit to Paris in the early 1760s, to le monde and the men and women of the French High Enlightenment who had at least one foot in it: Antoine-Léonard Thomas (1732–1785), a French Academician and master of the patriotic eulogy (a very popular genre in his day); Suzanne Curchod Necker (1737–1794), an intimate friend of Thomas, and the presiding figure in the last great salon of old regime France; and the radical philosophe Denis Diderot (1713–1784). We end with Louise d'Épinay (1726–1783), who achieved precarious acceptance in the circle of philosophes as one of their own, and who set down, in strictly confiden-tial letters to her friend the abbé Ferdinando Galiani, her feminist convictions.

Across this broad temporal sweep, from the 1640s to the 1770s, I have tried to keep our eyes close to the ground with a tight focus on particular texts, some of them well known, others off the beaten track, at least for historians. The charac-ters may seem to be an odd assortment, but they have not been chosen arbitrarily. It is not simply that, in their various ways, they all addressed the question of the manly mind; they did so in especially resonant ways, inviting us to learn a great deal about the immovable convictions and the ambivalences surrounding the subject and how these found expression in various literary forms. They take us into the social spaces most relevant for our purposes: Parisian high society, or le monde, literary circles in Paris, the political and intellectual milieus of English gentlemen at the turn to the eighteenth century; and what Hume called the middle station, the educated professionals of Edinburgh and other Scottish cities. They form a kind of virtual conversation across generations, eras, and national cultures. Whether the threads of connection were disagreements, or intellectual affinities and friendships, they guide us through the themes of the book over nearly a century and a half.

My scholarly engagement with gender issues began with work on the German Enlightenment and the ensuing Idealist phase of German philosophy. Somehow over the last dozen years or so, to give an estimate at the low end, I have migrated to the French, English, and Scottish Enlightenments.[2] Of the several national cultures of the Enlightenment, I have focused here on these three, largely because they represent with particular clarity the complex ways in which gender figured in larger questions about what constituted modernity and the moral meaning of its social and cultural changes. I do not attempt a systematic transnational comparison. The transnational dimension of the book lies in tracing the diffusion of the culture of politeness from the salons of splendid town houses in aristocratic Paris to the more modest but eminently decorous drawing rooms and parlors of, to recall Hume's phrase, the middle station. In the early modern era Great Britain and France served each other as foils in the formation of national self-images. One way in which Hume stands out—there are many—is in rejecting British stereotypes of French aristocratic society as a women-dominated world that made men "effeminate." More commonly France was made to epitomize a modernity that would marginalize, if not erase, the manly mind. We hear sporadic echoes of this self-serving stereotyping in recent Anglophone, and particularly American, caricatures of "the French" and, by extension, the "Europeans."

The study builds on, and would not have been possible without, the conceptual and methodological creativity of feminist scholarship over the last several decades. The critical tool has been constructionism, the basic insight that sexual and gender differences that have had the status of the "natural" are in fact constructions with which societies and cultures enforce norms that put unequal distributions of power beyond question. "Nature" is not a foundational reality, anterior to culture. Culture gives meaning to physical differences; to give the differences ontological status is to mistake the effect for the cause. By denaturalizing differences and the norms that govern them we open the putatively unquestionable to fundamental critique, and we make a society and culture self-critical right down to its roots. It would be hard to exaggerate the emancipatory potential of this conceptual shift. The historian contributes to it by thinking historically; she shows that constructions of a universal and unchanging nature were in fact historically contingent.[3]

Constructionism is, then, a method with a powerful potential for critiquing arbitrary power disguised in the seemingly objective language of the natural. At this point it is also something of a mixed blessing. It risks suffering the usual fate of innovative concepts that become shorthand banners and stop doing the work they should do. One thinks of hegemony, or secularization, or identity, or experience, or contingency, or indeed the concept of context itself. In principle the notion of a "construct" should be a point of departure for two historicist inquiries that, as the German sociologist and historian Max Weber argued, should be intertwined as tightly as possible.[4] One is explanatory: what have the relevant contexts contributed to shaping the text? The other is hermeneutic: how does the language of the text work to produce its meaning? When used as a convenient shorthand, "construct" may obviate the need for both inquiries; it seems sufficient simply to evoke the concept, when in fact it should be taken more as posing a question or set of questions than as providing a readymade answer.

To understand construction in a richly contextualized way, I have put the idea of labor at the center of the study. The term "labor" does not simply encompass a set of practices; it is the semantic locus for a cluster of meanings that inform practice and draw normative distinctions within it and between it and other modes of social life. It would be foolhardy to assume that in early modern Europe a society in which women practiced the same occupations as men, and on equal terms, was simply unthinkable. As early as 1673, Poullain de la Barre advocated precisely that. His argument had hardly any purchase over the next century, but in the 1760s and 1770s some French women were entertaining the same change in the division of labor in private discussion, if not in print. But in this study the primary meaning of "labor" is not employment, which *was* unthinkable for genteel women in the upper and middle reaches of society well beyond the eighteenth century. (In Edith Wharton's *The House of Mirth*, published in 1905, the tragic fate of Lily Bart turns on this social fact; her resort to employment puts her in a "false position" in the New York high society in which she had maneuvered so carefully to win acceptance despite her lack of fortune.) What I mean by labor here is simply the labor of the mind as a cognitive practice, the concentrated, sustained, and often physically as well as mentally exhausting intellectual effort that, it has been assumed for millennia, only men can accomplish, as opposed to what the French called the *aisance*, or effortlessness, which was considered natural to the female mind and became emblematic of what I am calling the social aesthetic of play in *le monde*.[5]

This angle of approach promises a deeper historical understanding of what representations of gender difference have meant and how they have worked to constitute social and cultural life. It will provide a resource for feminist theory, but I should reiterate that the book is an historical work of textual exegesis, to use the old-fashioned term; the measure of its usefulness will be whether readers are persuaded, or at least intrigued, by what it has to say about the historical meaning of texts familiar and unfamiliar to them. In the ways in which the exegesis historicizes gender differentiation, however, I hope to offer contemporary argument a more extended and richer genealogy. I have written the book with a growing awareness of the irony of normalization with which present-day feminists are contending. As feminist studies have been firmly institutionalized in academe, feminism's critical edge has been dulled, and it is losing its purposefulness as a political movement.[6] I want to contribute to moving the history of gender, as a practice of fundamental critique, to the center of historiography, where it can more effectively challenge routine disciplinary practices that have adapted to, but are far from fully absorbing, the conceptual and methodological challenges posed by feminist history.

Following Denise Riley, Joan Wallach Scott has questioned whether feminist constructionism can accomplish its purpose if it continues to use the categories "men" and "women," which work to perpetuate gender differentiation by grounding perceived sexual difference in the putative biological ontology of the body, the assumed irreducible reality.[7] I have worked in the spirit, if not the letter, of Scott's agenda by bringing a critical skepticism to the concept of intelligence itself, which has of course been central to the categories of men and women. I try to avoid the trap of accepting as a category of the self-evident, or the undeniably "real," what has to be explained as a discursive category open to critique. Perhaps the most obvious problem is with intelligence in the singular, which posits a unitary entity. Since the mid-nineteenth century, particularly in the United States, the use of quantified intelligence testing has encouraged this view of intelligence, though not without strenuous protests from skeptics.[8] In the early modern era metrics played no role in estimations of intelligence, but it was quite common to distinguish men and women by their degrees of intelligence. We find here a classic case of the tenacious logic of illogic in the construction of difference. It rests on a false and arbitrary analogy between the physical and the mental, and a resulting causal inference, no less false or arbitrary, from the one to the other. Given the visible physical strength of men, their brains—physical organs, but unseen—were assumed to be stronger than women's; they had more force, or energy, or power. And that in turn meant that men had greater strength of mind, particularly in what made a society and polity possible, the exercise of judgment in applying laws of nature and principles of morality and justice. Perhaps paradoxically, the unitary category, even as it might seem to level different kinds of intelligence by lumping them into a homogeneous mass, made it possible to arrange the kinds into a steep hierarchy. Men, but not women, ascended to the pinnacle of the hierarchy, where abstract thought and judgment reigned. One of the challenges we face today is to retain the critical work that abstraction does without undervaluing cognitive capacities that grasp the concrete particularity of our emotional and affective lives and the manifold talents and skills that go into human artifice.[9] The question is, of course, central to making men and women experientially, and not just legally, equal. It is also integral to understanding, and changing, arbitrary inequalities of class and status.

The larger issue is how the mind, understood metaphorically as a space in consciousness, is related to the physical organ we call the brain. In recent decades new imaging technology has produced remarkable discoveries of the division of labor among regions of the brain, of the electrochemical motion of its neurons, and of how the brain receives and acts on hormonal signals. We may eventually have digital simulations of chemical and electrical synapses connecting the roughly eighty-five billion neurons that make each brain unique. But conscious-ness, including the mind, is something else again. To the philosopher Colin McGinn there is no doubt that consciousness depends on the brain, and indeed that the brain is a necessary condition of its existence; but "there seems to be nothing about physical organisms," McGinn writes, "from which [consciousness] could conceivably arise"; indeed, "the operations of matter look like a singularly inadequate foundation for a mental life." McGinn aptly calls his position Tran-scendental Naturalism.[10] The passage from matter to the immaterial—from activ-ity in the brain to activity in the conscious mind (emotions, images, ideas, etc.)—remains incomprehensible to us and may be an insoluble mystery. We speak of the electrochemistry of the brain giving rise to, or generating, or produc-ing the feelings and ideas of the mind. The very profusion of possible verbs to describe the brain/mind relationship betrays our ignorance.

McGinn may be overly pessimistic. At this point agnosticism would seem to be the prudent position; neuroscience opens a vast new universe of scientific exploration, and there is no telling what it will and will not yield in knowledge of the mind. Nonetheless I find it essential to take McGinn's skepticism as our heuristic premise, if we are to be duly critical of leaps to conclusions that reduce the workings of the mind to brain functioning. It was precisely such materialist reductionism that informed much early modern medical thinking about intelli-gence, which distinguished between brain and mind but in effect reduced the latter to the former. The question early modern physicians asked was not whether men and women differed in mental capacities, or what the differences were, but what paradigm of the brain/body relationship best accounted for them.

In the very concept of intelligence (not to mention the measuring of it) we see the naturalization of something that could only be witnessed then, and can only be witnessed now, positionally. We see and hear performances of intelli-gence, without knowing what the thing (if it exists in the singular) is. More pre-cisely, we see what a society and culture endorse some people and not others to perform, and what kinds of performance they forbid them, or at least disapprove. The rules are more or less internalized; there is room in individuals' subjectivity to acquire a critical distance on them. People can, of course, adjust their perform-ances to different contexts, and can move from one to another.

Though my use of "performance" has obvious affinities with Judith Butler's notion of performativity, I am not advocating a way of conceiving a feminist political strategy. Nor am I following Stephen Greenblatt and other practitioners of the New Historicism, whose modus operandi I find incompatible with the kind of explanatory and interpretive historical analysis I attempt here.[11] I am tempted to suffice with the OED definition of performance as "the doing of any action or work" and "the quality of this, esp. as observable under particular conditions." But in the spirit of nineteenth-century positivism, the OED seems to have had in mind laboratory testing. For our purposes "observable" needs to be redirected to the ways in which we observe each other in the social relations of everyday life. In that capacity it implies—and I want to imply—that making one's cognitive capacities audible (as in speech) or visible (as in writing or gestures) is a performance, not always in the sense that it is calculated to please or impress, but always in the sense that it occurs with awareness of the socially and culturally specific expectations of others. It is not quite right to say that my historical subjects misunderstood the workings of intelligence, as though we now thoroughly understand what they didn't. They wrongly assumed that the nature of intelligence could be inferred from the performance of it. Neuroscience notwithstanding, we share this illusion with them. The critical point for our present purposes is that our historical subjects' conceptual leap from performance to the thing itself is historically specific, contingent on the social arrangements and cultural resources of a particular time and place.

Of particular interest here are what I am calling aesthetic and relational intelligence, which were often conceded to women. That women excelled in aesthetic sensibility—in the gifts of "taste"—was a truism from the beginning to the end of our period. This sensibility usually had to bow to the principled rigor of manly moral judgment; but as the aesthetic and the moral were so tightly interwoven in early modern thought, there was no dispelling the lurking implication that women should have a central normative role in defining public as well as private morality. I use the term "relational" purposely to link my work to Jerrold Seigel's history of the idea of the self and, as important, to suggest its relevance to arguments reverberating through feminism for at least the last four decades.[12] In a study published in 1982 the developmental psychologist Carol Gilligan argued that women have a distinctly "female voice" in moral reasoning. Whereas men think morally by conceiving individuated rational agents and removing contextual detail to clear the way for the application of abstract principles, women's moral thinking works through complex connections with others (hence "relational") and takes into account the particularity of contextual detail. The implication is that the two voices should be integrated in a fully human moral reasoning.[13] Though I admire Gilligan's book, I wish she had brought more critical distance to bear on her claim about the difference in voices by considering historical precedents for it that had labile gender implications. We are only beginning to understand how complex were the implications of making relational intelligence a distinctly female capacity. This way of differentiating feminine from manly minds can be traced back at least to seventeenth-century France, well over a century before modern feminism emerged. It operated within the broad semantic range of the word *esprit*, which could mean the immaterial soul, or the mind as a structure of cognitive faculties, or the reasonableness of the cultivated social being, or the alacrity and acuteness of wit, or aesthetic and psychological discernment, or sentiment.

Gilligan's contribution to theory has come to seem naïve as "difference" feminism has undergone several mutations, some far more radical than she had in mind, advocating a feminine alternative to reason rather than a feminine kind of reasoning. The opposition has been no less firm. To some any positing of female difference in reason merely has the effect of validating men's power to define what women are; but at the same time any purported universalism—even a concept of the human being that tries to transcend gender and sexual difference entirely—relies on a male model and justifies male control. Other feminists want to extend, not negate, the logic of a broadly liberal tradition of universal human rights based on a universal human nature. Still others have recently made their peace with abstract universals, with what might be called reluctant pragmatism. They accept the need for the regulative ideas that universalism provides, however exclusionary they may inevitably be in application.[14]

I should make clear that my ethical loyalties lie with making the practice of reason as gender-neutral and sex-neutral as it can be, despite the fact that historical contingencies still impinge on it and may always do so. In 1984 Genevieve Lloyd, in a classic work of modern feminist scholarship, demonstrated that in western philosophy women have symbolically represented what is outside the deep symbolic structures of the concept of reason. Women were relegated to the "nether world" that manly reason transcended. Some feminist literary scholars, taking their cue from various strands of postmodernism and postcolonialism, have abused this insight in applying it to the period of the supposed formation of the modern world, the eighteenth century in western Europe, and have described the ascent of a "logocentric" Enlightenment (with the privileging of Logos, or reason, camouflaging male hegemony). As an Enlightenment historian, I find this view woefully ignorant. When it takes cognizance of the wide variety of texts that constitute the Enlightenment, it simply lumps them together, despite the many objections in them to a rigid privileging of the authority of Reason that turned it into a desiccated, coercive, and dehumanizing power. I agree with Lloyd, who herself took pains to avoid the conclusion that the concept of reason inherently relegates women to a nether world.

—

The distance between the discipline I entered and the one I now practice can seem unbridgeable. When I was a graduate student, in the late 1960s and early 1970s, social history began its heady ascendancy. The middle years of my career witnessed the passages from social to cultural history and to the linguistic turn.

More recently I have taken part in the renewal of intellectual history, and have become increasingly interested in literary hermeneutics. I say this not to advertise my versatility, but to explain why the book cannot be easily categorized within a disciplinary subfield. Looking back, I do not see myself migrating from approach to approach, method to method. The evolution of my work is better described as a gluing together of pieces, and sometimes I have wondered whether the glue has been anything more than a rather vague determination to limit what I take on board to what will advance *historical* understanding. In this book, however, I want to demonstrate that border crossings among the pieces are possible and worth the effort. Like Samuel Moyn, I am interested in the integration of representations with social structures and practices, though there will be less attention here to the role of concepts in constituting societal structures than to the terms of exchange in structured social practices.[15] Within that theoretical agenda, I want to demonstrate that literary hermeneutics—what I am calling a rhetorical approach—are essential to the recovery of social meaning.

The labor/*aisance* dichotomy requires us to bring the social and the cultural into a working partnership. The dichotomy had an internal logic, by which I mean that, however arbitrary its point of departure in the underlying assumptions of gender difference, its apparently indisputable appeals to the work of "nature"—to the ways in which nature connected things causally and made sense of social difference—provided authoritative justification for the assignment of unequal intelligence to men and women. I want to give explanatory and interpretive bite to a truism often acknowledged in theory but more rarely found in practice: that the logic in question fused gender norms with status norms, the hierarchical norms of "honor" in early modern societies. If feminism seeks the emancipation of women, then advocacy of the emancipation of women's minds, however tentative from our standpoint, certainly merits, by itself, the name feminist. But feminist scholarship that has largely ignored the logic of the imperatives of honor is seriously flawed; it has given us presentist oversimplifications of early modern articulations of feminism, which are as striking for their self-imposed constrictions as for their emancipatory impulses. In the social and cultural processes in which perceived differences in male and female minds partook of the authority of "nature," gender norms and status norms reinforced each other. Our modern controversies about intelligence began not in the heads of enlightened philosophers, but in the networks of *le monde*, the Parisian milieus where the precious qualities of politeness (*honnêteté*), gallantry (*galanterie*) and worldliness (*mondanité*) were the currency of social distinction. In their putatively natural being, manifested in the *aisance* of their thought and speech, women were the exemplars of the unique honor claimed by *le monde*. Men had to perform their manliness in leisured conversation with aristocratic women. There was an inherent tension between this performance and the ethos of what I will call the manly mind, a certain sort of ideal intelligence formed by intense, disciplined labor in the Stoic tradition of askesis, in philosophical reasoning, and in the acquisition of learning.

We speak of a process of feminization that extended into the eighteenth century. Polite status required men to emulate their female counterparts in manners and above all in conversational sociability. But not to emulate them too much; the specter of "effeminacy," already a presence in the seventeenth century, stalked Shaftesbury's thought and became something of an obsession, the trope for a drumbeat of anxiety, in the eighteenth century, especially in Britain but also in France. In a persistent stereotype, the "fop" betrayed his effeminacy in his excessive delicacy, his overly demonstrative expression of feeling, and his preoccupation with the latest fashions (especially French). A widespread adaptation of civic humanism made effeminacy emblematic of the softening effect of excessive luxury in a rapidly commercializing civilization of speculation and consumerism.[16] Within a discursive tradition that descried the vitiation of "character," understood as the social representation of the inner autonomy of "virtue," our focus will be on strength of mind as the critical ground of character. Manly integrity was acceding to womanish dissembling, the corrupting art of presenting a false self; manly courage to cowardice; manly rigor and energy to vanity and indolence. Men of excessive sensibility had an "effeminacy of mind," the ever vigilant moralist Vicesimus Knox wrote in 1782, as seen in their flight from "vigorous pursuits and manly exertion."[17]

One of my aims is to contribute to changing an originally troubled relationship between intellectual history and feminist history into one of mutual support. Until quite recently intellectual history was not a pathbreaker in denaturalizing gender categories. Its practitioners either entirely ignored male-centeredness or accepted it on its own terms. But we have begun to recognize that, in the effort to make sense of processes and meanings of gender differentiation, the two fields need each other. My aim, I should stress, is not to add a "gender" dimension to what we already understand about the thought of a particular historical figure, but to follow, as far as it will take me, an angle of approach that gives us a new understanding of the central concerns of her thought.[18] This kind of re-reading can fairly be called "cultural," but without a thoroughgoing practice of intellectual history it cannot be accomplished. We need to understand how gender differentiation at once infused and was infused by a wide range of currents of thought in early modern European intellectual life. The most important of them will be familiar to students of the era: Malebranche's Augustinianism and Cartesianism; Mme de Lambert's classical ideal of virtue and friendship; Shaftesbury's Stoicism and English republicanism; David Hume's mitigated philosophical skepticism, as well as his reliance on the notions of sympathy and sensibility; Mme Necker's blending of sentiment and enlightened Calvinism; Diderot's shift, via a kind of Stoicism, from sensibility to vitalist materialism; Mme d'Épinay's Stoic logic for female emancipation. There was something protean about the Stoic tradition. If Stoicism typically guided men, and only men, though a rigorous askesis, a solitary exercise in rational reflectivity, it could also be a grounding for women's as well as men's moral autonomy. It will be a thread running through the book.

I also want to add to our growing awareness that, however clearly drawn gender differences were in the early modern era, they did not imprint one unvarying template on individual subjectivities. It is important to distinguish between how in "underlying normative structures" gender differences were conceived as binary opposites, and what they could be taken to imply, or how they could be normatively reconfigured, in discursive practice. If the question educated men faced was how to be polite without being stigmatized as effeminate, the corresponding question for women was how to display their intellectual abilities without seeming to be man-like and hence unnatural creatures, the freaks evoked by the term "learned woman" (*femme savante*). There were binaries: strength/weakness; hardness/softness; willed action on a resistant Nature/passivity as Nature's instrument; self-sufficiency/dependence; abstraction/sensate particularity; rational judgment/the fantasies of the imagination; labor/indolence. They operated in tightly clustered metaphors and had deep and tenacious root systems, as evidenced by their remarkable consistency over the period we cover, despite shifts in the medical paradigms that underlay them. Today the notion of "fluidity" in gender differences is becoming a commonplace. But the binaries still fix differences; compliance with the natural requires inward muting and silencing for both sexes. Precisely because the binaries are fixed, they at once overlie anxiety about identity and fuel it. "Manliness," Pierre Bourdieu has observed, "is an eminently *relational* notion, constructed in front of and for other men and against femininity, in a kind of *fear* of the female, firstly in oneself."[19]

And yet we know that in the early modern era, as in any other era, there was a measure of confusion in gender roles, and that is not at all surprising. The cognitive capacities and other attributes assigned exclusively *either* to men or to women are better conceived as currents and cross currents on a spectrum than as neatly divided into two different kinds. If taken in their apparent rigidity, the binaries leave no spaces for a middle zone of variations in construction as a social and cultural process; in the social configurations in which these variations operate; in the suppleness of their meaning in social exchange; and in the rhetorical performances that represent them. These are the spaces I have tried to explore.

The men and women of this book thought and wrote within large-frame structural changes in social relations and cultural practices. To encompass both "the constructed quality of the entire social world" and the importance of "material instantiation" and especially the "material social fabric," William H. Sewell, Jr., has proposed the term "built environment."[20] Our story progresses through episodes in the building of what our historical agents viewed as the modern, in the sense of the new or recent. Placing our texts within these experiences of change is essential to understanding the construction of gender differences as a process of diachronic change, or, to put it more simply, as history; and to learning how the binaries worked, or were subverted, in the lives and thought of my subjects. The main lines of the narrative are familiar, as they summarize extensive research in recent decades on polite sociability and literary culture. We begin with what I see as the paradox of unmodern modernity, a variation on Ernst Bloch's idea of "the synchronicity of the nonsynchronous" (*Gleichzeitigkeit der Ungleichzeitigen*).[21] In the seventeenth century the elite Parisian social circles known as *le monde*, despite their rigidly hierarchical values, brought men and women together in a "polite" and "gallant" sociability that required men, within the boundaries of this social space, to show a new respect for women and indeed to take them as models in the art of conversation, the central site for the performance of the refined mind, and the exemplar for tasteful style in writing.

In the course of the eighteenth century *le monde* remained predominantly aristocratic but included larger numbers of men of letters without aristocratic credentials, including the philosophes. Even Diderot, who prided himself on being an anti-Establishment figure, made occasional appearances at Mme Necker's salon and others. In Great Britain purveyors of polite manners had looked to France, but tapered French aristocratic norms to the lives of the expanding urban middle class in the liberal professions, commerce, and trade that was so artfully constituted as an audience, a modern public, by Joseph Addison and Richard Steele in their wildly popular *The Tatler* and *The Spectator*. Particularly in England and Scotland, as print became a commodity in an expanding consumer culture, women became a larger presence as authors and, as important for our purposes, as readers. Some of the new print materials—popular romances, devotional literature, pedagogical tracts, etc.—were aimed primarily at women; but other genres, including some novels, gave men and women an unprecedented common ground for intellectual exchange. Shaftesbury had detested this development. Several decades later Hume realized that, to win fame as a polite man of letters, an author had to bring educated and cultivated women into his audience.

As a master essayist Hume practiced what has aptly been called Enlightenment gallantry.[22] Among Anglophone authors he was the most acutely attuned to the *galant* style in French belles letters that extended back to the early seventeenth century. The career of this tradition figures large in this book, as it was one of the sites for argument about the meaning and value of modern changes for relations between the sexes. The argument was in part historical. Was modern gallantry—the kind practiced in *le monde* in the eighteenth century, and in the drawing rooms of the Scottish literati—a social expansion of the medieval chivalric code that gave women a new value and esteem; or another patronizing way of not taking the female mind seriously; or a corruption of chivalry, a thin veil for rampant licentiousness? At issue was what the proper relationship between men and women in the upper reaches of French, English, and Scottish societies should be. More precisely for our purposes, in the praise of more or less gallant politeness, and in the rebukes of it from various angles, we find guiding assumptions about how the intelligences of men and women ought to connect despite (or by virtue of) their supposed differences.

In one way or another, modern changes required delicate maneuverings within the gender binaries, and occasionally they opened, however tentatively, lacunae free of them and spaces to slip by them. This is where historical explanation and literary interpretation converge in the book. I will argue that the convergence makes texts revelatory in new ways. In the use of genres, in the choice of authorial style, and in the practice of literary criticism, we see dilemmas in the self-representation of both male and female character. The dilemmas give most of the chapters an ironic arch. Poullain de la Barre's first treatise called for women to assume work roles that would allow them to perform the same intellectual labor as men; in his second, he retreated from that position, bowing to status imperatives that the women he was addressing could not be expected to defy. Malebranche saw the presentation of self in prose style as so sinfully effeminate that he sought to eschew it altogether in his own writing; and as a result he became one of the master prose stylists of the French classical era. Shaftesbury sought to remold literary politeness. Faced with what he saw as effeminacy run rampant in modern commercialized print culture, he undertook creative but tortuously convoluted essays to reconcile the polite and the manly. David Hume performed a delicate balancing act, embracing women as readers, and often identifying with them temperamentally, but finding it necessary to reserve cultural authority in matters of taste—the authoritative judgment of the critic—to rare men. In her exercises in virtual authorship Mme Necker acknowledged "genius" as an exclusively male power but nonetheless claimed a kind of equality for a distinctly feminine literary criticism. Diderot, who saw effeminacy as a creeping social reality, not a specter, faced the task of making the imagination, traditionally considered more errantly volatile in women, a labor integral to a manly mind.

My concern with relational intelligence has led me to devote considerable attention to friendship as an intimate exchange of intelligence between men and between men and women. Again I find Scott's agenda challenging. Gender differentiation is "an attempt to resolve the dilemma of sexual difference, to assign fixed meaning to that which ultimately cannot be fixed," she argues, and hence we should regard identity not as in any way "fixed," but rather as ceaselessly fluid.[23] That opens the way to recovering transgressive fantasies of "wholeness" and "completeness" that keep impelling change precisely because they are indeed fantasies, never to be fully realized. Scott's notion of fantasy draws primarily on Freud and Lacan. Her own work confirms that her proposed way of employing psychoanalytical concepts, unlike earlier moves in that direction, would be thoroughly historical. Though I am neither inclined nor able to take this psychoanalytical route, I find Scott's notion of fantasies of wholeness of great interpretive value. For some men, of course, wholeness might seem to require standing firmly on one side of the gender divide. A striking case in point is Shaftesbury's fantasy of an exclusively masculine ethos in the practice of intellectual raillery among a circle of male friends. Removed from the softening influence of women, the fraternity would be at once genuinely polite and manly. But there is something of fantasy in Scott's sense, and of the felt need for fluidity, in the intellectual intimacies of friendships between men and women, as they were imagined and practiced. As different as are the texts of Saint-Évremond, Lambert, Hume, Thomas, Necker, and d'Épinay, they share a quest for a wholeness that would absorb gender differentiation into a holistic ideal of the human, even as they proceed from the reigning assumption of the reality of difference.

—

Contextual intellectual history is at once experiencing a renewal and undergoing skeptical questioning. To some critics we run the risk of trapping ourselves in a hyperparticularism, and to escape it we need what Darrin McMahon calls a "refashioned history of ideas." The critics are not calling for a return to what has been dismissed as the hopelessly idealist history of ideas with which, fairly or not, Arthur Lovejoy is said to have burdened American scholarship. What they have in mind would not be premised on any sort of idealist metaphysics, and would certainly not be limited to a sacred canon. It would explore continuities and ruptures in ideas over much wider temporal stretches than we find in most current scholarship, and it would assess them in a way that allows us to engage them for present purposes, perhaps even to evaluate their truth claims. At the same time contextualism itself is being reconceived as we ask how the social can be returned to intellectual history without falling back into a crude reductionism, making ideas a function of the interests of structural blocs like classes and professional groups.[24] Can we practice an intellectual history that explores the integration of representations and social practices? Can we recover the social meaning of ideas by seeing how they worked, sometimes with surprising suppleness, in processes of social exchange?

How these two ways of refashioning the field might be combined is an open question. In an effort to intertwine seemingly divergent positions, I read texts as the performances of rhetorical personae.[25] Performance in this sense is a subset of my notion of the "performance" of intelligence, but focused now on writing and print. I do not have in mind rhetoric as a formal academic discipline, based on classical texts and central to the academic education of boys and young men for centuries (though it is highly relevant that rhetoric in that sense was an exclusively male realm of public action). My approach is somewhat akin to Quentin Skinner's idea of the performance of "illocutionary acts." But whereas Skinner was concerned exclusively with historicizing the study of political thought, I want to broaden his idea to encompass the performed qualities of all kinds of intersubjective exchange in language.[26]

My working use of the term "rhetorical" may seem so broad as to be meaningless. For my purposes, however, it has the advantage of having a reach that is at once specific and capacious. In several of my selected texts—Shaftesbury's essays, for example, or Hume's *A Treatise of Human Nature*—the performance self-consciously enacts the art (or arts) of language use, particularly in the practice of a literary genre, the choice of authorial voice, and the presentation of authorial character in style. In some cases the practice of the art was quintessentially public, as oratory was in the ancient polis; the aim was to constitute or renew a civic culture. With other texts, I have extended the notion of rhetorical performance to writing that was not intended to be art, and indeed in some cases was not intended to be read by others. I have in mind, for example, Shaftesbury's solitary exercises in Stoic askesis and Mme Necker's voluminous journals, as well as the private correspondence of figures like Hume and Diderot.

I will hazard the claim that any verbal trace of an individual's subjectivity is a rhetorical representation of it. Even the most intimate revelation in a diary entry is a performance, if only as a dialogic effort to convince oneself. It is always, in Richard Holmes's apt phrase, "evidence that is witnessed," which is to say that the subject produced it with some awareness of the witnessing. And that is a way of saying that the traces are always "transactions of the social realm," ways of "giving social expression to the subjective interior."[27] The retreat to labor in solitude, so often considered essential to a manly mind, was a social act with a social message.

Approaching a text as a rhetorical performance does not require positing a unitary subjectivity, or a wholeness of the writing self. The performance may reflect a yearning for the absent, for an unachievable wholeness; and in any case—as Shaftesbury's and Diderot's texts demonstrate—it can be done in two or more voices in counterpoint. At the same time, this approach avoids what Fritz K. Ringer has called the "identificationist" fallacy, which he sees as a failure to maintain "hermeneutic distance."[28] The fallacy lies in assuming that in an intuitive act of empathy, one can relive the subject's inner states, the "experience" behind the text, and make those states immediate to the reader. There is an illusory premise, a notion of self-emptying, or self-abandonment, that purports to short-circuit the unavoidable fact that we must *translate* from the subject's meaning to our own. We are left with no way of recognizing when, in our effort to intuit the subject's self-understanding, we're really indulging in a presentist reading of ourselves into the historical Other. An effort to plumb alterity all too easily becomes a way of erasing it.

The only verbal access we have to the subjectivity of the historical subject is through rhetorical mediations. That means, of course, that we have to practice self-denial; but if we take an emphatically contextual approach, the mediations themselves abound in meaning. The performance of a rhetorical persona is *situated* in various directions, and as we examine its situatedness we engage in an interactive recovery of meaning, with the text pointing us to contexts that bear on it, and with contexts illuminating the historical meaning of the text. The rhetorical persona, by the very nature of its mediating function, has an intended audience. The social implications are, of course, obvious if the intended audience is an actual group of readers, as in much polite literature written for *le monde*. But authors often imagine audiences as rhetorical communities in the making, as Hume did in celebrating a middle station, or they try to constitute such communities, as Shaftesbury did in his essays, and in these cases too the question of audience has a social dimension. The other contextual strategy is biographical. To say that contextual biography is an inherently reductionist approach to ideas is to ignore the way the genre has been evolving. There are ways of practicing it that avoid one of the crudest forms of reductionism, making ideas instruments of social interests. In constructing a biographical narrative we can see class and status not as reified structural entities to which ideas are attached, but as relational processes in which we can learn more about what ideas meant by seeing what work they did in social exchange. In these ways, and in others, biography is in a state of creative experimentation; it has become one of the main ways of restoring the social to intellectual history.[29]

Though five of the book's chapters focus on single figures, they are obviously not full-scale contextual biographies. I have selected biographical episodes in which the themes of the book become sharply etched: Poullain de la Barre's disillusionment with university scholasticism; Malebranche's relationship to his own tortured body, which played no small role in his conversion to Cartesianism; Mme de Lambert's disgust with what she saw as the shameless decadence of false gallantry under the Regency; the life crises that led Shaftesbury to undertake Stoic exercises; David Hume's turn to polite essay writing in the wake of the failure of his *Treatise* to find a readership; the treacherous terms on which Thomas ascended to literary celebrity; Diderot's anxious efforts to find a husband for his daughter as he conceived his essay "On Women"; Louise d'Épinay's troubles with her prodigal son.

Can we read texts rhetorically, as I have done, and at the same time connect our reading to a refashioned intellectual history encompassing the longue durée? Perhaps the point is simply that the two approaches offer intellectual history a needed contrapuntal division of labor. But I find more possibility of convergence, or at least of the subfields touching on each other fairly habitually. The logic of situatedness takes us into the author's biographical circumstances, her passage through webs of social relations, the immediate field of argument she is addressing. But rhetorical readings also by necessity require a wide-angle lens, if we are not to remain on the textual surface. If we pay close attention to a text's rhetorical properties—its figurative language, its tropes, it use of conventions of genre, its changes of voice, and so on—we reach deeper into its layered meanings. We might call this the vertical route to horizontal extension; we are led out to the longue durée embedded in the text, or at least to the middle durée. The language of seventeenth-century politeness echoes through texts of the High Enlightenment, over a century later, which play with and sometimes bend beyond recognition their received connotations. We cannot understand Malebranche without Augustinianism; Shaftesbury and others without Stoicism; Diderot without a succession of medical mind/body paradigms. To do justice to the labor/*aisance* binary we have to be aware of the lineages of the family of words in which it operated, which have articulated gender differentiation since antiquity.

All this may not meet the aims of a refashioned history of ideas. I prefer to call it a history of language at work, a history whose tight focus on the form as well as the content of texts requires a long view.

Chapter 1

The Social Aesthetic of Play
in Seventeenth-Century France

In the second half of the seventeenth century French authors commonly gave their nation pride of place in the creation of a distinctly modern literature. The natural grace of literary French seemed to make it superior not only to other European vernacular languages, but also to classical Greek and, perhaps more striking, to the classical Latin on which boys and young men labored in the *collèges*, heard university lectures, and conducted academic theses and disputations. There was much arrogance and more than a little pretension to the assumption that French belles lettres were, or ought to be, the envy of Europe. And yet many of the innovations that came to characterize "modern" literature did have their origins in seventeenth-century France, and the reason is not hard to find. It was in *le monde*—the elite society of Paris—that the writing of prose and poetry entered into symbiosis with a new culture of orality, the polite conversation of the salons and other venues of sociability among the titled and the wealthy.[1] Out of this chemistry came a wide array of new stylistic forms and genres in the vernacular, among them the mock epic, the "gallant" love letter, the vernacular poem, the epistolary essay, the polite dialogue, and the novel. Strict traditionalists among "the learned" (*savants*) might disapprove, but they were scorned as mere "pedants"; there was no need to imitate classical literature unswervingly on the assumption that it could not be superseded. The eloquence of public rhetoric in the royal law courts and the pulpits was owed respect, of course, but polite conversation and writing prided itself on being unsullied by it.

This was the *goût moderne*, the "modern taste" developed by, among others, Vincent Voiture, Madeleine de Scudéry, Mme de Lafayette, and Bernard Le Bovier de Fontenelle. The eighteenth century witnessed a growing distaste for the *goût moderne* as the fluffy mannerism of a self-absorbed aristocratic society. Diderot and other philosophes equated its modernity with decadence; national rebirth required something quite different, an uplifting literature of high moral seriousness. Over the last several decades literary scholarship has taken exception to the self-righteousness of this verdict.[2] Two interlinked themes have emerged: that the *goût moderne* was modern in a far more positive sense than its eighteenth-century critics allowed, and that women—or more precisely, the women of *le monde*—played the central role in forming it and endowing it with cultural authority. In the French monarchy, Mlle de Scudéry has one of her characters observe in a conversational essay on "politeness" (*politesse*), the conversation of women is more "free" (*libre*) than in republics.[3] Scudéry's *Artamène, ou le Grand Cyrus* (1649–1653) and Lafayette's *Zaïde* (1669–1671) and *La princesse de Clèves* (1678) were founding texts in the history of the modern novel. Women's presence as listeners and readers was essential to the formation of a worldly literary culture and the fledgling literary public that emerged around it. Stylistic experiments in constituting a new relation between author and reader—a shift from the rhetorical imposition of authority to a more reciprocal intersubjectivity—simulated the reciprocity expected in the "sociable equality" of polite conversation, of which women were the acknowledged masters. If aesthetic judgment was not individualized in the modern sense, it nonetheless gave more play to the "free" subjectivity with which women, unencumbered by learned rules, seemed especially endowed.

The *goût moderne* confronts us, however, with a deep paradox that we have not taken sufficiently into account. It is all too obvious that leisure was the way of life of the French old-regime aristocracy. It is so obvious, in fact, that we rarely plumb the alterity with which that way of life confronts us. We observe seventeenth-century polite culture from our side of a great social and cultural divide. One of the defining assumptions of modernity is that labor, and especially intellectual labor in various kinds of professional work, is a vital route to personal and social self-validation. When we speak of labor that is dehumanizing, it is with the certainty that labor ought to confer moral dignity, and indeed that it is essential to the realization of human potentialities. The certainty owes its centrality in modern culture to a concatenation of social and intellectual changes, some of them already underway in the late seventeenth century. One thinks of the Protestant and particularly Calvinist ideal of the calling, the Jansenist recognition of the need for the motive power of self-interest in human societies, and John Locke's ethical thought.[4] The norm of utility in assigning personal worth—of social "usefulness" through labor—is one of the enduring legacies of the Enlightenment, and it has been powerfully reiterated, if also impoverished, in our current saturation in an ideology of immediate market utility. Modern advertising insinuates that disciplined labor is not only materially rewarding, but also emotionally satisfying and even liberating. Enthusiasts of contemporary crime novels and television series will agree, I think, that the detectives, so obsessed by their work that they have little or no personal life, are emblematic of this ethos. Only in work do they find the meaning they cannot do without.

Most pertinent for our purposes, the work ethos permeates the pursuit of equality in modern feminism; among the essential human rights owed to women is the right to equal access to labor and its rewards. The Declaration of Rights and Sentiments, approved at the Seneca Falls Convention in 1848, claimed for women equal rights to "life, liberty, and the pursuit of happiness"; and women's exclusion from most intellectual labor surely figured in its denunciation of men for endeavoring "in every way that (they) could to destroy woman's self-confidence in her powers, to lessen her self-respect, and to make her willing to lead a dependent and abject life." Feminists regularly appeal to the Universal Declaration of Human Rights, adopted by the UN General Assembly in 1948, because it makes no distinction between men and women in stating that "everyone has the right to work, to free choice of employment, to just and favourable conditions of work and to protection against unemployment."

In the light of these lineages of modernity, the norms of *le monde* and its literary culture were profoundly un-modern. The preeminence of this world rested on a perceived incompatibility between the socially validating freedom of play and the socially invalidating constraints of labor. In the spaces of polite sociability, labor was taboo. Women were the emblems and guardians of a social aesthetic of play that scorned utility, and that required that the performance of intelligence appear to be effortless, untainted by the concentrated and sustained effort that the term "labor" evoked. Hence the paradox of a profoundly unmodern modernity in which gender and status norms were so tightly interwoven as to be barely distinguishable. The paradox reminds us pointedly that, just as perceptions of social institutions and practices are refracted through the lens of gender distinctions, so too gender distinctions are refracted through the lens of status imperatives.[5]

To avoid presentism in studying seventeenth-century *mondanité*, I have made the social and cultural logic of un-modern modernity central to my reading of its texts. That is essential to understanding another paradox: that gender and status norms fused to set strict boundaries for women's performance of intelligence even as they made female thought and speech exemplary for men aspiring to polite cultivation. Awareness of this duality has been implicit, and sometimes explicit, to two rich scholarly traditions, and my agenda here is largely to synthesize them in an effort to grasp the ways in which seventeenth-century French discourses contributed to perceiving and valuing male and female performances of intelligence. The first tradition is one that intellectual historians have not sufficiently engaged: the large and growing corpus of literary scholarship on the texts produced by the sociable and literary culture of *le monde*. The second tradition can be broadly described as the historical sociology of knowledge. Beginning in late nineteenth-century German sociology, and flourishing today in scholarship in which sociology and cultural anthropology meet, it is indispensable to positioning our texts within structural and normative wholes.

Aisance and Labor

Jean-Louis Guez de Balzac's *Oeuvres diverses*, published in 1644, included an imagined "conversation" (*entretien*) with Catherine de Vivonne, marquise de Rambouillet, the daughter of a prominent Roman family and the wife of a royal councilor of state. More than a quarter century earlier the marquise had withdrawn from the court of Louis XIII, which she found tiresome and crude. In delicate health after bearing seven children, she preferred not to make the social rounds in Paris. Instead she created a kind of court that brought Parisian high society to her. She herself designed a new *hôtel*, begun in 1618, with high-ceilinged reception rooms leading into each other and a smaller chamber, known as the *ruelle*, where she received her guests reclining on her bed. The room was painted blue rather than the usual red or tan, with a matching décor, and the atmosphere was at once elegantly luxuriant and intimate, projecting aristocratic grandeur but offering a retreat from the demands of public life. This "Blue Room" became the fabled archetype for the salons of old-regime France.[6]

Balzac's *Lettres*, published in 1624, used the discursive latitude of the epistolary genre to conduct a high-spirited and mischievous discussion of a wide range of subjects, including politics. The book was a literary triumph in *le monde*, "so much in vogue," one of Balzac's adversaries observed, "that for a long time one has not seen such a small book make such a grand name."[7] In the ensuing *querelle* about Balzac's prose among men of letters a central issue was the relative value of tradition and modernity, imitation of the ancients and innovation. Balzac's critics among the learned attacked his unrestrained ornamental exuberance and his impertinent tone for perverting ancient Greek and Latin rhetoric. His defenders haled him for endowing authorship with an unprecedented free subjectivity.[8]

Balzac had had high ambitions to pursue a political career at court, but having failed to win Cardinal Richelieu's sponsorship he had retired to the family chateau in Angoulême in 1628, with only occasional visits to Paris thereafter. "I would rather ruin my little hopes than renounce entirely my liberty," he wrote his friend René Descartes on April 25.[9] Having marooned himself among provincials, he spent much of his time writing. In letters to friends in Paris he extolled the satisfactions of a solitary life of Ciceronian *otium*, or leisure, removed from the demands and intrigues of court life. If Balzac had renounced the life of the courtier, however, he could not live in isolation from Paris. Volatile and fiercely polemical by temperament, he would not have shone in polite sociability. But he remained virtually present in *le monde* through his letters to Jean Chapelain, a celebrated man of letters who was an *habitué* of the Blue Room and saw to it that Balzac's letters were circulated and sometimes read aloud there. Balzac wrote his "conversation" with the marquise knowing that, in a limited but real sense, it would be a public event, and that he was addressing the nascent public of *le monde*.[10]

The opening conceit of the *entretien* was that, having read selections he had provided her from the canonical Latin texts, the marquise now wanted to learn about the "private" life of the Romans, their "play" (*jeux*) and "diversions," and their "conversation" rather than their "ceremony." Balzac used the opportunity to suggest that the "pleasures" enjoyed in the Roman republic and at the Augustan court, which had been "virtuous," not "sensual," should inform the new conversational sociability of the Blue Room. The French, guided by the Romans, would develop a culture of "urbanity," a term Balzac coined, a "liberty" in social exchange that was "accommodating" without being "servile," that avoided both "vain ostentation" and "affected restraint," and that eschewed the burdensome "rules and precepts" of "public rhetoric." In the new art of conversation, as in Roman urbanity, there would be nothing "studied or acquired." And yet, even as he went so far in adapting to an aesthetic of play, Balzac, in the same polite prose, asserted his identity as a *savant*. He explained to the marquise that he was drawing on the fourth book of Aristotle's *Nichomachean Ethics*, where the "three virtues" needed for rational and self-disciplined conversation were spelled out. That was a daring move: Aristotle was held responsible for university scholasticism, for which *le monde* had contempt. Balzac claimed to take great pride in having acquired a recently discovered cache of Caesar's letters to Cleopatra, translated into Greek in an ancient manuscript, though he acknowledged that their authenticity would remain in doubt until an "infallible" philologist at the University of Leiden was consulted. The point was clear: there could be no knowledge of Roman private life—the knowledge the marquise had requested—without the labor of scholars.[11]

Balzac was somewhat fatalistic in adapting his literary talents to the demands of *mondanité*. Even as he supported the French monarchy against the Huguenots and other enemies, he retained his admiration for the civic life of the Roman republic. But he understood that under the political authority of the French monarchy and the cultural supremacy of *le monde* he could only dream of being a modern reincarnation of the Roman orator addressing "the people." It was a matter of rhetorical strategy; the eloquence of the Roman orator, intent on persuading his audience on a great public issue, had to accede to a seemingly light, informal, and discursive style that made "pleasing" the condition for instruction. In his heyday Guez de Balzac did please, but in doing so he walked a fine line between two social personas that were not easily combined: the *savant* laboring in his study, and the "polished" (*honnête*) man or woman enjoying the diversions of *le monde*. It was the difference between two meanings of the word *loisir*, or leisure. In the new social and institutional form the Blue Room gave to the aristocratic ethos of leisure, the usual entertainments acceded to a rarified play of *esprit*, precious precisely because it had no tolerance for any appearance of strenuous intellectual effort. In his provincial retreat Guez de Balzac tried to practice an *otium studiorum*; free from *negotium*, or the demands of public life, he had the liberty to work at his own pace, to let his work ripen. Such "leisure," he wrote in another *entretien*, was entirely different from "laziness" (*paresse*); while "we are in the power" of laziness, leisure allows us our "liberty."[12] Solitary reading and writing offered liberty in the control of one's time.

It was entirely compatible with Guez de Balzac's agenda that, like most other erudite men of letters, he considered women incapable of the manly labor of "study." There should be no violating the divide marking the different "duties and conditions" and "virtues" of the sexes, he advised Mme Desloges. "Pedantry" was even more intolerable in a woman than in a schoolmaster. The woman who spoke the language of philosophy (even the Platonic ideal of love), or who laid down rules about literary genres and style, was ridiculous.[13] As politely deferential as his conversation with the marquise de Rambouillet was, he took care to assert the cultural authority of his own, exclusively male world.

By the 1640s, however, the tone was being set by Vincent Voiture, a very different sort of man of letters. The son of a wine merchant who supplied the court, Voiture knew that despite his personal merit he would always be regarded as a plebeian by the aristocratic guests of Rambouillet. But his extraordinarily nimble and entertaining wit, made all the more piquant when he courted insolence, made him the central attraction of the Blue Room. It was essential to his carefully cultivated image that he not appear to be laboring as a *savant* or even as an author. As his nephew recalled in the preface to his posthumously published *Letters*, he always pleased the ladies, whose "very exquisite taste" was due to "the delicacy of their *esprit*."[14] He was perhaps the first complete *galant homme*, applying his gifts to amuse women with poetry, ballads, and charming, playfully flirtatious letters, all seemingly extemporaneous, though he may have prepared his verbal magic in private. His writings had no room for Guez de Balzac's view of learned "leisure" as a periodic Ciceronian retreat from public affairs; they record worldly "leisure" as a total way of life in which the value of the written word lay in its air of ephemeral entertainment.

By the 1660s salons, modeled on Rambouillet's, though usually on a less grand scale, were a fixture of the Parisian social scene. The classical "virtue" that Guez de Balzac had in mind in calling for a new urbanity was not explicitly repudiated, but it lost the moral rigorism of the ideal of republican citizenship as it was folded into what I am calling a social aesthetic of play. Mlle de Scudéry was a protégé of the marquise de Rambouillet and became a prominent salon hostess in her own right. She has Cleonte, one of the characters in her dialogue on politeness, observe that the word "urbanity" has acceded to "politeness" because the latter was better suited to the "natural conversation" of women; though acknowledging that the urbanity celebrated by Guez de Balzac and the Blue Room was clearly at the origins of modern politeness, Cleonte thinks the term should now be left to the learned and to "grand eloquence."[15] In the second half of the seventeenth century the discourse of *honnêteté* and *politesse* assumed a new level of self-consciousness; its family of words acquired a kind of coded meaning for the initiated, and as the self-justification of a privileged and exclusive world it became, in the broadest sense of the term, an ideology. A variety of literary forms—among them model letters and conversations, advice books, essays, dialogues, and novels—sought to capture the essence of *honnêteté*, drew the boundaries between what it encompassed and what lay outside it, and tried to identify its emblematic forms of behavior without reducing it to a set of rules or abstract principles.

The discourse of *honnêteté*, it should be stressed, was largely prescriptive. It tells us how a social milieu imagined and justified itself; how it thought it ought to be, and indeed how it thought it had to be if it was to sustain its claim to singular honor. Beneath the lacquered surface lay the actual workings of sociability in what Antoine Lilti has called "the space of *mondanité*." Lilti has shown in impressive detail that the high aristocracy dominated that space, linking the salons to the royal court through both patronage and a shared style of worldly amusement; and that in the multiple hierarchies of *le monde*, the arts of *politesse* at once enabled and veiled an intense jockeying for social and political power in the circulation of "reputations" and attendant rewards.[16] Lilti focuses on the eighteenth century, but there is no reason to think that seventeenth-century *mondanité* was any different. The prescribed norms surely governed behavior to some degree, but just as surely they allowed the *honnêtes* to delude themselves by conflating the reality into a normative imaginary. One might argue, in fact, that the imaginary marked the need for a respite from the competitive realities of aristocratic life. We cannot assume, though, that the respite actually eliminated the competitive maneuvers for reputation. It was just as likely to veil them. To captivate others on apparent terms of equality might be an act of aggression, an imposition of superiority; one could prevail by not seeming to want to prevail.

The term *honnête* could still be used to describe an upright man, or a man of integrity, but that meaning was overlaid by the emphasis on "pleasing" to win the approval of others. A *galant* was not primarily a seducer; he had mastered the art of pleasing women in erotically charged but inconsequential conversational play. In his supreme incarnation the *honnête homme* was a *bel esprit*, a brilliant performer entertaining with seemingly effortless wit. Moralists like La Rochefoucauld and La Bruyère pointed to the fine line between pleasing others and deceiving them, presenting a false self. Finding self-validation in the gaze of others was a far cry from having the inner core of integrity that the term "virtue" had long evoked. Even as they cast a cynical eye on the ways of *mondanité*, however, the moralists were immersed in them and contributed to defining their normative ideal. To them, as to so many others, the sine qua non of *honnêteté* was mastery of the art of conversation, and the raison d'être of conversation was to give and receive "pleasure." The verbal circulation of pleasure in turn required a collective equanimity and harmony, a commitment by all participants not to introduce a discordant note.[17] There could be no winning an argument, no closure in that sense. It was necessary, La Rochefoucauld wrote, to "observe the same precise sense of harmony (*justesse*) that the different voices and diverse instruments ought to observe in music."[18] *Honnêtes gens* were always "agreeable" and "obliging" (*complaisant*); they said nothing "shocking" or "wounding." They acted with a "sense of the appropriate" (*bienséance*), always finding the "juste" word or phrase, the one the moment required. They spoke with natural "ease" and "grace." They all did their part to ensure that social interaction was an "enjoyment," and indeed a "joy."

This is the coded lexicon of a social (and socially bounded) aesthetic, an emphatically aestheticized set of norms that made sociability a kind of play and virtue always "agreeable." To engage in this play was to maintain an illusion of equality within the interlocutors' self-enclosed space, however unequal they might be outside it. No matter what tensions and rivalries lurked beneath the surface, the sociability of polite conversation could not be sullied by the audible (or visible) exercise of authority, or indeed by the intrusion of power in any form into the free circulation of verbal gifts. The line of demarcation between insiders and outsiders was permeable, but paradoxically the ineffable moments of intersubjective and aesthetic experience conveyed by the "je ne sais quoi" (literally the "I know not what"), that indefinable something that distinguished a pleasing phrase, or a facial expression, or a gesture, kept the line clear. "The *je ne sais quoi*" is "so delicate and imperceptible," the Jesuit language critic Dominique Bouhours wrote, "that it escapes the most penetrating and subtle intelligence."[19] With the "je ne sais quoi" *honnête* society declared its effortless aesthetic to be beyond philosophical analysis and scholarly explanation. At a deeper level, it asserted its exclusiveness in the very act of admitting that even its language, as psychologically and aesthetically fine-tuned as it was, had its limits. The outsider betrayed himself by failing to recognize the limits—by trying to explain what insiders knew defied explanation.[20]

The novels of Scudéry and Lafayette—the most conspicuous examples of French literary modernity in the seventeenth century—were fashioned in this social and discursive space. We can clarify the social geography of the space by taking a critical look at the work of the literary and feminist scholar Joan DeJean. In her *Tender Geographies* (1991) DeJean argues that the early French novels were informed by a feminist ideology that was "sexually, socially, and politically subversive."[21] In *Ancients Against Moderns* (1997) she returns to this theme; "the most successful first novelists" made the early novel "a feminized, and often a feminist, and even a feminizing (in the sense of that which promotes its creators' feminocentric values), literary genre." In the controversy that the novels occasioned, DeJean contends, the issue was, contra Jürgen Habermas, more "gender" than "class."[22] Defenders of the novel formed a loose but vocal feminist movement; and this literary feminism aimed to effect a democratization of taste and criticism in an emerging public sphere.

For historians, and for literary scholars with an historical orientation, DeJean's work is fatally flawed by its presentism. The early novels surely were a feminized literary genre. Much of their material came from conversations among society women; they were written primarily for a female audience; their depictions of gallantry gave women a new respect and agency. Hence we can fairly call their values "feminocentric," but only so long as we keep in mind that, as will become apparent, the role of intellect in the female-centered world that produced the novels was at least as strictly circumscribed for women as it was for men. But DeJean's application of the term "feminist" to this context is highly problematic. Her declared aim was to combine literary history and history, with its attention to "a precise historical context," but that is precisely what she does not do, particularly when situating her subject in a social context. Rather than giving the term "feminist" contextual specificity in an old-regime social milieu that was jealous of its singular honor, and that was open only to the few commoners who could master its performative culture, DeJean wants to find the moment of origin for the modern feminist agenda for women's rights, which does indeed require a process of democratization. She in effect shunts aside the unmodern in seventeenth-century French literary modernity. Scudéry and Lafayette were society women living in something like a caste, permeable to some degree but, in the self-image that sustained it, contemptuous of other ways of life as vulgar. The notion that they aimed to democratize taste and criticism is simply wrongheaded.

Max Weber's conceptual precision about social hierarchy is a good place to start in correcting DeJean's work. To Weber there were two fundamental categories for understanding social hierarchy: classes and status groups (*Stände*). While one's class position was a function of the objective power of disposal afforded by command of economic resources, one's status position, or one's position in a hierarchy of honor (*Ehre*), was a subjective phenomenon, a matter of social and cultural perception; it depended on the norms and values that informed "the privileging of social estimation" and especially the value attributed to an entire "way of life" (*Lebensführung*). Class and status were ideal types, indispensable as analytical distinctions but always bound together to one degree or another in social reality. Elements of class and status mingled in myriad ways in old-regime society, and the elite that gathered in the salons is a striking case in point. The salons mixed people from the upper and lower ends of the steep scale of rank and wealth in the nobility of the sword; families from this ancient nobility with families of the judicial, or "robe," nobility with virtually hereditary rights to the expensive and lucrative offices of the royal parlements; robe and sword families with families in commerce and finance who had acquired titles as the Crown's sale of offices and noble titles commodified honor; scholars and men of letters drawn from all these groups.[23] The venality of offices introduced anxiety-ridden instability into what was supposed to be a clear hierarchical order of inherited ranks and attached moral qualities. As one historian has aptly put it, it "monetized status," converting "the attributes that determined one's identity into qualities that could not only be acquired but also purchased in a marketplace."[24] This confusing conflation of the calibrations of honor with economic (class) positions helps explain why salon society took such pains to demarcate itself as a status group, a circle whose members, however different in origins, wealth, and power, were united, and set apart from everyone else, by a unique social honor that could only be acquired with the personal mastery of worldly self-cultivation and self-presentation.

It was this honor that was performed in the social aesthetic of play. Its generic characteristics have been described in a remarkable essay published in 1910 by Georg Simmel, another German sociologist and a contemporary of Weber.[25] Titled "The Sociology of Sociability," the essay focuses on the "pure sociability" to be found in, among other historical examples, the aristocratic *mondanité* of old-regime France. Simmel finds "a special sociological structure corresponding to those of art and play, which draw their form from these realities [of the constellation called society] but nevertheless leaves their reality behind them." Pure sociability derives its substance from the actual social relations outside its space, but is "spared the frictional resistances of real life" (179). Its aspiration to "the pure, abstract play of form" cannot be reconciled with the values of modern rationalist utility, which sees in it only "empty idleness"(179). There is nothing specialized about this "play-form"; "all the specific contents of the one-sided and qualified societies" are "dissolved away." The required traits of character are "amiability, cultivation (*Bildung*), cordiality, and powers of attraction of all kinds" (180). These require an intense self-discipline, an inner "self-regulation" essential to participation in the form of play, from which both the individual's "interests" and his "most purely and deeply personal qualities" must be excluded (180–81). Discretion or "tact"—the suppression of the "purely subjective and inward parts of [the] personality"—is essential to the engagement in "nothing but the capacities, attractions, and interests of [one's] pure humanity (*reine Menschlichkeit*)" (182). In that sense the "social ideal" might be called "the freedom of bondage" (*Freiheit der Bindung*) (190). But precisely because the social interaction in this world is "artificial," it can be "a democracy of equals . . . without friction," "free of any disturbing material accent" (182–85). What matters in conversation is not the content, but the stylized form that makes it play; there can be no "serious argument," no attempt at an intersubjective "verification of a truth."

Though he does not use the term *honnêteté*, Simmel's essay offers a penetrating analysis of its preoccupation with *complaisance, bienséance, agrément, enjoue-
ment*, and related qualities, including *aisance*. He constructed an ideal type, and he
was aware that its actual social instantiations could ossify into "a conventionalism
and inwardly lifeless exchange of formulas" (193). He suggests, in fact, that this
may have happened in the French ancien regime. He is confident, though, that
some social spaces have approximated the ideal purity; and in fact he tried to
create such a space in the weekly salon he and his wife held in their Berlin home,
which one of his friends recalled as having been designed to achieve "the cultivation of the highest individuals."[26] We need to apply Simmel's paradigm cautiously,
keeping in mind how the logic of pure sociability functioned in a larger structure
of class inequality that Simmel simply assumed. Simmel was well aware that
"sociable equality" inside the group hinged on a strict exclusiveness, a sharp distinction between the rare few insiders and the great mass of outsiders. As the
essay nears its end, however, it becomes apparent that he viewed the historical
phenomenon of pure sociability through the lens of a late nineteenth-century
variant on the German ideal of individual self-cultivation (*Bildung*) in "pure
humanity." Like many of his German contemporaries, he posed against the
increasing specialization and commercial materialism of modernity a new aristocracy or, perhaps better, a new clerisy carrying the torch of aesthetic cultivation. As
he tried to enact this ideal in his own salon, he looked for historical antecedents.
He ends the essay on a swelling note: "the more thoughtful man" finds in sociability a "freeing and lightening," a "simultaneous sublimation and dilution, in which
the heavily freighted forces of reality are felt only as from a distance, their weight
fleeting in a charm" (193).

We need a skeptical antidote to Simmel's idealism, and it is to be found in the
work of the French sociologist and anthropologist Pierre Bourdieu. Bourdieu's
concept of the habitus is, to be sure, open to the charge of reducing the cultural to
a function of social power. I use it here simply as a reminder of the need to place
the internal symbolic structure of the discourse of *honnêteté* within the societal
structure in which it positioned itself.[27] *Le monde* presents us with a habitus in
Bourdieu's sense: a cultural preconscious formed in the induction from childhood into a total way of life. What interests us here is the binary duality of Bourdieu's concept of the habitus. It is, first, a "structuring structure," the internalized
symbolic organization of "practices and perceptions of practices." This is not
simply a matter of internalizing ideas, as in the commitment to a political ideology; it is the ground for the individual's consciousness of himself and others
as social beings. But Bourdieu is equally insistent that the habitus is, second,
a "structured structure," formed by the objective reality of hierarchy, its social
perceptions being "the product of internalization of the division into social
classes."[28] The "distinction" attached to the aesthetic is "rooted in an ethic, or

rather an ethos, of elective distance from the necessities of the natural and social world," "the objective and subjective removal from practical urgencies, which is the basis of objective and subjective distance from groups subject to those determinisms."[29]

We proceed with the understanding that the interaction Bourdieu posits between the subjective and objective, though it leads him to a reductionist concept of culture, is essential to the study of symbolic power.[30] But our focus here is on Bourdieu's structuring structure. We want to understand how the social and cultural logic of *mondanité* shaped and informed social relations within its own space. "In a cultural system," William H. Sewell, Jr., writes, "the meaning of a sign or symbol is a function of its network of oppositions to or distinctions from other signs in the system."[31] Pervading the discourse of *honnêteté* is a central axiom of opposition, the deep logic of what Bourdieu calls an "elective distance from the necessities of the natural and social world": the polarity between labor (*travail*) and *aisance*, or effortlessness. In his *Conversations*, Antoine Gombaud, chevalier de Méré, an elder statesmen of the salons, observed that the *surest* sign of failure to master the art of conversation was "a constrained manner, where one senses much work (*travail*)."[32] Méré's essays remind us again and again that in the ideal of *honnêteté* "free" (*libre*) and "natural" were virtually synonymous qualities. We must be careful not to read back into this language the eighteenth-century critique of aristocratic society and culture, and more broadly of *le monde*, that would find its most impassioned articulation in Rousseau's texts. In the discourse of *honnêteté*, appeals to the "natural" were not meant to censure the artificiality of polite sociability by invidious comparison with the more natural life of common people. Quite the contrary; the apparently natural *aisance* of the *honnête femme* and the *honnête homme* was precisely what marked their superiority over everyone outside their clearly delimited space. To be able to act naturally—to engage in the spontaneous play of the social aesthetic—meant to be free of the "determinisms" that labor to satisfy basic needs imposed on the great mass. Most obviously it marked the fact that one used one's time as one wished, rather than as material needs demanded. Ultimately this conception of natural freedom drew a line between the choices open to a uniquely human nature and the imprisonment of the human animal in material necessities. It stigmatized labor as the mark of subjection to material need. The ideological irony lay in the fact that a universal ideal—the freedom of the human being as such—justified the exclusion of most human beings from its practice. This self-image obviously put the *honnêtes* at a vast social distance from people engaged in any kind of manual labor. More to the point, it made the life of the leisured mind—the pleasure of *esprit*—qualitatively different from the rule-governed intellectual labor of the "learned" or "liberal" professions. Their *eloquentia*—their distinctly male forms of verbal authority— was laborious. We miss the point, then, if we think of the discourse as perching *honnêtes gens* at the pinnacle of an occupational hierarchy; its imagined world hovered above the entire social organization of labor.[33]

If men who practiced professions and occupied offices—university professors, magistrates in the parlements, military officers, clergymen—did not want to be branded bores, they had to leave their professional concerns behind them when they entered the salons. Even when Méré and others wrote for publication, they took pains to seem to be merely recording the "caprice" of their thoughts, without any planned order of presentation, as in the free play of conversation.[34] The social aesthetic would not allow any intrusion from the occupation world. At a deeper level, it would not allow conversational play to sully itself by taking on any appearance of labor in its practice, or indeed any hint that an investment of labor had been required to prepare for it. If we define intellectual labor as concentrated and sustained mental effort, that was precisely what the aesthetic excluded. To apply rules would be to degrade conversational play into something laborious and hence boring. Dwelling on one subject had the same effect; the orchestra could remain "diverting" only if it changed melodies constantly, like a meandering stream. The great gift of women—the "free" and "natural" air men had to acquire from them—was to leave the impression that everything they said was said spontaneously and effortlessly, or with "ease" (*aisance*). As Scudéry put it: "Although judgment is absolutely necessary so as to never say anything inappropriate, the conversation must appear so free that it seems that one rejects none of his thoughts, and that one says everything that comes to one's fancy (*fantaisie*)."[35]

As the aesthetic emphasis on appearance suggests, there was something illusory, perhaps even self-deluding, about this taboo on labor. In fact the play of *honnêteté*—the exclusive concern with giving pleasure, the care to avoid shocking or wounding others, the repression of any instinct to dominate—required a relentless exercise of self-discipline.[36] "How much art," La Bruyère observed in his *Characters*, "to return to nature! How much time, rules, attention and work to dance with the same liberty and the grace as one knows how to walk, to sing as one speaks, to speak and express oneself as one thinks."[37] The art might be considered an antirhetorical rhetoric—one that could not be learned in "the schools," but nonetheless had to be mastered. However noble his birth, the individual had to acquire the requisite self-discipline through long practice. It is striking, however, that the interpreters of *honnêteté*—Scudéry, Méré, and many others—insisted that the art of conversation could not be mastered by reading books. However important reading was in supplying a point of departure for conversation, and in providing the language of "judgment," it had to remain a "diversion." Otherwise one's speech would betray, in Méré's phrase, "the smell of study."[38] One could learn the art only as an apprentice to one of its masters, *within* the permeable but self-sufficient space of polite conversation. The social aesthetic needed nothing—not even print—that could be acquired in the world of labor outside it.

At its deepest level, the *honnête* performance of intelligence can be understood as the social exhibition of a dimension of selfhood. In his study of western European thinking about "the self" since the seventeenth century, Jerrold Seigel has identified a "relational" dimension in which the self "arises from social and cultural interaction, the common connections and involvements that give us collective identities and shared orientations and values, making us people able to use a specific language or idiom and marking us with its particular styles of description, categorization, and expression."[39] The worldly sociability prescribed in the discourse of *honnêteté* might be described as hyperrelational. In his *L'honneste femme*, first published from 1632 to 1636, the Franciscan priest Jacques du Bosc, in the tradition of Francis de Sales, sought to keep anchored in Christian ethics women's obligation to devote themselves to pleasing others, and to diverting themselves, in leisured sociability. Contrary to conventional wisdom that only men could be *honnête*, he argued that women could be paragons of *honnêteté*. Du Bosc assured women that a measured worldliness, with no taint of libertinism, was entirely compatible with being a devout Christian. The virtue enabled by God's grace provides "an interior joy" that does not make one "too melancholy" for "conversation." Quite the contrary; it is the Christian virtue of charity that "gives us the qualities that render a person amiable in conversation." "It is necessary, first," Du Bosc wrote, "to put virtue in the will; after that, knowledge (*la science*) in the mind (*esprit*); and finally, gentleness in the countenance."[40] But in the ensuing articulation of the code of politeness little serious attention was given to Du Bosc's effort to fuse a devoutness infused with divine grace and worldly self-fashioning. In the worldly ethos of constant "diversion," there was little room for the meditative tradition of solitary prayer, much less for the asceticism, of Jansenist women at Port-Royal and the followers of Mme Guyon's mysticism of utter abandonment of the self in surrender to the divine will.[41]

Nor was there anything of modern authenticity about the social aesthetic; any impulse to make transparent the depths of one's inner self had to give way to what Simmel called "freedom in bondage." More to the point here, *honnêteté* rejected what Seigel calls the "reflective" dimension of selfhood, which makes inwardness—introspective self-examination—the route to one's consciousness of one's self as "an active agent of its own realization," often in opposition to social expectations.[42] *Honnêteté* was openly hostile to the most rigorous tradition of intellectual labor inherited from the ancients: the Stoic tradition of askesis, the struggle for self-command at the rational core of human nature, the inner self, in the solitude of intense and repeated meditation. Since the late sixteenth century there had been a neo-Stoic strain in French philosophy, but it was obviously at odds with the feminizing of worldly culture, and particularly with its ideal of *aisance.* Neo-Stoicism kept virtue manly, as a labor of rational self-control, contrasted with the enslaving imagination that the term "effeminacy" evoked.[43] *Honnêteté* preferred the joys of sociability; to enter solitude by choice, and to try to plumb the inner self, seemed unnatural and futile. In his effort to graft polite learning onto modern urbanity, Balzac dismissed the Stoic idolization of the "reasonable and judicious" sage. The sage was not really meditating; he was in fact merely just "still" or "sleeping" (*dormant*).[44] Several decades later, in an essay on "pleasures," Saint-Évremond reported to a friend on how he was spending his time in the country. He sought constant diversion, not "profound" truths, not having any desire for "overly long and serious commerce with [himself]." "Solitude," he went on, has the effect of imprinting on us *"je ne sais quel* sad and somber (*funeste*) air by the ordinary thought of our condition. . . . To live happily, it is necessary to reflect little on life, but to go out often, as it were, outside of oneself."[45]

The discourse of *honnêteté* was no exception to the fact that collective self-imaginings are positional. Its claim to honor used several social referents as foils, defining itself as what they were not. Though *honnête* sociability was not informal by modern standards, it was clearly a relief from the rigid hierarchical protocol that Louis XIV instituted at court. But as at the highest levels of *le monde* the Parisian gentleman was also by necessity a courtier, dependent on royal patronage and vulnerable to royal reprisals, caution had to be exercised when it came to the court. Even Méré, who found the court pompous and intellectually vacuous, took pains not to challenge its social and cultural supremacy too blatantly. The discourse of *honnêteté* was less circumspect in fashioning its other foils, which were representations of exclusively male corporate cultures, identified above all by their control of public knowledge and their uses of public speech. There was the "eloquence" of the law courts, a formal and elaborate oratory, based on classical models, that contrasted sharply with the unstudied ease and simple grace of salon speech.[46] And there was the pulpit, another platform for male eloquence. By contrasting itself with these worlds, the discourse of *honnêteté* asserted its aesthetic superiority over male-controlled forms of expertise and the training in Latinity on which they were founded. It staked its claim to unique value by casting a critical and bemused eye on the rhetorical performances, sometimes ridiculed as "harangues" aimed to intimidate, with which men exercised public authority and ultimately wielded public power.

It is above all in the figure of the "pedant" that we hear the voice of women distinguishing the art of conversation from exclusively male speech. The pervasive caricatures of "pedantry" in the discourse of *honnêteté* echoed Montaigne's contemptuous views on that subject, recorded in an essay he wrote sometime in the 1570s; but they also marked a shift in gender values in aristocratic culture in the intervening century or so. Montaigne had ended "Of Pedantry" by observing that "the pursuit of knowledge makes men's hearts soft and effeminate more than it makes them strong and warlike."[47] In keeping with this view, he extolled the art of "conversation" as a "quarrelsome" exercise in "strong, manly fellowship" that "delights in the sharpness and vigor of its intercourse, as does love in bites and scratches that draw blood."[48] In the contempt for pedantry a century later, there is hardly a trace of this equation of manliness with an aristocratic martial ethos. The nobleman in military service, droning on about horses and campaigns, has joined the pedant as an example of distinctly male social ineptness—though, unlike the pedant, he still commands a certain tolerant respect. The social persona of the traditional scholar has become the example par excellence of crude and overbearing masculinity.[49] The reason for his social ineptness seemed obvious. After spending his boyhood being drilled in Latin grammar and translating arcane bits and pieces of classical learning, the pedant had acquired a doctorate at one of the university faculties. The quintessence of the type was the Sorbonne-educated theologian. He was still—as Montaigne had portrayed him—a boor and a bore, intent on impressing others with his esoteric and tunnel-visioned academic expertise. Far from exemplifying effeminacy, however, he was a reproof to the fact that the colleges and the university faculties were male ghettos. Having been formed in that world, the pedant was "intractable, arrogant, uncivil, impolite, opinionated."[50] His voice grated; he interrupted imperiously; he droned on. These were stereotypical traits, of course, but they pointed to certain realities of academic education. The battle-like exercise of "dialectic" in public "disputation," often before a large and rowdy audience, was still a characteristic feature of university learning and teaching. Since their origins in the late sixteenth century, the Jesuit *collèges* had also simulated a martial spirit by making debates between platoons of pupils central to their curriculum. There was, of course, an ancient pedagogical rationale for pitting boys and young men against each other in relentless argument, but it was one that the standards of *honnêteté* simply dismissed. The pedant's combativeness betrayed the excessive masculinity that conventional male education inculcated.

Pedantry was a serviceable social stigma, not a reliable social descriptive. It was not uncommon, particularly in the Jesuit *collèges*, for sons of the nobility to be introduced to classical Latin literature. There were *savants* who had been immersed since boyhood in academic Latinity, and who were active in the epistolary exchange of scholarly knowledge in the Republic of Letters, and yet were also accepted in *le monde* as *honnêtes hommes*.[51] They knew how to mute their learning when they engaged in aesthetic play. And yet there were tensions in their efforts to bridge the worlds of scholarly labor and leisured amusement, and even when they wrote in the *honnête* key, apparently speaking from within its habitus, they sometimes declared their independence from it. The tensions remain audible in Dominique Bouhours's *The Conversations of Ariste and Eugène*, published in 1671, though he assumed the literary persona of mediator between learning and *mondanité*. Having first attracted attention as a professor of literature at the prestigious Collège de Clermont in Paris, Bouhours became tutor to the two sons of Henri II d'Orléans, duc de Longueville. His publications from the 1670s onward made him a widely recognized authority on correct and elegant usage in literary French. *The Conversations of Ariste and Eugène* sought to convey in print the lightness of the art of conversation, and they continue to have literary importance as examples of the polite essay in a conversational mode.[52] The two characters Bouhours puts in dialogue are young *honnêtes hommes*, and though they often question each other's views, they do so in fluid and accommodating conversation, not in the battle formations of an academic disputation.

The *entretien* titled "The je ne sais quoi" is an extensive exploration of the meanings of a deliberately mystifying phrase that was much in vogue. By using the definite article Bouhours announced that the phrase, so often used sloppily, now required examination as an object in itself. It is an examination, however, that Ariste and Eugène conduct from within the social aesthetic of play. The *je ne sais quoi* is what "pleases" or, perhaps better, delights in a way that can neither be grasped intellectually nor captured in language. We recognize it only by its effect, an entirely spontaneous "sympathy" or "inclination" of "the heart." Experiencing it is an entirely "natural" moment of freedom; in it we are, in fact, free not only of "reason," but also of the need to exercise freedom of the will. This is a social epistemology that in effect bans philosophers and other *savants* from intruding their authority into the aesthetic of play; it will likely always be futile for them to try to understand, much less explain, the phenomenon. There are, to be sure, universal cases of the *je ne sais quoi*, but in matters of taste, as in individuals' face-to-face reactions to each other, all human beings have a particular *je ne sais quoi* that makes them pleased or displeased at first sight. It would be hard to imagine a more explicit defense of the modern literary subjectivity of the culture of *mondanité*. Appropriately Bouhours includes a comparison commonly used in *le monde* by the 1660s. There are, he acknowledges, "great beauties" in Guez de Balzac's works; but, turning a word against the author who coined it, he finds Voiture's works "infinitely" more pleasing because they have that "air *du monde*," that "tincture of *urbanité* that Cicero did not know how to define."

In the essay on the *bel esprit*, however, Bouhours cautiously became a critic of fashionable *mondanité*. He undertook an act of lexical policing, aimed at counteracting a "usurpation" of the phrase *bel esprit* by all sorts of people who did not merit it. The delicacy of his task lay in politely leveling a scornful critique of pretended *bel esprits* and, with it, a soft but pointed admonishment of *mondanité*, as he tried to regenerate the term by steering it into the intellectually more serious waters that the worldly shunned. "The true beauty of *l'esprit*," Ariste observes, "consists of a correct (*juste*) and delicate discernment" that reveals "things such as they are." If such discernment is "brilliant," it is also "solid," a matter of "judg-ment," with a "force" to "penetrate the principles of sciences and the most hidden truths."[53] Bouhours was trying to remove the true *bel esprit* from the *mondain* preoccupation with pleasing appearance, and that in turn required a male repos-session of the phrase. "The beauty of the *esprit*," he writes, "is a manly and gener-ous beauty, which has nothing of the soft and effeminate."[54] Later in the essay Bouhours has Eugène observe that "the *savants de profession* are ordinarily not *beaux esprits*," as they are always "buried" in study and, having little "commerce with *les honnêtes gens*," they lack "a certain *politesse* and I know not what of *agré-ment*."[55] Bouhours acknowledges the social ineptitude of the stereotypical pedant, however, only to give more credibility to his defense of learned men who are not at home in polite sociability but can nonetheless be polite authors. He breaks down genuine *beaux esprits* into three types with "talents" that are rarely com-bined: the worldly conversationalist, the statesman at the pinnacle of govern-ment, and the polite author. "There is nothing more opposed to study and public affairs," he writes, than "the spirit of conversation," which is "a natural spirit, an enemy of all labor and constraint." With the term "natural" Bouhours seems to follow the underlying logic of a pure sociability devoted to *aisance*. But as he continues *aisance* becomes a more dubious attribute: "those who have this talent are ordinarily idle people (*oisifs*) whose principal employment is to make and receive visits." Even as he hales Voiture as the supreme example of the *bel esprit* who writes effortlessly and delicately, he detaches the *bel esprit* as a man of letters from Voiture's conversational artistry. "The most brilliant and exact authors do not always shine in conversation"; they "examine things in depth," and in com-pany they speak seldom, "as they think too much about what they want to say."[56] Bouhours in effect extracts the man of letters from the symbiosis of orality and the written word that the aesthetic discourse of *honnêteté* made mandatory. Though the author's style must of course have "I know not what of the agreeable and the flowery to please people of good taste,"[57] the *bel esprit* is an emphatically male intelligence whose engagement in the labor of strenuous thought grants him a certain independence from the social aesthetic of play.

The *savant* Pierre Daniel Huet also moved fairly comfortably in *le monde* but kept himself at a remove from its ethos. In his *Treatise on the Origins of the Novel*, published in 1670, a year before Bouhours's *Conversations*, the implicit assertion of authorial independence we find in Bouhours's text widens into an explicit effort to reclaim the scholar's cultural authority.[58] A prodigy of Jesuit education, Huet became a scholar's scholar. Over the course of his career he would produce trans-lated editions of ancient and early Christian texts as well as his own Latin poems, and would devote serious study to philosophy, chemistry, mathematics, and anat-omy. In 1670 Louis XIV called him from Caen, where he had founded an Acad-emy of Sciences, to Paris to serve as subtutor of the Dauphin. In 1674 he was appointed abbot of Aunay in Normandy, and shortly thereafter he ascended to the bishopric of Avranches.

Neither his provincial origins nor his commitment to scholarship prevented Huet from being accepted in *honnête* circles in Paris. He became a regular visitor in Mlle de Scudéry's salon and a friend of Mme de Lafayette. He published his *Treatise* as an epistolary preface to Lafayette's novel *Zaïde, histoire espagnole*, which he had probably commented on in drafts as he wrote his treatise. Ignoring the tensions between a scholarly ethos of labor and a social aesthetic of play, DeJean seriously misreads this text and its larger significance in the debates it addressed. She makes Huet's treatise a key expression of respect for the feminizing (or feminist) impulse in the early novel.[59] Huet was pursuing a quite different and in some ways opposed agenda. He did, to be sure, give the novel literary legitimacy by placing it in a lineage that went back to the classical epic. And he did conclude with a paean to Mlle de Scudéry, confessing his "astonishment" that a "girl," not a man, had published three illustrious novels. Perhaps she had originally hidden her authorship, he suggested, and thus had deprived herself of "the glory that was her due" for working for "the glory of the nation," because "she wanted to spare this shame to our sex."[60] But Huet's overarching argument was that the novel was an "entertainment," though one that must be morally instructive. He was treading a fine line in a debate about the novel that would continue into the eighteenth century. In *L'honneste femme* Du Bosc had advised women that to be *honnête* they had to undertake serious reading, even in the works of *savants*; but he had warned them against reading novels, as their gallant love stories corrupted female readers insidiously, not only acquainting them with evil, but teaching them how to commit it.[61] Huet obviously disagreed. But what made the novel a moral necessity was the fact that people were naturally "lazy"; unable or unwilling to understand the truth, they were instructed in the effortless reading of a story, without getting behind the fact that the story was a fictional "lie."[62] This was to say that the novel adapted to human weakness, whereas serious study overcame it. For all his admiration for this new genre being developed by women, Huet could not refrain from regretting its recent ascendancy in polite circles. The novel reflected the unprecedented "forms" of *complaisance* with which men in France had to win the favor of women. It is worth quoting in full a passage DeJean has ignored:

> [Women] have made novels their entire study, and have been so con-temptuous of the ancient fable and history that they have not understood works which drew on them formerly for their greatest ornament. So as no longer to be embarrassed by this ignorance, of which they have so often the occasion to be aware, they have found that it would be preferable to disapprove what they are ignorant of, rather than to learn it. Men have

imitated them to please them; they have condemned what [women] would condemn, and have called pedantry what was an essential part of politeness, still at the time of Malherbe. Poets and other French writers who have followed [Malherbe] have been constrained to submit to this judgment, and several of them, seeing that knowledge of antiquity would be useless to them, have ceased to study what they dare not put in usage. Thus a good cause has produced a very bad effect, and the beauty of our novels has brought contempt for *belles lettres*, and thus ignorance.[63]

It is not surprising that in his later years Huet became estranged from *mondain* conversational sociability.[64]

The Intelligence of Women

The last question raised in Bouhours's *Conversations* is whether a woman can be a *bel esprit*. Surely he had heard the subject discussed in worldly circles. Eugène endorses the received view of women's intelligence:

> This beautiful fire and this good sense (*bon sens*) of which we have spoken so much does not come from a cold and humid complexion. Coldness and humidity, which render women weak, timid, indiscreet, light-headed, impatient, babbling . . . prevents them from having the judgment, the solidity, the force, the precision (*justesse*) that the *bel esprit* requires. This mucus (*pituite*) of which they are full, and which gives them that delicate tint, does not accord much with the delicacy and the vivacity of *l'esprit*; it blunts the point, and weakens [the mind's] lights (*lumières*): and if you reflect on it, what women have of the brilliant is in the nature of flashes (*éclairs*) which dazzle for a moment and have no point at all of consistency. They shine a little in conversation, and provided that one speaks only of trifling things (*bagatelles*), they do not speak badly, but beyond that they are not very reasonable. In a word, there is nothing more limited than the mind of women.

The friends admit exceptions to "the general rule," but agree that there is "some sort of opposition between the beauty of the mind and that of the [female] body."[65]

The passage is as compact an example of the durability of ancient perceptions of differences between male and female intelligence as one is likely to find. It is geologically layered. The bottom stratum of conventional wisdom, including humanist scholasticism, was formed by Aristotle's view of women as imperfect or incomplete men and Galenic humoral theory, which still dominated medical thinking and had long been integrated into neo-Aristotelian philosophy. In the tight body-mind nexus that this discourse posits, intellectual strength, or "force," is in some way a function of physical strength, which in turn is generated by the power of heat. By virtue of her role in reproduction, and in sexual intercourse as it was commonly perceived, the female is a passive instrument of nature; the male acts on nature, willing and reasoning to dominate it. Humoral composition makes the female brain, one might say, a soft cold sponge; the male brain is fire-hardened metal. No less than lifting a weight or pushing a plough, though of a qualitatively different order, intellection is an exercise of strength. In her social being woman's weakness of body and mind takes the form of a lack of self-command, and that is exhibited above all in her indiscrete and babbling speech.[66] Here we rise to the top geological layer, Bouhours's critique of his own era. He extends the ancient stereotype of the babbling or chattering woman—the woman unable to control her tongue—to what was being haled in other quarters as women's mastery of the art of conversation. Often extolled for its liveliness and subtlety, female *esprit* figures here as "flashes" that are ephemeral, irrational, and trivial. The epistemological assumption that runs through all the layers is that women lack the capacity for judgment. Bouhours draws on a standard philosophical concept of judgment as the grasp of universal principles and the prudent and consistent application of them to particular cases. It is above all in this power to abstract—to detach universal ideas from sensate particularity—that men demonstrate their superior intellectual strength. Paradoxically "solidity" lies in abstracting from the density of material being. Women are confined to the particular, in their thought as in their social being, which is to say that they cannot rise above trivia. Again Bouhours undercuts the feminizing lexicon of *honnêteté*. There is a clean difference between the "delicacy" conventionally attributed to women and the true delicacy of mind required of the *bel esprit*.[67]

The conventional wisdom had not gone unchallenged. In the traditional "argument about women" (*querelle des femmes*), stretching from the Renaissance to the mid-seventeenth century, women's defenders piled on historical examples to prove that exceptional women could be just as virtuous, and just as courageous, as men famed for those qualities, and, less often, that they could be just as intelligent as men with great minds. But this amounted to challenging male supremacy on its own terms; attributes considered "natural" to men remained normative for women.[68] As the discourse of *honnêteté* put a premium on the distinct kind of *relational* intelligence required in polite sociability and particularly in conversation, female-coded kinds of cognition were revalued in a new hierarchical order of capacities of intellection. Now the qualities considered "natural" to women became normative for men. Men had to acquire from women a "natural" way of speaking; a lively sensitivity; quick intuition; gentleness or softness (*douceur*); delicacy; grace; amiability. To fail to do so was to risk a loss of honor, a social derogation from the elite of worldliness. Bowing to the imperatives of honor, one might say, men had to give women the lead as cultural facilitators, mediators, and even arbiters.

At issue here was the relationship between intelligence and language facility, the mind and speech. For men educated in the *collèges* and the universities, learning language was a laborious process of acquisition. One of the justifications for the centrality of Latin in the curriculum was, in fact, that learning the language instilled in boys the endurance, the inurement to laborious effort, essential to a manly character.[69] While men were disciplined to use language as an instrument of thought, women's facility in their native tongue seemed to make words the "natural" and unmediated expression of thought. What had been dismissed as women's babble about social particularity, a world of mere appearance, was now admired as the performance of women's superior relational intelligence. To be socially efficacious thoughts must be communicable, and it was women who excelled in that kind of intelligence. Sometimes this was considered a natural gift, something women had by nature and men had to acquire. But if women had the gift, it was no less important that it had not been corrupted by the Latinate education of the schools.[70] Society women looked down on the training they neither could have nor, in their enjoyment of an exclusive liberty, wanted to have. It was not simply that they rejected academic jargon. They were free of the rules of traditional rhetorical performance, and of a manly labor of abstraction they considered laborious and therefore boring. While the French Academy sought a standard French for print, women continued to spell phonetically. It was precisely this "natural" naïveté that made women's speech and writing the model for the elegant simplicity of a polite style.[71] Natural simplicity grounded their new cultural authority as judges of literature. At once cultivated and uncorrupted by pedantry in any form, they were the arbiters of taste.

At work here was not "rhetorical re-description," if we mean by that phrase the technique (*paradiastole*) of effecting social change by replacing one term with another—from negative to positive, or vice versa—to describe an attribute or an action.[72] Instead there was a more subtle and, one might say, smoother process: the received terms were given new valuative and normative meaning. The revaluation is especially clear in the use of the word "delicacy," a female trait by tradition, to describe an essential quality of polite conversation and good taste.[73] Writing in the 1630s, Du Bosc sought to persuade society women that they could make polite conversation more intellectually substantive by doing serious reading, including the ancient texts. He knew that he was challenging conventional wisdom by claiming that female "delicacy" of mind included the capacity to understand the "sciences."[74] In the ensuing decades the discourse of *honnêteté*, in putting a premium on delicacy, often gave it a kind of acuteness of piercing strength. This linguistic shift made it questionable whether the intelligence that really mattered was about strength in the conventional sense, or indeed in any sense. Perhaps there were more valuable kinds of mental capacity in what had been considered female weakness.

The discourse was cutting the connection (literal and analogical) between male physical strength and mental energy. It implicitly contradicted the conventional notion that by virtue of women's role in reproduction, their minds were more subject to their physicality. In a sense, it reversed that assumption: the nature of women's physicality—the delicacy of their bodily makeup—gave them more freedom of mind in what mattered, in relational intelligence and the socially constructed "taste" of le monde, than men enjoyed. That was why schooling could not give men the delicacy of taste that distinguished le monde from the world at large. Only by attending "the school of women" could they become honnête. Delicacy in speech implied a cognitive advantage. Traditionally stereotyped as ephemeral prattle, women's speech was now admired for its greater "netteté" than men's; one of the attributes of their more natural speech was greater precision of expression. The implication was that, to a degree, women had the advantage in reasoning itself; the natural flow of their speech reflected the natural acuity of their thought. While in ordinary usage "delicacy" might continue to connote female mental weakness, a daintiness and fragility of the mind, delicacy now also attributed a superior cognitive perceptiveness and clarity to women. Other female traits gave reason a "beautiful" appearance, above all in its externalization in speech. They clothed it—not in the sense of providing mere ornamentation, but in the sense of softening it without diminishing its strength, enhancing its inherent persuasive power without making it overbearing or intimidating. It was in this positive sense that women were seen to be able to "insinuate" thoughts to others in a way that men could not.[75]

In this discursive context we can better understand what makes Fontenelle's Conversations on the Plurality of Worlds, published in 1686, such a tour de force. The son of a provincial noble family related to the Corneille brothers, Fontenelle had begun visiting Paris as a young man. He entered the literary world as a fledgling playwright and a contributor to the Mercure galant. Thanks to his connections, his literary gifts, and the grace and wit with which he exhibited his considerable learning, he rose into the highest fashionable circles and was much in demand in the salons. In the Conversations he undertook the formidable task of having a gallant gentleman explain the new science, from Copernicus's heliocentric cosmos to Descartes's vortices, to a young and beautiful marquise who is quite at home in le monde but is spending some time at her country chateau. They have five evening conversations in the garden, where they can converse unobserved as they gaze at the heavens. The gentleman obviously accomplishes his purpose. Having been introduced at the end to Descartes's vortices and the possibility of a vast plurality of solar systems, the marquise exclaims "I have the whole system of the universe in my head! I'm a scholar!"[76] "Scholar" is, of course, a surprising term for an *honnête femme* to apply to herself. The marquise uses it with more than a little irony, but not at all flippantly.

J. B. Shank has done us the service of rescuing this text from conventional misreadings and placing it squarely in the new discursive freedom of mixed-gender conversational sociability. Extricating the text from a now defunct teleology in the history of science, a linear narrative in which Cartesian science figures as a wrong turn, is only the first step. What Shank sees Fontenelle enacting so deftly is one of "the lost alternatives to Newtonian physics," another way of conceiving scientific inquiry that is by no means irrelevant today, and that can "open up perspectives on the lost social and political possibilities of the period as well."[77] Nor is the text, Shank argues, another conventional exercise in gallantry, paternalistically using the idiom of light flirtation to "popularize" scientific reasoning to a typical woman who cannot rise above sentiment.[78] The gentleman does, to be sure, try to engage in gallantry out of incurable habit. "It will never be said of me," he comments on the first evening, "that in an arbor, at ten o'clock in the evening, I talked of philosophy to the most beautiful woman I know."[79] But talk he does, at sophisticated conceptual levels, and that is because the marquise insists that she is capable of "enjoying intellectual pleasures." She repeatedly demonstrates her intelligence by grasping truths, by countering her interlocutor's speculations with skepticism, and by raising questions that move the conversation in fascinating directions. In this alternative view science requires rational clarity, but the essential measure of its "truth" is whether it gives "pleasure" to the imagination. Its beauty lies in the elegant simplicity of its laws, and in the apparently infinite diversity of forms and colors that clothe them. Science becomes a process of "imaginative picture making."[80] What we are witnessing, Shank emphasizes, is the aestheticizing not just of the presentation of science to neophytes, but of the basic process of scientific understanding.

Much of this is convincing, but when Shank follows DeJean's lead he pushes his argument too far. In the fusion of the aesthetic and scientific that we have lost, he argues, we find a mixed-sex partnership in "knowledge production"; and that in turn connects the text to "the feminist pedagogical project" of the era, whose key text was Poullain de la Barre's *On the Equality of the Two Sexes.*[81] "Production" carries the wrong connotations; it cannot be detached from labor, the disciplined making of a product. At issue, I should stress again, is not intelligence itself; it is a measure of Fontenelle's mastery of dialogue in its polite form that he gives us no reason to conclude that the marquise is any less intelligent than the gentleman (and she often seems quite a bit more sensible). The issue is the socially and culturally acceptable performance of intelligence. From that standpoint, Shank undervalues the ways in which gender and status reinforced each other to ban the appearance of labor in the social aesthetic of play. From the outset the marquise is assured that, though she will have to "[apply] herself a bit," it will not be necessary to "penetrate" obscure matters "by means of concentrated thought." She needs only "the same amount of concentration that must be given to *The Princess of Clèves* in order to follow the plot closely and understand all its beauty." She understands spontaneously, only "conceiv[ing] of those things of which she can't help but conceive."[82] Her imagination not only aestheticizes the suns and planets; it makes them dramatic characters she can approve or disapprove of. We have to keep in mind that it is not only the gallant gentleman who worries that these ungallant conversations will be an embarrassment to him. The marquise is no less concerned about her performance, even though it is physically removed from *le monde* and there is no one but the gentleman to witness it. When he proposes to make an outline of the zodiac in her garden sand, she shrinks back on the grounds of impropriety; "it would give my garden a scholarly air which I don't want it to have."[83]

In his Preface Fontenelle explained that he had tried to find "a middle ground . . . where it's neither too dry for men and women of the world nor too playful for scholars"; and that is precisely what he accomplished. He does not fuse the two worlds; he uses his middle ground to dance with such agility from one to the other that one hardly notices that he's dancing. "I hold her a scholar," the gentleman writes to his friend in the opening letter, "because of the extreme ease with which she could become one."[84] Left unsaid—but obvious to his audience—is that she could not become one without shedding her entire social identity. Women had to embody the principle of *aisance* in its full purity by not betraying any sign of labor in their way of thinking and speaking in their own world, detached as it was from occupational life. That was why, despite their intellectual equality and, in some respects, superiority, their presentation of self had to remain distinctly feminine. Scudéry warned the *salonnière* that she must avoid "speaking with a certain affected simplicity, which smells of the child," but also that, if she did not wish to appear "bizarre" by playing the man, she must not "[pass] judgment decisively on some difficult question."[85] Scudéry's point was not that difficult questions were beyond women's mental capacity, but that women could not appear to have worked through them to a conclusion. The man whose speech betrayed intellectual labor invited ridicule. The woman who committed such a violation of the social aesthetic undermined the group claim to unique status more directly. Her resulting stigmatization as a "learned lady" (*femme savante*) threatened her with a kind of social death.

The imagined world of *honnêteté* was a community of frictionless exchange, immune to destabilization because its speech could neither offend nor shock nor stray into argument. In principle, the kind of critique that would make a society and polity self-critical was banned. Women were the keepers of the ban.

Chapter 2

Poullain de la Barre: Feminism, Radical and Polite

From 1673 to 1675 François Poullain de la Barre published three books arguing that women were by nature as intelligent as men.[1] From our perspective other early modern feminist thinkers reflect the inhibitions of their times in one way or another, but Poullain seems to crash through his times to offer us nothing less than the full-blown agenda of feminism in our own era.[2] And yet, though we now have a better historical understanding of the intellectual chemistry that produced Poullain's feminism, the compound itself still seems to leap out of its historical context and address contemporary feminism in its own terms, without that quality of strangeness, requiring a strenuous leap of the imagination, with which we expect seventeenth-century thought to confront us.

That Poullain's historical significance remains less than fully contextualized is not due simply to the fact that he has acquired iconic status. The more serious problem is that, in part because he failed to command the public attention he sought, the historical traces of his life are so meager and scattered.[3] What we have is the skeletal narrative of a life: his birth into a Parisian family of the judicial nobility in 1648; theological studies at the Sorbonne from 1663 to 1666, almost certainly in the expectation of pursuing a university career; his disillusionment with Scholasticism and discovery of an alternative source of certainty in Cartesian philosophy; his withdrawal from Paris to village curacies in Picardy from 1680 to 1688; his relocation in December 1688, as a Protestant, to Geneva, where he married, raised a family, taught at the *collège*, and died on May 4, 1723.[4]

Despite the paucity of detail, we can push farther in historicizing Poullain's thought. There are, first, the autobiographical details *in* the texts, which tell us more about the experiential meaning, and particularly the social meaning, of Poullain's feminism than has been recognized. This biographical inquiry in turn opens another avenue of approach. To date, the texts have been read largely as exercises in formal argument. But we can also read them as sites for social and cultural representations in seventeenth-century discourses, hence recovering meanings that are more diffuse but also more resonant than formal argumentation. Of the various relevant discursive contexts, the most important for our purposes is the discourse of *honnêteté*.

On the Equality of the Two Sexes and his second book, *On the Education of Ladies for the Behavior of the Mind in the Sciences and in Mores*, are two distinct textual moments in a fusion of Cartesian philosophy and the discourse of *honnêt-eté*. Together they reveal the affinities that made the fusion possible, and the tensions that made it problematic as a point of departure for modern feminist thought. The second text—the *Education*—is not, as is generally assumed, a straightforward reiteration and elaboration of Poullain's basic position that "the mind has no sex," but a tentative moment in turning a utopian vision of gender equality, offered as a regulative idea, into a strategy for realizing that vision in a specific social milieu.[5] When we consider the two texts in sequence, we find Poullain shifting tack. One way—an emphatically historical way—to understand the contextually unique radicalism of *Equality* is to watch Poullain turning the salon culture's reconfiguration of gender distinctions in a new and startlingly unconventional direction. Not only did he draw radical implications from the discourse's devaluation of certain kinds of male intellectual labor; pulling the discourse out beyond the salons' well-guarded walls of social exclusiveness, he combined it with Cartesianism to project a sweeping transformation of the social organization of labor. As compelling as his argument may have been as an exercise in Cartesian method, however, it was problematic in application to a culture whose norms of exclusiveness rested on the banning of labor, including intellectual labor, from the practice of a thoroughly aestheticized art of leisure. It was one thing to appropriate those norms for the egalitarian vision in *Equality*, but quite another to come to terms with the issue of labor in *Education*.

Poullain was even more radical in context than has been assumed, and at the same time more distant from us, less familiar to us, and less detached from the constraints of his contexts than his application of Cartesian rationalism, taken by itself, might suggest.[6] This split profile tells us a great deal about the ways in which even the most radical applications of Cartesian doubt were socially refracted, and thereby constrained, as they became instruments of social critique; and about the inescapable entanglements of gender with class and, more important for our purposes, with status in the question of female emancipation in the ancien régime.[7]

Conversion

Sometime in the late 1660s, when Poullain was twenty or a little older and was pursuing his doctoral studies, he underwent a "conversion" (his term), both in his intellectual orientation and in his social persona. The intellectual turn is described in the fifth (and final) "conversation" of *Education*. Poullain came to realize that, outside the narrow academic career track he had entered at age nine, "everything" he knew was "of no use to the world," since "cultivated people (*les honnestes gens*) cannot endure our way of reasoning." Finding himself in "no little anguish," and listening to the advice of "certain people (he) talked to," he resolved to "start all over again." A "friend" took him to a meeting at which "a Cartesian spoke about something concerning the human body." Having already come to regard the Scholastic "sciences" as "particularly distasteful," he found the lecturer's "principles" so "simple" and so "true" that he "could not fail to agree with them." For six months he followed Descartes's "method," learning more than he had learned in the previous six years. One of his discoveries was that the "scholastic" view of women "as monsters, and as very much inferior to men," was completely wrongheaded.[8]

There is something stylized about this recollection, echoing as it does Descartes's autobiographical account of his "search for truth" in *A Discourse on Method*. We have reason to suspect that in his ardent identification with Descartes the young Poullain had cast his recent conversion to fit a received mold. And yet the details are revealing of Poullain's own experience. We learn that he came of age at a time when Scholastic learning, still deeply entrenched in the Parisian university faculties, faced a mounting challenge from the new natural philosophy and its offshoots. As in the case of many other educated young men in the 1660s, Poullain's disillusionment with Scholasticism and his attraction to the Cartesian alternative fed off each other. The study of Descartes was not simply another intellectual experiment; it proved to be a definitive way out of a personal crisis, an escape from the anguish of disillusionment. Having lost the sense of purpose he had had since childhood, he found a new one. This intense awareness of shedding an outworn tradition and embracing a new mission drives the feminist argument in *Equality* and the subsequent texts. Poullain's reasoning was that if Cartesian clarity can prevail on the subject of the equality of the sexes, which is "more prone to prejudice than any other subject," it can prevail against "custom" in any area of social life. He would show that women in their current state were not what "nature" intended them to be; they were what arbitrary male domination—the abuse of superior force, sanctioned by mere custom—had made them. Once emancipated they would prove to be men's equals, and perhaps in some ways their superiors, in every kind of work requiring rational intelligence.[9]

The recollection also suggests that, if Poullain's intellectual commitment to Descartes entailed a measure of solitary reading and meditation, it nonetheless took place in, and required, a juxtaposition of social milieus to be found only in seventeenth-century Paris. It was conversations, friends, and at least one public meeting that led him to Descartes. The young Poullain was from a well-established family, if not an especially prominent one.[10] At least from talk with friends and from his own reading, he was familiar with the conversational culture of the salons.[11] He was acutely aware that the turn to Cartesianism from Scholasticism was social as well as intellectual, from the emphatically male clerical society of the Sorbonne to the very different world of men and women gathered in the salons. Academic study, he writes in *Equality*, stamps men with "rudeness" and "crudity (*grossièreté*) in their manners": if scholars "want to go back into polite society (*le monde*) and cut a good figure there, they have to go to the school of ladies to learn politeness, the art of pleasing (*complaisance*), and everything else that is essential today to polished and cultivated people (*honnestes gens*)."[12] In the first conversation in *Education*, Poullain counters the stereotype of the haughty and affected *salonnière*, used to such satirical effect in Molière's *The Learned Ladies*, with the image of a "learned lady" who is "natural, polite, and easy to be with." A few pages later he makes this appeal to the ladies:

> What a singular service you and women like you could render our learned men (*sçavans*)! By admitting them into your circles, you would give them a beautiful means of civilizing what they know; by making them part of your conversations, you would communicate that gentleness that they lack and that is distinctive of you. You would inspire in them insensibly that gallant and cultivated (*honnêtes*) air that makes you so lovable; and thus ridding them of what is hard and crude in them, you would put them in a position to be well received in *le monde*.[13]

His conviction of transformation notwithstanding, Poullain is perhaps best understood as a liminal figure. Thoroughly alienated from academic culture, he had probably not been assimilated enough into the empire of women to be aware of dissonances between its self-representation and its actual social practices. He was something of a naïf; enraptured by the ideal of *the honnête femme*, he made its radical revaluation of women integral to his reconstrual of his own social self.

The Mind Has No Sex

How did Poullain blend the discourse of *honnêteté* with his Cartesian argument in *Equality*, and with what results? The first time it is used in *Equality*, the phrase "the mind has no sex" stands alone, as the marginal header for several paragraphs. There is a sense, of course, in which the statement is eminently Cartesian. Descartes replaced the Aristotelian teleological distinction between a vegetative and a sensitive soul with his famous mind/body dualism. His dichotomy was ontological; there was matter, which he defined as having extension, and there was the single, unitary soul or "mind," the thinking substance with no extension. The existence of the mind is not, in principle, contingent on anything with extension, including the human body. In this immaterial mind Descartes found our innate certainty—our clear and distinct ideas—of our own existence, of the existence of God, of the immaterial nature of our intellection, and of pure extension. Since the mind thus conceived is cleanly detached from corporeal substance, physical differences between human bodies, including sexual differences, are irrelevant to it.

In the passages Poullain's phrase introduces, however, we soon learn that the mind has no sex only when it is "considered independently." Having established the independence of "mind" as a concept, Poullain immediately proceeds to consider embodied minds, which differ despite the natural sameness and "equality" of all minds as such. He observes that "difference" between male and female minds is to be explained by variations not only in education and environment, but also in "the constitution of the body." This, too, was an eminently Cartesian step. Descartes's very insistence on the mind/body dualism had made it imperative to explain mind/body interaction. He did so by developing a psychophysiology based on a radically mechanistic conception of the body, including the brain. It was this new paradigm of the human body—a paradigm Descartes posed squarely against the received wisdom of scholastic medicine, despite its numerous borrowings from that tradition—that first attracted Poullain and others to the new philosophy. The human body, we should recall, was the subject of the "Cartesian lecture" Poullain attended with a friend.[14]

How did sexual differences affect the workings of the mind? On this subject Descartes's texts offered very little guidance. Their presentation of the new paradigm was fragmentary and simply ignored sexual differences. Hence in the years following Descartes's death in 1650, Cartesians had ample room to draw a wide spectrum of inferences. Most of them significantly qualified the principle of the sexless equality of minds by emphasizing that the physical weakness of women had its corollary in their mental weakness, usually explained by the softness of their brain fibers. Poullain derived from Descartes's mechanistic paradigm a quite different view of the mind/body interaction; and, no less important, he made the normative implications of the discourse of *honnêteté* integral to his use of Cartesian doubt to mount a radical critique of the social status quo. Women, he argued, "have an advantageous disposition for the sciences":

> Their brain (*cerveau*) is constituted in such a way as to receive even faint and almost imperceptible impressions of objects that escape people of a different disposition. . . . The warmth that accompanies this disposition brings it about that objects make a more lively impression on a woman's mind, which then takes them in and examines them more acutely and develops the images they leave as it pleases. From this it follows that those who have a great deal of imagination and can look at things more efficiently and from more vantage points are ingenious and inventive, and find out more after a single glance than others after long contemplation. They are able to give an account of things in a pleasant and persuasive way,

finding instantly the right turn of phrase and expression. Their speech is fluent and expresses their thoughts to best advantage. . . . Discernment and accuracy (*le discernement et la justesse*) are natural qualities [of a woman's disposition]. . . . It could be said that this kind of temperament is best fitted for social intercourse, and since man was not made to spend all his time shut away in his study, we should somehow have greater respect for those who have a superior talent for communicating their thoughts in an agreeable and effective way (*agréablement et utilement*).[15]

In Poullain's variation on Descartes's psychophysiology, what he called the distinctive "constitution" of the female brain was not a matter of softer fibers. Recent discoveries in anatomy, he argued in another passage, proved that male and female brains were "exactly the same." The gendered difference lay in the fact that women's sense organs were "more delicate," and hence that the images imprinted on their brains by their imaginations were stronger. Poullain's radical step lay in assuming that this "more lively" image-making capacity, rather than constricting or overwhelming women's capacity for abstract thought, gave them the intellectual "advantage." Taking up what was sometimes implied in the discourse of *honnêteté*, he made psychophysiological "delicacy"—the putative source of women's intellectual weakness—the source of their cognitive strength. A woman's more delicate sensations and stronger imagistic faculty did not make her mind less capable of rational intellection; they gave her thought more clarity, and in that sense more vigor. At the same time Poullain derived from women's physical delicacy and powers of imagination a natural "eloquence" and persuasiveness. It was not simply that their speech, like their thought, was clear. They had a natural gift for communicating their thoughts in "beautiful" forms: "their message is accompanied by such beauty and grace that it penetrates our minds and opens our heart to them." Female speech was the instrument of a superior social intelligence; one might even say that it was the social act intrinsic to the workings of that intelligence.

In Poullain's normative revaluation of female powers of cognition and communication, the implications of two meanings of the "natural"—the "natural" reason of Cartesian philosophy and the "natural" quality of the *honnête femme*—reinforced each other. Because women had not been corrupted by the formal education of "the schools," their minds naturally gave assent to self-evident truths to which the learned were blinded. And for the same reason, women's powers of intelligence were plain to see in the natural flow of their speech. Poullain's revaluation of female delicacy did *not*, it should be stressed, give a new lease on life to the conventional paradox that the strength of women lay in their weakness, which required them to develop the wily arts of manipulation and dissimulation summed up in the word "cunning." His claim was that, thanks to the greater delicacy of their sense organs, women tended to have greater clarity of mind in precisely those areas of intellectual labor which, on the traditional assumption, only men could perform. Nor did his appreciation of female eloquence have the effect of reconsigning women to a merely ornamental role, a world of pleasing appearance distinct from the male world of intellectual substance. By aestheticizing communication, women could give the rational thought of the sciences and their professional applications a new social purchase. The truly learned woman, like *the honnête femme*, would "insinuate" her thoughts in the positive sense. Rather than being imposed by sheer force of logic, or by overpowering rhetorical techniques, knowledge would be extended as a gift of beauty from one embodied mind to another. Above all in that sense women's intelligence—unlike the intelligence of the trained rhetor or the pedant—was naturally social.

This reading of *Equality* is confirmed by the actual agenda for social change that Poullain spelled out in his war against "custom" and "prejudice." The emancipation of women, to be sure, was only a means to a larger end, a step in realizing a rational distribution of life chances in the entire social organization of labor. There would be an end to the inheritance and sale of offices requiring education; for men as for women, a "wise selection process" would place every individual in the position for which his aptitudes best suited him. It is hardly surprising, however, that women figured especially large in this vision of careers open to talent; the belief that they were self-evidently unqualified for such positions was the most imposing obstacle to it. In the face of conventional wisdom, Cartesian logic did not suffice. Poullain had to harness to it the gendered inversion of the attributes of intelligence in the discourse of *honnêteté*. And that entailed doing something quite remarkable in the context of late seventeenth-century France—something that would have been virtually unthinkable to interpreters of *honnêteté* like Méré, Scudéry, and Saint-Évremond. The natural attributes of thought and speech that Poullain extolled were precisely the ones that had made women the guardians of an exclusive, self-referential code, marked above all by freedom from the constraints and indeed the appearance of labor. But now those attributes became women's qualifications for entering a world of labor that had been closed to them. Intellectual labor was no longer a social stigma, an activity threatening social derogation; it was the social arena in which emancipated women would prove themselves.

It is important to realize how far Poullain went in pulling the social aesthetic of *honnêteté* down from its elite perch of privileged leisure. Properly educated women, he argued, would be equal or superior to men in all areas of educated labor. He discussed many cases in point, including university teaching, scientific research, medicine, law, theology and clerical offices, military command, and government service. Women, he observed, were less likely to be attracted to fields like algebra, geometry, and optics, but that was not because they lacked the intellectual capacity to excel in them. The nature of their intelligence simply inclined them more to learning that drew them into social interaction, or what he called "the mainstream of conversation."

All this is to say that the utopian impulse in *Equality* took two forms. Inspired by Descartes's radical questioning of the very principle of "authority," Poullain wanted the dead weight of history to accede to the active force of reason. He rejected what he saw as an irrationally organized society, built on the arbitrary and hence unjust historical contingencies that lurked behind appeals to the sanctity of tradition. In a just social structure, education and its rewards would be open to talent and achievement; the ascriptive power of both gender and class would be annulled. Providing women equal access to educated labor would be the first step in a sweeping reorganization of the distribution of life chances—the step that would prove that the entire agenda could prevail over ingrained resistance to it. But in *Equality* female emancipation did not figure simply as the first step in a structural change; it was also the key element—the sine qua non—in Poullain's vision of a cultural transformation, a transvaluation of the values, and ultimately of the terms, of human exchange that informed the social exercise of authority. Here is where a coded social aesthetic became integral to a utopian logic. The issue of intellectual clarity aside, the aesthetic qualities of female intelligence would make work itself the social exchange it ought to be. Because they communicated so effectively as, and so effectively to, embodied minds, women would bring a new efficacy to the entire range of educated offices and professions.

With this positive evaluation of women's natural eloquence and powers of persuasion Poullain went far beyond echoing the ideal of *honnêteté*. He redirected the ideal to engage and change the social world it had been so intent on keeping at a distance. While the discourse of *honnêteté* challenged distinctly male forms of verbal authority—in the university, in the law court, in the pulpit, and so on—by excluding and ridiculing them, it also implicitly accepted their legitimacy outside its own space. Poullain sought to change those forms; he would humanize them—make them less acts of imposition and more acts of gentle attention and persuasion, as in pleasing conversation—by feminizing them.

Cartesianism for Ladies

In *Education* Poullain undertook to explain the "new method" for women's education that he had promised in *Equality*. His philosophical and psychophysiological arguments for gender equality did not change, but he opted for a new rhetorical strategy. Rather than simply continuing to address the reader directly, he made himself one of four characters engaged in a series of dialogues tuned to the standards of polite conversation. The result was a rather dogmatically Cartesian variation on the Socratic dialogue, ending in entirely predictable agreement.

Having failed to elicit a response with *Equality*, Poullain hoped the dramatic form of the dialogue would bring him more success. His literary imagination was not up to the task; there is nothing particularly dramatic, much less gripping, about these dialogues. In fact it must be said that, compared with the lively and playful repartee in Fontenelle's *Conversations on the Plurality of Worlds*, published eleven years later, Poullain's conversations are flat and, ironically for a Cartesian, didactic. And yet they are not without revealing tensions. *Education* was meant to show how the intellectual emancipation of women might find a beginning, a point of departure, in his own society. In creating his interlocutors, he gave that beginning a recognizable social location and sought to dispel the skepticism he could expect to confront there. Though the conversations advance to a forgone conclusion, there are moments along the way when, with a close reading, the tensions in his efforts to fuse Cartesianism and the discourse of *honnêteté* become audible.

This is not to deny that *Education*, like *Equality*, attests to strong affinities between the two discourses. They both offered alternatives to the institutionalized forms of expertise in seventeenth-century France.[16] Both assumed that the mind achieves a certain clarity and precision when it is freed from the pedagogical tyranny of "the schools" and follows its natural inclinations. They shared an undisguised contempt for the obscurantist jargon of Latinist scholarship and a preference for simple, clear use of the vernacular in print as well as in speech. They found ridiculous the conventional scholar's knee-jerk appeals to canonical texts and especially to the ancients. In rejecting such appeals as mere "pedantry," and in questioning what they saw as manipulative and intimidating forms of public and private communication, they opposed blind submission to "authority"; and at least to that extent, they both endowed individuals with a measure of intellectual autonomy.

But there are tensions, and these are reflected in the very dramatic structure of the conversations. Poullain introduces his dramatis personae with quick sketches, as in a play bill. There is Sophia, a "lady" (*Dame*) who is "so accomplished and so wise that she can be called wisdom itself"; Eulalie, a young lady "who speaks well, with ease and grace"; Timander, "an *honnête homme* who is persuaded by reason and good sense"; and Stasimachus, "the peacemaker, or the enemy of division, quarrels, and pedantry."[17] From the opening scene, when Stasimachus joins the other three at Sophia's home, we learn that he is the author of *Equality*. He has already guided his friend Sophia to the new philosophical wisdom, which she states with a simple and sometimes blunt certainty that may have unsettled some readers. Timander, like Stasimachus, has freed himself from the "pedantic" schooling to which he was subjected; but, as his objections to his friend's arguments make clear, he is noticeably less free of conventional social wisdom. With Sophia as his exemplar of an intellectually emancipated woman, and with Timander alternately aiding him and raising objections, Stasimachus undertakes the reeducation of the young Eulalie. The process begins with her initiation into Cartesian doubt, and culminates with his outlining an order of study for her, from geometry textbooks to several of Descartes's philosophical texts. Because she is naïve in the positive sense—because her natural gifts of comprehension and speech have not been corrupted by conventional formal education—Eulalie is an able and willing pupil. By the end she has joined Sophia on the path to wisdom. Having surpassed Timander in intellectual emancipation, she declines his invitation to be as open with her as Stasimachus is with Sophia— though at points along the way she has shared his misgivings about adopting the new philosophy.[18]

One might expect the educational program of *Education* to be designed to realize the larger emancipatory agenda of *Equality*—the transformation of the world of educated employments into a meritocracy that would be as open to talented women as it was to talented men. That is not the case. In *Equality* Poullain had explained why, despite his egalitarian convictions, he looked to "distinguished ladies" to prove that women could be as rationally educated as men. He was careful to note that his "observations about the qualities of mind" could "easily be made about women of any class," and that "the whole sex" was "capable of scientific study"; but because the "ladies" had "opportunity" and "external advantages," they were able to overcome the "indolence" induced by "pleasure and idleness" and demonstrate their intellectual equality with men. There is an implicit paradox here; if leisure was a habit that "women of quality" had to overcome if they were to undertake "study," it was also the sine qua non for study. Her advantages made Eulalie a promising subject of Stasimachus's guidance because they exempted her from the work burdens that left most women with neither the time nor the energy to educate themselves. Poullain would have denied that he was abandoning the larger goal; he saw himself taking the first step—the only step that was practically possible under the circumstances. And yet there is a yawning silence in the text, a disconnection between it and its predecessor. The author of *Equality*, one might assume, would feel compelled to note in *Education*, if only in passing, that the Eulalies of French society would some day enter the world of offices and professions, or at least that their education would eventually be organized with that prospect in mind. The text offers no hint of such a prospect. The silence marks Poullain's need to adapt his argument. The most radical change he had called for—his virtually utopian vision of a rational restructuring of social access to educated labor—could not be reconciled with the norms and taboos of an elite whose self-validation lay precisely in imagining itself hovering above the social organization of labor. Left unspoken is the irony that made this adaptation necessary: in the only social and cultural milieu that made Poullain's first step possible, the next step was unthinkable.

Less obvious is the fault line in the text between two different concepts of selfhood. In the relational selfhood attributed to the *honnête homme* (or *femme*), self-formation and self-validation require a kind of hypersociability, leaving hardly any room for the introspection that distances an inner self from the particular society and culture in which it is immersed. Descartes's philosophical calling was a reformulation of the reflective idea of self-formation as an "inner" ascent to wisdom through the meditative labor of "spiritual exercises." It was indebted especially to Stoicism, and perhaps influenced by Ignatius Loyola's *Spiritual Exercises* as well. Only with that context in mind can we understand what Descartes meant to convey when he wrote of "meditations" and offered "rules for the direction of the mind." He was calling his readers to engage in reflective intellectual labor, to be distinguished sharply from the mere social "pleasures" that Saint-Évremond extolled.[19]

Poullain did not, it should be stressed, evade the possibility that the reflective self of Cartesian philosophy was incompatible with the relational self of the culture of *honnêteté*. In fact he might be said to have confronted it quite directly. He did so, however, by focusing not on the labor that reflectivity required, but on the commitment to radical critique that it might entail. Could one be an uncompromising Cartesian doubter and an *honnête femme*—or, for that matter, an *honnête homme*—at the same time? Descartes himself had been notoriously cautious on this issue. The first maxim in his own "provisory code of morals," outlined in *A Discourse on Method*, offered a kind of compromise between critique and acceptance of the status quo. So long as he was on the path to truth, he would continue to "obey the laws and customs of [his] country," adhering to the faith in which he had been raised, and conforming his "practice" to the "general consent" of "the most judicious." In his own attempt at a Socratic dialogue—the unfinished *Search for Truth*—Descartes characterized the ideal seeker after Cartesian truth as an *honnête homme*.[20] He seems to have been using the phrase in its literal sense, to evoke a sensible and upright man. To judge by his own life, the *honnête homme* he had in mind need not be the totally socialized participant in conversational play that the term *honnête* had come to imply by the 1670s. Descartes had preferred Holland to Paris. In that commercial country, "in the midst of a great crowd actively engaged in business," he could enjoy the "conveniences" of "the most populous cities" and yet live "as solitary and as retired as in the midst of the most remote deserts."[21] Living in (relative) solitude, far removed from the salon culture as well as the learned societies of Paris, Descartes had simply avoided the demands of the new social aesthetic.

Poullain's Cartesianism was necessarily much more tension-ridden. Unlike Descartes, the author of *Equality* extended the principle of radical doubt from epistemology and natural philosophy to a critique of the social order. By the very nature of the imagined setting of *Education*, its interlocutors could hardly avoid asking whether a consequential application of social critique was compatible with the social identities they brought to its exercise. To judge by his initiation of Eulalie into Cartesian doubt, Stasimachus's answer is uncompromising. One of his conditions for undertaking her reeducation is that she be prepared to shed completely the habit of blind deference to authority that she originally learned as a child in relation to her parents and has continued to practice in submitting to "prejudice" in all its forms, including the authority attributed to superior social status, public rhetoric, and esoteric expertise. The "discernment" she will acquire will make her aware that conventional authority is nothing more than unexamined "custom," a social construction by which mere "opinion" perpetuates its dominance.[22] Eulalie, in other words, is being asked to undo an entire process of socialization. At issue was not simply the behavior, or "practice," that Descartes seemed to have in mind; it was speech as the externalization of thought, the act of asserting or withholding the inner self of the Cartesian rationalist in the social presentation of self. Should one's speech be devoted to helping others along the path to Truth, or should it simply be fashioned to "please" them, even if this *complaisance* required keeping silent about truths that might "shock" people and thereby explode the aesthetic illusion of the group?

This is the question that occasions the most obvious moment of tension in the text, at the beginning of the second conversation. Faced with the prospect of ridding herself of all untested opinions, Eulalie ("smiling") asks whether that means that we "have to give up the whole world," and whether there is not a "disadvantage" to "such a general renunciation." Timander joins in: will not the result be "a terrifying solitude (*une solitude épouvante*)"—a life spent seeking the truth "as if we were the only people in the world, with no possibility of ever talking about it to anyone?" At first Stasimachus remains uncompromising. It is not "I" but "reason," he tells Eulalie, that demands the renunciation. There is no middle ground; one either "submit[s] completely" or "withdraw[s] completely." Timander's concern about solitude can be dismissed as "excessive panic." It is Eulalie who begins to find a way around this stark choice. She imagines a kind of "conversation" that "opens the mind" with a mutual exercise in instruction, not possible in "the privacy of our own studies."[23]

Eulalie's remark prompts Stasimachus to resolve the issue by advocating a dual social existence, at once withdrawn from social custom and acquiescent to its demands. Stasimachus reminds his friends that, though we cannot suppress thought, we can "avoid argument" by remaining masters of "our speech and action." The proper strategy is to "consider [the truth] as if you were alone whether you are in fact alone or with other people." There are two kinds of knowledge: the "feelings and thoughts" we seek through "philosophy," which we "keep to ourselves" in the face of custom; and the "external" knowledge manifested in "outward actions," which is "of society" and "concerns the public and intercourse between people." One can live in both knowledge-worlds without being false to either. But isn't it "counterfeit and dissimulation," Eulalie asks, to be "able to speak other than the way one thinks"? Though at first Stasimachus remains uncompromising, he goes on to reassure her that there is a middle ground. Speech in society at large need not be an act of total conformity to opinions one no longer accepts. You can "insinuate" the truths to others, though you must proceed ever so carefully, keeping in mind the need to "moderate the dose" and "add honey to the medicine."[24] Stasimachus elaborates on this need for caution in the fifth conversation. When dealing with opinionated people, "we shouldn't show off our intelligence or reason constantly in their presence, because they will find us trying." We must take stock of others very carefully, "become accustomed to turning [our] thoughts so well that they always have several faces"; and "take more pain to excuse [the opinionated] than to condemn them."[25]

In a sense these exchanges deflect our attention from the actual social site of the problem. Poullain uses the phrase "the whole world" to refer to society at large, not to the elite society of salon conversation. For the most part, when he insists on the need to choose between intellectual independence and conformity he pits the individual against the mass. There are the "vast numbers of people" who are immersed in custom and opinion and manipulated by authority; and there are the rare individuals who can rise above that miasma. On one level, this abstract dichotomy between an imagined philosophical elite and the uninitiated mass allows Poullain to sidestep the immediate social question: whether Cartesian autonomy can be reconciled with the imperatives of conformity *within* an elite. Can the individual inject Cartesian critique, with all the egalitarian implications Poullain has drawn from it, into the rarified world of polite conversation without questioning one's interlocutors' very logic of self-legitimation and thereby making herself an outcast?

If the question is deflected, it is nonetheless there, posed not only by the characters and the setting Poullain has chosen, but also by the echoes of the social aesthetic of *honnêteté* in his framing of their choices. In the "world" in which his characters circulate there can be no open "argument"; it is forbidden to be "trying"; a certain serene equilibrium must be maintained within the constraints of custom. We can think of the unresolved tension at several levels. The self that withdraws into a Cartesian state of nature, where disembodied reason reigns, has to coexist, very uneasily, with the embodiment of self in the intensely and relentlessly socialized form of *honnêteté*. The Cartesian natural self connects immediately with objective (i.e., universal) truth. In that task the mastery of a social aesthetic—the mastery required to achieve self-validation within the community of *honnêtes gens*—becomes in principle an obstacle, though it may be unavoidable. A Cartesian philosophical conversation is about ascertaining and communicating truth; that aim may very well collide with the need to affirm the cohesion and harmony of a community, to practice an art whose claim to exclusiveness lies precisely in subordinating the "search for truth" to the shared appreciation of a codified and ritualized verbal exchange. Ultimately it is the difference between reasoning as a kind of internal dialogue and reason as the instrument of an emphatically other-directed sociability—between the spiritual self, as autonomous interiority, and the self externalized in relentlessly social speech.

Poullain does, to be sure, try to bridge these dichotomies with his little circle of three or four philosophical friends. In this context speech can be social in another sense; friends use it to aid each other in the search for truth. They help each other strip away the mere appearances, the chimeras of authority, in which society at large remains wrapped. There is something quite radical about this way of giving Cartesian truth-seeking a social dimension. By bonding both Sophia and Eulalie in friendship with Stasimachus, Poullain contradicts the longstanding assumption that truly "philosophical" or "spiritual" friendship is possible only between males. That defiance of conventional wisdom is punctuated at the end; it is Timander's intellectual inhibitions, and not Eulalie's, that explain why he fails to draw her into such a friendship. The circle of philosophical friends, however, is more a retreat from the demands of polite sociability than a base from which to challenge them. In their larger social world, the friends can only exercise critique obliquely, with a kind of conspiratorial insinuation. And, while that constraint applies to men as well as to women, it is women who have the most to lose. If she keeps within Stasimachus's recommended limits, the *honnête femme* runs the risk that her much-admired gifts for aestheticizing thought and speech will come to be seen, and resented, as a new form of manipulative dissimulation, still gendered female. Violating the limits—openly asserting the power of critique in intellectual argument—would not only condemn individual women to terrifying solitude. *Honnêtes femmes* could assert the power of critique—could speak that power— only at the cost of sacrificing their normative role in a discourse extending them a kind of intellectual equality and, in some respects, superiority. There is a sense in which their newly acquired capacity for critique lands them in a kind of social nowhere; there is no social space for it in the very world that puts a new value on female intelligence.

Underlying this equivocal solution to the problem of critique, though more obliquely recorded in *Education*, is the tension between a Cartesian self and the self of *honnêteté*. Can Cartesian radical doubt be integrated somehow into the aestheticized play of conversation? The difficulty of doing so is acknowledged, very discreetly, in Madeleine de Scudéry's imagined conversation on "politeness." In the course of advocating a kind of Cartesian doubt, Clitandre remarks that he "dare not name [the philosopher] before the ladies, although we are in a time when many beauties (*belles*) are amused to know the new philosophy"—and then proceeds to name him. Has not Descartes, he asks, disabused us of the long-held illusion that we see the same "star" in the morning as in the evening? When Théanor reminds him that Descartes also taught the doctrine of metempsychosis, Clitandre lays the blame for that folly on the great man's disciples. Théanor concedes the point; Descartes's "doctrine" could not be so "foolish," because "his morality (*morale*) is so beautiful."[26] The philosopher can be named in this circle, and at least some of his ideas can be discussed there, because he is, after all, an *honnête homme*.

The reference to the stars is revealing. There were salon women who engaged Descartes's concept of rational agency, but it was primarily his discoveries in natural science that became popular in the salons from the 1750s onward.[27] Fontenelle's *Conversations* suggests how the social aesthetic accommodated Cartesian science. In *Education* Poullain sought a middle ground between Fontenelle's exercise in the instructive diversion of conversational play and an ascetic insistence on strenuous spiritual labor. Stasimachus seems to provide this via media when he promises, early in the first conversation, that the "quest for truth" will bring a "pure and complete joy" that is spiritual, in that it "has almost nothing to do with the body," and yet also aesthetic. "Nature," he assures his friends, endows Truth with "beauties and graces that ought to render it adorable to all men." Hence there is no danger that women educated in the new philosophy will be corrupted by "meditation and study" and will succumb to the attendant boorishness of the "pedant." For "women who have leisure and means," Stasimachus claims, his method of studying science will provide "a gentle and pleasant intellectual exercise"—intellectually challenging, to be sure, but entirely compatible with "their usual diversions."[28] The rest of the text is sprinkled with similar assurances. With his method, "science" will provide his friends with "a gentle and pleasant intellectual exercise." Eulalie will find it "easy" to "withdraw" into herself and "admit nothing that is not clear and of which one does not have some idea." In the fourth conversation, Eulalie agrees; the new science would indeed be "a gentle, easy exercise for ladies."[29]

Does all this mean that the *honnête femme* can avoid the rigors of meditative labor? When Stasimachus extolls the ease with which the search for truth can be pursued, he means that the knowledge in question is relatively accessible. He is assuring women of quality that, thanks to the natural simplicity and clarity of Cartesian truth, they will not have to undergo the tedious initiation into obscurantist learning—the dogged training in classical languages, logic, formal rhetoric, and so on—that produces the pedant.[30] Their learning will be entirely compatible with both their femininity and their status as *honnêtes femmes*. At the same time, however, as a Cartesian, Poullain has to insist that, unlike the pseudoknowledge dispensed by learned authorities, truth is not something one can passively receive from someone else; it has to be acquired in a process of self-discovery, an exercise in reflective autonomy, and that requires no little effort. Hence if the Cartesian search for truth is "agreeable," and indeed a "pleasure," it is also "serious study," requiring "acute and clear thought." The difference is perhaps clearest in its figurative expressions. While the apt metaphor for *honnête* conversation was a stream flowing by chance, Poullain, following Descartes and the tradition of askesis, figured the search for truth as a purposeful, resolute ascent up a path.[31] Conversation offered a shorter and more "agreeable" path than the reading of massive scholarly tomes, but only if it was conducted in "a methodical and orderly way," as the "labor" of "solid reflection" following "principles and rules." There was no avoiding the fact that we must "labor to become learned."[32]

In Poullain's construal of Cartesian reflexivity, labor in this fundamental sense is the sine qua non for intellectual and spiritual autonomy. The required commitment to it is implicit to his analogy between the acquisition of knowledge and the acquisition of property. In a particularly interesting exchange at the end of *Education*, Eulalie and Stasimachus confront the possibility that, by giving preference to Cartesian philosophy, they are simply accepting a new authority. If they are disciples of Descartes, can their search for truth really be said to be an exercise in autonomy? Stasimachus assures his pupil that his loyalty is not to a particular thinker, but to the truth. In her usual laconic manner, Sophie, echoing Descartes, summarizes the point: "If by the force of meditation we gain entry to certain principles, even though we got them from a learned man, they are no longer his but ours. The effort (*peine*) we have given ourselves in understanding them is the price for acquiring them as property (*la propriété*), and they belong to us no less than the goods of the body of which we have become masters through legitimate means."[33] So it is in the "gift" (*donation*) of "sciences," Eulalie agrees; "However eager a person is to make us a part of their knowledge, we must collaborate (*concourir*) with her and accept through our own labor (*travail*) what she wishes to give to us."[34]

In the exchange of verbal gifts in the play of polite conversation, both the giving and receiving must be—or must seem to be—effortless. In the exchange of ideas in Cartesian philosophical conversation, the reception, even more than the giving, is a kind of labor of appropriation. Such labor is the condition for the "natural" freedom of the spirit that Cartesian meditation offers. Having made the point, Poullain does not ask whether natural freedom in that sense can be reconciled with the natural freedom *from* labor to which the discourse of *honnêteté* attaches singular honor. Instead he returns to an earlier theme: that the little circle of philosophical friends must be very cautious in their conversation with others. In these broader circles of conversation, Timander adds, perhaps naïvely, women are better at gift-giving (and receiving) than men. It is not simply that men defer to women out of politeness, without taking their ideas seriously. When joined with "intelligence," "beauty" gives women "such a powerful and absolute ascendancy" over the heart of a scholar that "he keeps nothing secret from them, and far from being as reserved with them as he is with men, he feels an indescribable (*je ne sçai quoi*) force to tell them all he knows." Eulalie agrees, "smiling"; "it is in such encounters that it must be said that there is in men and women not a demon but a corresponding genie."[35] Her remark heightens Timander's disappointment. In her eyes, now open for the first time, he is not, or at least is not yet, worthy of such an encounter. We are left wondering whether the little circle of three philosophical friends—Stasimachus, Sophie, and Eulalie—will eventually become a circle of four.

—

In 1691, in an effort to improve Genevan French (and perhaps to win sponsorship for a school he hoped to establish), Poullain published a little book on proper French usage. He dedicated it to Mme Perdriau, the wife of a Genevan councillor of state. It was in her home that he had been introduced into the city's patrician circles and had met his future wife. He fondly recalled that, in a typical conversation there following a dinner, Mme Perdriau distinguished herself "as much by the importance of the subjects (she) brought up as by (her) reasonings and by the turn and beauty of her expressions." There was nothing more important or beautiful or worthy of our "study" and "conversation," he recalled her saying, than "the truths of salvation"; and so we should "neglect nothing to acquire the purity of the language," since "it can serve to render the truth at the same time more agreeable and more useful."[36]

We glimpse in the dedication a world of bourgeois wealth and domesticity quite different from the Parisian salons. If there is any room in it for the free play of *esprit*, it is subordinate to a sober concern with the purity of religious truth. All the more striking, then, that Poullain made Mme Perdriau a kind of bourgeois— and Calvinist—*salonnière*. We do not know whether his radically unconventional commitment to gender equality survived the transition from Parisian polite sociability to the Genevan variety. But we can be sure that Poullain carried with him to Geneva, along with his Protestant convictions, the social aesthetic with which he had identified when he turned his back on the clerical scholasticism of the Sorbonne. In this bourgeois world of Calvinist religiosity, he retained his Parisian attachment to polite conversation and, with it, his appreciation of the indispensable contribution of women.

The social aesthetic of *honnêteté* played a constitutive role in Poullain's youthful feminist thought, crucial to understanding both the experiential grounding of its radicalism and its implicit tensions and inhibitions. The tensions lurk beneath the surface, in the interstices between formal argument and the uncontested norms and assumptions that shape an intellectual field. There is a sense in which Poullain's concept of equality, "abstract[ed]" from so many intellectual and cultural contexts, is "socially undetermined" and hence "applicable to all social and political practices."[37] But that misses an irony central to his radicalism: that his argument for granting women equal access to educated work roles drew so much of its rhetorical power from a discursive world that made freedom from labor essential to its self-imagining and its claim to incommensurable status. To do justice to the irony, we need to pay due attention to the differences between *Equality* and *Education*. And, however useful it may be to separate out gender and status conceptually, we must reentwine, and indeed reentangle, them if we are to understand the historical contribution of both *honnêteté* and Poullain to early modern feminism.

This is not, it should be stressed, a simple story of the imperatives of status constricting the emancipatory thrust of new thinking about gender. Arguably one of the instructive twists in the story is that a logic of elite status, pervasive in the discourse of *honnêteté*, played a vital role in *making possible* a new logic of gender—one that quite explicitly reversed the construed normative relationship between male and female intelligence. It is hard to see how Poullain could have formulated his concept of gender equality without the salons' efforts to justify themselves as a status community. The denigration of the kinds of intellectual authority represented by male corporate cultures; the revaluation of the relationship between female physical "delicacy" and intellectual strength; the new significance given to "natural" speech as an instrument and emblem of intelligence; the insistence that the value of intelligence and knowledge hinged on their efficacy in forms of social communication emphasizing reciprocity: these new cultural construals of gender were as indispensable to Poullain's breakthrough as was Cartesian method. Poullain did not simply reorient the discourse; he upended it, using gender norms designed to make women the guardians of a culture of leisure to advocate equal access for women to positions in the social division of labor. In his hands the reconstrual of gender norms leapt across the boundary that distinguished an imagined community of leisure, mixing men and women on new terms of communication, from the rest of society. It justified a vision of a society bringing together men and women on new terms of labor conceived as social communication. It is above all this reimagining that makes Poullain a remarkable figure for his time and place.

In this sense Poullain distilled a socially determined discourse into a "socially underdetermined" concept of equality. In *Education*, however, he can be said to have reacknowledged the constraints of the historically determinate. Its "conversations" reflect the fact that, in the social world he was addressing, women's ascent to intellectual equality with men was inseparable from, and indeed contingent on, their fulfilling their assigned role as the exemplars and guardians of an exclusive culture of leisure or, more precisely, of aesthetic play. Because that role was not compatible with the avowed practice of intellectual labor, it also forbade women from using their newfound intellectual equality to engage in critical thinking *as a social practice.* That is the irony that Poullain's blending of Cartesian rationalism and the discourse of *honnêteté* in a polite dialogue could not efface.

We risk limiting ourselves to two equally unacceptable alternatives. One is to discount the ideal of "the feminine" produced by the discourse of *honnêteté,* and by the women who had a central role in its formulation. Since the discourse banned even the appearance of intellectual labor, we might conclude, it has nothing to say to modern feminism. That would be unfortunate; we would deprive ourselves of an instructive historical precedent for reconstruing intelligence in terms of social communication. The precedent anticipates efforts in contemporary feminism to rethink the nature and value of intelligence. But for feminists seeking ways to avoid the no-win choice between equality and difference, its lesson may be as cautionary as it is inspiring. The other extreme would be to hail the female practitioners of *honnêteté* as modern feminists, ignoring their need to avoid even the appearance of engaging in the labor of the mind. That too has its cost, or at least its danger. Can a feminism arguing that women have the same capacity as men to engage in the labor of the mind, and that they ought to have the same right to do so, afford to trace one of its roots back to the ideal of the *honnête femme?* Perhaps; but only if the recovered ideal is handled with extreme care, keeping in mind its double-edged implications. The discourse of *honnêteté* confirms that, even in emphatically patriarchal societies, gender norms can be reoriented in an emancipatory direction. But the discourse is also an object lesson that, particularly when fused with gender distinctions, status imperatives have been insidiously powerful in segregating women from the freedom that labor has come to promise.

Chapter 3

Malebranche and the *Bel Esprit*

"Error is the cause of men's misery." With that somber appraisal of the human condition Nicolas Malebranche opened the first chapter of *The Search After Truth*, a prodigious treatise written in French and published in two parts in 1674–1675.[1] The title was a bold gesture, obviously meant to evoke the search for truth Descartes had recounted in his *Discourse on Method* nearly forty years earlier. The treatise immediately established its author as a presence to be reckoned with in the theology, metaphysics, natural philosophy, and moral philosophy of the final quarter of the seventeenth century. There would be ten editions in his lifetime. He would publish seven more books, all in French, and most addressed to educated audiences extending well beyond academic learning.

To judge by the multiple editions of his texts, Malebranche was a widely read author. Well before his death in 1715, he was regarded as one of the great stylists of French classicism. And yet he might be called an author who rejected authorship, and even as he developed an elegantly lucid and forceful style, he sought to resist the temptation of style. Central to this posture was his equation of French social modernity—the world of polite civility and its paragon, the *bel esprit*—with "effeminacy." Malebranche did not use the term "effeminacy" simply to characterize inclinations to be observed in certain men. He made it emblematic of the form that human corruption was taking in what he saw as the social condition of seventeenth-century modernity. As one of the great system-builders of his era, he gave the concept of effeminacy a new status, as a key term of moral diagnosis set within an all-encompassing philosophical and theological framework.

Montaigne's Sin of Style

The similarities between Malebranche's life and Poullain de la Barre's extend well beyond the fact that the two men were roughly of the same generation (Poullain was ten years younger) and that their first publications appeared within a year of each other. Both were born and came of age in Paris, in families that made their livings in the judicial apparatus of the French state. Both were disillusioned by their theological studies at the Sorbonne, though Malebranche, unlike Poullain, received a degree. Perhaps most striking, the two men had passed through the same crucible; for both, Descartes's new paradigm of the human body had been the point of entry to an intellectual vocation.

And yet it is precisely in their appropriations of Cartesianism that we see their intellectual paths beginning to diverge sharply. We are reminded that in the middle decades of the century Cartesianism was a protean force in French intellectual life.[2] What it generated depended on what it bonded with. Poullain found in Cartesianism a new justification for his commitment to developments in French Protestantism that point directly to the relatively undogmatic and humanistic Christianity of the Enlightenment. Malebranche incorporated his Cartesianism into the most powerful change in the French religious culture of his age: the reassertion of the theological and moral rigorism of the Augustinian tradition.

The Augustinian revival found its most radical expression in Jansenism, a movement defined by its refusal to accept the papal condemnation of several doctrinal statements in Cornelius Jansenius's *Augustinus* (1640). In the efforts to surround the convent at Port-Royal, the Jansenist devotional center, with theological defenses, Antoine Arnauld, Blaise Pascal, and Pierre Nicole were the leading voices. Malebranche steered clear of their theological dissent from orthodoxy, though he had close ties with some Jansenists and owed a considerable intellectual debt to Pascal and Nicole. He numbered Jansenists among the people whose ostentatious "air of piety" gave them a false authority in the world.[3] The publication of his *Treatise on Nature and Grace* in 1680 occasioned a rancorous public feud with Arnauld, the leading Jansenist theologian, that dragged on until the latter's death in 1694. If he found much to criticize in Jansenism, however, he shared its bedrock Augustinian belief in the innate and ineradicable corruption of human nature resulting from original sin. That is why we find him at the opposite extreme from Poullain in seventeenth-century French thinking about *honnêteté* and the questions about gender it raised. To Poullain the *honnête femme* and her male counterpart marked a welcomed process of feminization, a decidedly progressive development. To Malebranche they were emblematic of "effeminacy," a particularly pernicious display of the corruption inherent in postlapsarian man and society.

Malebranche's perception of effeminacy acquires particularly sharp edges, and an especially pointed social specificity, in his critique of Montaigne's *Essays* in Book Two of *The Search After Truth*. The subject of Book Two is the imagination, the faculty that imprisons the mind of postlapsarian man in error and hence is the cause of the misery of sin. Having described in considerable detail the workings of the imagination within Descartes's mind/body paradigm, Malebranche discusses three widely read classical authors as examples of the contagious power that its chimeras exercise through the written word. Though he takes Seneca and Tertullian to task for their all too imaginative rhetorical dazzle, he concedes in his introductory remarks that their prose has "certain beauties" that merit the "universal approbation" they have enjoyed for centuries. "I do not" he continues in the same remarks, "have very much esteem for Montaigne's books" (173). This may be the only sentence in *The Search After Truth* in which Malebranche, just for a moment, tries to sweeten the pill. In fact the ensuing discussion of Montaigne is a vehement and categorical indictment. Malebranche warns readers that the *Essays* are "criminally" seductive. They represent not the true "beauty" of a "solid mind," but the false beauty of an unconstrained imagination, expressed in the "free" and "pleasing" air of longwinded and cunningly vivacious prose. The "pleasure" of reading Montaigne "arises principally from concupiscence, and supports and strengthens only our passions" (184). It is "criminal" in the Augustinian sense: the illicit pleasure of sin.

The critique is meant as a warning to all readers, but it is phrased above all to confront the world of *honnêteté* with its deep complicity in Montaigne's criminality. Malebranche evoked that world at the very start of the critique by attributing to Montaigne "the pride of an honest man (*honnête homme*), if it can be put that way," with "a certain free air," an affected "negligence," and "the air of the world and the cavalier with some erudition"; and again at the end by imputing to him "the beauty, the vivacity, and breadth of the imagination . . . that passes for *bel esprit*" (184, 190). He was turning his irony on the fact that in polite circles Montaigne had become a virtually iconic figure, and that his *Essays* were admired as a model for the kind of free-flowing conversation that adepts at *politesse* liked to contrast with the excessively masculine aggression of the "pedant." Taking particular satisfaction in turning this image on its head, Malebranche charged that, in the case of Montaigne, the gentleman's aversion to pedantry was a false pose; behind it we find a "gentlemanly pedant of quite singular species." The gentleman's apparent nonchalance could not hide the fact that, indulging a vanity puffed up by "false science," Montaigne showered his readers with superfluous literary and historical references (188).

As fierce as it is, this skewing of Montaigne the pedant has a supplementary role in Malebranche's critique. His main purpose was to mold the conventional reservations about this admired but controversial author into an unqualified indictment of the subjectivity he exemplified and its representation in prose. To defenders of the faith it mattered little that Montaigne was in the end a fideist; they feared that his apparently limitless skepticism would poison the minds of simple believers. Jansenists like Pascal could not tolerate his brazenly self-absorbed egotism, though they conceded the lucidity of his language and the brilliance of his psychological insights. Literary critics differed on whether the natural "liberty" of his prose betrayed the "rudeness" of an earlier era or made him one of the language's great stylists. Malebranche echoes these appraisals, but rids them of their ambiguities in an assault combining theological doctrine, philosophical reasoning, and literary judgment. He attributes Montaigne's obsessive representation of his inner life in print to the egotism that makes us all corrupt. A reckless skepticism—the vehicle of that egotism—finds expression in the "vivid turns" of an imagination that has overpowered the author and in turn overpowers his readers (186–87). That overwhelming effect represents, in heightened form, the essential sinfulness of all authors' efforts at "style." It would be "useless to prove . . . in detail," he writes, "that all the various styles ordinarily please us only because of the secret corruption of our heart." But, he continues,

> we shall be able to recognize to some extent that if we like the sublime style, the noble and free air of certain authors, it is because we are vain, loving grandeur and independence. We would also find that this relish we take in the delicacies of effeminate discourses has no other source than a secret inclination for softness and voluptuousness. In a word, it is a certain attraction to what affects the senses, not an awareness of the truth, that causes us to be charmed by certain authors and to be carried away by them almost in spite of ourselves. (185)

What were the female traits exhibited in effeminate discourse? At the start of Book Two Malebranche had explained that one of the principal impediments to the discovery of truth was "the delicacy of the brain fibers." It was "usually found in women," and gave them "great understanding of everything that strikes the senses":

> It is for women to set fashions, judge language, discern elegance and good manners, they have more knowledge, skill, and finesse than men in these matters. Everything that depends upon taste is within their area of competence, but normally they are incapable of penetrating to truths that are slightly difficult to discover. Everything abstract is incomprehensible to them. . . . They consider only the surface of things, and their imagination has insufficient strength and insight to pierce to the heart . . . the style and not the reality suffices to occupy their minds to capacity. (130)

Several of these traits—women's inability to think abstractly or to deal with complex questions, the sensual cast of their cognition and its limitation to the superficial, their concern with fashion—were the standard fare of female stereotypes and had an ancient pedigree. But others evoked the new cultural authority of the *honnête femme*. Women were not only loquacious; they were judges of language. Their "elegance" and "finesse" were not simply personal attributes; they were particular manifestations of the larger competence conceded to their sex in setting standards of taste and judging style.

Considered within the larger argument of Book Two, these concessions of authority to women implied anything but a positive assessment. If Malebranche had read *On the Equality of the Two Sexes* (he almost certainly had not), he would have found Poullain's view that women's physical "delicacy" gave them superior powers of cognition and communication thoroughly wrongheaded. Likewise he would have dismissed Poullain's idealized image of the salons as progressive enclaves in a rigidly traditionalist and hierarchical society and culture. In contrast to Poullain, he employed Descartes's psychophysiological model to demonstrate that, as a rule, the power of women's imaginations made them intellectually and morally weaker than men. They were not only less able to counteract decadent social and cultural modernity; they were its chief agents.

His fellow Oratorian and friend Father Lelong tells us that Malebranche had a "lively imagination" and was well aware of its power. We hear Malebranche's own voice behind his friend's reverential prose: "his imagination was so fertile that he sometimes said that, had he wished to tell stories (*faire des contes*), he would have made them more pleasing than most that we have."[4] Hence there is reason to think that, when Malebranche turned to writing, Montaigne was not simply an example of what to avoid. He was so vehement in condemning Montaigne because he saw too much of himself in him. His struggle against that part of himself is evident, if only obliquely, in *The Search After Truth*. To readers expecting a classic example of a philosophical treatise, the text seems crowded with digressions inappropriate to the genre. Malebranche acknowledged that fault when, at several points in the text, he apologized to readers for having strayed from what should have been a straight-line philosophical argument. But the critique of Montaigne is not a case in point; it may betray Malebranche's own imaginative powers, but it is not a digression. Rather than distracting from the purpose of a philosophical treatise, it gives a pronounced social resonance to its core vision.

The Cartesian Augustinian

A biographer who wanted to take us behind the skeletal facts of Malebranche's youth and early adulthood, into the formative experiences of his interior life, would likely stray into historical fiction. At least in print, Malebranche saw no point in dwelling on the details of his life.[5] He had concluded from his study of church history and biblical criticism in the Oratorian seminary that all historical facts were merely contingent and hence trivial. As a devout priest who condemned Montaigne as a culpable egotist, he could hardly be expected to have laid bare the history of his own subjective life in his published works. Nor can we expect much from the surviving correspondence. Most of it was written when he was a controversial author known throughout Europe, and is devoted largely to the issues preoccupying the learned. For the earlier years we must dig out, and sometimes infer, what we can about his formation from biographical material set down in the immediate aftermath of his death by his friends Father J. Lelong and the Jesuit Father Y. M. André. Both knew the great man well, but as disciples as well as friends. There is more than a scent of hagiography in their accounts.[6] Fortunately, however, both men were also devotees of Cartesian science. They felt obliged—one might almost say compelled—to make the public aware of the obstacles that their friend's bodily "machine" had posed to his work. What they tell us about Malebranche's physical ailments and his ways of dealing with them is not irrelevant to understanding his intellectual development.

If Lelong and André were hagiographers, they were also close to their subject. They drew on conversations with Malebranche in which he reminisced about his life, and so we hear him, behind their reverent prose, mapping its turning points. We find two decisive moments. In 1660, at twenty-two, he entered the Oratory, an order founded in 1616 by Cardinal Pierre de Bérulle, a central figure in the French Counter-Reformation. Malebranche would live in the order's Paris residence on the Rue St Honoré from his ordination in 1664 to his death in 1715. Also in 1664, shortly after he was ordained, his reading of Claude Clerselier's edition of two of Descartes's fragments on the human body occasioned an intellectual reorientation.[7] This latter event might at first appear to have caused a rupture with the religious vocation that had just been sealed; in fact it gave a vital impulse to the direction he had already taken.

While devoting himself to a life of spiritual retirement Malebranche could also, under the order's protection, construct his emphatically Catholic philosophy and defend it in the often brutally polemical theological and philosophical battles of his day. But he could not have foreseen this latter advantage as an eighteen-year-old who did not strike his elders as having a particularly scholarly bent. He entered the order because the patrimony he enjoyed as the youngest son of a well-placed judicial family allowed him to eschew a worldly career. The cornerstone of that patrimony was his father's marriage to Catherine de Lauzon, the daughter of a family already established in the judicial corps of the parlements. Like his older brothers, Nicolas inherited a portion of the family's landed property in its native province, along with the honorific offices and titles attached to it. But the family owed its wealth, status, and influence primarily to its involvement in the French state, whose hierarchy exhibited at once the lineaments of a modern bureaucratic structure and an intricate configuration of old-regime corporate privileges and solidarities. Entry into this state elite required both merit, demonstrated in the study and practice of law, and the wealth and social connections that enabled families to invest in heritable judicial and administrative offices of the monarchy.

Malebranche's father and several of his uncles took this path, as did most of his older brothers.[8]

In the immediate aftermath of the death of both parents in 1658, there may not have been enough family capital to sustain the last two sons in legal careers. In Nicolas's case, however, his physical condition was probably the decisive consideration. The curiously elongated figure we see in portraits of him as an adult suggests, but also hides, his physical deformities. He had been born with what Fontenelle, in his eulogy, described as "a tortuously rounded spine" and "an extremely sunken sternum."[9] Lelong was more graphic; his spine had the shape of an S, and his arms hung down toward the center of his body "like a dangling pendant."[10] These deformities made him a chronically sickly boy, not deemed strong enough to attend one of the Jesuits' *grandes collèges* in Paris until age sixteen. To that point he had been educated at home, under the close guidance of a devout mother.

It is not surprising that Malebranche did not become an academic theologian, despite his having studied theology at the Sorbonne for three years. He had not distinguished himself as a student, probably because, like many other students of his generation, he was aware enough of the new science to find the Sorbonne's mix of Thomism and Aristotelianism unpalatable. Given his family's wealth and influence, he could have secured an ecclesiastical benefice. A maternal uncle occupying the comfortable position of canon in the Cathedral of Notre Dame proposed such an arrangement, but Malebranche demurred. As strongly inclined as he may have been to monastic asceticism, however, he could not withstand its rigors. The Oratory was a happy compromise, less entangled in worldly affairs and comforts than the beneficed clergy, but far less ascetic than monastic orders following the strict observance. Its priests were devoted above all to prayer and a renewal of the clergy, but their community was not cloistered, and, thanks to their family wealth, they led fairly comfortable lives.[11] Nicolas entered the order with an annual pension of 500 livres, derived from a property he had inherited from his father. He furnished his rooms with pieces he had brought from home.[12] He spent a good portion of his pension on books.

For Malebranche it also proved critical that Oratorians enjoyed a measure of intellectual independence not to be found in most other branches of the Catholic clergy. The intellectually gifted among them could devote themselves to their scholarly interests, though not to the point of neglecting daily communal devotions. The rooms in which Malebranche lived and received visitors were also his library. An inventory at his death listed more than 1,150 volumes—and that number does not include the books he had bequeathed to friends. As one would expect, there were works in theology and scriptural exegesis, editions of classical authors, and lexicons for the study of Hebrew as well as Latin and Greek. But the largest number of his purchases had been in mathematics, natural philosophy, anatomy, botany, and medicine. Virtually all the most important seventeenth-century progenitors of modern science were present: Bacon, Robert Boyle, Descartes, Galileo, Gassendi, Huygens, Kepler, Leibniz, Newton. Almost entirely absent were the texts—among them the essays and letters of Méré and Saint-Évremond, Scudéry's dialogues and novels, and Fontenelle's popularizations of science in the form of polite conversations—that the culture of *honnêteté* had produced.[13]

What happened in 1664? Why did the young Oratorian embrace Cartesianism? We can assume that Lelong tells us the story much as Malebranche had related it to him. Passing along the Rue St Jacques in search of new books, he came upon Merselier's just published edition of *The Human Being*. "The method of reasoning and the mechanics (*la mécanique*) that he perceived in paging through it," Lelong continues, "appealed to him so strongly that he bought the book and read it with so much pleasure that he found himself obliged from time to time to interrupt his reading because of the heart." Lelong and other disciples used Malebranche's reminiscences to fix his growing legend in print. The young man they described was destined to be the century's great metaphysician, the philosopher the True Faith badly needed. Appropriately, the legend has Malebranche begin the final turn to this destiny with an isolated act, the solitary discovery of philosophy's own turn, at last, to truth. No doubt Malebranche's reading of Descartes's *Treatise* did occasion an intense awakening, a Catholic's philosophical analogue to the Protestant conversion experience. But the image of the solitary reader can obscure the fact that in embracing Cartesianism Malebranche joined a movement in French Catholicism that had found its way into the Oratory well before 1664. In the 1650s the intellectual leaders of the Jansenist movement—Antoine Arnauld, Blaise Pascal, and Pierre Nicole—were already at work selectively grafting Descartes's philosophy onto their rigorous Augustinianism. They had close ties with several Oratorian scholars. The older generation at the head of the order—men who had been with Bérulle at the founding—had good reason to maintain an official line of scholastic orthodoxy. In the eyes of orthodox critics in the upper reaches of the ecclesiastical hierarchy, Cartesianism was becoming closely associated with Jansenist heresy. It posed a serious danger to an order committed to a teaching mission in strict obedience to church authority. But Clerselier's edition of the treatise fragments marked the fact that by the early 1660s some of the bright young men of the younger generation were going their own way. Clerselier was one of several Oratorian Cartesians among Malebranche's friends and colleagues. He certainly conferred with them after the awakening of 1664, and they had probably acquainted him with Descartes's thought in the years leading up to it.[14]

Still, for Malebranche one of the texts in question had singular appeal. In *On the Human Being*, Descartes had intended to describe "the body on its own, then the soul on its own," and to end by showing "how these two natures would have to be joined and united." But the fragment was limited to the first subject. It presented what Poullain heard, in less detail, in the lecture he attended while still at the Sorbonne. Descartes describes the body as a hydraulic force field powered by the heart, which he conceived as a kind of furnace, transforming the blood into vaporous "animal spirits" that passed along or through fibrous substances to and from the fibers of the brain. Conceived in this way, Descartes argued, the body was a machine; it had the same mechanical self-sufficiency that counterweights and wheels gave to a clock.

On the face of it, all this was too technical to inspire an inner awakening in a devout young man. It is easier to imagine Malebranche being mesmerized by the personal search for truth Descartes recounted so masterfully in *A Discourse on Method*, or by his *Meditations on the First Philosophy*. But we have to imagine how powerfully new and efficacious this mechanical model seemed to a man with Malebranche's physical ailments. His crooked spine and sunken sternum often made it difficult to breathe. The daily saying of mass exhausted him. He suffered from kidney stones and long fevers. He had, in the words of a colleague, "a violent stomach acid," a condition clearly not helped by his habitual coffee-drinking and tobacco-chewing. Over time the frequent vomiting of his meals damaged his throat.[15] The Aristotelian explanation of the body's vital physical and psychological actions by appeal to the immaterial forms of a "vegetative" soul and a "sensitive" soul did not help him come to terms, intellectually or spiritually, with this wretched state of physical being, and did not offer effective ways of ameliorating it.[16] What he learned from Descartes was that the body was a "form" in a quite different sense: a mechanical configuration of hydraulic forces and vibration-like effects, transmitting motion among its parts like any other machine. As a mechanical system, the body could be understood simply as the field of efficient causes constituted by parts in motion. This paradigm would later be framed within the theological doctrine of "occasionalism" that made Malebranche so controversial. If, as he insisted, all the body's occasional causes—its seeming infinity of transmitted motions—were caused directly by God, there was no need for the teleological mediation of "occult" forms. His own body was simply defective as such; he was neither responsible for its odd configuration nor ruled by it. He could observe it, and even wonder at it, with a certain scientific detachment, as he observed insects and plants. And, if he could not rebuild the machine, or even repair it, he could at least lessen the distractions its malfunctioning caused him. He consulted medical expertise, but in the end devised his own simple treatments. The main one was the daily drinking of a great quantity of water, apparently in an effort to keep the hydraulic system running as smoothly as possible.[17]

But Malebranche did not seize on Descartes's psychophysiological paradigm with the fervor of a convert simply, or even primarily, because it served his

medical needs. The paradigm became the point of intersection between his experience of his own body and his aspiration to grasp universal truths. His determination to hold himself in a state of spiritual detachment from an especially tyrannical
body marked, in heightened form, the conviction of so many of his contemporaries that Descartes's dualism—the radical ontological difference he posited
between body and soul—opened a new prospect. It seemed possible at last to
complement Augustine's theological and ethical teaching with an understanding
of the nature and workings of the material world. Indeed, Augustinian rigorism
and Cartesian dualism could be fused into an integral whole, with the soul at once
imprisoned in the body and capable of defying it in the realization of its own pure
spirituality. This was the vision that Clerselier evoked in appealing to the authority of Augustine in his preface to the edition, and that Malebranche's reading of
the treatise fragments impelled him to realize. If we imagine him, over the next
several years, simply reading Descartes's texts as one would read any other texts,
we fail to appreciate their spiritual import to him. He used Descartes's writings to
grasp clear and distinct ideas by "meditating with" the philosopher, in an intense
struggle waged against the body to return the soul to its prelapsarian union with
God (13). Likewise with Augustine; having known his thought largely through
his order's teaching and the compendium published in 1667 by André Martin, a
fellow Oratorian, he now applied the same powers of meditation to the original
texts.[18]

If we are to understand how Augustine and Descartes combined to shape
Malebranche's concept of effeminacy, we have to trace the fit among three dimensions of his thought: the psychophysiological paradigm he adapted from Descartes, his corollary theory of social power, and the place of language in that
theory. We can expect little help from recent vexed and tangled disputes about
the relationship between Augustine's thought and Descartes's. The disputes have
been a touchstone for a much larger quarrel, and have operated on an ideological
level that is more metahistorical than historical. At issue is how the ascendancy of a
secular "modernity" since the seventeenth century is to be judged; what responsibility, if any, Christianity has to assume for this development; and how Christianity ought to react to the challenge of secularism.[19] The battle positions would not
have made sense to Malebranche. He was, of course, aware that his own Catholic
orthodoxy, and indeed the fundaments of any species of Christian faith, were
under threat from more secular impulses, particularly in the "libertine" forms of
radical skepticism, neo-Stoicism, and neo-Epicureanism. But Descartes's thought
was not one of those threats. Malebranche found it perfectly consistent to be at
once an Augustinian and a Cartesian, using each thinker as his lens for reading the
other. In his view Descartes's philosophy provided the compelling philosophical
complement to revealed truth that Aristotelianism had signally failed to provide.
His Cartesian lens did modernize Augustine's thought significantly by drawing a

sharp line between the material and the spiritual, body and mind; by defining man's intellectual and moral freedom primarily in terms of his capacity to withhold consent from anything but clear and distinct ideas; by relating man to his world and to God through mechanistic causality; and by denying any immediate relationship between objects and the sensations they seem to produce. But in these Cartesian readings a thoroughly Augustinian economy of sin, trinitarian redemption, conversion, and prayer remained intact.[20] The result was *The Search After Truth*.

Original Sin and the Labor of Attention

Within the vaulting system of Cartesian Augustinianism Malebranche gave the concept of effeminacy a new philosophical and theological scaffolding, unprecedented in its theoretical justification of a moral indictment with quite specific social resonances. The connection between the overarching structure of his thought and his perception of effeminacy as a social phenomenon may at first seem suspiciously attenuated, but it becomes tighter when we trace the logic leading from one to the other.

For Malebranche, as for other Augustinians, the point of departure for understanding the human condition was "concupiscence," the natural and ineradicable corruption to which Adam and Eve's original sin had degraded all human beings. He shared this bleak Augustinian vision of man's radical alienation from his Creator with Pascal and other Jansenists. Like them, he pitted it against both Stoic conceptions of "virtue" as self-mastery and strains of Christianity that seemed to go too far in endowing human beings with a natural capacity to contribute to their sanctification, if not to achieve it through their own efforts. And yet Malebranche also sought to correct what he saw as dangerously oversimplified varieties of Augustinianism among his contemporaries. In the strongly Augustinian leanings of orthodox Lutheranism and Calvinism, man was seen to have been so thoroughly corrupted by original sin that he could do nothing to merit salvation; he was sanctified only by God's gift of grace, to which he became receptive in a wrenching conversion experience that made him aware of his utter helplessness. Within French Catholicism Jansenists tended to lean in the same direction, particularly in their vision of the monstrosity of postlapsarian human nature, the pitiful inadequacy of natural reason, and the inscrutability of God. Even closer to home, Jean-François Sénault, the then head of the Oratory, had argued in *Criminal Man; or, The Corruption of Nature by Sin*, published in 1644, that the Fall had corrupted all of nature, though not completely.[21]

Malebranche's Augustinian embrace of Cartesian dualism gave him a far more flexible way of thinking about original sin and its consequences for the material world and man's corporeal and spiritual being. As a material creature, man was at once an object of disgust and an object of wonder; and as a union of body and mind, he was imprisoned in the corporeal and yet capable of going remarkably far, even without grace, in reuniting himself with God through his grasp of the universal and immutable truths of reason. The key to these paradoxes was Malebranche's view of the Fall as a radical inversion of the relationship between body and mind, set in a Christian metanarrative but conceived in Cartesian terms. In their prelapsarian state, Adam and Eve existed in a union of pure intellection with God. Their raison d'être was to understand that union through the exercise of reason, the purely intelligible emanation of the Absolute. Their corporeal senses were essential but entirely subsidiary. By serving as the "faithful" instructors Adam and Eve needed for self-preservation in the spatial and temporal world of material particularity, the senses freed them to realize their purpose as spiritual beings participating in universal truth. In Cartesian terms, they put the body, an extended substance, in the service of the mind, a substance without extension. The senses were a kind of faucet, turned on when self-preservation required it, otherwise kept off so as not to distract from pure intellection. God's punishment for original sin was to put man at a great distance from his perfection by shifting the preponderance of cognitive power to the senses. As a result the natural instincts of self-preservation expanded into the virtually infinite exigencies of self-love, and the mind, vastly "weakened" in relation to the body, became so "dependent" on it as to be corporeal-like in its operations (xxxiii–xliii).

Ironically it was here, in this apparently unsparing way of conceiving man's corruption that Malebranche differed from radical Augustinians. In his view the *res cogitans* and the *res extensa*, considered in themselves, had not been changed by original sin. What had changed was the distribution of power in the immutable "laws" of their "union." To corrupt the substances themselves, Malebranche argued, God would have had to contradict the hierarchical order of degrees of "perfection" that he, as the universal Being, contains. That was impossible; his divinity would have been contradicted in the forms of its emanation. God could, to be sure, "unite minds to bodies," but he could not "subjugate them to bodies." Though the mind was "enslaved," Malebranche's partly figurative use of that term did not imply complete enslavement. He did not, of course, flirt with a heretical denial of the necessity of grace. But in his conception of the laws of union, the mind, uncorrupted in itself, could develop the habitual capacity of "silencing" the senses and "returning into itself," to the "secret" recesses of reason that sense knowledge normally hid. By doing so it could prepare itself to make the reception of grace morally efficacious, as weeded soil is prepared for grain seeds. The vital link between sanctification by grace and the mind's natural illumination was the Incarnation, the central mystery of trinitarian divinity. The grace that we receive though Christ's divine mediation enables us to take a pure "delight" in truths that, though perfectly rational, surpass our natural understanding. The Second Person of the Trinity is the Logos, the Word as Reason assuming a corporeal form "and instructing us in a sensible fashion by His humanity," adapting to our weakness without losing its purity.

And yet, though original sin could not be said to have left either mind or body in an essentially corrupt state, the resulting laws of their union made concupiscence a force so powerful that it came close to negating man's aspiration to return to union with God. This power Malebranche already knew from Augustinian teaching and his applications of it in his own examinations of conscience. But it was in the study of Descartes's mechanical paradigm that he came to understand, in scientific terms, how concupiscence exercised its power or, more precisely, how it actually worked. In his hands, Cartesianism became an epistemology and psychophysiology of sin. On the epistemological level, Descartes had demolished representational theories of cognition, including Augustine's. The axiomatic "error" in the postlapsarian state was the illusion that objects represent themselves to our minds as they exist. It is simply false to assume that the qualities—color, coldness, heat, smell, and so on—we perceive are in the objects, and that, in the form of sensations, these are transmitted directly to the mind. In fact the objects simply occasion the body to generate illusory images and ideas of them through its own internal dynamic. In our perceptions of our own bodies, as in our perceptions of external objects, we blindly assume to be "natural" truths, and indeed indisputable matters of common sense, what are in fact mere illusions, phantoms of the "darkness" to which our senses consign us. Immersed in these illusions, the mind finds it extremely difficult to rise out of them to grasp the properties of extension and mobility that constitute objects' real substance and explain their relations to each other.

In his awareness of the world surrounding him, man is not simply limited to perspectival knowledge; he is condemned to a pitifully myopic anthropocentrism. He makes his own body an "absolute standard against which one should measure other things" (26–27, 31). For his self-preservation, to be sure, he needs to be aware of the degree of force he faces in other bodies, and that requires that he perceive their sizes in proportion to his own body. But in the postlapsarian state that is all that his body's eyes, as opposed to the figurative "eye" of the mind, perceive. He fails to realize that, in the larger scheme of God's creation, the relative sizes we perceive do not indicate the relative values of objects; even a creature as tiny as the gnat represents the perfection of his work, since it has the same "infinity of parts" that far larger creatures have. The microscope gave Malebranche a glimpse into that infinity. It compensated for his corrupted human vision, so that he could admire all of creation from a position outside, as it were, the illusory world to which the overweening power of his senses confined him. While man "has only one crystalline lens in each eye," he reported, "the fly has more than a thousand." That men nonetheless had "disdain" for insects was one more proof that they lived in self-centered error (25–27, 31).

As dependent as it was on the body, the mind retained what Malebranche called a "freedom of indifference" (9). He made cognition and conscience, and indeed error and sin, virtually coterminous. Man was free to withhold consent until he had the "evidence" of clear and distinct ideas—ideas to which he could not refuse consent without experiencing both the painful "secret reproaches of reason" and "the remorse" of "conscience." The reproaches became audible as he retreated into the recess of reason within himself by engaging in what Malebranche called "the labor of attention" in "meditation" (9–10). He was indebted to Descartes for this concept of disciplined intellectual and spiritual labor. Ironically, through Descartes's mediation, he appropriated for his purposes not only elements of Ignatius Loyola's *Spiritual Exercises*, but also, despite his disapproval of pagan philosophy, the commitment to rigorous mental exercises in Stoic askesis.[22]

Here again, though, he folded Descartes into Augustine. In first sounding this theme in *The Search After Truth*, he quoted Augustine: "when man judges things only according to the mind's pure ideas, when he carefully avoids the noisy confusion of creatures, and, when entering into himself, he listens to his sovereign Master with his senses and passions silent, it is impossible for him to fall into error." The intellectual labor of meditation was, as Malebranche would put it in *Christian Conversations*, "the natural prayer that we make to the interior truth, so that it will reveal itself to us." Like any other kind of labor, "the attention of the mind" was man's punishment for original sin; but it was also a liberation from its effect, the tyranny of the senses (xxxiii–xliii). In his later, more didactic writings Malebranche would urge his readers again and again to traverse this route to a decorporealized awareness of God's illuminating presence within the mind.[23] Even as he assured readers that meditation would lead them from error to truth, he warned them that it was "painful" and "fatiguing" labor, and that the corporeal self would resist such effort with all its might. In a methodical, step-by-step progression, one scales a cliff of abstract universals, from rational certainty about the laws of God's creation to some understanding of God's perfection and man's participation in it. This is labor in which the mind has to claw its way out of illusions so deeply rooted as to be virtually beyond questioning. The qualities that the mind attributes to objects, and that it seems to experience so vividly, are its own physically generated projections onto particular being, distortions reflecting the corporeal self's incapacity to perceive things in any way other than in their relation to itself. Such projections are possible only because the archetypal ideas of the objects as beings with extension *are* directly present in us, as the universal and immutable ideas that are "in" the "substance of God" and that our pure intellection "sees immediately" as it turns to God. To think in God requires that we strip away layer upon layer of sense distortion that has hidden our immediate participation in God's intellection in the deep recesses of our minds. The mind must effect a wrenching inversion of the hierarchy of ontological value to which the senses work to confine it. It has to struggle to realize that abstractions are not, as we are so strongly inclined to assume, less real than the objects that, in our senses' representations, seem to act on us from outside. They are more real, the higher reality of our interior agency.[24]

For all its emphasis on human corruption, this was Augustinianism with a distinctly Cartesian confidence in the powers of reason. Malebranche's concept of meditation as a methodical progression marked his departure from the overarching pessimism with which Jansenists like Pascal and Nicole borrowed from Cartesian rationalism. Where they saw reason groping futilely in the face of the mysteries of God and his creation, Malebranche saw it advancing deep into the same mysteries. The meditator achieved certainty about physical nature by pondering the universal laws of extension to be found in the abstractions of mathematics and geometry—the circle and the triangle were his prime examples—and the universal laws of extension that their lines represented with the least possible use of the senses. This was the propaedeutic path to reunion with God, through pure ideas that, being "in God," were discovered in his illuminating presence in the mind.

Seen from this angle, the other implication of Malebranche's definition of concupiscence as a hierarchical inversion, not a corruption of substances, may at first seem puzzling. The body, too, represented the majesty of God's creation, though it did so in its configuration of mechanical forces rather than in any freedom from force. Malebranche insisted that the senses of postlapsarian human beings were no different from Adam and Eve's, and, in providing man with the sense data he needed for self-preservation, they still functioned remarkably well. Seen in this light, the human body deserved to be approached with awe precisely for what it shared with animals. As machines with intricate and seemingly infinite relations of "parts," all bodies exemplified the interactions of "occasional causes" through which God, the only sufficient cause, directly willed every motion in his creation. It was this "mechanical design" that enraptured Malebranche when he observed insects under a microscope; they are "so beautiful," he observed, that "it even seems as though God has willed to bejewel them in compensation for their lack of size" (31). The same sense of awe pervades his calls for a new "science of man," which would be "the most beautiful, the most pleasant, and the most necessary of all our knowledge" because, in addition to explaining the nature of the mind as such, it would fathom the wonders of the human body that Descartes had discovered (xxxix).

Concupiscence was man's deluded perception of finite particularity, which the mind's eye—its capacity to perceive the universal and immutable laws instantiated in particular things—could escape, though only with great difficulty. By itself, this epistemological explanation of a theological doctrine echoes centuries of Christian thinking about the compulsive egotism at the heart of human corruption. But in Malebranche's reading of it, Descartes's mechanical paradigm of psychophysiology went a momentous step farther. It made the infinity of parts of the human body comprehensible by dividing them into the fibrous substances of organs, veins, nerves, and muscles and the highly refined blood particles, the vapor-like animal spirits, that transmitted motion among them; and it interrelated these fibers and forces in a way that seemed to explain how they worked to keep the mind in error and why some minds were more enslaved to their bodies than others. The villain of the piece was the imagination, the faculty that turned sensations into images in the brain that in turn "modified" the mind. If the senses were "false witnesses," the imagination was their deafening voice or, to switch metaphors, the instrument of their coercive force. Its power lay in the "traces" or grooves the animal spirits imprinted on the brain. The deeper the traces, the more easily the imagination turned sensations into blinding images. And that, of course, depended on the relative softness or hardness of the brain fibers. The softer or more "delicate" the fibers, the deeper the traces (87–90, 110–11).

This was the logic that underlay Malebranche's description of women, in his indictment of the imagination in Book Two of *The Search After Truth*, as masters of language, manners, and taste, and as incapable of grasping anything "abstract." Precisely because the power of their imaginations made them so prone to error, women were also, in relation to men, more prone to sin. To say that they were unable to grasp abstractions was to say they could not perform the labor of "natural prayer" in meditation, and hence could not approach (re)union with God through self-illumination. "Effeminacy" marked the ways their example and influence weakened men in their efforts to disentangle the mind from the body, or indeed precluded such efforts.

As opprobrious as his judgments were, Malebranche was not a misogynist, if we mean by that term a hater of women as such. On a key issue, in fact, we find him arguing, albeit tentatively and somewhat tortuously, against what might more fairly be called a misogynist position. In *The Search After Truth* he applied Descartes's mind-body dualism to argue that the intergenerational transmission of original sin occurred in the direct communication between the mother's brain and the brain of the fetus. "One could say," he wrote, "that from the time we were formed in the wombs of our mothers we were in sin and infected with the corruption of our parents." He stepped back immediately from the possible implication that women bore sole responsibility for human corruption, or indeed that in pregnancy itself they were "criminal." If the woman is "righteous"—i.e., if she has the faith to love God—she remains righteous even as her brain's traces, without her volition, communicate concupiscence to the fetus (120–23). In his later "elucidation" of this subject, he took another step back; a strict interpretation of scriptural passages led to the conclusion that, because it takes both a man and the woman to effect procreation, they both "must be said to be the real causes of sin, each in [his/her] own way."[25]

Nor was Malebranche a biological essentialist. The relative strengths of the imagination and reason in a specific person, he explained immediately after listing women's distinctive traits, depended on the proportion between the volume and force of her (or his) animal spirits and the degree of softness, or delicacy, of her brain fibers. The differences in the proportion from person to person were virtually limitless, and they did not always follow gender lines. Rather than positing a rigid dichotomy between male and female cognition, he conceived something more like a continuum, with exceptional men at the "weak" end and exceptional women at the "strong" end. Hence "some women are found to have stronger minds than some men" (130–31). That was a conclusion about natural fact that he took quite seriously. Indeed it explains what would otherwise be an incomprehensible detail of his life. We know from his friends' reminiscences that Malebranche found it particularly satisfying that exceptional women of rank could understand his books without the guidance of a "master," and that "his most illustrious disciples" included women "distinguished as much by their merit as by their birth." Like Poullain and other admirers of the *honnête femme*, he found women to be especially promising pupils precisely because they were, by academic standards, ignorant; they had not been corrupted by the "blind prejudice" of "the schools."[26] But he did not see the delicacy of their imaginations as a source of intellectual clarity; unusually "strong, constant women" were distinguished by the fact that their imaginations were relatively lacking in delicacy and hence more easily disempowered.

The *Bel Esprit*

To extend our reach deeper into the meanings Malebranche attached to "effeminacy," we have to follow the social line of his thought, particularly as it focuses on language as the instrument of human intersubjectivity. Malebranche "ordinarily got bored in conversations," his friends recalled, but "he said an infinity of times that he never got bored when he was alone."[27] If he could not live a cloistered life, he could at least avoid unwanted contacts with the world outside the Oratorian residence, and with some of his neighbors within it, by withdrawing into himself. Explaining this inclination simply as a matter of temperament would leave us with an all-too-obvious half-truth. Malebranche's preference for solitude was grounded in the sharp dichotomy he drew between the silence of meditation and the noise of social communication, and that in turn marked a cultural tension in the worlds he inhabited and observed.

The upper reaches of seventeenth-century French society harbored a felt need for the state of silence in solitude. It stood in counterpoint to the aesthetic ideal of conversation, promising to some an occasional respite, and to others a permanent refuge, from the hyper-relational self that polite sociability required. We would seriously underestimate the tension between speech and silence if we conceived it simply as a line dividing worldly *honnêtes gens*, devoted to the art of conversation, from people with more devout sensibilities. The line also runs *through* the milieus of polite sociability, registering a strain internal to it. The life of Mme Madeleine de Sablé literally straddled the line. A habitué of the Blue Room, she experienced a conversion under Jansenist influence in 1652, at fifty-four, and built an apartment abutting the convent at Port Royal. Her new residence positioned her to alternate between participating in the nuns' monastic life and presiding over an elegant salon peopled by cultivated aristocrats of both sexes and Jesuit men of letters as well as Jansenist luminaries.[28] In the case of Mme Marguerite Hessein Rambouillet de la Sablière, a *grande dame* of *le monde* who had had strong interests in worldly literature, philosophy, and science (she had been a convinced Cartesian) and had been the patroness of Jean de la Fontaine, renunciation took the form of a far more radical break, in reaction to a humiliating marriage and a broken love affair. Following her conversion from Calvinism to Catholicism in the late 1670s, she entered a life of penitence. "I am in complete solitude . . . with God," she wrote joyfully in 1692 to her spiritual guide the abbé de Rancé. "Having talked too much," she informed the spiritual director Rancé had chosen for her, "I must remain silent."[29]

Malebranche saw this need for solitude in the women who sought his spiritual guidance. In his own order, the same need had found expression in the founders' strong attraction to the mysticism of, among others, Bernard de Clairvaux and Saint Theresa of Avila. Though he was wary of the theological implications of the mystical tradition, Malebranche advocated and practiced a form of spirituality that had strong affinities with it. The theologian who seems to have served as his director of conscience for the last forty years of his life was the abbé Pierre Berrand, a student of mysticism with a strong ascetic bent. Berrand taught "hatred" of the natural "self" (*le moi*) and the practice of solitary "prayer" in a systematic ascent through stages of meditation.[30]

Another figure looms large in this world of pious women and priests seeking to extract themselves from worldliness: Armand Jean Le Bouthillier de Rancé, the founder of the Trappist order. The sole heir of a wealthy family that had ascended to the pinnacle of the Parisian robe nobility, Rancé came of age with the titles and incomes of no less than five ecclesiastical benefices. His extensive classical education had equipped him to be a fashionable man of letters and a dazzling habitué of the salons. His ecclesiastical dignities did not prevent him from leading the life of a dandyish libertine in Parisian high society. "I am going this morning to preach like an angel," he wrote a friend, "and tonight to hunt like a devil."[31] In 1657, when he was twenty-nine, the sudden death of his mistress Marie de Montbazon, herself a notorious libertine, set him on the path to radical renunciation of the world. In 1686, in a letter to Mme de Lafayette, he would recall of this conversion that "agreeable conversation, worldly pleasures, plans for a career and a fortune, seemed to be such vain and hollow things that I began to look on them with disgust."[32] In 1664 his renunciation took a radical turn; he left Paris to take up his duties as abbot at Notre-Dame-de-La-Trappe, a monastery in the Perche valley that had fallen into ruin and had been reduced to six monks of dubious religious commitment. He replaced these remaining residents with a group of Cistercian monks of the strict observance. Taking the Anachronites, the hermit saints of the early Eastern church, as his models, he set about subjecting himself and his fellow monks to a life devoted entirely to penitence and expiation.[33] The major exception to Rancé's embrace of silence was his correspondence with several society women who sought his spiritual guidance, of whom Mme de la Sablière was one.

Some churchmen protested that Rancé's excessively severe rule created a climate of sadism and encouraged suicide. But notoriety only increased the fascination with La Trappe at the royal court and in Parisan high society, as well as in the clergy; the monastery became a kind of pilgrimage site for people in these circles. For some, visits to La Trappe probably offered little more than an opportunity for spiritual tourism. Others were drawn to Rancé's community precisely because it was so uncompromising in excluding the relentless demands of polite sociability. They felt a need for expiatory solitude, and wanted to experience it even though they could not devote their lives to it.

Malebranche was one of the latter. We have known from Lelong's biography that he was on close terms with Rancé, and that he made periodic "retreats" at the monastery. But one of the two surviving letters from Rancé to Malebranche, largely ignored to date, tells us much more. Dated April 9, 1672, the letter is in response to Malebranche's announcement of his "resolution" to become a member of the community at La Trappe. Not wanting to seem to have recruited Malebranche, the abbé urged him to keep secret their earlier conversations about his "plan." Though he approved of the decision in principle, he remained concerned that a man with Malebranche's frail health would not be able to withstand the harsh physical conditions (he notes "the horrors of the long winters") and "the deprivation of all human contact and consolation" at La Trappe. But if Malebranche remains unphased by "all the possible consequences of so great a renunciation," Rancé writes, he should "follow the stirrings of grace"; "a person taking so great a step must have complete trust in God and expect nothing from human help." He advised him, though, to visit La Trappe before making a decision.[34]

Malebranche obviously changed his mind, probably because in the end he had to acknowledge to himself that his poor health was an insuperable obstacle. But the very fact of his resolution in the spring of 1672 points us to the complexity of his vocation. That was the year in which Rancé introduced a new regimen at La Trappe, still harsher than the Cistercian strict observance. Henceforth the monks could no longer use their cells as private retreats; they could retire to them only for sleep, in complete darkness. Their entire waking lives would be spent in a collectivity of silence, without conversation of any kind. By 1672 Malebranche almost certainly had begun writing *The Search After Truth*, whose first volume would appear two years later. He knew from conversations with Rancé, and perhaps from visits to La Trappe, that, in sharp contrast to his own and other orders, the monastery was organized on the principle that the life of a monk was one of penitence in silent retreat, not study. Learning led to speech, and speech would transform the monk into a public spectacle.[35]

Malebranche was apparently willing to abandon his philosophical project, and indeed the entire world of learning, for a life in which reading would be limited to devotional material. Having turned back from a commitment to harsh asceticism, he would henceforth retire periodically to La Trappe, where he could lead a life of total silence in meditation and prayer, away from the world of conversation that he, like Rancé, found so morally "dangerous." "There is nothing that shrivels up the heart, and that is more ruinous to piety, than conversation," Rancé wrote in one of his "spiritual letters"; "those who greatly love conversing with God keep a great silence with human beings." His renunciation was categorical; "however regulated and innocent they can be, speech (*la parole*) and conversation open for us the portals for getting out of ourselves and fill us with phantoms and vain imaginings."[36]

It was this animosity toward social speech, no less radical than Rancé's, that informed Malebranche's righteous disdain for the social aesthetic of the *honnête femme* and the *honnête homme*. In characterizing the aesthetic as effeminate, he made it the site of both weakness and tyrannical power. It not only betrayed, in a particularly pathological social form, the abject dependence of weakened reason on overweening imagination; in doing so, it provided a heightened example of the exercise of blind and arbitrary social power through speech.

"All live by opinion," Malebranche wrote in his *Dialogues on Metaphysics and Religion*, and "all act by imitation."[37] Like sense knowledge, a social order is essential for our self-preservation; and, in that limited but essential role, it is constituted by the natural inclination God has implanted in us to imitate each other. In the postlapsarian world the disposition to love others as fellow rational beings has been overwhelmed by "self-love" (*amour-propre*), and the innocent desire to imitate others has degenerated into the corrupt desire to please them. With the love of God nearly extinguished, a boundless self-love fills the emptied space. The body's instincts for self-preservation have become the embodied social self's unbounded need to expand its power over others by pleasing them, and above all by winning their approval. This self "expands outward" not out of love for the other, but to have its illusory existence confirmed in the no less illusory image the other has of it. Self-love takes the form of insatiable egotism, blind in its appetites but calculating in its drive to satisfy them. The instrument of this egotism is language. Through the social exchange of sounds, the chimeras of the imagination become the symbolic power to which embodied selves subject each other.

This animus echoes Jansenist Augustinianism. We find a similar view of language as the vehicle of corrupt self-love and tyrannical imagination in, among other sources, Pascal's *Thoughts*, published in 1669, which Malebranche owned and had probably read in an unedited version. Perhaps his greatest debt was to another volume in his library: Pierre Nicole's *Moral Essays*, published in 1645, which includes an essay on "how the conversations of human beings are dangerous." "Opinion," Nicole explained, was the "contagion" effected by speech, which, as the chief medium of concupiscence, is "full of illusion and deception." "Silence" is "so useful" because it prevents "false ideas" imprinted on our minds in childhood and youth from being "renewed."[38] Malebranche emphatically confirmed this dichotomy, but within a new framework. He was engaged in building a "science of man," a project that in the Jansenist view represented the vanity of philosophy's claim to independent understanding of God's work. Here again his adoption of Descartes's mechanical paradigm, so much less qualified than Pascal's or Nicole's, gave him a simple but encompassing way of understanding how concupiscence worked, thus endowing an Augustinian vision with a new theoretical structure. In dichotomous contrast to communication in pure intellection, social intersubjectivity was the interaction of bodies imparting the force of motion to each other. It occurred entirely through the mutual interaction of bodies' sense representations, as each occasioned traces on the other's brain and a resulting "modality" in the mind. The chief instrument of this exercise of ego-aggrandizing social power is language, and particularly the physical force of sound in the spoken word. It is above all speech that transforms the delusions of each person into the collective delusion that Malebranche, following Pascal and Nicole, calls "opinion." Malebranche sees opinion as the product of "contagion" (161–72). He uses that term not metaphorically, but to designate the literal transmission of pathology from one body to another. To say that postlapsarian society is ruled by concupiscence is to say that opinion reigns; whether blatantly or more or less insidiously, we coerce each other into virtually complete entanglement in the net of false perceptions, norms, and values that the interactions of our imaginations have fabricated. In this process hearing—and here the echoes of Pascal are particularly clear—is reinforced by sight, in the gestures and looks that accompany the spoken word, and in the entire appearance and setting of the speaker. All speech is, in that severely opprobrious sense, rhetorical manipulation (80–81).

Malebranche's concept of "opinion" as social cacophony can fairly be described as a critique of ideology. In the intersubjective workings of imagination and sound we see ideology endowing arbitrary power with a not-to-be-questioned "natural" status, as the apparently legitimate exercise of authority and validation of social honor. Several of Malebranche's targets are the same male-specific uses of speech that the discourse of *honnêteté* contrasted invidiously with the natural freedom of the *honnête femme* and *honnête homme*, and he attributes the same faults to them. There is the preacher haranguing from the pulpit; the academic pedant precluding dissent by arming himself in Latin phrases and eso-teric appeals to ancient authorities; the nobleman overpowering his audience with the grace of his address; the magistrate wrapping his authority in the pomp-ous gravity of his legal rhetoric, reinforced by the physical setting of the law.[39] We might say that in this questioning of the public authority of men Malebranche goes much further than the discourse of *honnêteté*. What the imagination and language make "natural" he exposes as socially constructed, equating the perform-ance of authority with the abuse of power inherent in human corruption. His critique rests on an egalitarian logic conspicuous by its absence from the dis-course of *honnêteté*. It combines the ancient Christian idea that we are all equals in the eyes of God with Descartes's principle that rational truth, because it is univer-sal, cannot be appropriated by some to the exclusion of others. Reason, unlike material goods, is a universal resource. Every human being can grasp all of it without depriving anyone else of any of it.

In his actual social critique, however, Malebranche did not—as the principle's immanent logic might lead us to expect—see the women-centered culture of *honnêteté* as a relatively egalitarian alternative to male-exclusive forms of cultural authority. Quite the contrary: he applied the same dissection of social power to his attack on the corrupt and corrupting effeminacy of *honnêteté*, and he pursued that attack with a singular animosity. In the tenth "éclaircissement" of *The Search After Truth*, "the world" is used in its broad Christian sense, as the secular threat to the sacred, but at the same time takes on the seventeenth-century social speci-ficity of *le monde*, evoking the realm of imagination and taste over which women reigned:

> The carnal and sensual (*sensible*) human being cannot understand spiri-tual things because worldly knowledge, contemporary tastes, polite con-versation, refinement, liveliness and beauty of imagination, and the things by which we live for the world and the world lives for us, induce in our minds (*esprit*) a dull and frightening stupor with regard to every truth that we understand perfectly only in the silence of our senses and passions. (631–32)

Appropriately Malebranche fixed his sights on the *bel esprit*, the paragon of the aesthetic of social play, the master of the effortless elegance, the "je ne sais quoi," of polite conversation. Though he restricted himself to discussing the generic type, readers would have thought of celebrated figures like Voiture and Méré or, in his own generation, Fontenelle and Saint-Évremond. Malebranche's first profile of the *bel esprit* comes in his discussion of "effeminate minds" in Book Two of *The Search After Truth*. As an example of the "fine mind" devoted exclusively to "the art of pleasure," the *bel esprit* joins "the nobility, courtiers, rich people, [and] the young"; but it is his specific traits, inseparable from the milieu of salon society, that dominate the diagnosis of an effeminate "softness" of mind. Soft minds "are extremely sensitive about manners and style"; "an ill-spoken phrase, a provincial accent, a small grimace irritates them infinitely more than a confused mass of bad arguments." Nonetheless "these are the sorts of people who have the most esteem in the world"; far from being seen as effeminate softness, the *bel esprit*'s "free and easy air" is admired as "an effect and a mark of the beauty of his genius" (155–56).

The concluding image of the self-deluded dazzler is developed with greater psychological precision and a deeper moral bite in the *Treatise of Morality*, published in 1684, a decade after the first part of *The Search After Truth*.[40] The *Treatise* deserves more attention than the history of philosophy has given it; it was Malebranche's effort to make his thought accessible in a concise and well-ordered volume of ethical teaching, demonstrating how the power of concupiscent imagination informs and structures social relations. The *bel esprit* reappears toward the end of the first part, on "virtue," following Malebranche's effort to classify eight kinds of criminal imagination as variations on the relationship between animal spirits and brain fibers. As the quintessential example of "speaking well" and "agreeably" to satisfy the ego's craving for approval, the *bel esprit* now stands on his own (527–37). He is, from a moral standpoint, sui generis, a figure "more separated from God than any other," with "no appearance of returning," and indeed a figure more corrupt than the "deceiver" (*le fourbe*) and even the "debauched person" (532–33). What makes him unique is his entrapment in two kinds of insidiously tyrannical self-deception. Even as he feels his self-love sustained by his admiring listeners, who are "penetrated" and "dazzled" and "dominated" by his words, his need for their admiration makes him their "slave" (532, 536). And, unlike the deceiver or the debauched person, he sees no reason to feel remorse. How can he? How can it be a "crime," he asks, to "merit the esteem of *honnêtes gens*?" "It is not a crime to have intelligence (*l'esprit*)," Malebranche responds, "but it is an error to mistake the imagination for intelligence" (534). Rather than turning people to God, the *bel esprit* "prostrates weak imaginations at his feet, and makes of himself a veritable cult, a spiritual cult, a cult that is owed only to God" (535).

Malebranche speaks with a certain exasperation in the face of the *bel esprit*'s apparently triumphant power. The man who does not admire "lively and animated" speech, he will write later in the *Treatise*, is seen to "[make] himself odious and ridiculous." It is not clear whether, from this dissenting standpoint, Malebranche uses the term *bel esprit* to refer to women as well as men, as was the common practice in the discourse of *honnêteté*. What *is* clear is that this exposé slashes into vulnerabilities in the new polite sociability, the dissonances between norms and actual behavior that even some of its practitioners occasionally found hard to endure. Malebranche echoes moralists like Pascal and La Rochefoucauld, who likewise found something false and morally suspect about *honnêteté* and *politesse*. But, in an unprecedented way, he elaborates their moral insights into a sustained and systematic condemnation, its binary opposition between silence and speech set within the axiomatic metaphysical and epistemological distinction between, on one side, the rational and the spiritual and, on the other, the corporeal and its dominant faculty, the imagination. If the *bel esprit* in Malebranche's texts is male, he nonetheless uses the figure's "effeminacy" to reject the entire way of being intelligent that salon women represent and guide. The celebrated qualities of the *honnête femme*—her delicately perceptive mind, her softly animated voice, her pleasing facial expressions and bodily gestures—are all instruments of the pursuit of power. The *honnête homme* has not been improved by commerce with the female masters of *politesse*: he has been corrupted and debased by it.

It was the duty of human beings to work for each other's sanctification; and that required the mutual "natural" communication of rational ideas, without the power-laden social static of the imagination. The resulting exchange of the gift of *complaisance* was not an act of social representation, but a "secret" spiritual intimacy. Its most effective means was not "speech" (*discourse*), but "a modest and respectful *air*" which "marks sensibly that we give [others] the right (*droite*) to ourselves, that we freely accord them, in our mind and in our heart, the place they believe they well merit" (636–43). In Malebranche's usage, as in the language of *honnêteté*, "air" had a broad semantic range; a certain way of looking at the other, an agreement of facial expressions and gestures, a certain impression made by one's entire manner. For the *bel esprit*, male and female, it was a vital part of the aesthetic of self-representation, the physical accompaniment to beautiful thought in the art of conversation. Malebranche made the "air" of Christians the higher sign of friendship in silence.

The Author Despite Himself

On April 22, 1716, roughly six months after Malebranche's death, Fontenelle delivered his eulogy at a public assembly of the Royal Academy of Sciences. Father André, who attended the session, tells us that it "attracted much of *le monde*" as well as Academy members and disciples like himself.[41] The visitors from Parisian high society probably included women.

A eulogy by Fontenelle was a major event in the public life of the French capital. As the "perpetual secretary" of the Academy of Sciences Fontenelle had become its official promoter to the French public, and his eulogies of its members and other prominent men (and some women) may have been his most effective instrument. He was the unrivaled master of the genre, combining the ability to explain natural philosophy and mathematics in lucid prose with a rare skill in the narrative art of biography (what he called "history") and in psychological portraiture. We can assume that many of his listeners were particularly curious about how Fontenelle would portray a man whose intellectual career had converged with his own in some ways, but had stood in undisguised reproach to it in others.

Since his election in 1699, almost certainly with Fontenelle's support, Malebranche had been an active member of the Academy. It is not at all surprising that the two men had established a viable working relationship; they were fellow Cartesians, and they shared a wonder at the simple unity in infinite complexity that the new science and mathematics had revealed in the natural world. They were well aware, however, that they faced each other across the deepening divide between believers and nonbelievers. In 1686 twenty-nine-year-old Fontenelle had published his doubts about Malebranche's doctrine of occasionalism. He wrote in the voice of a modest young naïf, appealing to the philosopher to relieve him of his "uncertainty." Malebranche had not bought this pose; beneath "the appearance of a false respect" for God, he wrote in a published reply, the apparently "modest" author was denying his existence.[42]

Malebranche's riposte took aim at the young man's "manner" (*air*) as well as his reasoning. Fontenelle was the epitome of the *bel esprit*. Fontenelle's eulogy made it clear that he considered Malebranche one of the great minds of his generation, and conveyed his sincere affection for the man. But even from the distance of nearly three centuries we can hear the apparently gentle but quite pointed notes of mockery with which he laced his encomium to his deceased colleague. In the dispute with Arnaud, Malebranche had allowed himself to be drawn into a sterile sectarian war, a regrettable waste of time for a great mind. Having recounted Malebranche's career as a theologian and metaphysician, Fontenelle reminded his audience that the Academy "abstained totally" from metaphysics, "which would appear too uncertain and contentious," as well as from theology. It was as a "great geometer and a great physicist" that Malebranche had earned a seat in the Academy.[43] Malebranche would have been quick to reject this way of placing him in an intellectual division of labor. It in effect declared his life purpose as a Cartesian Augustinian—his effort to unite theology, metaphysics, and natural philosophy in a single system—to have been futile. Fontenelle's use of polite mockery is more generous, but no less attentive to irony, in his comments on the paradox of Malebranche's prose. Malebranche's approach to reading as an exercise in "assiduous meditation," he reported, excluded poetry as well as "pure erudition" in history and philosophy; "he never read ten lines of verse in succession without disgust." And yet even his most abstract philosophical arguments exhibited the "art" of an "author" employing a rich imagination for his purpose:

> There reigns in [*The Search After Truth*] a great art of putting abstract ideas into the light of day, of tying them together, of fortifying them by their association. One finds there a skilful mix of quantity of less abstract things, which, being easily understood, encourages the reader to apply himself to others, flatters him to think that he can understand everything, and perhaps persuades him that he understands nearly everything. The diction, in addition to being pure and polished (*châtié*), has all the dignity that the materials require, and all the grace that they can allow. It is not that he has taken any care to cultivate his talents of the imagination; on the contrary; he is always intent on decrying them; but he has naturally a very noble and lively imagination, which works for an ingrate despite himself, and which adorns reason in hiding itself from her.[44]

On one level Fontenelle's point was simply that there is no escaping rhetoric. However insistent the philosopher might be that his presentation of demonstrative reasoning is essentially different from a rhetorical performance, and however untainted he keeps his universal concepts, philosophical argument is itself a form of rhetoric. But Fontenelle's praise of Malebranche's "diction"—its polish, its dignity of manner, and its grace—pointed to a deeper paradox: that, despite his diagnosis of the imagination as the pathological faculty, the philosopher had quite naturally used his own imagination to embody disembodied truth in a rhetoric uniquely his own.

Was Fontenelle right? To take the question a step farther, was Malebranche an "author," despite all his efforts to avoid being one? In seventeenth-century French belles lettres the concept of the author, as Fontenelle used the term, took shape in the conceptual triangle formed by style, character, and rhetoric. We might think of "style" as representing the duality of "character"; it joined character as singularity of expression with character as the embodiment of the socially specific requirements of rhetorical convention. "Styles," wrote La Mothe Le Vayer in 1638, "are infinite and always different, like faces, which never lack some *air* that distinguishes them."[45] But if an author's style was uniquely his own, it also, as a condition of its efficacy, had to resonate through a rhetorical community constituted by shared social norms and standards of taste.[46] In his critique of Montaigne, Malebranche had condemned his style as the expression of both a unique (and uniquely self-absorbed) subjectivity and a social "air," the aesthetic of *honnêteté*. And he had gone much further; the "secret corruption of our heart" revealed in the "delicacies of effeminate discourse" was to be found in all styles. Did he succumb to the temptation of style even as he categorically condemned it?

In 1672, when he considered entering the monastery at La Trappe, Malebranche came close to permanently renouncing authorship. In the preface to *The Search After Truth* he questioned his assumption of an authorial identity in the very act of acknowledging it. "I chanced becoming an author," he told readers. He had undertaken the work for "[his] own instruction, in order to think well, and to set out clearly what I did think." This was to say that he had made writing a tool in the solitary labor of meditation. He saw publishing as a way of making meditation all the more rigorous; readers would confront him with "discoveries" that he had "neglected through laziness" or had "given up through lack of strength and courage" (xlii–xliii). Malebranche's projected readership is hard to identify. Men of the schools, blindly accepting the authority of the ancients; *honnêtes hommes*, too "effeminate" to engage in rigorous thought; cultivated women constitutionally unable to grasp abstractions: all would seem to have been disqualified from following Malebranche's meditations in print. Whoever the readers might be, they were not being asked to judge the results of the controlled empirical experiments that other seventeenth-century scientists were conducting. To Malebranche "evidence" meant clear and distinct ideas, and these were so difficult to grasp precisely because they were essentially different from the empirical knowledge acquired through the senses.

Malebranche aspired to create a community of *méditatifs*—people for whom print communication was an act of shared labor, a propaedeutic for each reader's retreat into the solitary labor that entry into the inner recess of reason required. His frustration in the face of this task was already evident in *The Search After Truth*. "I do not claim to teach everyone," he wrote at the beginning of his discussion of the imagination; "I teach the ignorant, and merely advise the rest, or rather, in this work I try both to teach and advise myself" (87). In the very act of assuming an authorial role, he seemed to be stepping back from it. In later works he chaffed at the need to use "ordinary" language, which he regarded as hopelessly "confused." In his efforts to make his thought more accessible, he often repeated what he had already made clear elsewhere; but he did so with audible annoyance. He would have preferred that the reading of his texts be a step-by-step advance in the labor of meditation. There should be no need to reexplain truths the reader had already grasped.[47]

On one level, Malebranche's vexed relationship with his readers, and with the act of writing, marks a clash between two ideal reading publics: the invisible society of relentlessly disciplined meditators that this Cartesian Augustinian sought to create, and the public of conversational freedom that the culture of *honnêteté* and its emblematic figure, the *bel esprit*, projected. In *The Search After Truth* there is a revealing shift of target in his retort to those who rejected

Descartes. Having begun by taking aim at "those of false learning, who pretend to know everything" and always echo Aristotle, he went on to dismiss people who "read [Descartes's] works as fables [*fables*] and novels [*romans*], which are read for diversion and not meditated upon for instruction" (12–13). The latter remark evoked the polite public being created by the new symbiosis of conversation and print. The scholar labored; the problem was that his labor made him blindly submissive to authority. Novel reading was no less a foil for Malebranche's conception of reading as meditative labor, but from another angle of contrast. It was the difference between apparent effortlessness and disciplined effort, and between print communication as a simulated conversation and as a means to withdraw from speech to inner silence.

This difference must be framed within arguments about the relationship between philosophy and rhetoric that seventeenth-century France inherited from antiquity. In the purist self-image of some of its practitioners, philosophical argument stooped to the use of words, with all their slippery and multivalent meanings, only because they were unavoidable. It had no truck with the manipulative arts the rhetor used to mobilize his listeners' passions. In the tradition of humanistic belles lettres, Guez de Balzac sought to counter this antirhetorical logic, claiming that the pagan eloquence of the ancients could be put in the service of Christian piety. When he described "the words of the good orator" as "contagious," he meant it positively; the words "pierce right to the center of the soul and mix and agitate (*remuer*) therein with thoughts and other interior movements." The "brilliant" and the "agreeable," Balzac wrote in the preface to his *Socrate chrétien*, "gains" rather than "forces" the soul, which "has a horror of entirely naked (*crue*) reason and the purely dogmatic genre."[48] Far from stripping the listener of her freedom, the aesthetic pleasure of rhetoric prevents bare rational argument, as well as purely dogmatic formulations, from coercing her.

Malebranche would have none of this; he stands squarely within the philosophical tradition. Indeed he might be said to have given a new edginess to its dichotomy between philosophy and rhetoric. His ultimately theological concept of reason as pure cognition "in God" made the rhetor's verbal trickery seem all the more sacrilegious. At the same time, he expanded the trope of the orator manipulating his audience into an all-encompassing social analysis and moral indictment of speech itself. While speech turned one outward in insatiable self-love, the labor of attention turned one inward, from the social shell to the inner recess. It made the meditator present to God within himself, in the form of universal reason, and hence present to his real self, the rational *res cogitans* seemingly trapped within the distorting mirrors of the *res extensa*.

Did this radical dichotomy leave any room in the turn inward for sense representation in the form of words? There was reason to think that print communication, as opposed to oral exchange, opened a space. In soundless reading, with the role of sight limited to the printed characters, reader and author could enter the same haven of silence. Words on the printed page were in that sense more immune to concupiscence precisely because they were "dead." And yet the examples of Tertullian, Seneca, and especially Montaigne were so alarming because these writers managed somehow to use dead words as the instruments of their lively, overpowering imaginations. "Their words, dead though they may be . . . enter, they penetrate, they dominate the soul in a manner so imperious that they are obeyed without being understood, and we yield to their orders without knowing them" (173). Hence as a tool of concupiscence "style" in the written word, one might conclude, differed from oratory only by degree. But the case of Montaigne—the fact that an imagination as "criminal" as his could infect others through print—raised a possibility that was still more alarming. As the representation of an authorial persona like Montaigne's, style could make the written word more poisonous than the orator's performance.

Intent on purging Montaigne from himself, Malebranche had more reason than most to prevent the imagination from "revolting" by "always subjecting it to reason," even as it gave his "expressions" such "beauty" and "precision." His effort as a writer to keep the imagination under tight control, but without entirely forgoing its help, has aptly been characterized as his "wager" that he could develop a "rhetoric of Christian charity." Postlapsarian man's weakness made it necessary to reinforce reason with a new rhetoric in which imagination had a role but authorial style had no place. The wager's underlying paradox was that Truth, though universal and hence accessible to all, is not transferable from one person to another; each person finds it within himself, in his own labor to remove the sense veil. Verbal communication of the truth runs two inseparable risks: distorting the universal by giving it the particularity of sense representation, and intruding power, in the form of apparent "authority," into what should be a completely autonomous interior search. How then can there be a rhetoric of truth? In the face of this challenge Malebranche tried to construct a completely depersonalized voice in writing—a voice without an authorial persona, detached from the particular attributes of any individualized character, whether that character, in its power over others, was represented in the conventionally male terms of public life or in what he saw as the still more coercive "effemimate" alternative to those terms in *le monde*.

Another way of putting all this is to say that Malebranche wagered that he could develop a counteraesthetic, an aesthetic of truth.[49] Such an aesthetic had to be asocial and even antisocial. Reading might be, to a degree, detachable from the ideological cacophony of oral communication, but it was in the end a social act. It was precisely the social character of reading that allowed the world of *honnêteté* to make it an extension of itself, and to celebrate a new symbiosis of print and orality in its reconfiguration of the gendered attributes of intelligence. For Malebranche the question was whether he could give his philosophical persona a rhetorical voice, even in the most minimal sense, without surrendering to and becoming complicit in the corrupted intersubjectivity effected in social exchange.

There were, in principle, two ways to win the wager. The first Malebranche took from Augustine, as translated by his Oratorian colleague Father Martin. He would limit himself to serving as the reader's "monitor" or, perhaps better, his "prompter," offering his own words simply as a way to prompt the turn inward to truth that the reader must pursue entirely on his own, by his own mental labor.[50] In theological terms, the prompter was the occasional cause through which God, the sufficient cause, effected the reader's conversion, understood as his return to union with God and to his selfhood as a spiritual being. While the prompter could not play the pedagogical master (*magister*), he also had to eschew the techniques of style through which an author, in the act of representing himself in print, commanded authority. Eschewing style in that radical sense meant not assuming a social persona, whether it be that of an orator inflicting power under the guise of public authority, or that of the *bel esprit* exercising power more insidiously in what appeared to be the reciprocal freedom of conversation, outside the jurisdiction of public authority. In this styleless writing—and here is the second strategy— Malebranche could harness his imagination to elicit and perhaps intensify the reader's "attention" to rational demonstration by using figurative language and other rhetorical devices, ever so sparingly, to "strike" the reader in a way that awakened his "secret ardor" for the truths of reason to be found within himself.[51] This was rhetoric without coercion, imaginative representation free of concupiscent impulses.

A recent study has shown us, in illuminating detail, the forms this rhetoric of Christian charity assumed in the figures, tropes, and other illocutionary elements of Malebranche's prose.[52] No less important is his use of the genre of the philosophical dialogue, particularly in two of the volumes he wrote in the quarter century or so after the appearance of *The Search After Truth*. He published the *Christian Conversations* in 1677 in response to a request by the duke of Chevreuse that he take up again all the principles pertaining to religion in *The Search After Truth*. In the *Conversations on Metaphysics, Religion, and Death*, published in 1688, he guides the reader through his entire Cartesian-Augustinian system in a logical progression from Descartes's mind/body dualism to the Incarnation.[53] These are two classic contributions to the Christian tradition of appropriating Socratic and Platonic dialogue, reaching "a final point of unity and order" in an ascent from reason to revelation.[54] But within the structure of the received genre, he was experimenting with the use of characters and the interplay of metaphysical and psychological elements in their dramatic encounters. The terms *conversations* and *entretiens* in the titles are in themselves a measure of his intent to turn the language of *honnêteté* against itself.

In the progress through a series of conversations, Malebranche the writer is, so to speak, invisible and indeed silent. Instead there is a character—named Théodore in both texts—who has undergone the labor of meditation and now serves as the prompter to his interlocutor, offering explications of truth that occasion him to undertake the same labor. In the first conversation we learn that the conversion process has already begun; earlier conversations with Théodore have made the interlocutor disillusioned with "the emptiness" and "the nothingness" of his life in the world. All that is happening in the conversations themselves, Théodore emphasizes repeatedly, is a physical exchange of sounds. Why, then, should the reader regard the use of language in this exercise in intersubjectivity as any different from the "confused noise" of power in social exchange? The answer lies in the capacity of the prompter to communicate without social motives, and without exploiting the illusion of social authority; and in the fact that the interlocutor's actual grasp of truth only occurs offstage, so to speak, in the solitary meditation he undertakes between conversations. Each conversation begins with the interlocutor assuring Théodore that, in the silent turn inward he has undertaken since their last meeting, he has made progress in grasping abstract concepts and is now ready to pose new questions.

On one level the conversational form structures a logically ordered exposition of rational truths. But the exposition is also driven by a kind of dramatic action, a dynamic in which characters engage each other psychologically even as they explore a world of ideas that are, in principle, universal and hence cleanly different from the particularity of the psychological. It is in this dramatic interplay, as well as in what Fontenelle calls his "diction," that Malebranche harnesses his imagination to his purpose. A psychological dynamic between particular selves becomes the occasion for a spiritual "friendship" between selves participating in universal truth. Even as he surveys a realm of truth above the social, the prompter becomes a character engaging other characters.

The two texts are variations on this basic rhetorical strategy, and the differences between them are worth examining. In the *Christian Conversations* Théodore's primary interlocutor is Aristarque, a disillusioned man of the world. We learn that Aristarque is a well-travelled military man and, more important, something of a *savant*. He has a friend, always offstage, who is a philosophical skeptic, and the friend's influence, combined with the fact that his mind, "too dissipated" by his travels, is unable to "listen with attention," makes him persist in resisting Théodore's promptings well into the text.[55] Aristarque's resistance gradually ebbs not simply because Théodore's words awaken his inner ardor for the truth, but also because a third character, Éraste, serves as a powerful reproach to his philosophical pretensions. When Théodore proposes that Éraste be brought into the conversation, he describes him as "a young man whom the commerce of the world has not at all spoiled, so that nature or rather reason alone speaks in him and we can recognize which of us two is preoccupied." Where Aristarque engages in intellectual maneuvers, Éraste "consults the master who teaches him in the most secret place of his reason" and "responds only in accord with him."[56] He speaks, as a character, the rational truth that one labors to find in the silence of meditation. His simple answers to Théodore's questions and completely candid admissions of ignorance guide Aristarque as he sheds both his intellectual baggage and his social shell. In the end, of course, it is Éraste who acts most consequentially. In the final conversation Aristarque reads Théodore a passionate letter from Éraste, explaining why he has decided to abjure any "particular vocation" in the world for a life of cloistered "privation" in search of the "essential things." Théodore urges Aristarque to do likewise, and to take his formerly skeptical but now chastened friend with him.[57]

Malebranche completed the *Conversations on Metaphysics, Religion, and Death* in the summer of 1687, during one of his retreats to an Oratorian residence outside Paris. By then two new developments had given him reason to conduct a somewhat different experiment in dialogic writing. Four years earlier he had published the *Christian and Metaphysical Meditations*, his most obviously devotional work and his boldest effort to develop a new rhetoric.[58] Rather than presenting his thought in a series of conversations, seemingly without an authorial presence, he presented himself engaging in a dialogue with Christ as the Logos, the Word Made Flesh. The reader witnesses meditation as natural prayer of a higher order, ascending to an aesthetic that transcends "sensible beauties." Christ enables us "to merit a grace of *sentiment*, or that interior delectation that makes human beings love, as by instinct, a beauty they ought to love by reason."[59] Malebranche was aware that his fervid prose would open him to the charge of authorial self-exhibition and rhetorical manipulation. In the preface to the *Meditations* he emphasized that all the truths to be expounded were Christ's alone, and that he alone was responsible for the book's "errors," since he "had no doubt whatsoever that [his] imagination had seduced [him], however much effort he had made to oblige it to be quiet and to reject its responses." In the meditations themselves he took pains to limit his own role to asking questions and humbly accepting Christ's answers. Conducting his task with this humility and caution, he felt justified in using "expressions" that were "alive and animated" as well as "clear and true (*véritables*)" in the service of a purely spiritual aesthetic.[60]

But Malebranche's Jansenist antagonists were quick to fault him for presuming to give the Logos so obviously a human voice and, worse, for concealing his advocacy of his own theological and philosophical views behind this questionable ventriloquism. It was probably with an awareness of his vulnerability on this score that, in the seventh of the fourteen conversations in the *Conversations on Metaphysics and Religion*, Malebranche brought a third character, Théotimus, to the support of Théodore. Unlike the Éraste of the earlier *Conversations*, Théotimus is an experienced *méditatif*. He proves to be a more sober prompter than Théodore, sticking more closely to the pure logic of the argument. He is the check on Théodore's—and Malebranche's—rhetorical imagination.

The most striking difference from the earlier *Conversations* lies in the psychological dynamic between Théodore and Aristes. In a more generous but still sharply critical way, the character of Aristes continues the indictment of the *bel esprit* and his world that Malebranche had leveled three years earlier in the *Treatise on Morals*. Aristes is receptive to Théodore's promptings in the conversation and yet still cannot help playing the *bel esprit*, with "that quality that makes [him] entirely brilliant (*tout éclatant*) in people's eyes [and] that makes those who know [him] want to possess [him]."[61] That is why Théodore insists at the outset that they withdraw from the "enchanted places" of their earlier meetings to Aristes's study. Perhaps the most dramatically subtle and effective moment in Malebranche's writings comes in the first conversation, when Aristes entreats Théodore ever so earnestly to "remove" him to "that happy and enchanted region" that has so "pleased" him in an earlier conversation. Théodore reads this as a "delicate" and *honnête* gesture of mockery, and, even as he forgives it, refuses to be drawn into Aristes's conversational game. To be drawn in would be to allow the counter-aesthetic of truth to be absorbed into the social aesthetic of play. "You are following the secret inspirations of your ever enjoyable imagination," Théodore responds. Rather than "leading you into a strange country," he continues, "I will perhaps teach you that you are yourself a stranger in your own country" by "returning [you] into yourself."[62] When Aristes reverts to his "flattering manners" in the sixth conversation, he receives a much sharper rebuke. He is acting like "most people," who "think only of some rejoinder which would make people admire the subtlety of their imagination." Théodore assures Aristes that he is not being "severe" to him in particular; it is in my own "heart," in "its depth of concupiscence and vanity," that "I read what I am telling you." But then comes this emphatically social provocation, like a clenched fist:

> My manners surprise you. They are harsh and awkward, rustic if you will. But what is this? Do you think that sincere friendship, founded on Reason, seeks detours and disguises? You do not know the privileges of the *méditatifs*. They have the right to tell their friends unceremoniously (*sans façon*) what they find fault with in their conduct.[63]

In his eulogy Fontenelle expressed admiration for all three of Malebranche's adaptations of the dialogic form. However skeptical he might have been about their metaphysical and theological contents, he found them elegant examples of the "natural disposition" with which Malebranche practiced "the art of the author," lending poetic "ornaments" to philosophy without allowing the voice of "the senses and the imagination" to intrude on its reasoning.[64] This tribute is, in one sense, misleading; the term "natural" obscures the fact that, in channeling his imaginative powers into his rhetorical strategy, Malebranche had taken a calculated risk. In his own writing, he approached the literary imagination less as an ingrate, to recall Fontenelle's term, than as a severe disciplinarian. Arguably his severity came at a price that Fontenelle's mix of praise and raillery left implicit. The way he perceived the social—the specific sites he fixed his critique on—sharply narrowed the parameters within which he could realize the ideal of Christian charity in the printed word. What the world of honnêteté celebrated as the natural freedom of conversation he saw as its opposite: the coercive power of speech, all the more tyrannical for being so insidious. Even in his "conversations," and indeed especially in them, he had to renounce the use of style in its polite conversational form, despite the fact that that form was conceived and practiced as an alternative to the public rhetoric that he too sought to avoid. The renunciation was double edged. It limited the writer's options, but also required him, within the limits, to reinforce demonstrative reasoning with spare but enlivening, and indeed animating, rhetorical techniques that make some of his texts stunning examples of the rational lucidity, psychological finesse, and simple elegance that came to define seventeenth-century French classical prose.

Malebranche had good reason to regard his writing as cleanly different from the style with which the bel esprit inscribed himself as a social being in print. And yet he too was an author, a writer with no choice but to represent himself, however obliquely, as a character and, perhaps more effectively, in the imagined interaction of characters; and in this practice of a distinctive style lay much of his communicative power.

When we consider Malebranche and Poullain together, we find two strikingly different perceptions of the feminization of salon society and culture. Poullain drew inspiration from an idealized salon world to frame his argument for female equality, though he also bowed to the strict demands that the actual culture placed on women (and men) of leisure. To Malebranche the same culture represented an especially alarming site of human corruption in the form of the honnête femme and her pliant pupil, the honnête homme.

Until the close of the eighteenth century, Poullain's argument for equality had hardly any purchase. It is the traces of Malebranche's vision that we find in eighteenth-century French thinking about gender. The fact that the overarching structure of his Cartesian Augustinianism was discarded makes all the more striking that his rigorist censure of effeminacy survived, though it was often hard to discern as it mixed with other variations on the same theme and most notably with classical republicanism. Malebranche was one of Jean-Jacques Rousseau's favorite authors.

Chapter 4

Love, Gallantry, and Friendship

There was much discussion of friendship in seventeenth-century France, where it remained an adhesive essential to the workings of hierarchy and patronage but also began to allow mutual individuality, sometimes at a private distance from social conventions.[1] Not surprisingly, one of the issues was whether a man and a woman could be friends without becoming lovers. La Bruyère was cautious about the extent to which the gender difference could be rendered irrelevant: "Friendship can subsist between people of different sexes, exempt even from all crudeness. A woman, however, always regards a man as a man, and reciprocally a man regards a woman as a woman. This liaison is neither passion nor pure friendship; it makes a class apart."[2]

Scudéry may have agreed, but in her essay on *politesse* she observed that what she found most "agreeable" was a gathering of five or six men and women friends for a good meal, enjoying an *honnête liberté* and conversation in which one says what one wants to say and what one thinks. "The *esprit* glows more brilliantly than elsewhere, though there is no design at all to appear."[3] Scudéry's comment reminds us that men and women found a respite from the performative demands of *le monde* in private friendships, relationships of *amitié* with far more intimate exchange than polite conversation allowed but without the passion of *l'amour*. They were not lovers; they simply spoke freely, confided in each other, and took pleasure in each other's company. Whenever the play of *esprit* in the salons was prized for its natural spontaneity, the implied contrast was with the stiffness of court manners and the grandiosity of public eloquence. These private friendships were more natural still, a kind of retreat from society rather than play on its stage.

In much of public discourse, however, the ideal of friendship had been shaped by a classical tradition that educated men were taught in Latin texts in the *collèges* and the universities. They learned that the highest order of friendship—the bond of complete equality between the virtuous—was reserved to the rare few among men. The ur-text was Aristotle's *Nichomachean Ethics*. To Aristotle most friendships were of the "lesser" kind, in that they were instrumental relationships in which each served the other's needs or gave him pleasure. These were the relationships of asymmetrical interdependence, including marriage, that constituted society. Erotic love was friendship of this lesser order, distinguished by its extreme dependence and transience. The higher form of friendship—what I will call the friendship of heroic virtue—was reserved almost entirely to rare men who loved each other from positions of autonomous selfhood, purely as virtuous human beings, without a self-interest in the satisfaction of need. Such friendship required "rational choice" about the character of the other, and hence it was a "state" of mind, not a "feeling." It helped men in their prime "to do noble actions." Many, perhaps most schoolboys were introduced to this ideal in Cicero's *De amicitia*, which made it rhetorically much more compelling than did Aristotle's dry prose. True friendship was rare, they read; and it was to be found only among an aristocracy of citizens, the most "illustrious" of the well-born and propertied patriciate that presided over public life. Only this kind of friendship is "natural" rather than calculating, as it is "an inclination of the soul joined with a feeling of love." The friends' love for each other was grounded purely in mutual admiration of moral character. It allowed for a certain private psychological intimacy, but this was intimacy without the "weakness" of women and others driven by need. Cicero, following Aristotle, emphasized that the "love" in such friendships was made possible by the intellectual and moral autonomy of each friend. It was because they did not need each other that they could love each other. What was to be said, Cicero asked, about a man who could not bear the absence of a friend who was called to "duties"? He "is not only weak and effeminate, but, on that very account, is far from reasonable in his friendship."[4]

Seventeenth-century humanism had its own idealized community of friends, the Republic of Letters, which attached virtue to learning and especially Latinate erudition. It drew more on the Stoic tradition of askesis, but joined the solitary acquisition of learning with the communal sharing of it across Europe's political and religious battle lines. Conversation in this tradition brought reciprocal moral improvement through reasoned learned exchange.[5] The conversation was often virtual, an epistolary exchange conducted in a stylized "passionate rhetoric of affection" that was understood to be clearly distinct from erotic passion. It could degenerate, of course, into the petty feuding that the word "pedantry" evoked, but that did not prevent the Republic's members from priding themselves on the civility, fraternal openness and equality with which they shared knowledge and conducted arguments. The Republic was an emphatically male community; learned women were considered freakish.[6]

One might think that the culture of *le monde*, regarding as it did philosophical abstraction and displays of learning as male-specific disqualifications, would make some greater measure of equality between autonomous men and women in friendship possible. But the code of gallantry, integral to the social aesthetic of play and often considered its highest form, had more ambiguous effects. The *galant* was a master of the art of pleasing women in speech and in manner. This was an aesthetic of performance with erotic innuendos, or at least an erotic sub-text, a game of words and gestures and glances that might end in seduction but in the ideal was pleasurable precisely because it had no consequences. Though far removed from the exaltation of sexual purity in chivalry, it retained a measure of the chivalric element of self-denial. Part of the pleasure for both sexes lay in knowing that the erotic desire for the other would never diminish but would never be satisfied. At least rhetorically, the man embraced a role of servitude, a state of total dependence on the woman's response, in a kind of fictive bracketing out of the power men enjoyed over law and property.

The role of gallantry in producing modern civilization would be much debated in the eighteenth century. Some credited it with allowing women to transform men into members of a civil society that elevated both sexes morally; others blamed it for trivializing sociability, reducing it to dissimulating appear-ances, and for making men effeminate. Recent scholarship has provided a more balanced view that gives us some insight into how gallantry at once perpetuated and questioned received assumptions about gender relations and gendered differ-ences in intelligence. Gallantry was, in Alain Viala's apt phrase, a "culture of respectful desire."[7] In the very long view, its play precluded the brutal treatment of women as mere prey in the satisfaction of male sexual desire; ritualized flirta-tion gave women a certain freedom of choice in the realm of the erotic and the passionate. Arguably gallantry also filled a psychic need for the sons and daugh-ters of titled and propertied families, most of whom had no choice but to honor the financial and political imperatives of lineage by entering arranged marriages, a lynchpin of old-regime social hierarchy. There was, to be sure, a small group of Parisian society women caricatured as *les précieuses*, Scudéry prominent among them, who imagined an alternative world where they might reject such marriages for a community of female friends devoted to the most refined taste in conversa-tion and writing, and perhaps practice a voluntary lay celibacy.[8] More commonly for both sexes, though, gallantry—whether in ritual performances or in extramari-tal love affairs—offered emotional compensation for marriages with incompatible and sometimes odious partners.[9]

To judge by Scudéry's essay "Of the *galant* air," cultivated women of her generation feared that a plague of "false" gallants (*mauvais galants*) was ruining the genuine article. An "infinite number of young people" were professional gal-lants who cared only about "making their entry into *le monde*," taking up "the most bizarre fashions," ceaselessly making the rounds of "all the houses whose doors are open," talking much without having anything to offer but "trifles" (*baga-telles*). If brusque and arrogant lovers were intolerable, so were the "universal sighers" and the cheerful gallants (*enjoués*), neither flirts nor lovers, going from *ruelle* to *ruelle* speaking of love only with ridicule.[10] Scudéry's character Sapho finds corruption in all this; the mutual respect required in true gallantry is degenerating into formulaic behavior that makes men ridiculous and denigrates the women it is supposed to honor. With that danger in mind, Scudéry wanted to play down erotic idolization, which in fact serves men's contempt for women, and to insist on the need to engage women's reasonable agency. She acknowledges that, in addition to all the other qualities required of a *galant*, the man must "have had at least once in his life some light amorous inclination." Not so for a woman; it suffices that "she have the intention of pleasing in general, without loving anything in particular." Women "would in no way allow that uncivil familiarity that most of the new *galants* want to introduce in *le monde*."[11] Nonetheless, she added, we should not reproach the woman who cooperates in gallantry, not being able "to prevent herself from loving another more than herself."[12]

The larger significance of Scudéry's essay lies in its evocation of a group of men and women trying to lift gallantry above a conventional rhetorical code they found tiresome and degrading. It was often implicit to the code that no kind of friendship with a woman could operate outside the erotic; female intelligence was valued only when it was coupled with physical beauty. If eroticism was to remain inconsequential, it required an implicit ironic distance, but the ways of assuming that posture clearly varied. Irony could take the form of patronizing deference, a homage whose subtext was that, in intruding nothing serious or labored into the exchange, the *galant* graciously lowered himself to female intellectual weakness, confirming his own superiority of body and mind by not using it to his advantage. But there were also subtleties in gallant irony that widened the conventional parameters for intellectual affinity between men and women. We have to keep in mind that from the midcentury on gallant conversation was in symbiosis with a new gallant style in polite literature, some of it printed. However frothy that literature may seem to us, it allowed something unprecedented: a bond of shared psychological insight through literary texts that made new kinds of friendship possible.[13] Scudéry's Sapho raised the possibility of "a type of gallantry without love (*amour*) which sometimes even mixes with the most serious matters, and which gives an inexplicable charm to everything one does and says."[14]

The Loves and Friendships of Saint-Évremond

There is perhaps no better example of the unmodern modernity of the culture of *honnêteté* than Saint-Évremond, a casual gentleman of letters and an internationally renowned master of the French art of conversational sociability in the second half of the seventeenth century.[15]

Literary scholarship on Saint-Évremond has revealed a critic more intellectually serious and substantive than he wanted to appear. To be sure, he did not think of himself as practicing "critique," which he dismissed as a severe and joyless academic trade. If he had contempt for the critic's "exactitude," he also would have nothing to do with the "austerity" of abstract reasoning in philosophy. But he was in fact a thoughtful and discerning judge of literature, and his efforts to weave his way through the disputes that became known as the battle of the ancients and the moderns are noteworthy.[16] While he did not subscribe to the ancients' view of the classics as the pinnacle that could never again be reached, he was in fact well versed in classical literature, in part from his education in a Jesuit *collège*, in part from continual rereading of a wide variety of Latin texts.[17]

Still, Saint-Évremond's mostly brief and casual writings are classic examples of the social aesthetic of play shaping a new polite literature. Most of his writings were in the discursive style of letters to friends. Writing was a form of play, a way to "divert" himself and a few other gentlemen, though some of the pieces seem to have circulated broadly in manuscript. It was friends who published some of his epistolary essays during his lifetime; shunning the identity of an author, he did not authorize them. If his *aisance* and *négligence* were a pose, they were also an exercise in the literary modernity of the seventeenth century. He often made it clear that he was making no claim to objective authority; readers were simply being offered his personal opinion. He was despite himself one of the creators of the essay genre. In his very denial of labor and seriousness he was contributing to a new subjectivization of critical judgment. It is not surprising that David Hume, whose polite essays often had the discursive style of simulated conversation, enjoyed reading Saint-Évremond.

His relations with women, like his writing, are more complicated than they might at first appear to be. With what might be singular clarity, they reveal two needs that were fused rhetorically in the ideal of gallantry but came into tension in social practice: the need for a *galant* love (*amour*), so saturated with erotic passion that it enslaved the man even as he remained aware of his superiority, and the need for intellectual equality with a woman in what Saint-Évremond, defying conventional male wisdom, called a "friendship of the mind." With most women he was an inveterate practitioner of gallantry, albeit a somewhat eccentric one. He aged into a grizzled man with a large goiter between his eyes, notoriously slovenly in his dress, preferring a skull cap to a wig to cover his sparse white hair. That he could ignore his appearance is a measure of the admiration he drew from both sexes as a master of the art of conversation, the flashing wit that could be caustic but was more often agreeable. However much the art required manipulative mastery of a code, in his practice of it gallantry was more than a matter of following convention. It was integral to his psychological and emotional makeup, a kind of second nature that seemed to him essential to discernment in matters of taste. He simply could not feel truly alive without being in a state of homage to a beautiful woman, a female to whom he enslaved himself emotionally in return for her gift of the "pleasure" in sheer beauty that made life bearable.

Saint-Évremond was a master of the ironic subtext to gallant flattery, the implicitly detached awareness of merely playing a game. At times the ironic distance in his prose went beyond the conventional variety and became a critical distance with a moral bite, contrasting the superficial traits of the *galant* with the qualities that true character required. Consider his portrait of the Countess d'Olonne, the young wife of one of his friends, published in 1659. The Countess already had a reputation as a particularly libertine *galante femme*, fickle and mercenary with her lovers. Saint-Évremond had been a regular visitor at the d'Olonne home. Now he assumed the persona of "a Spectator" who had "taken care to maintain his liberty" of judgment by keeping his distance from a woman he described, in the gallant key, as irresistibly beautiful and charming. He acknowledged that, in addition to having no need to hide defects in her beauty, as she had none, she was a master of politeness in conversation, with a "fine intelligence" and vivacity of *esprit*. But the piece was not the usual Voiturian exercise in gallantry; it was an appraisal of "character" in the tradition of Theophrastus, allowing for more frankness. The implicit message was that gallant qualities of beauty, charm, and even *esprit* could not make up for faults of character. Saint-Évremond confronted the lady with her faults. She was easily swayed by "mediocre people"; she was incapable of serious reflection; her opinions were "more strongly imagined than solidly known"; and she was haughty and too quick to take offense.[18]

Another portrait, titled "The idea of a woman who is not found at all and who will never be found," is perhaps Saint-Évremond's most unconventional and thoughtful comment on women of character.[19] It was probably written in the late 1660s when he was living at The Hague, and it records his need for the society of a woman different from both Dutch Protestant women, whom he found sociable but uninspiring, and affected Parisian ladies. Its language is worth close scrutiny, as it judges gallantry largely from outside its code. Saint-Évremond begins in a tone of relief: this woman, whom he calls Aemilie, does not need the usual adulation, as "she is obliged only to herself for the justice that is rendered to her."[20] To put it another way, she has an interior sense of self-worth; it does not require the (apparently) admiring gaze of others. Her *esprit* "has extension without being vast, never going so far into general thoughts that she cannot return easily to particular considerations." In her conversation "she says nothing with study and nothing by chance"; she deals with "the most serious matters" without any apparent "effort."[21] Sensibly devout, with no ascetic impulse, she avoids "the horror of solitude" and "has no wish to detach herself from civil life." In Aemelie, Nature "has made a sensitive heart, which should feel, and has given reason, which should command, an absolute empire over her movements (*actions*)." She "attracts you, she retains you, and you always approach her with desires you would dare not make visible."[22]

The encomium ends somewhat tortuously, with an intriguing departure from its title. Aemilie is not an unrealizable ideal; she is "rather the idea of an accomplished person": "I have not at all wished to find [such a person] among men, because they always lack in their commerce an indescribable *douceur* that one encounters in the commerce of women; and I have believed it less possible to find in a woman the most forceful and sane reason of men than to find in a man the charms and *agréments* natural to a women."[23] Though Aemilie is naturally sociable, she does not need the approval of admirers; she is *honnête* without being drawn into the hypersociability that *honnête* culture demanded. She is in that sense an autonomous being, fully engaged in the particularities of social life but self-governing in her rational agency. Saint-Évremond describes an intelligence that is at once effortless and cultivated. It is posed against, at one end, frivolous society women and, at the other, the "austerity" of scholarly and philosophical reasoning.[24] With the phrase "accomplished person" Saint-Évremond makes the essay about the *relational* intelligence that men as well as women ought to have but is more likely to be found in women. The ideal of the *honnête femme*, now cast as *any* accomplished person, becomes a human aspiration.

Joan Scott identifies in feminist movements a "fantasy" promising "wholeness and completeness," though never fully realizing the promise.[25] I find something analogous here in the figuring of a friendship between a man and a woman, joined in reasonable sociability as self-governing persons, each making the other whole. Only in this conjoined wholeness can a man integrate rational intellection into a holistic ideal of the intelligent social being. This requires not repressing erotic passion, but containing it within the imagination. It is their shared reason that allows Saint-Évremond and Aemilie to have a truly natural relationship in which the erotic remains subliminal. Desire accedes to respect for the accomplished person that perhaps only a woman can be. To disdain abstraction was not to embrace the irrational; he had in mind a sociable but autonomous reasonableness, practicing the appropriate, the *bienséance* of *honnêteté*, but at the same time, under cover, one might say, of the freedom of *esprit* that seemed so natural to Aemilie, exercising a critical distance within the worldly ethos of honor.[26]

Saint-Évremond's most formative education had been in the company of Anne Lenclos, who had nothing of the devoutness of Aemilie. Lenclos was born into a family of the lower nobility which could boast lineage but lacked the wealth to make good matches for its daughters. Her upbringing had been a classic tug of war between two utterly mismatched parents, an extremely devout and strict mother and a father who spent much of his time in Paris's libertine circles. Henri de Lenclos had made something of a career in the military but had to flee the country in 1633 after murdering a man who was going to testify against him on the charge of adultery. His wretched marriage had probably reinforced his contempt for conventional religion and his devotion to libertine philosophy, especially that of Epicurus. He dearly loved his daughter, who seemed so much like him, and he won the battle for her mind. When she was merely eighteen, her mother (piety notwithstanding) arranged for her to be the well-kept mistress of a member of the Paris parlement. When her mother died in the spring of 1643, Lenclos became the mistress of her own fate, despite recurrent efforts by "the devout" to suppress her intellectual and sexual libertinism. Perhaps because scandal made her persona non grata in polite society, she took the unrespectable route and became a courtesan, while continuing to cultivate her literary taste and philosophical interests.[27]

Over the next two decades Lenclos, who became known as Ninon, became a unique presence in seventeenth-century Paris. The evening gatherings at her residence attracted a wide variety of men, from scions of some of France's wealthiest and most prominent families to impoverished gentlemen. It hardly mattered that she was, by all accounts, not a beauty. Few came for sex; what most guests enjoyed was a unique "liberty" of manners and conversation. At the center of it all was the elegant and intellectually scintillating conversation of Ninon herself. She seems to have managed to keep in separate departments her impassioned love affairs and sex for pay, which she provided to some men and refused to many others.[28] Even in mercenary sex she was the chooser, not the chosen. That way of being a courtesan gave her a financial independence that very few unmarried and unwidowed women enjoyed, which in turn allowed her to pursue her tastes as well as her amorous pleasures as she pleased. She and Saint-Évremond became friends when he was soldiering in the Thirty Years' War and had frequent stays in Paris. The nature of their relationship is not entirely clear; in a letter to her in 1669, he recalled that he had "always played with her neither the simple friend nor the true lover."[29] What is certain is that he became one of her self-appointed tutors, completing her education with readings in the classics and modern literature. Tutor and pupil seem to have dealt with each other on terms of intellectual equality. In his final years, in a renewed correspondence with Ninon, he looked back nostalgically on a truly natural freedom at her gatherings that the salons, for all their preference for natural spontaneity, did not allow. With Ninon, he recalled, he had known both the delights of erotic love, if only vicariously, and the more satisfying pleasures of friendship with a highly intelligent and free-thinking woman.[30]

The configuration of several key words in Saint-Évremond's writing—nature, pleasure, liberty, and friendship—was to some extent philosophically grounded. Sometime during his years in Paris he had had long conversations with Pierre Gassendi, the well-known neo-Epicurean philosopher, and he came away from them convinced that, as there were strict limits to what could be known, any other philosophy was vain and futile. In an essay titled "Sur les plaisirs," he divided seekers after pleasure into three types: the sensual, abandoning themselves grossly to their animal appetites; the voluptuous, whose sensual impressions "go all the way to the soul"; and the "delicate," who give a greater role in their taste to *esprit*. It was the "delicate" who had given modern society politeness, gallantry, the refinements of luxury, and what he called *l'erudito luxu*, following Petronius, the author of *Satyricon*, his favorite Latin text.[31] In a rare statement of self-reflection, he summarized the state of mind he sought as an Epicurean: "I wish that the knowledge of feeling nothing (*sentir*) that disturbs me, and that the reflection of myself free and master of myself bring me the spiritual *volupté* of the good Epicurus, which is not, as the vulgar imagine, a state without sorrow and without pleasure, but the sentiment of a pure and delicate joy that gives repose of the conscience and tranquility of esprit."[32] The "spiritual pleasure" he sought was to be found above all, and perhaps only, in friendship. In contrast to "justice" in civil society, friendship was indispensable because it was "the work of Nature"; its sentiments were "the movements most natural to Man," at the opposite pole from the self-interested and overly prudent calculations of the courtier.[33] In the confiding of secrets and opening of the heart one experienced "the entirely natural sweetness of a liberty." This "liaison between two souls" required fidelity and confidence in the other's discretion, and allowed for reasonable differences of opinion; but there must also be a "warmth," an "ineffable charm": "In my view, the private commerce with a woman, beautiful, *spirituelle*, reasonable, renders such a liaison sweeter still, if one can be assured of its permanence. But when passion mixes in with it, disgust puts an end to the trust in love, and if there is only friendship, the sentiments of friendship do not hold out long against the movements of a passion."[34]

For much of his life Saint-Évremond refused to accept this double bind. He sought a wholeness with a woman that combined the sweetness of friendship of the mind and the desire of passionate love (*l'amour*), irresistible and beyond fulfillment. He owed his second great opportunity to exile. In 1661, soon after assuming personal rule, Louis XIV had Nicolas Fouquet, his minister of finance, imprisoned for life. It was not simply Fouquet's great wealth and power over state finances that made him an overmighty subject; he threatened to overshadow his king as a collector and patron of the arts, surrounding himself with some of the most celebrated men of letters of the day and cultivated gentlemen, including Saint-Évremond. The gatherings at the magnificent chateau Fouquet had had built on his estate at Vaux-le-Vicomte seemed unrivaled for their polite taste, their promotion of literary fashions, and their dazzling fêtes.

But Fouquet's seized papers were said to include an indiscrete letter by Saint-Évremond, disapproving of French foreign policy, and he had to flee into exile in late 1661. In November 1662, he moved from The Hague, his first haven, to London, where he would spend the rest of his long life. Thanks to his published writings and his reputation as the epitome of the *honnête homme*, he was welcomed by admirers among the English aristocracy. With a pension from the king and what remained of his small personal fortune, he continued in the intensely sociable life-style of a gentleman of leisure. In 1689 the government of Louis XIV finally granted him permission to return to France, but he decided to remain in London. Having spent twenty-seven years in the very different political climate of England, he preferred not to live under the thumb of the Sun King. He had developed a certain fondness for the ways of his adopted country, and may even have found its weather to his liking. But it was the fondness of an inveterate Frenchman who saw no need to integrate into his host culture. He was an ambassadorial icon for men and women in London's high society who were eager to emulate French refinement of manners and conversational wit. He did not learn English.

In 1675, when Saint-Évremond was sixty-two and had been in London for thirteen years, he was drawn into the powerful magnetic field of twenty-nine-year-old Hortense Mancini, Duchess Mazarin, another celebrated (and despised) woman, though one quite different from Ninon.[35] Hortense was one of two daughters whom Girolama Manzini brought from Rome to Paris in 1653 at the summons of her fabulously wealthy brother Cardinal Mazarin, in the hope that he would secure them the advantageous marriages that she, the widow of a scholarly Roman baron, was in no position to arrange. For eighteen months Hortense and her older sister Marie lived in the Convent of the Visitation, whose nuns were known to educate well-born young girls in French, literature, and the arts as well as religion.[36] They spent the rest of their youth at Mazarin's lavish palace and the royal court at the Louvre, the two centers of power around which *le monde* revolved. In 1658 her sister Marie grew rebellious, to the point of endangering state interests, by entering a tender love affair with the young Louis XIV. It took a prolonged effort by Mazarin and Queen Anne to sever the relationship and marry the king, in a proper exercise of dynastic politics, to the Spanish princess Marie-Thérèse.

Hortense was seven years younger than Marie, apparently more pliant, and reputedly the most beautiful of the five Mancini sisters. She became Mazarin's favorite. In 1659, when Hortense was thirteen, Charles II, still in exile in France and a first cousin of Louis XIV, proposed to her, but the state negotiations broke down. Two years later she was married to Armand Charles de La Porte de La Meilleraye, a nephew of Cardinal Richelieu, and reputed to be one of the richest men in Europe, who acquired the great bulk of the Mazarin fortune and the title of duke on condition that he assume the family name. The new duke was a bizarre caricature of the Counter-Reformation Catholic, confirming virtually all stereotypes of the excess to which popery led. He insisted that his wife spend a quarter of each day in prayer. His dreams were haunted by celestial apparitions, among them conversations with the angel Gabriel. He woke his wife and the servants in the middle of the night to recount these chimerical tête-à-têtes. To protect his milkmaids from evil thoughts, he advised them not to spend too long in the grossly physical act of milking cows, and they were to assume modest postures when churning milk.[37]

The duke had reason to be watchful of his wife, whose upbringing had immersed her in the arts of flirtation and amorous intrigue. But his jealousy was obsessive; he had to be present at virtually every contact she had with a man. When he traveled to distant provinces on official duties or to visit his estates, she had to accompany him, even when she was pregnant. This manic possessiveness went hand in hand with reckless use of his wealth. Since the marriage contract did not explicitly give Hortense control over her part of the combined fortunes, the new duke could do with it as he pleased. She watched him squander much of it. Not surprisingly, all sorts of dubious people profited from his eagerness to lavish wealth on the Church. The only form of wealth that mattered to him was landed property, and he made bad investments in it. No less compulsive was his passion for litigation, on which he spent a great deal of his own and Hortense's fortunes in the belief that to litigate was to accept God's will, win or lose.

On the night of June 13, 1668, Hortense, with the help of her brother, fled to Rome, where she took refuge with her sister. Her ensuing lengthy travels to find a safe haven enraged the duke, who believed all gossip about her debauchery. To the horror of many, including the king, he chose the Mazarin art collection, the largest in Europe, for his revenge. For an entire day and much of an evening he raged through the painting galleries, throwing black paint over all the naked flesh on display and slashing the tapestries with a knife. He used a hammer to dismember the statues. Louis XIV, who regarded the Mazarin galleries as a national treasure and was well acquainted with her husband's obsessions, provided Hortense with a modest pension. Her insistence on her right to live separate from her husband, and her efforts to secure what remained of her inheritance, entangled her in a legal morass that would drag on for decades. In 1672 she settled in Chambéry in the Duchy of Savoy, where she could be sure that Duke Charles-Emmanuel, who found her enthralling, would protect her. Her home became a gathering place for men of letters and artists. With the duke's death in 1775, his widow made it clear her presence would no longer be tolerated.[38]

Shortly before moving to London, Hortense wrote a memoir, perhaps with the help of César Vichard de Saint-Réal, a writer and a *galant* entirely devoted to her.[39] It was a cleverly executed effort to dispel the aura of scandal now surrounding her. She was one of the first women to publish her life story during her lifetime with her name on the title page. Knowing that that very act might feed the scandal, she addressed the memoir to an unnamed gentleman, perhaps the duke of Savoy, who had "done [her] great favors" and had requested the story of her life. She could not turn him down, despite her "natural reluctance to talk about [her] own affairs." She had not written a "novel," though the events of her life might resemble one, and she had no desire to "[make] a public sensation." [40] The story that followed was unusually personal and replete with titillating detail, but in the voice of a woman on whom more suffering and injustice had been afflicted than anyone could be expected to endure. She had, to be sure, abandoned her four children as well as her husband, but as the victim of a despotic and pathologically ambitious uncle and a deranged husband she had had no choice. What finally made her leave, she claimed, was maternal instinct; the squandering of her money was threatening to leave her son, who ought to have been "the richest gentleman of France," penniless. Sparing no details, she recounted her horror at her husband's religious fanaticism; perhaps already contemplating a move to England, she wanted to dissociate herself cleanly from popery. Most striking was her effort to counter her image as a dissolute and empty-headed product of the French court. She recalled being an intellectually curious and serious little girl, a kind of prodigy. She would later recall that at Chambéry, she had spent much time cultivating her mind with serious reading of the classics and modern literature.[41]

In keeping with her image as both a heroic adventuress and a helpless victim, the duchess entered London with her retinue on December 31, 1675, on horseback, her man's riding habit and long cloak muddied from the long and wet winter journey. Charles II, who remained enamored of her, provided a pension and an apartment at Whitehall, the royal residence, and she also set up her own household at a residence of the duke and duchess of York in St James Park, which with her presence came to be called "the little palace."[42] Courtiers who hoped to redirect the Crown's pro-French foreign policy worked to have her replace the Duchess of Portsmouth as the king's "official" mistress, but their efforts were thwarted by Hortense's open preference for the count of Monaco.[43] To Saint-Évremond, the duchess's presence in London was a godsend, the chance for a second youth. He could at once continue to enjoy London and feel himself to be living back in the France of his youth. His conversation made him an attraction at her evening gatherings, which he would recall as having the same atmosphere of social and intellectual "liberty" Ninon had created. The timing of their friendship at once vitalized him and gave him a "sweet" melancholy. He was entering old age, and knowing that she would not take an old man as her lover, he could safely idolize her erotic power as well as her qualities of mind. In a "Portrait" he wrote in 1676 Hortense was at once well read and the epitome of *aisance* in the social aesthetic of play, her "acquired knowledge" showing "no trace of the study she has employed in acquiring it."[44] His ending of another letter, written in 1677 or 1688, reworked the same theme: "You inspire passion in all who are capable of it, and reason delivers to you those whom passion no longer touches."[45]

As with Ninon, Saint-Évremond assumed the role of tutor. He had the duchess read the "sayings" of the ancients and gently lectured her on the wonders and limitations of classical literature. They read together *Don Quixote*, his favorite book, and Montaigne's *Essays*, which he found inexhaustibly fascinating. But even in the late 1670s his ideal and the reality were diverging. The duchess was too fond of gambling, a habitual aristocratic diversion, and she drank to excess. Soon after her arrival in London, a professional gambler named Morin came on the scene, presiding over basset, a fashionable card game. In the early years she may have been able to converse about philosophy and literature even as she played the game (she was entranced by Fontenelle's *Conversations on the Plurality of Worlds*), but she became addicted to it, and her home became known more as a casino than as a venue for intelligent conversation. Saint-Évremond made no secret of his disdain for Morin and his like, and he conveyed to her with fond frankness his disgust with this "spoiled" situation.[46] What I want in friendships, he wrote her, is that "les *lumières* precede the movements, and that an esteem correctly formed in the *esprit* goes on to be animated in the Heart, and takes there the warmth necessary for friendships, as for love."[47] Instead he found himself being treated as a silly and irritating old man, caught in the very fusion of erotic passion and friendship of the mind he had imagined. He could not do anything right with her, he complained; if he was passionate, she treated him as an old fool; if reason regulated his sentiments, she said that he loved nothing, and that there had never been such indifference as his. "I prefer to see you," he wrote, "and suffer." But at times he withdrew, feeling ridiculed and embittered by the loss of their intimacy.

In the earlier years Saint-Évremond had obviously turned the duchess into an idol of the feminine, but his admiration for her was not mere fantasy. She was a remarkable woman, highly intelligent and well cultivated, gifted with a rare capacity to make people feel free and happy in her presence. She had the fortitude to endure cheerfully the insecurities and hardships of a runaway wife in the early years of her liberation and, for the rest of her life, to retain her personal independence in the face of her vengeful husband, his zealous supporters, and his fierce lawyers. Her defense of her cause did much to bring the legal plight of unhappily married women into public discussion. But she had been brought up in a world of luxury and unceasing entertainment, and she saw no reason to remake herself. Over the years she lost her pensions. Though she moved to smaller residences, she fell deeper and deeper into debt, with Saint-Évremond one of the creditors. Accustomed to gallant homage, she became trapped in it as she felt herself losing her fabled beauty with age. As she entered her fifties she grew increasingly depressed. She wished to die, Saint-Évremond would recall, while she was still the most beautiful woman in the world.[48] In the spring of 1699 she withdrew from society with two of her servants, and on July 2, 1699, at fifty-three, she died. Saint-Évremond later confirmed rumors that by refusing all medical care and food, and by drinking relentlessly, she had committed suicide.[49]

Sometime in the mid-1680s, when Saint-Évremond was in his early seventies, he and Ninon Lenclos renewed their correspondence. She had become, as she put it to him, a "personage," renowned for her good taste and sparkling conversation. Her days as a courtesan had been forgiven, or at least forgotten; and she was friends with prominent society women. She consoled him for the loss of the duchess.[50] The two friends looked back nostalgically on the passions and pleasures of earlier years, and could not help but regret that they were now imprisoned in aged bodies. But they urged each other to accept the ineluctable fact of aging, as the duchess had not been able to do. "One finds you light in your love affairs," he wrote her, but "always reliable and sincere in friendship."[51] They agreed that the most precious pleasure of life was friendship of the mind, the rare practice of intellectual equality between a man and a woman. Saint-Évremond probably had known it with Ninon Lenclos, however rose-colored their later view of it was; he had tried but failed to relive it in his years with Hortense; and it became, in the memories of old age, the greatest of all pleasures.

The Dissent of Mme de Lambert

The marquise Anne-Thérèse de Lambert formed a very different ideal of wholeness in friendship. Her *New Reflections on Women*, a brief but rhetorically dense essay, appeared in 1727, but it drew on the gatherings the widowed marquise had held on Tuesday and Wednesday afternoons from 1698 onward.[52] The salon had attracted a veritable *Who's Who* of the leading men of French letters, including Bouhours, Marivaux, and Fontenelle, who became a friend of the hostess and the salon's mentor. She managed to give the salon an aristocratic style while devoting most of the time to serious and sometimes carefully supervised discussion of scholarship and belles lettres.

The immediate provocation for Lambert's *New Reflections* was the derision being heaped on the women novelists of her day, which she took to be emblematic of the degradation of women of *le monde* under the moral profligacy of the Regency. "I have been wounded," she writes, "that men know so little their interest as to condemn women who know how to occupy their *esprit*," and that so many women are leading "a frivolous and dissipated life . . . not sustained by any principle." The derided novelists are in fact "respectable authors who have believed that they have in them qualities which enable them to conduct great things, as the imagination, sensibility, taste; these are the presents they have received from nature."[53] Lambert speaks not as a *salonnière* successfully continuing the legacy of earlier generations, but as an impassioned critic of the reigning decadence. She grounds her argument in a nostalgic vision of a golden age of salons, where the culture of *honnêteté* and gallantry was to be found in its pure form, and "where the Muses mingled with the Graces" and "the highest women in the land were not ashamed to consort with people with *esprit*."[54] In her own era women, faced with men's anti-intellectual ridicule of their intelligence, prefer to compromise their honor by enjoying the unashamed pursuit of vice. To regain their empire women must embody the aesthetic as well as the ethical, beauty as well as virtue; but virtue alone is "durable," and that is what must somehow be revived.[55]

We now have a promising new way of thinking about the significance of *New Reflections* for the history of feminism.[56] As the text amply demonstrates, Lambert contradicts Malebranche even as she seems to show him great respect. She appropriates his thought in a way that completely inverts the conclusions he drew about women's bodily weakness, their powers of imagination, and their authority in the realm of taste. Lambert drew on the assumption in the discourse of *honnêteté* of women's greater physical "sensibility," which underlay the admiration for their relational intelligence and above all their cognitive intuition and "delicacy," and which had gained new authority in Cartesian science, including, ironically, Malebranche's version. Contra Malebranche, women's greater sensibility does not make them mentally and morally weaker; it becomes a cognitive "advantage," a complement to their rational intelligence that makes it all the more "vital." "Men do not realize," she writes, "the grandeur of the present they make to women when they concede to them *l'esprit du goût*."[57] Taste is a function of the imagination, which not only gives women a quickness of understanding, but also enables them to grip the soul with its *agréments*. When Lambert writes that "we [women] give ourselves over more certainly to *agréments* than to truth," her point is that the capacity to persuade is integral to intelligence, and that it is an aesthetic capacity with which women, by virtue of their apparent weakness, are especially endowed. "We go as surely at the truth by the force of the warmth of sentiments as by the extent of the correctness of our reasonings; and we arrive always by them more quickly to the end that knowledge deals with." Hence men's exclusion of women from the study of the arts and sciences is simply unjust. Indeed women have the right to publish their labor and enjoy the public recognition she calls "glory." She is not, of course, commenting on all women, but she is issuing a striking challenge to status as well as gender norms in claiming a place for women's intellectual labor within the milieu of *le monde*.

In this reading, the fact that Lambert had been inculcated since childhood with the values of *honnêteté* did not make her, as has often been claimed, a "conservative" thinker. Quite the contrary; she was "an *honnête* feminist." Her view that in the *commerce du monde* women had a certain attentive *politesse* that taught them to manage the *amour propre* of others would have been familiar to *honnête* readers. It was another way of stating the value of women's relational intelligence. But her advocacy of women's intellectual emancipation was eclectic, drawing on her own reading in the classics, including Stoic texts, as well as her engagement in salon conversation. Using the logic of natural rights in Poullain's *Equality*, with which she had at least a second-hand knowledge, she argued that men have "usurped" authority over women by "force" rather than "natural right."[58] Against the view that women's tastes were entirely subjective and hence arbitrary, she maintained that there is "a correctness (*justesse*) of taste," "costing nothing to reason," though there can be no "rules."[59] She uses *justesse* frequently, with the inference that "judgment" is not a process of abstraction reserved to men; there is a kind of judgment combining mind and sentiment in women's discernment in matters of taste.

As we penetrate the rhetorical layers of the text, however, we realize, first, that Lambert's feminism was as much anti-*honnête* as it was *honnête*; and, second, that, paradoxically from a modern feminist standpoint, the radicalism of her views rested on sentiments that were anything but egalitarian or democratic. Perhaps most striking is that, even as she draws on the values of *honnêteté*, she faults some of its key words for justifying the oppression of women. She charges that, in men's "arbitrary" ridicule of women novelists, the stigma of "pedantry," the alter ego of *honnêteté*, becomes an excuse for an anti-intellectualism that derides intellectually engaged women.[60] Though far from rejecting the rules of propriety (*bienséance*), she writes that women's *esprit* would know how to spread its wings, were it not recalled immediately by "what one calls *bienséance*."[61] She rejects the common hyper-relational view of the *honnête femme*; intelligent women need solitude not only to study and write, but for the intellectual nourishment that vitalizes their relations with others.[62] Such views point us to the deepest level of Lambert's dissent: she denies the equation of freedom with natural *aisance* at the heart of the *honnête* revaluation of the female mind. It is not true that women think spontaneously rather than reflecting, as if "nature . . . does the reasoning for [them] and spares [them] the trouble of doing [their] own." Women *think* through "sentiment." "I don't believe that sentiment destroys the understanding," she writes; "it furnishes new *esprits* that illuminate ideas by making them more alive, more precise (*nettes*), more disentangled (*démêlées*)."[63]

To Lambert intelligence is an inherently social (or relational) capacity, and its most ennobling social site is friendship. This theme of the essay has received little attention, despite the fact that half of the text is devoted to it. It is a reflection of Lambert's milieu of conversational sociability, so different from Malebranche's world, that the litmus test for the intellectual emancipation of gifted society women becomes what she calls "a metaphysic of love." The relationship between love and friendship, particularly between men and women, had long been a subject of conversation in her salon, as it had been among the *précieuses* several decades earlier. In 1703 Louis-Silvestre de Sacy, perhaps her closest friend in the salon circle, had published a *Treatise on Friendship*, dedicated to Lambert with the acknowledgement that he had gotten the principal ideas from her.[64] Several years later Lambert published her own *Treatise on Friendship*. In a gesture of cryptic candor, she admitted that "[she] gives herself too much in friendship," and that "those who think in a vulgar way regard her as a type of dupe." She was offering "maxims" of "prudence" based on "her own experience," but largely repeating the conventional wisdom that among men and women friendship had no place for erotic passion.[65] A friendship between a man and a woman based on shared virtue and enjoying an intimacy of minds (*esprit*) was "the most delicious" of "all unions." But it was "rare and difficult"; "one must be on guard against oneself, for fear that a virtue evolves into a passion." [66]

By the time she wrote *New Reflections* Lambert had enlarged her thinking on the relationship between friendship and love in a metaphysic of love, intertwining the many strands in her intellectual and emotional formation as a woman closely engaged with the scholars and men of letters in her circle. The contrast with Saint-Évremond's aspiration to wholeness through intellectual and erotically soaked intimacy with a woman is marked. She imagined a moral union that had no place for erotic passion, even if confined to the imagination. One strand of Lambert's metaphysics was clearly the Platonic ideal of love, which had been passed down in salon circles for several generations. More striking was her blending of two traditions one might have thought to be incompatible: the classical ideal of a friendship of heroic virtue, and a de-eroticized code of gallantry. Lambert knew her Cicero and, through him, her Aristotle. Fundamental to her argument was the distinction between the moral autonomy of virtuous people and the instrumental dependence of people tied by needs. And yet, even as she excluded intimacy between women from the friendship of virtue, she feminized that ideal. The union of virtue became a "union of hearts," in which reason was made substantial and fortified by sentiment, the expression of the bodily sensibility that women had in a larger measure than men. Lambert was insistent that there could be no sensual pleasure in friendship as love; it was duty—duty to the friendship—that bound people in these rare unions. That is where gallantry became crucial to the metaphysic of love. Lambert had nothing but contempt for what passed for gallantry in her day—the rituals that facilitated and only thinly veiled rampant promiscuity. Virtue would be sustained by the "resistance" to the satisfaction of passionate desire that she found in the code of true gallantry.[67] Resistance was a key term in the essay. It made the practice of virtue and the guarding of honor, of *honnête* social reputation, virtually identical. Only a rare few *honnêtes* people in *le monde* were destined to experience the "*immensity* of happiness" in such friendship.[68]

Resistance was a kind of delicate repression of desire; without it there could be no "delicacy" in the intimacy (it would descend to gross sensuality), and without delicacy there could be no mutual nourishment in taste. In friendship as love a man and a woman were not simply in agreement on moral principles and the joint practice of them; they also trusted each other to constrain the passion of the embodied self, drawing on, but not acting on, the impulses of the sensible body. In this mutual distancing from a decadent *mondanité* women, in friendship with men, could produce as authors and enjoy the "glory" they, like exceptional men, merited.[69]

Chapter 5

Shaftesbury's Quest for Fraternity

The surviving papers of Anthony Ashley Cooper, third earl of Shaftesbury, are voluminous, as one would expect of a man of his birth and standing. His grandfather—the first earl—was one of the most gifted politicians of his age: a man of principle who molded his Calvinist heritage and ancient and modern civic humanism into a coherent advocacy of English liberties; a gifted parliamentary orator with a keen-edged wit; an exceptionally competent administrator; a charming, if coldly ironic, conversationalist; and a ruthless manipulator. In the spring of 1660, in recognition of his contribution to the restoration of the Stuart monarchy, Ashley Cooper was raised to the peerage and appointed chancellor of the exchequer. His resignation as lord chancellor in 1673 marked the fact that he could no longer keep his balance on the tightrope he had been walking for the past several years. Even as he served the king, he was becoming the leading figure in the "country Whig" opposition that sought to use the authority of Parliament to protect Protestant England from popery, arbitrary royal power in the French style, and the corrupt and corrupting court that inevitably came with it. How great a role he played in organizing failed plots to exclude the Catholic duke of York from the line of succession to the throne, perhaps with armed rebellion as a final resort, is not clear. But he fell under suspicion, probably with reason. In late November 1682 he fled to Holland, where he died in Amsterdam two months later.[1]

At fifteen the first earl's son Anthony, the only surviving heir, had suffered an illness, or perhaps an injury, that seriously incapacitated him for public life and made him increasingly reclusive. His father's hopes for founding a political dynasty had to be invested in a grandson. In 1676 the first earl brought his four-year-old grandson Anthony—the future third earl—into his own household. Supervision of the boy's education was entrusted to John Locke, one of the first earl's closest advisors on a wide range of matters, including politics.[2]

Shaftesbury grew up knowing that he was being groomed to fill his grandfather's shoes and, from 1682 on, that the responsibility for vindicating his grandfather's political principles in the face of his merciless vilification by Royalists and

Tories fell squarely on his shoulders. From the moment he returned to England from his grand tour of the continent in 1689, he was pressured by friends and allies of the family to enter Parliament. He pleaded youth and inexperience, but in 1695 was elected to the House of Commons from the seat of Poole in Dorset. On the death of his father in 1699, he ascended to the House of Peers and inherited Wimborne St. Giles, the family seat.

The great bulk of Shaftesbury's papers show us a Whig grandee performing daunting familial and political responsibilities. In the mid-1790s he began a friendship with Robert Molesworth and entered his circle of parliamentarians and men of letters intent on protecting from royal encroachments the Settlement of 1688, with its balance of power between king and Parliament. He threw himself into the political mêlée during his term in the House of Commons, and in later years, as a peer, he did his best in elections to keep in Whig hands the area of south England under his family's sway. His letters to friends and allies are filled with observations on the state of domestic and international politics. Well before the War of the Spanish Succession in 1702, he had been a passionate advocate of a European alliance to meet the menace posed by Louis XIV's France.

Shaftesbury was assiduous in overseeing Wimborne St Giles, left in disorder for the two decades before he inherited it. As an improving landlord he urged his tenants to practice what he called "the *Bolder Husbandry* newly afoot amongst us."[3] A letter of instructions to his butler grew from a little over three pages in 1700 to 150 pages in 1707. In 1699 he purchased Little Chelsea, a residence about three miles from the center of London, to which he added wings, a library, and meticulously planned gardens. He went into debt to secure generous dowries for his four younger sisters.

There is also in Shaftesbury's papers, however, a stunningly incongruous item, a set of mental "Exercises" in two volumes under the Greek title *Askêmata*.[4] They record a turn in his life that would seem to be so at odds with his social persona and his public position that one has to wonder whether there were two Shaftes-burys, and whether they could yield to each other enough to form an integrated personality. The apparent split between the public and the private man first became apparent in 1695–1696, when Shaftesbury began to suffer severe attacks of the asthma that would kill him in 1713, at forty-two. The affliction gave him an unassailable reason to decline to stand again for Parliament in the election of 1698. Rather than retiring to his estate in Dorset, he went into a self-imposed exile in Rotterdam, where he already knew some of Locke's friends among the city's English expatriates and Huguenots. In response to pleas from his steward and his friends about damage to his political reputation and urgent family responsibilities, he returned to England, reluctantly, in April 1699. In August 1703, again exhausted by responsibilities and asthma, he made a second retreat to Rotterdam, this time for nearly a year of more resolute solitude.

It was largely during these two stays in Rotterdam that Shaftesbury wrote the *Askêmata*. As the Greek term indicates, the notebooks record his exercises in Stoic meditation. Shaftesbury could look back on roughly a century and a half of "neo-Stoic" thought, made possible by Renaissance humanists' discovery and editing of the few surviving texts. Justus Lipsius (1547–1606) and others were concerned to reconcile one of the great schools of philosophy of pagan antiquity with Christian (especially Protestant) doctrine, natural law theory, and the demands of proto-absolutist states.[5] Though Shaftesbury owned several of Lipsius's works, they had no discernible influence on the meditations recorded in his notebooks. That underscores a crucial point: Shaftesbury was *not* a neo-Stoic. He was intent on becoming a Stoic "proficient," practicing, as a way of life, a wisdom incomprehensible to "the profane," an alternative to both revealed religion and natural law, and within a tradition of English "liberties" quite at odds with continental state building. To that end he engaged directly, in the original Greek, the three surviving texts of Stoicism: the *Discourses* of Epictetus, as recorded by his student Arrian; the *Encheiridion*, the record of Epictetus's synopsis of rules for meditative exercises; and Marcus Aurelius's *Meditations*.[6] The notebook entries are organized around numerous Greek quotations copied from these texts, with frequent cross-referencing. Shaftesbury wrote for himself, often in the internal dialogue central to Stoic practice, pitting the autonomous rational self against the self-inflated, self-deluded man of the world. He had no intention of publishing the notebooks, or indeed of revealing his practice even to his closest friends. He had the pages bound for his own repeated use in meditation.

Shaftesbury undertook the exercises recorded in his notebook to effect a "Revolution" of his "self," a remaking of his consciousness to achieve the state of "tranquility" and "equilibrium" of Stoic *apatheia* (128, 203). The effort required him to learn to "despise" the ties that bound him to the "profane" world of family, friends, and public life. It was a "struggle" allowing no "Relaxation," no "resting" from solitary and intensely introspective self-disciplining (321). He must become "indifferent" not only to his public reputation, but also, as painful as it might be at first, to his friends' estimation of him. Family, estate, friends, political aspirations: these were the "outward" dependencies, the enslaving objects of uncontrolled desires, from which he had to free his interior life. Writing at Wimborne St. Giles in December 1699, just a few months after returning to England, Shaftesbury lamented his relapse into "an anxiouse Care" about his family and his household, with all the "Crosses, Disappointments, Re-jolts" it brought (169). If he cannot return to the "state" achieved in Rotterdam, he has only two choices: to "wholly retire," or—and here he may draw on a mystic text—to *"be present, as tho' not present; act, as tho' not acting; use, as tho' not using"* (169–70).

As the second option suggests, Shaftesbury committed himself in 1698, and again in 1703, not to a permanent withdrawal from "the World," but to a "Retreat" from it. The exercises were the therapy needed to reassume his worldly responsibilities on the radically different terms of Stoic detachment. The scathing Stoic language of rejection—the expressions of contempt for all matters "external," often in tropes of visceral disgust—was a received rhetorical means to the therapeutic end. But often Shaftesbury's language also conveys an alienation so deep, and a criticism of his social and public self so self-lacerating, as to make reengagement with the world seem virtually impossible. During the second retreat he castigates himself for worrying about the impressions he makes in conversations, and concludes that, while that "habit" lasts, "the only Safety is in Retirement." Having become re-enmeshed in "Compassion. Sympathy. Relation. Family. Publick," and knowing that his physical decline probably leaves him "short remaining Time," he wonders whether he has the strength to return to his Stoic "Experiment." All the more shameful, then, that he has "become an Appendix to a Grange! An Apurtenance to an Estate & Title!" (217–21). What is the point of "Pedigree, Coronet, Seat, Garden, Name, Title," he asks himself. Nothing more than "to make a Rattle" (223–25).

Following his return from his second stay in Rotterdam, Shaftesbury did reengage the world. He did so not as a peer active in parliamentary politics, but as an author of several essays on philosophy, literature, criticism, and the nature of authorship itself. Published separately from 1708 to 1710, the essays appeared together in 1711 in a volume titled *Characteristics of Men, Manners, Opinions, Times*.[7] With self-consciously experimental and devious rhetorical strategies, sometimes tortuous in execution, Shaftesbury sought a route from the revolution of self in the *Askêmata* to a reform of English literary culture and public discourse.

One of the threads connecting the notebooks and the published essays, and marking the path from the one to the other, is a dichotomy between manly intellectual labor and effeminacy. It speaks for the pervasiveness of the dichotomy's foundational oppositions that Shaftesbury's version of it, at this ground level, is quite similar to Malebranche's. Still more striking is that the thought of these two critics often converged in their use of the concept of effeminacy as a reproach to the moral decadence of modernity. Both saw effeminacy as a relational performance in which the apparently "free" rituals of women-centered politeness hid the manipulative exercise of power and made the apparently powerful as servile as the people dazzled by them. For both, servility took the collective form of "opinion," an ever-fluctuating product of social imagination; and the labor needed to position oneself beyond opinion's reach had to be undertaken in solitary meditation on the inner self, the locus of the divine presence within.

For Shaftesbury, however, England was the nation positioned to reject an effeminate modern politeness, its servility pervading absolutist political culture and epitomized by Louis XIV's France, for a morally regenerated politeness, no less modern but emphatically manly. In England the politeness he detested seemed all the more dangerous because it was entering a symbiosis with the burgeoning commercialization of print culture. The new politeness he imagined would suffuse a new public and civic discourse. It would find its inspiration in the ancient Greek polis, ground itself in the labor of Stoic reflectivity, and be responsive to the relational demands of a distinctly British tradition of political liberty—the tradition into which Shaftesbury had been born, and for which he had been groomed.

Though drawn to self-concealment as a writer, Shaftesbury would have found something quixotic and uncivil about Malebranche's Christian aspiration to write and be read without assuming the social persona of author. He came to believe that authorship could translate the moral autonomy achieved in self-lacerating solitude into a literary performance of citizenship in a public space of open contestation. Only by freeing themselves of effeminizing contamination by a women-centered discourse of sociability could authors make print the vehicle of a new kind of emphatically social communication—the kind that English political liberty required. His Stoic vision might be said to overlap with Augustinian moral rigorism in some ways, but in the end its implications were quite different. He did not see style as essentially corrupt, another stain of postlapsarian concupiscence; there was, he was convinced, a style in essay writing that could banish what he saw as the effeminate styles corrupting modern literary culture. The point was to create a new manly style, cleansed of effeminacy but still, in its representations of virile argument in an open society, educating readers in the amiable fellowship of polite civility.

The Turn to Stoicism

In the decade or so from his return from the continent in the summer of 1689 to his departure for Rotterdam in the summer of 1698, Shaftesbury had to find his way through a tangle of crises. Two threads in the tangle—his troubles with his parents, already evident at the beginning of the period, and the onset of asthma at the end of it—might be considered private matters, but for a man of Shaftesbury's birth and upbringing they were inseparable from his engagement with the intellectual issues of his day and his public responsibilities in the volatile political arena of post-1688 England. The commitment he made to Stoicism registers the urgency of his need to find a new moral grounding for his inherited principles.

Shaftesbury came to pose his Stoic practice squarely against what he considered the pernicious implications of modern philosophy, which he in turn saw extending from one of the two divergent lines of ancient Greek philosophy. The first line, he explained in a letter to Pierre Coste in 1706, ran from Socrates to the Stoics; the second from Democritus to Epicurus:

The First therefore of these two Philosophys recommended Action, Con-
cernment in Civil Affairs, Religion &c: The Second derided All, and
advised In-Action & Retreat; & good Reason.—For the First maintained
yt Society, Right and Wrong was founded in Nature, & that Nature had a
Meaning, & was Her self, that is to say, in her Wits, well Governed &
administer'd by one Simple & Perfect Intelligence. The Second again
derided This, & made Providence & Dame Nature not so Sensible, as a
doating old Woman. The first therefore of these Philosophys is to be
called ye Civil, Social, Theistic: the Second, ye Contrary.[8]

These lineages made Hobbes and other seventeenth-century philosophers neo-
Epicureans; they had simply turned the moral emptiness of Epicurus's universe of
random atoms into a no less empty mechanistic vision of life, with all of nature,
including human cognition and behavior, reduced to matter in motion. One of
Shaftesbury's grievances with the new Epicureanism was that its preoccupation
with natural science and epistemology deprived philosophy of the central moral
place it had had in the ancient polis, and indeed made it an exercise in irrelevant
speculation. Intent on explaining the workings of material forces in nature and the
human mind, modern philosophers failed to tell people what they wanted and
needed to know: how to live a good life and be truly happy (282–87). Instead
they reduced all choices and acts, however virtuous they might appear, to the
motive force of self-interest. They could do so because, in the absence of "one
Simple & Perfect Intelligence," there was no moral certainty and indeed no stable
ground of moral meaning. The result was bottomless relativism. Moral principles
no longer had a compelling ontological objectivity; they could be dismissed as
the contingent rules of particular communities, mere products of "custom" or
"fashion" or "opinion."

Stoicism told Shaftesbury that Nature was an objective moral order of which
human society was an integral part, and that human beings, in their deepest
subjectivity, were attached to it by an innate and therefore natural inclination to
be sociable and a capacity to be virtuous. To be a "self-legislating" person, one had
to build an inner "economy" organized around the natural love for a Supreme
Intelligence imparting order to the universe and providing a transcendent
grounding for society as a natural order. A "theist," as Shaftesbury applied the
term to himself, conceived God as the rational One, the universal intelligence on
which all connections within "the Whole" depended. "If there be a Deity," he
reasoned in one of his early notebook entries, with modern Epicureanism in
mind, "there is no Chance or contrary ill Design"; "if all be from one Wise &
Good Design, then all is to one & the same End, and nothing is supernumerary or
unnecessary." There is "a Concatenation & Connexion: all things are related to
one another, depend on one another, and every thing is necessary to every thing"

(112). The wise and virtuous man accepts his assigned place in an intricate and virtually infinite web of interdependencies and performs the duties assigned to him in its providential order. Paradoxically this service to others required a kind of moral fencing off from the "outward things" of the world. The Stoic has learned not to try to bring within his power of will anything that in the natural state of things lies outside it. Only within the circle of his moral efficacy as a rational will can he act naturally on his "affections," or inclinations, for others. All efforts to gratify the self by pleasing, impressing, or dominating others perverted natural affection into unnatural desire. The core self is scattered abroad; self-legislation dissolves into a self-inflicted enslavement to insatiable needs and dependencies on others and to the tyrannical "opinion" others purvey. Hence the Stoic can engage the world virtuously only because he has achieved an affective detachment from it and from the desires it generates. This is *apatheia*, the equilibrium of the interior self.

Shaftesbury's commitment to this ethic intensified as his relationship with John Locke grew increasingly conflicted. The importance of Locke in his life would be hard to exaggerate. In 1667, while still a medical student, Locke had supervised a risky surgery that had probably saved his grandfather's life. Locke had found a suitable wife for his father, and had supervised her pregnancies. Perhaps the most indelible features of Shaftesbury's mind and character had been imprinted by Locke's close tutelage of his boyhood education. As the boy matured in the 1680s, the relationship between mentor and pupil became a cordial friendship, though the former pupil may have chafed at standing in the older man's shadow. It was Locke who assumed the task of reminding the young man several times that it was time to find a wife and produce an heir. Upon Locke's death in 1704, Shaftesbury freely acknowledged his "gratitude" to the great man in a letter to their common friend Jean Le Clerc. It had been his good fortune, he wrote, to have Locke as his "friend and foster-father." Recalling the deceased as a friend might be considered mere convention; calling him a foster father was an admission of an immense debt.

And yet on December 2, 1704, just a few weeks before writing the letter to Le Clerc, Shaftesbury had sent a bitterly sarcastic denunciation of Locke to another friend. The friend had sent him an excerpt from a letter in which Locke, in the near approach of death, had testified to his belief that a good life merited an eternal reward. Laid low by asthma for the previous several months, Shaftesbury thought he too was dying. And so he made his own letter a kind of farewell summarizing his own credo, a "Counter-Charge" quite "different . . . from the admired one." What provoked him was Locke's implication that virtue was to be practiced not for its own sake, but as a calculated investment in an afterlife. He himself had sought to "do the most good," "throwing aside Selfishness, Mercinariness, and such servile Thoughts as unfitt us even for this World and much more for a better." He had been "true to his own and Family-Motto wch is. LOVE, SERVE."[9] The reference to family was an especially mean-spirited gesture, suggesting that Locke had betrayed the first earl's principles as well as Shaftesbury's own. In 1709, again in the privacy of a letter, Shaftesbury laid out the full indictment. Locke was not simply one of the villains in the story of modern philosophy; he was the chief culprit. He had "struck at all Fundementals, threw all Order and Virtue out of the World"; to him virtue has "no other Measure, Law, or Rule than *Fashion* and *Custom*."[10]

These attacks were provoked in part by Locke's defenses of Christianity in his later years. But Shaftesbury's underlying grievance was already beginning to surface in a letter he wrote Locke in 1694, the year in which the second, revised edition of *An Essay on Human Understanding* appeared. Having heard that his young protégé was writing a philosophical essay of his own, Locke had written to inquire about it. Shaftesbury dodged the question, but in a way that left little doubt about the direction his thought was taking. He would not emulate Hobbes's and Descartes's efforts to raise "new Notions . . . to amuse the world . . . or for tryall of their acuteness." "What I count True Learning, and all wee can profit by," he informed Locke, "is to know ourselves"; for that "there is no Labour, no Studdy, no Learning that I would not undertake."[11] He was already moving in a Socratic and possibly Stoic direction. By way of Hobbes and Descartes, he was reproaching his mentor. From that point on their correspondence became infrequent and avoided substantive intellectual matters.

His willful misreadings of Locke's thought stand in contrast to his faithful renderings of Stoic teaching in the notebooks. As early as 1694 we can hear the sense of personal injury, the hurt from a disorienting betrayal, that drove him to denigrate his mentor as he sought a way to self-knowledge as the ancients had conceived it. Locke the educator had reared him to be a gentleman of virtuous character. Locke the philosopher threatened to unmoor him from the moral certainties of his youth, and indeed from any access to moral meaning, just at the time when he urgently needed them. Though Locke's argument against innate ideas was aimed directly at Descartes, it struck Shaftesbury as not essentially different from Cartesianism and other forms of modern Epicureanism in its preoccupation with abstruse issues in epistemology at the expense of ethical guidance. Still more disappointing, perhaps, were the issues about selfhood and personal "identity" that Locke had raised in the first edition of his *Essay* and pursued a bit farther in the 1694 edition. What constituted a self, Locke speculated, was a continuity of self-consciousness through memory, which tied together past actions as well as past mental states. Moral selfhood lay not in a self-reflexivity exercised in detachment from the body, but in a self-consciousness that always remained embodied.

Locke's underlying point was that a self so conceived was morally responsible for her past as well as her present actions.[12] But Shaftesbury shared with several contemporary critics of Locke a concern that such a self, so inextricably embodied, could not develop a conscience independent of material existence. He had his own reasons for feeling forsaken by Locke's materialist psychology. In 1694 Shaftesbury was a twenty-three-year-old young nobleman beginning to assume responsibilities that proved difficult and at times intractable. He had been raised to honor patriarchal authority not just as an abstract principle of social order, but as a sacred injunction to filial piety. With his grandparents that duty was easily fulfilled, but his parents were quite another matter. At some point during his second stay in Rotterdam Shaftesbury, emulating Marcus Aurelius, considered how providence had benevolently arranged "the whole of [his] Birth Education & Circumstances." He was grateful for "providentiall Deliverances" not only from the political corruption of his era, but also from the "early Family-Troubles" when he fell "into other hands" after his grandfather's death (460–61). The other hands were those of his parents.

On his return to Dorset in 1689 Shaftesbury preferred to live at Ivy Church, the home of family friends, making only occasional visits to his parents at St. Giles. When at Ivy Church, he explained to Locke, he felt "att home."[13] In his relations with his parents lay his greatest danger of becoming so anxiously entangled in "outward things" as to have no inner core. He oscillated between a dutiful son's sense of obligation and the impulse to wash his hands of them. The St. Giles he had returned to was depressingly different from the household of his boyhood. It would be hard to imagine a greater contrast to Shaftesbury's grandfather than the second earl. His debilitating illness had led him to withdraw not only from public life, but from the minimal sociability expected of a man of his station. In a long letter Shaftesbury had written to his father just after returning from the continent, the strain between them is already audible. Shortly after his grandfather's death his father had sent him, against Locke's advice, to Winchester College; and now his brother Maurice was following in his footsteps. The letter is a patronizing lecture on the proper education of younger sons of the nobility, delivered to a man who ought to know these things but did not. Barely hidden beneath his disappointment with his brother's schooling lay his resentment about his own sufferings at the college. He had been sent off to an institution dominated by royalist and high church families, and had had to endure his schoolmates' vilification of his purportedly traitorous grandfather. What he recalled in his letter was the subculture of carousing; "only those that studdie and are diligent and scarcely they too Escape the Mother vice of Drinking." Winchester had threatened to undo all the molding of character Locke had supervised. The fact that he was kept there three years, despite his complaints, made his father seem all the more inadequate and blameworthy. When his father failed to follow his advice about Maurice to the letter, he threw up his hands in exasperation. He would no longer offer rational advice; he would only "act in [his parents'] concerns" as "one that is obliged to be according to his duty the executor of what his father and Mother should command him to doe in any case."[14] Duty was reduced to the minimal obedience that society and the law required.

By the mid-1690s his estrangement from his mother was the more serious problem. In 1691 Lady Dorothy had entered a long illness that seems to have been as much psychological as it was physical. Lacking confidence in the second earl, Lady Dorothy's sister had insisted on bringing her to her own home. Lady Dorothy, convinced the second earl was letting his steward pilfer the estate, pressed her son to intervene. But he would not, and he became the target of her anger.[15] By early 1696 he could no longer conceal his bitterness. There may have been a time in his youth, he wrote to his mother, when he had behaved badly toward her, but in recent years she had had ample "Proofs" of "my intire Submission, and Willingness to doe any thing that may regain me your ffavour." To no avail; while he had become "sensible of what it is to bee a Son," she still lacked "the Heart of a Mother." Even as he dealt Lady Dorothy this stinging slap, he confirmed his need to do whatever filial piety required. In October 1696, he wrote to her that he had succeeded in winning over his father to her cause, and that he begged her forgiveness for former offenses and dearly wished to be "restored to [her] Favour and affection." By February 1697, she was at last satisfied with his "many Extraordinary Submissive Letters."[16] One reason he felt free to leave for Rotterdam at the end of July 1698, we can speculate, was that with her death just two weeks earlier his need to atone had ended.

Stoicism gave Shaftesbury a justification for being at once dutiful and detached—for honoring his most immediate and exigent social obligations without scattering his inner self to the winds. It is a measure of the importance of this resolution that in August 1698, soon after arriving in Rotterdam, he recorded an exercise on "Naturall Affection"; and that it is the first substantial entry in the bound volume. The point of the exercise was to grasp a central tenet of Stoic ethical teaching: that "affections" for others that are considered "natural" in "the imperfect & vulgar sense" are in fact "un-natural," and that by becoming ensnared in them the individual loses his "Liberty" as a rational, self-legislating self (79). Shaftesbury begins by reasoning that affections can be "natural" only if they proceed from natural affection for the species, or "the whole of Mankind," which in turn must flow from disinterested love for the Supreme Intelligence. There can be no natural affections if one pursues the goods or the approval of others; only by despising needs and desires can one have affection with "true Liberty." With this kind of detached affection, always exercised with an overriding awareness of "the Economy of the Whole," one avoids being "disturbed within thy Self, wholly dissatisfied with Providence and the Order of Things, Impatient, Angry, full of Complaint, Bitterness, Vexation, Discontent" (71–83). The proficient achieved not a renunciation of ties and duties, but an iron discipline in keeping them in their proper subordinate place in a hierarchy of affections ascending from family, friends, and fellow citizens to the natural order and the Deity. He could then perform his duties with a certain serene invulnerability, an inner tranquility that no demands by others, and no disappointment in others, could disturb.[17]

We know from the notebooks that engaged detachment, or detached engagement, became, in principle, his rule of social behavior. With the onset of his asthma, however, the quest for an inner citadel of invulnerability came to require a more severe detachment. The asthma was a recurrently incapacitating and at times death-threatening condition. It confronted him with the possibility that the debility of his own body precluded the achievement of inner freedom. We begin to see how emphatically masculine, and how opposed to what he saw as effeminacy, his labor of interior liberty became. In his exercises in self-laceration in the notebooks, he often recoils from the nightmare of "effeminacy." In perhaps the most explicit of them, he asks himself "As how then *not a Child*? How *least like a Woman*? How *far from a Beast*?" and continues: "How properly *a Man*? . . . *A Man*; & not a Woman; effeminate, soft, delicate, supine; impotent in Pleasure, in Anger, Talk: pusillanimouse, light, changeable &c . . . The Contrareys. *Manhood. Manlyness, Humanity—Manly. Humane Masculine*" (395). There is nothing original about this coding of male and female; aside from its other pedigrees, it had been conventional wisdom in civic humanism for roughly two millennia. Women are by nature "soft" and "impotent" in temperament as well as body. Like children, they cannot control their animal appetites, their passions, their speech.

The vehemence with which Shaftesbury applied these dichotomies, and the existential meaning they acquired for him in the face of his illness, return us to his upbringing under Locke's guidance. Locke's pedagogy was designed to form a gentleman who was both "polite" and "manly." His guiding assumption was that it was as easy to produce "a Sound Mind in a sound Body" as it was to channel water into various courses. If the child's environment was properly controlled, the result would be "a strong Constitution able to endure Hardships and Fatigues." This did not, Locke noted, require the "affected Stoical austerities" of a Seneca. If the child learned, by degrees, to endure pain and face dangers with "noble and manly Steadfastness," he would remain in "the quiet Possession of a Man's self, and an undisturb'd doing of his Duty." Developing this "Armour" against weakness would free him of fear.[18]

Shaftesbury came of age aspiring to exemplify this standard of manly character, and until age twenty-five or twenty-six he seems to have maintained the sound body it required. But no amount of self-inuring to physical hardships could dispel the emotional tyranny of his asthma. His term in Parliament taught him that the illness could be triggered by psychological and emotional exhaustion. He had to be very careful not to become too caught up in politics and other matters. The choice of Little Chelsea as his second home was a compromise; roughly three miles from the center of London, it was near enough to allow him to visit the city periodically but kept him at a safe distance from its thick coal dust and smoke.

Shaftesbury knew he would never again have a sound body. More frightening was the possible effect on his mind and character: that the illness would make him perpetually fearful. Surely the specter of his father loomed when he contemplated that prospect. In the face of it, Stoicism offered a way to develop, despite his physical weakness, a higher order of manly strength, free of effeminate fears. There was no point in feeling cruelly singled out by the affliction; Stoic wisdom taught him to take it as a needed reminder of the flux and decay of animal life to which all human beings were subject. Rather than hardening himself to physical conditions, as Locke advised, he had to take special precautions. He could do so without self-recrimination because the illness gave a new, relentless urgency to his need to conceive a self cleanly detached from the body. In the notebooks, following Epictetus and Marcus Aurelius, he asks "By what, but by coming out of [the body]? By not being *It*; but *in it*: and only so far in it & joyn'd to it as Nature has made me" (346). He told himself repeatedly that his body was "no part of Himself." "Lent" for a higher purpose, the body was to be cared for like "Lodging an Inn, a Passage-boat, or Ship, a Post Hors" (229–30). From the standpoint of the mind as the "acting Principle" of a human being, the body was nothing more than a "carcass." How is "the Carcass to be subdued," he asks himself in a notebook entry. By "giving me withall my Reason and those suitable Facultyes by wch I can abstract My Self; by wch I can separate from this meer matter, & redeem my Self from ye Carcass. For how else *redeem my Self*?" (346, 420).

The term "redeem" notwithstanding, this is not the harsh Christian asceticism to which Malebranche was attracted. To neglect available means to "care" for the "mere matter" would be to violate one's duty to the Supreme Intelligence. But Stoical mind-body dualism, in Shaftesbury's radical appropriation of it, not only opposed Locke's epistemology with a conception of innate cognitive and affective capacities; it spurned the environmental logic of character Locke had applied to his charge's upbringing. In the logic of Stoicism, Locke was guilty of a fundamental error: assuming that the body, an "outward thing" largely outside our circle of moral control, could be harnessed to the process of character formation. Asthma brought home to Shaftesbury the contrary Stoic wisdom: that the moral autonomy at the core of true character developed in a process of abstracting the self from the body. This was what Shaftesbury called the "Work" of the aspiring proficient, the relentless exercise of the "acting Principle." It was "manly," as opposed to "effeminate," because it required a constant struggle against bodily weaknesses and desires. "That which to an Effeminate Person is insufferable Pain and Trouble," Shaftesbury wrote in a notebook entry, "is to a Man Laboriouse or Warlike a Subject of Delight & Enjoyment" (136). Surely, he had reasoned in an earlier entry, "the Nature of Man" was not "*to whine and to bemoan, to be Peevish &*

Malignant, to be Effeminate & Soft. Impotent towards Pleasure, and Impatient of Pain Labour or Hardship"; "if Man-hood be the contrary to this; if it be in Action & Exercise, in Reason and in a Mind y* this consists; then is it here that the Man is either sav'd or lost" (129–30).

Shaftesbury's physical debility gave him special reason to figure the building of manly character as an abstracting of the moral self from bodily existence. If the practitioner was sometimes figured in Stoicism as an Olympic athlete, it was nonetheless imperative that he concentrate his notion of male strength entirely in mental activity. In principle this detachment of pure mind from body left women with their own, gender-specific moral duties, rather than consigning them to an immoral state. But the clear implication, sometimes made quite explicit, was that women's state was inferior both naturally and morally, a subrealm of bodily and psychological weakness and attendant lack of the self-discipline that distinguished the truly virtuous. The perversity of modernity lay in the fact that women were powerful in their weakness; sociability positioned them to denaturalize men, to vitiate their natural capacity for self-discipline. Every time he felt he was slipping back into dependencies on "the World," Shaftesbury became merciless toward himself; there could be no "Relaxation," no "loss of Attention," no "Dissolv(ing) in Effeminacy" (402). Redeeming the modern male self meant purging the feminine that had seeped into it.

The French Menace

During his second stay in Rotterdam Shaftesbury recalled in his notebooks "how near to real *Madness*" he had been just before it (257–58). Clearly family difficulties were only one precipitate of his asthma. Another was his political engagement as an MP from 1695 to 1698. Several years later he would tell his physician that during those years he had spent many a late night in the tobacco smoke of committee meetings, "often carry'd into an eagerness of Dispute."[19]

Shaftesbury's initiation into active politics occurred in one of the more turbulent parliamentary sessions of the late seventeenth century. He entered the House eager to fight for his grandfather's "country Whig" causes: against the increasing presence of placemen, pliant to the Crown's wishes, in the House of Commons; against a standing army; for tighter restrictions on the royal prerogative and greater toleration for Dissenters. But in the wake of the Revolution of 1688 the role of the Whigs had altered. Having cohered as a movement of opposition, they had become the governing party. Disillusioned with Whig leaders he branded "Apostate," Shaftesbury often found himself isolated and maligned. It was now the Tory opposition that was decrying the court's corruption of Parliament. Shaftesbury had even thought of joining the Tories in 1695, but that was not a realistic option; as the grandson of the traitorous first earl, he was persona non grata in Tory circles. More painful was the censure aimed at him by fellow Whigs frustrated with what they saw as his recalcitrance. His friend John Toland would later recall the rumors in Whig circles that he was "splenetick and melancholy," and "too bookish, because not given to Play nor assiduous at Court."[20]

Soon after his return to England in 1699 Shaftesbury had to adapt to ominous developments in international politics. As another war with France approached, he shared with many other Whigs the conviction that the Catholic and absolutist monarchy of Louis XIV, driven by its ambition to subject all Europe to a "universal Monarchy," posed a grave and immediate threat. With his recognition of James II's son as the legitimate king of England in 1701, Louis committed himself to ending the Protestant succession, the most sacred principle of 1688, and war became inevitable. Now the quarrels of domestic politics paled before the need for Crown and Parliament to unite in the conduct of a war of self-defense. Shaftesbury put the case bluntly in *Paradoxes of State*, a pamphlet he published in January 1702. Since 1688, he argued, English constitutional liberty had been firmly established and party distinctions had acceded to the only "real Distinction," which was "between those that are in a *French*, and those that are in an *English* Interest." In these circumstances court and country had the same objectives. Nearly a decade later, in the opening essay of a book on the visual arts, he evoked the vision he saw triumphing as the War of the Spanish Succession came to a close:

> When the free spirit of a nation turns itself [to the improvement of art and science], judgments are formed; critics arise; the public eye and ear improve; a right taste prevails, and in a manner forces its way. Nothing is so improving, nothing so natural, so congenial to the liberal arts, as that reigning liberty and high spirit of a people, which from the habit of judging in the highest matters for themselves, makes them freely judge of other subjects, and enter thoroughly into the characters as well of men and manners, as of the products or works of men, in art and science. So much, my Lord do we owe to the excellence of our national constitution, and legal, monarchy; happily fitted for us, and which alone could hold together so mighty a people; all sharers (though at so far a distance from each other) in the government of themselves; and meeting under one head in one vast metropolis; whose enormous growth, however censurable in other respects, is actually a cause that workmanship and arts of so many kinds arise to such perfection.[21]

Shaftesbury's implicit but obvious foil to English government by law and with a large measure of civic liberty was French absolutism. Now that the threat of French political and military hegemony had been met, England must seize the opportunity to demonstrate to Europe that modern polite culture need not take the French form; it could foster the spirit of "liberty" rather than snuffing it out. The English monarchy should take a lesson from the overweening tutelage of culture that its French counterpart practiced. Courts that seek to direct their nations' cultural genius "do more harm than good"; "it is not the nature of a court (such as courts generally are) to improve, but rather corrupt a taste." With the growth of her constitution, England "has in proportion fitted herself for other improvements," demonstrating "the rising genius of our nation."[22]

In this essay, as in others published since his second return from Rotterdam, Shaftesbury wrote as a critic of his nation's fine arts. But it would be misleading to say that his aspirations to serve his country had shifted from high politics to high culture. He sought to promote a politics of culture that would be the correlative to a distinctly English politics of government. If England's cultural liberty depended on its political liberty, so too its political liberty must be sustained by the free atmosphere, or "spirit," of its cultural creativity.[23] In his view of the court as the greatest threat to this agenda, he emulated his grandfather's "country" opposition to court corruption, which in turn had adapted to seventeenth-century English conditions one of the central themes of classical civic humanism. In this tradition "effeminacy" was one symptom of the larger process of corruption caused by the spread of "luxury." The private pursuit of wealth and attendant material comforts and pleasures had the effect of making men, like women, inclined to a life of luxury. Men became "soft" or weak; blind to the common good; unable to discipline their wants and desires; and for all these reasons lacking the physical and moral strength and the courage needed to defend their county. The clearest case in point was the decline of the Roman republic and its replacement by the imperial regime of Augustus. The luxurious and effeminating corruption of the Augustan court had its counterpart in the court life of modern monarchies.[24]

Even as Shaftesbury echoed this discourse, he modernized it. Unlike many proponents of country ideology, he did not simply use the idealized standard of the ancient polis to condemn features of seventeenth-century modernity. As nostalgic as he often was for the golden ages of Greece and Rome, he hoped that their examples would inspire his contemporaries to create something new, a reformed politeness in life and letters, a distinctly modern symbiosis of sociability and cultural vitality. Likewise he added new chapters to the traditional republican narrative of corruption. It did not suffice to warn in broadly moral terms that England could suffer the fate of Athens or Rome. He had to explain—to himself, and eventually to others—the more recent roots of the modern illness, and its new manifestations.

In both the essays and the notebooks Shaftesbury used the term "gallantry" as a shorthand for the pathology of modern politeness, thus putting men's interactions with women at the center of his diagnosis. Tracing gallantry back to the chivalry of medieval court cultures, he made it an expression of the "Gothic" barbarousness that had not yet lost its grip on Europe. In the draft of a letter to his friend Lord Somers in 1705, this Gothic genealogy conveys a particularly harsh message. The letter was meant to accompany an essay he had printed privately, for a small circle of friends, under the title "The Social Enthusiast." Shaftesbury had good reason to insist that Somers keep this "Tale of Philosophy" to himself. It would pair his disgust with the "Effeminacy" of "Gallantry" with a radical anticlericalism, a sentiment that he used an apparently soft irony to keep in check in his published writing. He could offer guidance through the "strange Mist" of politics, he assured Somers, because he now had little to do with it and had been "poking out (his) way" in "other dark Mystery's." This was the voice of the detached Stoic, only recently returned from his meditations in Rotterdam. Shaftesbury evoked an ancient Greece and republican Rome in which philosophical discussion of the great issues—the nature of the universe, the "ends of Man," the difference between good and evil—had been integral to the sociability of "men of breeding," including "Men of note" in government. In his search for an equivalent modern audience for philosophy, he told Somers, he had "e'en desperately ventur'd it with the Younger Men, and laid his Scene in the midst of Gallantry and Pleasure." But in that setting philosophy, like everything else in the culture of gallantry, was subject to "the Rule" of "the fair Sex." Just as priests had been given absolute power over our souls, the ladies had been given absolute power over "our understanding." And so in modern times philosophy, like religion, had "gone to wreck"; "t'is a Lottery Chance what Lady disposes of our Interest, or what Priest takes last possession of our Soul."[25]

The reference to "Chance" linked modern politeness to the Epicurean ascendancy in modern philosophy that Shaftesbury blamed for marginalizing ethical wisdom. At stake was the individual autonomy needed to form right judgments both in government and in matters of taste. We no longer "possess our own Opinions," Shaftesbury observed, and the only cure was a return to the philosophical reflectivity that the gender relations of modern polite society made impossible. With his Stoic exercises surely in mind, he warned that "A great deal must go to make our Opinion our own and free it from Affectation and Dependency. Formality, Pomps and Ceremonies must be broken through, Prejudices torn off, and Truth strip'd as naked as ever she was born."[26]

If modern politeness, as Shaftesbury perceived it, had its roots in medieval Europe, the center from which it now radiated across Europe was France under Louis XIV. Again Shaftesbury acted on a family legacy. In the mid-1670s his grandfather, having left the Privy Council and become a leading member of a nascent opposition to Charles II's policies, had helped orchestrate a shift in English perceptions of the European scene. It was now France under its absolutist king, and not the United Provinces, that threatened to impose a "universal monarchy" that would suppress English liberties. Louis XIV's military might was matched by France's cultural imperium, as the English court set the example in aping French manners and fashions.[27] The third earl was intent on inverting the imperium; what was so widely admired about France was precisely what made it such a menace to the rest of Europe. He was well aware that, for all the strength of English patriotism in the face of French military aggression, English gentlemen, eager to prove themselves masters of the new refinements of politeness, looked to France for instruction. Since the mid-seventeenth century the literature of *honnêteté* had been quickly translated for sale across the Channel. Shaftesbury found its social code and culture of deference completely at odds with the English spirit of liberty. In a notebook entry he had given this contrast greater social specificity and psychological depth. Learning "to be with Self; to talk with Self" required the purging of a dangerous "*Sickness*": "that fond Desire of Company, that seeking of Companionship, & Want of Talk & Story":

> See the Nation & People y^t are the most insatiable in this way, & hunt after Conversations, Partyes, Engagements, Secreceys, & Friendships of this kind, with the greatest Eagerness, Admiration, Fondness. and see in what Place this reigns the most. The Court, & Places near the Court: the Polite world; the Great-Ones. Of what Characters, Life, Manners are commonly that Sort who can never rest out of Company, & want ever to be communicating their Secrets? Call this to Mind: and remember that *real Friendship* is not founded on such a *Need*. Friends are not *Friends* if thus wanted. This is Imbecility, Impotence, Effeminacy: and such is all that *Ardour & Vehemence* in behalf of Others. (213)

Shaftesbury evokes here the ancient ideal of friendship of manly heroic virtue, free of need. The conversational sociability of the Paris salons was not, as it was often projected in the discourse of *honnêteté*, a "natural" and "free" respite from the hierarchical formalities of the court. It was the expansion of the court's web of dependencies and intrigues into a morally pathological world of hypersociability. If friendship was a relationship of reciprocal freedom, then the apparent freedom and ease of polite conversation was a travesty of friendship. It was driven by an insatiable need to have oneself reflected in the gaze and speech of others, with no room for the inner reflectivity that grounded friendship in equality. To some extent Shaftesbury's indictment echoes satires by late seventeenth-century French moralists and especially La Bruyère, whose *Characters* he had read (241). But La Bruyère censured French polite society from the inside, as a man who accepted the code of politeness, and found social value in it, even as he remained aware that its performances fell well short of the inner integrity for which the word "virtue" ought to be reserved.[28] To Shaftesbury the performances were not simply empty of virtue; they made the development of manly virtuous character impossible.

Again we find Shaftesbury modernizing the country critique of the court in English civic humanism. In his view of French polite society extending out from Versailles, one form of effeminate corruption is "luxury" in the traditional sense, a "soft" weakness for material comforts and sensual pleasures. But Shaftesbury's explicit censure is reserved for the addiction to "Company" in polite sociability. In a notebook entry he singles out people who have "feign'd to themselves a wrong Self" and devote themselves to "Study of *Gracefullness* & the *Decorum*" and the proper performance of "every Motion, Station Attitude." These are to be distinguished from "the sordidly sensual and meer Voluptuouse," but they are nonetheless "effeminate" (380). It was the combination of these dangers that he saw always lurking in the English court and the high society that surrounded it in London. He prided himself on resisting the temptations of this world. He could not play the courtier, he repeatedly told friends at home and abroad, and he was no gallant. When he finally decided to seek a wife in 1708, it was in response to the entreaties of friends and associates that he produce an heir. By then he thought of himself as having put libidinal urges behind him, and he did not want to burden a spouse with his illness. But once he committed himself, he took the choice of a wife as an opportunity to defy the social expectations of his world. His wife had to be a woman of simple character as well as a good "breeder." His dilemma, he wrote to his friend Benjamin Furley in November 1708, is "that there are so few of my own degree, or of those Circumstances that can justify my marriage, who have any sort of Education that promises good." He had in mind an education in the domestic virtues of a wife and mother, unspoiled by the frivolous sociability of the London season. If that meant forgoing a good match in financial terms, so be it. He made it a condition of friendship with several intimates that they accept this resolve, however much they had hoped the marriage would bring a substantial fortune into the family. His bride was Jane Ewer, the youngest daughter of a gentry family of modest wealth he had known since boyhood. Thanks to her quiet country upbringing in "a good family," he wrote Molesworth, she was free of "Air, and Humeur, and the Witt of general Conversation, and the Knowledge of the Town, and Fashion, and Diversions."[29]

Shaftesbury, one might say, sought a modern equivalent of the virtuous matron of the Roman republic. Beneath this reverence for republican virtue, however, lay a critical shift in his commitment to civic humanism, especially evident in the notebooks.[30] Like Locke's pedagogy, though with different ethical and political emphases, civic humanism saw the building of character as an environmental process. Socialized into a particular community and the political institutions that maintained it, the citizen acquired character by internalizing communal values, rather than forming character from within, from the ethical impulses he found in a core self. The danger Shaftesbury saw in the modern world, and especially in France, was that the values being internalized were the "fantasies" of mere "opinion," the contagion of socially dictated self-delusions. The modern epitome of the socialized person was not the virtuous male citizen, but the *honnête homme*, the master of the effeminate extroversion of French politeness. Polite sociability, properly practiced, was the modern medium for liberty; but it could only be so—it could only avoid effeminate extroversion—if it developed a new moral self-awareness. It was in this sense that Shaftesbury wanted to put philosophy back at the political and cultural center of lives of men of breeding. In a modern commonwealth governed by polite gentlemen, some gentleman had to exercise a radical liberty, a capacity to judge conventional wisdom from a position of complete self-command and with the critical distance it afforded. Despite having "repented" from a previous "relaps," he writes in a notebook entry, he had once again

> engaged, still sallyed out, & lived abroad, still prostituted thy self & committed thy Mind to Chance & the next corner, & so as to be treated at pleasure by every one, to receive impressions from every thing, & Machine-like to be mov'd & wrought upon, & govern'd exteriourly, as if there were nothing that rul'd within, or had the least controul . . . all is lost, thou art over-powerd & canst no longer command they self. (188)

The internal askesis of Stoicism was essential to a free commonwealth precisely because it was a process of desocialization. Only the man of manly character—the man who had recovered his interior self in askesis—could truly "possess" an "opinion." To live by common "opinion" was to be dragged along by the "train" of appearances, as random as Epicurus's atoms, that were produced and multiplied in everyday social intercourse. Here lay the critical difference between manly "activity" and female passivity. The man of character did not allow the myriad *visa*, or representations, that opinion flung at him from without to overpower him and deprive him of a core self. He had the mental strength to "conquer" these "fancies," rejecting some and transforming others into instruments of his self-empowered rational will. He acquired that strength in the Stoic "Hardness and Labour" of "inversion"—the labor Shaftesbury practiced repeatedly in the notebooks. Inversion, he wrote, was the "transforming of the Fanceys and Appearances and the wresting of them from their own naturell & vulgar sence into a meaning truly Naturell & free of all delusions and imposture." This "right Modelling or Molding of the *Visa*," he added, was the "Contest concerning Liberty" (296–97).

Friendship

There is something puzzling about the fact that Shaftesbury included "An Inquiry Concerning Virtue" in *Characteristics*. The original version of the essay had been published in 1699, apparently without his consent, by John Toland, a friend from whom he would soon be estranged. Arguably the revised version in *Characteristics* had the obvious purpose of staking out his philosophical and ethical position against both theological orthodoxy and the various strains of modern Epicureanism, and hence was an appropriate preparation for "The Moralists," the fifth and final essay. And yet the "Inquiry" is the misfit of the volume, and Shaftesbury clearly wanted the reader to regard it as such. In it Shaftesbury assumes the impersonal voice of the philosophical mind, ordering his paragraphs as a series of syllogisms.[31] In the other essays that voice moves offstage. Onstage the persona of the critic conducts experiments in essay writing. The final step in experimentation is the set of five "Miscellaneous Reflections" with which he ends the volume. Now he poses as a critic of the author of the essays—which is to say that, splitting his authorial self in two, he conducts a self-critique analogous to his Stoic self-dialogue. He takes the essay form to an extreme: an apparent simulation of the random freedom of polite conversation, emphatically modern in the way it caters to "the fashionable air and manner of the world."[32] It comes as no surprise, then, when in the third Miscellany he assumes a position of patronizing irony toward the "Inquiry." In the first three essays, the self-critic observes, "what he offers by way of project or hypothesis is very faint, hardly spoken aloud but muttered to himself in a kind of dubious whisper or feigned soliloquy." In the "Inquiry" "he discovers himself openly as a plain dogmatist, a formalist and man of method, with his hypothesis tacked to him and his opinions so close sticking as would force one to call to mind the figure of some precise and strait-laced professor in a university" (396).[33]

In the very act of affirming his commitment to the philosophical content of the "Inquiry," Shaftesbury dismisses his treatise as an exercise in scholastic pedantry. He can admit to this lapse in gentlemanly behavior because in the other essays and the "Miscellaneous Reflections" he returns to his proper voice, addressing other gentlemen as though engaged with them in polite conversation. But the relationship between this self-critical author and modern politeness turns out to be more troubled and conflicted than this simple contrast between pedant and gentleman suggests. Even in the "Inquiry," Shaftesbury is careful not to identify himself as a Stoic. There, and in the rest of the volume, we find frequent references to several classical authors, Horace foremost among them, but almost none to Epictetus and Marcus Aurelius. The more knowledgeable among Shaftesbury's readers would surely have detected a strong Stoical influence; but they would have had no reason to conclude that the author was a "proficient" trying to practice Stoicism as a way of life. Shaftesbury, we know from the notebooks, was convinced that, if Stoic reflectivity was to reform modern culture, it would have to be conveyed in semicamouflaged forms. But how do that? Much of his experimentation was designed to answer that question. What made it so complicated was that he regarded modern politeness with deep ambivalence. If it had the potential to be the ideal medium for the practice of modern liberty, it was in its present "gallant" manifestations the medium of enslaving effeminacy. The ancients, and particularly Socrates and Xenophon, provided the antidote, but it had to be adapted to modernity. What form of communication would channel the potential for freedom in polite conversation—its reciprocity and its rejection of imposed authority—into public discourse, while purging it of effeminizing gallantry? What form would keep communication polite, or civil, while making it a performance in emphatically male contestation, replacing insipid *complaisance* with productive argument?

At the center of the way Shaftesbury posed and resolved these questions is male friendship, as he experienced it, and as he imagined it as the social site for a new literary strategy. There was nothing new about his casting of most of the essays as letters to friends, or about his use of imagined dialogues between friends to develop his themes; these had been common tropes of philosophical dialogues and polite essays in the seventeenth century. Shaftesbury, however, was not simply choosing among literary forms. His use of tropes of friendship was unprecedented in its intricate layering of voices and stylistic tonalities. In the formal properties of the essays, as well as in their content, we witness a man trying to find a viable route from his solitary and secret labor of meditation to the public labor of authorship. It was through his emotional investment in friendships, and through his efforts to come to terms with the dilemmas with which they confronted him, that he constructed an authorial persona that was at once philosophical and conversational, ethical and aesthetic, manly and polite.

Like other English gentlemen of his era, Shaftesbury engaged in several kinds and degrees of friendship. During his second stay in Rotterdam he had secluded himself from society far more strictly than on his first retreat. Pierre Bayle was one of two exceptions—the other being Benjamin Furley, the expatriate English Quaker with whom he was on close terms. In a letter from St Giles to Jacques Basnage on January 11, 1707, he eulogized Bayle as an exemplar of "Philosophical Liberty" and religious toleration to whom he owed a singular intellectual debt. In their conversations, he recalled, they had subjected each other's ideas to relentless scrutiny, though they "agreed in fundamental rules of morall Practice." For Shaftesbury their "constant disputes" had been "improving Conversation," which in turn "served to improve our Friendship."[34]

The immediate purpose of this encomium was to condemn by contrast the "animosity and hatred" that fueled religious polemics. In making religious

tolerance central to "Philosophical Liberty," Shaftesbury offered a modern variation on the Aristotelian and Ciceronian ancient ideal of "philosophical" friendship, or friendship of virtue.[35] His larger point was that in the modern Republic of
Letters, as in the ancient polis, it was possible to have a pure friendship between
moral and intellectual equals, able to argue to each other's benefit because they
occupied a common ground of moral truth. In fact, though, most of Shaftesbury's
other friendships were not with scholars like Bayle, but with English gentlemen of
landed and commercial wealth, some of them engaged in parliamentary politics.
John Cropley, his oldest and closet friend, was from a family in commerce and
law, and was Shaftesbury's chief contact in the House of Commons. Thomas
Micklethywate was a lawyer's son for whom Shaftesbury spent several years trying to secure a government post. Robert Molesworth's father had made his fortune in commerce and land in Ireland, and he himself had a prominent career in
Irish and English politics.

The setting for these and other friendships was not the scholarly seclusion
that Furley's home and library in Rotterdam offered, or the circle of friends like
Bayle to whom he was introduced there, but the sociability of country homes and
men's clubs in London. We gain some access to the latter world in what is perhaps
the most personally revealing letter Shaftesbury ever wrote. It is dated January 22,
1705, and is addressed to a "Brother" in a London men's club Shaftesbury himself
may have founded. After a "long silence," the Brother has intimated once again
that Shaftesbury acted foolishly in his relationship with a young man nicknamed
"Bawble." Shaftesbury recalls meeting this "Bawble of a Friend" soon after returning from Rotterdam in the summer of 1704. While the other members of their
"private Community of Friends" have washed their hands of the young man,
Shaftesbury has maintained his attachment to him, despite his "Rake-hell-
Character" and his manipulative wiles. Shaftesbury now wants to put an end to
the matter by being unusually candid about what he has to that point refused to
acknowledge, though he fears that by doing so he will "make the matter worse."
To a degree he blames his Brothers; he had abandoned his initial "Dislike and
Aversion" for Bawble because the young man was already their friend and he
accepted their assurances of his "boyish Innocence." But he also admits that he
succumbed to the "Pains" and "Arts" the young man had used to "Court [his]
Friendship":

> At length, Time, Custome, Familiar Appelations, Names, Manners, With
> a hundred little things (such is Human-Nature) began to work on Me . . .
> (and) taught him to take possession of my Heart. *The Bawble* gain'd. I
> play'd too; awkward as I was, & grown grave. With Play came things
> Seriouse. Then Vows, Professions, Services, endearing Actions; till my
> easy Breast quite open'd, & I receiv'd him in, after the long Resistance I

had made. This is my Story. Thus I lov'd. too easily perhaps & to my Cost; as I now find. but not so easily can I *unlove*. I never yett Lov'd any Soul in any degree that I could afterwards cease to love, or love but in a Less.

"Forgive me," he concludes, "if I have writt any thing amiss, think it not so intended"; "do or think what you will, You can never make me Love you less."[36]

The letter has the ironic implication, perhaps intentional, that Shaftesbury's love of Bawble is an indulgence in effeminate weakness. The concluding remarks may convey a fear that his Brother would take his description of the "courtship"— the metaphor of seduction, assigning himself the female role—to imply that there was something homoerotic about his attachment to an apparently endearing young man. Battling against confinement to the body, Shaftesbury accepted the natural duty to procreate but regarded any kind of sexual pleasure, with a woman or with a man, as degrading. He would have been indignant about any imputation that for him the relationship with Bawble had a homoerotic element. The parenthetical remark is important; in attributing his weakness to "Human-Nature," he in effect heads off any speculation about a possible latent homosexuality in his own makeup. In other texts it is quite clear that he regarded homosexual love, which was not uncommon in the libertinism of his day, as morally disgusting to an extreme. Particularly striking is his view of men's "love of boys" in ancient Athens. This form of "corruption," he argues, was not as common as mistranslations made it appear; and, more important, the two Athenians he looked to for inspiration— Socrates and his disciple Xenophon—neither approved nor practiced it.[37] We cannot rule out the possibility that he was in denial about his own homosexuality. But it makes more historical (and psychological) sense to say that Shaftesbury, like most of his contemporaries, could not acknowledge to himself that he sometimes entered emotional grey zones between what he considered the normal and the perverse: heterosexual love, the only natural outlet for sexual desire; and the violation of nature in homosexual love. Even as he acknowledged the playful emotional intimacy of his friendship with Bawble, it was unthinkable that there could be something homoerotic about the emotional attachments between avowedly heterosexual male friends.[38]

More relevant is what the letter reveals about Shaftesbury's social world. He was, as he describes himself at the beginning of the letter, a great "builder of Societys." By trying to bring his friends together in "private" communities, he lived his belief in the innate sociability of human beings. These were not societies of "rakes." London did, of course, have libertine clubs devoted to debauchery; but the clubs in which Shaftesbury sought emotional sustenance, though certainly not as purely philosophical as his conversations with Bayle, preferred conversations with intellectual substance to debauchery. And whether or not Shaftesbury's

friendships had a homoerotic element, they were intensely emotional attachments to which he held firm and sometimes clung. Far more than his family, his
friends constituted his community of intimacy and emotional attachment.

That community figures large in Shaftesbury's Stoic exercises. The notebooks
are ordered only partly chronologically, the other ordering principle is thematic,
often without dating. Hence it is difficult to trace the development of his thought
over the eight years or so in which he wrote them. But it seems clear that on the
subject of his own friendships he confronted and then solved a dilemma with high
emotional as well as intellectual stakes, and that the solution became his central
route to theorizing and practicing a new kind of polite but manly essay writing.

"Why should it disturb me that I am thought singular?" he asks himself in a
notebook entry in Rotterdam in 1698. Surely, he continues, it is ridiculous to fear
"Censure" from people who admire, among other types, the man ambitious for
wealth or "popularity," the libertine, the miser, the "Gallant," the country sports-
man, the courtier, the lover of "poetry and fashionable Literature." Only by
despising such censure can a man have "Generous Affection and Exercize of
Friendship" (132–37). It soon becomes apparent, however, that the exercise of
friendship was the greatest dilemma for this practicing Stoic. Sometime in 1699,
soon after returning to England, he again ponders the "matters of outward independence" he should "despise." The "chief" one is "the Plays, Divertions, Talk,
Secrets, Confidences, & whatever else makes up that sort of Convers. Which thou
art so fond of, with a certain Sett of Friends." It is in this kind of interaction that
he finds himself most tightly in the grip of self-deluding "fancies," and most guilty
of dissembling in the need to please and impress. His betrayals of his Stoic inner
self on such occasions are not simply verbal; he regrets his entire self-
representation as an apparently well-bred man, including his "Carriage," his
"Countenance," his gestures as well as his tone of voice. In quitting such behavior,
he had already asked in 1698, will he not "Loose the Esteem of Friends?" So it
must be, he seems to conclude; "is it not better to be truly Sociable, retaining true
Simplicity and Gravity, than by being what the world calls Sociable, to give up
these, & live a stranger to Social Affection?" (63–65, 189–91).

Why could he not simply reveal his Stoicism to his friends and try to induce
them to take the same path? Was that not the most sincere and generous friendship he could give them? Part of the problem lay in his Stoic order of priorities in
the exercise of truly natural "affections." If he tried to show true affections for his
friends before he had fully developed true affection for himself, he would do
them more harm than good. He was, in that sense, not ready to reveal his newly
recovered self. But that only reinforced the major obstacle: his conviction that
modern society was not ready to subject itself to a self-critique grounded in Stoic
reflexivity. His friends were no exception; and indeed, precisely because they were
polite gentlemen by modern standards, they might be extreme cases in point. His

experience with Joseph Cropley may have contributed to this sense of futility. Soon after returning to England in 1699 Shaftesbury seems to have persuaded Cropley to take up Stoic exercises. In a letter dated September 1, 1699, Cropley sheepishly confessed that he was making "but slow proficiency," and indeed had fallen "so wide" in his effort to "remove hope and fear" that he had regressed into his "old distemper." He assured Shaftesbury and "all friends" that he would give "full satisfaction" another way—by taking up riding.[39]

The notebooks make clear that for several years after committing himself to Stoic reflectivity, Shaftesbury was caught on the horns of a dilemma. If he kept his Stoicism entirely to himself, as he seems to have done after his experience with Cropley, he would have no social outlet for his spiritual and moral renewal and, worse, would be able to consort with his friends only by dissembling. If he propounded his Stoicism to them, he would make himself vulnerable to "ridicule" for being ponderously didactic, excessively "grave," and inexcusably *Morose* (201). It will be a good sign of his progress in proficiency, he wrote in 1698, if his friends find that he is grown "Dull, Heavy, Stupid" and "has lost what he had either or Witt or Humour" (350–55). But in fact he could not live with that prospect. It was one thing to avoid effeminate French-style politeness, but quite another to disqualify himself from the status of a gentleman by the standards of his own male world. Could he be at once philosophically "severe" and the man of "Quality" and the "Good Companion" his friends expected him to be?

What is striking is Shaftesbury's growing awareness that he was in danger of drawing an uncrossable line between the inner dialogue of self-examination and the interchanges of social performance, even and perhaps especially among his intimates. Again it was partly a matter of bodily presentation; he needed to find "Perfection of Carriage & Manners" that avoided both offensive "Ruggedness" and "the Suppleness of one who only studdyes how to please" (238). The crux of the matter, however, was to develop a via media between what he saw as the crudely male and the effeminate, in conversation and in a kind of essay writing that took the "Ease, Freedom, Liberty" of conversation as its natural form.[40]

Shaftesbury found his ancient model in the apparently light but ethically serious wit of Socrates and his disciple Xenophon. That in itself signals his pursuit of another and arguably more modern route out of what he saw as modern women-centered decadence. As he pondered the dilemmas of friendship in the notebooks, he began to work through them in the notes he made largely during his two stays in Rotterdam for a related project that remained unfinished: a biography of Socrates from the ancient texts, and especially from Xenophon's *Memorabilia* and *Symposium*, that would be at once scholarly and pitched to a polite readership.[41] It was a measure of his need to keep masculine self-representation polite, even as he made his politeness unambiguously male, that he consulted, or at least planned to consult, "the politer Novells" of Mme de Lafayette and other

French women novelists for help on the proper "Style" for the biography and accompanying translations. Where he found his "third" way, however, was in Socrates's philosophical conversations and Xenophon's renderings of them. What he so admired in Socrates was, as he put it in a notebook entry, an "innocent & excellent Dissimulation" (241). And Xenophon, Shaftesbury's model for a gentlemanly philosopher engaged in public life, had caught this liberty perfectly, as a "Man of the World" writing "not with the utmost rigour of Philosophy or as a treatise merely of that kind," but to make philosophy agreeable "even in Courts & polite places where it least has to do." Shaftesbury was particularly taken with Xenophon's rendition of Socrates's bantering conversation with the glamorous courtesan Theodote; there could be "nothing softer nor no raillery and abuse more fine."[42]

The result was rhetorical experiments that transformed the conflicting pulls of his psychological dilemma into complementarities of style. For the performance of his inner self he found what he called a "Curtain," an innocent dissimulation (424). At the same time he assuaged his fear of being ridiculed as a ponderous philosopher with a ridicule of his own—a soft but pointed conversational raillery—that would give his philosophy a polite demeanor, and hence enable him to guide others to Stoic truth without resorting to uncivil efforts to impose it on them. His choice of the term "raillery" is in itself indicative of the new kind of politeness he had in mind. A French word that had entered English usage in the mid-seventeenth century, it marked the English elite's appetite for the literature of honnêteté. One of the issues in that literature had been whether a polite raillery was possible. Could one make fun of an interlocutor without offending him? Could one subject another's thoughts to skeptical irony without introducing a discordant note into a conversational culture devoted to completely harmonious complaisance?[43] Shaftesbury sought to break through these inhibitions with a distinctly English, and male, use of conversation for serious intellectual exchange, even as he took pains to sand down the combative edge needed to make disagreement efficacious. By the time he wrote his notebook entry on "Character," sometime during his second Rotterdam retreat, he had found a way not simply to engage his friends, but also to involve himself once again in his "times," now as a "Character" and a "Voice" combining "true Gravity & Simplicity" with "Humour and a kind of Raillery." Rather than being "two different Souls, two different Men," the one a "facetiouse Comick" and the other confined to "rediculouse Seriousness & Solemnity," he would mix philosophical gravity and raillery in a "conversible, communicable" manner, as "Communication & Transition in a Free Mind." "In this Balance," he instructed himself, "seek a Character, a Personage, Manner, Genius, Style, Voice, Action" (426–28). Here lay the translation of inner freedom—the freedom of wholeness and self-command—into the externalities of public engagement as an author.

Shaftesbury began to justify this authorial character, and to an extent to practice it, in "Sensus communis, an Essay on the Freedom of Wit and Humour in a Letter to a Friend."[44] Though first published in 1709, a year after "A Letter Concerning Enthusiasm," "Sensus communis" is the thematic prolegomena to all the essays. In the opening paragraphs a literary convention—the essay in the form of a letter to a friend—is given a new dramatic twist as Shaftesbury uses it to confront the social dilemma in which he has found himself. The addressee has expressed surprise that "so grave a man" as the author had spoken "in commendation of raillery" in a recent conversation. The author now wants to persuade his friend that he really meant the commendation, and "can continue still to plead for those ingenious friends of ours who are often censured for their humour of this kind and for the freedom they take in such an airy way of conversation and writing" (29–30). In fact, he is defending a "just raillery," a bantering wit that inserts philosophy into male camaraderie by a kind of humorous stealth and makes apparently "airy" conversation a group effort to advance closer to truth in reciprocity and by degrees (30).

This strategy, he makes clear, is a concession to modernity. As in the letter to Lord Somers in 1705, he looked back wistfully to the ancient polis, where philosophers had formed "youth of the highest quality" for the hardships of war and for "the fight against luxury and corruption in times of prosperity and peace." But he knew that, his friendship with learned men like Bayle excepted, modern society and culture had no equivalent place for philosophical wisdom. What makes the friend he addresses a receptive interlocutor is the fact that he is a "gentleman" who has "had little to do with the philosophy or philosophers of our days" (57). He has not been corrupted by neo-Epicurean excuses for materialism and selfishness. The author's projected context for a just raillery, he explains, is necessarily a "constricted" one. He has in mind "the liberty of the Club," "a select company of friends" who "meet knowingly and with that very design of exercising their wit and looking freely into all subjects" (36).

The club serves here as a microcosm for an active polity of gentlemen, and as a training ground for their exercise of liberty of thought and communication in public discourse. It is the site for the fusion of cultural and political liberty. In the face of mere "opinion," a rhetoric of raillery had become Shaftesbury's way to infuse the Stoic's rational discipline, his practice of autonomous selfhood, into a distinctly modern social and political arena of debate. It is striking that in this quite different setting Shaftesbury took aim at the same male-exclusive rhetorical performances that Malebranche critiqued. "Orations" were impositions of power in the guise of public authority, "declamation" by people "who assume to themselves to be dictators in [their] provinces"; their "power" was to "terrify, exalt, ravish or delight rather than satisfy or instruct" (33–34). He had in mind the performances of preachers as well as royal officials. "Where absolute power is," he observed in obvious reference to France, "there is no public" (50). His other target, however, was the "scurrilous" satire that had become so fashionable in the remarkably open public of England. This was a "gross sort of raillery," an "illiberal kind of wit." It allowed the author to hide his real view, and, for all its apparent bitterness, it was a kind of public gallantry, with authors, eager to please, assuming a servile posture toward their readers even as they seduced them into a no less servile acquiescence (31, 61–62). Paradoxically, then, this apparently no-holds-barred form of polemic was a variety of the *complaisance*, the obsession with pleasing, that Shaftesbury found so objectionable in female-centered modern politeness. The politeness he advocated would polish minds in a practice of "liberty" that was (politely) agonistic; "we polish one another and rub off our corners and rough sides by a sort of amicable collision" (31).

For all their shared contempt for effeminate conversation, Shaftesbury and Malebranche had radically different alternatives to it. In Malebranche's ideal of friendship as mutual help in sanctification, the bonding act, the truly "loving" (*aimable*) sign, was not speech as a vehicle of social representation, but a silent look of respect. Shaftesbury sought to turn sociable speech among gentlemen to his purpose. As the vehicle of manly argument, raillery would be polite and indeed amiable; but it would also be the instrument of a certain intellectual combativeness for substantive ends, thus making the polite conversation of gentlemen a social space, and a political space, free of authoritarian imposition. "A free conference," he wrote, "is a close fight" (34).

Critics, Markets, and Labor

Shaftesbury originally published "Soliloquy, or advice to an author" in 1710, just a year after "Sensus communis," and he had good reason to place it immediately after the latter essay in *Characteristics*. It is, rhetorically and stylistically, an exercise in the kind of manly raillery he advocated in "Sensus communis." Having achieved a new political "liberty," England must now sustain it with new forms of cultural freedom in polite letters and the other fine arts. The contrast between the effeminacy of women-centered politeness, epitomized by Parisian high society, and manly politeness—the kind of which English gentlemen must now be made capable—remains central.

But in "Soliloquy" Shaftesbury shifts the focus for this cultural agenda. The social site of intellectual liberty is still gentlemanly friendship, but the imagined interlocutors in this conversational essay are "authors." He frames his "advice" to them within the triangle formed by three issues that figured large in English public discourse at the start of the eighteenth century: the emergence of the professional critic as a distinct kind of man of letters; the commercial expansion of the print market; and the implications of that expansion for standards of taste.[45]

Shaftesbury begins by telling the reader that he will not be the typical giver of advice, using the occasion to "show [his] own wisdom at another's expense." There will be no pedantry. Shaftesbury will "make advice a free gift," though that "is no easy matter." He will follow the ancient poets, who "professed" their mastery while "profess[ing] only to please," without "lay[ing] their claim openly," with "a certain knack or legerdemain in argument."[46] How to avoid didactic advice but press an argument: that is the rhetorical challenge of the essay. As a free gift, Shaftesbury's advice is a polite alternative to the imposition of authority. As an argument, its purpose is not to please but to persuade, to lead authors and their public to accept authoritative standards.

It was already apparent in the *Askêmata* that Shaftesbury's Stoicism had a strong neo-Platonic tinge. He believed that rules and standards for right aesthetic perception, like the obligations of virtue, are objectively given in nature's harmonies and proportions.[47] The issue was how authors could be guided to represent this order in their work, and the central figure, the author's indispensable guide, is the critic. Shaftesbury advocates a "philosophical" criticism, resting squarely on, but not explicitly identified as, Stoic self-knowledge and self-mastery. True critics are a kind of public conscience, at once aesthetic and moral. They will rescue authorship from the effeminacy that an expanding print market has diffused out from conversational sociability to polite letters. With women as its arbiters, a commercializing print culture is producing rampant subjectivism, most evident in the egotism of a false polite refinement. Following the lead of critics, authors will subject themselves to the kind of rigorous self-examination that Shaftesbury had learned to practice.

Shaftesbury was well aware that, in assigning critics a virtually heroic role, he was defying widespread contempt for them among the authors of his day. "It is at present the boast of almost every enterpriser in the Muses' art," he observes, "that, by his genius alone and a natural rapidity of style and thought, he is able to carry all before him," that "he plays with his business, does things in passing at a venture and in the quickest period of time." The task of the critic is to expose the laziness behind this transferal of a playful aesthetic of sociability, its ease and grace floating on mere "vanity," onto the printed page. His polite rhetoric shading into provocation, Shaftesbury quotes Juvenal in Miscellany 5: "*Great is the concord among the effeminate.*"[48] Contempt for critics, he charges, is a flaccid way of avoiding self-reckoning. Authors see critics as "dreadful specters," "persecutors," a "merciless examining race." But it is precisely this "critic's eye" that is needed to assure "accuracy of the workmanship" (104–5).

In the early eighteenth century England well outstripped its continental neighbors in the pace and scale of the expansion of its print market. The expansion was part of a larger growth in consumerism, in turn linked to speculation in a new credit economy. Shaftesbury joined a chorus of literary voices warning of the decline from aesthetic and moral standards to a delusionary obsession with fashion and celebrity. The cries of alarm would be confirmed with a vengeance by the South Sea Bubble in 1720, and would find perhaps their ultimate satiric voice eight years later in Alexander Pope's *Dunciad*, with its swarm of Grub Street "dunces" worshiping at the feet of the goddess "Dullness."[49]

Updating the ancient republican theme of corruption, this view blamed the growing presence of women in the print market for perverting reading into frivolous luxury consumption. Perhaps more than any other author of his day, Shaftesbury sought to puncture any illusion that polite letters was an exception, hovering above the spreading mercenary vulgarity. The reigning polite style was, by his standard, no less "vulgar" than scurrilous satire. The polite aesthetic has become marketable, a commodity pitched to widening circles of polite society; and English authors emulating the *bel esprit* have become its entrepreneurs. His professed confidence that in the face of this trafficking critics and the authors who follow their guidance can institute authoritative standards of taste is belied by his split image of the reading public. He warns "our potentates and grandees" that "the public itself" points out authors of true "merit" and will resent a failure to support them (94–95). The growing market, it would seem, can give a latent consensus its public voice. And yet the public is also a mass of fickle consumers, and authors are their provisioners. The early Greek poets "formed their audience, polished the age, refined the public ear and framed it right." Our modern authors "regulate themselves by the irregular fancy of the world"; "the audience makes the poet, and the bookseller the author." They prey on the modern "need" for reading. Intent on stoking this luxury addiction, they make "an exact calculation in the way of trade to know justly the quality and quantity of the public demand, feed us thus from hand to mouth, resolving not to over-stock the market or be at the pains of more correctness or wit than is absolutely necessary to carry on the traffick" (118–19).

The intricate and at times tortuous path of argument in "Soliloquy" reflects Shaftesbury's efforts to stitch these images together. His difficulty in doing so is registered most strikingly in a sudden change of rhetorical persona that occurs roughly two-thirds of the way through the essay. To that point he had conducted a conversation with authors, implying that he was one of them. Now he anticipates an objection: why should a man who writes for "self-entertainment" have any wish to appear before the public, much less to put his writing on the market? His own "acquaintances," to be sure, include "certain merchant adventurers in the letter-trade who, in correspondence with their factor-bookseller, are entered into a notable commerce with the world." But he has no desire to be an "author" in that sense. He writes solely for his gentlemen friends, and print is simply a technological convenience that spares them the difficulties of his handwriting. His amanuensis is another matter; he may choose to make handwritten copies and sell them, but that "is a traffick [Shaftesbury has] no share in, though [he] accidentally furnish[es] the subject matter" (136–37).

There is more than a hint of conventional aristocratic disdain for buying and selling in this posture. But it rests on anxieties that cut deeper. Stoic meditation had given Shaftesbury a heightened awareness of what was at stake in the issue of taste. In a free state, judgments about the quality of the arts must derive their authority from the moral centeredness and autonomy that only Stoic introspection could develop; and in turn the cultivated ability to discriminate in aesthetic matters, precisely because it was an exercise in rational judgment, was indispensable to the formation of the gentleman-citizen. With the essays, however, Shaftesbury complicated his own role in this process of cultural and civic regeneration. He was now committed to expanding out from the privacy of friendship to self-representation as an author before a reading public. Even as he seemed to step into a new print culture, he stepped back from it.

His shift in voice marks a retreat, momentary but revealing, into a preoccupation in the *Askêmata*: how to bridge the gap between the self-command achieved in anxiously guarded solitude and the conventions of male camaraderie that threatened it. Within the bounded male circle, but not in a larger public arena formed by the print market, he could be sure of remaining polite while professing, somewhat obliquely, a philosophical seriousness—something he has found hard to do face-to-face. In the very process of venturing out from an imagined private circle of manly gentlemen-friends, he insists on remaining uncorrupted— immune to the temptation to indulge in effeminate self-display—by remaining within the circle.

What Shaftesbury added to the standard censure of effeminacy was his historical perspective on politeness, shaped to justify his Stoic alienation from both the "Gothic" past and the commercial present. He traces modern politeness to the "gallant" idolization of women in medieval chivalry and its jousting rituals. It is striking that he finds this genealogy particularly evident in the pleasure women take in vulgar modern "fighting plays." Beneath their air of *complaisance*, women have been perverted into enjoying cruelty by the unnatural power bestowed on them (122–23, 446–47). But the deluded worship of women and subservience to their whims pervades the apparently more refined tastes of politeness as well. That is one reason, and perhaps the chief, why the judgments of real critics are so arrogantly dismissed. "I have seen many a time a well-bred man," Shaftesbury observes, "who had himself a real good taste, give way, with a malicious *complaisance*, to the humour of company where, in favor chiefly of the tender sex, this soft languishing contempt of critics and their labours has been set afoot."[50]

Throughout the essay Shaftesbury uses his notion of polite gallantry to figure the newly commercialized relationship between author and reader.[51] The author writing for a reader/consumer, like the gallant lover, is driven by an effeminate need to please. They have in common the compulsion to inflate their sense of power even as they "prostitute" themselves. Moral selfhood is dissipated as the embodied social self, assuming an authorial voice in print, scatters into free-floating fragments in servile obedience to others. It will not do, Shaftesbury warns, for authors to object that, like lovers, they find inspiration in solitary communion with nature. The more an author exhibits himself before the market of polite readers, as gallants exhibit themselves before the ladies at court and in polite circles, the more he reveals his lack of a core self (79). If the analogy between author and lover is figural, it also posits what Shaftesbury sees as a causal reciprocity. *Complaisance* and market display—the dissimulated appearances of female-centered politeness and the manipulations of market dependencies—have fused in modern literary culture.

"That [authors'] vein of writing may be natural and free, they should settle matters in the first place with themselves" (124). The philosophical critic sets the example. He has himself mastered "self-dialogue," "the preliminary of self-study and inward converse," and by following him in that practice, the author learns to be self-critical, to proceed from "search and scrutiny of [his] opinions and the sincere consideration of [his] *scope* and end" (132). Shaftesbury extends to authorship the strategy he wants to adopt in friendship: withdrawal to meditation to ensure integrity in social intercourse. What he is advocating, he takes pains to explain, is not another form of submission to authority as such. "To bid me judge authority by morals," he writes, "while the rule of morals is supposed dependent on mere authority and will, is the same in reality as to bid me see with my eyes shut" (132). The author follows the critic's principles in taste because he has learned from him how to practice "impartial censure" as an autonomous self. The strict solitude of his self-examination must be spiritual as well as physical. Only in that way can he make himself aware of the social impingements that pull him into false presentations of the self in the circulation of opinion. This accounts for the most curious feature of Shaftesbury's conception of authorship. While self-dialogue is essential preparation, it cannot be conducted with the act of writing in mind and cannot be displayed in the writing. Even in his apparent solitude the author, like the gallant lover, always imagines the presence of the other; and thus, even as he seems to withdraw into self-converse, he is driven by an effeminate obsession with pleasing. He has nothing purely "for himself" on which to plant his feet as he engages in the sociability of authorship. Paradoxically it is the invisibility of self-examination that gives the authorial voice an authoritative moral transparency.

Arguably Shaftesbury, in his determination to purge writing of the false appearances of effeminacy, substitutes a no less deceptive performance. He deliberately hides the inner self behind a persona in the conversational rhetoric he called raillery. Like Malebranche, he saw modern polite taste as women's affair;

but in sharp contrast to Malebranche, he thinks that he has found a way to make taste a manly prerogative, in the politeness of a robust civic culture. He aspires to make writing a deeply social act, braiding the sinews of a new male sociability. If the moral authority of the author requires that he represent his character through the writing, however, it is also premised on his absence from the writing. Somehow his inner self must remain invisible in the text even as it externalizes itself through rhetorical skills. His manliness—his conquest of the effeminate inclinations all around him—requires that he be at once desocialized, as a self detached from all the "externals" of social exchange, and a social being represented in a public medium.[52]

What mediates the tension in this duality is Shaftesbury's concept of aesthetic labor, which he pits against the aesthetic of play in false politeness. "A legitimate and just taste," he writes in the third Miscellany, "can neither be begotten, made, conceived or produced without the antecedent labour and pains of criticism."[53] Labor makes authorship morally possible, is integral to its practice, and gives authority to its products. In "Soliloquy" his description of the required self-dialogue directly echoes the *Askêmata*, though still without Stoic references; and indeed, without acknowledging his own efforts to become a proficient, it demonstrates the same solitary exercises in inversion he has been practicing. Turning from his readers to speak to himself, he enters a laborious trial: "let me see how I can bear the assault of fancy and maintain myself in my moral fortress against the attacks which are raised on the side of corrupt interest and a wrong self" (131–35). As in the *Askêmata*, the inner dialogue of inversion is between the true moral self and the false social self, personified by "the Lady Fancies," those "very powerful solicitresses." Obliquely, without seeming to "importune," "the enchantress Indolence in all the pomp of ease and lazy luxury" hides the truth that "life and happiness consist in action and employment." The "Queen of Terrors" represents death "in such a hideous form" that people are driven to luxury and "effeminacy and cowardice instantly prevail" (140). Dispelling the Fancies is a labor in language, and in the disciplining, the stripping down, of language. Inverting the relationship between true and false self means forcing the seducers to abandon their impostures and speak a plain language open to refutation. This is the manly labor of self-command that will make possible an agonistic, though still polite, rhetoric in print.

The rhetoric in turn is a labor in rational argument. To underscore this point Shaftesbury offers a brief explanation of the origins of rhetoric in the early Greek polis. The first rhetors were not seductive manipulators, but masters of an art of "persuasion" developed in "free communities," where the people had to be convinced before they acted. "Hence was the origin of critics," guardians of the arts and sciences, including "the gravest philosophers." Always ready to "explode the unnatural manner," they insured against "the effeminate kind" of "style" as well as "Bombast" (107–12). Again Shaftesbury seeks an alternative to two forms of communication that suppress natural freedom: a public discourse that imposes power in the guise of authority, and the illusion of power-free and conflict-free *complaisance* in *honnêteté* and its English emulations. Authoritative standards must arise from rational argument, not blind submission to authority; and the antirhetorical rhetoric of social play, which aims to please rather than to persuade, must accede to the discursive but purposeful rhetorical effort to persuade.

It is in this labor of persuasion that the core rational self, from its citadel of autonomy, reveals itself and acts socially, without succumbing to the impostures that socially generated opinion seeks to impose on it. And that is why the labor must show itself in the product. It could not, of course, take the form of scholarly pedantry. Shaftesbury was too much the well-bred gentleman to advise authors to take on that social stigma, though he himself was a serious scholar, and perhaps singular in that regard among men of his standing. In the notes for his planned "Socratick History" we find him practicing close textual criticism of the original Greek texts and evaluation of commentaries on them, from the Romans to his own day. But the notes in the text itself were to be of a discursive nature, "agreeable and pleasant" to a polite readership; the actual scholarly notes were to be consigned to a separate section in small print.[54]

And yet the labor of self-dialogue must have its correlative in the labor of style. In "Soliloquy" Shaftesbury compares his ideal modern author, laboring under "a critic's eye," to the literary "workmen" in "the days of Attic eloquence," determined to "discover the pains they had taken to be correct":

> They were glad to insinuate how laboriously and with what expense of time they had brought the smallest work of theirs . . . to its perfection. When they had so polished their piece and rendered it so natural and easy that it seemed only a lucky flight, a hit of thought or flowing vein of humour, they were then chiefly concerned lest it should in reality pass for such and their artifice remain undiscovered. They were willing it should be known how serious their play was and how elaborate their freedom and facility that they might say, as the agreeable and polite poet, glancing on himself: *He will give the appearance of playing and yet he will be in torture.* (105)

The quote is from Horace, the ancient author Shaftesbury used most extensively in the essays to keep his Stoicism camouflaged. In Shaftesbury's reading of the poet's career, he had succumbed to the effeminate debauchery of the Augustan court but had returned in later life to the republican ethos of his youth.[55] He was proof, like Xenophon, that one could be a polite Stoic (114, 121).

Doubtless by modern democratic standards Shaftesbury's thinking about taste is elitist. But his social standpoint becomes more complicated when we take into account his insistence that the author display his "workmanship" in the writing, and when we realize how powerfully his concept of aesthetic labor was driven by a need to reassert gender distinctions. Though he equates true taste with breeding, he does not stigmatize intellectual labor as incompatible with the natural freedom of the well-bred man. Quite the contrary; intent on purging English gentlemanly culture of an effeminate aesthetic, Shaftesbury sees labor as emancipatory. Labor is his antidote to the feminine—and French—servility that pervades the exclusiveness of conventional aristocratic society.

The Moralists

"The Moralists, a Philosophical Rhapsody" is the longest essay in *Characteristics* and, appropriately, the final one. Here, far more than in any of Shaftesbury's other essays, we find the confluence of the two ancient philosophical traditions that shaped his thought: Stoic ethics, with its emphasis on the willed "action" of virtue, and a neo-Platonic aesthetic ideal of disinterested contemplation of beauty, transmitted to him in part by the Cambridge Platonists. Shaftesbury aims to demonstrate that moral goodness and beauty have the same universal formal properties of right proportion and integral harmony, reflecting the unity of a Supreme Intelligence; that the moral and aesthetic fold into each other to such a degree as to be virtually one; and that human beings have an innate, or "co-natural," rational and emotional capacity to make both moral and aesthetic judgments.

But the essay is far more complex and elusive than this distillation might suggest. It is "an undertaking of greater weight" than the "Inquiry," Shaftesbury comments in the fifth Miscellany; in addition to being at "bottom, as systematical, didactic and preceptive," it "assumes withal another garb and more fashionable turn of wit," "conceals what is scholastical under the appearance of a polite work," and "aspires to dialogue," including "even the poetic or sublime, such as is the aptest to run into enthusiasm and extravagance."[56] Shaftesbury is obviously aware that his prose is threading needles. If the essay has the philosophical substance of a treatise, it is nonetheless a contribution to polite letters. And yet if it is polite, it nonetheless risks assuming the voice of the religious enthusiast, a figure often used as a foil in polite culture's definition of itself.[57]

In the order of composition, "The Moralists" was the first of the experimental essays Shaftesbury wrote in search of an alternative to the genre of the philosophical treatise. The original, shorter version, titled "The Social Enthusiast," was the "Tale of Philosophy" Shaftesbury had offered to Lord Somers in his letter of 1705. The letter alerts us to the need to keep the social and cultural dimensions of the essay at the center of our effort to understand it, and above all to grasp the

centrality of Shaftesbury's gendered perceptions of modern polite culture to his
larger vision. Pairing "effeminacy" with "superstition," he had blamed the exclusion of true philosophy from polite sociability on the "the Rule" of "the Fair Sex."
This was the bitter legacy of "gallantry."[58] In the opening pages of the expanded
essay he elaborated this view. "Our modern conversations," Philocles tells his
interlocutor Palemon, have "such a scrupulous nicety" that "they lose those masculine helps of learning and sound reason." Even women may "despise us . . .
for aiming at their peculiar softness" and "affect[ing] their manners and be[ing]
effeminate." "Our sense, language, and style, as well as our voice and person,
should have something of that male feature and natural roughness by which our
sex is distinguished."[59]

Shaftesbury takes up this rhetorical challenge. Philosophy can escape its academic ghettos and find its proper place in modern culture and civic life only if it
becomes an accepted subject of polite conversation among gentlemen; and that
can happen only if conversation is deeffeminized or, to put it positively, remascu-
linized, so that men are free to conduct philosophical inquiry in their "natural"
voices, as a civil but "rough" combat in rational argument. To be more precise, the
"style" of the essay must represent philosophical inquiry as a relational process
among male friends, a process in which the terms of male friendship are integral
to the intellectual effort. It must present the inquiry as at once a pleasure of male
friendship among gentleman and an exercise in the social labor of communication, both verbally and in print. The reader witnesses characters who are sufficiently individualized to be believable protagonists but at the same time pursue
their argument within a shared culture of polite civility.

On the face of it Philocles, the essay's narrator, is an odd choice for such a
task. Even as he diagnoses the problem posed by "our modern conversations," he
is very much a part of it. We learn that he is inclined to a Pyrrhonian skepticism
that denies the possibility of any rational certainty, and that his skepticism is less a
firm philosophical position than a role in a culture of conversational play.[60] In the
fifth Miscellany Shaftesbury describes him as "an airy gentleman of the world
and a thorough *railleur*."[61] In this instance *railleur* evokes not the serious raillery
Shaftesbury wants to introduce, but the intellectual trickery of a man who takes
nothing seriously. Recalling their conversation, Philocles acknowledges Palemon
had sized him up correctly:

> Above all things I loved ease and, of all philosophers, those who reasoned
> most at their ease and were never angry or disturbed, as those called
> skeptics, you owned, never were. I looked upon this kind of philosophy as
> the prettiest, agreeablest, roving exercise of the mind possible to be imag-
> ined. The other kind, I thought, was painful and laborious . . . to drive
> always at a point and hold precisely to what men at a venture called "the

truth," a point, in all appearance, very unfixed and hard to ascertain. (241–44)

We can now appreciate the full scale of the challenge Shaftesbury faced. To give the wisdom of ancient philosophy a central place in the polite conversation of well-bred gentlemen was to insert serious labor into a culture that defined itself by its exclusion of anything that might seem laborious.

The voice of this labor is Theocles, the third interlocutor, who clearly represents Shaftesbury's own philosophical position. In parts 2 and 3, in conversation with Philocles, Theocles drives, politely but fixedly, toward the truth, though sometimes with the rapturous invocations of an "enthusiast" rather than with the conceptual precision of a philosophical rationalist. He seeks to refute in one broad swipe an irrational Christian theism, with its belief in revelation, in an anthropomorphic God, in miracles, and so on; the self-deluded imaginings of the religious "enthusiast"; modern rationalist philosophies whose laws of mechanistic causation seem to deprive the universe of moral meaning; and the radical skepticism that denies the possibility of any certainty. His alternative is a philosophical theism that is at once ethical and aesthetic, with virtue and beauty following the same laws of unity, harmony, and right proportion. One path to this theism—a classic Stoic path—is from the narrowly perspectival to the universal. How do we account for the apparent irregularities and asymmetries in Nature, including what appear to be the cruelty and evil with which it confronts us? If we transcend our blinkered perspectives as tiny parts of the universe to contemplate the universe as an organic Whole, these anomalies are only apparent; they point us neither to a limited Divinity, which is a hopelessly contradictory concept, nor to a malevolent one. There can only be one reason that the dynamic processes of Nature display such intricate order: they are emanations of an all-encompassing and completely unitary Supreme Intelligence.

Shaftesbury's other path to his philosophical theism is more noticeably akin to neo-Platonic concepts of ideal forms. The rational mind penetrates to the inner "forming forms" behind the external appearances of Nature. The core self is one such form, the inner force that accounts for the fact that the "I" remains the same self despite the constant transformation of its physical existence. In the continuity of a unitary self we experience most immediately the immanent presence of the Supreme Intelligence in its emanations. The inner self becomes the most unassailable proof that God, so conceived, exists.

The essay would be straightforward enough if it simply laid out this philosophical vision. But its aim is not simply to state truths; Shaftesbury wanted to dramatize the process of philosophical inquiry in the interaction of characters. To do so he had to adapt the dialogic form of the ancients to a modern context of polite sociability; and as he acknowledged in the fifth Miscellany, that required several stratagems, all signaled in the essay's subtitle: "A Philosophical Rhapsody, Being a Recital of Certain Conversations on Natural and Moral Subjects." The term "rhapsody" designates the mixed generic properties of the essay as well as its evocations of the sublime. There are two dialogues: one between Philocles and Palemon, the other between Philocles and Theocles. The latter has occurred first but is recounted second. The reader does not witness the dialogues immediately, as an audience witnesses a play. Philocles narrates, or recites, his recent conversation with Palemon, who has insisted that there be a "monument" to their "unseasonable" exchange, "so opposite to the reigning genius of gallantry and pleasure"; and we learn that, in a tense moment in the exchange, he was prompted to narrate his earlier lengthy conversation with Theocles. In both narrations Philocles intersperses his own retrospective thoughts with verbatim quotations. There are shifts in place, and in social setting, as well as in time. Palemon and Philocles have been together in a coach in a park, where Palemon has "taken the fancy to talk philosophy" in "a circle of good company" that includes women. Their one-to-one conversation begins only after they have left that scene. Philocles and Theocles begin their conversation among other gentleman at a dinner at a country house, but withdraw to a wooded hill to continue it the next morning.

What are we to make of these highly self-conscious and at times convoluted formal strategies? To a large measure they reflect the fact that Shaftesbury "aspire[d] to dialogue" with a clear purpose, at once philosophical and intensely personal, but also with a certain anxiety. He discusses the genre at some length in both "Soliloquy" and the fifth Miscellany, and particularly in the latter his doubts about his own use of it in "The Moralists" are quite explicit. In his aspiration to revive ancient Socratic dialogue, Shaftesbury sought the perfect bridge between his meditative privacy as a Stoic proficient and his public voice as an author. The question was not simply how the philosophical author could represent the self-mastery he has achieved in "inward rhetoric" without coercing his reader into passive imitation. Shaftesbury's other concern was to provide a defiant alternative to the mutual narcissistic servility that he used the term "effeminate" to evoke, and that he found in the modern relationship between author and reader in the expanding market for polite letters. Pure dialogue—a text with nothing but the interlocutors' speech—seemed to avoid both pitfalls. It effected the fiction of immediate witness, as in the theatrical illusion of hearing "real dialogues" on stage. With the author seemingly "annihilated," there could be no "pretty amour and intercourse of caresses"; both "self-interested parties"—author and reader— "vanish at once" (233–34).

The author's self-concealment is reinforced by the fact that his artistry is completely invested in creating individualized characters, each as unique in temperament as human faces are in appearance, and all representing the particular "manners"—the social norms and behavior—of his readers. It was in this social sense that Shaftesbury wanted to revive ancient dialogue as "natural conversation set in view" (462). Because the characters are so recognizable, the reader—in this case, Shaftesbury's fellow gentleman—is drawn into the intellectual substance as well as the dramatic action of the dialogue. He has to "make the effort of reading characters directly from their speech," and in doing so he engages and eventually forms judgments about the thoughts they advance. This witnessing of dialogue induces inner self-dialogue; readers learn to "carry about with them a sort of pocket mirror," a way of internalizing the dialogic split between the voice of rational self-command and the voice (or voices) of the false self, the creature of untamed imagination, enslaved to "opinion" (462–63). This extension of self-critical autonomy to a reading public is, of course, socially limited. The dialogue Shaftesbury conceives is "natural" in the sense that it represents the conversational world of gentlemen equals that it seeks to reform. Within that circumscribed context, he can use his individualized characters to demonstrate his rhetorical strategy of distinctly male raillery.

If Shaftesbury's theory of pure dialogue inspired him, it also put him in something of a quandary. He doubted that modern polite gentlemen could sustain the kind of labor he was demanding of them. Would his readers engage characters who, though men of "note or fashion," "[reasoned] expressly and purposely, without play or trifling, for two or three hours together on mere philosophy and morals" (459)? And could they bear to look at themselves in the pocket mirror? To make the conversation "natural," after all, meant to confront his readers with the obsequiousness that was integral to modern polite manners. These concerns also explain why Shaftesbury opted not to make "The Moralists" a pure, unmediated dialogue. Instead he placed the dialogues within a narrative essay that would demand less effort from his readers and avoid making them squirm as they held the mirror to themselves. When he played the critic to himself in the fifth Miscellany, however, he acknowledged that this adaptation betrayed the author's "timorousness" (459). His choice of terms is remarkable. He fears that he has surrendered to the effeminacy of his audience, and perhaps—this is no more than implicit—that in doing so he has acted effeminately himself. And he feels compelled to assure his reader that, though the result may have seemed like one of those essays that "come abroad with an affected air of negligence and irregularity," he had no intention of writing "after that model of incoherent workmanship."

In a sense, Shaftesbury was being too hard on himself. The resort to essayistic strategies was, by his standards, a regrettable concession, but it was also a means to the ethical autonomy he sought to induce. The overarching argument of the fifth Miscellany is that, if an author is to be accountable to just criticism, the reader must exercise *the liberty to read, that is to say, to examine, construe and remark with understanding.* He must have "the upper hand" (434, 441, 444). The reader in question, of course, is an imagined reader, not the actual polite reader demanding entertainment and caressing. He is the ideal gentleman-citizen of Shaftesbury's distinctly English political culture of republican civic values. Like Malebranche, Shaftesbury insists that autonomous judgment replace blind and passive submission to authority. But unlike him, he cannot use dialogue to guide the reader to unassailable truth, conclusions his rationality leaves him no choice but to accept. That kind of closure is not possible in a dialogue that eschews the transcendent truth claims of Christian theology.[62] It is also not compatible with a political culture of open-ended contestation about civic issues. In the practice of raillery as polite but rigorous manly combat, there can be no sage so intellectually superior to his interlocutors that he imposes his judgment on them with finality. Theocles is not the pure voice of reason; he worries constantly that he is succumbing to the temptation to fall completely into either the "flat" logic of demonstrative reasoning or ecstatic aesthetic "enthusiasm." He needs formidable opponents like Philocles who are not "overtame and tractable" and will not simply surrender to his vision.

All this explains Shaftesbury's most intricate strategy: the elusive multivocal part played by Philocles as interlocutor and as narrator. If Philocles's radical skepticism is the mere posturing of an "airy" railleur, it nonetheless poses relentless challenges to Theocles's philosophical optimism. He does seem to convert to Theocles's theism at the end of their dialogue, but only after adeptly meeting his friend's requests to be "govern[ed]," and indeed to be pulled back from the equally perilous precipices of overly "cool" reason and excessively "warm" enthusiasm. Having taken these pains to keep the combat open-ended, Shaftesbury still saw the need to use Philocles's retrospective narrative of it to Palemon to ensure that effect. Though he had apparently assented to Theocles's theism, Philocles nonetheless returns to a polite performance in skepticism in his conversation with Palemon. He has resumed this position, he finally admits, because he fears that under Theocles's guidance he had succumbed to "downright enthusiasm." Looking back on the conversation, he is deeply impressed by the fact that Theocles expressed such "philosophical passion" without assuming "that savage air of the vulgar enthusiastic kind," the "fierce unsociable way of modern zealots" (246). But in the end Philocles is no convert; he retains a certain resistance to Theocles's vision.[63] He is, one might say, the inner voice of the conventionally polite gentleman in Shaftesbury's own self-dialogue—the voice he has muted but cannot entirely silence.

It is on the subject of "enthusiasm" that "The Moralists" is at its boldest. Shaftesbury's aim was to guide the reader into a new kind of spirituality that rejected the coldness of modern mechanistic philosophy, emptied of man's natural affections for Nature and God, but also shunned the excessive heat of the enthusiast's conviction of being a receptacle of supernatural inspiration. By the early eighteenth century, "enthusiasm" was a widely used smear word, spreading from Protestant sectarian conflicts to philosophical polemics. It declared an opponent's words to be incomprehensible, the self-absorbed rantings of a fanatic, and hence denied them legitimacy in public discourse.[64] When Shaftesbury posited a "noble" enthusiasm, he knew he was entering treacherous waters. He took pains to assure readers that the aesthetic passion he had in mind was cleanly different from enthusiasm in the conventional sense, even though it drew on the same vital force in human nature. His Stoicism made the difference all the more important. Enthusiasm was at the opposite pole from Stoic wisdom; not the self-knowledge gained in strenuous introspection, but enslavement to the "externals" of physical being and social pressures. Self-delusion took many forms, from the profoundly unsociable rantings of the sectarian who claimed to have achieved self-transcendence as God's instrument to the pompous pronouncements of Anglican clergymen intent on suppressing freedom of conscience. In Shaftesbury's broad conception of it, enthusiasm was the place where the radical fringes of Protestantism and the orthodoxy of the established church met in the imposition of authoritarian claims to revealed truth, allowing neither free inquiry nor individual autonomy.

In the state of enthusiasm the imagination operates free of rational control, and the individual's capacity for self-governance is negated by passions run wild. Passively reflecting the appearances around him, the enthusiast becomes a mere appearance himself. He is without a core rational self. A chain of associations linked this enthusiastic state of mind with effeminacy: self-inflation rather than self-containment; passivity rather than active exercise of will; servile fear rather than a rational reverence; indolence or laziness rather than disciplined mental labor; unrestrained sensuality rather than spiritual purification. These negative images pervade "The Moralists," as they do the other essays in *Characteristics*. In the essay "A letter concerning enthusiasm," published in 1708 and placed first in *Characteristics*, Shaftesbury had begun to argue that the same inner force that powered zealotry could assume a "noble" form, expressing the "sublime in human passions" when "the ideas or images received are too big for the narrow human vessel to contain" (27–28). Enthusiasm conceived in this way, as rationally controlled imaginative intuition, was Shaftesbury's antidote to the moral and spiritual emptiness of neo-Epicurean mechanism. He saw it as vital to our capacity to envision the divine order and represent it in the arts. In "The Moralists" he wanted to show that, understood as inspiration in this sense, enthusiasm was integral to true spirituality; but he proceeded with an acute awareness that no more than a thin, wavering line divided the enthusiasm he wished to justify from the kind that he hoped his new culture of manly politeness would expunge.

There was the danger that Theocles's paeans to the awesome beauty of Nature would be seen not as sublime expressions of a theistic vision, but as pantheistic mysticism, giving divine status to nature itself. But even if Shaftesbury kept his philosophy at a safe distance from this precipice, he was in near danger of falling over another one. Was there not something erotic about his "love" of Nature? His insistence on rational rigor notwithstanding, was he not indulging in effeminate sensuality and in the "indolence" it produced? Shaftesbury posed this question in the opening pages of the essay. Philocles observes that the philosopher is a "lover," no different from the lover of "poetry, music . . . or the fair" (232). They are all "virtuosi," "enamoured" of objects that will give them pleasure. To put it another way, they are all driven by desires that the Stoic must deny. We learn later that Theocles has separated his theism cleanly from sensual desire and pleasure by drawing a Platonic distinction between two kinds of "love." Philocles must learn that "there is no principle of beauty in the body"; beauty lies not in "the matter," but in "the art and design." The "vulgar" lover is captivated only by "the faint shadow" of true beauty. The philosophical lover apprehends the *"form or forming power"* that gives an object a pleasing surface. In his grasp of inner forms in nature he experiences enthusiasm as a "reasonable ecstasy and transport." Here, in this true self-transcendence, is where the aesthetic, the moral, and the spiritual coalesce. The ascent to love of the Divine lies through disinterested contemplation of the forms, which "[lie] very absconded and deep." As in the arts, such contemplation is a kind of labor; it requires the long, hard acquisition of "true taste" (320–22). The inspired artist—the noble enthusiast—partakes of the Divine by representing in sense imagery the forms that emanate from it.

Shaftesbury's determination to separate the labor of true enthusism from effeminate indolence helps explain why he opted for a narrative essay. As narrator Philocles recalls two moments of crisis in the dramatic action—moments when dialogue ascends to a higher level, but only after it has survived a near breakdown of male friendship. At the end of Part 1, when Philocles admits that he has been merely playing the role of skeptic, Palemon is "offended" and "coldly" asks his friend whether "[his] fine skepticism . . . made no more distinction between sincerity and insincerity in actions than [it] did between truth and falsehood, right and wrong, in arguments" (242). As Shaftesbury explains in the fifth Miscellany, Philocles "must . . . feel the anger of his grave friend before he can be supposed grave enough to enter into a philosophical discourse" (460). Eager to reassure Palemon on this score, Philocles agrees to write an account of his conversation with Theocles. With this turn the recollection of a polite performance ends and Philocles must labor in solitude. It is a measure of Shaftesbury's concern to convey the full meaning of the turn that in the 1709 version he expanded on the original description in "The Sociable Enthusiast." Now, Philocles remarks in the new version, he will have to proceed "upon harder terms than ever." And he continues: "Your conversation, Palemon, which had hitherto supported me, was at an end. I was now alone, confined to my Closet, obliged to meditate by myself and reduced to the hard circumstances of an author and historian in the most difficult subject" (246–49). Effeminate play is over; by agreeing to write, he has committed himself to the hard reflective labor that Shaftesbury demands of authorship.[65]

The second moment comes at the beginning of Part 3, following a debate deep into the night among the gentlemen gathered at the country house. The others will depart in the morning, and Philocles rejoices that Theocles finally has been left to him alone. But he awakes to discover that Theocles is taking a solitary walk and has "left word . . . that nobody in the meantime should disturb my rest." This solicitude offends Philocles. Overtaking Theocles on a nearby hill, Philocles complains that he is not "so effeminate and weak a friend as to deserve that [Theocles] should treat [him] like a woman." He did not deserve "to be thought fitter for the dull luxury of a soft bed" than for "study with an early friend." And so Theocles must make "amends" by "allowing [him] henceforward to be a party with him in his serious thoughts," "his hours and exercises of this sort" (246–47).

Here again an advance in philosophical labor pivots on a dramatic moment of near breakdown in communication between the characters. The contrast is between womanish indolence and the active intimacy, at once intellectual and emotional, that male friendship should provide. There is an element of teasing in Philocles's demand that his friend make amends, but it also signals that raillery is over and what follows will be more a joint exercise in the rigors of meditation than the kind of lively argument the group of gentlemen had conducted. Theocles and Philocles, to be sure, continue to figure themselves as "lovers," entranced by the sublime beauties through which the Divinity makes its presence felt in the natural order. For a moment immediately following Philocles's rebuke, the friends' conversation becomes distinctly flirtatious. Theocles suggests that Philocles's anger is fueled by his "jealousy" of his own relation with the "sylvan nymphs" of the hill scene. Philocles's response is to figure the friends themselves as lovers: "My jealously and love regard you only. I was afraid you had a mind to escape me; but, now that I am again in possession of you, I want no nymph to make me happy here" (296–97). The coy language of love would seem to suggest that an erotically tinged aesthetic of nature draws on an erotically charged desire to possess the other, not physically, of course, but spiritually.

From this point on, however, the self-consciously rapturous invocations of natural sublimity, though meant to persuade, are not what clinches Philocles's assent to Theocles's vision. That is the task of a rigorously logical combat between the resistant skeptic and the philosophical theist, interspersed with flights of enthusiasm. Theocles in effect takes Philocles through a Stoic meditation on the logical reciprocity between unitary selfhood and unitary Divinity. " 'If you conclude that there is not a universal One,' Theocles points out to Philocles, you must also conclude that 'there cannot be any such particular one as yourself' ":

> But that there is actually such a one as this latter, your own mind, it is hoped, may satisfy you. And of this mind it is enough to say that it is something which acts upon a body and has something passive under it and subject to it, that it has not only body or mere matter for its subject but in some respect even itself too and what proceeds from it, that it superintends and manages its own imaginations, appearances, fancies correcting, working and modelling these as it finds good and adorning and accomplishing the best it can this composite order of body and understanding. Such a mind and governing part I know there is somewhere in the world. (302)

It is not simply that we can be certain of the centered unity of our own selfhood through time, as immaterial beings, only by being certain of God's existence. Conversely the reflexive turn inward—the exercise of the power of the immaterial mind to subject the body—grounds our awareness of God's power to inform nature with rational order. Accepting the requisite "labour and pains" of this reciprocity of rational conviction, they can proceed from their grasp of the "forming forms" that constitute their selves to an intuitive awareness of the inner forms behind the mere "representative beauty" that captivates the senses. Shaftesbury is careful to single out female beauty. The two friends will find pleasure in the physical beauty of a woman only because it "shadows" the spiritual beauty behind it (322–24).

Particularly at these junctures Shaftesbury's effort to convey philosophical argument in the "natural conversation" of polite gentlemen breaks down. The sociability of an imagined club accedes to the rigors of a philosophical friendship. Shaftesbury is intent on defining selfhood in the emphatically male terms of his ideal of virtuous character, as the mental strength achieved in an askesis of self-examination, in contrast to enslavement to the *visa*, the "fancies" of the bodily self. Theocles invites Philocles to ground their friendship in a shared labor of inversion. He knows that Philocles can hardly decline, despite his inclination to remain uncommitted within the performance of skepticism as a kind of intellectual and social play. After all, the skeptic's one certainty, or at least the closest thing he has to a certainty, is that by virtue of his mental activity he has a unified and continuous self. Shaftesbury aims to refute skepticism on its own grounds, requiring it to affirm, from its admission of the irrefutable fact of self-consciousness, that the existence of Divinity is no less irrefutable. He also wants to settle accounts with the modern philosophers he lumps together under neo-Epicurean materialism.

With Locke in mind, he denies that the psychophysiological processes of memory constitute a continuous self; pure intellect—the autonomous power of reason—makes the self "one and the same" through time, "when neither one atom of body, one passion nor one thought remains the same" (303–4).

Shaftesbury's amatory language is at once erotically evocative and de-eroticizing in its irony. In the aesthetic enthusiasm he embraces, the only permissible objects of erotic desire are purely intellectual forms; eros finds release in philosophical contemplation.[66] It is an ecstasy of the laboring mind, grounded in, and leading to, an awareness, at once rational and intuitive, that what puts one in the immediate presence of God is the inner forming, the action of the immaterial self. That is why a "reasonable ecstasy" is the very opposite of the enthusiast's self-deluding claim to supernatural inspiration. We know God by grasping our rational core.

—

In 1748 the young Adam Smith began offering a series of lectures on "Rhetoric and Belles Lettres" to the educated public of Edinburgh. He used the opening of the eleventh lecture to sum up his guiding principles: that a good prose "stile" is a "natural" one, a presentation of "character" as "agreable company," and that in writing, as in "conversation" and "behaviour," a man presents himself naturally by "never seem[ing] to act out of character."[67]

The rest of the eleventh lecture is a slashing critique of Shaftesbury, in whose prose Smith found neither "the character of a gentleman" nor any other character. What makes Smith's critique so sharp-edged is the way he configures Shaftesbury's intellectual inclinations, his biography, and his physical debility. Because of his family and Locke's tutelage, Smith tells us, Shaftesbury was brought up "without being attached to any particular men and opinions." To paraphrase Smith's point, Shaftesbury had not been formed in any social world committed to a particular tradition of thought or religious belief, and so his authorial voice was characterless. That deficiency was reinforced by his "very puny and weakly constitution." Having too "delicate a frame" to engage in the fatiguing labors of "abstract reasoning and deep searches," he largely ignored modern developments in philosophy, natural science, and mathematics. Instead, like other men with his "feableness of body," he cultivated "the fine arts, matters of taste and imagination," which require "little labour." In keeping with his upbringing as well as his physical debility, Shaftesbury "seems . . . to have formed to himself a [Platonic] idea of beauty of Style abstracted from his own character." Though he "modernized" the Platonic tradition "a little" to suit prevailing taste the result was style as "affectation," "pompous, grand, and ornate."[68]

Smith had in mind primarily the "The Moralists," though "Soliloquy" also annoyed him. His appraisal of Shaftesbury's thought and writing seems fair enough on at least two counts. Shaftesbury *was* willfully dismissive of modern philosophy. However justified his moral indignation may have been, it does not excuse his gross oversimplification of a wide variety of thought, including Locke's. More to the point here, Smith applied to Shaftesbury's prose the standard set by Addison's *Spectator*. Addison merited the accolade of being "a most polite and elegant writer" by "always display[ing] the modesty of his character."[69] A period-specific perspective, to be sure, but that is not to say that the modern reader can simply remove Smith's Spectatorial lens and come up with an appraisal that does more justice to the historical Shaftesbury. She is likely to share Smith's verdict, and that is because *The Spectator* ushered in a new way of modeling writing on conversation, polite but far more embedded in the everyday usage and the social diversity of a great city and hence far more socially animated and inclusive. "Soliloquy" does have a certain appealing discursive ease, but it is too self-consciously contrived, too obviously preoccupied with its own formal experimentation, to carry off the kind of conversational simulation Shaftesbury wanted it to have. In the dialogic parts of "The Moralists" the irony is that he failed where he most wanted to succeed. Even his efforts to extrude his own philosophical reflectivity from the text by having individualized characters engage in socially "natural" conversation have something artificial and stilted about them. The raillery often seems bloodless, in part because there is so little of the particularity of character needed to give it life, and in part because the dramatic action is so obviously a vehicle of philosophical edification. We are a long way from Diderot's *Jacques the Fatalist and His Master*, and still farther removed from *Rameau's Nephew*.

But if Smith takes the modern measure of Shaftesbury's style, he also diverts us from understanding what was significantly original about Shaftesbury's experiments in essay writing and why they often seem too contrived and indeed tortuously self-conscious to accomplish his purposes. In claiming that Shaftesbury the author spoke from no particular social context and hence exhibited no character, Smith obviates the need to understand Shaftesbury's writings contextually. We would not know from Smith's critique that, as a boy and a young adult, Shaftesbury had been anchored in a social world committed to the values of civic humanism; or that his family situation was difficult and at times oppressive; or that he lived a gentlemanly politeness even as he sought to immunize his fellow gentlemen from French *politesse*; or that when his tone became haughty, at least to our modern ear, it was partly in defiance of the commercialization of polite letters. The contrivances of Shaftesbury's style are not characterless flights of an aesthetic imagination shunning rigorous labor; they mark his dauntingly complicated and laborious efforts to plot a philosophical and literary course, penetrating deeper into some of his life's contexts to make himself invulnerable to others.

Smith's blind spot about Shaftesbury's Stoicism might seem especially puzzling. It is also ironic; in the final edition of *The Theory of Moral Sentiments* he himself would give his moral theory strong echoes of the Stoic concept of self-command. The lecture on Shaftesbury was, of course, written roughly four decades earlier, but the text on which he focuses—"The Moralists"—seems to be a fairly obvious brief for a Stoic ethic. Here again Smith was too put off by Shaftesbury's Platonism, with the result that he completely ignored the philosophical bedrock of his theistic vision. Though Smith does not use the word "manly," his critique unmistakably faults Shaftesbury's thought and prose for a lack of precisely that quality. To be fair, he could not have read the *Askêmata*. If he had read it, he would have seen a quite different effect of Shaftesbury's illness. His asthma heightened his need to dispel his fear and loathing of effeminacy by laboring, in the inner recesses of his self, to build a manly character, a space of rational self-command. His challenge—and his dilemma—as an author was to find a medium for that character in print. He had to make authorship a gentlemanly act without succumbing to the narcissistic servility with which modern authors pretended to exhibit their inner selves to the polite world and its print market.

Coming at Shaftesbury's authorial experiments through the angle of effeminacy, we see the full irony of his contribution to modern public discourse. If we simply extract the content of argument from his texts, we miss the radical thrust of their form. His stylistic strategies, as often as they miscarry, are consistently aimed at creating spaces for individual autonomy and freedom of expression. He was unyielding in his critique of male-specific rhetorical impositions of arbitrary power in the guise of authority in politics, religion, and the fine arts.[70] That was, for a gentleman of his standing, a remarkably bold and even subversive project. But he saw two kinds of modern servility: passive submission to the prevailing representations of public authority, and the servile deceptions parading as effortless freedom in a women-centered polite discourse that took French politeness as its model. With the latter, modernity itself seemed to pose the most seductive enervation of the will needed to constitute a political and literary culture of open but civil contestation. Hence there could be no place for female intelligence in Shaftesbury's vision of a new public culture of liberty. This was not a matter of inconsistency; it was not that he failed to extend to women a principle of autonomy he considered essential to realizing human potential. In the very radicalism of his critique of the conventional dynamics of social power, he amplified an essentialist dichotomy between male and female. His formation of a self; the moral meaning he drew from his Stoic practice; his concept of intellectual and spiritual labor; his conception of truly natural sociability: all pivoted on that dichotomy. So did his concept of style. It was calculated not only to ensure the extrusion of women from a political culture of engaged citizenship, but also to remove their contaminating presence from English polite letters.

Chapter 6

The Labors of David Hume

"Of Moral Prejudices" is one of the apparently slight pieces David Hume published in his second volume of essays in 1742. Hume was intent on undoing the mortifying mistake he had made by publishing *A Treatise of Human Nature*, a massive and in parts opaque tome, in 1739–1740. Expecting the *Treatise* to effect a revolution in philosophy, he had watched it "[fall] *dead-born from the press, without reaching such distinction, as even to excite a murmur among the zealots.*"[1] With "polite" essays he hoped to win the attention of the educated reading public that had remained oblivious to his absurdly overreaching literary debut. Although "Of Moral Prejudices" restates one of the central themes of the *Treatise*, it does so largely in parable-like stories rather than in formal philosophical argument. Perhaps for that reason, it has been one of the poor cousins in most of the philosophical scholarship on Hume.

As discursive as it is in form, the essay effectively positions Hume's new philosophy between the poles of the philosophical landscape in his own era. He begins with a swipe against the "Set of Men"—Bernard Mandeville was probably foremost in his mind—who ridicule everything that has "hitherto appear'd sacred and venerable in the Eyes of Mankind." Their rationalizations of selfishness threaten to pervert a "free Constitution of Government" into "one universal System of Fraud and Corruption" (538–39). But most of the essay is devoted to "another Humour," which Hume traces to the ancient Stoics. "I mean," he writes, "that grave philosophical Endeavour after Perfection, which, under Pretext of reforming Prejudices and Errors, strikes at all the most endearing Sentiments of the Heart, and all the most useful Byasses and Instincts, which can govern a human Creature" (539). He illustrates this "most egregious Folly of all others" by juxtaposing two parables. In the first, Eugenius, who had devoted his youth to the "the most unwearied Labour" in the study of philosophy, cannot philosophize his way out of the acute grief he suffers at the loss of his wife, "the virtuous and beautiful *Emira*." His "Darling" among his children is the daughter who most reminds him of her mother. Though "he conceals this

Partiality as much as possible," he is not so "affectedly Philosophical, as even to call it by the Name of *Weakness*" (540–41).

The second parable is in the form of a letter that Hume claims to have received from a friend visiting Paris. It tells the story of "a young Lady of Birth and Fortune," completely independent, who has witnessed "the many unhappy Marriages among her Acquaintance." She has resolved not to marry, and "being a Woman of strong Spirit and an uncommon Way of thinking," she "cou'd not suspect herself of such Weakness" as to abandon this resolution. Still, she wants to devote herself to the education of a son, a task that will compensate her for renouncing sexual passion. She cultivates the friendship of a thirty-year-old man, "the last Branch of an antient Family," who feels duty-bound to marry to prevent the family's extinction. Having determined that he will be a suitable mate, she reveals her plan: he will father her son, but will have nothing to do with his upbringing. The son is born, and she is willing to continue a friendship with the father but finds him "too passionate a Lover to remain within the Bounds of Friendship." She tries to buy him off with a substantial Bond of Annuity, on condition that he never see her (or the boy) again. He resorts to a law suit before the Parlement of Paris, claiming that as the father he has a legal right to educate his son as he pleases. Her counter-argument is that, "by express Agreement before their Commerce," he had renounced all claim to any offspring (542–44). A deal is a deal.

The case "puzzles" philosophers as well as lawyers, the correspondent tells Hume (544). What matters to Hume is the moral lesson, not the legal issue. It is stated succinctly in his introduction to the letter: "not to depart too far from the receiv'd Maxims of Conduct and Behaviour, by a refin'd Search after Happiness or Perfection" (542). The contrast between the Parisian heroine and Eugenius turns on what should and should not be considered "weakness." Eugenius has the wisdom to understand that his tearful grief over the loss of his wife is not a weakness, as an affected philosophical Stoicism would have it. The real weakness lies in the philosophical heroine's equation of the cold detachment of an excessively rationalistic pursuit of perfection with strength.

In 1740–1741, immediately preceding Hume's 1742 essay volume, Samuel Richardson had published his epistolary novel *Pamela; or, Virtue Rewarded*, whose extraordinary popularity and intense impact, especially on female readers, marked the ascendancy of the cult of sentiment and sensibility.[2] Over the next several decades it became a truism that women's civilizing agency had the morally and socially efficacious effect of feminizing men, making them softer, more tender and delicate in feelings, though there were accompanying fears that feminization carried too far produced effeminacy. The portrait of Eugenius may be said to have been a brief but pithy announcement of the arrival of the man of sentiment. It seems to dissolve Shaftesbury's dichotomy between philosophical labor and effeminacy. The second parable leaves us less certain of the essay's gendered meaning. The text gives us no reason to think that Hume is defending a patriarchal legal right over offspring. In fact we have reason to wonder whether he does; in the essay "Of Love and Marriage," he wishes that husband and wife could live in a state of "perfect equality, as between two equal members of the same body" (560). Nor can we read Hume's female character as another skewering of the *femme savante*. Her fault is not that she has a "Philosophy," "an uncommon Way of thinking"; at least in the permissive setting of Paris, that is to be expected. The problem is that in her excessive attachment to her philosophy—her determination to apply it so consequentially—she ignores natural human desires and feelings. Still, there is surely some significance to the fact that Hume chose to use a "philosophical Heroine" to issue this warning. He could, after all, have taken aim at a misguided philosophical hero, a male contracting with a woman to secure an heir. That might have given the parable more social credibility, especially in Anglophone circles. Did he consider it more unnatural, and hence more effective for his purposes, for a woman to be so coldly rational as to ignore "the most endearing Sentiments of the Heart"?[3]

Hume has given modern feminist scholars ample room to conduct an interesting debate about the gender implications of his thought. Some find Hume distinguished from other eighteenth-century philosophers by the protofeminist implications of his emphatically social and relational theory of cognition. Others look more to his essays and point to statements in them that seem to make him a typically masculinist thinker of his day.[4] When our aim is to recover Hume's historical meaning, the choices the debate poses are more a hindrance than a guide. They cover over the intricate skein of views on gender differences, manliness, and effeminacy that had formed by the 1740s, and they ignore how Hume's own views found expression in an imagined new pairing of leisured taste and intellectual labor in the affluent professional classes of urban Scotland and particularly Edinburgh. Hume may have been more careful than any other author of his generation in treading his way through the skein—so careful, in fact, that his path seems at times to weave tortuously around the core issues. In an essay in the 1742 volume he grants to "Women of Sense and Education" superiority in the judgment of polite writing (536). It would seem to be in keeping with this nod to women's cultural authority that in another essay in the same volume he writes that "any author who speaks in his own person," including the philosopher and the critic, must do so in "elegant" language. And yet, he continues, he must also speak in a "sense strong and masculine" (192). Hume's experiments in essayistic style aimed to accomplish both.

It has become a commonplace that Hume used the essay form to make the implications of his philosophy accessible to a broad educated audience of women as well as men. But there are more direct ties between the *Treatise* and the essays, and among the essays, than have been recognized. The ties become more visible when we trace them in a longer and wider context. Philosophers have been exploring the complex ways in which Hume at once rejected and adapted Stoic thought, but with little attention to his engagement with Stoicism as a formative experience in his efforts to reconcile solitary labor and polite sociability in the way of life of the modern philosopher.[5] That he conducted an argument with civic humanism and republicanism is well known; but the full scale and import of the argument becomes clear only when we give close scrutiny to his engagement with Shaftesbury. No less important is the French connection. From his youth onward Hume read widely in the French literature of the late seventeenth century and early eighteenth century. He had an unusually tolerant admiration for the rarified refinement, both in manners and in literature, of *le monde*; and several of his favorite French authors, including Fontenelle and Saint-Évremond, had been major voices in the discourse of *honnêteté*.[6] Their language echoes through the essays, as part of a rhetoric that tried to appropriate it, in a suitably adapted version, for a world whose self-validation would rest on a new social configuration of aesthetic play and labor.

Writing the *Treatise*

In March or April 1734 Hume, twenty-three, passed through London en route to Bristol, where he hoped to lead a more active life in employment to a sugar merchant. He took the occasion to write a letter to a London physician, seeking his diagnosis of a "Disease" of mind and body he had been suffering for the past five years.[7] Such correspondence was common between patients and their physicians, but Hume clearly had never met the intended recipient and, still more unusual, wrote anonymously. He admitted embarrassment at combining anonymity with so much self-revelation to "a perfect stranger," a man he knew only by reputation, but hoped that as a fellow "Scotchman" the physician would pardon his audacity. As the letter progresses the full source of Hume's embarrassment becomes apparent. The letter is not simply an autobiographical sketch and a history of symptoms and previous treatments; to describe "the present condition of [his] Mind," Hume has to lay out the immensely ambitious philosophical project to which he had committed himself at the age of eighteen, "with an Ardor natural to young men." "A new Scene of Thought" had suddenly "open'd" to him, and had "transported [him] beyond Measure." He would rebuild philosophy from its foundations by "deriv[ing] every Truth in Criticism as well as Morality" from the careful observation of "human Nature."[8] This was the effort that would result, five years later, in the *Treatise*. In 1734 Hume was despairing of whether he could pull it off. All he had from three years of effort were random scribblings on "many a Quire of Paper." It was a crisis that an ordinary physician, acquainted

only with his own profession, could not manage; Hume needed to consult someone who was also "a man of Letters, of Wit, of Good Sense, & of great Humanity,"
someone who could understand the "Motions of the Mind" he was experiencing.[9]
The addressee may have been George Cheyne, whose *The English Malady* had
appeared in 1733.[10] Another possibility (to which I am more inclined) is John
Arbuthnot, physician to Queen Anne and a member, along with Alexander Pope,
Jonathan Swift, and John Gay, of the Scriblerus Club, a literary society that usually
met in Arbuthnot's room in St. James Palace.[11]

Hume's life had begun to veer from the expected path for young men of his
background while he was a student at Edinburgh College.[12] As the younger son
with a "slender" inheritance he was expected to follow his father in reading the
law, but he had "an insurmountable aversion to everything but the pursuits of
philosophy and general learning" (xxxiii). Having left the university in 1729, at
age eighteen, he spent the next several years at Ninewells, the family home, and in
Edinburgh and devoted himself to reading "the celebrated books" in Latin,
French, and English, and learning Italian. It was during that broad course of study
that he was transported by the "new Scene of Thought."

His affliction had begun with "Scurvy spots" on his fingers, which prompted
the first physician he consulted to warn him "against the Vapours." Hume rejected
this prognosis. But then came "Ptyalism or Watryness in the Mouth," diagnosed
as "the Disease of the Learned" and treated with bitters, antihysteric pills, a daily
pint of English claret, and daily horseback riding; then a "Palpitation of the Heart"
and "a good deal of Wind in [his] Stomach," but "without any bad Goût, as is
ordinary"; and most recently, daily rides to "a mineral Well of some Reputation,"
more bitters and antihysteric pills, and "Anti-scorbutic Juices" (14–16).

Scurvy spots, ptyalism, the vapours, distempers, antiscorbutic juices: the
young man obviously knew his way around the medical nomenclature of his day.
One wonders why he is consulting Arbuthnot; he seems to have become his own
physician. By the 1730s Edinburgh College was on its way to becoming one the
great centers of medical education in Europe, and Hume was surely aware of the
basic elements of its medical culture. Among the popular medical books he read
was Bernard Mandeville's *A Treatise of the Hypochondriack and Hysterick Passions*,
published in London in 1711 and reprinted in 1730. Having thrown over ancient
and scholastic humoral theory, British medical thinking now operated largely,
though not entirely, within a loosely jointed psychophysiological paradigm combining Newtonian mechanism and Lockean cognitive psychology. The paradigm
left room for a quite eclectic array of treatments, including the taking of bath
waters, sundry diets and exercise regimens, and a great variety of medications, or
"tinctures," especially for the stomach and the bowels. Its several guiding assumptions pervade Hume's recounting of his symptoms. The new medicine's preference for observational practice over academic theory corresponded well with

Hume's own commitment to the empirical study of human nature. The emphasis in diagnosis was on the history of symptoms and reactions to treatments, set within the history of the patient's life circumstances. This was a thoroughly naturalistic psychophysiological concept of disease; it put the nervous system, the brain, and the mind, organic malfunctions and mental and emotional states, in such close interaction that they were usually lumped together in a capacious category of symptoms and their causes. When Hume writes of a "lowness of Spirits," he is using the common medical term for a psychological symptom that was assumed to accompany physical symptoms in many diseases.[13]

Looking back on the history of his "ruin'd . . . Health," Hume has a particular bone to pick with the Stoic strain in ancient philosophy.[14] It had induced him to undertake "the Improvement of [his] Temper & Will," along with "[his] Reasoning and Understanding."

> I was continually fortifying myself with Reflections against
> Death, & Poverty, & Shame, & Pain, and all the other
> Calamities of Life. These no doubt are exceeding useful,
> when join'd with an active Life; because
> the Occasion being presented along with the Reflection, works
> it into the Soul, & makes it take a deep Impression, but in
> Solitude they serve to little other Purpose, than to waste the
> Spirits, the Force of the Mind meeting with no Resistance, but
> wasting itself in the Air, like our Arm when it misses its Aim. (14)

Like Shaftesbury, Hume turned to solitary reflection in the Stoic tradition to build a character, a strength of mind, temper, and will that would allow him to engage life actively while remaining tranquil in the face of its "Calamities."[15] But the effort had backfired; it had withdrawn him from activity into something like a vacuum of solitary interiority, where the mind is cut off from willed action and simply flails within itself. The failure is one of emotional power as well as intellection, and it is the combination that makes him so anxious. It is a measure of his anxiety that he speculates that in his own "Coldness & Desertion of the Spirit" he resembles the French mystics and "our Fanatics here" (17). By 1734 Hume had probably shed the entire structure of Christian belief in which he had been raised. Like many of his contemporaries he read the "enthusiasm" of the mystic or the fanatic—the self-delusion of being the vessel of a divine inspiration—as a medical problem, the symptom of a pathology and perhaps one of its causes. From that standpoint he likens "profound Reflections, & that Warmth or Enthusiasm which is inseparable from them" to the mystics' "rapturous Admiration"; both "might discompose the Fabric of the Nerves & Brain." And yet, if the mystics are to be believed, they can come "out of the Cloud" (17). He may not be so lucky; having strained so hard in body as well as mind, in emotional fervor as well as rigor of thought, he may have damaged his constitution beyond repair. Is he permanently stuck in his exhaustion, never to return to his former fervor? If he is to resume his grand project, he has concluded, he needs a respite, a temporary change in his way of life. The distemper has been exacerbated by his alternations between intense study, in a solitude comparable to that of the Stoic or the mystic, and "idleness." Now he must find a way to alternate "Business & Diversion," and to that end he has resolved to "seek out a more active Life" and lay aside his "Pretensions in Learning." But he is interrupting his philosophical efforts "in order the more effectually to resume them" (17). Ultimately, he knows, he has to find a balance between the unavoidably solitary mental labor of the philosopher and the sociability needed to prevent that labor from becoming sterile self-absorption.

Meanwhile, though, Arbuthnot must advise him on whether he is taking the right path; whether he can hope for a full recovery, "so as to endure the Fatigue of deep and abstruse thinking"; and how long it will take (18). In the light of the history he has given, it is an odd request. The medical regimens seem to have worked (or perhaps illusory symptoms had eventually dissipated). A "very ravenous Appetite" has transformed him from a "tall, lean, & raw-bon'd" youth into "the most sturdy, robust, healthful-like Fellow you have seen, with a ruddy Complexion & a chearful Countenance." He eats and sleeps well. He has never had the "lowness of Spirits" that physicians often find accompanying physical symptoms in such distempers. In modern terminology, he has not been, and is not now, depressed, though he remains anxious. In fact his family "cannot observe the least Alteration in [his] Humor, & rather think [him] a better Companion than [he] was before." Indeed "now every Body congratulate me upon my thorow Recovery" (15). He finds all this thoroughly frustrating.

If Arbuthnot received the letter, he might be pardoned for not taking seriously the worries of a man who seems to have already been cured. As Hume himself puts it, there is "a small Distance betwixt me & perfect health" (17). But that is precisely what makes his situation so worrisome. If he is so healthy, why does he still suffer an incapacity, a "Weakness," that threatens to dash all his aspirations, and indeed to make the sense of identity he has been trying to assume for the last several years seem ridiculous? Why does he lack the strength to think through and set in words the implications of his philosophical epiphany? Here is his description of this "cruel Incumbrance":

When one must bring the Idea he comprehended in gross, nearer to him, so as to contemplate its minutest Parts, & keep it steddily in his Eye, so as to copy these Parts in Order, this I found impracticable for me, nor were my Spirits equal to so Severe an Employment. Here lay my greatest

Calamity. I had no Hopes of delivering My Opinions with such Elegance & Neatness, as to draw to me the Attention of The World, & I
would rather live & dye in Obscurity than produce them maim'd & imperfect. (16–17)

Hume describes a failure of endurance, a collapse of strength at the peak of
effort. The problem is not simply that he cannot break down his ideas "in
gross"—the overarching arguments of his philosophical revolution—into a logical sequence of steps in demonstrative reasoning. Seemingly without being aware
of the shift he is making, he moves from the thought itself to the style of its
expression, what he calls "such Elegance & Neatness, as to draw to me the Attention of the World." While he wants to emulate Shaftesbury's effort to make the
writing and reading of philosophy integral to a polite culture, his self-assigned task
is far more daunting than Shaftesbury's. His revolution aims at rethinking from
the ground up the very questions of epistemology and natural philosophy that
Shaftesbury had dismissed as obscurantist and irrelevant to the leading of a virtuous and happy life. We need only consider some of the headings of the *Treatise*
that appeared five years later: Of the connexion or association of ideas; Of the
infinite divisibility of our ideas in space and time; Of the component parts of our
reasonings concerning causes and effects; Of the relations of impressions and
ideas. The difficulty is compounded by the fact that his imagined audience is far
broader than Shaftesbury's little circle of polite but manly gentlemen, or a small
coterie of philosophers. He seeks what he would later call "Fame," and that
requires that he write in a way that will both instruct and entertain an expanding
public of educated readers that includes women.

"Weakness," of course, was a gender-charged term. The psychophysiological
medical paradigm was another way of naturalizing the ancient dichotomy
between male strength and female weakness of mind as well as body, even as it
assumed a continuum that allowed for male and female exceptions. The focus was
on, in Hume's phrase, "the Fabric of the Nerves and the Brain," with the nerves
carrying stimuli to the brain and in turn sending the brain's messages throughout
the body's organs. Unlike Cartesians, who thought of nerves as hollow tubes
through which the "animal spirits" traveled, the Newtonian alternative likened
them to strings vibrating in response to sense impressions. These alternatives
hardly differed in their gender implications. Men's nerves were, as a rule, tough
and elastic; women's were softer and more "delicate," and hence weaker. The
difference might give women a greater sensitivity to beauty and to the affective
nuances of human relationships, but it also made them unqualified for strenuous
intellectual effort. In his discussion of women's propensity to "the Hysterick Passion," Mandeville had been quite unqualified on this point. Women were of "a
more Elegant composure," and "Beauty is their attribute as Strength is ours":

"their frame, though less firm is more delicate"; "they are unfit both for abstruse and elaborate Thoughts, all studies of Depth, Coherence and Solidity that fatigue the Spirits, and require a steadiness and assiduity of thinking."[16] Hume, in the spirit of politeness, might be said to have qualified confidence in this distinction; at least as readers, women's natural elegance qualified them to understand philosophy if it was presented in an "elegant" style. But he also accepted the distinction's axiomatic assumption. Implicit in the letter of 1734, the assumption is stated almost casually, as too obvious to dwell on, in an essay titled "Of the Rise and Progress of the Arts and Sciences," published in the same volume as "Of Moral Prejudices." Modern gallantry, he argued, works to alleviate men's natural "superiority" over women, which they enjoy by virtue of their "greater strength both of mind and body" (133).

Such statements have to be set within a field of public discussion that was already forming in the 1740s and would be fully articulated in succeeding decades. In Great Britain, and particularly in Scotland, it was common for male authors to argue that the feminization of social exchange—the civilizing of males—had been integral to the moral progress of the species in modern commercial societies. But when did feminization in this positive sense shade into a dangerous spread of effeminacy? Even among the more optimistic contributors to the discussion, there was a strong undercurrent of anxiety about this possibility; and of course there was the occasional jeremiad, the appeal to save manliness before it was too late.[17] Hume's example of an "effeminate" national language was not English or indeed French; it was Italian, and Italy's loss of martial spirit and patriotic courage was not due to any "enervating" effect of "luxury, or politeness, or application to the arts" (275). In 1734, despite his preoccupation with his moments of intellectual weakness, Hume did not fear that he had an effeminate constitution. His health problems, after all, had not prevented him from becoming a sturdy and robust fellow. Nor did he fear that his own commitment to polite elegance put him in danger of degenerating into effeminacy, or of being perceived to be doing so. It is remarkable, in fact, that in the essays of the early 1740s Hume seems oblivious to the cultural anxiety about the decline of manliness. In "Of the Delicacy of Taste and Passion," the lead essay of the first volume, he seems perfectly comfortable with introducing himself as a male of unusually "delicate" sentiments, a Eugenius of polite letters (3–8).

What, then, was Hume's fear in the 1734 letter? He worried that he would have to wait a long time for a recovery and that it might not be "perfect"; his "Spirits" might never regain "their former Spring & Vigor" (18). His underlying fear, however, surfaces when he recalls being diagnosed with the Disease of the Learned, despite his lack of "lowness of Spirit": "Though I was sorry to find myself engag'd with so tedious a Distemper yet the Knowledge of it, set me very much at ease, by satisfying me that my former Coldness, proceeded not from any

Defect of Temper or Genius, but from a Disease, to which any one may be subject" (14). The "weakness" manifested in his writing block might not be a symptom, but a natural given of his constitution or "temper." In a sense he *wants* to be told that he has an illness, however long the cure may take. The alternative—that his weakness is a natural trait—would condemn him to a life of permanent disappointment. His underlying question to himself is whether he has a rare manliness, a strength of mind and body exceptional even among men. If he has not been endowed with that strength by nature, there's nothing he can do to acquire it. It is a question of "genius" (*ingenium*). He may simply be unequipped by nature to convey philosophy in a polite style even as he resolves some of its most intractable issues.

In Great Britain as in France, the term "genius" had been gaining new currency in discussions of the fine arts and taste since the mid-seventeenth century. By the 1730s it was beginning to convey something of the cult of the creative genius that would become common in the second half of the century: a creature inspired by the "fire within" in some magical way, shunning conventional society and on the edge of madness, so different in kind from ordinary men as be nearly superhuman. Hume's use of the term remained rooted in a more sober body of classical ideas that any schoolboy would be familiar with. Individuals were endowed with particular natural talents, or *ingenia*, to a greater or less degree, and their *vocatio* lay in developing those talents and finding a suitable social outlet for them.[18] A genius was simply someone who possessed a talent or set of talents to an exceptional degree. His classical learning aside, the young Hume may have asked himself whether he had genius in this sense when he encountered the Abbé Du Bos's widely read *Critical Reflections on Poetry and Painting* (1719), a book to which we shall return. Du Bos's concern was with great painters and poets, but his extensive discussion of genius applied to any intellectually demanding vocation. A genius must bring the requisite qualities with him into the world, Du Bos insisted. He must also, of course, devote years to disciplined training, mastery of the rules and techniques; but no amount of laborious effort could compensate for the lack of natural gifts.[19]

One of Hume's notes on reading Du Bos is "For a young Man, who applies himself to the Arts and Sciences, the Slowness with which he forms himself for the World is a good Sign."[20] By 1734 his "cruel Incumbrance" had made him begin to doubt that, for a man of his ambitions, any effort at self-formation, however deliberate, mattered.

⁓

Several tedious months as a clerk in the sugar trade in Bristol resolved Hume to return to philosophy and letters. In midsummer of 1734 he moved to Paris, the center of polite learning. He delighted in the city but found it too expensive. He settled in La Flèche, whose Jesuit College had a fine library. In September 1737, he returned to London to revise the manuscript of the *Treatise* and find a publisher. The surviving correspondence from those three years tells us almost nothing about how the *Treatise* developed out of the many quires of paper Hume had scribbled by the spring of 1734. But the letter to Arbuthnot is a marker, compensating to a degree for this empty space. When we juxtapose it to sections of the *Treatise*, we get some sense of how Hume came to realize that he had misunderstood his encumbrance. By the time he wrote Book 1 (or perhaps as he wrote it), he was convinced that his paralysis had not been due to weakness, but to overreaching for an illusory strength, conceived as a capacity for abstraction in narrowly rational terms. In fact his very efforts to exercise that strength had landed him in "false philosophy," a misguided reliance on reason alone that threatened to plunge philosophy into self-destruction even as it debilitated the psyche of the philosopher.

Hume wants to show that what the American philosopher Thomas Nagel has called the "view from nowhere"—the fully autonomous position reason claims to have assumed when it has detached itself from bodily, psychological, and social existence—does not yield certainty and is in fact not autonomous at all. Only when the essentialist quest for certainty ends, as it must, in radical skepticism, denying any certainty about anything, is the philosophical consciousness jolted into moving from "false" to "true" philosophy, from pathological self-delusion to an acceptance of limits beyond which philosophy becomes a kind of "enthusiasm." For much of Book 1 Hume assumes the persona of the radical skeptic. This is a rhetorical performance, and indeed a self-dramatization, as much as it is a philosophical exercise. Hume is recalling former states of mind, but often uses the present tense, as though admitting the reader to the workings of his consciousness as he writes. The rhetoric makes the reader experience, vicariously and yet with the immediacy of personal testimony, the psychic ordeal Hume himself has undergone. Hume draws him, step by logical step, toward a seemingly inexorable plunge into radical skepticism, pulling him right to the edge of the cliff, confronting him with the impending free fall into a black hole. His first target is the essentialist view of the object world in terms of cause and effect. As commonly applied, the idea of cause and effect assumes that reason, in observing motion and impulsion, can grasp the ultimate substance or "force" of objects and the ultimate principle of relation between them. In fact we only know cause and effect, as we know anything else in the science of man, from the "facts" of our experience, and from experience we must conclude that our certainty lies in the feeling that informs a habitual expectation, grounded in the imagination, that we necessarily share with all others in "the custom of common life." By "custom" Hume means the fund of shared, habitual "sentiment" that constitutes our indispensable beliefs, the ones we need to function in the physical world and as moral agents in interaction with others.[21]

Hume's larger point is that radical skepticism is the unavoidable inversion of the essentialist error. Though the two errors might seem to lie at opposite extremes of the philosophical tradition, they conspire with each other, in a kind of dialectic of the deluded search for rational autonomy. The process of inversion becomes apparent in the discussion of "personal identity," when his next swing of the skeptical wrecking ball takes reflexive essentialism as its target. "Some philosophers," he begins, assume that we have access to a "SELF" that is unitary (a core substance, material or spiritual, that does not change over time) and has "simplicity" (its indivisibility insures against its being conflated into other selves).[22] As in our conception of cause and effect, we mistake relation for identity. Instead, he argues, still in the voice of the radical skeptic, all we have access to is "particular perceptions," and these consist of "nothing but a bundle or collection of different perceptions, which succeed each other with an inconceivable rapidity, and are in a perpetual flux and movement."[23] It is the affective force of the imagination, using the perceptions stored in memory, that forms this inchoate bundle into the usable fiction of an integral self continuing over time. Understanding this indispensable but fictive sense of selfhood, to the extent we can understand it, is not a matter of penetrating to an ontological core of reason; it requires empirical observation of our own psychology and that of others, and of the affective logic of our own and others' moral sentiments.

To judge by the letter to Arbuthnot, Hume was beginning to become disillusioned with essentialist reflexivity as early as 1734. We need only recall the image of the mind "wasting itself in the Air, like our Arm when it misses its Aim." He had turned his back on the vaguely Stoic regimen he found in Cicero, Seneca, Plutarch, and others, having tried in vain to commit himself to "that grave philosophical Endeavor after Perfection" of "our philosophical Heroine" in "Of Moral Prejudices." The error now is not helpless self-absorption, but blindness to human affective needs. But these errors are intimately connected, and their linkage has been established in the *Treatise* and especially in the discussion of self-identity in Book 1. His reference to "some philosophers" widens his attack to encompass not only ancient conduits of the Stoic tradition, but also modern philosophers, including Descartes, Spinoza, and Malebranche. The essentialist quest has not simply failed; it has backfired, and it inevitably backfires for anyone who attempts it. In the purely rational effort to find a reflexive certainty every apparent success accedes to doubt, and the doubts spiral ad infinitum into what he calls "philosophical Melancholia and delirium."[24] There seems to be no hope of certainty about anything, and indeed no way of establishing degrees of probability, though life itself—the daily living in a material world and in a web of social relations—would be impossible in such a state of mind.

The philosopher escapes his delirium by acknowledging that, like it or not, he is a participant in custom and perceives the world through its lenses, albeit with a more critical eye than others. All the knowledge that allows us to function as social beings, including rational understanding, is grounded in the imagination, the very faculty that had traditionally been blamed for the human capacity for self-delusion and had been found to be particularly tyrannical in women. In social life sentiment takes the form of "sympathy," or fellow-feeling, the imagination's capacity to experience virtually what others are experiencing. In modern commercial societies, with their complex division of labor and proliferation of social identities, it is the pervasive circulation of sympathy among people that gives society its coherence.

The possible implications of all this for rethinking the received values assigned to male and female qualities of intelligence, and especially moral and aesthetic intelligence, are huge. Arguably Hume anticipated precisely what people committed to developing a feminist theory of cognition and moral sensibility are trying to do, and so not surprisingly an impressive group of feminist philosophers have become Hume advocates in recent decades. Hume—a giant in the philosophical pantheon—offers them a way to dig back into the core of the philosophical canon and appropriate an imposing chunk of it, rather than critiquing it from its edges as hopelessly masculinist and logocentric. If there was an eighteenth-century philosopher who rejected the logocentric privileging of reason, it was Hume. Hume does not deny, of course, that the imagination can run amok; but far from being a corrective to this danger, the supposed autonomy of the view from nowhere is an example of it, an enthusiasm camouflaged as rational autonomy. He sometimes speaks of faculties, but posits no hierarchy of faculties. He conceives a circulatory process of cognition, not a scale of cognitive powers. Ideas and concepts are built from sense impressions, and in turn articulate themselves as sense images. The "true" philosopher does practice skepticism in the face of conventional wisdom, but it must be a moderate skepticism. When he justifies his power and authority to criticize by claiming to have climbed to a view from nowhere, outside the cognitive world to which ordinary human beings are confined, he is simply flailing within his own involuted consciousness. The immanent thrust of Hume's epistemology is that men and women occupy a single realm of cognition; there can be no essential gender difference. Intelligence, considered holistically in this way, is inherently social; and hence all knowledge is inherently social or, perhaps better, relational, both in the process in which it is acquired and in its myriad refractions through custom. It would seem that Hume's casual acceptance of male strength and female weakness of mind in his defense of gallantry is merely an historically contingent failure to apply his epistemology consequentially. Indeed Hume might be said to provide an imposing new philosophical foundation for making women the norm for a needed revaluation of cognition as an inherently social capacity—the view Poullain de la Barre had advocated over sixty years earlier.

There are moments in Hume's texts from 1741 onward when we find him applying, or failing to apply, the arguably protofeminist argument of the *Treatise*, particularly on the issue of taste. But his careful rhetorical maneuverings do not fit well into the pro-and-con positions of the feminist debate. We have first to underscore an irony: that in one regard, Humean feminists have not fully appreciated the new departure Hume advocates. Hume's new understanding of cognition serves a larger ambition; he wants his readers to reconceive philosophy as a way of life and as a kind of labor. Philosophy may still be a manly effort, but it is decidedly not a meditative askesis, figured as a struggle against the female-coded indolence of the embodied mind. Hume has rejected the entire tradition of meditative askesis, whether it be Christian or secular. He has become disillusioned with the very notion of an inner striving to overcome the impulses of the natural man, trapped in the mere appearances of the material world and the body, to reach a core self of pure intellection.

In the conclusion of Book 1, immediately following the section on personal identity, Hume returns to a first-person narrative of his own psychic drama, shifting voices as he ponders "the voyage [he has] undertaken."[25] He begins by speaking from the "splenetic humour" in which he finds himself when he concludes that his only choices are "a false reason and none at all." On this "barren rock" he resolves to perish, rather than venturing upon the "boundless ocean" of speculation. What encumbers him is no longer a weakness of intellection, as in the 1734 letter; he finds himself trapped, by the very tenacity of his doubting reason, in the "forlorn solitude" of a "philosophical melancholy and delirium." He feels himself to be "some strange, uncouth monster" who can neither run into "the crowd" nor "make a company apart." His "weakness" now seems to lie in his need for "the approbation of others," the lack of which seems to make all his opinions "loosen and fall of themselves." It is "nature herself" that "cures" him by pulling him back into "the lively impression of [the] senses" in the common acts of sociability: dining, playing backgammon, conversing merrily with friends. Returned to "the common affairs of life," he cannot continue to pursue his futile speculations.[26]

At first he feels that he must complete this liberation—this return to an "indolent belief in the general maxims of the world"—by throwing off philosophy altogether. Why should he "abuse" his time in "subtleties and sophistries" in "dreary solitudes"? Why must he "strive against the current of nature," which leads him to "indolence" and "pleasure"? And yet he begins to tire of "amusement and company," and now "nature" intervenes again; certain sentiments "spring up naturally," this time to lure him back into a more self-constrained engagement in philosophical speculation. The fact is that he is "naturally *inclin'd*" to satisfy a curiosity about the disputed subjects of philosophy. Likewise he "[feels] an ambition to arise in [him] . . . of acquiring a name by [his] inventions and discoveries." Should he attempt to banish these inclinations, he would "*feel* [he] shou'd be the loser in point of pleasure; and this is the origin of [his] philosophy."[27]

Hume's return to the subject of ambition, in a section of Book 2 on "the love of fame," occasions his first full explanation of the concept of "sympathy" as a form of social communication. "Our reputation, our character, our name," he writes, "are considerations of vast importance." So often censured as a form of pride and a motive for dissemblance, ambition becomes the impulse to satisfy a natural need—one of those currents rising from nature's wellspring to give form to society—by achieving a public character. The desire for "the approbation of others" is not a weakness, as Hume had thought in his splenetic mood, but an indispensable source of strength. It is not just in "reasoning" but also in the mutuality of sympathy—seeing into the other, and imagining how she sees into you—that our judgment of "our own worth and character" acquires "authority."[28] The once anxious young philosopher, worried that he is not up to the task, has come to realize that it would be at once unnatural and unsocial of him *not* to be a philosopher. The reasonable pursuit of ambition is integral to the social process in which a man builds a sense of social selfhood, a conviction that, epistemological skepticism aside, he possesses a self in the form of character.

Hume ends the conclusion to Book 1 by inviting the reader, if he too is so inclined and finds himself "in the same easy disposition" alternating application and good humor, to follow him in his speculations in the remaining three books. The true skeptics study philosophy "in this careless manner."[29] The phrase "in this careless manner" might seem to evoke the apparent ease (*aisance*) and effortlessness of the *bel esprit* in "the modern style." One thinks of Fontenelle in the *Conversations*, explaining to the marquise that the cosmos he is about to describe to her does not require concentrated thought. And yet Hume has begun the conclusion by stating that his voyage "into those immense depths of philosophy"—the voyage he will undertake in the next three books—will require "the utmost art and industry." The apparent contradiction dissolves when we page back to his earlier discussion of skepticism. Why, he asks, despite the speculative free fall into complete uncertainty, do "we retain a degree of belief, which is sufficient for our purpose, either in philosophy or common life?" As we ascend the ladder of abstract reasoning, he explains, "the action of the mind becomes forc'd and unnatural, and the ideas faint and obscure":

> The mind, as well as the body, seems to be endow'd with a certain precise degree of force and activity, which it never employs in one action, but at the expense of all the rest. . . . No wonder, then, the conviction, which arises from a subtile reasoning, diminishes in proportion to the efforts, which the imagination makes to enter into the reasoning, and to conceive

it in all its parts. Belief, being a lively conception, can never be entire, where it is not founded on something natural and easy.[30]

Hume does not deny that philosophy requires intense labor. He wants it to avoid the unnatural labor that has been central to its self-definition for so long. In cognition the imagination, where the mind flows in its deepest pools, is the shaping force. It is also the connecting force, making the development of moral character in shared, though from a strictly rational standpoint illusory, certainties a natural process and in that sense an "easy" one. The "careless" philosophy that Hume advocates rejects slippage into indolence, if by indolence is meant a lazy acceptance of all the conventional wisdom of custom and forgoing of rigorous criticism; natural inclination calls the philosopher back to critical labor. It is careless in the sense that it will not labor to advance beyond a certain level of abstraction from custom; that it is content to rest on foundational illusions that are grounded in particular perceptions and that make common life possible. It is in this sense that Hume makes the startling claim that true philosophy has more affinity with "vulgar" notions than with a false philosophy of essentialism or radical skepticism. The philosopher does not occupy a meditative chamber from which the vulgar are excluded, as the Stoic tradition and Shaftesbury's version of it would have it; he proceeds from certain felt beliefs that he shares with the vulgar. The vulgar, in this positive usage, are the educated but nonphilosophical members of society, in the circles that were commonly called "polite," operating on the customary certainties that philosophers must also operate on. Philosophy is not a withdrawal from the social; it is an integral part of a social process of communication. In the *Treatise* Hume repeatedly uses the term "vivacity" to describe the force of this process. The test of a "truth" is not its abstract logic, which cannot move anyone to do anything, but the "vivacity" with which it is conveyed in the social circulation of sympathy. In this rhetorical force Hume has found a new grounding, at once philosophical and psychological, for the "eloquence" he was unable to achieve in 1734.[31] His failure had not been a matter of weakness, but of unnatural aspirations, straining in vain against the natural flow of sentiment and its verbal representations in style.

The Essayist

In February 1739, Hume returned from London, where he had arranged for the publication of the first two books of the *Treatise*, to the family home at Ninewells.[32] In 1741–1742 he made his debut as an essayist with the twenty-seven essays, all more or less "polite" in style though quite varied in depth and scope, that appeared in the two-volume *Essays, Moral and Political*.[33]

Hume committed himself to essay writing as he faced up to the immensely disappointing fact that the first two books of the *Treatise* were, by his own standards, a failure. He had not pulled off the effort to combine philosophical profundity with polite stylistic elegance. Rather than vaulting him to great fame, his "performance," as he called it, had failed to earn him any public character as an author. For the rest of his life he would be convinced that the publication of the *Treatise* had been premature, the mistake of a brash youth who had not been ready to cast his thought in an accessibly elegant style. He poised himself to make a new start, announced in the "Advertisement" for Book 3. His subject now was "Morals," which in his empirical approach required less "abstract reasoning" and thus, he hoped, "may be understood by ordinary readers, with as little attention as is usually given to any books of reasoning."[34] But the volume fared no better than its predecessors.

One of the prominent men he had turned to for vindication was Francis Hutcheson, the professor of moral philosophy at Glasgow, a man Hume greatly admired. When Hutcheson had written him that the manuscript of Book 3 lacked "a certain Warmth in the Cause of Virtue," Hume had replied in exasperation that he had examined the mind as "an Anatomist," not "a Painter." The "Air of Declamation" Hutcheson seemed to be calling for would be "esteem'd contrary to good taste," which he could not ignore. To paraphrase, he would not act the pedant or the preacher using "warm" rhetoric to impose his authority. And yet, he noted, he "intend[ed] to make a new Tryal, if it be possible to make the Moralist & Metaphysician agree a little better."[35] As the trial evolved into the essays, he found that the anatomist who aspired to win an audience of "good taste" could not do without the painter. And so long as his painting took the conversational form of the essay, with its imagined reciprocity between author and reader, it need not resort to pedantry or preaching. Hume had not concluded that in its basic argument the philosophy of the *Treatise* had been wrong. The question was how to communicate the implications of the philosophy in a new form, for an audience that read for entertainment as well as instruction. In fact, even as he tried to put the *Treatise* behind him, Hume was acting on its principles: that the search for truth or, more precisely, for compelling belief was a process of social communication; that the fundamental bond of sympathetic intersubjectivity was the imagination; that for the philosopher, as for anyone else aspiring to win the approval of a polite public, an effective style, though it could not dispense with abstract reasoning, had to enliven it with the vivacity of the imagination's impressions and sentiments. His challenge was not just to get the reasoning right, but to assume the right rhetorical persona.[36]

Hume's fear that with the *Treatise* he had gone off half-cocked had been confirmed by a substantial review of Book 1 published in the London periodical *History of the Works of the Learned* in November 1739. The criticism Hume probably found hardest to swallow was that his book "abounds in Egotisms," as though

the author were writing "his own Memoirs." The self-dramatization that concluded Book 1—the descent into philosophical delirium and the rise out of it—
was mocked as self-pitying exhibitionism.[37] Hume was being told that even in his
very efforts to enliven his philosophical abstractions with a personal voice in the
dramatic mode, he had violated the restraint expected of a polite author. James
Boswell, a man who chastised himself repeatedly (and with good reason) for his
"rattling" speech in company, would state the rule of "*retenue*": to be polite was to
master the "nice art" of "neither being too free nor too reserved," and of knowing
"how much [one] ought to show and how much to conceal."[38] Hume the writer
had yet to master the art. He needed to find an alternative both to excessively
abstract philosophy and to what polite readers would regard as intrusive self-
revelation, an opening into individual interiority that cracked the smooth surface
of mutual agreeableness.

In a letter from London on December 3, 1737, Hume had confided to Home
his "Shamefacedness" about returning to Edinburgh "at [his] years without having yet a settlement or so much as having attempted any."[39] He was now twenty-
six, and he was in danger of leaving behind his youth without prospects for establishing himself as an adult male. When he returned to Scotland in February 1739,
it was to Ninewells to live with his brother and sister; he lacked the means to set
up a household in Edinburgh, much less to support a family there. With the first
two volumes of essays he began earning enough money with his pen to support
himself. Hume would later dismiss some of them as "trifling," and in a sense they
were. He was obviously flattering the audience he knew he needed. But Hume's
turn to the essay form was not simply a quick way of securing the respectability
expected of a man of his family background and education. These are apparently
light Addisonian essays that we, like his intended readers, cannot pass over
lightly.[40] Hume aimed to show how his science of man could underpin an entirely
new normative order for a modernizing society. He joined a challenge to aristocratic social and cultural supremacy that can be traced back in Great Britain at
least as far as Defoe and the *Spectator*; that would be carried on by the next
generation of Scottish literati as well as by, among other English authors, Samuel
Johnson in his *Rambler*; and that from the 1790s onward would harden into a
political ideology challenging aristocratic supremacy.[41] Hume's essay "Of the
Middle Station of Life," published in the 1742 volume, was just one moment in
this long-term process, and if it had been written three or four decades later we
might read it as a not particularly noteworthy statement of what was becoming
conventional wisdom in widening circles of educated and propertied Scottish
commoners. But written as it was in 1741, or perhaps earlier, it was a remarkable
performance, a foretaste of things to come, but one perhaps unprecedented in the
fullness of its coverage of virtually the entire gamut of claims in a social ethos in
the making.

Set in our long-term perspective, Hume's claims can fairly be called "bourgeois," but for mid-eighteenth-century Scotland bourgeois is a treacherous and potentially misleading label, evoking as it almost unavoidably does class formations of modern industrial capitalism that were not yet in place. Hume's use of "Middle Station," common at the time, is more faithful to eighteenth-century perceptions of hierarchies that were still, to varying degrees, corporate in structure. Hume saw commerce as the driving force in the European advance from barbarism to civilization, but it is striking that his essay on the middle station makes no mention of merchants and tradesmen. He wrote from within his own social milieu in Edinburgh and other university towns, the hubs of the Scottish Enlightenment. Hume's middle station was formed by the educated or learned professions: university professors, lawyers, physicians, natural scientists, clergymen, architects, portraitists and other artists, and of course men of letters, who usually also had professional positions. In the wake of the Union of 1707 and the elimination of the Scottish Parliament, the high aristocracy no longer had a seasonal presence in the town and educated commoners, along with men in the lower ranks of the nobility, many of whom also needed professional incomes, were coming out from under their shadow. Shaping this rising elite were the Scottish universities, which had entered a process of reform aimed at producing professionals who were also "polite" gentlemen, many of them sons of lairds with landed estates, and at integrating their faculties as well as their graduates into a new urban civic life dedicated to "improvement."[42]

The place of women in this culture is not easy to fix, particularly since so much of the literature on the subject was prescriptive rather than descriptive. Marriage was coming to be regarded as a companionate union, a bonding of "friends" whose complementary natures matched the rough division between the publicness of male professional work and the privacy of female-managed domesticity. As household managers women performed "a form of labor that was superior to labor." Their self-discipline and practicality in that role stood in contrast to the aristocratic woman's devotion to amusement and self-display, though it had nothing to do with labor for money.[43] And yet the public/private distinction must be used with some caution. There were senses in which women of the middle station, precisely in their companionate and complementary roles, were being drawn increasingly into areas of public or at least quasi-public life. As alarmist as they were, the continuing lamentations about effeminizing "luxury" did not evoke a mere specter; as Scotland was increasingly integrated into Britain's commercial empire, the escalating consumer revolution, sustained by domestic production as well as imports from across the globe, *was* extending to cities like Edinburgh and Glasgow. If the role of women in it was often exaggerated (men, after all, also consumed, and often for themselves), it was nonetheless large and visible. The age witnessed the ever-changing fashions turned out by increasingly sophisticated textile industries, and the spread of fine china tea sets and place settings and ornate cutlery; of intricately carved writing tables and elaborately embroidered sofas; and of a host of other domestic furnishings that exhibited a fair measure of affluence and made the home a proper setting for drawing-room sociability among families bound together by marriage, friendship, and professional ties.[44]

To many observers, the epidemic of consumerism confirmed that women had an innate instinct to manipulate mere appearances, to gain power through self-display, and that they were by nature given to sinking into the undisciplined materialism, and indeed the gross sensuality, that terms like "indolence" connoted.[45] And yet these women of the middle station were also decision-making market agents in their own right. Their very responsibility for making the home a site of respectable domestic comfort and polite sociability required it. They also had to be fashioned from an early age to be the "friends," as well as the helpmates, of educated men. Increasingly importance was being given to women's learned ability to engage with morally and aesthetically elevating forms of polite letters that had their place in polite conversation. They could not aspire to be "learned," but that prohibition left considerable room for cultivation of their minds. It was not simply that they acquired various "accomplishments"—playing a musical instrument, for example, or drawing. In some families they were encouraged to read histories and even novels, provided that, like Richardson's *Pamela*, they were morally uplifting. These were the kinds of mothers and daughters, "virtuous" but also "educated," whose company Hume so much enjoyed. Shared reading, in fact, was becoming a powerful and sometimes volatile bond in male/female friendships in mixed-gender sociability, with the result that the terms "friend" and "friendship" were now commonly used to encompass intellectual affinity and affection between men and women outside marriage. In October 1754 Hume would see nothing untoward about sending a copy of the first volume of his *The History of England* to Mrs. Dysart, the wife of a clergyman. In his accompanying letter to the lady, whom he addresses as "Your affectionate Friend," the banter of gallantry camouflages the seriousness of his concern about her reaction. Now that long nights and wind and rain have set in, he expects her to "peruse [it] first with Pleasure, then with care." He hopes she, her husband, and Alexander Home, another friend, will fall into "disputes" about his political principles.[46]

As this glimpse of the sociable Hume suggests, he was not as marginal a member of the middle station as might at first appear to be case. When he wrote the early essays, to be sure, he was describing a social milieu in which he aspired to win full-fledged membership. His religious skepticism doomed his candidacy for a professorship in moral philosophy at the college in 1747, and for a position at the University of Glasgow in late 1761. In January of 1762 he was elected librarian to the Faculty of Advocates, an office he would hold for five years. What induced him to take the position was the 30,000 volumes in the library; he would later recall that he was paid "little or no emolument" (xxxvi). And yet by the early 1750s Hume was able to support himself respectably with his writings, and despite his shocking views on religion he was becoming a celebrated figure in the genteel circles of Edinburgh's middle station. His combination of intellectual acuity and affable simplicity of manner gave him a strong presence, and at times a guiding one, in the series of men's clubs which served as the hubs of Edinburgh's intellectual life and its culture of civic improvement. He prided himself on being a favorite among "the Ladies" and was in great demand for suppers and other social events. It is a mark of his local social eminence that in 1770, at age sixty, he began the building of a house at St. Andrew Square. St. Andrew was one of the first squares in the area of expansion toward the Firth of Forth, to the north of the cramped, smoky old city. The Georgian architecture of this New Town was a monumental announcement of the city's new prosperity and the epitome of modern elegance. "I wish you saw my new House and Situation in St Andrew Square," Hume wrote to his London publisher; "You would not wonder that I have abjured London forever."[47]

With his projection of a middle station, Hume sought to do with the essays what he had failed to do with the *Treatise*. He would draw learning into a larger rhetorical community of politeness whose center of gravity lay not in the aristocracy, or in Shaftesbury's select circle of gentlemen of leisure, but in professional men and their families, including their wives and daughters. The early essays were Hume's forum for establishing a public character by identifying with this group. He used the singular "station" to evoke a singular community of labor, refined leisure, and friendship where virtue, wisdom, and ability were most likely to be found. This was a highly distilled image of a social formation, more the imagining of a social space than a map of all its features, lofty, prosaic, and disreputable. As he well knew from his college years, the study of the law could be deadly boring; and there was a grinding routinism to its practice. The Law Faculty's high degree of intergenerational continuity and endogamous marriage combined with the importance of family connections in the making of legal careers mark the social closure typical of an old-regime corporate body.

To Hume, as to his friends in the law, there was no contradiction between proving individual merit and capitalizing on inherited advantages. Within their profession's admittedly narrow social parameters for entry, advocates shared an intensely competitive ethos—in their search for clients, and in their aspirations to ascend to the bench and perhaps beyond it. In 1763 Boswell would be reminded of the nimbus of virtue with which lawyers surrounded this motive force of ambition when he wrote to his mentor David Dalrymple, a lord on the Court of Sessions, that he had "a most independent spirit" and could not "bear . . . to hang on like a *young Laird*." Dalrymple responded with a stinging rebuke. It was imperative to have an "object" in life; "the condition of an idle man" was "ridiculous" for anyone, but "in a gentleman it may be said to more than ridiculous; it is contemptible, as implying a want of Ambition or of ye desire of excelling."[48] But money-grubbing and the manipulation of clients, particularly in the lower ranks of the profession, often made for less harmony between ambition and virtue than Hume attested. In all the professions the rewarding of talent and industry did not always square with the protocols of patronage, both within the profession and in the larger society and polity. Connections and especially family connections, formed the lower rungs of patronage ladders that extended up to "the Great" at the heights of government and political eminence.[49] At their Scottish pinnacle stood the third duke of Argyll, whose power as London's chief agent made him known as "the uncrowned king of Scotland," and who took a special interest in university and clerical affairs.[50]

If the essay on the middle station is fantasy, it is calculated fantasy. Hume's selectivity projects a solidary social block, its moral self-estimation demarcating it from both its inferiors and, by the conventional criteria of social honor, its superiors.[51] In fact, the overarching theme of the essay was a paradox: that this professional culture could credibly claim the intellectual and moral high ground precisely because it occupied the social middle. There was nothing egalitarian, much less democratic, about his perspective. To Hume, as to the *honnête homme*, the labor of the uneducated marked their imprisonment in the iron laws of "the animal Life" (533). It was "the Great," the titled aristocracy of vast wealth, that Hume took as his foil for celebrating the middle station. Even as his style took on something of the apparent effortlessness of the *bel esprit*, Hume flatly rejected the notion that true natural freedom was freedom from labor in a world of social play. Leisure is now an earned respite from work, not a way of life free of work. It was precisely their drive to engage in the division of labor, and their manner of engaging in it, that gave professional men a kind of freedom the great could not enjoy.

Hume's friend Hugh Blair would posit the same basic principle in sermons given at St Giles Church in Edinburgh: "Industry," Blair wrote in the published version, "is the law of our being; it is the demand of Nature, of reason, and of God."[52]

> By the destination of his Creator, and the necessities of his nature, man commences, at once, an *active*, not merely a contemplative being. Religion assumes him as such. It supposes him employed in this world, as on a busy stage. . . . It rebukes the slothful; directs the diligent how to labour; and requires every man to *do his own business*.[53]

Disciplined work habits were construed as a kind of self-determination, allowing the individual to appropriate his own natural resources—his talents or "powers"—for a willed purpose, rather than leaving them subject to the "chance" operation of nature's blind forces. In enlightened Calvinism this logic reshaped the meaning of life as struggle; the struggle between sanctification and sin— between God's saving grace and Satan's seductions—acceded to the struggle between the imperatives of character, conceived as habituated action, and the threat of its dissolution in the inertia of indolence and in its result, the depressive's state of hypochondria or melancholy. Depression was a descent into melancholic self-absorption, an irrational incapacity to heal oneself in channeled diligence and the self-validation it offered. The only guarantor against it was "improvement" conceived as a linear progress, like the process of collective improvement to which it contributed.

For Blair and other moderate literati the pursuit of ambition still needed a sacred frame. The believer's active pursuit of his own life plan had moral meaning only because, in the new economy of salvation, the specialized division of labor— the structural context of his pursuit—was the instrument of a Providential Design. In this distinctly Protestant Enlightenment, one might say, the division of labor became the key social mediation between the Absolute and the individual life course.[54] Hume, of course, was distinguished from the moderates by the fact that he was not a Christian, but an uncompromising naturalist. His occasional mentions of Providence are empty gestures to convention. There is a direct, though implicit, experiential line of continuity from the essay on the middle station to the *Treatise* that merits more attention. The same "natural" forces—the same intellectual curiosity and ambition to win others' approval (sympathy) as a public character—that Hume had embraced in himself as he assumed the identity of a philosopher, are now extended to the specialized labor of the middle station. He elaborates this theme in his essay on "The Stoic," one of a set of four in the 1742 volume on philosophical traditions, Stoicism, Epicureanism, Platonism, and Skepticism. Hume's purpose was not to provide accurate historical profiles of the ancient schools of philosophy, but to personify what he considered the four basic philosophical temperaments, inviting his readers to ponder their relevance to their own lives. Returning to the theme of the conclusion to Part 1 of the *Treatise*, he has the Epicurean denounce the Stoic delusion that rational askesis can make one happily independent of external objects. Intent on "feasting on [his] own thoughts," the Stoic falls into a "lethargy" or "melancholy," as the young Hume had done (140). In "The Stoic" Hume counterbalances that verdict, but only by offering a notably soft or "mitigated" Stoicism for his own era. That the Stoic aim in reaching the pure rational self was to become aware of the presence of the Divine within is simply not mentioned. Hume's is the Stoicism of an emphatically relational self, a Stoicism modernized to serve as the philosophy for a work ethic encompassing all kinds of specialized and skilled labor but attributing the highest felicity to the intellectual labor of the educated. Even the workman, Hume writes, does not regard the "labor and attention" his work requires as "burdensome and intolerable." The labor itself "is the chief ingredient of the felicity to which [he aspires]," and "every enjoyment soon becomes insipid and distasteful, when not acquired by fatigue and industry." How much more so for the "industry" required for "the cultivating of our mind, the moderating of our passions, the enlightening of our reason" (149). Intellectual labor develops self-command, which secures a serene independence from sensual pleasure in "external objects" that "chance may, in a moment, ravish from you." And yet, rather than producing the callous indifference to others of the philosophical recluse, it is the chief vehicle for "the social affections," the source of energy for "the social virtues," "the tender sentiments of sympathy and affection" (151). There is a vital synergy between labor and sympathy, the imaginative ground of social cohesion in a society with an increasingly complex division of labor.

The full implications become apparent when we return to the essay on the "Middle Station." We find a striking inversion of the logic of status and, with it, a shift in emphasis in the logic of gender. In juxtaposition to the improving pleasure of polite taste in the middle station, which is tuned to "the calm Voice of Reason," "the mere Pleasure" in which "the Great" are immersed is neither rational nor cultivated (546). Nor does it have commanding moral credibility. Like other critics of le monde, Hume sees, behind the apparent reciprocity of aristocratic complaisance, instrumental relationships structured by asymmetrical needs and power. To "mere men of the world," one companion is as good as another; the resources of their superiority—the favors they are in a position to bestow—make them oblivious to the differences in character that ought to "make one man preferable to another." The "Virtue" of true friendship among equals was possible only in the "narrow circle[s]" of friends formed in the middle station, where there was a reciprocal sharing of refined taste and sentiment (546–48). Expanding the Aristotelian and Ciceronian ideal of "philosophical" (as opposed to instrumental) friendship to encompass an entire new social milieu, Hume now makes shared aesthetic pleasure the medium, and indeed the moral bond, in more informal, even intimate, friendships formed in the sociability of polite men and women. Confident of the "Sincerity" of their friends, people learn to read character in a way "the Great" cannot. They polish each other, but not just in the external forms of complaisance; they develop each other's character, understood as the reliable representation of a moral core. It is not the publicness of the salon, or of the court, but the quite different exclusiveness of the domestic gathering or the select club that promotes this kind of self-improvement.

Another paradox of Hume's soft Stoicism becomes evident when we cross-reference "The Stoic" and "Of the Delicacy of Taste and Passion." In the latter essay he again denies that happiness can be achieved through complete "independence of every thing external." What one can do is develop a "delicacy of taste" or "sentiment" (as opposed to "passion") by "plac[ing] his happiness on such objects chiefly as depend upon himself." "We are pretty much masters," Hume writes, "what books we shall read, what diversions we shall partake of, and what company we shall keep" (5). There is a sense in which the ideal gentleman of the middle station chooses the social context for his self-improvement; unlike the aristocrat, he is not assigned to it by a code of honor. This form of autonomy goes hand in hand with the freedom of the market agent to choose his reading material and his leisure activities. Reading, of course, is done in solitude, and talk about it is in company; but it is neither "moping" reclusiveness nor the *bel esprit*'s way to superficial mastery. As solitary as the act of reading is, it is itself an engagement in social interaction. Encounters between authors and readers through print are refined simulations of sociability and indeed, metaphorically if not literally, its highest form.

It was the natural drive to self-improvement and socially recognized achievement that made the middle station "the most numerous Rank of Men, that can be suppos'd susceptible of Philosophy." Hence "all Discourses of Morality ought principally to be address'd to them" (546). Again Hume's observations pivot on the sense of identity he had achieved in the struggle to write the *Treatise*, culminating in the realization that his fear of weakness had been rooted in a false conception of philosophy as meditative askesis. Following his conviction that philosophy must operate within custom, Hume pulled the philosopher off his metasocial perch and into the middle rank. The philosopher not only spoke to its members; he spoke for them, as the advocate of their values and way of life. And yet there was also a sense in which philosophers, along with poets and scholars in "the higher Parts of Learning," were of a "mold" so much "finer" than men in the "common Professions" that they formed a breed apart. An Addison or a Pope or a Newton was "a Kind of Prodigy among Men." In such cases the "richest Genius" afforded by "Nature" had to be cultivated "from the earliest infancy" by education and example and brought to "a Degree of Perfection" by "Industry" (549). It is striking that, in his effort to reconstitute philosophical and critical authority, Hume gives equal importance here to the formative contributions of nature and industry. He makes it essential to the philosopher's claim to persuasive authority that he be blessed with exceptional inborn gifts, affording him greater "delicacy" and wider vision than other educated men. But the philosopher's authority also rests on the fact that he too has to labor strenuously and continually. Being of the same industrious species, though of lesser qualities, professional men can be counted on to recognize the superiority of the prodigy. As high above them as he stands, he is one of them.

Hume's life was a sustained commitment to living this ethos, as his correspondence makes abundantly clear. It was not simply that, intent on proving himself despite the *Treatise*, he spent much of his adult life laboring at the art of polite writing, first with several volumes of essays, then with the two *Enquiries* with which he sought to make the core argument of the *Treatise* palatable to an educated public, and finally with his monumental six-volume *The History of England*. The alternative to making a respectable living with his pen, as his own man, was to join the swarm of clients of "the Great," hired pens in the service of a party, and Hume had a horror of that fate. In a world structured vertically by networks of patrons and clients, he took pride in staying out of the clutches of the powerful. One of their grounds for an "amicable connection," he wrote Rousseau in July 1762, was their shared "Disdain of all Dependance."[55] When Hume did accept appointments, it was only after being assured that his intellectual independence would not be compromised. Friendship, on the other hand, was a critical need, and he took obvious pleasure in writing letters to friends that conveyed the warmth of his affection with mockery and teasing, tongue-in-cheek admonishments. His friendships were his rebukes to the degrading culture of clientage.

Hume knew, of course, that in rejecting clientage he was making himself directly dependent on the print market and its reading public, and that that also brought its frustrations. At the same time, however, in "My Own Life," the brief self-eulogy he wrote just before his death, he had no inhibitions about presenting himself as a professional writer living from his earnings; there was nothing of the casual ease of the persona of the *honnête homme* writing for the sheer amusement of it, disdaining any effort for commercial gain, or of Shaftesbury's rejection of the market for a highly select group of gentlemen-friends. What is perhaps most striking about "My Own Life" is the unabashed pride with which Hume chronicled a life of labor, a writing career structured around his climb to market success. It was in the period from 1745 through 1747—when he served as the tutor to Lord Annandale and then as secretary to General St. Clair—that, thanks to his "frugality," he reached a "fortune" of nearly a thousand pounds. "I called [it] independent," he noted, "though most of my friends were inclined to smile when I said so" (xxxv). It was the *History* volumes, despite (or perhaps because of) the attacks they brought on him from all sides, that finally made him financially comfortable. When he retired to Scotland in 1769, it was with "the satisfaction of never having preferred a request to one great man, or even making advances of friendship to any of them" (xxxviii). He writes with an audible sense of self-vindication.

—

Hume's most explicit announcement of his rhetorical agenda was "Of Essay Writing," which appeared in the 1742 volume but in fact seems to have been written to introduce the essays as a whole. Assuming the voice of a philosopher of the "new Age," he proposed to serve as the "Ambassador" from the "Dominion" of "*the learned*," whose work "cannot be brought to Perfection, without long Preparation and severe Labour," and "the conversible World," which "joins to a sociable Disposition, and a Taste of Pleasure, an Inclination to the easier and more gentle Exercises of the Understanding" (533). Hume casts derision on the learned men of "the last Age," who were "shut up in Colleges and Cells, and secluded from the World and good Company . . . without any Taste of Life or Manners, and without that Liberty and Facility of Thought and Expression, which can only be acquir'd by Conversation" (534). He is evoking the figure of the pedant, now the foil to the politeness of a middle station rather than to an aristocratic mystique. "Even Philosophy," he writes, "went to Wrack by this moaping recluse Method of Study, and became as chimerical in her Conclusions as she was unintelligible in her Stile and Manner of Delivery" (534–35).

Speaking as a philosopher of the "new Age," Hume goes on to extend "particular Respect, to the Fair Sex, who are the Sovereigns of the Empire of Conversation." Were it not for the fact that the learned "are a stubborn independent Race of Mortals, extremely jealous of their Liberty, and unaccustom'd to Subjection," he would give the women of this empire "the sovereign Authority over the Republic of Letters" (535–36). Admitting coyly that he has nearly "worn out" his conceit of the philosopher-ambassador, he shifts to a "serious" voice and states his opinion simply: "Women of Sense and Education (for to such alone I address myself) are much better Judges of all polite Writing than Men of the same Degree of Understanding":

> My fair Readers may be assur'd, that all Men of Sense, who know the World, have a great Deference for [women's] Judgment of such Books as ly within the Compass of their Knowledge, and repose more Confidence in the Delicacy of their Taste, tho' unguided by Rules, than in all the dull Labours of Pedants and Commentators. (536)

Hume was a master of the qualifying phrase. His essay is a *locus classicus* for the palpable condescension toward women in an emerging bourgeois culture, the patronizing male posture of pseudorespect that Mary Wollstonecraft would excoriate in her *Vindication of the Rights of Woman* in 1792.[56] Even as it shifted away from the aristocratic ethos it claimed to be challenging, this new order of politeness extended it. Women remained by nature unguided by the "Rules" that learned men, by virtue of their commitment to labor, knew to be necessary. But the aristocratic woman who is stigmatized as laboring derogates herself primarily as a person of quality displaying her rank in a public setting; the laboring woman of the middle station derogates herself primarily as a woman, her natural place outside the public gaze. Learned and weighty books that the *honnête femme* would have dismissed as the drudgery of commoners are now beyond "the Compass of [women's] Knowledge." And yet this change in gender configuration is multivalent, especially in the British context. It also had the effect of easing the constraints on men to avoid the stigma of effeminacy, even as they retained a manly voice. Hume performed a softened manliness in the very process of advocating it. He did so quite early in the century, and in sharp contrast to a figure like Pope. In "Of the Delicacy of Taste and Passion," defying the stereotyping of polite and elegant men as effeminate, he writes that a man with "a delicacy of taste," cultivated in study of the sciences and the liberal arts, is distinguished not only by "a certain elegance of sentiment," but also by "soft and tender" emotions (5–7).

Hume makes this persona essential to the essay as a simulated conversation, an exercise in soft persuasion rather than an imposition of authority. But how seriously intellectual were women allowed to be in Hume's notion of "gallant" social intercourse? The fineness of the line he was drawing is nowhere more evident than in a brief essay—a trifle, he would later say—in the 1741 volume titled "Of the Study of History." Hume was obviously trying to draw women into his readership. He "earnestly" recommends to his "female readers" the study of history, "as an occupation, of all others, the best suited both to their sex and education, much more instructive than their ordinary books of amusement, and more entertaining than those serious compositions, which are usually to be found in their closets" (563). This is the voice of the modern gallant, assigning women to a conversational realm of instructive (but not too "serious") entertainment, suitable to "the tenderness of their complexion, and the weakness of their education" (565). Unlike abstract philosophy, the vivid depiction of characters and events in historical writing stimulates the capacity for moral judgment. Here again Hume is applying his conviction, applicable to men as well as women, that the efficacy of knowledge is a function of the vivacity of expression. But in trying to cure women of their fondness for romances and novels, Hume sees himself pulling them out of a "falseness" that makes them susceptible to seductive gallantry and into "matter of fact." When he chides them for their preference for "*secret history*," the stories of behind-the-scenes intrigues and scandals, he aims to endow them with a knowledge of public history they can share with men (564). Women would do well to become familiar with "the policy of government" as well as the history of advances in the arts and sciences. They must know the history of Greece and Rome as well as that of their own country. He recommends Plutarch's *Lives* and, more striking, Machiavelli when he writes as an historian rather than a politician (567).[57]

The sheer blatancy of Hume's condescension, particularly from a modern feminist standpoint, can distract us from the fact that, against the backdrop of one of the most pervasive conventional discourses in early eighteenth-century Britain, he conducts a positive revaluation of women.[58] Hume did not join the chorus of censorious critics of aristocratic decadence in the civic humanist tradition. Quite the contrary; he teased and provoked the tradition, flatly rejecting its ethos of manly virtue and its animus against women. The timing makes that all the more striking. With the bitter disillusionment generated by the investment collapse that ended the South Sea Bubble, and with the increasingly evident abuse of patronage and credit in Walpole's Whig regime, the republican themes of "luxury" and "corruption" now made the specter of capricious females, effeminizing men in their craving for luxury and in the very way they set the tone in mixed-gender sociability, integral to a moral critique of rampant commercialism. In fact in the 1720s and 1730s this patriotic discourse carried further a process that can be traced back to the late seventeenth century: the assertion of a manly, no-nonsense British national character by contrast to the effeminacy of French polite culture.[59] Hume was well aware that one of the first texts to braid together all these themes was Shaftesbury's *Characteristics*. He did not share his friend Adam Smith's contemptuous estimation of Shaftesbury's style as pomposity in lieu of character. To judge by his letters, in his relations with women in his social circles Hume used a caricature of himself as the gloomy philosopher—the persona he had emphatically rejected—as a way of mocking gallantry even as he feigned regret at being unsuitable for it. Such is the impression we get from Hume's letter in September 1743 to William Mure of Caldwell, one of his closest friends. Mure should tell his sister Miss Betty that he is "as grave as she imagines a Philosopher to be." He laughs "only once a fortnight" and "look[s] sullen every Moment"; "none of Ovid's Metamorphosis ever show'd so absolute a Change from a human Creature into a Beast; I mean from a Gallant into a Philosopher."[60]

There is something of playful self-mockery in his prose, but for a serious purpose. In fact in "Of Essay Writing" Hume not only practiced but also defended precisely what Shaftesbury found so detestable about modern literary culture: its commercial vulgarity, the style of "complaisant" gallantry pandering to female consumers. In his way of commercializing gallantry, Hume was in effect commodifying his polite style and his authorial person. What disgusted Shaftesbury seemed quite justifiable to Hume, and not simply because he needed to earn a living with his pen. Hume set modern gallantry within an historical perspective quite different from Shaftesbury's, with a new configuration of nature and civil society, luxury and politeness, and status and gender, anticipating the importance given to women's civilizing agency in later Scottish conjectural histories of stadial progress.

In the essay "Of Refinement in the Arts," published in 1754, Hume would lay out his defense of "luxury" as the mark of superiority of modern urban societies over the ancient polis. Here again he took the opportunity to refute "the men of libertine principles" who praise "vicious luxury." But most of the essay is aimed at "men of severe morals [who] blame even the most innocent luxury" for all civil corruptions (269–76). This challenge to conventional wisdom supports a realignment of the entire semantic field of the debates on luxury. Hume distinguished between the natural "indolence or repose" that is needed to sustain "an assiduity in honest industry" and the "languor and lethargy," or the "Idleness," that deprives both labor and leisure of natural enjoyment. Reconfigured in this way, "indolence"—so often gendered female and made a symptom of effeminacy— takes on a positive meaning as the leisure that complements work and gives it added vigor. Far from "enervating" people, the material comforts and conveniences provided by the mechanical arts make it possible for the "refined" or "liberal" arts to flourish. The result is that "*industry, knowledge,* and *humanity*" form an "indissoluble chain" throughout society in "the more polished" and "more luxurious" ages. As cities and their conversational sociability grow, people pursue "taste" in their intellectual inclinations as well as in their material goods. "Both sexes," Hume writes, "meet in an easy and sociable manner; and the tempers of men, as well as their behaviour, refine apace" (270–71).

"Of Refinement in the Arts" should be read as a supplement to the relatively long essay "Of the Rise and Progress of the Arts and Sciences," published in the 1742 volume. It was above all in the 1742 essay that Hume turned the tables on the British variation on civic humanism; and he did it at its most politically sensitive point, the combined smugness and anxiety in the British dismissal of French claims of cultural supremacy since the late seventeenth century. Only ancient republican liberty, he acknowledged, could have served as the original "proper *nursery* for the arts and sciences" (17–19). But in the modern era the baton had passed to "civilized monarchies," states that had once been despotic but had developed a rule of law that guaranteed their subjects a large measure of security (124–25). Pace Shaftesbury and others, France did not stand as a warning to Great Britain as the prime example of female-centered degeneration from the virtuous polities of the ancients. It commanded the summit of distinctly modern cultural achievement.

What is perhaps most remarkable about this argument is the way it reworked the trope contrasting the natural sincerity of Shaftesbury's virtuous gentleman and the insincerity—the contrived, calculating manipulation of mere "appearances"—of the *honnête homme* or *femme*. The theme is adumbrated as early as the fall of 1734 in Hume's letter to his friend Michael Ramsay summing up his impressions of the French from his brief stay in Paris and his first few weeks in Rheims, where he had received invitations from "the best families." He had not found English conventional wisdom confirmed. Though French "manners" were often "too remote from the Truth," the French in fact had more "real Politeness of the Heart," more of "a Softness of Temper, & a sincere Inclination to oblige & be serviceable," than the English. The "outward Deferences & Ceremonies" of politeness, Hume reasoned, were matters of "Custom," and "whenever any Expression or Action becomes customary it can deceive no body." Hume was drawing an implicit analogy between the illusory but necessary foundational beliefs we derive from epistemological Custom—the belief in cause and effect, in an integral self, etc.—and the not-really-sincere but still necessary performances required in polite society. Like the sets in a theater, such performances "are not designed to be believ'd." Though the ceremonies of politeness ought to be "contriv'd," and though "they do not deceive, nor pass for sincere," they "still please by their Appearance" "& lead the Mind by its own Consent & Knowledge, into an agreeable Delusion."[61] Paradoxically, the pleasing presentation of self, because it is practiced self-consciously by all the participants in polite conversation, is not dissimulating artifice. The effect—the elicited consent—is so free of coercive imposition as to be virtually natural.

At issue here was a longstanding question about the ethical status of *complaisance*. Was it a civilizing art that men must learn from women, its masters and guardians in the discourse of *honnêteté*, or was it a pernicious manipulation of appearance that effeminized men by making their presentations of self as false as women's? Hume's underlying point was that *complaisance* was, at worst, morally neutral, and that in any case it was socially efficacious. He returned to this theme eight years later in his defense of modern gallantry in the 1742 essay "Of the Rise and Progress of the Arts and Science." This time he took on Shaftesbury directly, citing him in a footnote as an example of "some of the more zealous partizans of the ancients [who] have asserted [gallantry] to be foppish and ridiculous, and a reproach, rather than a credit, to the present age" (131). He agrees with Shaftesbury that modern gallantry is a creation of monarchies and their "elegant" courts; and yet he makes it "*natural* in the highest degree," "*generous*," and "compatible with *wisdom* and *prudence*" (131–33). Again he argues for the need for "the appearance of sentiments" (132), thus validating the self-conscious screening of the self, the contrived social representation of affect. Hume might be said to offer a variation on the French aesthetic of social play. His emphasis, however, is less on the natural freedom of play itself as it is on the role of social artifice in counteracting one set of natural passions with another. The science of man tells us that human beings, though naturally inclined to "mutual sympathy," also have natural inclinations to vices like pride, selfishness, licentiousness, and the abuse of superior strength. These are checked, and even tamed, by the "studied display" of "directly contrary" sentiments (132). Social artifice is so deeply grounded in the natural as to be virtually indistinguishable from it. Modern politeness is "naturally . . . ornamental," though it does indeed "[run] often into affectation and foppery, disguise and insincerity" (130–31). Gallantry alleviates men's natural superiority of body and mind over women by "a studied deference and complaisance for all [their] inclinations and opinions" (132–33).

In a sense, then, the polite leisure of the middle station, like the leisure of the *honnêtes*, is an artifice, a performance of equality among unequals, whether the inequality is in social rank or in gender. And yet for Hume it is a natural artifice.

Though "studied" and indeed contrived as a compensatory social form, polite leisure is a social site for communication of natural affection and, in an appropriately disciplined way, of desire between the sexes. There is still another sense in which this kind of leisure is natural; through the ethos of personal and collective improvement, it bonds in an "easy" but purposeful symbiosis with labor in modern culture. Hume's phrasing is telling; the "garniture of reason, discourse, sympathy, friendship and gaity" provides both "*entertainment* and *improvement*" to "the youth of both sexes" (133–34). The "wisdom" of this form of leisure lies both in making young women accomplished in the polite arts, and in forming young men, through their interaction with women, to devote themselves to the rational discipline of a life of labor in the very process of refining them for the pleasures of polite entertainment. Aesthetic play serves labor, just as labor earns one the right to play.[62]

Hume used the discursive freedom of the essay to weave his thought along the evasive line seen to separate the polite gentleman, polished by women to emotionally sensitive delicacy and even softness, and the effeminized male, a violation of nature, a female temperament in a male body. He wanted his gentlemen of the middle station to be polished in a way that refined their manly industry without dissolving their drive for it—the drive to act, to produce, to win recognition—into effeminate indolence, or what he now called idleness. Women would be the agents, however indirectly, of this precarious process, without being producers themselves in the public world of labor. They would enjoy a certain equality, and even a certain superiority, in the appreciation and evaluation of the intelligence required in polite performance. Would they also be given authority to define the rules of performance in the public media of print and the visual arts?

The Vicissitudes of Taste

Hume had originally planned a separate treatise on criticism as well as one on politics, but the ambition faded as he shifted to writing essays and history. He sufficed with an essay titled "Of the Standard of Taste," written sometime in the mid-1750s.[63] Despite the straightforward confidence that its title suggests, it is a tentative and elusive piece.[64]

The essay's title stops well short of his earlier claim "That Politics May be Reduced to a Science," thus signaling that taste is a particularly hard case. And yet, to recall Ernst Cassirer's distinction, Hume made a case for "practical generality" in aesthetic judgment even as he denied it "theoretical generality."[65] If there could not be purely objective authority, there nonetheless could and must be, within the constraints of custom, a culturally authoritative entitlement to identify general precepts and set rules. Hume was clearly trying to counter subjectivism

and relativism—the combined voice of the philosophical skeptic and the indis-
criminate consumer—by constructing an authoritative aesthetic voice. One
implication, kept implicit in the essay, was that this strategy would settle once and
for all gender-framed issues of taste to which Hume had been introduced by the
seventeenth-century French discourse of *politesse*, and with which he had already
engaged in passing in the early essays. And yet, even as he kept aesthetics refracted
through custom, he edged out of custom to something like a view from nowhere
in his argument for a rational analytic for evaluating literary texts. In both lines of
argument, women's very gift for appreciating beauty disqualified them from the
public exercise of aesthetic authority. To the extent that Hume prevented the lines
of appreciation and judgment from diverging entirely, it was by keeping them on a
common ground of critical labor that only very exceptional men could perform.

The timing of the essay is important. Britain in the decade and a half from
1748 to 1762 witnessed a spate of lectures and publications on taste, with a large,
if not predominant, Scottish presence. In 1747 Home arranged for the young
Adam Smith to give a series of public lectures in Edinburgh on rhetoric and belles
lettres. Smith's analysis of prose style explored the intimate relationship between
aesthetic cultivation and the representation of character. In 1755 the new Edinburgh Society for Encouraging Arts, Sciences, Manufactures, and Agriculture in
Scotland—a spin-off of the Select Society—proposed to award a medal for "the
best essay on taste." The winner was Alexander Gerard, a professor in Aberdeen,
and Hume helped prepare Gerard's manuscript for publication in 1759. In 1757
Hume had published his own essay. In 1759, with Hume's "Of the Standard of
Taste" very much in mind, Edmund Burke added an introduction to the second
edition of his *A Philosophical Enquiry into the Origin of Our Ideas of the Sublime
and Beautiful* (1757).[66] Kames himself weighed in in 1762 with his long-awaited
magnum opus, the two-volume *Elements of Criticism*.

In the discursive field formed by these texts and several others, two meanings
of "taste" seemed to pull against each other, and one of the underlying questions
was how they might be aligned or at least conceived as steps in a single process.[67]
In its semantic roots in the French tradition of aesthetic play, taste was an immediate experience, a spontaneous pleasure taken in the beauty of things. It required
the "delicacy" of sensibility that was often seen to distinguish women from men.
But "taste" was also used to designate a capacity for deliberate judgment, an
application of general rules to the particular, made in some detachment from the
object in question. The challenge was to reconcile the immediate and indispensable experience—the element of sensate, affective spontaneity in aesthetic
pleasure—with the need for rational judgment. Could the philosophical critic
establish rules and fix hierarchies without draining the spontaneity out of the
aesthetic experience? How could the sober application of general rules be made
compatible with delight?

"Morals and criticism," Hume had written in the introduction to the *Treatise*, "regard our tastes and sentiments."[68] The many French and British attempts to define taste and set the agenda for philosophical criticism from the late seventeenth century onward rested on an awareness that the authority at issue was moral as well as aesthetic, but there was a wide spectrum of views on the degree of consanguinity between the two. We can suffice here with a heuristic mapping, considering as three separate strands claims that often crisscrossed and became laced in the literature. In what might be called hard-line classicism, judgments in the appreciation of beauty and in the exercise of virtue were fused to the point of virtual identity; art, like ethics, followed the universal laws of Nature, discernible in the pure and unchanging forms behind the apparently infinite particularity of appearances. This was Shaftesbury's conviction, mixing neo-Platonism and Stoicism; and a variation on it, from a different philosophical angle, is to be found in Pope's *Essay on Taste*. Hume's philosophical principles obviously implied a flat rejection of this position. His entire philosophy, in fact, became pivotal for a growing reversal of the relationship between subject and object. Our psychological engagement with objects, and not their essential "nature," became the shaping force in aesthetic judgment. In his early essays, and particularly with his notion of the paradoxical naturalness of "appearance" in polite sociability, he might be said to have straddled two weaker claims. One had it that aesthetic and moral judgments, though not to be collapsed into each other, were in some sense homologous; and hence that aesthetic cultivation contributed powerfully, and perhaps indispensably, to the formation of moral character. The other view was a defense of modernity in the face of a neoclassical purism that seemed to have become anachronistic. The inner purity of intention—the unselfish devotion to duty for its own sake—that had been deemed essential to classical "virtue" was not to be expected in modern commercial societies, whose motive force was the self-interested pursuit of wealth and honor. But commercial modernity compensated for this apparent decline with polite manners, which disciplined people to treat others civilly and with the reliable predictability of character, as though they were virtuous. If this position was a retreat from the classical ideal, it nonetheless made aesthetic cultivation essential to the observance of "propriety" in civilized society.

What was it that made, or should make, the judgment of the philosophical critic authoritative? Even in arguments for universal critical standards that were assumed to be self-evident to any unprejudiced mind, there remained the fact that the critic exercised his authority over a particular "public" of viewers, listeners, and readers. Was there a sense in which their collective enjoyment of a work of art—the fact that they all found pleasure in it—was the ultimate ground for determining whether the critic's judgment was valid? In the preface to the 1701 edition of his works, Nicolas Boileau had declared that "a work that is not approved by the public is a very poor work." He could put such faith in the public, however, because he was convinced that something is beautiful because it is true (and hence has universal validity), and that a truth properly represented or expressed could not fail to please people. The flip side of this logic was that fashions, however long they might reign, should not inhibit the critic from voicing his dissent; "it is quite possible for the bulk of mankind over a long period of time to mistake the false for the true, and to admire bad things."[69]

Far more subversive of critical authority were the *Critical Reflections* published in 1719 by Jean-Baptiste Du Bos, a man of letters who frequented Mme de Lambert's salon and had had extended stays in England and Holland in the French diplomatic service.[70] The book defies the usual categorizations. One of its purposes was to defend the ancients against disparagement by the moderns, which was quite in keeping with the French Academy's mission to maintain standards in the arts. Though he cited Boileau approvingly in several places, however, Du Bos repeatedly dismissed critics and their rules as useless and sometimes detrimental to the appreciation of painting and poetry. All that mattered was, quite simply, whether people found pleasure in the work in question, and that depended on whether the work affected the senses in a way that engaged an "inner motion" or "inward sense in every person, which we know not how to explain." Reason was notoriously fallible in such matters, and in any case was irrelevant. Du Bos did not go as far in subjectivizing and democratizing taste as some of his most provocative statements seemed to imply. By "the public," he was clear to explain, he meant "such persons only, as have acquired some lights, either by reading or by being conversant with the world."[71] Du Bos acknowledged that the presence of women in the public for art had been growing since the sixteenth century, particularly in Paris, most recently with the inclusion of educated and polite bourgeois women. His book marks an early step in the transition from French aristocratic *politesse* to a widening consumption of tasteful things. There was something in it of the contempt for pedantic academic rules, the insistence on the "je ne sais quoi," that marked the unique social honor of the *honnêtes* who frequented the salons. In that sense it was indebted to the subjectivism of women-guided literary modernism in the seventeenth century. At the same time, Du Bos's subjectivism, however limited, nodded to the widening sphere of leisured pleasure afforded by a commercializing society.

Hume read and made notes on the *Reflections*, probably sometime in the mid-1730s when he was residing in France, and there are echoes of the book in his essay on taste. By the 1750s, however, he and other advocates of standards in taste had to contend with two far more unsettling figures, both intent on deflating the aesthetic as well as the moral pretensions of societies in which there seemed to be no limit to the spread of "luxury" in the form of consumerism. With the publication of an enlarged edition of his *The Fable of the Bees* in 1723, Bernard Mandeville became a specter haunting debates about the state of morals and taste in commercializing societies; and the Scots literati, including Hume, missed no opportunity to refute him, even as they came to terms with his economic logic. Mandeville's central point was that, however morally lamentable and even vicious the proliferating luxuries of the modern era might be, the demand for them had the immense public benefit of generating wealth, creating employment, and improving the material conditions of the laboring masses at the broad base of the social pyramid. The increase in vice, it would seem, was well worth it. No less shocking was the corollary: that moral and aesthetic standards were simply self-serving froth, the coinage of hypocritical self-justification for the wealthy and powerful at the top of the heap.[72]

In 1750 Jean-Jacques Rousseau won the prize for the Dijon Academy's essay contest on the question "Whether the Arts and Sciences have contributed to the purification of morals." Rousseau drew on Mandeville, but where Mandeville shocked with his cynicism, the Citizen of Geneva confronted readers with a stark moral rigorism in the tradition of civic humanism. Luxury, the dissolution of morals, and "the corruption of taste" were all of a piece. To reproach modern societies Rousseau evoked the "natural" virtue of the citizen-soldiers of the ancient republics, content to satisfy limited material needs and, in their "rustic" simplicity, innocently transparent to each other. The multiplication of artificial needs had released the opposite, omnipresent human selfishness, a "rage for distinction" and the wealth that displayed it.[73] The arts as well as the sciences were the most insidiously pernicious luxury, since they provided specious excuses for deception and for the injustice of gross disparities in wealth.

Rousseau obviously rejected Shaftesbury's contention that human nature was innately social and altruistic, but his very phrasing and choice of targets suggest that he was also challenging Hume's defense of luxury and, most striking, his defense of "appearance," as opposed to real virtue, in polite sociability. The arts and science were not the products of disciplined intellectual labor, as Hume would have it; they were "born in idleness [which] they nourish . . . in turn."[74] Ambition was not a vehicle of freedom, but a symptom of corruption. To ascend the social ladder one must please others, and to please one must dissimulate, present a false self. This was to say that there was nothing natural, much less morally efficacious, about *complaisance*. It was the chief emblem of the vice—the calculating compulsion to please—that made modern society an arena of vicious competition behind a "uniform and deceitful veil of politeness." "One no longer dares to appear what one is," Rousseau lamented; there are "no more sincere friendships." Print had made matters worse: there is now a "flood of print," aimed to win popular approval with a "false delicacy." Rousseau obviously had in mind the commercialized print gallantry Hume was practicing. "The "ascendancy of women" required authors and artists to "[sacrifice] their taste to the Tyrants of their freedom."[75]

The substantial Scottish contribution to the midcentury debate on taste engaged all these issues. If it was European in that sense, it also had a certain local immediacy. Hume's paean to the moral superiority of the middle rank notwithstanding, there was a growing awareness among the Scottish literati that its constitutive elements—the educated professions—were not up to their assigned role. Hume's use of "the good lawyer," along with the good physician, in his claim that "the middle station should be the most favourable to the improving our natural Abilities" was understandable but ironic. Since the seventeenth century the Scottish Faculty of Advocates had prided itself on being the paradigmatic liberal profession. To acquire liberality of mind in this sense meant to be groomed in the erudition of Protestant humanism. Learning in law and learning in the humanistic wisdom and elegance of the ancients were two sides of the same coin, fused by the texts and principles of Roman civil law.[76] One could be a practicing, sleeves-rolled-up professional and a learned man, an *érudit*, at the same time. In the course of the eighteenth century, as politeness became the gentlemanly norm and erudition lost its purchase for new generations of lawyers, the pairing of "liberal" and "profession" had to be reconceived. In 1748 Henry Dundas, the new lord president of the Law Faculty, told his colleagues that, in addition to learning Roman and natural law, advocates should master "the other Sciences and accomplishments becoming the Character of a gentleman," and that above all "rational and manly eloquence" should distinguish their profession.[77] But Adam Ferguson, appointed to the chair of moral philosophy in Edinburgh in 1764, saw little improvement; in one of his unpublished meditations on the adverse implications of the modern division of labor for civic culture he singled out law along with medicine. Practitioners in both professions tended to lack a "Liberal extensive view," and their intellectual tunnel-visioning made them socially "lame."[78]

In the light of the new standards of polite letters, the tradition of erudition seemed a species of pedantry, specialized to the point of being laughably esoteric, and too obviously the product of tedious mental labor. It mimicked, rather than counteracting, the sheer tedium of the law itself. There was a larger issue at stake about the middle station as a whole. How could its members credibly assume the cultural and moral authority Hume and others assigned to them if in fact the very nature of their professional practice belied the projected symbiosis of intellectual labor and refined leisure? What was lacking was precisely the polite taste that Rousseau found so corrupted. The solution, Kames argued in the introduction to *Elements of Criticism*, lay in reforming the university education of professional men to make it "liberal" in the modern sense, and in that project criticism must play a key role. The critic's task was to offer young men "a clear perception of what objects are lofty, what low, what proper or improper, what manly, and what mean or trivial." The problem now was that students passed directly from language training to "the most profound philosophy." Cultivation of the fine arts, guided by criticism, would provide the needed "middle link." In the process of developing moral character, "taste" in this sense also formed the polite gentleman, able to engage in "elegant subjects for conversation" and to "[act] in the social state with dignity and propriety." Thus conceived, the acquisition of taste in university education, by "[furnishing] an inviting opportunity to exercise the judgement," would bridge the gap between professional labor and polite leisure. They formed a continuum in the self-disciplined exercise of the male mind.[79]

It is in these contexts—the longstanding debate about whether the pleasure of taste could or should be subject to critical authority, the more recent radical questioning of claims for the moral efficacy of the fine arts and taste, the immediate Scottish concern that the claim of the professions, and especially the law, to be "liberal" was losing credibility—that Hume wrote his essay. He surely discussed these matters with Kames, but he just as surely disagreed with his former mentor. Taking up the hard-line position, Kames argued that our conviction that in taste, as in morals, there is a "right" and a "wrong" judgment is entirely justified. Our aesthetic standards are "rooted in human nature, and governed by principles common to all men."[80] This was precisely the kind of essentialism Hume had tried to demolish with his argument in the *Treatise* that all our knowledge, and hence all our judgments, are mediated through the indispensable shared beliefs of custom. At once agreeing with and stepping back from Kames's conviction, Hume found "the principles of taste" to be "universal, and nearly, if not entirely the same in all men" (241). The qualification assumed considerable significance in the concluding pages of the essay, where Hume expanded the idea of "custom" from its epistemological use to include "the different humours of particular men" and "the particular manners and opinions of our age and country." It is regrettable, Hume observes, that certain "peculiarities of manners" of past ages blind the "common audience" to the true aesthetic value of a work. An author's description of "vicious manners," or his personal commitment to religious "bigotry" or "superstition," is an aesthetic as well as a moral "blemish," and it is "eternal." There are barbarisms for which no contextual excuse can be made. But when differences in aesthetic judgment are due to "diversity in the internal frame or external situation as is entirely blameless on both sides," then "we seek in vain for a standard, by which we can reconcile the contrary sentiments" (243–47).

The tentativeness of the argument makes it all the more striking that the bulk of the essay is a brief, at a more modest level of generality, for the authoritative judgments of rare critics, "easily to be distinguished in society, by the soundness of their understanding and the superiority of their faculties above the rest of mankind" (243). Hume was surely taking aim at Mandeville and Rousseau, but his immediate task was to respond to his Scots colleague Alexander Gerard, who seemed to reach a conclusion similar to his own but by a quite different route. Gerard's crucial move was to posit universals: qualities of beauty inherent to objects, and principles of beauty inherent to the human mind. With that foundation established, he anatomized "the sentiment of taste" into two qualitatively and sequentially different acts of cognition: "the sensibility of taste . . . generally accompanied with lively passions," which "women have always been considered as possessing . . . in a greater degree than men," and authoritative judgment in taste. By itself, he warned, the sensibility could easily degenerate into "a blind, enthusiastic feeling." Judgment he defined as a "reflexive faculty," "an exercise of abstraction, which every man of tolerable acuteness employs for himself," the capacity to apply "general rules of established authority."[81] If perfect criticism was "philosophical," it was also, Gerard insisted, "composed" from "general approbation." This was a backhanded gesture to the mass market and its consumers, women as well as men, reminiscent of Boileau's. General approbation, as Gerard uses the term, is not what people preferred, but what the critic, proceeding from the universal qualities of objects and minds, knew they ought to prefer. Principles of taste could rest only on "unperverted" sentiments.[82]

Hume's essay also argues for standards of taste, though so cautiously that one wonders whether he is convinced of what he is doing. In its structure it recalls the passages in the *Treatise* about his nearly irrecoverable plunge into anxiety. Here too, in his cogent précis of the radical skeptical argument that taste is completely subjective and hence relative, he brings the reader to the abyss, then pulls him back. In a way, he is more philosophically aggressive than Gerard. Not content that every man of tolerable sense exercise criticism, he profiles the true philosophical critic, who he thinks is a very rare bird. At the same time, though, Hume is, at least at the outset, much more philosophically modest than Gerard. He cannot take Gerard's essentialist route. The philosopher has to accept his containment within custom; he cannot posit anything intrinsic to objects or to the mind.

Like Gerard and other contemporaries, Hume knows that taste without spontaneous delight would be deadening. The true critic must have "that *delicacy* of imagination . . . which is requisite to convey a sensibility of the finer emotions" (234). This strand of his argument is entirely in keeping with his view that knowledge is inherently social, and that it is generated in imaginative sympathy. It is not only a radical departure from the rationalist tradition; it seems to imply that critical judgment itself—and not only sensibility—must be feminized. That impression is strengthened by the fact that Hume considers delicacy a capacity of the bodily organs—thus echoing the psychophysiological logic that made women judges in matters of taste in the discourse of *politesse*. But fifteen years earlier Hume had proposed that learned men draw the "materials" for a science of man from their engagement in the conversable world, with its "Taste of Pleasure" and its "Inclination for the easier and more gentle Exercises of the Understanding." Now, one might say, he masculinizes what he had seemed to feminize.

Criticism—the judgment of aesthetic value—cannot be just a matter of exceptional delicacy; it requires "a more accurate definition of delicacy" (234). To that
end he shifts the critic's laboratory from the world of sociable play to the habit of
labor, to serious study. In fact he argues for two new laboratories in which the true
critic must rigorously train and discipline himself. One he calls "*practice* in a
particular art." Labor in one art is required to assign correct aesthetic value to
works in all the arts, and hence the labor of artistic creation and the labor of
criticism are inseparable. The other laboratory is the historical test; the critic finds
his guide to the rules of taste in "the durable admiration which attends those
works that have survived all the caprices of mode and fashion, all the mistakes of
ignorance and envy" (232–33). Though he does not use the term, Hume makes
the critic the learned guardian of a literary canon, a series of monumental works
that have continued to be valued over centuries.

In all this Hume can be said to have remained within his delimited philosophical sphere of "custom" and "experience." In fact, in a mischievous turn reminiscent of Du Bos, he takes the opportunity of the essay form to invert philosophical
convention and once again poke fun at metaphysics. Over the centuries, he
observes, it has been in "theories of abstract philosophy" and "systems of profound theology"—emanations from the view from nowhere—that the caprices of
fashion have reigned. Aesthetic approval is, by contrast, a constant; through the
centuries culture after culture, despite their differing contextual parameters and
constraints, continues to admire the same works (242–43).

And yet Hume cannot stop there. He has not yet removed himself and his
readers far enough from the abyss of relativism in modern commercial societies.
In addition to deep learning in a canon, strenuous practice of an art, and great
delicacy of the imagination, the critic must have uncommon "soundness" of
"understanding." Now Hume changes keys, so to speak; in the end the critic has
to abstract, and indeed not only from the work of art, but also from himself.
"When any work is addressed to the public," he writes, "I must . . . [consider]
myself as a man in general, forget, if possible, my individual being and my peculiar
circumstances." "Every kind of composition, even the most poetical, is nothing
but a chain of propositions and reasonings; not always, indeed, the justest and
most exact, but still plausible and specious, however disguised by the colouring of
the imagination" (239–40). Here, in abstract detachment from the critic's own
particularity, the act of discriminating judgment finally takes form. Hume has
made a puzzling move for a philosopher who has rejected the illusory autonomy
of purely abstract cognition for an authoritative process of cultural judgment
within the constraints of custom. He drifts—or, perhaps better, is pulled—out of
custom and into the view from nowhere he has found "false" in principle.

Hume leaves implicit that his redefinition of aesthetic delicacy as a rare power
disqualifies even the most cultivated women from the public exercise of critical

judgment. Female delicacy may make women more capable of enjoying beauty, but only the labor of the male mind can make them understand why they should (or should not) enjoy it. They can, of course, participate in polite engagement with a canon, and indeed are indispensable to keeping the engagement polite; but they cannot become learned masters of the canon. And precisely because their intelligence is so naturally sociable, so immersed in immediate imaginative sympathy, they cannot detach themselves from their particular characters and circumstances—and hence cannot credibly pass judgment.

The Philosopher and the Countess

As late as 1770, when he was building his new house at St Andrew Square at age sixty, Hume wrote to a friend that "the taking of a Wife" was "the first . . . great Operation of human life," and that he still hoped to do so "in time." The remark may have been tongue-in-cheek, but there is reason to believe that over the previous years Hume had at least considered undertaking a serious courtship several times. Why didn't he? It was not because he was socially inept with women; he prided himself on being a favorite among the Edinburgh "ladies," who enjoyed his combination of simple good nature and gallant but often self-mocking wit. In the early years of his writing career he probably saw marriage as incompatible with his determination to remain independent. Aside from depriving him of the flexibility to work when he pleased, the obligation to support a family would have made it much harder to avoid the snares of clientage.

But these concerns leave us on the surface of Hume's fear of dependence. In January 1748, he reported to a friend that "the most extraordinary adventure in the world" had befallen the third earl of Marchmont, who had been "entirely employed in the severer studies." The widowed earl had fallen passionately in love with "a fair nymph," the teenage daughter of a bankrupt linen drapier, and she would soon be the countess of Marchmont. "They say many small fevers prevent a great one," Hume wrote; precisely because he had "always liked the persons & company of the fair sex," he "hope[d] to escape such ridiculous passions."[83] In his philosophy, of course, Hume had put constraints on abstract reasoning by grounding it in the passions. But the lead essay in his first essay volume—the one on "Delicacy of Taste and Passion"—was a warning against excessive "delicacy of passion," which brought a kind of "violent" enslavement, carrying its victim "beyond all bounds of prudence and discretion." One such enslavement—perhaps the most violent—was the erotic passion that had seized Marchmont. For Hume it threatened a loss of self-mastery and of the disciplined conduct that a serious life of work required, a collapse into bottomless indolence, so closely tied to effeminacy. When Hume wrote in "My Own Life" that the pursuit of "literature" had been "the ruling passion of [his] life," he meant to suggest that, in at least this one case, a dominating passion had been productive and admirable (xxxii). But his phrasing also intimated that the sovereignty of that passion was indivisible. The relentless self-discipline of writing could not coexist with an overpowering erotic "fever." And so, one might say, Hume's strategy was to spread the fever thin—to break it up into "small fevers"—by playing the lovable gallant with many women, in relationships that could grow into real friendships but, precisely because they occurred in a larger circle of polite sociability, would stop well short of the kind of emotional exclusivity and physical fixation that an unleashed need for sexual intimacy would demand.

In the twenty-six months he spent in Paris, from October 1763 to January 1766, this strategy may have momentarily collapsed, though, unlike Lord Marchmont's, Hume's passion (lust may not apply here) was for a woman far superior to him in social rank. In March 1761, from Paris, Marie-Charlotte-Hippolyte, Comtesse de Boufflers-Rouvera, sent Hume a remarkable letter—so remarkable that she admitted that she had long had "conflicting sentiments" about writing it, fearing that "the excess of [her] veneration for [his] attainment" would violate "prudence and propriety." She wrote as a female reader who had been transported by the reading of his *History*. Apologizing for her "presumption," she became virtually rapturous about Hume's "wonderful" gift of painting with "a grace, a naturalness, an energy surpassing the reaches of the imagination." It was almost as though she had read his little essay on the value of the study of history for women and had pitched her admiration accordingly. She requests that her letter be kept in "the most profound secrecy." But following her signature she adds that she has heard he has thought of coming to France and that she "may be able to help make [his] sojourn agreeable."[84] And so the letter has two registers: asking Hume, quite out of the blue, to enter a secret epistolary intimacy and inviting him, apparently as an afterthought, to enjoy the countess's hospitality in her own social world. Hume knew that she was not writing simply for herself; she spoke for many others in *le monde* and the intellectual circles of Paris who were eager to host this now celebrated British author.

The countess's marriage in 1746, at twenty-one, was anything but a love match; her husband was a cavalry captain who spent most of his time in the provinces. In 1752 she had become the mistress of the widowed prince de Conti, a prince of the blood and one of the wealthiest men in France, and she remained his friend and consort long after he had moved on to other mistresses. At the Temple, the prince's Paris residence, he had constructed, in the spacious grounds within the walls of a medieval Templar fortress, a modern building complex that included a town house for himself, a separate residence for his consort, a great assembly room, and a theater. The Temple was said to rival the king's residence in its lavish entertainments, and the countess, their guiding hand, was known as its "Idol." The couple periodically retired to L'Isle Adam, one of the prince's several chateaux, on an island in the Loire River just ten leagues east of the royal palace at Compiègne. It was a retreat from the city, but hardly a withdrawal from society. They were usually surrounded there by numerous guests, who were entertained with elaborate fêtes.

Though she was obviously a very public person, any attempt to portray the countess's character enters a marshland of spiteful rivalries and venomous gossip. Mme du Deffand—perhaps her greatest rival among the *salonnières*—judged her knowledgeable but utterly self-centered, with an "ethics . . . most austere, always mounted on high principles," which she liked to proclaim "like a flute which is pronouncing laws and delivering oracles."[85] Perhaps all that can be said with confidence is that she played her public role with extreme self-consciousness, regarding her relationship with the count as a "sacred" duty requiring irreproachable conduct even as, and perhaps because, she was uncomfortably aware that it was hard to reconcile her high-minded principles with the fact that she was, after all, a married woman.

The countess was one of the presiding figures of *mondanité*. This was *le monde* on a much larger scale than it had been in the seventeenth century, and arguably with greater diversity, offering more room to bourgeois wealth and to *philosophes* who had the requisite connections and, so long as they met the standards of politeness and *esprit*, were free to air their ideas with the powerful. But it remained dominated by the high aristocracy, which kept it closely tied to the court, where the most valued offices and other perquisites were to be secured. What mattered was "reputation," a highly competitive commodity exhibited in well-made marriages, in lavish but tasteful display, in the gracefully charming performance of social etiquette, in the presence of the most sought after guests, and, in some circles, in a capacity to engage in serious intellectual conversation.[86] The social aesthetic of play still reigned; in principle, the freedom to devote oneself entirely to entertainment was a unique form of honor reserved for those at the tip of the social pyramid, and any sign of serious work was considered inappropriate on most occasions. But *le monde* was also a big tent under which women as well as men could share their interests in belles lettres, including philosophy, and, with due caution, could discuss the political issues of the day. The countess was an "idol" in both these milieus. On Monday evenings, she and the prince presided over a supper for fifty to one hundred aristocratic guests in the Temple's assembly room, with the men arranged in ranks and the women sitting in a circle. But there was also a small weekly "Salon of the Four Mirrors," where the women served tea in the English fashion in lieu of servants, whose presence might have inhibited free conversation. On Friday evenings the countess customarily hosted a few select friends in her own residence. She had trained herself assiduously in the several personas such a position and its various skills required. "In society," one of her "Rules of Conduct" reads, "charm, ease, courteousness." "In discourse," another reads, "clarity, truth, and precision."[87] The countess was at once a consummate mistress of polite entertainment on a grand scale and a serious reader who relished intellectual exchange with the men of letters she admired. One of her other sobriquets was "the learned Minerva."

Hume reacted to the countess's invitation with mixed feelings. Despite the fact that his "principale Friendships" were in Scotland, he had written to Smith in July 1759; "it is too narrow a place for me," with too much animosity toward his radical views on religion. London was not an appealing alternative; he detested the haughtiness of its literary world, its prejudices against Scots, and above all the ferocity of its political partisanship. Paris he regarded as the center of civilization, "the Place in the World which I have always admird the most."[88] Under the sponsorship of the countess he would have access to the court as well as to the most brilliant salons. And yet, in a studiously gallant response to her invitation, he held her off. The state of war between their two counties, he explained, "sets at a distance" the prospect of his coming to Paris. When the countess made a gala visit to London in the spring of 1763, he stayed on a pleasure trip with friends in Scotland, though he apologized profusely for his absence. When he finally set sail for France in October 1763, six months after the signing of the peace ending the Seven Years War, he may be said to have fulfilled his implicit promise to the countess, but on his own terms. He had seized the opportunity to serve as secretary to the earl of Hertford, the new British ambassador to the court of France, having received assurances that his duties would not interfere with his literary life, and knowing that his official position would spare him from being regarded as a man seeking the patronage of "the Great" in Paris. The obstacle of the war aside, he had had reasons to be uneasy about entering a relationship with the countess and becoming her sponsored guest. He had had experience, of course, with women friends, but this was not an ordinary "polite" woman of the middle station, or indeed of the aristocracy. He continued to worry about his independence, knowing that in the intense competitiveness among *salonnières* a man of letters of his stature might be exhibited as a trophy.

In her invitation the countess had adroitly anticipated other possible sources of his unease. She had been reluctant, she assured him, to abandon "that reserve and privacy . . . more suitable to my sex." She realized that the "sublime qualities" she attributed to him were "far above the understanding of a woman." And yet, within those limits, she was an intellectually serious woman, able to appreciate "the clearness, the majesty, the touching simplicity" of Hume's "style," despite "the dissipated life one leads in this country"; "there are few good books in any language or in any genre that I have not read, either in the original or in translation."[89] She obviously was aware of British stereotypes of French society women—the *femme savante*, the shameless libertine—and knew how to counter them. In his initial responses, nervous about her adulation, Hume found it necessary to tamp down her expectations. He was a scholar from a remote country,

"more accustomed to a select society than to general companies."[90] He was head-
ing off the possibility that she would find him not a man of the world, but a bit of a
pedant.

Hume was entering a political minefield. The prince had gone into loyal opposition as one of the key figures in Anglophile circles, and as a supporter of the
parlements in their constitutional quarrels with the Crown. To judge by his surviving correspondence, Hume was largely oblivious to these fissures, though they
cut through the world that was fêting him. That is a measure of how important
the image of the never-failing civility of the French was to him as a reproach to
English partisan zealotry. Here too the countess's first letter had struck the right
note; she regretted that she did not have the eloquence to do justice to his "divine
impartiality" as an historian of England. But one of Hume's purposes in going to
Paris was to win international acclaim, and especially French acclaim, as a Scot
and for Scotland. He believed that Scotland, and not London, had become the
center of a great literary renascence, comparable to the French literary achievement under Louis XIV. Scots men of letters were outdoing the English in literary
English. He hoped that French critics would confirm that view.

In exceptional men who could evoke virtue with eloquent immediacy the
countess found confirmation of her own commitment, in principle, to moral recti-
tude. Bound to a life of performance under the public gaze of *mondanité*, she
needed an inner refuge, a kind of alternate world of sincerity and genuine intimacy of the heart. In *mondain* circles seventeenth-century classicism still had a
strong grip, but by the 1760s the literary culture of *sensibilité* was no less appealing. Since the summer of 1759 the countess and the prince had been protectors of
Rousseau. For the prince this was at least in part a political maneuver—a safe way
of thumbing his nose at the court, so long as he did not proceed too openly and
could hold the Citizen of Geneva within certain bounds of discretion. The countess found in Rousseau an intimate "friend," albeit a very prickly one. Like other
society women, she was driven by a certain discontent with the calculated maneuvering that the pursuit of reputation required, and with the superficiality of the
daily routines of politeness. To a degree, dealing with this recalcitrant man was an
exercise in self-reproach. Even as he took great satisfaction at being on seemingly
equal terms with great personages, Rousseau flailed their way of life and, professing horror at becoming dependent on the great, made them practically beg him to
accept their help. While the countess took pains not to make him feel dependent,
she made arrangements to protect him from his reckless and self-destructive
impulses. When his paranoia occasioned an ugly public exchange of accusations
with Hume in 1766, she was reluctant to condemn him, though she eventually
ceased communication.

With Hume the countess hoped to form something like the same kind of
friendship, a special bond with a man of genius who combined reason and virtue

with sublime eloquence and a sensitivity unusual for a man. Hume had entered a stage of his life when the amusements of *mondanité* were precisely what he wanted, though he was aware that he was indulging himself shamelessly in the adulation he encountered virtually everywhere. As early as 1756, at forty-five, Hume had spoken of the prospect of retiring to "some provincial town in France," where he could live off his earnings to date and "trifle out [his] old age . . . amidst a sociable people."[91] By 1762, when the sixth volume of the *History* appeared, he felt himself to be entering a state of retirement, though he was only in his early fifties and, despite his growing rotundity, was in good health. In a letter to David Mallet in November 1762, he described himself as very happy to be in the "indolent" and "idle" state of not writing and determined to remain in it, despite his friends' predictions that he would not be able to stay away from writing for long.[92] His practical reasons for not writing a final volume of the *History* may have been something of a dodge. The fact is that he was heartily sick of the partisan attacks on him, and, at a deeper level, he felt that, having accomplished his life's work both in philosophy and history, and having achieved the fame he had so wanted, he deserved a restful "old age," free of the goad of ambition and the labor of writing. In the decade between 1762 and 1772, the year he became gravely ill, he devoted most of his literary efforts to revising his essays and his philosophical *Enquiries* and preparing definitive editions. In France he found what he yearned for: the opportunity to spend his remaining years studying for the sheer pleasure of it, with ample time for the quiet solitude of reading and for intellectual exchanges, both integral to a life of refined leisure.

For his first several months in Paris, the pleasures of such leisure were precisely what Hume reveled in. To Smith he reported at the end of October that he "retain[ed] a Relish for no kind of Flattery but that which comes from the [great] Ladies."[93] "No body ever led a more dissipated Life than I do here," he wrote to Andrew Millar two months later. As late as April 26, 1764, he wrote Blair that, now that he was "A Man in Vogue," there could be no doubt of his gift for "Gallantry and Gaiety" with the ladies.[94] He would probably spend the rest of his life in Paris. "Do you not think it happy for me," he asked, "to retain such a Taste for Idleness and Follies at my Years?" He only wished some of his "old Friends" could join him in the amusements, "tho' I know none of them that can on occasion be so thoroughly idle as myself."[95] The letters have more than a little self-mockery; Hume was well aware that there was something ridiculous about the fuss being made over him. His irony has a soupçon of guilt about plunging into "dissipation" and "idleness," a word he had earlier used to distinguish inexcusable laziness from productive manly industry. But there is also an underlying theme of defiance; Hume was flaunting his liberation from the ethos of "industry" to which his Scottish friends were so committed. He would not be contrite, and his friends, however alarmed they might be, would have to make the most of it.

From December onward, as he began to tire of the large "companies" at court, and as he became involved in the life of the Temple and spent time alone with the countess there and at L'Isle Adam, their relationship evolved rapidly. The protocols of gallantry gave way to assurances of intimate friendship and they tried to make verbal rituals serve an intimacy that had become emotionally, if not erotically, charged. In his letters to her in the summer of 1764, when he was a guest of the court at Compiègne and she was at L'Isle Adam, he began to express the depth of his feelings, but cautiously, with protective irony. At Compiègne, he wrote her, he had "given [himself] up almost entirely to study and retreat," to which he returned "as it were [his] natural element." He imagined her doing the same, as she too had resolved "to tie the broken thread of [her] studies and literary amusements," and wished they could share their thoughts "for half an hour a day." But he remained determined, he told her only half seriously, to shake himself loose from her spell.[96] In her response the countess acknowledged his spell, which had had the effect of making her confront her alienation from her own world. "Your coming here," she wrote, "only gave me distaste for most of the people I have to live with." She regretted that when he left Paris, as he inevitably would, books would not replace him:

> The worst of it is that I cannot limit myself to a simple esteem or a cold admiration. As soon as these sentiments are aroused in me, my sensibility is touched and my affections engaged, with the result that I suffer real sorrow when circumstances bring about separation from those who have merited such progress over my heart. . . . In truth I am afraid that my reflection, and my prudence, are not useless to me at present so far as you are concerned . . . for today I permit myself to assure you that I love you with all my heart.[97]

With whatever implicit restrictions, they had admitted that their attachment, though still grounded in friendship, was now spilling over its boundaries. At this point, Hume's frustration with the fact that Conti monopolized so much of the countess's time surfaced. It was not simply, he explained with a calculated air of detachment, that, now that he had reached "a time of life when [he could] less expect to please," "common sense" required him to "keep at a distance from all attachments that can imply passion." "It must surely be the height of folly to lay myself at the mercy of a person whose situation seems calculated to inspire doubt, and who, being so little at her own disposal, could not be able, even if willing, to seek such remedies as might appease, that tormenting sentiment." Clearly a half hour a day was not enough. This time Hume did not fear, as we might have expected, that a "ruling passion" for a woman would dissipate his work discipline. He wanted to satisfy a passion that might not rule him but was certainly driven by an intense need, if only by spending long hours with the countess. He clarified his stance ambiguously. Though he sometimes entertained "the chimerical project of relaxing the severities of study, by the society of a person dear to me, and who could have indulgence for me," he took comfort in being "a person free as the air we breathe," and in knowing that "wherever such a blessing might present itself, [he] could there fix [his] habitation." He was at once threatening to leave Paris and withdraw into studious solitude and admitting that that was not at all what he wanted.[98]

The countess responded that she did not see why she must choose as he wished. Her devotion to the prince was unselfish and "sacred," "the most pleasing of sentiments, the foundation and the support of all the others." But her duties did "not absorb [her] wholly; they [left her] in [her] heart for other sentiments, and [she was] able to command the greater part of [her] time and give it [him]."[99] In his response Hume doubted that she could fulfill that promise, though their circumstances might "alter." And then he assured her of his devotion; "You have saved me from a total indifference towards every thing in human life. I was falling very fast into that state of mind, and it is perhaps worse than even the inquietudes of the most unfortunate passion."[100] What the countess took from the letter was his stubbornly unreasonable demand on her, and she responded with bitter cynicism. Surely he did not want to confirm her "in the idea which I hold, that your sex like to be handled roughly":

> For to confess to you my opinion of men, the majority seem to me to have servile souls. One can be seduced by them, but one can scarcely, it seems to me, esteem them. . . . Sometimes it is discernment that they lack, sometimes delicacy, and almost always generosity. . . . For you towards whom love bore me as a consequence of esteem, you, I separate from this crowd of slaves, and I attribute to you an entirely different character.[101]

The countess threatens here to trivialize their relationship by relegating Hume to the culture of gallantry and its sugarcoated power games. We see, from the woman's standpoint, the cynical, alienating side of that culture. Gallantry was not a matter of men obligingly feigning intellectual equality with women, as Hume had described it in his essay on the rise and progress of the arts and sciences. It was a matter of women having to hide their contempt for men's inadequacies, for their petty egos, their selfish weakness, their obtuseness. The prince was a rare exception, and so might Hume be, if only he could rein in his expectations. Hume responded with an abject retreat, perhaps the most passionate letter he ever wrote. Though in everything else she had unlimited control over him, nothing she could do would prevent him from being her friend. He realized, he wrote, that he was tempting her "to tyrannize over [him], in order to try how far [he] will practice [his] doctrine of passive obedience." He was willing to be her "slave," and surely did not deserve her contempt for that.[102]

This surrender is all the more remarkable in view of the fact that at the beginning of the letter of July 6, 1764, the countess had humiliated Hume on a matter of great importance to him. In the summer of 1764 they had made a secret pact: he would tutor her in philosophy, and she would tutor him in taste. He asked for her judgment of a play titled *Douglas*, written by his nephew John Home, which Hume had been ardently promoting for the past decade. It was an emphatically Scottish tragedy set in ancient times, with a young and valiant hero, Norval, who was abandoned as a child, returning disguised as a shepherd to his birthplace and his mother Lady Randolph. Hume and his Edinburgh friends had high hopes that the play would be acclaimed as a rebuke to the usual shoddy fare on London stages; it might even provide the momentum to launch a Scottish national theater. If they were confident of the play's genius, they also felt compelled to help Home polish its rough edges. The stage performances left audiences in tears and, as a bonus to Hume, provoked a staunch condemnation of stage plays by the orthodox clergy. Now Hume wanted the imprimatur of the countess, probably in the hope that she would recommend the play to critics in Paris who would confirm, for an international readership, its great promise.

The countess began her comments on the play by acknowledging Hume as her "master of philosophy and ethics." Now she wanted to make him her "disciple," on "a genre in which speculation does not exceed the very limited capacity of us poor women." She proceeded to tear the play apart. She took offense at the character of Lady Randolph, perhaps alluding to her own efforts to maintain an unsullied reputation in a labyrinth of scandal. Lord Randolph, she wrote, "has such a good opinion of women that he believes immediately (in truth, from a letter) that his wife, after twenty years of irreproachable virtue, has instantly fallen madly in love with a young villager of whom she could be the mother." And how could the Lady "ignore the fact that for a woman it does not suffice to be innocent, that it is also necessary that appearances are favorable to her"? Her other criticisms were about style and structure. The play confirmed for her that "the tragic muse will never establish itself on [Hume's] island." Shakespeare was indeed a genius, and his "faults" could be excused by his "ignorance" and his "century." There was no excuse for the "extravagant" performances of his successors. In this case "the pathetic (one encounters it sometimes) is in the verse and not in the subject." Scenes designed to move her to tears had had no effect on her. And the plot, "puerile" throughout, had no denouement; "the piece finishes" simply "because everyone dies."[103]

Hume's reply was repentant. He knew that he had disappointed her—that her "verdict," as he called it, was not just on the play, but on the deficiencies of his own taste. He acknowledged that most of the criticisms were "well-founded," and enlarged on them. Still, he hoped she would read the play again, since he remained convinced that it was "a work of merit, from the sensible pathetic which runs through the whole." And he questioned her severely analytical approach to it; "The value of a theatrical production can less be determined by an analysis of its content, than by the ascendant which it gains over the heart, and by the strokes of nature which are interspersed through it." He acknowledged, though, that on a second reading she might not change her mind: "Your nation, your sex, and, above all, the peculiar delicacy of your taste, give you a title to pronounce on these subjects."[104]

The exchange about *Douglas* has little or no literary significance, but its negotiation across the gender line is an ironic sequel to Hume's thinking in "Of the Standard of Taste" about pleasure and authority, delicacy of sentiment and soundness of reason. The countess had obviously been groomed in French classicism; for all her Anglophilia, she had no doubt that in the seventeenth century France had earned the right to be Europe's arbiter of taste—and that Shakespeare, for all his natural genius, was no Racine. Even as her feminine persona precluded any claim to be the kind of learned critic Hume had envisioned in his essay, she based her judgment precisely on the logic of a canon—a pantheon of time-tested works—that Hume had advocated. More striking, there is a sense in which she in effect echoed Hume's argument that the critic must also judge the work with a certain analytical detachment, testing it by reducing it to the abstractions of "a chain of propositions and reasoning." In *Douglas* there was no chain of reasoning; the characters acted nonsensically, and then everybody died. Hume gave priority to the emotional power of the composition, which is to say that, like Du Bos, he (though a great admirer of Racine) made affective pleasure the key to aesthetic value. In conceding to the countess female delicacy of taste, even as it took the form of analytical judgment, he might be said to have refeminized, within the prevailing gender distinctions, the delicacy of taste he had masculinized in the essay. It would be easy enough to pronounce Hume guilty of self-contradiction, and even of hypocrisy, in his efforts to take issue, very tentatively, with the countess without alienating her. It could be, though, that he meant what he said. He may now have expressed a sentiment that, in his preoccupation in the essay with dispelling the specter of aesthetic relativism, he had had to suppress to make credible his endowment of the rare critic—the male critic—with authoritative judgment.

In mid-August a petty quarrel occasioned more declarations of devotion. The countess, it seems, had committed a small and uncharacteristic indiscretion in Hume's quarrel with Alexander Murray, one of her Scots cousins. Hume's letter of August 18 begins with a sharp rebuke, but then describes the anguish of being "very angry" with "the person whom we passionately love." Satisfied by her explanation of the incident, he apologized profusely and "beseech[ed]" her to "continue to like me a little: for otherwise I shall not be able in a little time to endure myself."[105] Convinced of "the sincerity of [his] affection," she acknowledged that he had "acquired complete ascendancy over [her]."[106] They seemed to have reached a modus vivendi, however shaky; they would be far more than friends, though not lovers. In the four days Hume spent with the countess at L'Isle Adam in early October, their intimacy came closer to crashing through that distinction.

But then the unforeseen occurred, and for both of them it entirely altered the situation. The countess's husband died, freeing her to marry again. As Hume immediately realized, the countess was now bent on reaping the deserved reward for years of devoted service, for herself and for her son. The prince, after all, was the only other man of true character in her life; hence she could have no qualms about legitimizing beyond question her position at the summit of *le monde* by marrying him. Nothing, Hume knew, would deflect her from the pursuit of that goal. At first he was bitter about being neglected, and his gallantry turned frosty and wounding. When the countess returned to Paris on the coming Saturday, he wrote her, "I hope that your etiquette, which allows you to receive relations and particular friends, opens a wide-enough door for my admission."[107] She had fallen back, he was telling her, into the false world from which he had rescued her. Soon he accepted the only role he could assume: the devoted confidante, counseling her as best he could, even ready to mediate with the prince, but waiting for an opportunity to pull her away from him. On December 10, 1764, he wrote her a long letter of advice, summing up what he had already told her in conversations. It is unusually revealing of the ideal of friendship and sociability, part Scottish and part French, he hoped to realize with the countess. Hume began by assuring the countess that he understood her determination to escape, through marriage, "a state little befitting [her] worth and merit." But the prince, who was by breeding a man "covetous of honour," could not marry a woman lacking his royal lineage. Without causing a "rupture," she should "gradually diminish" her connection with the prince and "betake [herself] to a private, and sociable, and independent life at Paris." It would be "an exchange of tranquility for luster," and it would restore the "former tone" of her "temper" as well as her health. She need not fear that "the dignity of [her] character [would]," "in the eyes of the world," lose "its luster." Men would see that she "set the just price upon [her] liberty," and that, "however the passions of youth may have seduced [her], [she would] not now sacrifice all [her] time, where [she is] not deemed worthy of every honour." He knew he was proposing something she was likely to find preposterous:

> And why should you think with reluctance on a private life at Paris? It is the situation for which I thought you best fitted, ever since I had the happiness of your acquaintance. The inexpressible and delicate graces of your character and conversation, like the soft notes of a lute, are lost amid the tumult of company. . . . A more select society would know to set a

juster value on your merit. Men of sense, and taste, and honour, and letters, would accustom themselves to frequent your house.[108]

Hume wanted to reproduce, in the more cosmopolitan and aristocratic setting of Paris, the "narrow circle" of true friends, bound in tasteful intimacy, he had claimed to find in the middle station in Edinburgh. The difference was that the reigning presence would be a countess who could fuse the social aesthetic of play with substantive intellectual conversation, a kind of leisure that was serious but in no need of manly "industry" to justify itself. The countess would at once nourish his mind and spare him the severe and punishing study to which he had devoted so much of his life. What Hume could not accept, and perhaps could not understand, is that, while he was eager to give up his writer's life of work, she could not give up her life of *mondanité*. At stake was not simply whether her service to the prince would be justly rewarded, or whether her role would now be morally validated. To say that as the prince's consort the countess had a profession would be absurdly anachronistic. This was still a world that held itself above labor. But her devotion to him was a vocation for which she had formed herself as a social being over many years. She could not retreat into the "private" life Hume evoked because she could not give up her vocation without losing her character and indeed her sense of self. She had been shaped by a world of reputation in which being a private person was not a guarantor of independence. It was the equivalent of being no one.

Meanwhile Hume's friends in Edinburgh, reading his letters and hearing the rumors flowing across the Channel, had become worried that he was being corrupted by the Parisian world of amusement and particularly by the countess. His old friend Gilbert Elliott, who had been in Paris that August, perhaps spoke for Hume's other Scots friends in warning him that he was "standing on the very brink of a precipiece." "Love the French as much as you will," he had counseled, "but above all continue still an Englishman."[109] Calling Hume an Englishman was obtuse; he reacted by lashing out at the English, drawing on all the grievances built up over the years, and vehemently denying that he, a Scot who had suffered much at their hands, owed them anything. The fact was that the English would not allow Scots to be English. "I am a Citizen of the World," Hume declared; and if he were to "adopt any Country," it would be France.[110] It was a heartfelt tirade, but it also allowed Hume to ignore Elliott's unstated but obvious reference to his relationship with the countess.

In a letter dated September 5, 1765, Hume asked Adam Smith, his closest friend, who was in France but had not yet reached Paris, for his "judgment" about where he should settle. He was inclined to remain in Paris, but worried that "Offers" that would make his life "agreeable" there "might encroach on [his] Independence, by making [him] enter into Engagements with Princes & great

Lords & Ladies."[111] He could not imagine enjoying the ease he needed at this stage of his life without forfeiting the independence that hard work guaranteed a man of his station. Apparently Hume had not sought Smith's advice as he was deciding, two years earlier, whether to go to Paris. Perhaps he had feared that Smith would marshal arguments against the trip that he could not ignore. That is precisely what Smith did now. Zeroing in on Hume's fear of dependence, Smith's letter was meant to give him a cold splash of reality, evoking an image of *le monde* that had been forming in British culture for nearly a century:

> Notwithstanding the boasted humanity and politeness of [the French], they appear to me to be, in general, more meanly interested, and that the cordiality of their friendship is much less to be depended on than that of our own countrymen. They live in such large societies and their affections are dissipated among so great a variety of objects, that they can bestow but a very small share of them on any individual. Do not imagine that the great Princes and Ladies who want you to live with them make this proposal with real and sincere affection to you. They mean nothing but to satisfy their own vanity by having an illustrious man in their house.[112]

To an extent Hume was armed against Smith's verdict on *le monde*. In his essays and his correspondence he had, after all, gone against the grain of British (including Scottish) moralism by extolling the unrivalled taste and the harmony that reigned in Paris. But over two decades earlier Hume, like Smith now, had distinguished between the merely instrumental friendships of "the Great" and the real friendships—friendships built on and fostering independence—in the middle station. His relationship with the countess had made Hume aware that, contra Smith, the psychic costs of the competition for reputation in *le monde* heightened the need for an intimate and even passionate private life; and that, at least for the ladies among the great, friendships with illustrious commoners like himself were impelled by real esteem and affection, and not just vanity. But at this moment Smith's warning may have had a stronger purchase on him.

If he responded to Smith, the letter has not survived. In any case, it became obvious that fall that the countess would persist in her campaign, whatever emotional and physical cost it might exact. Faced with the prince's gracious but implacable refusal to marry her, she fought against bitterness and returned to being the friend and consort who gave the needed female direction and luster to his relentless public life. In January 1766 Hume finally left Paris for London and thence, in August 1769, for Edinburgh.

Chapter 7

Genius and the Social: Antoine-Léonard Thomas and Suzanne Curchod Necker

On August 25, 1770, Antoine-Léonard Thomas delivered the first part of an address on "the character, the mores and the intelligence (*l'esprit*) of women in different centuries" before a public audience at the French Academy. The entire address was published as an *Essay* in 1772 and as part of Thomas's *Essay on Eulogies* a year later.[1] An obscure figure now, Thomas was one of the most acclaimed authors of the French High Enlightenment, a "genius" in the new meanings the term acquired in the second half of the eighteenth century, and, in the wake of Rousseau, that marvel of a commercialized print culture, the "celebrity." In the 1760s the academy's patriotic eulogies of great men had become major events in the life of literary Paris and the overlapping circles of *le monde*, and Thomas was the acknowledged master of the genre.[2] His *Essay* and its reception allow us to gauge what had changed since our point of departure, the seventeenth-century intersection of Parisian literary culture and *mondanité*. Almost a century had passed since Poullain de la Barre, an admirer of the *honnête femme*, had published *On the Equality of the Two Sexes* and Malebranche had begun his denunciation of *mondanité* in *The Search After Truth*.

Despite the praise that had been lavished on Thomas as "the Plutarch of France" and "the Cato of the Century," the critics of the *Essay* drowned out the admirers.[3] The antiphilosophe party denounced it as another coup by the "sect" of philosophes, paying tribute to certain salon women who had coddled them. The circle of men and women associated with the *Encyclopédie* seemed to have taken another step in the corruption of French society by the fashionable "philosophical spirit."[4] The reaction was not entirely paranoid; Thomas's appointment to the French Academy in 1767 *had* been a victory for the philosophes and their supporters. And yet the philosophes themselves—Denis Diderot, Friedrich Melchior Grimm, Louise d'Épinay, and others—were even more dismissive of the *Essay*. Aside from the pedantic monotony of its prose, they complained, the essay left the reader, in d'Épinay's words, "not know(ing) what the author thinks, and whether his opinion on women is other than the received opinions."⁵ The modern reader is likely to agree; the essay abounds in puzzling compounds of discourses that would seem to resist commingling.⁶

For the historian Thomas's confusion is something of a blessing. The value of his essay lies precisely in its equivocations and the mixed reactions they provoked in print and private letters. In the text itself and the brief *querelle* it occasioned we have a high-resolution snapshot of the recognizably modern topography of gender discourses forming in France on the eve of the revolution. It took the revolution itself, of course, to break certain silences at what we now consider the feminist end of the spectrum. In the 1770s it still seemed virtually impossible to entertain publicly the prospect of women exercising active rights of citizenship. And yet the basic logic of gender equality was being articulated, quite rarely in print but more commonly in private conversations and correspondence.

My aim here, though, is not to sight anticipations or breakthroughs retrospectively. I want to understand how the discursive field that formed in France in the third quarter of the eighteenth century at once reflected and changed gender logics we have been tracing over a century or more. The central thread of the story remains the opposition between manly intellectual labor and the *aisance* of a social aesthetic of play, the apparent effortlessness that still figured in aristocratic circles as the emblem of a unique social honor, embodied in the *honnête femme*, but, in a widening culture of letters, was now indicted as the most telling symptom of corrupting effeminacy. Among men of letters the conviction was spreading that concentrated and sustained intellectual labor should be the sine qua non underpinning critical authority in matters of taste. The dichotomy between labor and *aisance* still operated within configurations of the discourses we have traced: republican virtue and corruption, Augustinian moral rigorism, Stoicism, sensibility. It still played a role in estimations of a variety of literary genres and styles: the philosophical treatise, the dialogue, the polite essay, including the essay in literary criticism, the published letter, and now the patriotic eulogy that became so popular in France from midcentury onward. As they had been for the past century, two social practices, gallantry and friendship, were sites of contention and rapprochement in discussions of gender.

In France, however, the larger framework for these configurations changed from the midcentury onward under the impact of three new cultural developments. Extolling the "*nation*" became something of a requirement for serious authors.⁷ It rarely took the form of an open assault on the aristocracy's political supremacy, but frequent moralizing about a decadent aristocracy implied a radical questioning of its cultural authority and, by extension, its moral authority, to which the nobility had to respond with reformulated conceptions of merit and patriotic virtue.⁸ A pivotal step in this direction was the French Academy's decision in 1758, under the leadership of its permanent secretary Charles Pinot Duclos, to shift the themes for its prizes in eloquence and poetry from doctrinally grounded moral lessons and encomiums to the king to patriotic eulogies of "the celebrated men of the nation." The intent, Jean Le Ronde d'Alembert would recall, was to find figures "in all the estates and in all talents, from the warrior to the philosopher [and] simple men of letters." By publicly venerating such people the academy would "fulfill (*remplir*) the wishes of the Nation."[9] This was the rhetorical agenda Thomas made his own and realized with unique success. Inseparable from it was the new assertiveness of "men of letters" as the voice and conscience of the nation, the supreme embodiment of an ideal of patriotic virtue in which the true mark of nobility was "utility," not lineage. The exemplar was the orator of the ancient polis, whose sublime eloquence transcended mere rhetoric; the printed word could be a virtual oratory following this classical model.[10] Ironically this reconception of the Republic of Letters as a national clerisy, bonded rhetorically with a nationwide audience of readers, found its most ardent expression in the cult of the manly genius laboring in solitude. It was an atmosphere in which educated women aspiring to engage seriously in intellectual life and to be recognized as authors had to proceed cautiously, even as in private they asserted their right to do so.

Recent readings of the *Essay* on women have largely ignored an obvious biographical fact, one I find essential to understanding it. "In this century, and even in this capital," Thomas wrote toward the end of his essay, "there are [several] women who combine a truly cultivated reason with a strong soul, and who by these virtues heighten (*relevant*) their sentiments and their honor" (158). It was common knowledge that the inspiration for this tribute was Suzanne Curchod Necker, wife of the Genevan financier. She and Thomas had become close friends sometime in the mid-1760s, soon after she had started what would be the last great salon of the old regime, featuring, among others, Jean-François Marmontel, Georges-Louis Leclerc, Comte de Buffon, Denis Diderot, Friedrich Melchior Grimm, André Morellet, Jean Le Rond d'Alembert, the abbé Guillaume-Thomas Raynal, and of course Thomas. The friendship between Thomas and Necker, as they conceived it and practiced it, will be our main angle of approach to the *Essay*. It lies behind Thomas's equivocation in the *Essay* on the fundamental question whether gender differences were due to nature or environment. From the alienation the friends shared, and from the ideas that bonded them, we learn why the cult of genius had such purchase and why, in their hands, it placed so much emphasis on solitary and relentless labor. All this was intertwined with a disagreement with Diderot and others about friendship itself, conducted along the wavering line between the demands of manliness and the stigma of effeminacy.

Friends

Sometime in early 1771 Voltaire received a poem on "the happiness of wisdom" from Mlle Mariette Moreaud, the nineteen-year-old daughter of a wigmaker in La Rochelle. He was charmed by it and told her so in a letter. News of this female literary prodigy in a distant provincial town who had won the imprimatur of the doyen of the French Enlightenment soon spread through literary circles in Paris.[11] Among the men of letters Mlle Moreaud contacted to express enthusiasm for their work was Thomas. If he seeks something more than conventional friendship, he tells her in the first of his surviving letters (none of her letters to him survived), dated May 10, 1766, the blame lies with her precious sensibility. Mlle Moreaud apparently objected to the flirtatious note. In his next letter (May 31, 1766), Thomas imagined that he and she already formed a union of "sensible souls" who "[live] by sentiment," and added that despite his inclination to solitude he too treasured the happiness of family life. He appealed to her sympathy; unlike her he was, at age thirty, plagued with bad health, a theme that would carry through the correspondence.[12]

She might find it necessary to regard their epistolary discovery of each other as no more than a friendship, he wrote her in June, but he preferred the word "union," which "expresses better this melding of two souls who search for each other." It was actually a blessing, he assured her, that they could not see each other face to face. It was better that he just saw her "soul."[13] In a letter dated October 8, 1766, he tried to counteract her timidity about talking about herself. The two of them were among the few people who could despise "cold conventions of pride" and "abandon" themselves naturally in friendship. Surely it should not always be necessary to represent yourself, "to not be oneself, as if one did not wish at all to exist." He elaborated: life among the "corrupted and frivolous people" of Paris withers the soul more than it preserves it; he has to see people he does not love, make boring visits; to appear often in "societies where everything is said to the mind (*esprit*) and nothing to the soul." When he returned home, discontented with others and with himself, he consoled himself alone or with a friend and "redefine[d] his soul in writing to her."[14]

In the fall of 1766 and the winter of 1767, as Thomas's letters to Mlle Moreaud became less frequent, he apologized for not writing, pleading that he was overwhelmed with work and that his recurrent depression made writing impossible for months at a time. Her soul recalled him to life from a feeling of "nothingness," he wrote on February 7, 1769, after an apparent silence of fifteen months. He found himself cut off from the external referents of language, the objects that occasion its creative use. He offered her extended advice on the literary career she should pursue to win the attention of modern readers, who were so easily distracted. If she offered a poetry that was "philosophical" and "strong," she would ascend to a rank far above all the other women who had written verse. Responding to her objection that she did not want to be stigmatized as a philosophical woman, he insisted that philosophical was precisely what she should be. She would excel not only by feeling much, but also by thinking deeply. She had the rare gift of being able to render philosophical abstractions into powerful images. He wanted her to become "the Pope of her sex."[15]

For the most part Thomas's letters to Mlle Moreaud are a banal rhetorical performance of a rarified, febrile ideal of friendship between a man and a woman, an ideal in which in principle performance had no place. The rhetoric subsumed psychological particularity under an aspiration to a kind of spiritual communion of sentiment. Unattainable in everyday social relations, transparency may have been practiced most safely and with the least inhibition under the condition of epistolary distance. One of its foils was the falseness of gallantry, though it was not without its flirtatious subtext, even when, as in Thomas's second letter, there was an avowed denial of flirtation. The "union" of "souls" had its erotically suggestive base chords. In principle, though, union evoked the purity of an incorporeal communion, free of the asymmetrical power and the unequal dependence that erotic desire intruded into intimacy.

And yet Thomas's letters to the young lady reveal more than the usual rhetorical play. We begin to see the role that disaffection with the society and culture of *mondanité* played in making spiritualized friendship so appealing. Such relationships invited scandal, of course, but they also offered a quiet escape into shared solitude. In the end we find that Thomas's flattery was not as conventional as it might at first appear to be. At times, to be sure, the tone of his letters exemplifies the condescension of what has aptly been called Enlightenment gallantry, the patronizing deference on the part of men who had no doubt of their own intellectual superiority.[16] In fact in the letters we see how easily such deference found a new idiom in the literary language of sensibility. The equality implied by "union" rests uneasily with the tutorial role Thomas assumes as he gives the young lady several extended lectures on Descartes and Leibniz. But Thomas's paternalism makes it all the more startling that he urges his potential protégé to become the Pope of her sex. If his tutoring had been more conventional, he would have advised her to write books on education, or uplifting novels for young women, or charming verse in the female voice. Instead he chose Alexander Pope, a fixture in an emerging canon of great modern authors, celebrated as the philosophical poet par excellence. Thomas did not expect Mlle Moreaud to become an original philosopher; her gift lay in making difficult philosophy accessible in figurative language. But by assuming that she could grasp and communicate the abstractions of philosophy, Thomas attributed intellectual capacities to her that were still almost universally denied women. He may have been flattering her shamelessly, but for our purposes that hardly matters. In his advice to Mlle Moreaud we see

Thomas's ideal of a female author, and it is quite unusual in the intellectual range and public scope it allows her.

By the time Thomas wrote his last letter to Mlle Moreaud, he probably no longer needed her epistolary friendship. As his life in Paris became "more and more solitary," Thomas recalled, he spent virtually all his time in his own home and Mme Necker's. It was in private retreat, with Necker sometimes visiting him, and not in salon company, that the friendship had developed. Their "opinions, ideas, sentiments" were in perfect accord, and Necker "inspired [Thomas] with still more contempt for all that [he] disdained or [could] not endure."[17] On December 28, 1768, Thomas described his relationship with Necker to his friend Nicolas Barthe:

> You know how I love her and I believe that her soul is made for mine, I never go there without pleasure and I never leave there without regret; but this is a sweet sentiment which occupies me without agitating me, it is not at all like that other woman whom I have not yet seen again at all, and whom I did not see for so long a time only to be tormented; the sentiment that she inspired in me was a continual storm. I hope that I will see her less, or that I will be happier in seeing her.[18]

The need to exclude agitation was mutual. Necker had probably made it clear early in their relationship that for her marital infidelity was unthinkable. There was surely an element of calculation in this; she would do nothing that might cause her husband scandal and damage his career. But she also thought of a woman's devotion to her husband as a voluntary exercise of her duty to God. The couple freely exhibited their mutual admiration in company, to the annoyance of their more cynical guests. As for Thomas, we know from his letters to Barthe that, epistolary flirtation aside, he saw sexual pleasure as a distraction from his ambitions, a drain on his capacity to work. When "you let yourself be softened by women," he had written Barthe, "the soul is enervated with the body"—and "the genius [loses] this male pride and this enthusiasm which is its character." His language evokes the usual specter of effeminacy in civic humanism: the loss of work discipline under the softening hand of women, the smothering of intellectual and spiritual energy by the indolent pleasures of luxury. The only exception to sexual asceticism, he told Barthe, was the pleasure of a truly "passionate" love,[19] but he seems to have been relieved that that was precisely what Necker would not allow. Like Hume before he met the Countess de Boufflers, Thomas needed guarded tranquility to pursue ambition. Industry allowed no inner storm.

It was an unusual friendship, an affinity of great power despite the friends' obvious differences in background and in rank. Even as they practiced the performative rituals and maneuvers of *mondanité*, they were, in the privacy of their interior lives and the intimacy of their friendship, profoundly estranged from that world. It was above all this conflicted self-consciousness that bonded them. How it related to their chronic physical problems cannot be determined with any precision, though it seems clear that they both used their sense of themselves as victims of weak and hypersensitive physical constitutions to keep *mondain* social demands at arm's length and even to censure *mondain* performance implicitly with a counterperformance of passive resistance, the withholding of the suffering body.[20] Nor can we be precise about how their estrangement drew on or contributed to the recurrent bouts of depression they confided to each other, those descents into an existential anxiety, a sense of inner nothingness that made them indifferent to everything. If the root origins of their physical and psychic syndrome cannot be traced, however, its cultural expression is quite legible, as it drew on the discursive resources available to them and their contemporaries. Not surprisingly, Rousseau has a large presence, though they both had reservations about him as an author and as a person. It was above all in Rousseau's writings in the 1750s and early 1760s that the moral critique that *mondanité* had engendered within itself, like an undertow, since the seventeenth century found a powerful new rhetorical expression. In the impassioned righteousness of a man who in principle turned his back on *le monde*, Necker and Thomas found a voice for their estrangement within it. Theirs was, one might say, *mondanité* with a dark Rousseauian shadow.

"Rarely," Mme Necker observed in one of her journal entries, can one "hazard . . . speaking one's intimate sentiment"; but such moments were so much more "piquant" and "new" than "the language used in *le monde* . . . which is only the superficial surface of thought."[21] The historian cannot help wishing she could have been a fly on the wall listening to the many private conversations in which Thomas and Necker drew on their shared estrangement to build this bond of intimate sentiment. Committed to high intellectual seriousness, they were dismissive of the abuse of rational intelligence in superficial and excessively nimble wit. At the same time, they held themselves apart from what they saw as the false sensibility that had entered *mondain* sociability.[22] In a tribute to Mme Geoffrin, Necker's mentor as a *salonnière*, Thomas described her as "a character to herself, a merit so rare in *le monde*," who in sociability, unlike the intimacy of friendship, took care to avoid "all lively emotions." Thomas's praise for Geoffrin was a reproach to *sensibilité* à *la mode*. If false sensibility was melodramatically gushy, its opposite might be worse; in the essay on eulogies Thomas derided the "hypocrites of sensibility . . . [who] speak icily (*glacé*) of their tender friendship . . . and vaunt their profound sorrow with a motionless visage."[23] He and Necker had clearly reached this verdict together. Necker spoke and wrote to Thomas of the "affectation of *sensibilité* being carried to a peak" in their era, particularly among women.[24] To her, Rousseau's emotional self-revelation was uniquely authentic,

but in the novels and conversation that attempted to emulate him it was becoming a mere fashion, absorbed into and coopted by the *mondain* imperatives to
perform, to impress others.[25] Ironically the friends saw the new eagerness to
exhibit feeling in company not as a liberation from the constraints of politeness,
but as a new phase in the *mondain* affectation of the natural and the spontaneous.

This reaction makes it all the more significant that in the *Essay* Thomas nonetheless classified friendship with love; they were both "virtues of sensibility"
involving "the affectionate and sweet passions" (120). The choice of adjectives is
his first signal that, despite his reverence for civic virtue, he will not advocate an
ideal of friendship rooted in Aristotelian virtue ethics. Typical of the tortuousness
of the *Essay* as a whole, the discussion of friendship registers the tensions in
Thomas's efforts to articulate what he found in his friendship with Necker, at
least when he was not in mute self-withdrawal. He imagines a conversation with
Montaigne, whom he reproaches for "doing little justice to women" (120). Readers would have recognized the aptness of his choice of interlocutors. One of
the features of Montaigne's essays that made them an odd model for the polite
conversational essay was his bluntly expressed animus toward women, and particularly his belief that there could be no true friendship between men and women.
Thomas begins by suggesting to Montaigne that there is something contradictory
about his position, listing the reasons that men have less inclination or need than
women for the sweet joy of friendship. Men are more occupied and distracted,
and more free (*libre*); they are more capable of expanding their ideas at a high
level and deploying all their sentiments; in all their occupations they are more
conscious of their powers. Women are weaker and have more need of support;
they have secret sorrows of the soul they yearn to share; they are almost always
forced to play a role in the world and hide sentiments and ideas that weigh on
them; they value persons rather than things. Precisely for these reasons women
"would seem to have to feel more forcefully the liberty and the pleasure of a secret
commerce, and the sweet confidences that friendship gives and receives" (121).

Montaigne takes this to be an argument "from Nature," though in fact it can
as easily be read as an argument from social conditions. Becoming a kind of
surrogate for Rousseau, he responds that women must be judged by "the society
of the great cities"; and he asks whether the "frivolous and vain . . . desire to
please" does not "desiccate their soul" and "extinguish in part their sensibility
itself," and whether constant flattery does not render them incapable of "subordinating themselves to those sacrifices day by day, and to that happy equality, that
friendship imposes" (121–22). Endlessly vying with each other for reputation,
they are driven by "always calculating amour-propre." They lack "the energy in
the soul," "the depth of spirit as character," "the manly and austere language of the
truth," and the "courage" that friendship requires. This is heroic male friendship
in a part-Aristotelian and part-republican key, implying the civic virtue of an

exclusively male citizenry. Having posed "society" against what he takes to be Thomas's appeal to nature, Montaigne ends with a gallant pair of similes that collapses the social back into the natural. Nature makes women "like flowers that shine sweetly." It has made men like trees that grow strong in storms; their vigor puts them in even greater danger of being broken by the wind, and so "they have more need to support each other, and to sustain themselves in unity" (122–23).

Thomas leaves us with an anemic conclusion. "Perhaps it follows," he writes, that friendship would be "more rare" in women; but when it is found in them, it would also be "more delicate and more tender":

Women have a sensibility for detail that takes account of everything. Nothing escapes them; they intuit friendship that remains quiet; they encourage timid friendship; they console gently friendship that suffers. With finer instruments, they guide more easily a sick heart; they repose it, and prevent it from feeling its agitations. They know especially how to give value to a thousand things that otherwise would not have any value. Hence one must perhaps desire a man for a friend on great occasions; but for happiness all one's days, one must desire the friendship of a woman. (123–24)

If we dismiss this preference as another gesture of male condescension toward the weaker sex, we miss the significance of Thomas's qualified devaluing of heroic male friendship, the kind he has Montaigne advocate. There are two striking features of Thomas's concept of a "secret commerce" with "sweet confidences." Having begun by seeming to imply that the reciprocal willingness to admit need, weakness, and a kind of dependence is distinctly female, he has, by the end, drawn men into the same psychological terms of commerce. Women, Thomas suggests, can offer their male friends an emotional empathy and a solace that they need, and that male friends, by their very commitment to the autonomous commitment to truth and practice of courage, cannot be expected to provide. Equally striking is the value Thomas gives to psychological and social particularity over universal, or at least general, philosophical principles. He imagines friendships of character, but character operates in webs of contingent specificities, with moral meaning to be found in the everyday details of sociability. Appearances that might seem trivial become carriers of emotional and moral meaning. This is a different kind of equality in friendship: not the union of strong minds in heroic virtue, offering mutual support from positions of strength, but the sharing of emotional needs and anxieties. It has, one might say, a Humean texture. All this is left largely implicit, within a dialogic strategy that, by its very juggling and conflation of languages, allows Thomas to keep a certain public distance from what we will find to be Necker's more direct questioning, in the privacy of her journals, of arguments for women's inferiority. But it reminds us of how protean the discourse of sensibility was. We can imagine Thomas's idyll of women's "more delicate and more tender" friendship taking its place in a larger rethinking of the conventional dichotomy between male strength and female weakness, male rational self-mastery and female emotional self-indulgence.

Amphibians

A manly mind was an independent mind, one that formed and articulated judgments from a position of intellectual and ultimately moral autonomy. In a philosophical tradition that Stoicism had done much to shape, such a mind could judge independently because it grasped and applied abstractions in solitary meditation, as if it were detached from the social and political meshes in which "opinion" was formed and exercised its tyranny. For late eighteenth-century men of letters, this ideal remained appealing, even as polite sociability and the culture of sensibility drew them into a mixed gender world of relational intelligence, including sympathetic friendships with women. At the same time the ideal of manly independence of mind had to be reconciled with the social and political dependencies that making a career in *le monde* entailed. As Thomas's career demonstrates, that was no easy matter. Necker too had ascended into *le monde*, though by a different route. As an outsider, determined to succeed as one of the preeminent *salonnières*, she knew that for a woman of her standing reputation depended on "appearance," in dress, in manner, and above all in speech, which mattered as much as, and perhaps more than, her "inner" moral disposition, and made her subject to "opinion."

Biographical detail maps the routes through which men like Thomas navigated a kind of independence, even as they accepted dependency as crucial to their ascent. His main sponsor was Jean-François Marmontel, whose rise from obscure origins to the Parisian pinnacle of belles lettres made him at once a self-satisfied man of the world and a guarded critic of *le monde*. Marmontel climbed the usual rungs: as the prodigy of a provincial Jesuit *collège*; as a protégé of Voltaire, who encouraged him to seek literary success in Paris: as a client, first in the entourage of a wealthy tax farmer, then under the protection of the royal court in the person of Mme de Pompadour. He began to win literary recognition with four modestly successful tragedies from 1748 to 1763, and achieved celebrity with his *Moral Stories*. In 1763, at forty, he was elected to the French Academy, the supreme honor in the French world of letters. In the salons he deftly performed his role as polite author, and he designed his *Stories* for the pleasurable instruction of society women. And yet Marmontel also had a defiant side, however muted.

He became involved in the philosophes' radical *Encyclopédie* project, and he even spent a few days in the Bastille.[26]

Thomas had a similar meteoric career. Born on October 1, 1732, one of seventeen children of a modest merchant family in Clermont-Ferrand, he was educated at the local *collège* and then the *collège* Sainte-Barbe in Paris. After a brief apprenticeship with a *procurateur*, he abandoned the law for a teaching position at the *collège* de Dormans-Beauvais. He became the presiding figure in a small literary cenacle, mostly of young *collège* instructors, who in their free time gathered in the woods to read Rousseau as well as Homer.[27] He would have remained an instructor, beneath public notice, if the academy prizes had not catapulted him to fame. With his first success, the eulogy of Count Maurice of Saxony, in 1759, he began to establish himself as the peerless tribune of patriotic virtue. The French Academy awarded him no less than five prizes for eloquence from 1759 to 1765.[28] Thomas's Eulogy of Sully in 1763 seemed to have largely dissipated Grimm's view of his prose as mere "verbiage." "The orator has taken a great step," he wrote in the *Correspondence littéraire*, by shedding the vapid "declamations" of *collège* rhetoric for "taste" and "true eloquence." Though he still has "a little of [the schoolboy's] puerile and petty finery," his eulogy "may be the first academic discourse" that "has had the approval of the enlightened public, and even that of the people."[29] Thomas was shedding the stigma of pedantry and being welcomed into the worldly ranks of the philosophes. At the same time the prizes lifted him into the intricate patronage networks through which reputation circulated in the old regime. Thomas's mastery of the eulogy, combined with the support of Marmontel and others, won him benefactors and protectors in high places. Intent in principle on remaining independent, he received the usual pensions, sinecures, outright gifts. His ascent reached its acme in January 1767, when he was elected to the French Academy.

Like Marmontel, Thomas can be fairly placed in the generation of "mandarins" who "grew fat," or at least well-nourished, in Voltaire's Enlightenment church in the closing decades of the old regime. They have been sharply distinguished from the much larger crowd of aspiring authors who came to Paris seeking fame and fortune and found themselves in a literary underground, scratching out livings as hired pens, using scabrous pamphlets and *libelles* to pour out a "gutter Rouseauism" that demonized the aristocracy of the court and *le monde* as parasitical and degenerate.[30] But if we take this dichotomy to refer to social psychology, and not just to social position, it does not do justice to the conflicted sense of self Thomas retained well after he achieved celebrity.[31] His psychological makeup is better understood by reference to d'Alembert's remarkable "Essay on the Society of Men of Letters and the Great," published in 1753. D'Alembert divided the "men of letters who court the great" into four "classes." His first class was "the slaves," who, unaware that they were slaves, were beyond rehabilitation.

Second came the authors who might be called rationalizers, though d'Alembert did not use that term. They were "indignant" about the "disagreeable" role they had to play; but having "convinced themselves" that it was the only way to "fortune," they calculated the "*complaisances*" and "intrigues" (*bassesses*) required to purchase "the smallest service." Less numerous were the species of "amphibians," perpetually undecided. Having "formed in the morning the project of being free," they "return in the evening to being slaves." They were "at one and the same time bold and timid, noble and self-interested," seeming to "reject with one hand what they try to seize with the other." The last class was the worst: the authors who "incensed the great in public" and "tore them apart in private," and who "with their equals show off a philosophy that hardly costs them anything."[32]

Thomas obviously was not a hypocritical radical in d'Alembert's sense, but neither should he be placed among the hopeless sycophants. Even at the height of his career he was an undecided amphibian. "It is only too ordinary," he remarked in an address to the academy in 1770, "that talents lack places."[33] He knew of the magnetic attraction of Paris for bright young men from the provinces; the hunger for fame; the craving for an intellectual "liberty" that life in a provincial town and a professional career would not provide; the danger of literary ambition ending in poverty and degradation. Like Hume in the early 1740s, men of letters of his generation and the young men who ached to follow them saw ambition as a legitimate and indeed noble motive force. But this was ambition in a different context and a different key. In his 1741 essay on "the middle station of life" Hume had perched practitioners of "the liberal arts and sciences" above "the common professions," but had bound them all together as a "middle station" with a shared ethos of talent and industry. For young men with Thomas's ambitions, men who aspired to "celebrity" in Voltaire's church, the "party of humanity," a life in letters and a life in a profession—the law, let us say, or commerce—had nothing in common. To enter a profession was to be confined to a mere "*état*," a conventional station that "suffocated" men of exceptional talent. Men of letters hovered above that world of narrowly focused labor. For Hume the route to "independence" had lain through success in the literary market, and he was proud to have travelled it so well. For Thomas and his fellow writers commercial success was not the goal, in part because the state of the market still made it very unlikely, and in part because, for all their resentment of "the great," nothing short of recognition among the *mondain* of Paris could confirm their sense of singular worth.

Among the authors who publicly expressed their contempt for this kind of success was Thomas's protégé Jacques Delille, also a native of the Auvergne, who had been a younger member of the literary cenacle in Paris in the late 1750s. He would follow Thomas into the academy in 1769, with Voltaire's support, on the strength of his translation of Virgil's *Georgics*. In 1760, at twenty-two, Delille submitted a poem titled "Epistle to the Utility of Retreat. For Men of Letters" for the academy's prize competition. Thomas found it strong—so strong, in fact, that he feared it would eclipse his own entry.[34] Delille's poem was a slashing Rousseauian indictment of *mondanité* and its corrupting tyranny over men of letters. It begins with one friend asking another why he has made the error of retreating from "the ocean of the world." The rest of the poem is the solitary's uncompromising response. *Le monde* is "the imposture world," where the "vulgar" *bel esprit*, one of those "rampant parasites," "degrades [his] century by living to please it and devoting his pen to frivolity," and where art is perverted into performances in fakery. Transported to its "lazy circles," Malebranche or Pascal or Newton would yearn for "the refuge where the soul lives and thinks." "Do you want to subject your manly character," he asks his friend, to "what is called the art of pleasing (*complaisance*)"? Only silence nourishes the profound sentiment of "manly eloquence." Only in retreat does the genius "dare elevate himself and listen to himself," because only there does his soul belong entirely to himself. In *le monde* women, "once content with being seduced, exercise their empire over talents," and "effeminate at once *les esprits* and *les moeurs*." Do not lower yourself before "the great," he tells his friend; such adulation "debases the soul and enervates genius." He himself will continue to embrace solitude and true friendship.[35]

A more scathing condemnation of *mondanité*, or a more radical denial of its claim to the unique honor displayed in the social aesthetic of play, would be hard to imagine. Though Delille's poem is arguably entirely derivative, its intense and rigid moralism may make it a singular moment in the process in which the social, cultural, and aesthetic values of mid-seventeenth-century France were being shaken. The once touted figure of the *bel esprit* has become the lazy parasite. There is nothing here of Hume's effort to practice a feminized but still manly politeness in his writing as well as his social comportment. In *le monde* women "effeminate" men. The use of the verb (perhaps the first instance of it) underscores Delille's conviction that the demands of *complaisance* stifle genius by emasculating it. The only recourse was retreat to silent solitude and the mutual support of private friendship, which Delille separates from worldly sociability and the power it gives women. True friendship is not only private in practice; it is a deliberate mutual withdrawal into independence from polite sociability and its women-centered play of power.

Arguably Delille's poem was just a youthful gush of indignation; he went on to a comfortable academic career, cutting something of a gallant figure in *le monde*; and looking back across the shock waves of the revolution, he wrote a nostalgic poem of adulation to polite conversation as reciprocal truth-seeking in "harmonious accord."[36] More striking is that in 1772, at age forty, Thomas used his concluding critique of eighteenth-century society in the *Essay* on women to issue a similar indictment, though with his own emphases. If Thomas's language was less inflammatory than Delille's, it was no less subversive of aristocratic cultural and social authority. In modern polite sociability Thomas saw "the fury of appearing, the art of putting everything on the surface," a ruthless competition for distinction and the power it brought (154). It was all a calculating game of false self-representations. One had to master the trick of "conquer[ing] ceaselessly without having the air of combat." Women read to amuse and be amused, not to learn. With the increased mixing of men and women "the two sexes denatured themselves," the men obsessed with appearing agreeable, the women with gaining independence (150–58). As in Delille's poem, *complaisance* denatures men, which is to say that it effeminates them. Thomas's main difference with Delille was one of emphasis in judging the responsibility of women for this emasculation. Delille depicted the women of *le monde* as the power-hungry agents of corruption. To Thomas they were victims of the corruption they had done so much to create; they had deprived themselves of the natural joys of marital love and child-rearing. Echoing Rousseau directly, he lamented that only a rare few society women dared breastfeed their infants.

One has to wonder how a man so apparently faithful to his youthful Rousseau-ian moral indignation, and so aware of the plight of the have-nots in literary Paris, avoided reproaching himself for complicity with the world he condemned. Perhaps at times he did reproach himself. It was the self-image of the academy that allowed him and other members to see themselves as innocent exceptions. Since the early 1750s d'Alembert had led the effort to profile the academy as a unique institution, a proof that the Republic of Letters was not simply an ideal; that unlike other French institutions, including the provincial academies, it was meritocratic in its selection process and egalitarian in its internal proceedings.[37] Thomas did much to perpetuate this image in his academy speeches in 1769 and 1770. Part not-so-oblique censure of the court and the corruption over which it presided, the image was also part self-delusion. The fact is that the academy was not only a carefully monitored institution of the Crown, but also an integral part of *mondanité*. A significant number of academicians were Crown appointees selected more for their inherited titles and their offices in church and state than for their literary accomplishments; and most of these used their membership to protect the dignity of the Crown, the church, and the nobilities of robe and sword.[38] In November 1766, as he was vying for an academy position, Thomas described himself to Mlle Moreaud as "running around, making visits, seeing cardinals, princes, ministers, men of letters, friends and enemies, going back and forth between Paris and Versailles."[39] Rivalry among *mondain* sponsors and fac-tions at court, in the government, and in the salons played a major role in both the selection of members and the awarding of prizes. The prizes did facilitate the publication of some daring material, but academy members also sought to avoid recklessness by practicing a measure of self-censorship. In 1769 Thomas toned down two sections of his *Essay* d'Alembert deemed too daring.[40]

These conflicting pulls are evident in the zig and zags of Thomas's own career. The first published expression of his moral outrage was his "Epistle to the People," a hackneyed contrast between the virtuous simplicity of working people and the vices of courtiers that, having won the first honorable mention for the academy's prize in poetry, was published in 1760.[41] With Marmontel's help he was appointed to a sinecure as the private secretary to the duc du Choiseul-Praslin, the recently appointed secretary of state for foreign affairs. The price for this financial security was that he had to lodge at Versailles, and his time there confirmed that it was a den of iniquity. In 1763 he found himself squeezed in a battle between court factions about an academy position that had just come open. Choiseul-Praslin's faction was intent on denying Marmontel the appointment and wanted to push Thomas as their candidate, despite his youth. He refused to cooperate, deferring to his older friend and patron. This act of self-denial cost him his position but earned him much admiration in salon and literary circles. That made all the more embarrassing his publication of a funeral eulogy of the Dauphin, the son of Louis XV, who died in December 1765. Thomas had undertaken the eulogy in part to satisfy the Comte d'Angiviller, a courtier involved in the education of the king's children and another high-placed friend of Marmontel. He assumed the voice of an "obscure but true and free citizen . . . animated by love of the State," but when he turned the Dauphin into a model student of an Enlightenment education, defying the court and touring the provinces to learn the real situation of the nation, and full of respect for men of merit, he fell into sycophancy.[42] Having welcomed Thomas into their fold, Grimm and Diderot met this performance with undisguised disgust. In the *Correspondence littéraire* Diderot addressed Thomas directly. "Never has the art of speech been so disgracefully prostituted."[43]

To a degree Thomas redeemed himself with two speeches in 1769, one distinguishing the "friendship, peace, wise liberty" and especially "equality" practiced in the academy from "this active laziness and this shock of little movement that one calls *le monde*." In his own reception speech he offered the usual assurances. True enlightenment strengthened authority; enlightened change had to be gradual; there could be no "fanaticism," the "most dangerous enemy" was "impatience for the good." But in its main thrust the speech apostrophized men of letters as a unique community of citizens, a disinterested national clerisy, morally superior to wealth and pedigree and power, who alone could provide the detached criticism that would discredit outworn traditions and guide needed innovations.[44] In 1770, in a speech welcoming the archbishop of Toulouse to the academy, Thomas went back on the offensive with a defense of the academy's priority of intellectual merit over birth and its duty to improve government by playing a critical role. The speech was ill-timed, as Antoine-Louis Séguier, the *avocat general* of the Parlement of Paris and an academy member, was in the audience. Séguier had recently threatened philosophical writers with severe measures, and felt personally attacked. At Séguier's insistence Maupeou strongly reprimanded Thomas, even threatening the Bastille, stopped publication of the speech as well as Thomas's eulogy of Marcus Aurelius, and forbade him to speak in public for the next two years.[45] To some Thomas was a philosophical hero, a modern Cato; to others a man who lacked the courage of his convictions; to others an arrogant philosophe who had gotten his comeuppance.

Thomas was not simply maneuvering through dangerous political waters, dodging the risks of overly explicit defiance on one side and censure for toadying on the other. His very way of life marked an underlying psychic split, an amphibian state of mind. His career demanded that he be in Paris for months at a time, but he took every opportunity to escape to spas and country residences. In Paris he lived in the modest household maintained by his mother and his two sisters. He could not avoid making the social rounds, but he did not master the art of conversation at polite gatherings. Necker noted in an incisive portrait of her friend in her journal that when he came back into society after a bout of work, he was "like an exile who returns to his country after a long absence and is frustrated by the fact that he recognizes no one"; and so "he floats without ever being able to mix." It was not easy to maintain a friendship with a man "made more to die like Cato and Regulus than to live in the eighteenth century."[46]

But the friendship was maintained, and that was because the friends found in each other's company consolation for afflictions and a haven from the regimen of *mondanité* that seemed to aggravate, if not cause them. In accounts of her state of health in letters to friends in Switzerland, Necker complained of what her husband called "painful nervous anxieties" and insomnia, and sometimes felt herself to be close to death.[47] As with Thomas, it is impossible to separate out the physical, the psychic, and the psychosomatic. It is clear, though, that in her bouts of depression she, like Thomas, feared descending into an "abyss" of "nothingness," a state of psychic nullity. It would be simplistic to say her physical ailments or mental afflictions were caused by her anxiety as a self-conscious outsider in *mondanité* and the salons. But in the outsider's efforts to be an insider, even as she found so much of the insiders' way of life intellectually shallow and morally objectionable, we find obvious strains that contributed to her afflictions.

We know much more about Necker's conflicted interior life than we know about the much-published Thomas's. From about 1770 onward she kept an extensive journal, ranging from intimate self-examinations to drafts of essays, with frequent corrections and additions. She had most of the contents burned, considering the material "useless" or fearing that it would make her appear "ridiculous," and the rest she entrusted to her husband. For reasons that are not clear, Jacques Necker, who had prevailed on his wife not to publish during her lifetime, published three volumes of "extracts" from the surviving journals in 1798, four years after her death. The two volumes of *Nouveaux mélanges* that appeared in 1801 brought the total number of pages to roughly 19,000. As the full surviving entries in the archive of the Necker chateau in Coppet in Switzerland remain inaccessible to scholars, we are left wondering how representative the extracts are. Necker tells us in his introduction to the first volume that he had decided against organizing the extracts topically so as to avoid giving the false impression that in writing his wife had ever taken account of "the public"; he had wanted "to preserve that perfect reality whose character can belong only to solitary writings."[48] And yet many of the selected extracts contradict that claim. Thanks to Necker's editorial eclecticism, the extracts document, almost despite him, his wife's virtual authorship. Unfortunately his apparently insouciant editing also makes the volumes a perilous source. The extracts are not dated; they were arranged with no thought to chronological order. They come at you like scraps of paper floating in the wind. In places it is hard to know whether Mme Necker was recording opinions and beliefs to which she was committed or simply bits of salon conversations she found noteworthy. Likewise it is sometimes not clear where one entry ends and another begins. We have to approach the journal extracts as a wide but at times treacherous opening into the mind of a highly intelligent and well-read person, a woman who was, intellectually as well as socially, a central presence in one of the social spaces where *mondanité* and the world of letters met.[49]

Even if we bring due caution to the journals, they leave no doubt that this woman, one of the most prominent salon hostesses of her generation, felt herself to be an outsider, a perpetual candidate for admission, always aware that in the eyes of many she could never qualify, and always doubting that she wanted to qualify. Her father, a village pastor in the Vaud, had educated her as though she were a son, having her learn, among other subjects, Latin, Greek, and physics. In Lausanne, where she became president of a circle of young women wanting to restore the ideal of the *précieuses*, she was free to exhibit her learning and was admired for her precocity. With the death of her father in January 1760, when she was twenty-two, she had to resort to tutoring to support herself and her mother. Her mother died in 1763, and she became the companion of a rich young Parisian widow who brought her to Paris, where she met Jacques Necker. She never ceased to consider herself an exile in Paris; "I am forced to hide the most natural movements," she wrote to a Swiss friend, "in order to avoid the criticism of pedantry; I continuously enact a sort of assault against my heart and its emotions, and at the very instant when I feel free, I find that it has lost its usual elasticity."[50] Here and elsewhere Necker viewed *le monde* through a certain nostalgia for the Swiss sociability of her youth, which had celebrated her learning and allowed her to freely express her feelings as well as her thoughts. The lurking criticism of her "pedantry" was not aimed simply at the intellectual pretensions of a *femme savante*. It marked her vulnerability to ridicule as a prudish Calvinist, a provincial

Swiss bourgeoise, and a former tutor who had had to work for a living. Her wealth and her salon did not erase the fact that, by virtue of her upbringing and her commitment to serious study, she was comparable to the academic pedant. It was a vicious circle; the more naturally she acted as she had been raised, the more unnatural—the more lacking in *aisance*—she would seem by the standards of the social aesthetic of play.

If she failed in the eyes of many, it was not for want of trying. Several of her entries read as paraphrases of the code of conduct for the *honnête femme* in the literature of the seventeenth century. By reading extensively in this literature she hoped to overcome her handicaps, to absorb through print the art of pleasing, the *aisance*, and the "je ne sais quoi" most of the women she dealt with had been bred to. She would be "the manager (*administrateur*) and the mistress of the house," preventing the conversation from "taking a boring, or disagreeable, or dangerous turn."[51] One cannot, she reminded herself, prepare for conversation. And yet she did use the journals to prepare. Many of the shorter entries are not quick notes to herself or sketchy observations, but aperçus crafted in the hope that she would have occasion to offer them with apparent spontaneity, as flashes of insight, in her salon.[52] Repeatedly she urged herself to practice intense and unflagging *attention* in conversation.[53] She may have borrowed the term from Malebranche, an author she greatly admired, but in this usage she sought to master precisely the kind of ego-stroking *complaisance* Malebranche condemned. In her dogged *attention* to stroking the other's amour propre, the outsider was making the extra effort to please. Necker labored in private to appear effortless in company, in a futile effort at methodical effortlessness. The contradiction did not go unnoticed. She was criticized for being hopelessly incapable of grace and ease and light wit. Marmontel, a sympathetic friend and an admirer of her moral qualities, regretted that she had "neither the air nor the tone of a woman . . . formed in the school of the monde"; "her mind (*esprit*), like her countenance, was too calculated (*ajusté*) to have grace."[54]

Just beneath the surface of Necker's futile social ambitions, however, lay a stringent moralism, and in the journals it occasionally took the form of contempt for the world that looked down on her failed efforts to join it. "Each day," one entry reads, "adds to my disgust for the great world (*le grand monde*); everything appears to me contrived (*factice*)."[55] If in her salon she tried, in vain, to avoid the stigma of the *femme savante*, she often assumed that persona in the journals.[56] She did dismiss some "publishing women," but it was for exhibiting mere *personalité*, her term for egotistical self-display, without the effort to demonstrate an "*enchaining*" of rational ideas. Educated women should join rigorous reasoning to "eloquence, as much as that is possible." Obviously trying to perfect her writing, she devoted many entries to questions of composition and style, finding minute errors in the prose of, among others, Rousseau and Thomas.[57] The journals include draft essays on several philosophical and literary subjects. In some of the longer entries she assumed quite purposefully the authorial voice of the literary critic and showed considerable insight in that genre.

The Labor of Genius

When we combine Thomas's published writings with the friends' correspondence and Necker's journal entries, we see how each contributed to shaping the other's thoughts and sentiments on a cluster of ideas. At its center is a variation on a theme of their era: the need for a new public rhetoric in print, an alternative to what was called *le goût moderne*, the "modern" (as opposed to neoclassical) style of polite culture that had gained ascendancy in *le monde* in the seventeenth century. If the friends' ideas were largely derivative, even banal, in their reliance on a commonly used family of words, there was nonetheless a certain creativity to the way in which they formed, largely in private, a logic of resistance to the imperatives of *mondanité*. The axial distinction was between the genius, the writer of unrivaled intellectual creativity and expressive power, and the *bel esprit*, the virtuoso of the culture of *complaisance* and *aisance*. Their thinking is in fact one of many measures of the wide purchase that the figure of "genius," posed against the *bel esprit*, had gained by the 1760s.

Tearing down the mystique of the *bel esprit* had been common in critiques of *mondanité* since Malebranche and La Bruyère, but by the mid-eighteenth century the normative framework had changed. In Malebranche's Augustinian vision of a postlapsarian world governed by concupiscence, the *bel esprit* had embodied the sins of egotism, self-delusion, and hunger for power in relations with others. In the predominantly literary reaction against *le goût moderne* in the first half of the eighteenth century, the concern was not with inveterate sinfulness, but with the need for stylistic forms that would express a high seriousness of moral purpose, and for a standard of personal merit gauged by the individual's contribution to public utility—and the *bel esprit* failed on both counts. To say that Malebranche's moral rigorism was secularized is not to imply that it slackened. To attack the *bel esprit* was to assert an ethic that questioned the very legitimacy of an aristocratic order in the decades prior to the revolution. In this sense the new critique, while hardly ever engaging political issues directly, had immense political implications. Necker and Thomas joined many others in debunking Fontenelle, whose life and writings now seemed to epitomize all that was wrong with the tradition of *honnêteté*. Necker assured Thomas that his own genius drew from his "substance," in contrast to Fontenelle, one of those people who were "empty of any conscience, any center, any consistency in *l'esprit*, because they have none in character."[58]

"Genius" in this usage differed markedly from the genius Hume had feared he lacked in 1734. Now the term evoked one of the rare Herculean figures scattered across the centuries, a man whose powers of thought, feeling, and expression were so strong as to be more than just exceptional.[59] The genius often figured at the center of the new secular ethic; his magnetism seemed essential to the transformation of France into a new civic community, a fatherland (*patrie*) or nation of citizens. "Extremely subtle aperçus," Necker observed, become a kind of superficial "legislation" by force of repetition; the genius can "replace everything and substitute his laws, like a conqueror, for those of the old government."[60] A "revolution" might require a century of preparation, but it is the genius who "finally produces all those great changes that astonish us."[61] It was, perhaps, a measure of the felt need for great changes, for the rebirth of a corrupt society, that so much hope was invested in the power of one man. There was a wide spectrum of opinion, though, on what generated or constituted that power. At one end the emphasis was on the making of the genius, particularly through education and rigorous intellectual application. Against this Lockean view others, wanting to exempt the genius from the rules to which ordinary mortals were subject, emphasized that the genius was born, not made; that his virtually superhuman creative powers allowed him to make his own laws, at least in the aesthetic realm; and that he produced in a process of spontaneous combustion, a kind of seizure of creative energy, as though inspired. Not surprisingly, as Thomas and Necker remind us, these apparently irreconcilable views sometimes mingled; the cultural resources they drew on were not neatly separated. The friends took elements from both ends of the spectrum, though they gave more emphasis to the labor behind creativity than to its spontaneous outpouring.

For Thomas "work is the sole measure of life," Necker observed in a portrait that was both admiring and disapproving.[62] If work gave meaning to a manly life, it was also a debilitating compulsion, as we see in Thomas's troubled friendship with Nicolas Barthe. Thomas had admitted to Mlle Moreaud that the friendship was an enigma.[63] The son of a wealthy merchant family in Marseilles, Barthe had been sent to Paris to study law, but he already had literary ambitions and joined Thomas's little circle of *collège* instructors. Perplexed by Thomas's stubborn loyalty to him, Mme Necker tolerated him in her circle, perhaps to avoid offending Thomas, but found him to be "the proof that it is necessary to have much empire over one's *esprit* and one's character when one does not wish to become the prey of one's imagination, the joke of others, and the torment of oneself."[64] Despite his very modest accomplishments as a writer of comedies of manners, Barthe moved in high circles in the nobility. He was a notorious womanizer and a bon vivant, a regular member of Paris's most famous gastronomic club. Though anguished and volatile, he managed nonetheless to cultivate the persona of a worldly and charming man of letters.

Each served as a warning to the other, and perhaps also as an envied alter ego, though in their moments of mutual exasperation Thomas clearly held the upper hand. In the 1760s Thomas became the academy-certified genius and Barthe assumed the role of needy disciple and sometimes abject supplicant. He complained repeatedly that he could not sustain his own work without Thomas's presence and constant approval. As early as May 1760 we find Thomas lecturing Barthe on his voluptuousness, which he saw as incompatible with the man of letter's mission to serve humanity.[65] When Thomas failed to write or critiqued Barthe's outlines for plays in merciless detail, Barthe complained bitterly, though in the end, no matter how much praise he received from others, he could not do without his friend's approval. Thomas became increasingly impatient with Barthe's failure to complete projects. "It is so sweet to let yourself go, to cede to the moment, to not fight yourself," he wrote Barthe on December 28, 1768; "you will accomplish nothing."[66] In fact, though, as he confided to Barthe, he had the same failures of manly self-disciple, though for different reasons. What he called the excessive "movement" of sociability and ideas in *le monde* withered his inspiration, but his retreats to solitude, whether in Paris or at the baths in Mont-Dore, often backfired, particularly when he had to struggle against his physical debility. "I consume myself, I desiccate myself, I bore myself," he wrote on August 19, 1769; "my spirit languishes, my body is weak, and my soul, half the time, is devoured by melancholy."[67] For all his subservience, Barthe might be said to have had the last word. He himself was lazy, he freely admitted, but his friend was at the other extreme; he had too much "impetuosity in the career of glory." In a letter in April 1769, Barthe feigned an apology for not being "a great man"; Thomas would have to settle for him until he found a friend who was "a compound of Rousseau, Diderot, and La Fontaine." "You have only one fault," Barthe concluded, "that of not being at all happy."[68]

Mme Necker was aware of her friend's syndrome of compulsive work, physical debility, and paralyzing depression. Thomas's ambition, she warned him, exceeded his physical capacity.[69] She saw reclusiveness as the necessary condition for the work of genius, but there were times when his self-absorption threatened to deprive her of the very intimacy she sought in the friendship. In another letter to Thomas in 1770 she asked him to "conquer [his] taste for interior solitude"; "with this silence, with this somber air, constrained and reserved, it seems that one breaks all ties."[70] He had to recognize that he was, after all, only a "half-Stoic."[71]

⸺

Thomas was an extreme case, almost a caricature, of an ethos gaining purchase in eighteenth-century France. It owed less to Rousseau than to two other prominent figures: Charles Pinot Duclos and d'Alembert. Duclos became the *sécretaire perpetuel* of the French Academy in 1755, and d'Alembert followed him in that position in 1767. Duclos's *Considerations on the Mores of This Century*, published in 1750, immediately won widespread attention in educated circles and went through four new editions from 1764 to 1772. In both the *Considerations* and d'Alembert's "Essay on the Society of Men of Letters and the Great" we find a socially and culturally more radical impulse than has been recognized.[72]

Duclos did not share the common view among men of letters, particularly in the upcoming generation, that ordinary bourgeois professions (*états*) were deadening to the spirit. In the *Considerations*, in fact, he used the criteria of the "intelligence" a profession required and its relative usefulness to society to place the man of letters in the same honorable bourgeois ranks as the legal official, the merchant, and the inventor.[73] Duclos had come to Paris in 1713, at age nine, as the prosperous descendent of judicial and commercial families in Brittany. He spent five years in a Parisian school whose pupils were largely sons of the minor nobility, and in the brief autobiography he wrote late in life he would recall his bourgeois pride in excelling titled scions in his studies.[74] On the completion of his schooling in 1720, he took up the study of law but entered a dissolute life with friends in the aristocracy and in lower circles of libertine Paris. Thanks in part to his literary talent, he began to acquire patrons in the high aristocracy and among influential *salonnières*. Whether he retained his independence from the great, as he would claim in his autobiography, is open to doubt. In 1739, with little in print, he was appointed to the Academy of Inscriptions and Belles-Lettres. The autobiography is more reliable in describing a gradual transition in his way of life, as he channeled the judicial and commercial work ethic of his family into serious literary labor. Though he frequented several salons and was a lively talker, his brusque frankness disqualified him from being a *bel esprit*. His real education took place in the cafés frequented by *savants* and writers, and particularly the Café Procope, where he took part in the debates and acquired a reputation as a master of the bon mot.[75]

By 1750 Duclos was at once a well-positioned man of the world and a man of letters disillusioned with *mondanité*. In the *Considerations* he proposed to develop, through the lens of Parisian *mondanité*, a "science of mores." Though Duclos claimed to be writing about France, his book was entirely Paris-centered; it excoriated Parisian high society for its duplicity in the veiled struggles for the power afforded by reputation, its "mania" for evanescent celebrity, and its idle and boring conformity to convention and fashion.[76] Duclos was not simply lashing out at contemporary manners. He took from his predecessors in the first half of the century, and especially from the abbé de Saint-Pierre, the axiomatic principle that the measure of an individual's social and cultural value was "utility," the importance of his contribution to the larger community. Seen in that light, Duclos argued, the claims to superiority of a leisured aristocracy were both unfounded and unjust. By imposing their standards of "taste" on public opinion, they usurped rights to cultural and ultimately moral authority that ought to belong exclusively to the men of letters. It was the fact that their works were "labored on with care" that qualified men of letters alone to judge each other's work.[77] Duclos was emphatic on this point. Works of value demanded work; they could not just materialize from "amusement." To Duclos the cult of the *bel esprit*, to which he devoted an entire chapter, epitomized the tyranny of superficial standards of mere social performance. The only putative "*état*" of the so-called *bel esprit* was laziness (*oisiveté*). The disciplined labor of the true man of letters, among whom he included the practitioner of "the art of criticism," made him the example par excellence of the self-legislating citizen. His personal autonomy was grounded in his capacity to transform his natural force of intelligence into a product of strenuous labor.

Two years later d'Alembert carried the offensive against aristocratic *esprit* and *aisance* several steps farther with his "Essay."[78] At thirty-six, the author was already an internationally renowned mathematician and physicist. He was perhaps uniquely positioned to write the essay. The illegitimate son of a celebrated society woman and an artillery officer, he had been placed in a foundling home. His father's family rescued him, arranging for his upbringing by a glazier's wife named Mme Rousseau, and seeing to his education at a Jansenist *collège*. Even as he continued to live in a small room in Mme Rousseau's house, he rose into Parisian high society, thanks to his social charms and to the fact that he had become one of the protégés of Pierre Louis Maupertuis and the *salonnières* Mme Geoffrin and Mme du Deffand. In the mid-1740s, as he mixed with Diderot and other radical philosophes, he became involved in the *Encyclopédie* project. His cordial relations with men in the high aristocracy and government gave the project a critical measure of protection. At the same time, though, he was insistent on standing on his own accomplishments as a mathematician and scientist, which he knew to be, in contrast to achievements in letters, indisputable. In 1753, the year he wrote the "Essay," he reluctantly allowed Mme du Deffand and her circle to press his candidacy for the academy, protesting that he would not practice the usual sycophancy to gain admittance.[79] He was at once a striking exemplar of the principle of merit and a man with extensive personal experience of the workings of patronage and the advantages of having powerful contacts.

D'Alembert began the "Essay" by rejecting the extreme position taken by Rousseau in the Dijon prize essay. Enlightened knowledge had not caused the corruption of humanity. It was, rather, the route out of barbarism.[80] But it could be, and indeed in eighteenth-century France it had become, corrupted by social conditions and mores. Hoping to avoid the spiteful rivalries and factionalism to which they were so prone, men of letters had turned to the great as disinterested and qualified judges. This was a calamitous mistake; the education of the great qualified them to be nothing more than "demi-connoisseurs" or "amateurs." The ability to produce "polite works of society" (*honnête d'ouvrages de société*) does not qualify one to be a judge. The "aristarques" should be put to the test, like the men they patronized. Let them put in print the opinions they express in conversation, so that the "public" can judge them.[81] If the qualified public was not to be found in "a small circle of friends or *complaisans adulateurs*," it also could not be extended to the people at large. It was constituted by men of letters who had labored to transform their inborn talent, the "impulsion of nature," into mastery of the secrets of their art.[82] At times d'Alembert seems to be simply repeating Duclos's critique. He too saw the *bel esprit* as the epitome of the problem. Like Duclos he imagined men of letters forming a new community of the accomplished, a "public" of autonomous professionals, its members judging themselves by their own hard-won standards. Only with this unity among themselves could men of letters "come to give the law to the rest of the nation on matters of taste and philosophy."[83] The autonomy had to be social as well as intellectual; to claim their right to a collective assertion of cultural authority men of letters had to themselves effect a structural change, a collective withdrawal from degrading dependency to positions of social independence. In the midcentury context of *mondanité* this was a remarkable conclusion, and d'Alembert tried to give it moral cogency by assuming the persona of the Stoic sage. The debt to Stoicism does not become explicit until the beginning of the penultimate paragraph, when he writes that "Such are the reflections and the wishes of an author without a household, without intrigue, without support, and as a consequence without hope, but also without cares and without desires."[84] But this Stoic ethic of inner autonomy achieved through self-denial runs through the entire essay. By claiming to be free of needs himself, d'Alembert sought to make credible his appeal to other men of letters to liberate themselves from the dependence that the satisfaction of needs imposes. Such dependence, he insists, inevitably corrupts the work as well as the man; the benefactions of the great "communicate to the soul a degradation which insensibly degrades ideas, and of which the writings show the effect in the long term; for the style takes the coloration (*teinture*) of the character."[85] D'Alembert did not call for an end to the distribution of positions and monetary rewards by high-placed patrons; but he wanted much less of it, on the reasoning that the result would be to encourage authors to win opulence through true merit, without intrigue and sycophancy. Men of letters would not be required to be indigent; the meritorious could, in fact, ascend to opulence. But "poverty" had to be one of their mottos (*mots de la devise*); they had to be prepared to accept it rather than sell their souls.[86]

Duclos and d'Alembert were not renouncing ambition, but trying to rechannel it. Authors were no different from other people in requiring the approval of others, and ambition in that form was a socially efficacious motive. The question was how to distinguish "reputation" properly earned from one's peers from the kind granted arrogantly and in ignorance from "the great," and, for d'Alembert, how to detach proper reputation from "considerations," the gifts of money and positions that kept men of letters slavishly dependent on their putative social betters. Like Hume, both men wanted the man of letters to be able to pursue literary ambition with manly "independence." Unlike Hume, however, they did not project an alliance of letters with the polite sociability of a new middle station. Preoccupied with *le monde* and *mondanité*, d'Alembert saw social retreat as the only escape from the corrupting grasp of lineage, wealth, and power. Both the natural force of talent and the labor required to develop it had to be quarantined from social corruption. His variation on neo-Stoicism did not require Shaftesbury's regimen of meditation on ancient Stoic texts. But unlike Shaftesbury, who kept the regimen while maintaining the comfortable life of a landed aristocrat and London gentleman, d'Alembert's independent authors would have to be willing to accept a significant measure of material deprivation as the condition of their creative integrity.

The radical implications of d'Alembert's argument become fully apparent in the way he accepted the necessity of an elite of birth and wealth. He did not concede to the elite a natural right to authority and power by virtue of breeding, or a natural ability to govern. It was simply the opulent visibility of birth and wealth that made their pretended superiority an undeniable social fact, though it was merely "external" and "perhaps entirely unjust."[87] Though less radical, Duclos also deflated the aristocratic mystique, and the pretensions of wealth, by devaluing some words and revaluing others. "Amusement" was now a negative term, evoking not the unique social and aesthetic value of a kind of play, but its social uselessness and aesthetic sterility. "Work" (*travail*), a stigma in the "free" space of the discourse of *honnêteté*, now connoted the release of the natural force of intelligence and its transformation into a socially useful product. A career in letters was a "profession," which was to say not that authors were consigned to a narrowing occupation, but that authorship was a vocation or, perhaps better, a calling, though the reorganized and autonomous Republic of Letters would have some of the features of a recognizably modern profession. Duclos's use of the term, like d'Alembert's, evoked total commitment to authorial labor, whatever position the author might occupy for some measure of financial security. The true author was the opposite of the mere "amateur," whose aversion to labor became disqualifying.[88]

These texts were not seeping up from a netherworld of radical discontent in the world of letters. Their ideas became current in the French Academy and in salon conversations. Though still powerful, the logic that made play in the aristocratic social aesthetic emblematic of the highest forms of social honor was being widely questioned; and it would eventually be marginalized. In 1749, in the fourth volume of his *Natural History,* the naturalist Buffon had included a section on "Homo Duplex" that made the dichotomy between the disciplined labor of reason and the counterprinciple of laziness integral to human interiority, without distinction between male and female. The first he called "the soul, that spiritual principle, that principle of all knowledge." It was in a ceaseless struggle with "the animal and purely material," which dominated in "lazy people, and even men whom no work commands." In this latter state we find ourselves the instruments of the senses and the imagination; despite our thoughts, "we are forced into inaction, although we have the will to act."[89] Buffon in effect transformed conventional gender dichotomies into a struggle central to the human condition. In doing so, he at once confirmed the equation of reason and disciplined labor and set severe limits to its efficacy. One implication was that men, no less than women, were sometimes helpless against the pull of inaction, when their rational self-discipline simply was not strong enough. The other was that women, no less than men, did struggle; that they too had "the reasonable faculty," the power to understand and to act on their understanding.

In a volume of *Pensées* published in 1774, d'Alembert went much farther, in effect claiming for talented women the same intellectual autonomy he had sought for talented men in the 1750 "Essay." Arguing for the emancipation of women from "slavery" and a "type of degradation," he dismissed "the jargon, humiliating for them and for us, to which [men] have reduced their commerce with [women]." It was a simple matter of the physically powerful oppressing the physically weaker. The fact was that women not only "would succeed better than us in works of taste and *agrément*, especially in those in which sentiment and tenderness have to be the soul"; "as for works of genius and sagacity, a thousand examples prove that the weakness of the body is not an obstacle in men; why then would a more solid and male (*mâle*) education not put women in a position to succeed?"[90]

But these interventions by Buffon and d'Alembert were rare moments in eighteenth-century anthropological thought. On the whole the revaluation of intellectual labor gave no reason to question, much less dissolve, the fusion of status and gender that banned women from any serious exercise of it. Old and new medical theories about gender differences; male resentment of what was seen as the abuse of female power and intrigue in the literary world, especially in the person of the *salonnière*; a bourgeois cult of domesticity that, in the very process of touting bourgeois industry by contrast with the decadence of aristocratic life, also emulated the aristocracy in making female "public" labor a disqualifying stigma: these were perhaps most important in keeping the ban intact. The essays Duclos and d'Alembert published in the early 1750s may have owed their popularity partly to a telling silence. They said nothing, positive or negative, about women as patrons among the great, or as *salonnières* with protégés, or as authors. Nor was the theme of literary corruption and decadence cast in the paradigm of effeminization, despite the fact that both authors saw authors' striving for opulence as a symptom of the reigning luxury. These silences were surely due in part to caution; neither man wanted to offend prominent women who were promoting their careers. One has to remember, too, that they did not yet have to deal with Rousseau's frontal attack on "the ascendancy of women" in his *Letter to M. d'Alembert on the Theater*, which did not appear until 1758. Just as striking, however, is that in these texts the great *salonnières* were not explicitly excepted from the indictment of the great for abusing their clients' dependence; that no space was opened for women in the authorial community of labor; and that, in sharp contrast to the discourse of *honnêteté* a century earlier, no cultural authority was ceded to women even in matters of taste. That the imagined Republic of Letters would be a male republic seemed too obvious to be stated outright.

Thomas and Necker shaped their concepts of selfhood and genius in this intellectual universe, but they were not wholly of it. In the privacy of her journals, Necker thought that educated and cultivated women *should* aspire to be authors in the Republic of Letters; Thomas, as preoccupied with manliness as he was, advocated opening a significant public space for female authorship. Like Duclos and d'Alembert, the friends were concerned with personal autonomy; but their emphasis was on a labor of selfhood, the self-examination and meditation needed to defend an inner core from the centripetal pulls to which the social self was subject in *mondanité*. Perhaps distinct to them was the spirituality they wanted to inform their practice of intellectual labor. When Necker and Thomas assured each other of the "purity" of their friendship, they meant that they were bound by a conviction of unitary selfhood, a spiritual core that no social pressure could pull apart or dissolve.

The conviction rested on two traditions of spirituality that we often see as divergent, one Stoic, the other Calvinist and ultimately Augustinian. The friendship, in fact, is a case study in how these traditions could enter dialogue and find common ground. Necker's father had raised her in the enlightened Calvinism that had taken root in Geneva and several other Swiss cities in the early eighteenth century.[91] Recoiling against the psychological materialism of Diderot and others, she held fast to her Calvinist spiritual heritage by insisting on the immateriality and the immortality of the soul.[92] One of her moral precepts was to be in a constant war with herself to extirpate the passions. But despite her admiration for Malebranche her faith had no place for original sin or sanctification through grace. Now the inner struggle rested on the assumption that human beings were, by nature, capable of moral self-perfectibility, and that it was their duty to strive for it.

Necker's early reading of the Stoics had helped form her aspiration to inner self-mastery and the self-discipline of labor. Thomas was not a practicing Stoic like Shaftesbury, but he ignored eighteenth-century efforts to discredit Stoicism by collapsing it into Spinozist atheism.[93] His version of neo-Stoicism found its clearest expression in his eulogy of Marcus Aurelius, to whom he attributed an "enthusiasm of virtue." The labor of Stoic meditation had allowed Marcus "to assure [himself] of [himself]." Perhaps under Necker's influence, Thomas grounded Marcus's conviction of selfhood in "a religious emotion," a belief in a God as "the universal mind," stamping its unity on all that exists, including the inner self.[94] In several journal entries Necker tried to articulate how she experienced God's presence in her in the form of an anterior sentiment of existence, mysterious but unshakeable, an "unknown point."[95] On that intuition rested her conviction of the inner core that she called the self, as opposed to the performative social being, the personality. Like Thomas, she too found meditative reflectivity imperative and thought of it as a kind of askesis, an inner struggle to achieve mastery of desires and impulses.

Thomas and Necker found their existential bedrock in the conviction of a transcendent self, anterior to any awareness of bodily existence, to any sense knowledge, and above all to a merely "external" existence, a false self existing only in the gaze of others. They reinforced each other's belief that, even as this self became particularized in social being, it remained unitary because of the indwelling presence of the Absolute in human interiority. Ultimately the sentiment of unitary selfhood was experienced in solitary self-examination. For Necker this self-awareness was solidified in a process of "self-ownership" through the solitary labor of reading and writing, which was itself a kind of meditation in which thoughts and sentiments found in print penetrated the self and became integral to it.[96] Necker was close in spirit to Malebranche in this use of *attention* as solitary meditation, in contrast to her resolve to devote complete attention to interlocutors in salon conversation. Such labor was the key to self-perfecting; it was a strenuous effort of acquisition, the kind of effort that had to be hidden in polite sociability. It was in this sense that Necker called solitary reading "the secret of liberty."[97] In the labor of selfhood, reading went hand in hand with habitual writing, which confirmed that the sentiments one sought to express were not superficially derivative, but had become one's own.[98] Truly "natural" self-expression lay not in the apparent ease of a social performance, but in the communication of something integral to the self labored on in solitude. The implication was that social knowledge—knowledge acquired in social interaction—deprives us of the self-distance needed to enter into our spiritual self, the unitary soul. Necker wants to keep thought from being the mere stuff of performance, to make it instead a force that, rather than making an impression in the *mondain* sense, has a moral effect that ripples out beyond the arena of performance.

For geniuses like Thomas, the process ended in the manly eloquence that would move people to create a new civic community. Having undergone the arduous mental labor of acquisition, the genius could advance a great public end. His concentrated force could pull people into a *patrie* or a nation, a community united in civic action. Without such labor, thinking degenerated into the hyper-social performance of itself that the friends called mere *personnalité*. The friends were reversing the order of priority between the spoken word and the written word in *mondanité*. The *bel esprit* wrote in symbiosis with a self-referential space of conversational sociability, never violating its parameters of the thinkable and the expressible. To Necker and Thomas such a man, for all his vaunted versatility, was fixed in his context, imprisoned within his performative role.[99] "The *homme d'esprit*," Necker observed, "always remains in his place . . . he receives his colors from all the objects that surround him, and in turn he gives them back to the [objects]." "The man of genius always dashes forward, upward or in advance"; "and yet his ideas still precede him: one could say that he runs after them."[100] The great mind—the genius—broke out of social fixity. He could think outside society even as he remained in it. To speak to the "soul" and the "reason" of a public, Necker observed in another journal entry, one has to labor in retreat.[101] That summed up the paradoxical relationship between the solitary and the social, the private and the public, in the friends' ideal of the modern author. Solitude was the condition of the genius's societal mission. Only a work forged in solitary labor, withdrawn from social representations and unmediated by them, could galvanize a society into a civic community.

There was a political as well as a civic dimension to all this. Largely implicit, it became audible in the friends' fondness for the term "enthusiasm." Against the mere wit of the *bel esprit* they posed the eloquent enthusiasm of the genius. This was common practice. They were well aware that, in the tradition of religious and philosophical polemics, enthusiasm conjured the specter of uncontrollable social and political disorder, the preacher's emotion-laden abuse of figurative language to effect a contagion of collective frenzy, a mob running amok.[102] That Necker and Thomas nonetheless took up the new, positive usage of the term is a measure of their animus toward the self-referential trivialization of language in the conversational culture of *mondanité*. In the final chapter of his *Essay on Eulogies* Thomas did not hide his envy of the oratory of the ancient republics, where eloquence flourished under "liberty" and was indispensable to decision making in the state. He reluctantly accepted the fact that in modern monarchies with the rule of law eloquence had to make do without either of these conditions. It could not be "political." Rather than communicating his natural impulsion of passion with a certain "abandon," the orator had to respect the constraints of politeness, the need to "please" and above all to not offend people of rank. And his oratory was in fact not really oratory. Rather than performing before a physically present assembly of "the People," he was limited to silent communication with isolated readers. All the more reason that his eloquence had to be driven by a unitary idea, developed in "profound meditation," and suffused with ardent and even "impetuous" sentiment. He advised aspiring authors to be as passionate as they could be within the limits of modern politeness: "Dare to mix a manly tone with songs of your century." Perhaps recalling the Dauphin eulogy, he warned them above all against flattery, which had banished "truth from the courts in every century"; and against "the softness (*mollesse*) of our mores," which "banishes [truth] from our societies."[103]

While they lamented the excessive abstraction of philosophical systems, Thomas and Necker were far from endorsing a radical repudiation of rationalism as such. They wanted a rhetoric that would move the wills of listeners, or readers, immediately, like an electrical current, breaking through the distortions of socially generated opinion, but without collapsing individual wills into a collective hysteria.[104] It would effect a kind of contagion, but without forming a mob. Necker called for a rhetoric centering on "a great intermediate idea," uniting sensations and thoughts, reason and imagination. The challenge was to put figurative language in the service of what she and Thomas repeatedly called a "chain" of ideas, a logic of argument which individual listeners were free to accept or reject.[105] The eloquence of the genius—the eloquence Thomas already practiced—would be edifying, ennobling, inspiring, majestic, sublime, even commanding, but not manipulative or overpowering. They had in mind a moral revolution, not a social upheaval.

What role did Thomas's essay assign women in this regeneration of language and society? He lamented that there were fewer women authors in his own century than there had been in the Italian Renaissance. In his concluding paragraph he called for more women to publish their way of thinking. The prevailing view, which Mme Necker seems to have shared, was that no woman could do the intensely concentrated and grueling labor that genius required. But the labor of the genius was creativity on a grand scale, beyond almost all men as well as women. To Thomas and Necker intelligent and educated women were no less capable than their male peers of engaging in intellectual labor as a process of understanding and communicating, and of doing so as writers as well as readers.

—

Necker surely approved of Thomas's fantasy, but in the privacy of her journals her own efforts to define female authorship reflected a subjectivity that remained fissiparous despite her belief in an integrating sentiment of selfhood. In "On a New Kind of Spectator," one of her most intriguing essay fragments, she tried to turn her acquiescence to her husband's wishes into the happy paradox of a "solitary book."[106] She imagined a time in her life when she "would perfect by style and reflection [her] wavering (*chancelantes*) and passing (*passagères*) ideas," forming them into "ideas fixed and for [herself] on all the objects of life."[107] She had in mind a remarkably variegated book, with chapters on reading, on taste, on celebrated men and women, on the correspondence of Voltaire, on the styles of Rousseau and Thomas, on style in general, on epistolary style, on Greek and other tragedies, and so on. She seemed content, and even considered herself fortunate, to be the sole reader of her own writing, though she held out the possibility that it would be published someday. She would read the book as if it were the work of another, to be meditated on to take the ideas fully into her possession. With the "style" she had in mind, she would neither report to the public on "what happens outside [its pages]," like the English *Spectator*, nor indulge in self-absorption, as in Montaigne's essays. She would deal with the external, but only as "it is seen within the self," "traced in the brain."[108] Her distinctions may not convince, but they leave us with the clear impression that she sought in writing and in style a new way of combining the interior and the external, self-reflection and engagement with public intellectual life.

Necker was clearly planning an ambitious undertaking, a sustained commitment to the solitary labor she extolled so often in the journals. In other journal extracts we find a different Necker, or perhaps two different Neckers. Nowhere are the differences more apparent than in a much longer and more intricate essay draft that was left uncompleted and in the printed extracts was titled "Beginning of a Eulogy of Mme de Sévigné."[109] Sévigné had been a well-connected society woman of the late seventeenth century and a close friend of Mme de Lafayette. The publication of her many letters, most of them written to her daughter, had begun in 1726 and was completed in 1754. The volumes became immensely popular in *mondain* circles. In 1734 no less a personage than Jean Bouhier, an erudite man of letters and a member of the French Academy, had praised the letters for their "effortless" and "natural" style and had placed them "in the rank of the classic books of our language."[110] That status was disputed, in part because to some readers the letters' charms were overridden by the fact that Sévigné was an uncritical product of an unenlightened age. There was her adulation of Louis XIV; her religious intolerance, most deplorable in her approval of the Edict of Nantes; her aristocratic pride of lineage. Some critics found her expressions of love for her daughter a sublime example of what maternal love ought to be; others thought them gushy and boringly repetitive. Precisely what made the letters so charming—the preoccupation with details of family and friends and society gossip—opened them, from a literary standpoint, to the charge of being trivial. There was general agreement, however, that the fact that these were private letters, and that Sévigné had had no intention of publishing them, was precisely what made them so appealing. They were to be admired for their naturalness and spontaneity, their lack of authorial self-consciousness. Here lay the paradox of the literary value attributed to the letters: Sévigné was a master of a new literary genre, the intimate epistle, because (like her contemporary Saint-Évremond) she had had no wish to be an author. An *honnête femme*, she had been posthumously made an author despite herself; and readers had the sense that they were in her immediate presence, as though listening to her conversation rather than reading her. There was no mediating authorial labor. For that reason she could be forgiven, at least to some extent, for her lack of critical judgment. In Voltaire's view her letters were to be enjoyed, even savored for their moments of "taste," despite the fact that she had poor judgment, or no judgment at all, when it came to the "taste" required to evaluate literature.[111] The *Encyclopédie* circle could not forgive her seventeenth-century prejudices, but they split in the evaluation of her style and the character behind it. To some the letters were nothing more than a "curdling sack" (*caillette*), the "padding of futile ideas of society" found in seventeenth-century polite conversation.[112]

What delighted Necker was that, after centuries of celebrating "great men" who "inspired admiration or fear," a woman had been given "the rights to celebrity" simply because "her pen was consecrated solely to friendship."[113] The popularity of her letters marked "progress in the finesse of our taste"; letter writing was now recognized as a legitimate literary "genre" with its distinct "epistolary" style. Necker went on to "hazard a parallel" of the letters with "those of the greatest ancient and modern writers." Precisely because they were so intimate and "naïve," she claimed, they compared favorably with the letters of, among others, Cicero, Pliny, Pascal, Fontenelle, and Saint-Évremond. She made this argument, she wrote, "without fear," knowing it might be dismissed in scholarly and literary circles as laughable.[114]

Necker was taking sides in arguments about Sévigné's letters that had marked the lesions in French literary criticism for nearly a century. Her defense of Sévigné often seemed to parrot earlier admirers of the letters. And yet if she had completed and published the essay, it would have marked an important moment, perhaps an unprecedented one, in French letters: the assertion of a female right to a voice in the public discourse of literary criticism, a genre that most male authors, including Hume, considered an exercise in authoritative judgment reserved to men.[115] It was, of course, a paradoxical assertion: here was a woman exercising (virtually) her right to make public literary judgments, and indeed to argue that the genre of the epistle ought to have a place in the French literary canon, but doing so for a female writer whose greatness seemed to lie precisely in the fact that she had not aspired to be an author and not made the effort to be one.[116]

If Necker's assertiveness seems at times to scatter into confusion, that is because it was inflected through the three Sévignés with whom she identified; the natural and spontaneous writer, not expecting to be published; the *honnête femme*; and the woman of character, rising morally above *mondain* performance. At times the essay, like some of her shorter journal extracts, seems to embrace the seventeenth-century ideal of the *honnête femme*. She pays tribute to the kind of effortlessly charming woman she wished she could be, the woman groomed in the social aesthetic of play. Sévigné simulates in writing the apparently spontaneous, or unreflective, play with fleeting detail in the art of conversation. It is a measure of Necker's inner tensions that in a journal entry she regretted precisely this female form of expression; "the sensibility of women delivers them almost entirely to the present," and hence "they have never written anything but letters"; "they stop at the first step," while men, knowing "how to live at a great distance from themselves," push on and reach "the goal."[117] In the draft essay she reverses herself, arguing that it is precisely the exclusive attention to the present moment that gives Sévigné's letters singular literary value.

If for Necker Sévigné is in some ways a representative character, the epitome of the *honnête femme*, her letters are also an example of style as the direct expression of the singularity of character. She was immersed in *le monde*, but she also achieved a higher greatness despite it. Ultimately her literary superiority is grounded in precisely the moral integrity that Necker found so lacking in seventeenth-century *honnêteté* and its *bels esprits*. We find in her letters authentic "sentiment," and that is because her "natural style" is the immediate representation of her noble "character." Her naturalness, one might say, lies in expressing her character openly, as it really was, and not in performing in a seemingly natural way. Strikingly, Necker largely ignores the questions that had been raised by Sévigné's fervid maternal attachment; her relationship with her daughter becomes an exemplar of intimate friendship. Sévigné writes as though she were speaking to a dear friend, with a vivid but measured use of images that "penetrates insensibly into the soul of the reader, and that finally unites intimately [the reader's] thought and that of the writer."[118] The quotidian particularity of Sévigné's style turns writing into the immediate communication of the intimacy of friendship, rather than a form of representation mediated by social conventions. That is why, despite her conformity to conventions, she is an "original" author for all ages, unlike her seventeenth-century male predecessors. It was a bold claim. Most of Necker's contemporaries would have agreed that the *mauvais génie* Voiture had a contrived style. She would have faced more skepticism for ranking Sévigné above Pliny, whose "excessive self-love *(amour propre)*" she finds in every line. In contrast Sévigné "forgets herself entirely"; "all her and our attention is directed to the person to whom she writes."[119]

In extolling Sévigné's epistolary genius, Necker had several targets in mind: the egotism of the male author seeking immortality in print; the social aesthetic of play in its contrived and superficial forms; the false expression of "sentiment" and "sensibility" in her own era; the abstract profundity of philosophical reasoning. She does not, it should be stressed, limit Sévigné to the mere immediate expression of a sensibility empty of thought. Contrary to the view of *"sensibilité"* as "a social virtue," she writes, it is a "reciprocal term" that "marks a return to the self," as "sentiments are the effect of several imperceptible reflections."[120] She sees such reflections as quite different from the abstractions of philosophy:

> It has been said that the talent of a sublime writer consists above all in seeing the objects as a whole (*en grand*) and by abstraction; that is to say, in distancing themselves from us. Reading Mme de Sévigné produces a contrary effect; she relates us more closely to general ideas; she shows them in their daily use, she reconciles (*apprivoise*) us with them, if one can put it thus; finally she attaches there our heart and our eyes. . . . These letters are also without interest for philosophers, whose hearts, desiccated by abstractions, become indifferent to the objects surrounding them; who think they can enlarge themselves by hurling themselves out of their sphere, and who, like gods, wish to take the measure of things outside themselves; but it is in ourselves that we must search for [that measure]; it is sentiment which gives it, which multiplies our relations (*rapports*), and thus which alone can extend our existence.[121]

Necker describes a symbiosis of the intellectual labor of solitary inwardness and the relational awareness of self and others in a plurality of social connections, and especially in intimate friendship. Perhaps because it is only a draft, the essay brings into bold relief the paradoxical dilemma of women who imagined themselves performing their intelligence in print. It stakes a virtual claim to women's right to exercise cultural authority in print as literary critics.[122] This, though, in an essay that restricts female literary genius to the epistolary genre, and indeed denies such genius literary ambition. And yet within that severe restriction the essay is a tentative but remarkable effort, an imagined manifesto for a female literary subjectivity in epistolary form. Necker wants to secure women a separate but equal literary sphere. It would be only one of many literary spheres, the rest apparently male domains; but within it the writing of the female genius would be equal to (or superior to?) that of her male counterpart because it would capture an individual interiority in its immediate engagements with the persons and things that fill a life from moment to moment. In a process she leaves unexplained, the turn inward and the social specificity of relations with others, and particularly with friends, combine to manifest the talent of the writing self. When we recall that Thomas, in his defense of men's friendships with women in the simulated dialogue with Montaigne, emphasized the unheroic experience of affective communion, we get a glimpse of how the two friends shaped each other's thinking. In the reciprocal actions of sentiment, one becomes aware of the grounding of the self and truly gets outside oneself, in sympathetic interchanges with others.

Necker is not simply saying that such writing does not aspire to objectivity; it questions the value of objectivity, and it mocks the centuries-old male claim to know how to achieve it. A natural style represents the fleeting particularity that gives life meaning. To a degree the woman who achieves lasting literary originality without trying remains bound to, and indeed exemplifies, the received aesthetic of play: the expectation of *complaisance, aisance,* tasteful attention to sensory and affective detail. But she also transcends her prescribed identity, posing, perhaps unwittingly, the moral and emotional authenticity of a distinct subjectivity, her delight in the quotidian detail of social relations, against men's pretensions to think outside both their interior awareness and their social transactions. The essay was, in this admittedly limited sense, a woman's gesture of defiance against the aridly purist conception of manly intellectual labor. By way of sentiment Necker tries to unite in reciprocity a felt conviction of centered selfhood, developed in isolation, and an enactment of character in the no less affective practices of social exchange. Her variant on a longstanding notion of women's superior relational intelligence, one might say, gives it a new literary status.

At the very end of the draft it becomes apparent that Necker's defiance was driven by a grievance against her putatively enlightened age, and against many of the men she hosted in her salon. She regrets that so many "women who are interesting because of their intelligence (*esprit*) and their character" would be "covered with contempt" if they tried to overcome the "obstacles" facing them. This is not just a matter of societal habit; "even the *philosophes,* those enemies of prejudice, conserve that of their sex." Though claiming to recognize only individual merit, they "divide human beings into two very distinct classes." "If nature had marked gradations among beings," she writes, "it would have been by the multiplicity of personal relations (*rapports*), and not by the ranks that force has determined." There was a fundamental hypocrisy in the Enlightenment's ideal of productive labor and ennobling ambition. Savages who mistreated their women were unwittingly in "error." In civilized society "it is not an error, but a barbarism to humiliate women, because love of self (*amour-propre*) is the only recompense that society has not at all stolen from them."[123]

There, with almost two lines of dots in the printed version, the draft ends unfinished.

Gallantry Corrupted

Even as Mme d'Épinay faulted Thomas's *Essay* for leaving the reader wondering where he stood on the question of women, she protested its "ceaseless attribution to nature of what we obviously receive from education or institutions, etc." The part of the text that might seem to confirm this latter reading emphatically is titled "The Nature of the Sexes." Raising the question whether women's intellection was equal to men's, Thomas went through a familiar inventory from "the natural weakness of [women's] organs." At times, in fact, he offers a litany of virtually every essentialist stereotype of women we have encountered in this study. Thomas questioned whether women had the powers of concentration needed to sustain "a long chain of ideas"; whether their "more delicate fibers" allowed them to pursue the naturally more "active" life of men; whether they were capable of evoking the sublime; whether "their imagination, although vivid, resembled a mirror capable only of reflecting everything, but creating nothing" (107–10); whether they could summon the "spirit of method" and the "excess of work" needed for erudition (111–12). In a comment in striking contrast to Poullain de la Barre's valuation of women's social intelligence a century earlier, women's ephemeral "crowd of little pieces of knowledge," the attention to immediate detail that made them such sympathetic friends, now seen from another angle, seemed to disqualify them from governing (112). Given what we know of Thomas's struggles with physical weakness and paralyzing bouts of depression, all this is not surprising. He was, after all, a man who practiced sexual asceticism to avoid falling into what he saw as effeminate indolence. He needed clear and irremovable gender boundaries. It seems fair to say that there was an element of self-fantasy in his concept of manliness. Suffering bouts of depression and physical debility, he projected a man of iron mental and physical strength, unwavering concentration, immense powers of labor—a man whose labor would not be constrained by mere physical and psychological frailty.

Thomas concluded his thoughts on "the equality" or "superiority" of the sexes by acknowledging that he had given only a partial treatment of the subject. Treating it well would require the combined insights of the physician, the anatomist, and the philosophe (132). The fact that he put medicine first is telling. By the early 1770s conceptions of sexual differences were positioned within at least two medical paradigms, both positing the natural physical and mental inferiority of women on materialist assumptions, but with different logics and implications. In the logic of mechanism, still quite common in medical thought, women differed from men in the degree of strength of the fibers through which forces—sensations, emotions, ideas—were transmitted. This view was being challenged by proponents of vitalist materialism, who had begun to argue that men and women had incommensurably different organic "organizations" or constitutions.[124] The physical and mental inferiority of women was not a matter of degree, but of kind. Sexuality was becoming the key to biological determinism in the strongest sense.

Necker was certainly familiar with the medical paradigms, and in her journals she sought ways to counter their implications. As the extracts make clear, the subject of gender equality was being discussed, at least at her salon.[125] Necker remained torn between her eagerness to fit the conventional mold of the *honnête femme* and her literary ambitions, which implied a quite different appraisal of female intellectual capacities. Refraining from publishing, she assured Thomas that she was quite content to share vicariously in his rise to immortality, as a lesser intellect; but that was because she knew herself to be one of the few who could understand his genius.[126] Her modesty in the face of genius had its note of envy. She yearned to connect with a public, as Thomas did. She approved Buffon's dismissal of the common notion that "one must write as one speaks." For well-educated women, as for their male counterparts, conversation was "careless" (*négligé*), whereas writing was a difficult art requiring constant revisions.[127] In our long-term perspective, the implications, though left unstated, are of course huge. They cut the symbiosis between the *aisance* of conversation and style in the culture of *honnêteté*. In writing, educated women should not be free from labor; they should be free to labor, outside the constraints of effortlessness in polite conversation.

Necker faulted women in particular for publishing only to "shine," to exhibit their "personality" rather than to instruct others. But if properly educated in a wide range of fields, including history, ethics, and literature, women could order their thought into a "chain" of ideas; and in literary studies they could aim at "perfecting their style and acquiring eloquence, as much as that is possible" (M3, 30–32). Several other entries elaborate Necker's critique of the philosophes' gender prejudice at the end of the draft essay on Mme de Sévigné, even as they follow a line of argument quite different from her homage to Sévigné's naïve and effortless genius. If women dabble in everything and have no sustained focus, that is simply because they are trained from an early age only to please in the present moment.[128] The cultivation of their sensibility prevents them from having men's ability to "know how to live at a great distance from themselves."[129] In a long entry she constructs a hypothetic plea for the "cause of women." The first part would show that "men cannot attribute the superiority of their talents to the difference in organs." The cause is "education." The second part would demonstrate that the objects of women's education "modify [their] *esprit* and their inclinations (*penchants*) without demanding any less intelligence and capacity." In the third part, she would cite "several treatises" that, if women are not as given to application as great as men's, "they are more continually virtuous and more patient, a kind of constancy that is of considerable value in work (*travail*)." "Perhaps," she speculates, "the force that supports sorrows is the same that gives genius."[130] She cannot deny the fact of men's greater physical strength, but she undercuts it by suggesting that intelligence is also a function of moral resources peculiar to women. Here her rejection of Diderot's materialism is critical. If the moral cannot be reduced to the material, then it is possible that the moral perseverance of women in the face of the suffering peculiar to their sex can contribute to intellectual strengths that are independent of their physical weakness.

Thomas wrote his *Essay* with medical theorists looking over one shoulder and Mme Necker looking over the other. The section on the "Nature of the Sexes" is relentlessly tentative. Rather than claiming to be asserting undisputed scientific fact, it moves from "perhaps" to "perhaps." In the *Essay* as a whole, the section is an oddly placed insert. Having carried his history of eulogies of women through the Italian Renaissance, Thomas abruptly stops the narrative to consider the nature of the sexes; then, with an equally abrupt "Return to History," he devotes most of the rest of the volume to French history since the sixteenth century. Thomas claimed to be offering tableaus, not a history. He saw his characterizations of successive centuries as a series of synchronic pictures, not a diachronic analysis of process. In fact, though, the tableaus form an historical plot with a discernible shape and movement, and in its course Thomas offers causal explanations of beginnings, ascents, and declines. As he reads them, the eulogies that crowd his footnotes tell us not only how societies and cultures formed exceptional women, but also, in the way they honored them, what they valued and denigrated. Thomas's subject is not, of course, women, but very small numbers of highly privileged women; and though the eulogies of them surely reveal something about their exclusive social circles, Thomas's generalizations will strike the modern historian as arbitrary. What matters for our purposes is not the result of the method, but its underlying logic. Women, like men, are no better or worse than their times. Changes in context, not universal and timeless natural determinants, drive the story. Thomas strikes a counterpoint to the essentialist argument even as his text seems to endorse it, however tentatively, and at points assumes it.

There is nothing original about his overarching narrative. It begins with women in savage societies subjected by their physical weakness to abject drudgery, a kind of slavery, beneath human dignity, requiring no intelligence. Even in "temperate countries," where women were not "completely deprived of their liberty," "severe legislation" made them "dependent," "opinion" tyrannized them, and they were forbidden "public esteem" (52–54). With the gendered division of labor in commercializing European societies, women were esteemed for their domestic virtues. Chivalry and its attendant gallantry gave them a new dignity as the guardians of a spiritualized love and a refined sociability. But in eighteenth-century France gallantry was dead; women were now the master practitioners of excessive and duplicitous sociability, infidelity, and unashamed voluptuousness. From being slaves of opinion, they had become indifferent to it.

As a text-based story of ascent and decline, Thomas's history obviously differs from Rousseau's metanarratives. Though it is suffused with the usual censure of luxury and corruption, it is not simply and at times not even primarily another version of the declinist narrative of civic humanism. He does give the formulaic account of the passage from the moral austerity of the Roman republic to the vicious corruption of the empire, taking the opportunity to credit Stoicism with providing both men and women with a rational ethical philosophy as republican virtue, which had to be inculcated almost from birth, died out. But when Thomas turns to Europe in the wake of the barbarian invasions, he shifts to the alternative narrative of the advance to modern "polished" civilization, a centuries-long process in which women gained in dignity and freedom, in contrast to their unchanging enslavement in the Islamic world. The peak—the golden age of western culture—was the Italian Renaissance in the sixteenth century, when highly educated women played a remarkable role as active creators of culture. To Thomas Renaissance Italy was the golden age in a narrative of regeneration, not inexorable decline, the utopian model for the recovery of French society and culture from its recent plummet into corruption. Its unrivaled glory lay in the fact that the women honored in its eulogies were admired, not maligned, as *femmes savantes*; and that they had "sought, to *assurer* in everything the equality of their sex, to prove that they had as much spirit as courage" (93). Thomas attributes the Italian "revolution" in letters and the arts to a seemingly miraculous concatenation of circumstances. Though chivalry had begun to die out in Europe, it had left "a tincture (*teinte*) of Romanesque gallantry in manners" which "was transferred to works of the imagination." At the same time the new interest in language was so strong that classical learning ceased to be an exclusively male property. Learned women became masters of Latin, Greek, and even Hebrew. "The spirit of religion that animates women in all times" took a new turn. Having made women "martyrs, apostles, and warriors," it now made them "theologians and scholars." Gifted women distinguished themselves in a wide range of fields, including theology, jurisprudence, and philosophy, and some became masters of eloquence. For once, one might say, women could be learned without being stigmatized as pedants. That was in part because in the world of the new humanism "people of imagination and enthusiasm" preferred Platonism, with its "spiritual and sublime metaphysic," to the cold, dry dialectal "logic that enchains" of scholastic Aristotelianism (91–98). This celebratory portrait takes on larger significance when Thomas comes to seventeenth-century France: there too cultivated women were not stigmatized by association with the crude male culture of the universities and the "cloisters."

In the ascent to the Italian Renaissance from the tenth century onward two aristocratic codes of honor, male martial courage and female purity, happily fused, and the result was the constancy of sublimated passion that gallantry originally required (85–87). The question was whether in modern civilization this motive force of "honor" was an adequate replacement for virtue conceived as disinterested devotion to the good for itself; or whether it was merely a thin vale for egotism and deceit. Thomas winds his way to his own era through the reigning narratives of the decline of virtue and the progress of civilization. He seems to begin by repudiating Shaftesbury in favor of Hume. To Shaftesbury chivalric men had been so foolish as to place women on pedestals, handing them an authority to judge in morals and taste that exceeded their powers. He saw a straight line of descent from this "Gothic" barbarousness to the pathological effeminacy of modern polite society, exemplified by the French monarchy and its court culture. Thomas certainly had read Shaftesbury's *Characteristics*, and in the *Essay* he may have been knowingly taking issue with him. To him gallantry, in its original practice, had been a progressive force for both women and men.

The refining role Thomas attributed to gallantry seems reminiscent of Hume's view. In fact, though, his judgment of the result—the modern era—is radically different. Hume had credited the French monarchy with leading the way in the advance of civilization that he found in modern politeness and especially in its gallantry. Thomas's story became an indictment of the monarchy for perverting chivalric "honor" into vice. Under Louis XIV the happy fusion of chivalry and gallantry dissolved as the court nobility, having nothing but titles without power, "were reduced to a grandeur of representation, rather than a real grandeur," and gravitated to the "society" of the capital. As "luxury" spread in *le monde*—we can hear the return of civic humanist moralism—"corruption and audacity of mores" became "almost regarded as a privilege of rank." "Gallantry became a fashion," and "the *aisance* of manners [became] a grace" (140). Under the reigning literary *politesse* of Voiture and novelists like Mademoiselle de Scudéry and Mme de Lafayette, the specter of pedantry returned and women almost had to hide their learning (142). Then came the Regency, another "revolution" but one with a downward spiral, when "voluptuousness" became the fashion and part of the veil that covered gallantry was ripped away (150). In this world Thomas found nothing of the happy fusion of artifice and nature that Hume imagined, nothing of the self-conscious custom of pleasing sociability that he found so benign. There was simply "corruption" without "shame," at once "profound and frivolous," in which "the two sexes denatured themselves." Gallantry became "a vile sentiment which assumed all weaknesses, or gave birth to them" (151). It was hardly surprising that under these conditions there were fewer eulogies of women than ever before. "The eulogy is produced by enthusiasm"; it cannot thrive in an age of pervasive cynicism and satire. It was no wonder that women themselves "praise[d]" this "general spirit of society": it was "their work" (157).

That many readers found all this confused is not surprising. I have simplified the text by abstracting plot lines from discourses that often swirl together in Thomas's profusely figurative rhetoric. Acutely aware of the minefield he was navigating, he could not settle on a single voice for his moralism; or at least he dared not assert it unambiguously. His long-term historical framework is nonetheless critical for understanding the larger significance of his tribute to Mme Necker. He was not simply expressing his gratitude for their friendship. When Thomas haled Necker for "honoring another century than ours," he made her a reincarnation of the *femme savante* of the Italian Renaissance (158). She and women like her would "recover" their rightful "empire"—the moral and aesthetic empire over which they ought to reign—by purifying themselves of *mondain* corruption (159). They would be able to "think" with Montesquieu and converse with Fenelon, even as they were loving wives and "mothers who dare(d) to be mothers" (158). No doubt "society" would be "less active"; but "the interior of families" would be "sweeter." Theirs would be a life of social grace without affectation, "where one exists only for oneself, and not for the regard of others, where one enjoys day by day friendship, nature, and oneself" (159).

—

In the *Essay*'s concluding encomium to "the ideal woman," Thomas portrays a woman mastering all the "charms of society," its taste, grace, and wit (*esprit*) without falling into "false sensibility" or denying her need for repose in friendship, while cultivating philosophy and letters "for themselves" and not "for reputation." Such a woman would, "at the risk of displeasing, know how to maintain her esteem for virtue, her contempt for vice, and her sensibility for friendship in her home and outside it, and despite the desire to have an extended society, in the midst even of that society would have the courage to publish a way of thinking so extraordinary, and the greater courage of sustaining it" (161). It was this concluding tableau of "the ideal woman" that Louise d'Épinay, a woman of letters in her own right, found the only agreeable part of the *Essay*, though she regretted that the author offered it as a chimera.[131]

From our current perspective, there is something odd, if not contradictory, about calling at one and the same time for women to retreat (partially) to domesticity and to publish in a wide range of fields. It probably also struck some of Thomas's contemporaries as odd. The call for more female authors confronts us with something puzzling: a blatantly un-Rousseauian twist in a text so indebted to Rousseau. Like Rousseau, Thomas pitted domesticity against the hypersociability of *le monde*; but he also imagined it offering educated women a kind of autonomy, developed and protected in the solitude of the home, and allowing them, from that position, to question the "opinion" to which women were subjected. This was a call for a certain independence for women, a right to introversion over extroversion, to "being" within themselves, and not always to "pleasing" or "appearing" as required in the gaze of others.

All this is not to deny that the more typical visions of a regenerated *patrie* had society women withdrawing from the stage lights into the privacy of domestic life. That was certainly Rousseau's view. In this friendship we see the worldly and the domestic, the public and the private, configuring in a different way. For women of the *haute bourgeoisie*, no less than for aristocratic women, the choice was not between confining women to the privacy of the domestic sphere and giving them access to public occupations still reserved to men. Gender and status norms still fused to make remunerated work unthinkable. For women of this exalted station, the issue of labor had a different valence. The question was whether well-educated women could be liberated, in the privacy of their homes, from the imperatives of a world that banned intellectual labor. For women, as for men, domesticity did not preclude authorship; it was the retreat—the space of solitude—that made serious authorship possible. This too was utopian. From our perspective Thomas used his Stoicism to square the circle. He tried to reshape an emerging bourgeois ideal of domesticity, floating the hope that women's domesticity, conceived as their habitual withdrawal from the performative imperatives of *aisance*, would become the site for their authorial labor.

Chapter 8

Minds Not Meeting: Denis Diderot
and Louise d'Épinay

Of the readers who found fault with Thomas's essay, none was more patronizing than Denis Diderot. His reaction was quick and persistent, though also somewhat disjointed. His critique appeared under the title "On Women" in the *Correspondance littéraire* in April 1772, immediately following the appearance of Thomas's book, and in expanded versions over the next several years, adding material from Diderot's contributions to the abbé Raynal's *Histoire des deux Indes*.[1]

To Diderot Thomas's failure in writing about women lay in his insufficient capacity to *sentir*. The verb *sentir* evades translation, particularly in Diderot's shifting usages. Often rendered simply as "to feel," it connotes an immediate and spontaneous understanding or knowing, a sensual and affective intuition as well as an act of intellection. In the opening of his essay Diderot seemed to be taking his cue from Grimm's introduction to it, which blamed the essay's banality on the fact that Thomas's Platonic relationship with Necker lacked the "tender delirium" of a "profane love." "It is said," Grimm added, "that he has a chest too delicate to quit Platonism."[2] The imputation of impotence was a choice bit of Parisian gossip, offered from within a high society rife with venomous rumors and behind-closed-doors ridicule, where a culture of sexual liaisons had little patience with holier-than-thou claims to purely spiritual friendship. Diderot sufficed with the less waspish comment that Thomas had not "experienced (*éprouvé*)" sexual passion "enough" (165). Though the initial version of "On Women" was available only in manuscript copies distributed to princely courts outside France, Diderot was writing for a wider imagined audience and his larger subject was the nature of cognition. Thomas lacked the sexual experience needed for a manly understanding, a capacity to know (*sentir*)—and for men that was the only form the truth about women could take. Thomas "thought much but knew (*senti*) not enough." Wanting his book "to have no sex," "he succeeded only too well." The book was "a hermaphrodite, which has neither the vigor of a man nor the softness of a woman" (165–66).

Diderot was not just sweetening the pill with his opening assurance that he "liked" Thomas and "respect[ed] the pride of his soul and the nobility of his character" (165). To him Thomas *was* a noble character, a man using his gifts to uplift his country from its corrupted mores. In principle (practice was often another matter), he shared with Thomas an ideal of sublime civic rhetoric aimed not at pleasing its listeners, but at moving them to emulate Roman civic virtue.[3] With the notable exception of the eulogy of the Dauphin, he admired Thomas's eloquence, as it exemplified this moral sublimity and civic idealism with which he too wanted to counter the decadence of the *bel esprit*'s hollow performances and the insipidity of the *goût moderne*. He and Thomas thought of genius as a manly gift and aspired to meet its exalted standards, though Diderot probably gave more credit to inspiration in the genius's creativity.

And yet in "On Women" Diderot obviously chose a style and a form of argumentation that was the antithesis of Thomas's. To him Thomas's prose was monotonous because it was sexless; his own would have the "suppleness proper to speaking of the infinite diversity of a being extreme in her power and in her weakness" (166). "In the absence of reflection and of principles," Diderot tells us, "nothing penetrates to a certain profundity of conviction in the understanding of women" and "the ideas of justice, virtue, vice, goodness, and malice float on the surface of their soul" (179). It is a sentence Malebranche or Shaftesbury could have written, a commonplace about women's inability to practice the laborious reflection needed to grasp abstract principles of morality and justice. While Thomas entertained this position as a possibility still to be investigated by physicians and philosophers, Diderot took it as a fact beyond questioning.

The tone of Diderot's essay is audacious—we hear the pronouncements of a man who has come to know women thoroughly, as far as they can be known—and at times the prose seems to dart unpredictably, almost errantly, from thought to thought, progressing by mysterious association, as in the conversational performances that his friends found so entrancing. This is the truly daring speculation of the philosophe, perhaps the genius, not the conventionally bounded and formalistic cleverness of the *bel esprit*. Diderot was well aware of his effect. In 1759 he described to Sophie Volland an evening spent at the Baron d'Holbach's country house in which he had seemed to his audience "extraordinary, inspired, divine"; he had been "the fiery center" of the gathering's "enthusiasm."[4] He seemed to write as he spoke, in a trance-like state. His voice in "On Women" is reminiscent of the authorial persona he had assumed in his eulogy of the epistolary novelist Samuel Richardson in 1762. Diderot had tried to grip his readers with something of the immediacy of Richardson's prose, his gift for giving the reader the unmediated feeling of experiencing morality (or immorality) in action in the ordinary circumstances of life. He had "set down . . . these lines," he told his readers in the last paragraph, "without coherence, plan or order, just as they came to me in the

tumult of my heart." In the end it was futile to try to evoke Richardson's characters; "the pen falls from my hand."[5] There is something of the same impression
of disordered and ultimately futile outpouring in "On Women." "The symbol of
women in general," Diderot writes, "is that of the Apocalypse, on the front of
which it was written Mystery" (180). And yet there is also something methodical
about the essay; under its apparent disorder it follows the logic of a plan Diderot
laid out immediately after his opening skewering of Thomas. Women are aston-
ishing, he writes, in the passions of love and jealousy, in "the transports of maternal tenderness," in "the instances of superstition, the way in which they share
epidemic and popular emotions." He does not use Thomas's essay, as some readings assume, merely as a jumping-off point to air his own views on women. In his
seemingly disordered way, he addresses Thomas point by point.

Any attempt to stitch Diderot's thoughts on gender and sexuality into a consistent whole is likely to yield no more than a crazy quilt of readings.[6] There is no
subject on which this famously unsystematic thinker was more eclectic. The Diderot of this chapter is something of a heuristic figure: not the author of a corpus
with consistent thematic lines, but the author of a single text, "On Women"
(though several of Diderot's other writings are brought in to the extent that they
help us understand it). Of all the texts we have considered, this one may have the
strongest claim to our attention as a complex rhetorical performance. At least by
the standard of length, it is a "minor" piece. Aligning it with more substantial
texts has required selective quotation, at the expense of attention to its rhetorical
structure, the specifics of its rebuttal of Thomas, and its location in the
eighteenth-century historical debates about women and gallantry.

Mistreatment of the essay has been especially noticeable in the last several
decades of feminist scholarship on Diderot.[7] Several scholars have followed the
lead of the French philosopher Elisabeth de Fontenay in her article "Diderot
gynéconome," published in 1976. De Fontenay argues from forays into "On
Women" and several other texts that, despite gender prejudices typical of his era,
Diderot developed a "hegemonic reversal" of the conventional wisdom on male
and female cognition. His view of the uterus as inherently different from male
reproductive organs, and not as an interior inversion of them, opens a way to deny
the male solipsism of the Cartesian cogito and its corollary mind-body dualism.
Seeing women not as males manqué but as incommensurably different sexual
beings, with cognitive powers (powers to *sentir*) grounded in uterine energy,
makes it possible to think of female cognition as qualitatively different, possessing
its own value, and thus to undercut the false universalism that makes maleness the
norm that women cannot meet.[8]

There are good reasons for skepticism about this way of thinking about female
intelligence, but my objection here is to the stunningly arbitrary absorption of an
eighteenth-century text into a late twentieth-century debate within feminism. A

reading so much against the grain of the text makes it unrecognizable. Lieselotte Steinbrügge's reconstruction of the text is a cogent antidote, but it distills an argument rather than considering the essay as a rhetorical performance in a dense biographical and sociocultural context.[9] The text presents us, in fact, with two rhetorical performances, one expressing an unusually frank and unblinking sympathy for the plight of women, the other a performance in manly thought and writing that can fairly be called misogynistic. The sympathetic Diderot spoke in the voice of a bourgeois father outraged by the oppression facing his daughter. He accepts social convention only for want of choice, and is provoked by the blatant injustice of it all to evoke alternative worlds. The misogynist based his authority on the privileged insights of a new kind of genius, the great clinician ascending to heroic status in cutting-edge medical philosophy for his practice of a distinctly male labor of the imagination. The father speaks of what ought to be, in the anthropomorphic voice of humans as moral beings. The clinician speaks of what is, what the amoral laws of nature dictate implacably. Thinking outside his own and his species-situated knowledge, he sees Nature simply as an economy of energy and naturalizes gender differences and inequalities as irremovable facts of life, within a new framework of scientific knowledge about male and female bodies and minds.

Perhaps more than any other author of his era, Diderot, as he evolved from his early Shaftesburyian moral idealism to neo-Stoic materialism, allows us to map the field of perceptions and choices about male and female attributes of intelligence in the French High Enlightenment. His thinking at once rested on conventional gender stereotypes and took a radical turn in the separation of manly intellectual labor from the dangerously errant female imagination. Arguably the literary and sociable culture of sensibility, even as it rejected the superficiality of *honnête* performance, heightened the possibility of reshaping the configuration of gender and intelligence that the discourse of *honnêteté* had opened. From a purely logical standpoint, sensibility had the potential to transform a negative stereotype of women into a positive. Regarded by the standard of abstract reasoning as a mark of women's intellectual weakness, affective cognition, shaped by the imagination, might now be valued as a power more natural to women than to men, especially in matters of taste, literary judgment, and social morality. Unlike David Hume, who tried to walk a fine line on this issue, Diderot sought to resolve it. He was ambivalent about abstract reasoning and at times contemptuous of it, but the imagination he privileged was an exclusively male domain. He separated out within the imagination, so often seen as the faculty of undisciplined and potentially anarchic female fantasy, a distinctly manly labor of scientific and poetic genius.[10]

Diderot's Paternal Voice

What does it mean to say that Diderot was a "bourgeois" father, or a bourgeois in any sense?[11] His own father was a master cutler whose surgical instruments were

much in demand. In Diderot senior's hometown of Langres, his substantial property, the strict propriety of his household, his reputation for honesty and good
judgment, and his orthodox piety made him an eminent figure. He had the solidity for which the provincial bourgeois—when he was not being ridiculed as a
philistine—was appreciated. And yet there is arguably something preposterous
about giving his son a bourgeois identity. When his father sent him to Paris in
1728, it was probably in the expectation he would study for the clergy. What
ensued was the familiar story of the young man freed from provincial life in the
great metropolis. Like Thomas and his friends nearly twenty years later, Diderot
had no interest in pursuing a conventional profession (*état*); he had a passion for
"letters" and an ambition to achieve literary fame. Diderot senior allowed his son
to change to law in 1732, but soon came to realize that he had entered the
dissolute life of the literary underground. He confronted the young man with the
choice of taking up a useful profession or forfeiting his allowance. The wayward
son chose to live hand to mouth, earning what he could from translations, anonymous reviews, tutoring, and sermons written for hire. In 1742 he returned to
Langres seeking permission to marry Anne-Toinette Champion, who worked
with her widowed mother in a small lace and linen shop in Paris. His parents flatly
refused; she was socially too far beneath him, and in any case he was unable
to support a family. Diderot returned to Paris, having escaped from the brief
incarceration his father had arranged for him in a monastery, and married. Fearing
disinheritance, he kept the marriage secret, going so far as have his wife keep her
maiden name. It was nearly six years before his family learned of the marriage.[12]

Father and son eventually reconciled, but with little effect on Diderot's life in
Paris. His daughter would later recall that he was too possessive to allow his wife
to mix with male customers in a shop, and too habituated to a bachelor's life on
the margins of literary Paris to give it up. His wife, isolated in their apartment,
became embittered. In the late 1740s he became enamored of Mme Madeleine
d'Arsant de Puisieux, the exceptionally well-educated daughter of a family in the
lower nobility. The attraction was intellectual as well as physical. Puisieux may
have been the first woman Diderot encountered who was both at ease in the
conversational culture of *le monde* and intent on being recognized as an intellectually serious author. She shared Diderot's inclination to radical materialism and to
a libertinism in defiance of Christian morality, though her open advocacy of liberty and equality for educated women may also record her reaction against Diderot's views.[13] In 1755 he began a more enduring relationship with Sophie Volland,
to whom he wrote the voluminous letters that are now a treasure of eighteenth-
century correspondence. In later years, as he achieved literary fame, he continued
this way of life, married in law but a bachelor in practice, busy with his writing and
publishing projects, his literary circles, and his letters and visits to Sophie and her
mother and sisters, who had become a kind of surrogate family. Much of his time

was spent at his friends' country residences. Though his failed home life did not prevent him from occasionally extolling the family as the sacred ground of natural moral sentiment, his more cynical view was that for many men and women, perhaps most, marriage was an unbearable prison, if only because monogamy flew in the face of the natural impulse to inconstancy.[14] And yet Diderot's values were less antibourgeois than one might suppose.[15] He was a guilt-ridden rebel against paternal authority, intent on winning his father's approval well after his death in 1759. He often made an idol of the bourgeois patriarch in his writings: a man whose life revolved around family and sober work; the righteous but tender pater familias, propertied but preferring a simple domestic life to the frivolity, excessive display, and licentiousness of aristocratic culture. In his play *Le père de famille*, performed in 1758, he contrives a happy reversal of a father's opposition to his son's determination to marry a poor young woman from an obscure family. Originally misled, the father proves to be benevolent and just; and the son, now regretting his impetuous and volatile behavior, submits to his wisdom. In *Entretiens d'un père avec ses enfants*, written in 1771, a prudent father argues that the law must be followed, even if natural justice might demand that it be ignored, and his idealistic son takes the opposite position. The father is given the last word.

In 1761 Diderot began taking more interest in his only surviving child, Angélique, who at nine seemed ready to be educated properly. He entered a prolonged battle with his wife, who was raising their daughter in orthodox Catholic piety and, he feared, would transmit to the girl her own crude irascibility. Father and daughter went on long walks, as Diderot tried to improve her manners and emancipate her from religious superstition and bigotry. His wife's resistance was powerfully reinforced by the disapproval of his younger brother, a canon in the cathedral at Langres whom Diderot, with some justification, would make legendary in his correspondence as an utterly unyielding bigot. To their horror Diderot gave Angélique instruction in sexual matters and, as she approached marriage, had her attend anatomy lectures. Aside from seeking a victory over superstitious dogmatism, Diderot wanted his daughter to acquire habits and skills of self-cultivation that his wife had not had when they married and had had no opportunity to acquire. He inculcated in her a love of serious reading, or "study," and, impressed by her musical talent, had her take harpsichord lessons. He was concerned less that these accomplishments would qualify her for the social rounds in bourgeois society than that they would give her a retreat from them, a space of solitary repose to be herself. She responded affectionately to his attention, and he delighted in his role as a wise and caring father.

By 1767 Diderot was assuming the responsibility of finding Angélique a husband.[16] At one point he seems to have entertained the hope of marrying her to Grimm, twenty-one years her senior and long attached to Madame d'Épinay. It may have been a mere playful fantasy, and in any case it went nowhere. But it gives us a glimpse of his ambivalence. Even as he sought to place Angélique in a secure and respectable bourgeois marriage, he wanted to keep her in his own unbourgeois world, where he would see her often and she might continue to develop her talents in the company of his unconventional friends. He soon returned to convention, though not to the kind of arranged marriage that took no account of the girl's wishes. On May 4, 1770, he wrote his sister that Abel-François-Nicolas Caroillon, the twenty-eight-year-old son of a prosperous merchant family in Langres with close ties to the Diderot family, had asked for his daughter's hand. His decision, Diderot told him, would depend on Angélique; he was "too good a father to give her to someone who would not be agreeable to her." She did find Caroillon agreeable, and the couple married on September 9, 1772, four months after "On Women" appeared. His brother had refused to attend, and his wife had forbidden him to invite any of his friends. Having done his duty, Diderot was in despair. Hopelessly estranged from his wife, he no longer had a family. "I am desolated in being alone," he wrote Grimm on September 18, pleading for his company, "and that is all I feel."[17]

Four days after the wedding he had sent Angélique a solemn letter, an impassioned catechism of good behavior that he instructed her to reread at least once a month. In giving you to Caroillon, he wrote, "I have resigned to him all my authority," and "now I have only the right to counsel." In the very act of letting go of his legal control, he was intent on holding on to his moral authority. "If you occupy yourself with increasing [my love for you]," he wrote, "if you ask yourself: what would my father think of me if he saw me, if he heard me, if he knew, you will always do well."[18] Her marriage would not prevent him from dwelling in her as her conscience. For the emerging division into private (female) and public (male) spheres in bourgeois life this letter would seem to be a locus classicus. "Affairs outside [the home] are his," Diderot wrote; "those within are yours." Surely thinking of his own domestic situation, he continued: "You will render your home so agreeable to your husband that he will be away from it only with regret, if you are sweet, pleasing, and gay." And she must avoid giving "a false appearance" of herself, as women are rightly judged "by appearances."[19] But there is an undertow of alarm in this apparently assured advice to a beloved daughter. Diderot was warning Angélique against the perils of her marriage. He saw the strict privacy of the home as protection against the corruption that lurked in bourgeois life, no less than in le monde. She should accommodate her husband's "reasonable" tastes. Above all she must always "restrain her society"; "where there is much of the world (beaucoup du monde), there is much of vices. A numerous society is necessary only to those who are bored and who are not content with themselves." Diderot sees a vicious circle: women throw themselves into society because they are bored at home; and they are bored at home because they have become addicted to social circulation. He had provided Angélique with a resource against this fate, and she must use it habitually. Once she had fulfilled her domestic duties, she must retreat into serious reading, of which she had happily done enough to have taste, and to her music. It is striking that the value of her accomplishments does not lie in providing companionship to her husband. Diderot's point is that Angélique will avoid "the boredom, the disgust with all occupation," that would lead to "dissipation," by having the resources to be alone with herself at home. With reading and music she would "fortify her soul" by "adorning her spirit."[20] She should remain at home not only to perform her domestic duties, but also to have time for self-sufficient intellectual application; domesticity is the condition for refuge from the constant performance that scatters the self. There is an ironic affinity here with Mme Necker's view of the domestic space as a retreat from false and excessive sociability, though the social context is several tiers below the pinnacle of *le monde*, and though Diderot had no intention of encouraging his daughter to be even a virtual author.

By the time he wrote the letter Diderot had reason to wonder whether he had given his daughter to the wrong man. In the hope of keeping her near him, he had promised to find Caroillon a good position in Paris, but that was proving difficult despite his contacts with people in high places. He had a repulsion against playing the client and was thoroughly sick of "running around the court, the city, and the countryside." That made it all the more exasperating that in the course of the property negotiations the Caroillon family was becoming, as he saw it, grasping. On August 27, 1771, he wrote his sister in Langres that he wanted his daughter to be married out of "love," but that the "imbecile" who wanted to be his son-in-law "proposes to make her a peculation for profit (*intérêt*)." His daughter was a "person"; he would not have her "haggled over" as a piece of property, and she was of the same mind. "Neither she nor I nor her mother will be surprised to learn how he proposes to dispose of her once she belongs to him."[21] His visits to the couple's home in the months immediately following the wedding confirmed his worst fears. He wrote Grimm on December 9, 1772, in a state of "desolation" that must be taken seriously, though in parts the letter reads like something out of a Molière comedy. Caroillon's "project," he lamented, was to "transform [his] daughter into an incorrigible little mistress of the second order." He was making his wife a "doll," and she "has to spend the day decorating herself to please him." Must Angélique have one dress for every hour of the day, just to satisfy the vanity of "this little florist," and must they all be "crinolined, gauzed and baubled from head to foot?" He had "accustomed this child to reflection, to reading, to the pleasure of a retired life," he lamented, "with contempt for all the frivolities that devour the entire life of women." Her husband wanted to make her "a little fool, dull, impertinent, who unceasingly only knows how to well place a pompon, to simper, to lie, and to smile." Her husband appreciated the value neither of her domestic skills nor of her reading and her music. He "does not know that when he has inspired in her the taste for appearance, for twaddle, for dissipation; that when she will have forgotten everything, when she will not know what to do by herself, when she is bored at home, she will have to gallop and prowl about and will go where they all go."[22]

The Diderot of these letters is a caricature of the possessive father. At bottom he simply could not endure the fact that another man—a young fool—now had possession of his daughter. But in the letters we also see that Diderot, for all his concern with securing his daughter a comfortable bourgeois life, was no ordinary bourgeois. His ideal of simplicity and integrity was formed in a profoundly alienated social vision, directed not only against the aristocracy, but also against the bourgeois obsession with aping it. In his novel *Jacques the Fatalist and His Master* he wrote that there would be more "real original[s]" among French men "if education to begin with and then the great ways of the world did not wear them down like coins, which lose their stamp from the effect of circulation."[23] The mixing of people of different stations in so many social spaces did not have the effect of lowering the mental barriers separating people in a steep social hierarchy; every station became obsessed with emulating the station above it, with the result that people's natural characters as individuals were effaced.[24] This was what his son-in-law, with the aid of spreading consumerism, was doing to Angélique. He was making her a puppet in the emulation game. As Diderot's language of ownership and transaction, giving away and taking possession, suggests, the structuring power of this infantilizing of women lay in property and its laws; and that is what he focused on in "On Women." Women's frivolous and ultimately licentious manners were rooted in the fact that they were legally helpless minors. Having idealized the patriarchal bourgeois family, he flatly condemned its reality. Losing possession of his daughter made him rage at possession itself. He did not need his daughter's marriage, of course, to become aware that the law kept women in a helpless condition. He knew his wife was a victim as much as she was his tormentor, and he knew the dilemmas of women at much higher social levels. "On Women" became an occasion to vent his sense of the injustice of it all:

Time will continually weaken the tyranny [of the father] that you leave; time will continually increase the tyranny under which you are going to enter. One chooses a husband for her. She becomes a mother. . . . What is then a woman? Neglected by her husband, abandoned by her children, nothing in society, religious devotion becomes her unique and final resource. In almost all countries the cruelty of the civil law against women unites with the cruelty of Nature; they have been treated as imbecile children. In polished societies there is no sort of vexations that men have not been able to practice with impunity against a woman; the only recourse available to her results in domestic trouble and is punished by a contempt more or less marked, depending on whether the nation has more or less mores. . . . Women, how I feel for you! There would have been only one compensation for the wrongs done you, and if I had been the legislator, perhaps you would have obtained it: liberated from all servitude, and put above the law, you would have been held sacred in whatever place you had appeared. (173–76)

The sudden shift from the second to the third person reinforces Diderot's claim that women are legally objectified. The law empowers men to be tyrants; in modern societies it requires women to endure what Diderot later in the essay calls "oppression" (177). As Diderot explains elsewhere, the civil law's enforcement of church dogma forces both men and women to remain together, when in fact marriage is an institution that suppresses the individual's natural desires. Soon the sexual attraction between husband and wife wanes, for the simple fact is that both sexes are naturally inconstant. Like several other philosophes, Diderot thought that women should be free to divorce and remarry.[25] This rejection of indissoluble marriage is a main theme of his *Supplement to the Voyage of Bougainville*, in which an imagined Tahiti is the utopian counterpoint to Europe and its sexual unions are a reproach to the family as Europe knows it. The Tahitian Orou find it shocking that in European marriage as a permanent union people possess each other; a being endowed with natural freedom cannot be owned by another. On Tahiti sexual unions are of short duration, and the pleasure of the couple requires no fidelity for justification. The only requirement—a severely limiting one, to be sure—is that it be for the purpose of procreation.

But Diderot is a cautionary case, a reminder that the ideas of eighteenth-century radicalism did not form a package whose contents always, or even often, included the female emancipation sought by modern feminism.[26] He joined several other eighteenth-century materialists, and most notably La Mettrie, in advocating women's right to sexual pleasure,[27] and, like several other philosophes, he called for new property rights for women in marriage. But these positions did not seem to require a rethinking of the conventional wisdom that women were inferior to men in intelligence and incapable of performing the same kinds of educated labor. As striking as the depth of Diderot's moral sympathy and his outrage at women's plight is his conviction that this situation cannot and should not be seriously altered. All he can offer is a fantasy, and one in which women are freed by being given a sacred status outside society. Strikingly in the final, enlarged version of the essay written in 1780, Diderot omitted the phrase "put above the law" and proceeded immediately to an appeal to history to prove that women's subordination to men was "a well-known, general, and constant law of Nature" (176). Taken by itself, this observation is another truism of gender discourse: men, the stronger sex, naturally rule (and oppress) women, the weaker sex. What underpins the truism in Diderot's hands, however, is a new and radical way of positing women's weakness within an economy of Nature's power that simply must be accepted, no matter how unjust or immoral it may seem; and hence Diderot takes a step farther in naturalizing conventional perceptions of gender differences by making them the necessary epiphenomena of a sexual ontology. Gender differences become an irreducible fact of life, beyond the reach of moral agency.[28]

Diderot's Clinical Voice

The rhetorical power of "On Women" lies in part in the audacity of Diderot's personal testimony. When he tells us that many women never reach orgasm, even in the arms of men they adore, he leaves no doubt that he is speaking from his own experience. Likewise when he comments that "I have seen an upright (*honnête*) woman shudder with horror at the approach of her husband," and adds "I have seen her plunge herself in the bath, and never feel herself cleansed of the stain of duty" (166–67). When confronted by a woman in the grip of hysteria, he too has sometimes shivered. The text's claim to authority also rests, however, on a commitment to radical materialism, a philosophical discourse that had wide purchase among the philosophes associated with the *Encyclopédie*. A silent presence pervading the essay, it becomes audible when the piece is placed in the cluster of texts Diderot wrote in the late 1760s and early 1770s: *The Dream of d'Alembert* (1769), *Elements of Physiology*, a fragment on "genius," *Refutation of Helvétius* (1773), *Paradox of the Actor* (1770–1773).

Diderot had embraced materialism with the zeal of a convert. In the mid-1740s he had been drawn to Shaftesbury's "theistic" argument that under the providential hand of the Absolute One human nature had an innate proclivity to the practice of virtue in benevolent sociability, and that the moral beauty of virtue had its aesthetic counterpart in the great poet's evocation of ordered sublimity in nature. By the late 1760s he had completed his shift to a monist and vitalist materialism, admitting no transcendent power, no Absolute existing outside Nature and intervening in it, no soul and indeed no mind in the sense of a nonmaterial substance (Descartes's *res cogitans*), nothing but matter.[29] Diderot had assumed this position as he conducted a two-front war. As a radical member of Voltaire's church he battled religious and especially Christian "superstition" *à l'outrance*. To admit the existence of a soul was to allow the enemy to keep a grip on human subjectivity. Diderot would leave no door open for coercing people into absurdly unnatural behavior by appeal to a supernatural power that somehow dwelled within them, or to which they were somehow accountable. It was precisely on this issue that he and Madame Necker disagreed in her salon. The second front cut through the broad discourse of materialism, where the issues were how to account for motion in matter, for any form of sentience, and ultimately for moral awareness. In 1773 Diderot would spell out his convictions in his initial reactions to Helvétius's *Of Man*, published in 1773–1775. A mechanist and an avowed Lockean, Helvétius denied that differences among human beings "depended on the unequal perfection of their organs."[30] All were born with roughly equal aptitudes of intelligence, but the extent to which these developed now depended on the "accident" of environment. Accident had to be replaced by purposeful education, which could make any person virtuous and give him the capacity to grasp the truth; it might even make him a rare genius. Helvétius's environmentalism, Diderot objected, was a threat to human freedom because it would produce people denatured by society and its institutions. He had thought of himself as battling against the denaturing of his daughter under her mother's tutelage, and he worried that that fate would nonetheless befall her in marriage. His philosophical alternative to mechanistic determinism was vitalist materialism, which gave priority to the forces inherent in organic life, the springs of self-action within the body's complex of organs. Virtue was a matter of character, and the individuation of true character, as opposed to the conformity that passed for character, was a function of the organic organization of the individual from birth. It was this organically developed character that gave uniqueness to an authorial style.[31]

Such debates in natural philosophy helped frame the arguments about the nature of genius. Diderot was quite firm in taking the vitalist side, but that did not make his several attempts to define genius any less elusive.[32] For him understanding or simply contemplating genius was an act of reflectivity. He kept feeling the pulse of his own subjectivity, where he found two conflicting impulses to self-presentation, now denying each other's moral legitimacy, now trying to come to terms. What is remarkable is his ability to record with unflinching scrutiny his efforts to understand genius through intense examination of his conflicted self and the processes of his own creativity. It is this acute self-awareness—this capacity to keep listening to the argument within himself—that animates his experiments with various dialogic forms, including the dual voices we find in "On Women." On one side of his internal argument Diderot was the man of feeling in the culture of sensibility, like Hume's Eugenius: expressing his own emotions openly and spontaneously, empathic to the point of being able to enter others' emotional states. In the higher order of this kind of emotion-soaked spontaneity, the creative act—the act of genius—was a kind of ecstasy or transport, akin to inspiration. The other Diderot was a man of detached and impersonal reason, the impartial spectator observing the action on stage. Genius in this key was self-controlled, calm, cold in its powers of judgment. Though neither impulse decisively conquered the other in the nearly two decades from the mid-1750s to the early 1770s, there was a noticeable shift in emphasis.[33]

In 1755, in an *Encyclopédie* entry on "genius" that he may not have drafted but almost certainly edited, he made Shaftesbury the model for creative genius. Given that the clear distinction between the manly and the effeminate was integral to his identity, one might have expected him to take up approvingly Shaftesbury's preoccupation with effeminacy, but he entirely ignored it. What mattered was the difference between philosophical reasoning and rhetorical creativity. Locke, who had "seen" so much correctly, had been a methodical philosopher with an "arid" (*sèchement*) prose style. Shaftesbury had been "a genius of the first order," despite his many philosophical errors. Where Locke had merely "seen," Shaftesbury had "created" and "edified"; and he had done so in "brilliant systems" of "sublime truths" evoked with "charm" and "eloquence."[34] It would be hard to imagine a greater contrast to Adam Smith's verdict on Shaftesbury's prose style. Genius was "a pure gift of nature," an overpowering force of the imagination, which animates thought with "sentiment," with "an excess of desire," with "the heat of enthusiasm." It took the form of a torrential style, the simulation in writing of a trance-like flow of inspiration. It had no use for either abstract rationality or the rules of mere "taste."[35]

Diderot was unaware of Shaftesbury's *Askêmata*, and he ignored the more or less oblique indications in Shaftesbury's essays that he was a practicing Stoic striving to achieve the rational self-command of the sage. Imagination, sentiment, sublimity, inspiration: in Diderot's hands this lexicon made Shaftesbury a genius in the register of literary sensibility, with its revaluation of "enthusiasm" to mean a kind of emotion-laden creative transport in which the creator, in the very act of wielding awesome indwelling force, acts as an instrument of natural forces beyond his rational control. The same themes are sounded in Diderot's "Eulogy of Richardson," also published in 1757. Hoping to counter common criticisms of Richardson's novels that had prevented full recognition of his genius, he tried to recreate for his reader, and for himself, his first readings of the novels, when "[his] soul was held in a perpetual agitation." As Diderot had stressed in the *Encyclopédie* entry, a genius like Richardson "breaks through" the conventional prescriptions and formalities; that is why he is only recognized "long years after his death." Now Diderot's emphasis is on the moral force and efficacy of genius. Rather than formulating an "abstract and general rule of conduct," Richardson has the extraordinary gift of putting moral maxims "in action" by representing the characters' inner life and its motivating passions in their speech and behavior, and by placing them in the ordinary but revealing details of common life. We feel the characters' emotions from inside them, as it were, as though provided with a "torch" to find our way around their motivational "cavern." By making his readers "feel" the psychological "truth," the novelist "sows in [their] hearts the seeds of virtue which rest there at first idle and still." With this unmediated evocation of emotion Richardson activates the innate moral proclivities that Shaftesbury had insisted on. This is fiction as high moral edification, enabling readers not only to "know" (*sentir*) immediately, almost instinctively, virtue (or viciousness and injustice) in others, but also to act virtuously themselves. As a man in his mid-forties, Diderot wondered whether it was too late for him to be a French Richardson. Richardson's genius is overpowering; it "stifles any genius of mine." "The years of toil and the harvest of laurels fall away," he concludes, "and I go forward to my last hour, abandoning every project which might also recommend me to future ages."[36]

In the ensuing years Diderot seems to have undergone a change that was as much social as it was philosophical. True to his bourgeois origins, he was critical of the affected and frivolous language with which *le monde* maintained its exclusivity. In an *Encyclopédie* entry on "jargon," he called it "a certain song of society" which "sometimes has its pleasure (*agrément*) and finesse," but "is a substitute for true *esprit*, good sense, judgment, reason, and knowledge of persons, which has a great use in the world." "One can pardon it in women," he writes, but "it is undignified of a man."[37] Like Necker and Thomas, Diderot grew skeptical of sensibility as it was absorbed into this *mondain* culture of performance and became fake self-exhibition. Performances of sensibility were not trustworthy manifestations of virtue, as he had assumed in the eulogy of Richardson.[38] His disillusionment went hand in hand with an inclination to a modified Stoicism. He never fully embraced Stoicism; rational self-command through askesis seemed to him unnatural and hence unattainable. But as early as his *Encyclopédie* entry on Stoicism, published in 1765, he expressed a deep admiration for the true Stoic sage, though as he found moments of sectarian nonsense and demagogic posturing in the history of the movement.[39] At times Diderot seems to be entrenching himself at this neo-Stoic end of his internal argument. In the character of Bordeu in *The Dream of d'Alembert* he playfully caricatures the real Théophile de Bordeu, a prominent physician in Paris with whom he was well acquainted, but nonetheless makes him the voice of scientific authority. "The superior man," Bordeu observes, "who has unfortunately been born with this kind of disposition [toward sensitivity] will constantly strive to suppress it, dominate it, master its impulses and to maintain the hegemony of the centre of the network." In this way, Bordeu continues, "he will keep his self-possession amid the greatest dangers and judge coldly, but sanely"; "People with sensitivity, or fools, are on the stage, he is in the orchestra, he is the sage."[40] In this and other statements Diderot distances himself radically from his earlier portrait of Richardson. One has to wonder whether he is deliberately overcompensating as he confronts his disillusionment.

More revealing of his unceasing self-doubt is a brief fragment on genius he wrote sometime after 1757. He begins by acknowledging the futility of his effort; genius is "secret" and "indefinable." What follows is an inventory of what genius is not, running through most of the family of words for defining and gendering work, intelligence, language, and style that we have traced through this study.

Genius is not "imagination," which may produce little or nothing. And yet it is also not, at the other end of the cognitive spectrum, "judgment," which often produces things that are slack (*lâches*), limp, and cold. Diderot's genius seems to transcend the conventional distinction between male and female cognition. At the same time he stands outside the performative intelligence of politeness; his genius lies neither in "taste" (something socially acquired, not a "force (*ressort*) of nature") or *esprit* (pretty but small) or "heat" (self-deceiving). And pace Richardson, it is certainly not "sensibility," which pulls people out of themselves into a drunken or mad state and makes them "stammer like children, whether they are writing or speaking." Having once revered demonstrative sentiment as the transparent medium of virtue, Diderot is now inclined to dismiss it as a degradation of language into infantile babble. What, then, is genius? "A certain conformation of the head and the *viscères*, a certain constitution of the humors"; and, no less important, *l'esprit observateur*, which is something utterly different from "that petty daily espionage of words, actions, and looks, that tact so familiar to women to a degree superior to the strongest heads, to the greatest souls, to the most vigorous geniuses," in "a miserable petty daily study whose utility is domestic and trivial." The "spirit of the *observateur* . . . is exercised without effort; without contention; it does not examine, it sees; it instructs itself; it extends itself without studying. . . . It is a kind of sixth sense others do not have."[41]

Diderot is obviously moving toward a concept of genius as not only natural, but as a bodily power, a rare organic constitution. He is at pains to avoid unacceptable implications of the entire available language. He cannot attribute genius to "study," or to a capacity for close examination. In that direction hovers the rote labor of the pedant. The genius would be nothing more than a laborious thinker who learns and applies rules, or whose originality derives from erudition. But Diderot obviously cannot collapse the profile of the genius into the figure of the man of taste in the polite sense, the *bel esprit*. Taste is not the natural and effortless gift it might appear to be in polite culture; it is a dubious gift, as its acquisition merely enables one to satisfy social expectations. The antidote to polite taste might seem to be sensibility, but in fact it too would trap the genius in social conformity: the fashionable but childish and vapid displays of emotion that debase language itself. While Diderot avoids the usual equation of manly intellectual strength with the power to abstract, he gives sensibility a female coloring that implies weakness. It is not simply that he despises the trivial particularity of women's language in domestic chatter. What is implied in the fragment is made explicit in the *Paradoxe*: his gendering of sensibility itself. "Sensibility is never without weakness of organization," he wrote in the latter text; "the tear which escapes a man who is truly male touches us more than the crying of a woman."[42] As he swung away from the genius of sensibility, he had this specter of female weakness—of effeminacy—clearly in mind.

It is in this context that we must understand Diderot's fascination with the thought of Bordeu, the chief advocate of the vitalist medical philosophy emanating from the Montpellier school. The vitalists saw themselves as an Enlightenment vanguard, advancing from their materialist rejection of metaphysics—their reduction of emotion and thought to corporeal sensibility—to the science of man that Hume had envisioned in his *Treatise*. They were intent on tearing down the mechanistic paradigm, in which organs moved in response to the external forces transmitted through fibers. To Bordeu the key concepts were "sensitivity" and "irritability"; each organ had its own irreducible force, activated but not transmitted by irritation; and the vitally enervated organ was in that sense self-acting.[43] If this was medical theory, it was also a moral anthropology with increasing emphasis on the biological/moral (and mental) differences between men and women.

We can be more specific about Bordeu's influence. The concept of the *l'esprit observateur* in Diderot's fragment on genius echoes the description of the *grand observateur* in "philosophical" medicine in Bordeu's *Encyclopédie* entry on "*Crise*," published in 1754. Most of the entry is a disquisition on the multitude of ancient and modern theories on the timing, duration, and causes of fevered crises in the course of an illness. Bordeu argued that medicine could achieve authoritative knowledge, despite this pluralistic and excessively hypothetical legacy of theory, if it built a new foundation of medical observation. He stressed the critical role of thorough empirical observation, in part to counter the radical skeptics who denied physicians' claim to "see" with scientific authority, and in part to warn physicians against simply applying theories from classical medicine and modern mechanistic science, all floating in "the immense space of generalities." The ordinary practitioner must accumulate proofs for medicine as a whole, largely by recording his unbiased observations in journals that would be available to "the whole world."

Bordeu, one might conclude, hoped to restructure medicine into a professional hierarchy based on strictly empirical science as it is now practiced. In fact he conceived of medicine as an "art," even in its ordinary practice, and made its prime faculty the "imagination." This was what made Bordeu's essay pivotal for Diderot. In Diderot's aesthetics there was, to be sure, a positive side to the errancy of the female imagination; it allowed women to engage deeply in the moral community created by the novels of Richardson and others. But when he thinks of the bodily and mental differences between men and women, it is with a concept of bimorphism that makes women's imagination anarchic. Bordeu's concept of the *observateur* allowed him to distinguish between a manly imagination and a feminine imagination, and thus to give men, or at least some men, an imaginative intelligence, intimately connected with rationalism, to which women could not aspire. This was not the imagination Diderot dismissed as unproductive in the fragment on genius. It was intensely self-disciplined, perhaps best described as a

labor of the imagination, in contrast to the gendered stereotype of the imagination running wild and producing mere phantasms. Nor was it the imagination of
sensibility in the conventional sense, the outpouring of feeling that Diderot came
to dismiss, though Bordeu described the practitioner as entering a kind of
"ecstasy" in the interaction with his patient. It is useful here to distinguish
between sensibility in manners and organic sensitivity in the psychophysiological
interaction of human bodies. Bordeu had the latter in mind. What produced the
practitioner's empirical data was his ability, partly from natural talent and partly
from training and experience, to enter an interbodily communion with the
patient, with his own acute organic sensitivity registering the sensitivity of the
other and identifying organic disorder, the pathological excess of vitality in an
organ that upsets the equilibrium of the entire "organization." In this communion
the physician was in a "passive" state, in the sense that he "observed" by being
completely receptive to the emanations of the patient's sensitive forces, without
applying theories or rules.[44] He simply listened to a semiotics of bodily signals. In
Diderot's terms, he did not examine; he saw.

The rare "great observer," the genius who became "a legislator of the art,"
built on his own and others' insights as practitioners. But he ascended from passive to active labor, the "exact painting" of "the effect he has produced," "express[-
ing] the traits reflected on" in "a manner that could enlighten the reader about
them as Nature would do." It was the liberating effect of this kind of "philosophical or transcendent medicine" that would end the debates about *crise* once and for
all. In constructing for himself and his colleagues a new authority, the "philosophical physician . . . broke through the ordinary boundaries and elevated himself
above even his own profession." His breakthroughs involved not only the strenuous labor of reflection, but also the labor of communication. In his writing, the
"art" lay in explaining *crises* in a precise imagistic language, a kind of painting, as
though Nature itself were doing it.[45] It was a labor of imaginative precision in the
use of imagistic rhetoric.

What Diderot found in the medical philosophy of Bordeu and other vitalists
was a poetics of science, of unprecedented exactitude, but exact precisely because
it harnessed the powers of the imagination and relied on its images. Bordeu's
own writing was often imagistic, in studied contrast to the technical language of
conventional medical treatises, and Diderot used a similar rhetoric of metaphor
and simile in "On Women": women figured as symbols of the Apocalypse; they
formed an aviary of conversational song; the man who wrote about them had to
"dip his pen in the rainbow and scatter on his line the dust of the wings of the
butterfly" (179). More important for understanding "On Women," Diderot's
own claim to authority on the subject of the male and female body partook of
the authority of Bordeu and his colleagues. It was not simply that he knew his
observations to be rooted in the insights of a medical vanguard that seemed to

have grasped the amoral authority of nature. Vitalist medicine gave him a way to join together two epistemological implications of his philosophical materialism that are arguably irreconcilable. If men, or at least some men, can understand the laws of Nature's power in their unqualified amorality, that is because they can step outside their species as well as themselves; their minds transcend the anthropomorphic tunnel-visioning in which moral meaning is imputed to Nature. But for men to understand the workings of Nature in women, if only in a way that leaves much mysterious and frightening, it must be as sexually embodied and sexually active human beings, one of two incommensurably different sexes. Their knowledge of Nature at once escapes the situatedness of their species being and is situated, and therefore limited, by their sexual being. Thomas's essay had failed on both counts.

At the same time, Diderot carried organic vitalism well beyond the claims of Bordeu's generation, anticipating in some ways the medical anthropology that Bordeu's pupil Pierre Roussel and others advocated from the mid-1770s onward. Like this next generation Diderot, in the course of positing a strict gender bimorphism, sexualized human cognition, perhaps to an unprecedented degree, as a function of the self-generated force of the reproductive organs. Bordeu had certainly pointed the way by making seminal excretion the model for the excretions of any gland, and by sexualizing all glandular activity by describing it in the language of erotic sensitivity. Still, Bordeu conceived of a "federation of organs," a decentralized organology dividing the body into "departments," each with a ruling organ that sometimes emitted too little or too much vital force. Diderot took from Bordeu's phallic analogies what can fairly be called a theory of genital determinism. Women were cognitively weaker than men—they were unable to reflect deeply and understand principles—not because their nerve fibers were weaker (or softer), but because their brains were so subject to the controlling force emanating from their uteruses. "The woman carries inside herself," Diderot writes, "an organ susceptible to terrible spasms, disposing of her and arousing (*suscitant*) in her imagination phantoms of all kinds" (170). "It is from the organ specific to her sex," he adds, "that all of [women's] extraordinary ideas start." This is the flipside of the physician's imaginative powers of observation: the uncontrolled imagination, spasming in response to uterine impulses.

Hence Diderot's argument for the natural growth of the individual as a unique organism, an argument for freedom in the face of Helvétius's mechanistic environmentalism, has an iron corollary: that the vital power of Nature dictates and we have no choice but to obey it. Vitalism implies a determinism of its own. This implication informs Diderot's retort to Thomas's comment that in everyday life he prefers the friendship of a woman to that of a man. It is one of those moments in the essay when Diderot pounces on Thomas's words as he pores through the text line by line. "There are women who are men and men who are women," he writes; and he "avows that [he] would never want as [his] friend a woman man" (180).

Conceiving themselves as heroic authors wielding a manly eloquence, Diderot and others of his generation (including Thomas) had a heightened contempt, echoing Malebranche, for what they saw as the effeminate politeness of salon wits. In an entry in the *Encyclopédie*, Diderot had explained why "effeminate" was and should be a term of opprobrium. Men should not act with the "weak and delicate character" of a woman, just as women should not act like men. This was not a prejudice, he implied, as there was a fitting reciprocity of disapproval; we do not like to encounter either a woman or man with the "exterior qualities" of the other sex. "Experience has made us attach to each sex a tone, a walk, movements, outlines that are proper to them, and we are shocked to find them displayed."[46] Precisely because he spoke and gestured with such "vivacity," Diderot was highly sensitive to the risk of appearing effeminate himself. Art critics found that a portrait of him by Louis-Michel van Loo, exhibited at the 1767 Salon, captured "the *esprit* and the fire of the genius." He emphatically disagreed, protesting that Van Loo had given him "the air of an old coquet who still makes herself attractive." He wanted his grandchildren to remember him not as "this smiling, affected, effeminate old flirt," but as a man with "a large forehead, penetrating eyes, rather large features, a head quite similar in character to that of an ancient orator, an easygoing nature that sometimes approached stupidity, the rustic simplicity of ancient times."[47]

The wording of the *Encyclopédie* entry is quite familiar. It reminds us that for centuries effeminacy, denatured as it was assumed to be in its manifestations, had been seen as socially acquired, the result of being too much under the influence of women or too eager to please them. It was a question of the improperly socialized body and temperament, their exterior qualities unnatural in the weak sense that they violated a set of distinctions that society, as a matter of deep custom (to use Hume's term), expected to be maintained. In the reaction to Van Loo's portrait Diderot's notion of effeminacy seems to mix this socially formed character with a biologically determined character, inscribed in physical features. In "On Women" the awkward pairing of nouns in "woman man" is not fortuitous. It signifies a denaturing in the strong sense. It is not that some men acquire a womanish character; it is that some men are inherently not men; that they are, their sexual organs notwithstanding, organically female. In a new gender discourse that posits the physical and mental incommensurability of men and women, the woman man is a freak of nature.

There is a certain irony to Diderot's use of the new philosophical medicine of Bordeu and likeminded colleagues. They came to Paris seeking a fame they could not enjoy in provincial cities; and they succeeded, in part through their writings for the educated public and in part by securing a *mondain* clientele, especially women, and winning acceptance in their social circles. Bordeu himself was known to be a *galant*, and his prose often has the flowery ornamentation of gallantry. In "On Women," Diderot appropriates the vitalist's medical authority to justify an emphatically unpolite and even antipolite essay, a repudiation of the entire tradition of polite writing going back to the seventeenth-century *honnêteté* of a Fontenelle or a Saint-Évremond. There is nothing here of the tendency to turn women's weakness into intellectual acuity and moral strength in the discourse of *honnêteté*. To appreciate the full force of Diderot's stylistic transgression, we need only recall David Hume's adaptation of the French polite style in his effort to cultivate female readers in an alliance between the learned and the "conversible" worlds. Diderot's prose is essayistic in an altogether different key. Instead of discretion—the *retenue* expected in prose as well as conversation—we find a performance of blatantly intrusive self-revelation, an insistent frankness (*franchise*) for which politeness has no place. Particularly striking is Diderot's candor on sexual matters, including male and female orgasm. Immediately after describing the wife bathing compulsively to wash away the stain of conjugal duty, he writes:

> This sort of repugnance is almost unknown to us; our organ is more indulgent. Many women will die without having experienced the extreme of *la volupté*. This sensation, which I gladly regard as a passing epilepsy, is rare for them, and never fails to happen when we summon it. The sovereign happiness flees them between the arms of the man they adore; we find it beside a woman who tries to please but displeases us. Less mistresses of their senses than us, the recompense for them is less sure and prompt; a hundred times their attempt is disappointed. Organized completely to the contrary of us, the mobile that solicits sensual pleasure (*volupté*) in them is so delicate and the source of it is so distant that it is not extraordinary that it does not come at all or is lost. (167)

The text is a marker of transition, still indebted to the Galenic tradition, but drawing the common notion of a uterine *furie* or *manie*—a trope of Nature at its most terrifying, its force uncontrollable—into a new paradigm of incommensurability between men and women in body and mind.[48] Women's loss of self-control is evident both in the "fury" of their orgasms *and* in their inability to have organisms. To paraphrase Diderot's logic about the latter: men can have orgasm, even with women to whom they have no affective attachment, because their sexual organ, being an external bodily part, is relatively accessible to their wills; women have so little control over their pleasure because their sexual organ, in addition to being very delicate, is an internal bodily part and therefore out of reach. Men's "indulgent" capacity to experience orgasm indiscriminately does not make them playthings of their sexual drive; it demonstrates their independence from their affective impulses. We need not dwell on this psychophysiological logic; one could as easily argue its opposite.

What is striking in the essay is the weight Diderot puts on male self-control, physical, emotional, and mental, and on the division into two separate and unequal cognitive communities. The division is inherent in Diderot's rhetorical positioning. The "we" or "us"—the audience Diderot positions himself in and evokes through most of the essay—is men, to the exclusion of women. That is the underlying reason that the essay is not, and cannot be, polite. The cognitive division, of course, implies that there is no unsexualized, or gender-neutral, knowledge of human nature. Diderot in effect discards one of the central tenets of gender discourse since antiquity: that there is universal knowledge, the knowledge of abstract laws and principles, and that men have far greater access to it than women because they (men) are far more able to detach their thought from their bodily existence. Diderot's "we" know only from their partial position as sexualized males, and indeed, to judge by Thomas's failure, as actively sexualized males. And yet their maleness still gives them far greater freedom not only to satisfy their sexual appetite at will, but also to understand "ideas" of morality and justice through "reflection" and "principles." In some sense male erotic power grounds a rationality which, however limited, achieves a measure of detachment. If men have to think through their bodies, women's bodies hinder them from thinking, as opposed to being tossed about by their imaginings. As a form of self-control, Diderot suggests, men's sexuality sustains and perhaps even makes possible their labor of reflection.

In the imagining of polite social spaces in modern civilized societies, a veil was drawn over the asymmetries in power that divided their participants in the larger society. In principle the polite man addressed women as if they were equals, even when the underlying assumption was that they were not. In print, as in conversation, the reciprocity might take the form of patronizing intellectual gallantry, as Hume deliberately practiced it in some of his essays. While Hume and others saw this politeness as an efficacious illusion, Diderot was intent on ripping off the veil to reveal the sexually driven power struggle just beneath the surface of modern civilization. His candor about the female experience of intercourse took on a sympathetic note when he described women's difficulties in reaching orgasm, but it turned frightened when he considered women having orgasm. He writes of "violent movements" and "frightening spasms," in contrast to the male's "indulgent" self-control. The uterus in spasm is a raw physical force that seems to be beyond control and hence to threaten chaos. It is the awesome force of Nature surging up from its depths, breaking through the paper thin glaze of civilization. The spasms are frightening not because they empower women as autonomous agents, but because the female body is seized by them, made an instrument of the power of Nature. In this sense, the surge of force within her is the most dramatic sign of her weakness; it deprives her of all physical and mental control.

And yet, paradoxically, women transmute their uncontrollable erotic energy into a deeply fearsome power to manipulate and destroy. This theme enters early in the essay, immediately after Diderot describes women as "beautiful as the seraphim of Klopstock and terrible as the devils of Milton" (166). It has echoes of his fear for his daughter. "The distractions of an occupied and contentious life," he writes, "break up [men's] passions"; the woman "covers [her passions]," and her "idleness or the frivolity of her functions" allows her to fix on them. In extreme cases, he continues, the impassioned woman seeks "entire solitude" (166). Whether women act alone or in concert, however, they unceasingly threaten to upset the social order through which men, exercising their responsibility to Nature's laws, maintain in human law the unequal distribution of power between the sexes. Women practice "impenetrable" dissimulation; they are "cruel" in their "vengeance," "constant" in their "projects," and "unscrupulous" in their choice of means (168). Driven by "a profound and secret hatred against the despotism of man," they seem to form among themselves a "tacit conspiracy of domination," like that of priests in all nations (168). We have reached the point in the essay where its two voices meet, but not on equal terms. The anthropomorphic lament of the father about the injustices, both social and moral, to which women are subjected is silenced by the clinical eye, reminding us that in the larger scheme of the natural order, it is the "is" of power, not the "ought" of morality, that must be followed. With the potentially uncontrollable erotic force it has given women, one might say, Nature threatens to tear down the order it has given society in making the weaker sex subordinate to the stronger. In the end, though, Nature will not tolerate this outcome. It will not act on Diderot's fantasy by putting women "above the law." Instead it uses patriarchal law, especially the laws of marriage and property, to enforce its implacable will.

Obviously Thomas is unaware of the danger, and of the constant need for male-ruled society to ward it off. Diderot seems to have been particularly exasperated by Thomas's discussion of the "religious" virtues of women. Once again Thomas had walked a tightrope. In "exalting religious ideas," he wrote, "the woman would be closer to superstition and the man to fanaticism": but when the woman is fanatical, she is more "ferocious," and "what makes a part of her charms will contribute more to her furies." These remarks, however, end a discussion in which women's religiosity is generally presented in a positive light; they have "more than men . . . religious virtue," partly because they "naturally have more sensibility," and partly because their conditions of life make them more likely to turn to a Supreme Being. Diderot had long advocated the emancipation of women from a religiosity that pathologized emotional needs and perverted sensual pleasures, and now he integrates the trope of the "ferocious" female fanatic into his larger materialist vision. The essay is filled with examples of self-deluded female religious fervor: the Delphic Pythie, the mystic Madame de Guyon, Saint Theresa. While Thomas defended a female religion of sensibility, Diderot focuses on its excesses and uses the logic of genital determinism to explain them. "It is from the organ peculiar to [a woman's] sex," he writes, "that all her extraordinary ideas derive." There lies the pathology of female sensibility. "Nothing is more contiguous," Diderot adds, "than ecstasy, vision, prophecy, mad poetry, and hysteria." "Vapours" was still the common term of usage to describe what seemed to be states of convulsion, and it was usually applied to men as well as women. Diderot is at the beginning of a shift in medical discourse that would replace vapours with "hysteria" and would make the latter an exclusively female disorder, usually traceable to uterine spasms.[49]

The frightening power of this erotic self-delusion is not to be found simply in an individual woman at a particular moment. Diderot goes on to evoke the image of such women being sucked into "an epidemic ferocity"; "the example of one pulls in a multitude." Diderot draws on two standard tropes with a long history: the female hysteric self-deluded by her religious beliefs, and "enthusiasm" as a contagion effacing individual wills in a frenzied crowd.[50] In this epidemic ferocity, the imagination, through which uterine spasms become mental phantasms, gives women a collective social and cultural power, or, more precisely, a collective power to destroy the cultural and social achievements of civilization. Implicit is the vitalist idea of the physical communicability of organic sensations, not by actual physical contact, but across the spaces separating people in contiguity. Contagion in this sense is made possible by the victims' shared source in the power of Nature, so frighteningly apparent in female orgasm. The epidemic is not metaphorical, like the female "conspiracy" against men. The followers in these mass hysterias are literally ill, in the grip of a pathology. Their sensitive communicability produces the opposite of the physician's "ecstasy" as "observer." In the one, the vibrations of sensitivity are channeled into rigorous clinical knowledge; in the other, they run amok to produce an epidemic that threatens the foundations of social order.

—

In the expanded version of "On Women" Diderot, speaking in the new clinical voice, carries his outrage to another register, quite different from that of the anxious father. The added paragraphs are still another example of the easy eclecticism one often finds in eighteenth-century conjectural history, combining a declinist republican narrative and a civilizational narrative of stadial progress. Diderot's use of the stadial narrative is almost certainly indebted to the opening chapter of John Millar's *The Origin of the Distinction of Ranks* (1769).[51] If Diderot seems to be echoing Millar, however, he also takes a sharp turn in another direction. From this angle we can appreciate the full implications he drew from his radical materialism.

The differences between Millar and Diderot reflected the fact that they had been formed in quite dissimilar Enlightenments. As a student at the University of Glasgow Millar had become closely acquainted with conjectural history and its stadial paradigm from the lectures and conversation of Adam Smith. He was one of the many protégés of Lord Kames, and in addition to committing himself to David Hume's basic philosophical principles, he acquired at least a measure of Hume's skepticism about the declinist narrative of civic humanism. He had grown up in a distinctly Scottish Enlightenment, which had little space for the radical inclinations the young Diderot pursued in the cellar of the Parisian world of letters. He moved in a professional world, a network of lawyers, clergymen, scientists, physicians, and university teachers, products of the reformed universities and the vibrant civic life of Edinburgh, Glasgow, and Aberdeen. These literati can fairly be called moderate in part because they bore the imprint of an emphatically Protestant culture, even as they battled Presbyterian orthodoxy. Though most of them were on good terms with Hume, they rejected the hostility to Christianity he shared with Diderot and other philosophes. They believed in individual self-perfection within a Protestant framework of salvation; in belief sustained by emotional certainty rather than rational proof; and in the hand of Providence in history and their own lives.[52] They were critical of aristocratic pretensions and concerned about the corrupting effects of excessive "luxury." But they were solid members of the "middle station" Hume had seen forming in the early 1740s, dependent on aristocratic patronage to some degree, but not required to perform in a Scottish equivalent of le monde to pursue their ambitions. Their pride in the enlightened civilization taking shape in Scotland largely precluded the kind of social alienation that animated Diderot.

That pride is evident in Millar's chapter on women, though it is tempered by alarm that the further advance of commercial civilization may turn apparent progress into regression. The narrative inserts the question of gender relations into the usual stadial plot. In barbarous ages, before pastoral life and then settled agriculture, the men were hunters and warriors and the women beasts of burden who performed the "abject," mindless labor. In the work they did, as in their reproduction of the species, women were mere instruments of nature, hardly above animal status.[53] It was in the early stage of manufacturing and commerce that women came to be regarded as the "friends" of men in companionate marriages. Their new human value was a function of the dignity of their "private" labor, the active agency required by their household responsibilities as wives and mothers. As Millar put it, they were taught "to look upon idleness as the greatest blemish in the female character."[54] The freer intercourse of the sexes allowed them to indulge their passionate inclinations with some discrimination, without opening the gates to licentiousness. Corruption came with the increase of commercial wealth in modern times. People sought escape from boredom in "licentious and dissolute manners," including promiscuous mixed-sex conversations in the public settings of modern politeness. The result was the threat of an ironic circularity in what might appear to be a linear advance of progress; reduced to animality in the state of barbarousness, women might return to that status with their sexual behavior in modern civilizations. As Millar and other Scottish commentators saw it, this looming irony had reached its height in modern-day France and parts of Italy; and England might be entering the same route. If Paris was the pinnacle of elegance, it was also the most alarming warning of its dangers in excess. "It should seem," Millar observed, "that there are certain limits beyond which it is impossible to push the real improvements arising from wealth and opulence."[55]

To the Scottish literati the stadial narrative seemed to legitimate the monogamous and permanent marriage-type of an emerging bourgeois Europe. It grounded the notion of complementary male and female intelligences in a compelling paradigm of the modern division of labor. If gender complementarity was "natural," it was also required by the increasing complexity of the labor division, which motored progress but also, in the best of worlds, would keep the brakes on it, preventing a moral regression as progress threatened to exceed its morally efficacious limits. That men labored with large issues in the public world, and that women labored in the domestic space where affective cognition and delicate attention to detail were required, was not only the natural order of things; it was also the most "useful" order, in Enlightenment cultures in which utility was the watchword. Women were humanized—they escaped the animality of abject toil—as they internalized and practiced the work ethic that Hume had been so precocious in celebrating in 1742. What mattered, it was implied, was not that their work reflected their inferiority, their weakness of mind and body; it was that they had been brought into a unity with men in a shared ethic of self-disciplined and purposeful agency.

The overarching assumption was that the patriarchal structure of monogamous and permanent marriage was the end-point of the stadial march of progress, the limit to the moral and social improvement of the species.[56] In the relevant Scottish texts, we find that assumption soaked in complacency about the modern condition of women. There is little attention to the legal fact that this was a world of male-controlled property in which women, for all the new respect and admiration granted them, were seriously lacking in social as well as civic rights. In stark contrast Diderot, in the rhetorical persona of the outraged father, confronted his readers with the social reality of women's legal helplessness. If the Scottish literati were all too comfortably bourgeois, Diderot was, in the outer reaches of his outrage, unnervingly antibourgeois.

And yet in "On Women" this outrage took second place to a radical departure from the civilizational paradigm. Millar and other Scots assumed a "human nature" common to both sexes, but their main interest was in how that nature was differentiated into male and female characters with changes in economic and social structures. The key was the "free intercourse" that developed between the sexes with increasing commercial exchange. In their long-term historical perspective, there was a reciprocity to the *process* in which both men and women came closer to realizing the full potential of their psychological, emotional, and intellectual capacities; and the excessive freedom allowed by modern opulence—the freedom from the moral self-disciplining of labor—threatened a reversal of the course of that reciprocity.

With his brief excursion into conjectural history in the added section of his essay, Diderot seemed to adopt a similar view of process and hence of historical contingency in gender differentiation. To a point the Scot and the philosophe found the same pivots for the condition of women in a stadial plot of economic development and accompanying changes in the division of labor; and the key distinctions were among the animal slavery of drudge labor, which gave women hardly any value in the eyes of men, the respect attached to socially useful labor in the home in agricultural and early commercial societies, and the idleness of modern opulence, which brought sexual dissolution. Here again, though, the issue of gallantry was a touchstone for contrasting views of modernity as characterized by social and intellectual exchanges between the sexes. In the spirit of Enlightenment Protestantism, Millar did worry that "in modern Europe, the chief effect of debauchery, beside the encouragement given to common prostitution, has been to turn the attention, from the pursuits of business or ambition, to the amusements of gallantry; or rather to convert these last into a serious occupation" (155). In the long view, however, he credited the gallantry produced by chivalry with giving a new "air of refinement to the intercourses of the sexes," with greater respect for women, that still had "considerable influence" in his own day. "A valuable improvement" had arisen "from the extravagance of Gothic institutions and manners." Diderot shared with Millar the belief that at a certain stage of luxury the surplus of wealth made people "disgusted with work," and they had to multiply their amusements and pleasures to avoid boredom (179). One thinks of Diderot's fear for his daughter. Speaking with an insider's knowledge of the overcivilized France Millar had evoked, he condemned the attribution of unique honor to the social aesthetic of play for providing an excuse for decadence. A society without labor, in its various male and female forms, inevitably became corrupt. The protocols of gallantry had become a flimsy cover for a shameless licentiousness that threatened to make the very notion of virtue meaningless.

It was in this shift to modern corruption that Diderot's voice changed registers. The stadial plot of contingent process acceded to a categorical essentialism.

Diderot's vitalist materialism, disdaining even enlightened forms of Christianity, ceased to assign any role to historical process when it came to women; under the veneer of civilization women were now, as they always had been, savages, mere instruments of natural force. Their intelligence, unlike men's, was more animal than human. It was in the grip of their sexual energy. It was intelligence as the cunning of Nature's morally blind power.

What Thomas (and Millar) failed to understand is that male and female sexual power are in a ceaseless struggle, with men striving to use marriage and other legal institutions to maintain a social hierarchy conforming to Nature's unequal distribution of physical and mental strength, and with women intent on upturning it. Women, Diderot writes, "have conserved *amour-propre* and personal interest with all the energy of Nature, and more civilized than us on the outside, they have remained true savages within." They are "all machiavellians more or less" (179–80). So much for the civilizing role of gallantry. Society is entering a state of total "depravity" in which the typical woman has no natural modesty. Raised to practice "coquetry" with all men, and no longer inhibited by fear of scandalizing "public opinion," she "continues on to gallantry, so fickle in its tastes . . . and ends by counting as many lovers as acquaintances, whom she calls back, puts at a distance, calls back again, according to the need she has of them and the nature of the intrigues in which she is precipitated" (180–82). In a calculated exercise of female sexual power, the tables are turned; men are reduced to mere instruments of female needs and whims, in a completely unnatural society. Again Diderot shocks by his literalness, in a passage that was probably a direct response to Millar. He claims to see no distinction between prostitution as a trade and gallant amusements. Gallant licentiousness *is* itself prostitution—and, far more than the public prostitution of the streets, it is multiplying adultery. The only difference is that women moving from one extramarital affair to another, or conducting several at once, are selling their favors for power rather than cash. There will only be a "frivolous" distinction, Diderot predicts, "between the gallant woman and the courtesan, between free vice and vice reduced by misery to demand a payment (*salaire*); and these subtleties will make a systematic depravity easier to identify" (183).

—

In the final paragraph of the essay Diderot seems to indulge in a bit of literary gallantry himself, swiveling suddenly from his nightmare vision of female-driven depravity to a gesture of homage to women's essential contribution to the elegant simplicity and clarity of modern literary style. He begins by echoing a familiar contrast in the seventeenth-century discourse of *honnêteté* between the "natural" conversational culture of *le monde* and academic learning. While men read books, women read in "the great book of the world"; their "ignorance," precisely because it is without system and is always at the dictate of the moment, disposes them to a prompt reception of truth, without "subjugation" to "any authority" (184). Diderot seems to return us here to the *mondain* appreciation of women's intelligence with which we began: precisely because by both nature and social rank they are free from sustained intellectual labor, women are the model for the conversational intelligence to which men aspire, and for the style meant to emulate it. Thomas is an "ingrate," as he has not said a word about "the advantages of the commerce of women for a man of letters" (184). But Diderot goes on to say that women's "decency" (in sharp contrast to their licentiousness in corrupted gallantry), "does not permit them to explain themselves with the same frankness as us [men]." Instead women "make themselves into a song (*ramage*) with which one says honestly (*honnêtement*) what one wishes when one has been whistled into their aviary." Or women are quiet, or "often they have the air of not daring to say what they say" (184–85). Whether women "sing" in men's presence, or keep silent, or speak timidly, they create the conditions for men to speak in manly voices.

In a virtuoso reading of a wide variety of Diderot's texts, Jean Starobinski has shown the rich ambiguity with which he used the figures of "song" and the "aviary." Diderot liked to think of the Parisian salons as one large aviary, an image that in his hands had both positive and negative resonances. Starobinski finds Diderot to be condemning "the restraints imposed on women," and at the same time welcoming a "change in the general tone of conversations," thanks to "the effort for better self-expression between men and women."[57] That would certainly be in accord with Diderot's sympathy for the condition of women, so frankly expressed in parts of "On Women." But the remainder of the paragraph in question suggests a different reading. Having mischievously (or maliciously) used Rousseau and Marmontel as examples of authors who have spent much time in the arms of women, Diderot continues:

> They accustom us still to put agreement and clarity into the most dry and thorny materials. One addresses speech (*la parole*) to them ceaselessly; one wants to be listened to by them; one fears tiring or boring them; and one acquires a particular facility to express oneself that passes from conversation into style. When they have genius, I believe that in them the imprint is more original than in us. (185)

The paragraph is a classic example of the calculated elusiveness of Diderot's apparently spontaneous style. He surely did have in mind a paradox, an aviary formed by the beauty of women's speech, but one that, in a departure from the social aesthetic of play, formed the setting for serious intellectual engagement. When he imagines the engagement in the final lines, he discards the themes of *honnêteté.* Women's natural facility in language—the facility that had made them the arbiters not only of conversation, but also of polite writing style—dissolves in a tribute, a gesture of gratitude, to their silence and veiled words. It is doubtful that Diderot has a reciprocal engagement in mind. For women to understand, they must be pleased and even entertained; and that means that men must address them clearly and agreeably. It is not by speaking with an *aisance* that prose should emulate, but by listening that women help men to speak and write clearly. Men must simplify their thought, adapting it to women's weakness and limited attention span. Male frankness occurs in the solo performance of a man before women.

Even in descriptions by admiring friends, we should recall, Diderot is not a brilliant conversationalist. He is a brilliant talker. Madame d'Épinay was entranced by the talk despite her feminist views, but Mlle de Lespinasse, perhaps the most perspicacious of the last generation of old-regime *salonnières*, complained that he forced himself upon one's attention.[58] One has to wonder whether the "genius" Diderot attributes to some women in the last line is a power of creativity, or simply a capacity to receive male-created imprints in ways peculiar to their sex. Women do not develop a literary style out of their conversational gifts; as passive listeners, they help men develop one.

Mme d'Épinay's Feminism

"I will say to you, as is our custom, everything that will pass through my head," Mme d'Épinay wrote her friend the abbé Ferdinando Galiani about Thomas's essay on March 14, 1772, "provided that my opinion remains between you and me." Secrecy was imperative. She knew that as a woman she would be censured for "assum[ing] in the world such a slashing tone" toward a man of Thomas's stature. She dismissed him as a hybrid of the opposite types he prided himself on not being: the pedant and the superficial *bel esprit.*[59] Much worse, she would have been ridiculed, in conversation and perhaps in print, for her views on women. Galiani responded to her request for his opinion with a brief dialogue between a Neapolitan chevalier and a Parisian marquis. The chevalier argues that women are "naturally weak and sick," as evidenced by their menstruation, their pregnancies, and their breast feeding; the marquis objects that gender differences are due almost entirely to "education." The dialogue is a light repartee between easygoing friends, with neither making any strenuous effort to persuade the other.[60] D'Épinay avoided Galiani's repeated requests for her opinion of it.

On March 22, 1772, d'Épinay wrote Galiani that she would soon send him Diderot's critique of Thomas's essay. The critique had "some very precious things," she wrote, and "was worth the pain of being read."[61] Was she expressing her sincere admiration for a text she had read selectively, bracketing out the parts she could not agree with? Or did she mean the words "precious" and "pain" as a double entendre, conveying her animus toward a text she found thoroughly wrongheaded? We are left wondering.

There is no doubt, however, that d'Épinay and Diderot were in irreconcilable disagreement.[62] In "On Women" Diderot incorporated the conventional notion that men alone had a capacity for abstraction into a biologically determined epistemology in which male and female intellection—in reasoning, in feeling, and in imagination—was a function of incommensurable sexual energies. Perhaps without their realizing it, he and d'Épinay clashed on something fundamental: what distinguished a true philosophe from conventional minds. To d'Épinay it was not a heightened capacity to *sentir* that made the philosophe, but the sharp critical edge of a rational mind that could slash through prevailing gender prejudice about the supposed natural inequality of the sexes. Her reasoning would become integral to the logic of nineteenth- and twentieth-century liberal feminism: that there was one human nature, with no difference between men and women in intellectual makeup, and that the failure to draw the implications for women of this universal truth was philosophically inconsistent and hence indefensible.

D'Épinay's letter to Galiani of March 14, 1772, critiquing Thomas's essay, had been preceded by a straightforward statement of her views on January 4, 1771, roughly a year before the essay appeared.[63] The timing tells us that there was nothing impromptu about the critique; Thomas provided a provocation to commit to paper convictions she had been developing since the 1750s. Her use of the received language repays close attention. In the earlier letter, as in the later one, d'Épinay insists that the protection of her "reputation" requires strict secrecy. "I love to chat (*causer*) with my friends in complete security," she writes, "and I do not wish to have a role to play."[64] Chatting here is a medium of intellectual intimacy between friends, not women's prattle about trivia. Nor is it the performance of a role that society imposes on her as a woman. She goes on to say that she is very ignorant, as her entire education was directed to "the agreeable talents" (*les talents agréables*), of which she has lost the use. "*Agréables*," of course, points us back to the discourse of *honnêteté*, but d'Épinay goes on to dispel the illusion of intellectual reciprocity between men and women that the discourse had often imagined. The reputation of a woman as a *bel esprit* seems to her a mockery, "invented by men to revenge themselves for the fact that [women] have as a group (*communément*) more *agréments* than them in *esprit*." Women's intellectual *agrément*, unlike their pleasing manners, is a social capacity to communicate ideas effectively. But, she continues, the phrase *bel esprit* applied to a woman is almost always an "epithet," joined to the idea of a *femme savante* with superficial knowledge. Women, by the very fact that they are women, cannot acquire sufficient knowledge to serve their fellow beings in "useful occupations." They do not have "the theory" needed in the science of government, in politics, and in commerce, "almost the only great causes by which instructed or learned people can truly be useful to their fellow men, their station, and their country." In belles lettres and philosophy they are forbidden "profound study," and so "they are reduced to music, to dance, and to innocent verses, a puny resource!"[65]

> Let us conclude from all this that a woman is very mistaken and acquires only ridicule when she puts herself on display as a *savante* or a *bel esprit* and believes she can sustain that reputation; but she has very good reason, nonetheless, to acquire as much knowledge as she can. Once she has fulfilled the duties of a mother, a daughter, and a spouse, she has good reason to devote herself to study and to work (*travail*), because that is a sure means to live with herself, to be free and independent, to console herself for the injustices of fate and men, and that one is never more cherished, more esteemed by them than when one no longer has need of them. Whatever the case, a woman who, with *l'esprit*, with character, who still has only a light tincture of the things she has to renounce knowing in depth, would still be a very rare thing, very amiable, well regarded, provided she is not pretending.
>
> And so! You have fallen asleep? Let's move on! Wake up! You see, I have finished my chatter (*bavardage*). You should thank me that it has not been longer this time, as I find many other things to say on this subject.[66]

It is typical of d'Épinay's style in letters to her male friends, and apparently in conversation as well, that she moves from high seriousness to a banter that turns on self-deprecation. Having pressed her thoughts, she makes them out to be mere chatter, the trivial language of women (though she also assures Galiani that she has much more to say on the subject of women). There was a real and irremovable sense of inadequacy behind her self-belittling. She turned forty-three in 1771, and by then she was an experienced woman of letters; but she remained acutely aware that she could never acquire the formal education of her male friends and colleagues. And yet her self-deprecation was also a kind of dodge for violating the rules of feminine decorum; from behind it she could voice a sharp critique, one that encompassed most of her friends among the philosophes.

The 1771 letter has a strong note of fatalism. Women must be content to be intellectually useful in small ways, within the constraints that their lack of education imposes. Fifteen months later her tone is quite different. There is no professed humility in her scathing dismissal of Thomas's essay as hopelessly lacking in philosophical acuity. She mocks his claim to prefer a woman to a man for a lifetime friendship. Now she appeals to a principle of Nature she considers obvious: that men and women, sharing the same humanity, "have the same nature and the same constitution":

The proof of it is that savage women are as robust, as agile as savage men. Thus the weakness of our constitution and our organs belongs certainly to our education, and is the result of the condition that we have been assigned in society. . . . The virtues that one has wished to give women in general are almost all the virtues against nature. . . . It would doubtless take several generations to return us to what nature made us. We would perhaps gain; but men would lose too much. They are very happy that we are not worse than we are, after all they have done to denature (*dénaturer*) us with their beautiful institutions, etc.[67]

This is as simple and straightforward a statement of the universalist logic for feminism over the next two centuries as one is likely to find. In d'Épinay's hands too, of course, Nature is a construct; but now the construct evokes a state of equality, relegating conventional gender differentiations to the status of unnatural impositions of power. She does not qualify her position, though she remains aware that the women of her own era are severely handicapped intellectually. Women will cease to be physically and mentally weaker than men when they are given the same upbringing and education. They draw on the same "essence of humanity in general in fighting against pain, difficulties, obstacles, etc." The fact is that "if men were deprived, like women, of serious occupations, excluded from affairs (*affaires*) and made strangers to all great objects, they would exhibit this same unquiet disposition that, in [Thomas's] eyes, is extinguished by the nourishment that the role [men] play in society gives them."[68] Intellectual concentration, in other words, is a socially acquired power, not a gift of nature. This time d'Épinay's concluding banter is pointedly sarcastic: "I know at least that [women] are as much chatterboxes (*bavardes*) as the philosophes."[69] With this barbed teasing she draws her male friends and colleagues into the stereotype of women's speech. Diderot would not have been pleased to hear himself referred to as a chatterbox.

D'Épinay may seem to have been excessively cautious in her insistence on secrecy. In that regard she stands in contrast to the women (and some men) who edited the tolerated but closely monitored *Journal des Dames* from the early 1760s to the mid-1770s. Where she shunned any publicity, they made journalistic publication a weapon against the establishment, including d'Épinay's circle of philosophes. The difference lies in part in how they saw the larger social hierarchy. The *Journal* editors championed a large measure of equality for women of all social ranks, including the rights to freedom of speech and to active participation in public affairs, within an agenda that demanded a new civic respect for bourgeois and even plebeian men and women and made them heroes and heroines of the principle of patriotic utility.[70] Like her male friends among the philosophes, d'Épinay feared drawing those below her into any public action, though she felt they were owed far more respect than the aristocracy typically granted them. While she couched her argument in universalist terms, she spoke for the small minority of women who would be able to enter "serious occupations" while cooks, maids, tutors, and governesses took care of things at home. But this was not *mondain* snobbery. D'Épinay's unwillingness to publish her views on women had little to do with fearing a loss of "reputation" in the highly competitive circles of the Parisian elite of birth and wealth; she had little connection with that world. Her concern was that most (if not all) the philosophes with whom she was acquainted would find her views on gender absurd; she did not want to lose the hard-won intellectual credibility she enjoyed among them.

By the standards of contemporary feminism, d'Épinay may seem not only timid but also misguided. For nearly two centuries the implications of her universal principle—the idea of a shared human rationality—have come nowhere near full realization, even in the liberal tradition that has been most committed to them. To be sure, she did not oppose gendered difference with an argument for the complete sameness of male and female rational intellection. Even as she rejected the worldly notion that women's natural role was "to please," she was confident that women had the gift of making intellection more "agreeable"— which was to say that in their hands reason was more effectively communicable. At the same time, though, she accepted a false (i.e., male-specific) universalism at its point of deepest logical connection. We have to take seriously her insistence that women are by nature as strong physically as men—that it is their upbringing, not their hormonal makeup, that accounts for the difference. Obviously she accepts a male definition of physical strength, or power, that privileges male size and musculature and ignores, for example, the strength required to bear a child. More important, d'Épinay accepted the arbitrary analogy between the physical and mental, and the resulting false causal inference from the one to the other, that has justified characterizations of women as inferior for millennia. To do otherwise, she would have had to reject assumptions still lodged very deep in the epistemic logic of her society and culture well beyond the 1770s. D'Alembert, to be sure, challenged the logic as early as 1774, just two years after d'Épinay penned her second letter to Galiani. But as late as 1787 the young lawyer Maximilian Robespierre voiced the more typical view in an address to the Arras Academy, even as he argued on principle that women should be admitted to royal academies. His advocacy of women was ultimately grounded in "natural" physical differences: the "strength and profundity" of men's genius suited them for the study of "the intricacies of the abstract sciences"; given women's capacity for "delicacy and being pleasing," they should contribute to fields demanding "only sensibility and imagination," including literature, history, and morality.[71]

There is a more intriguing historical question: how d'Épinay went as far as she did in breaking through the conventional wisdom of her era and her context, though her upbringing stacked the odds against this outcome. What made her radical in this limited but important sense? We have not come full circle back to Poullain de la Barre's *Equality* a century earlier. D'Épinay did precisely what Poullain could not do. They were both liminal figures in relation to *le monde*, but the differences in their positions and their intellectual milieus made for divergent angles of vision. Poullain drew his inspiration for revaluing the qualities of the female mind from aristocratic women engaged in the social aesthetic of play, and for that reason he had to retreat in his second tract from his original call for women to have access to the same occupations as men. It was a condition of d'Épinay's feminism that she rejected that aesthetic, including the ideal of *aisance*, though she certainly enjoyed, and indeed found her sense of self in, the playful sociability of her own milieu. Her feminism is modern in part because, in its advocacy of personal and social self-validation for women through "study and work," it posed itself against the social aesthetic of play. She did not credit *le monde* for having made possible a positive, though constrained, revaluation of female intelligence. She found in it a foil to the "study and work" she wanted for herself and expected of others.[72]

What we know about d'Épinay's youth and early adulthood comes largely from a novel titled *The History of Madame de Montbrillant*, which she began writing around 1756 and returned to intermittently until 1762 and perhaps beyond.[73] It is a sprawling text (553 pages in its modern edition), reflecting in its scale the influence of Richardson and Rousseau, and as she crowded it with letters, diary entries, and free-standing stories, it may have spun out of control. Though there are fictional characters and events, the text is in its main outlines autobiographical. Three of its characters are, under the thin cloak of fictional names, Grimm, Diderot, and Rousseau. We cannot assume, of course, that the autobiographic detail is reliable, but we can be fairly certain that, on the whole, the novel conveys to us d'Épinay's retrospective understanding of her amplifying sense of self; and, though it ends in 1762, it gives us some notion of the formative experiences that led her to authorship and to feminism.

D'Épinay's childhood and youth can hardly be said to have prepared her to be an advocate, even in secrecy, for women's emancipation. Her father, a military commander, died in battle in 1736, when she was nine, leaving a meager inheritance. She moved with her mother to Paris to live in the household of her aunt, the wife of a wealthy *fermier général*. Though she never lost a certain affection for her mother, she remembers her as the kind of woman she eventually determined not to be: a slave to "opinion," cringing and hypocritical, obsessed with the appearances of respectability and reputation, intent on making her daughter ingratiating whatever the moral cost, a caricature of female *complaisance* and *agrément*. She raised Louise in strict piety and was adept at making her guilt-ridden. Louise's aunt, puffed up with her wealth, knew how to keep her niece aware that she was merely a poor relation. By the time she was married to her cousin Denis-Joseph Lalive de Bellegarde in 1745, at age nineteen, she had had little opportunity to develop a sense of self-worth. She was passionately in love, and at first the marriage seemed a blessing. She gave birth to a son in 1746. Her husband had received a lucrative post as a *fermier général*: she could look forward to a life of financial security and comfort. But it soon became apparent that Denis-Joseph was a familiar type in the old regime aristocracy, a man who found his wife silly for being upset about his mistresses (he was, after all, simply following "custom") and who was above petty considerations of money, squandering huge sums on gambling and presents to his mistresses. Louise contracted syphilis from him. In 1749, with the help of her father-in-law, she succeeded in arranging a separation of property, which protected her and her children to some degree from her husband's profligacy, but left her in a precarious financial situation that would subject her to intermittent crises for the rest of her life. She had acquired a certain contempt for ostentatious wealth, and for pretensions to aristocratic libertinism.

She was twenty-three in 1749, a young woman still under the thumb of her family and especially her mother, who did not hesitate to wield her authority long after her daughter was married. There is nothing in her life to this point to suggest the feminist we find in her letters to Galiani over twenty years later. We begin to see her developing a certain independence when she took a lover, Claude-Louis Dupin de Francueil, who proved hardly more faithful than her husband but introduced her to friends in the Parisian world of letters, including young men eager to make their mark. Thanks to the connection with Francueil she attended the regular dinners held by Mlle Quinault, a celebrated actress, where she heard the ideas of, among others, Diderot, Rousseau, the novelist Crébillon *fils*, and Charles Duclos.[74] It was, ironically, Rousseau, with whom she, Diderot, and Friedrich Melchior Grimm would have a bitter quarrel that began at the end of 1757, who introduced her to Grimm, who would become her lover. Having been introduced to d'Holbach's circle at dinners at his country residence, she began to entertain her growing circle of friends at La Chevrette, her father-in-law's imposing chateau just north of Paris. Though she was leaving behind her impoverished education for the intellectual world of the Enlightenment, she was still not her own person. Still eager to please, she may not have rejected the advances of men in her new circle as firmly as she should have. In any case, some of them, and most notably Duclos, a rejected suitor, spread rumors that she was a deceitful tease, a coquette of the worst sort. Small wonder that she was later horrified when friends betrayed confidences that might damage her reputation.

It was above all Grimm who gave her the self-confidence needed to assume the role of female philosophe. Friends since the late 1740s, they became lovers sometime around 1755. To most of the people who dealt with him Grimm was not a lovable man. He was vain, aloof, stiff and uneasy in company, imperious, severe in his judgment of others' work. But he was also highly competent, a man one could trust to get things done, and he was loyal to friends. He somehow managed to win the confidence of both mother and daughter, and played a key role in dealing with Louise's husband to secure their property. As their friendship turned to love, they also became intellectual companions. He gave no credence to the rumors of her promiscuity, and she in turn admired his powerful intelligence, the justifiable pride behind what others took to be his arrogance, and his need for solitude, a respite from social conventions, that she shared. With others his literary acumen was merciless; with her he was generous, even lavish, in praise. It was perhaps no accident that in a self-portrait she wrote in 1755, the year they became lovers, she resolved to become "a woman of great merit."[75] He encouraged her ambition to be a writer, and she drew resolve from his support.

During her stay in Geneva in the late 1750s Jean-Étienne Liotard painted two portraits of Madame d'Épinay. In one she is a fashionable lady of high society, with powdered, upswept hair and a plunging décolleté, gazing sideways playfully, confident that her pose will draw admiration. The other portrait is far less conventional. She sits in a chair holding a book in her left hand, with her thumb keeping her place. One has the impression that the sitting has interrupted her reading. Her hair is undressed and largely hidden by a simple white cap. Her head inclines to the right and the tip of her right index finger presses lightly on her chin. Her face would be unremarkable were it not for the gaze, frank, thoughtful, quizzical, and slightly mischievous.[76] The first portrait places her in the gay but mannered world of *le monde*, in which she had participated only occasionally, and which she, partly under the influence of Rousseau, found increasingly frivolous and false. Her frankness and mischievous humor did not square with the protocols of polite conversation.

At La Chevrette d'Épinay hosted not another salon, but a gathering place for a far more unbuttoned and convivial sociability. Its guests included, in addition to Grimm, Diderot, and Galiani, Marmontel, the d'Holbachs, and the Marquis de Saint-Lambert, a poet and contributor to the *Encyclopédie*. They gathered for days at a time, some working in their rooms during the day, and all dining, talking, listening to music, and watching the painters among them at work in the evenings. D'Épinay may have acted as hostess, but she was also actively engaged in the life of the mind with her largely male friends. Unlike Necker in her salon, her friendships formed an intellectual community in which she could break out of the constraints of politeness. The friends respected neither the social forms nor the intellectual parameters of the salons; Diderot and d'Holbach defended their atheism, and Galiani regaled the others with lascivious tales and outrageous mimicry of prominent personages.[77] Aware of her lack of formal education, d'Épinay learned through conversation, as a listener and occasional contributor, and undertook her reading accordingly. As she gained intellectual self-confidence, she participated—with characteristic self-deprecation but firmness of views—in convivial but sometimes heated intellectual contention that the social aesthetic of play had banned. The intimacy of friendship in this register allowed her an intellectual collaboration on something like equal terms. Grimm called her "one of the sisters of the philosophical communion."[78]

Still, though she worked continually at writing, she was cautious about assuming the public role of author and remained in the shadows of her fellow philosophes. *My Happy Moments*, a collection of short pieces, appeared in a small edition in 1758, printed by a friend in the village of Montbrillant near Geneva, where she was staying at the time. A year later the same press issued *Letters to My Son*, a more substantial and philosophical piece. Her contributions to the *Correspondance littéraire* were anonymous. The novel she began in 1756 was on the scale of Rousseau's *Julie*; but it remained unfinished and none of it was published during her lifetime. *Conversations of Emilie*, first published in 1774 and in an enlarged edition in 1782, was a pedagogical dialogue, a subject considered proper to female writers; but it finally brought her recognition in the wider world of letters when, three months before her death in 1783, it became the first book to receive the French Academy's Montyon Prize for a work of "utility" to the nation and humanity.[79]

As Grimm's closest friend, Diderot might have been expected to form a natural bond with d'Épinay. But he was a jealous friend, and he persisted in believing rumors about d'Épinay's promiscuous duplicity and refused to socialize with her for several years after her liaison with Grimm began. When they finally met in 1760, the barriers fell quickly. To d'Épinay Diderot was a kind of apparition, a singular voice in the philosophical commune. Dazzled by his conversational pyrotechnics, she found listening to him "ravishing," and his "self-possession" was "an inspiration." He had given her "a new capacity to enjoy all [her] advantages"; "I find myself more strongly attached to my duties, to everything I do. I work more easily: in short I am more *myself* than I was."[80] Particularly striking is that she found in this friendship a way to build a secure and authentic sense of self through work. She took to calling Diderot "the philosophe," admiringly but with a certain bemusement about his daring speculations on so many subjects. Diderot found her both intelligent and amiable and was soon declaring to her the intense warmth of his attachment. She, Grimm, and Diderot had often made a foursome with Galiani at La Chevrette. For a time Diderot, who shared her unhappiness with Grimm's career ambitions, consoled her for her lover's prolonged absences on diplomatic missions.[81]

It was Grimm's *Correspondance littéraire* that brought his lover and his friend into something like a professional collaboration. The newsletter was a uniquely secretive publishing project, available only in manuscript, and carefully limiting its readership to the several European courts that paid a hefty subscription price.

Though it catered to the courts' need to be in the know about gossip in *le monde* and Parisian literary circles, it also contained intellectually substantive material. With Grimm often away, Diderot and d'Épinay served as the unofficial editors of the *Correspondance littéraire*. She contributed anonymous book and theater reviews, some of them probably coauthored with Diderot. They seem to have become comfortable in disagreements. She did not accept his arguments for atheism, though she certainly found his critique of dogmatic Christianity liberating. In Diderot's *Entretien d'un père* a wise father, made executor of a deceased priest's will, finds in the priest's safe box a hitherto unknown will that excludes from his sizeable legacy all of his desperately needy country descendants. Reluctantly he applies the will to the letter, compelled to put positive law over natural law in denying an inheritance to the poor. In an alternative version of the story, d'Épinay declared that she would burn the will without remorse and give the legacy to the poor.[82] In 1771, in appraisals placed back to back in the *Correspondance*, they agreed to differ on La Harpe's "eloquence," she finding it moving, he faulting it for its coldness, its lack of "feeling."[83] In the same year, as Thomas was finishing his essay on women, their collaboration peaked. While working together on the journal they managed the formidable task of bringing Galiani's book on the grain trade to press, though Diderot, exasperated with his work load, complained of the incompetence of this "meddlesome little woman."[84]

In her editorial work, as in the new sociability of free conversation and uninhibited friendship at La Chevrette, d'Épinay was exposed to the entire gamut of Enlightenment ideas. Her feminism was a compound of multiple elements, including the tradition of natural law theory she used to justify her views of justice. At least as powerful in forming her feminist conviction were three other discourses with which we are familiar. It is no small matter that she opened them up to encompass women despite their male exclusivity.

The first was the pervasive norm of "utility" or "usefulness" that underlay a new patriotism in France. It is this theme that distinguishes d'Épinay sharply from the Marquise de Lambert (though it gives her some affinity with Necker), and that makes her feminism distinctly modern. She sought self-validation, and wholeness, not only from the intellectual labor of reading and writing in solitude, or from serious conversation, but from serious public occupation. Saddled with a husband who spent recklessly to live the life of the aristocratic libertine, she was utterly realistic about her own and her family's social position. In the eleventh of her *Letters to My Son*, she disabused him of the notion that he would inherit a fortune and could rely on "a name." "You are a man without birth (*naissance*)," she wrote, "and can merit the approval (*suffrage*) of the public only by your efforts and by your success . . . if you do not work with all your forces to acquire useful and honest (*honnêtes*) talents, you will pass your life in need, as you will pass it in contempt."[85] She herself was always in a precarious financial situation, but as she became engaged in the world of letters she knew that the obstacle to her "success" was not her lack of fortune, but her sex. She was accepted among the most original and high-minded men of letters of her generation, but she did not fully belong.

To say that d'Épinay's protest against this injustice pivoted on the eighteenth-century principle of individual merit, judged by the standard of utility or "usefulness," is true but insufficient. We hear in her use of these familiar terms essentially the same logic as in Hume's paean to "industry" in the middle station of educated professionals thirty years earlier, though she may not have been aware of that essay; but Hume had in mind an exclusively male professional world. She was certainly familiar with Duclos's and d'Alembert's calls in the early 1750s, when she was educating herself assiduously, for a republic of letters in which merit, exhibited in strenuous intellectual labor, would be the measure of the individual's social value; but that too was, with rare exceptions, assumed to be a male preserve. Not surprisingly, she has nonetheless been seen as a "bourgeois" feminist, but in fact she was at once bourgeois and counterbourgeois. Though she considered motherhood a sacred duty, she cut sharply against the grain of the reigning assumption in the discourse of merit that the only natural site for women's exercise of intelligence was the home.

This dissent from conventional assumptions of a gendered division of labor in a new order of "utility" was due in part to the fact that she absorbed, however incompletely, a republican ethos. The time she spent in Geneva, from October 1757 to October 1759, in the hope of improving her frail health was pivotal. Geneva brought to full clarity the conviction that her social position, her marital experience, the two-faced libertinism of so many men in her life, and her growing frustration as an aspiring woman of letters relegated to the fringe, had been forming in her over the last decade: that the idle, unabashedly ostentatious life of *le monde* must accede to a meritocratic society, with individual merit judged by "patriotism," or devotion to the common welfare. That is evident in the eleventh of the published letters to her son, written in Geneva in April 1758. She found it heartbreaking to watch her son emulating his father in a pseudoaristocratic life of Parisian pleasures and fashions, all flaunting unearned privilege. She had hoped that among the citizens of Geneva he would renounce that way of life, but he did not, and in the eleventh letter she made one more try.[86] To make her moral lesson credible she had to maintain an ideal of the city that Rousseau had probably done much to imbue in her. In fact over the previous several decades there had been mounting tension between the governing magistracy of wealthy patricians, many of them with close connections to Paris, and a bourgeois citizenry of artisans and shopkeepers who resented the patricians' emulation of the opulence of *le monde* and wanted to democratize the constitution.[87] She must have known of this conflict from Rousseau and, at the other end of it, from Voltaire, who invited her frequently to his home just outside the city and considered her that rarity, a truly "philosophical woman."

But in the letter to her son Geneva is a moral exemplar with no place for these complications. She had brought him there, she writes, in the hope that he would be "struck by the contrast between the dissipation of Paris, of the frivolity and looseness of our mores which sacrifice and pardon everything for *agréments*, and the regularity of a city where one has regard only for personal merit, and where one cannot remove oneself from virtue without renouncing esteem and public consideration." Geneva was a city of "real merit," of "useful talents," of "candor and simplicity of mores."[88] There is an irony, of course, to the fact that her feminism formed within this quasi-mythical image of a republican city. She separated out two elements of republican discourse: its emphatically masculine ideal of citizenship, which she implicitly rejected; and its condemnation of rampant luxury, with which she was in complete sympathy. Her imagined republic is a work-driven meritocracy in which women would enjoy equal citizenship.

What allowed her to make the discourses of merit and republicanism inclusive? D'Épinay needed to draw on another resource, one that seemed to offer to her and many of her contemporaries a universal human standard. It is another irony of our story that she drew on Stoicism, which had had anything but a feminist impulse in the thought of Shaftesbury and her friend Diderot. In the summer and fall of 1756, as she was deciding to seek medical treatment in Geneva, she conducted a correspondence with Théodore Tronchin, the Genevan physician of European-wide reputation who would treat her. Tronchin had strong Stoic inclinations. The best road to happiness, he wrote her, requires not becoming the slave of one's needs; "our happiness is within ourselves and weakens with support from without." He advised her to avoid "fleeting attachments"; "commit to friendships only to the degree that they are committed to [you]." D'Épinay demurred on this take-no-risks strategy. "It is impossible for me," she wrote, "to renounce either loving tenderly some of my fellow beings or a certain benevolence for mankind in general." To her friendship was the "only remedy we possess against the ills of this world."[89]

D'Épinay had in mind the exercise of relational intelligence in a friendship of reciprocal regard. For that, the self had to turn into itself to secure its moral autonomy. She did not evoke the classical ideal of friendships of heroic virtue, or the pure union of souls extolled in the culture of sensibility. Her point of departure was the Stoic idea of "the respect we ought to have for ourselves, in consideration of the excellence of human nature," which alone could provide "the tranquility of a good conscience." That was her message to her son in the twelfth and last of the *Letters to My Son*, written while she was still in Geneva. This time she simply ignores the boy's refusal to heed her and gives him a lesson in the philosophy of "the sect of *Portique*," which had "a great superiority over all the others" in considering "the excellence of human nature." The letter is a flat denial of the priority given to *complaisance* and *agrément* in the culture of *honnêteté*. "A man accustomed to finding in himself the most redoubtable judge," she writes, "and to preferring the interior certitude of his uprightness (*droiture*) to all the homages of the universe, cannot be an ordinary man." Unlike those whose "virtue depends on circumstances or a judgment of others," she continues, "the man who puts a high price on the opinion he ought to carry of himself is the master of his fate; his virtue is in his power." "The good man"—the man who always heeds his "interior censor"—"perceives himself always with *complaisance*."[90] *Complaisance* means here the opposite of the art of pleasing others; it connotes an inner satisfaction that makes social approval and reputation superfluous.

Given the course of life her son was entering (in 1769 he was imprisoned for indebtedness, and upon his release he continued his reckless gambling), the letter is perhaps best read as d'Épinay's fantasy of wholeness. Counseling herself, she finds in the respect for the human being within her, of the mind capable of making rational choices, the only way to achieve "a sure means to live with herself, to be free and independent." That conviction does not depend on a prior assertion that women can be as strong mentally as men because they can be as strong physically. What is required of women, as of men, is simply to "devote [themselves] to study and to work," to labor to acquire knowledge and to act on it. Nor is d'Épinay's interior spectator the same as Diderot's. Hers is the inner voice of moral autonomy, not of the manly intellectual disengagement of the clinician. Passages in *Conversations* echo the twelfth letter to her son. They have to be coupled with her instructions to her daughter's governess, published in 1758, which seek a balance between practical respect for social expectations and moral autonomy. The governess must correct her charge's mistakes "without pedantry, convincing her instead with reason, with evidence, and not with precepts and maxims." The meaning of "pedantry" has widened out from scholastic obscurantism to any irrational and coercive dogma the Enlightenment rejected, any abstraction hardened into doctrinal blindness. "For the essential things, but which are purely exterior and a matter of convention in the world," she writes, "inspire in her the love of her reputation and fear of the public; but never inspire in her either fear or the desire to please or displease any person in particular by her steps."[91]

A contemporary feminist might be put off by d'Épinay's faith in a gender-neutral reason, and by her respect for convention, particularly as it applied to women's sexual behavior. But in the context of her time she was advocating an emancipation of the mind that would make women, as rational moral agents, the equals of men. I find her not falling into a logocentric trap, but taking the necessary first step, and her commitment to it makes a fitting end to our story. The notion of a manly mind would no longer make sense.

Conclusion

Intelligence is a mystery, if we mean by that term the way neural activity in the brain is metamorphosed into concepts, images, memories, fantasies, intuitions, the logic of argument, and all the other elements of intellection we locate in the metaphorical space we call the mind. What we see and hear is the performance of intelligence or, more precisely, of various cognitive capacities. That has been our working premise in this volume. The assumed differences between the male and the female mind that pervaded early modern European culture had been handed down from antiquity; the men who oversaw pubic life—clergymen, bureaucrats, jurists and lawyers, teachers and university professors, scholars and men of letters—had absorbed them in their school and university years. But continuity is not truth; nor were these classical ideas necessarily handed down unconsciously or unaffected by the new contexts of performance available to educated women and men in seventeenth- and eighteenth-century western Europe.

In medical anthropology as in literary criticism, and in the philosophical treatise as in the polite essay, gender differentiation was integral to a rhetorical culture that was in turn rooted in a social epistemology of gender in everyday life. The norms of the gendering process were so tightly interwoven into the fabric of the everyday and into the social grammar of language as to largely preclude the critical distance needed to question them. To say that they were normative constructions is also to say that they had a prescriptive circularity; enforced performance was taken as proof of natural essence. This way of conceiving gender differentiation is essential to giving the historical study of thinking about intelligence a critical edge, as a practice in the social history of ideas. It accomplishes, I believe, what a radical historicism ought to do. The more we can uncover the historical contingency of assumptions about the natural that seemed unquestionable to historical agents, or of an apparent logical coherence to which they gave no less certitude, the more skeptical scrutiny we can bring to them; and the more aware we become of the need to bring the same critical skepticism to what seems to lie beyond questioning in our own era.

Running through most of our texts is a cultural logic of illogic in gender differentiation that feminist scholarship has been critiquing since the 1970s. Conceptions of intelligence that apparently rested on obvious facts of biological nature actually built on logically arbitrary analogies and inferences. In gender discourse, as in racial discourse, we see how easily facticity—the actual physical differences between men and women—slides into a normative ontology of assumptions about men's and women's essential states of being (who they were and must be, not just as embodied creatures but as persons). Throughout this book I have tried to keep our eye on a bedrock of binary oppositions between strength and weakness, action and passivity. Differences in the metaphorical space we call the mind were inferred from a logically (and empirically) unwarranted correspondence between the relative physical strength of men and women and the cognitive capacities of their brains. Men's willed action on nature was productive; it transformed nature into culture. In their reproductive function, and by extension in their entire mode of being, women were instruments of nature. Feminists of various persuasions—from Poullain de la Barre and Mme de Lambert to Mme Necker and Louise d'Épinay—had to negotiate new paths through, or detour around, this facticity become ontology.

Our main concern, however, has been with the higher levels of this seemingly logical edifice, where the unequal division of power and authority between men and women in social and cultural as well as legal and political discourses was taken as a matter of common sense. In educated and cultivated milieus the key measure of men's mental strength—what made their minds manly—was the capacity to perform a particular kind of strenuous labor, requiring both power and endurance. The labor might take the form of linguistic and textual erudition in the scholastic and humanist traditions, but it was above all an effort in abstraction, the climb from bodily cognition of the particularity of material and social life to the heights of universal truths or at least general principles. By contrast, women's intelligence was in effect confined to the immediate and fully embodied knowledge of particularity; their minds were delicate, sensitive, limited to the inherent particularity of emotions and passion and to a merely local knowledge of detail— and in all those senses women were weaker in mind as well as body. Men's role was to judge, applying the general to the particular; women's was to please within the sense world of particularity. From seventeenth-century learning and philosophy to the emerging bourgeois culture of the second half of the eighteenth century, men's exercise of authority was grounded in mental labor that women could not perform, the labor of the manly mind.

Especially striking was men's claim to authority over standards of taste, despite the fact that the choice, consumption, and display of objects of aesthetic pleasure were often conceded to be women's realm. In men's intellectual labor the inward-looking exercise of reflectivity in Stoic and other meditative traditions often went hand in hand with the grasping of laws, at once objective and morally normative, governing the reality external to human subjectivity. Mme Necker had the latter in mind when, in the privacy of her journals, she dismissed the "philosophers, whose hearts, desiccated by abstractions, become indifferent to the objects surrounding them; who think they can enlarge themselves [*s'agrandir*] by hurling themselves out of their sphere, and who, like gods, wish to take the measure of things outside themselves." Here was the deep paradox that Necker, this quote notwithstanding, was reluctant to challenge: because men could enlarge themselves by hurling themselves outside the dense particularity of material and social being, they could achieve a higher level of self-consciousness than women. That is to say that they were capable of superior moral intellection, however sensitive women might be to the immediate and concrete details of moral life.

It is a measure of the tenacity of the binaries as unexamined epistemological givens that new medical paradigms did not change them, but rather confirmed them in the course of reformulating them. Galen's hot and cold humors, Descartes's fibers conducting animal spirits, the fibers vibrating in reaction to Newtonian mechanical forces, the self-impelled organs of vitalist medicine: all explained the same putatively ontological differences of gender. The binaries lie somewhere between Hume's two meanings of "custom," one epistemological and the other social; in that loosely empirical sense they can be fairly said to constitute a social epistemology. They remained unquestioned even by men who prided themselves on radically questioning conventional wisdom, and indeed they were integral to the thought of some of the men who have been said to have constituted the "radical" wing of the Enlightenment. Diderot is a striking case in point.

There may be, inevitably, a degree of presentism in this approach; we smugly declare our predecessors to have been hopelessly wrong, trapped in ideologically loaded discourses from which we have shaken ourselves loose. That is not at all what I mean to imply about ourselves, here and now. There is no reason to assume that we've somehow risen above logics of illogic, and there is good reason to suspect that we're living with new ones. The proper role of "historicist" understanding, as I define it, is to listen closely to the past, rather than using it to talk to ourselves. This kind of engagement with the past induces us to ask whether we too are caught in logics of illogic. Why shouldn't we be?

Distilling the logic of illogic does not, of course, provide us with the specificity needed to provide an historical explanation that takes social configurations and processes as its context, or to penetrate a text as a situated rhetorical performance. Even as we historicize, however, we have to resist mapping contexts and texts onto conventional narrative forms of history. In the 1770s, the decade in which our story closes, we do not find the culmination of a process, or a linear narrative of contention in which one view of gender emerges victorious. Nor do we have a circular denouement. Louise d'Épinay, like Poullain de la Barre in *Equality* a century earlier, argued for women's equality of access to intellectual labor; but with the critical historical difference that, while Poullain drew inspiration from the social aesthetic of play in *le monde*, d'Épinay saw that same world as at cross-purposes with her aspirations to both friendship and autonomy. There had been no layering of discourses. They formed something more like a palette in which we can discern a spectrum of positions. At the close of the eighteenth century we can distinguish between the strictly rationalist feminism of equality based on sameness—the position of a d'Épinay or a Condorcet—and a feminism which, while insisting on women's equality as rational moral agents, flipped over the received stereotype of the female imagination, transforming it from a potentially wild, ravaging force that had to be vigilantly contained into a power to envision new possibilities of social order. They both ran up against a new scientific wisdom of biological essentialism and determinism, to which Diderot had already pointed. Not surprisingly, the middle ground—the ideal of gender complementarity in a modern social division of labor—had been most fully developed in David Hume's Scottish middle station. I have tried to add to our understanding of its roots in Hume's intellectual and social balancing act as a philosopher of the science of man and a polite man of letters.

If we do not have a narrative in the strong sense, we do have a story with an ironic twist. What occurred in *le monde*'s imagined social aesthetic of play was a significant revaluation of female intelligence. Aesthetic authority became a function of *aisance*, and women, as the embodiment of *aisance* in their self-presentation and especially in their speech, were made the arbiters of taste and the life of the mind where it mattered most, in polite social exchange. Only men could master the public eloquence needed in the pulpit and the law court, but it was women who had a natural facility in language. Women's talk might still be dismissed as evanescent babble about the trivia of domestic life, love affairs, and ever-changing fashions, but in worldly circles their facility in language was now seen as a social art, the paradox of natural artifice, at once prescribed as performance and idealized as "natural," the highest exemplar of purely human freedom. It was a physical facility, but as important, it had not been spoiled by the formal education reserved to men, who had to learn from women how to act naturally and above all to speak naturally in polite sociability. As female "delicacy" of body, temperament, and mind was endowed with a new intellectual acuity, in taste and in social interaction, it was not clear whether the relative physical strength of men mattered in the constitution of intelligence and hence whether one could still assume the supremacy of the manly mind. At the heart of this revaluation was the belief that what I have called relational intelligence, with all it implied about psychological insight and the capacity for social communication, was more natural to women than to men. Its corollary was that women had distinct gifts of taste, which was to say that they were the purveyors and guardians of the aesthetic symbols by which the imagined world of *le monde* defined itself and maintained its coherence. The mutual nourishing of tastes was an unprecedented form of relational engagement between men and women.

It is tempting from our present standpoint to see this revaluation as a missed opportunity. Could it not have provided the point of departure for a full-scale intellectual emancipation of women, at least in the upper reaches of society? The temptation should be resisted; in fact, intellectual emancipation by the standards of contemporary feminism was largely precluded, and that was because gender was so tightly fused with status. The point is lost when we work within the usual triad of race, class, and gender. Status tends to be subsumed under class and is visible only in its shadows. Class was, of course, important; everyone in this study occupied a class position, which was a major determinant, if not the primary determinant, of social power or the lack of it. But that, by itself, helps us very little in grasping the meaning of their self-representations, and it may lead us to crude reductions of meaning to collective interests. It is in the specific criteria for "honor," or the relative social and ultimately moral value of groups, linked in multitudinous ways to rungs on the class ladder, that we find the norms that combined with the logic of gender difference to define and patrol the parameters of women's intellectual performance. Placed in this framework, Mme de Lambert was a more exceptional case than has usually been assumed, and a strikingly ironic one. There was no democratic impulse to her feminism. Indeed she looked down on the common lot of *le monde* with a sense of spiritual superiority. Deeply offended by what she saw as the reduction of intelligent women like herself to sexually dissolute behavior in her own era, she took the audacious step of publicly condemning the stereotype of the *femme savante* as a serviceable trope for male arrogance. The art of much of her counterargument lay in enlisting the semantic field of *honnêteté*. It was no minor point to argue that, as women infused rational abstraction with affective cognition, they were able to make ideas "more alive, more clear (*nettes*), more disentangled (*démêlées*)." But she cut deeper into conventional wisdom; in a singular, if not unique, move, she denied the truism that in women thought flowed naturally and hence there was no need for the labor of reflection.

The historical question is how gender combined with other norms in the discursive webs of cultures. Paying due attention to "honor" is critical to reading some of the key texts of early modern feminism. Perhaps the most striking example is Poullain de la Barre, who has too often been read as a modern feminist tout court. His *Égalité* was indeed a remarkably modern feminist argument, even more radical in context than has been assumed, and all the more striking in that it inverted rather than denied the discourse of *honnêteté*. In *Éducation* he retreated; even as he insisted on the labor required to achieve a Cartesian ownership of ideas, he bowed to the need to assure society women that their honor would not be compromised by the practice of laborious thought. Madeleine de Scudéry well understood that the performances expected of women in *le monde* did not confirm that they had lesser intellectual capacities. At stake was an implicit social calculus. Excessive gallantry—gallantry practiced to the point of self-caricature—degraded women; but if they failed to honor the ideal of gallantry, they risked forfeiting the respect owed them. For all her intellectual and literary ambition, Mme Necker tried, perhaps futilely, to avoid the stigma of the *femme savante*. The point is not that these women and others have been mislabeled as "feminist." But in most cases their feminism was not modern for the simple reason that it did not, and perhaps could not, claim for women the social performance and practice of intelligence that modern feminism considers essential to female emancipation. To avoid presentism in the study of early modern feminism, we have to take more into account distinctions of honor that were of the utmost importance to women's as well as men's social identity. At least until the middle decades of the eighteenth century, utilitarian notions of labor as a route to self-validation must be assiduously bracketed out.

From the formative years of the social aesthetic of play onward, it was, of course, challenged from its edges. In the seemingly effortless voice of the *honnête homme*, scholars and men of letters—our examples have been Guez de Balzac, Bouhours, and Huet—questioned the intellectual authority with which *honnêteté* endowed well-born women. In the course of the eighteenth century the labor/*aisance* dichotomy was revalued in a groundswell change as bourgeois society began to assert itself publicly and the commercialization of print expanded, particularly to female readers of polite literature, from the novel to the essay. For the emerging bourgeois cultures of England and Scotland, and for the increasingly assertive men of letters in France, aspiring to form a national clerisy, intellectual labor was transformed from a stigma to the sine qua non for the exercise of public authority of virtually any kind, including authorship. Industry, self-discipline, ambition within reason: these became the watchwords of virtue. Male intellectual talent was an "impulsion of nature," to recall d'Alembert's phrase, and only by developing it with strenuous application could one validate oneself as a social being and qualify to speak authoritatively in a public role. To students of the eighteenth century this is now common knowledge, supported by voluminous research, and the ascendancy in public rhetoric (social practice is another matter) of its corollary implications—that the proper site for women's natural talents was the home, and that it would be unnatural for them not only to be employed outside the home, but also to engage in serious labor of the mind within it—is also well known. What I have examined is the process in which, in the rhetorical world of bourgeois polite culture, a new dichotomy between male labor and female *aisance* was configured, not without tensions and strains. Polite literature, rooted as it was in mixed-gender conversational reciprocity, had no place for the male-exclusive rhetorical imposition of authority. In the bourgeois world, as in *le monde*, politeness required that authors instruct by pleasing. But in the logic of the manly mind, a feminized society would be morally rudderless. The more feminized literary culture seemed to become with commercialization, the more necessary it seemed to assert the authority of the male voice, whether by insisting on it or quietly implying it.

Nowhere is this reaction against the threat of feminized relativism more apparent than in the much-discussed subjects of taste and the role of the critic. Women might have a distinctive capacity for aesthetic pleasure, but only men could be critics with authoritative standards acquired in intense and sustained labor. Despite its polite discursive style, Hume's "Of the Standard of Taste" rests on, and in the end justifies, the assumption that the remit of the critic, a man of rare gifts and learning, was to instruct women as well as men in what they ought to take pleasure in. And yet Hume's later relationship with the Countess de Boufflers reminds us that, in the interplay of gender and status norms, the line between the exchange of intelligence in aristocratic self-projection and in an imagined bourgeois culture could waver. The friendship he sought with the Comtesse, once she had taken his advice and left her position at the pinnacle of *le monde*, would be one of serious play, a kind of tasteful leisure, requiring intellectual conversation that was substantive but did not have to justify itself as industrious. Unlike Adam Smith and other friends in Scotland, Hume fantasized being a Scottish Parisian, or a Parisian Scott.

The manly but polite mind had to wend its way between idle dilettantism, which was marked feminine, and the excessive masculinity of the pedant. Here again gender and status reinforced each other. The trope of the pedant evoked the entire culture of school Latinity, university learning, and the combative academic argument with which disputes in theology and philosophy were conducted. Precisely because it was an exclusively male world, its denizens were too crude, too socially inept, to acquire the honor of "polite" identity conferred by mixed-gender conversational sociability. The pedant was the product of both hothouse fraternity and reclusive solitude. Not surprisingly, in the eighteenth century the trope remained central to the self-affirmation of *le monde*, as Mme Necker learned to her chagrin. More striking is that it also had strong purchase in bourgeois politeness. If Hume contrasted the labor of the learned professions with aristocratic leisure, he also posed mixed-gender conversation in the spaces of politeness against pedantry. Hume's pedant was a foil to a polite but industrious middle station, rather than to an aristocratic mystique of unalloyed *aisance*. The pedant's excessive masculinity did not lie in the performance of labor as such; it was now the unsociable—and hence unnatural—solitude of the labor, and the failure to counteract the danger of tunnel-visioning with the liberality acquired in polite leisure, that made pedantry a serviceable stigma. "Even Philosophy," Hume writes, "went to Wrack by this moaping recluse Method of Study, and became as chimerical in her Conclusions as she was unintelligible in her Stile and Manner of Delivery." He would leave unsaid, but implicitly acknowledge, that in writing the *Treatise*, for all his rejection of chimeras, he had not sufficiently distanced himself from the moping recluse.

From the mid-seventeenth century onward the specter of effeminacy arose where the requisite qualities of *honnêteté*—its art of pleasing, its grace, its *aisance*—seemed to turn into a weakness of mind and temperament that made men unnaturally feminine. Effeminacy was the collateral damage, one might say, in a world that insisted that men learn from women how to be fully socialized beings. With Shaftesbury we encounter something new that would pervade eighteenth-century discourse, or, more precisely, we encounter new variations on ancient themes. Effeminacy became the emblem for virtually all the ills of what was conceived as corruptive modernity. Most striking is its use as a trope for the softening (i.e., weakening) effect of modern consumer culture, and above all for authors pandering to an expanding print market. The figure of the self-caricaturing gallant in aristocratic sociability now had its counterpart in the bourgeois author too eager to please an ever widening reading market with an increasingly large presence of women. In this discursive context we find moments in the development of the essay as a genre and a performance of style. Shaftesbury tried to insert his Stoicism into public discourse by simulating manly fraternity, in essays that made civil but virile argument, sharply contrasted with the banning of argument in *mondain* politeness, their stylistic signature. Hume sought a via media as the "ambassador" from the "learned" world to the "conversible" world. Diderot made "On Women" an antipolite essay, a back-of-the-hand slap at the entire polite tradition.

In view of the pervasiveness of a discourse of effeminacy, it is not surprising that it was labile, serving quite different purposes in different contexts. We need only consider two near contemporaries, Malebranche and Shaftesbury, to see how contextually flexible the dichotomy between the manly mind and the effeminate mind could be. Both men condemned what they saw as a feminized modernity, and both launched full-scale attacks on the effeminized mind. Facing the challenge of ascending to rational abstraction despite the sensual and emotional needs of the body, they both were convinced that the route to reason lay through solitary askesis, the hard labor of meditation. And yet effeminacy served as their trope for entirely different diagnoses of and prescriptions for the ills of modernity. The Oratorian priest formed his vision of modern society within an internally consistent framework of Cartesian Augustinianism. In meditation he sought an "intimate union" with the God of the Augustinian Trinity; the taste and style exhibited in the aesthetic of social play, and manifested more incurably in the *bel esprit* than in any other social type, were sins of an ineradicably corrupt human nature; the apparent mutual *agrément* of French polite sociability was in fact a selfish competition for power, with speech as its insidious weapon. He sought to create a power-free community of *méditatifs*, using print but avoiding style and the very identity of author. Shaftesbury, an English nobleman in the Whig tradition, contemptuous of the mixed-gender polite social world and often pushing against the political winds of his day, cultivated moral autonomy in Stoic askesis. The Absolute One of which he considered himself an instrument was pure Reason itself, with no Christian garb. There was no ineradicable corruption in human nature; society was capable of a renewal inspired by the ancients but assuming modern forms, antidotes to the effeminacy of corrupt modernity. Seeing the aesthetic and the political nurturing of liberty as inseparable, he advocated a "philosophical" criticism in literature, resting squarely on, but not explicitly identified as, Stoic self-knowledge and self-mastery. Authorship had to be rescued from the effeminacy that an expanding print market had diffused out from conversational sociability to polite letters. That required a manly style of fraternal raillery, replacing effeminate *complaisance* with productive argument. Following the lead of Stoic-grounded critics, authors would subject themselves to the kind of rigorous self-examination that Shaftesbury had learned to practice. The self-disciplined autonomy they would acquire in that reflexive process would be exercised in a commitment to aesthetic objectivity as well as disinterested civic action. In comparisons like these, we see how indispensable intellectual history is to the understanding of broad cultural phenomena, in gender as in other constructions.

To Shaftesbury gallantry and real friendship between men—the only friendship worth pursuing—were polar opposites. It was the unbridgeable distance between dissimulation and integrity, slavish emulation and moral autonomy. That was an extreme view; what we find in the eighteenth century is a complicated debate about the role of gallantry in the formation of modern societies, with quite different judgments about how it had informed and should inform intellectual exchanges between men and women. To Diderot, as to Shaftesbury, the medieval chivalry from which gallantry had derived had been a great historical violation of the laws of nature that ought to govern society; it gave the weaker (but cunning) sex the power to define and police the terms of exchange in modern sociability, and that had had disastrous effects on the male mind and on public culture. Women like Mlle de Scudéry and Mme de Lambert distinguished between corrupted gallantry and the true gallantry of a receding golden age, when cultivated women had enjoyed a new respect on matters of taste and, often implicitly, moral values. It was Hume who tried to find a new justification for modern gallantry in a tortuous configuration of nature and society. He made gallantry a natural artifice, so inbred that habit was indistinguishable from natural impulse. It became the essential way in which bourgeois men, in their relations with women, developed liberal-mindedness in retreat from their professional lives. If this ideal was conde-scending toward women, it nonetheless made possible, pace Shaftesbury, their intimate friendships with cultivated men in taste in literature and the fine arts.

But could cultivated men and women form intimate friendships, meetings of minds as well as sentiments, as opposed to relationships dominated by erotic passion? By examining this kind of friendship in the ideal and in practice, I have argued, we avoid simplistic (and jargonish) uses of notions of patriarchalism and masculinism. Throughout the early modern era, to be sure, the classical ideal of friendships of heroic virtue that excluded women was very much alive. But as we find in Mme Lambert's ideal of virtuous friendship, even that tradi-tion, tempered with sensibility and practiced with sublimated passion, could be conceived as a foundation, in her historically specific situation, for an ideal of human wholeness that one could not attain simply as a member of one's sex. In a mix of intellectual chemistry and emotional intimacy in the register of gal-lantry, Saint-Évremond sought something like the same wholeness. In this light the friendship between Thomas and Necker becomes an especially interesting case. What makes it unusual is that it was formed within the cult of the solitary manliness of genius, as a reciprocal labor of selfhood. The conditions of the friendship were shared alienation from *le monde* and hence shared solitude (which prevented the reclusive solitude that often paralyzed the manly Thomas). Ironically its nourishment in mutual psychological need and depen-dence, lived in the detail of everyday life, offered a route to mutual indepen-dence from the hyperperformative culture from which they could not walk away. Louise d'Épinay, on the other hand, cherished friendships free of the protocols of politeness—and, despite the occasional misogyny of Diderot, her feminism found a vital resource in those friendships.

Concepts of nature and society were central to early modern thinking about the mind, as they are today. We can safely generalize that material nature was conceived as the primal source of energy, anterior to the formative powers of the social. We can trace a divide between the manly mind's reflexive detachment from the social and women's confinement to society's natural solidarities. But what moral status did the economy of nature have, if any? Was there a "natural" social use of that energy? In what sense did the individual find "freedom" or "liberty" in the natural? In the ideal of the *honnête femme*, society women's antirhetorical rhetoric made thought as well as feeling into beautiful speech with spontaneous immediacy. It seemed to be an admirably natural performance of what distin-guished the truly human from, in Hume's phrase, "immers[ion] in the animal Life." The natural meant the effortless social exhibition of innate gifts of mind and speech. To Shaftesbury such performances were utterly artificial and, in men's emulation of them, effeminate; a natural social order emanated from a supreme

Intelligence, which bound the individual to a hierarchy of "affections" in which women occupied a low place. To Hume the vital natural energy—the one generating social virtue in the middle station—was channeled into the intellectual labor of the manly mind; though at the same time, in an appreciation of French aristocratic liberality that cut against the English and Scottish grain, he wanted the natural and the social to meld in mixed-gender polite sociability. To Diderot in his vitalist phase the "natural" meant an economy of implacably amoral laws which made women at once mentally impoverished human beings, incapable of self-disciplined intellectual labor, and dangerously cunning animals.

The larger point is that the historical strategy of denaturalizing what past societies and cultures believed to be natural is essential to critique, but has to be used with care. If applied with too broad a brush, it threatens to flatten the immensely varied landscape in which intellectual historians work most effectively. Perhaps the most striking case in point is the Stoic tradition, which I had not expected to become a thread running through the book. The *Askêmata* make it abundantly clear that Stoic askesis was foundational for Shaftesbury's concept of the manly mind. What is usually left implicit in the meditations becomes explicit in his published essays: a renewed English civic culture, exclusive to men, had to be built on the Stoic ideal of moral autonomy. Though never a Stoic practitioner, the Diderot we have profiled here pitted the Stoic tradition, in the form of detached self-containment, against the effeminate exhibition of weakness, or lack of self-control, and the infantilizing of language that he found in excessive sensibility. Hence it may at first be surprising that for two of the early modern feminists considered here—Mme Necker and Louise d'Épinay—Stoicism was also foundational. In a sense it gave these women a solution to the same problem facing men: inner self-mastery in the face of the scattering effect of modern sociability, its threat to the dignity of rational self-possession. One might object that Stoic reason remained an instrument of domination, requiring women to measure up to a male standard. But the objection lacks historical awareness. It slights the fact that in Stoic reason some women found a refuge from the gendered expectations pressed on them.

In rhetorical performances in public and private texts, I have tried to demonstrate, we find mediations between a person's subjectivity, most of which is inaccessible, and her presence on the page, which is only apparently straightforward. We have traced the tensions in *mondain* women's efforts to engage in the labor of writing without appearing to violate the norms of polite effortlessness. Mme de Lambert's essay on women is a remarkable text because to a great extent she resolved that tension rhetorically, coupling an *honnête* voice and a more radical critique. Roughly a half century later Mme Necker wavered between regretting women's preoccupation with the immediate present, the quotidian particularity of social relations, and particularly of friendships, and perching that same attention above men's pretensions to think outside their social selves. To her Mme de

Sévigné's letters were literary masterpieces precisely because they spontaneously conveyed the social particularity of friendship, without the mediating labor of authorship. It was precisely that labor that Louise d'Épinay wanted to perform, if only in genres restricted to women. As she advised her daughter's governess, a woman should respect convention to some degree; but she should not lead her life desiring to please others.

Some of our male authors experimented in prose because modernity confronted them with challenges in representing the manly mind. One thinks of Malebranche's rejection of style, or of Shaftesbury's efforts to develop an exclusively male style. That Shaftesbury was, in our parlance, a male chauvinist, or that his obsession with having a manly mind was in some way due to his physical weakness as an asthmatic, is certainly relevant to understanding his thought. But it does not suffice. Precisely because he was obsessed, he had to engage in a labor of language, seeking a way to assert a fraternal politeness in a new world of commercialized politeness, where women had a large presence. It is the rhetorical complexity of that effort that still makes his essay experiments, contra Adam Smith, fascinating. By contrast Hume's essays fascinate by their effort to accommodate a female reading public without seeming to descend to effeminate ingratiation, and Diderot's "On Women" by its blatantly antipolite assertion of the manly mind.

There is an irony here too. We owe to the manly mind in its various guises—commanding, self-satisfied, condescending, uncertain, defensive, accommodating—some of the key texts in the development of modern literary genres and prose styles. The pertinence of the ancient rhetorical technique of personification is perhaps obvious: history has its cunning.

Notes

Introduction

1. Charles-Louis de Secondat Montesquieu, *My Thoughts*, trans., ed., and intro. Henry C. Clark (Indianapolis, 2012), 291. The quote, taken by itself, oversimplifies Montesquieu's thoughts on women and gender.

2. Anthony J. La Vopa, *The Self and the Calling of Philosophy, 1762–1799* (Cambridge, 2001), esp. 150–80, 345–67; La Vopa, "Thinking About Marriage: Kant's Liberalism and the Peculiar Morality of Conjugal Union," *Journal of Modern History* 77, 1 (March 2005): 1–34; La Vopa, "Women, Gender, and the Enlightenment: A Historical Turn," *Journal of Modern History* 80, 2 (June 2008): 332–57.

3. William M. Reddy, *The Navigation of Feeling: A Framework for the History of Emotions* (Cambridge, 2001), 34–62, summarizes recent skepticism about constructionism in anthropology. On the limits of its usefulness in historical analysis, see William H. Sewell, *Logics of History: Social Theory and Social Transformation* (Chicago, 2005), esp. 152–96.

4. Fritz K. Ringer, *Max Weber's Methodology: The Unification of the Cultural and Social Sciences* (Cambridge, 1997).

5. Helpful on long-term distinctions among work, play, and leisure is Victor Turner, *From Ritual to Theater: The Human Seriousness of Play* (New York, 1982), 20–60.

6. Sarah Knott and Barbara Taylor, "General Introduction," in *Women, Gender and Enlightenment*, ed. Knott and Taylor (Houndmills, 2005), xix–xx; La Vopa, "Women, Gender, and the Enlightenment," 332–33; Joan Wallach Scott, *The Fantasy of Feminist History* (Durham, 2011), 23–29.

7. Denise Riley, *"Am I That Name?" Feminism and the Category of Women in History* (Minneapolis, 1988); Scott, *Fantasy*, 8–11.

8. Lorraine Daston, "The Naturalized Female Intellect," *Science in Context* 5, 2 (1992): 209–35; John Carson, *The Measure of Merit: Talents, Intelligence and Inequality in the French and American Republics, 1750–1940* (Princeton, 2007).

9. For a summary of recent debates in cognitive psychology on the relation between emotion and cognition see Reddy, *The Navigation of Feeling*, 3–33.

10. Colin McGinn, *Problems in Philosophy: The Limits of Inquiry* (Oxford, 1993), 27–31.

11. See the critique of the "New Historicism" in Sarah Maza, "Stephen Greenblatt, New Historicism, and Cultural History; or, What We Talk About When We Talk About Interdisciplinarity," *Modern Intellectual History* 1, 2 (2004): 249–65.

12. Jerrold Seigel, *The Idea of the Self: Thought and Experience in Western Europe Since the Seventeenth Century* (Cambridge, 2005).

13. Carol Gilligan, *In a Different Voice: Psychological Theory and Women's Development* (Cambridge, 1982).

14. See, e.g., Martha C. Nussbaum, "The Feminist Critique of Liberalism," in Nussbaum, *Sex and Social Justice* (New York, 1991), 55–80; Lynn Hunt, *The Family Romance of the French Revolution* (London, 1992), 199–204; Joan Wallach Scott, *Only Paradoxes to Offer: French Feminists and the Rights of Man* (Cambridge, 1996), esp. 18. A subtle defense of "critical reason" in contemporary argument is Amanda Anderson, *The Way We Argue Now: A Study in the Cultures of Theory* (Princeton, 2006).

Louise M. Antony and Charlotte E. Witt, eds., *Feminist Essays on Reason and Objectivity*, 2nd ed. (Cambridge, 2002), is an excellent introduction to recent feminist debates about reason.

15. Samuel Moyn, "Imaginary Intellectual History," in *Rethinking Modern European Intellectual History*, ed. Darrin M. McMahon and Samuel Moyn (Oxford, 2114), 113–26. See also Sewell, *Logics of History*, esp. 318–72.

16. J. G. A. Pocock, *The Machiavellian Moment: Florentine Political Thought and the Atlantic Republican Tradition* (Princeton, 1975), 462–504; Christopher J. Berry, *The Idea of Luxury: A Conceptual and Historical Investigation* (Cambridge, 1994); Joan B. Landes, *Women and the Public Sphere in the Age of the French Revolution* (Ithaca, 1988), esp. 23–28.

17. Quoted in Philip Carter, *Men and the Emergence of Polite Society, Britain, 1660–1800* (Harlow, 2001), 132.

18. Genevieve Lloyd, *The Man of Reason: "Male" and "Female" in Western Philosophy*, 2nd ed. (Minneapolis, 1993), esp. ix. See also Lloyd's probing of the workings of metaphor in gendered concepts of reason: "Maleness, Metaphor, and the 'Crisis' of Reason," in Antony and Witt, *Feminist Essays on Reason and Objectivity*, 73–89.

19. Pierre Bourdieu, *Masculine Domination*, trans. Richard Nice (Stanford, 2001), 53. See also Gerald N. Izenberg, *Modernism and Masculinity: Mann, Wedekind, Kandinsky Through World War I* (Chicago, 2000), esp. 4–19; Judith Surkis, *Sexing the Citizen: Morality and Masculinity in France, 1870–1920* (Ithaca, 2006), esp. 10–12; Adam Phillips, *Terrors and Experts* (Cambridge, 1995), 77–82; Peter Hanns Reill, *Vitalizing Nature in the Enlightenment* (Berkeley, 2005), 220–29.

20. Sewell, *Logics of History*, 362–69.

21. Ernst Bloch, "Nonsynchronism and the Obligation to Its Dialectics," *New German Critique* 11 (Spring 1977): 22–38.

22. Barbara Taylor, "Feminists Versus Gallants: Sexual Manners and Morals in Enlightenment Britain," in Knott and Taylor, *Women, Gender and Enlightenment*, 30–52.

23. Scott, *Fantasy*, 5.

24. Particularly helpful is Ruth H. Bloch, "Theory: A Culturalist Critique of Trends in Feminist Theory (1993)," in Bloch, *Gender and Morality in Anglo-American Culture, 1650–1800* (Berkeley, 2003), 21–41.

25. My approach is similar to that of Sabine Arnaud in *On Hysteria: The Invention of a Medical Category Between 1670 and 1820* (Chicago, 2015). See esp. her "Introduction" (1–8), which argues for "a history of the enunciation of texts."

26. Quentin Skinner, *Visions of Politics*, vol. 1, *Regarding Method* (Cambridge, 2002). Though Skinner may have modified his original distinction between intended "meaning" and "motive," I still find that it precludes much that can be done in a social history of ideas without being reductive.

27. Richard Holmes, *Footsteps: Adventures of a Romantic Biographer* (New York, 1985), 66–69, 90–106; Nancy Struever, "Philosophical Problems and Historical Solutions," in *At the Nexus of Philosophy and History*, ed. Bernhard P. Dannhauer (Athens, Ga., 1987), 91; Anthony J. La Vopa, "Doing Fichte: Reflections of a Sobered (But Unrepentant) Contextual Biographer," in *Biographie Schreiben*, ed. Hans Erich Bödeker (Göttingen, 2003), esp. 144–51. See also Susan Manning, *Poetics of Character: Transatlantic Encounters 1700–1900* (Cambridge, 2013), 23. Manning's book opens a highly original rhetorical approach that is relevant to intellectual historians as well as literary scholars.

28. Fritz K. Ringer, *Fields of Knowledge: French Academic Culture in Comparative Perspective 1890–1920* (Cambridge, 1992), esp. 94–108, 314–23; La Vopa, "Doing Fichte," 136–37.

29. Pathbreaking in this regard is Jerrold Seigel, *Marx's Fate: The Shape of a Life* (Princeton, 1978). More recent examples include Barbara Taylor, *Mary Wollstonecraft and the Feminist Imagination* (Cambridge, 2003); Nicholas Phillipson, *Adam Smith: An Enlightened Life* (London, 2010); Peter N. Miller, *Peiresc's Europe: Learning and Virtue in the Seventeenth Century* (New Haven, 2000); April Shelford, *Transforming the Republic of Letters: Pierre-Daniel Huet and European Intellectual Life* (Rochester, 2007). I have argued for the value of new biographical approaches in intellectual history, including the history of philosophy, in "Doing Fichte."

Chapter 1. The Social Aesthetic of Play in Seventeenth-Century France

1. There is a considerable body of scholarship on seventeenth-century Parisian high society and its culture, most of it in literary studies. Four books have been particularly important for my purposes: Domna C. Stanton, *The Aristocrat as Art: A Study of the Honnête Homme and the Dandy in Seventeenth- and Nineteenth-Century French Literature* (New York, 1980); Myriam Dufour-Maître, *Les précieuses: Naissance des femmes de lettres en France au XVIIe siècle* (Paris, 1999); Alain Viala, *La France galante: Essai historique sur une catégorie culturelle, de ses origines jusqu'à la Révolution* (Paris, 2008). Benedetta Craveri, *The Age of Conversation*, trans. Teresa Waugh (New York, 2005), is an invaluable synthesis of scholarship on the salons and their *salonnières*, deftly using biographical portraits and written with admirable subtlety.

Also relevant for my purposes are E. Bury, *Littérature et politesse: L'invention de l'honnête homme, 1580–1750* (Paris, 1996); Jean-Pierre Dens, *L'honnête homme et la critique du goût: Esthétique et société au XVIIe siècle* (Lexington, 1981); Marc Fumaroli, "De l'âge de l'éloquence à l'âge de la conversation: La conversion de la rhétorique humaniste dans la France du XVIIe siècle," in *Art de la lettre: Art de la conversation à l'époque classique en France*, ed. Bernard Bray and Christophe Strosetzki (Paris, 1995), 25–45; Fumaroli, "L'empire des femmes," *La Diplomatie de l'esprit. De Montaigne à La Fontaine* (Paris, 1994), 321–39; Elizabeth C. Goldsmith, *Exclusive Conversations: The Art of Interaction in Seventeenth-Century France* (Philadelphia, 1988); Michael Moriarty, *Taste and Ideology in Seventeenth-Century France* (Cambridge, 1988); Christoph Strosetzki, *Rhétorique de la conversation: Sa dimension littéraire et linguistique dans la société française du dix-septième siècle* (Paris, 1984); Faith E. Beasley, *Salons, History, and the Creation of Seventeenth-Century France: Mastering Memory* (Hampshire, 2006).

2. Elena Russo, *Styles of Enlightenment: Taste, Politics, and Authorship in Eighteenth-Century France* (Baltimore, 2007), is an especially important recent study of "the modern taste" (*goût moderne*) of salon *honnêteté* and the reaction against it in the eighteenth-century Enlightenment.

3. Madeleine de Scudéry, "De la politesse," in Scudéry, *"De l'air galant" et autres conversations: Pour une étude de l'archive galante*, ed. Delphine Denis (Paris, 1998), 137–38.

4. On Calvinism and Locke see Michael Walzer, *The Revolution of the Saints: A Study in the Origins of Radical Politics* (New York, 1970), 199–231; Charles Taylor, *Sources of the Self: The Making of the Modern Identity* (Cambridge, 1989), 159–76, 211–47.

5. Though the need to relate gender to status as well as class is often acknowledged in historical scholarship, the triad is seldom given in-depth contextual analysis. Notable exceptions are Mary Terrall, "Émilie du Châtelet and the Gendering of Science," *History of Science* 33 (1995): 282–310; Paula Findlen, "Women on the Verge of Science: Aristocratic Women and Knowledge in Early Eighteenth-Century Italy," in *Women, Gender, and Enlightenment*, ed. Sarah Knott and Barbara Taylor (Houndmills, 2005), 265–87; Norma Clarke, "Bluestocking Fictions: Devotional Writings, Didactic Literature and the Imperative of Female Improvement," in ibid., 460–73, and Clarke, *The Rise and Fall of the Woman of Letters* (London, 2004).

6. Craveri, *Age of Conversation*, 27–35.

7. Quoted in F. E. Sutcliffe, *Guez de Balzac et son temps* (Paris, 1959), 30.

8. I have summarized here one of the themes in a rich and subtle study of the *querelle*: Mathilde Bombart, *Guez de Balzac et la querelle des lettres: Écriture, polémique et critique dans la France du premier XVIIe siècle* (Paris, 2007).

9. Quoted in Sutcliffe, *Balzac*, 38. On Guez de Balzac's life see Antoine Adam, *Histoire de la littérature française au XVIIe siècle*, vol. 1, *L'époque d'Henri IV et de Louis XIII* (1948; Paris, 1997), 241–58.

10. See esp. Alain Génetiot, *Poétique du loisir mondain, de Voiture à La Fontaine* (Paris, 1997), 431–40.

11. Jean-Louis Guez de Balzac, "Suite d'un entretien de vive voix, ou de la conversation des Romains: À Mme la marquise de Rambouillet," in *Les entretiens*, ed. Bernard Beugnot, pt. 1 (Paris, 1972), 74–82, 94–96. On Balzac's achievement in combining the humanist rhetorical tradition and the aristocratic culture of conversation see Marc Fumaroli, *L'âge de l'éloquence: Rhétorique et "res literaria" de la Renaissance au seuil de l'époque classique* (Geneva, 2002), 695–706.

12. Balzac, "Qu'il n'est pas possible d'escrire beaucoup et de bien escrire," in *Les entretiens*, 1:209–16. Similarly, Jean de La Bruyère, *Les caractères de La Bruyère* (Paris, 1843; repr. 2006), 308. See also Marc Fumaroli, Philippe-Joseph Salazar, and Emanuel Bury, *Le loisir lettré à l'age classique*, ed. Philippe-Joseph Salazar and Emmanual Bury, 213–31.

13. Quoted in Ian Maclean, *Woman Triumphant: Feminism in French Literature* (Oxford, 1977), 138.

14. Vincent Voiture, *Lettres de V. Voiture*, ed. Octave Uzanne (Paris, 1880), 4. There is an excellent brief portrait of Voiture in Craveri, *Age of Conversation*, 45–67. See also Génetiot, *Poétique*, 439–40.

15. Scudéry, "De la politesse," 122. The fullest portrait of Scudéry is Alain Niderst, *Madeleine de Scudéry, Paul Pellisson, et leur monde* (Paris, 1976). See also Daniel Gordon, *Citizens Without Sovereignty: Equality and Sociability in French Thought, 1760–1789* (Princeton, 1994), 107–11; Goldsmith, *Exclusive Conversations*, 41–75. Richard Scholar, *The je-ne-sais-quoi in Early Modern Europe: Encounters with a Certain Something* (Oxford, 2005), 204. Scholar's book has been helpful, but I have not followed his narrative of a shift in the primary term of "quality," from *honnêteté* to *urbanité*, then to *galanterie* and finally to *bel esprit* (203–11).

16. Antoine Lilti, *Le monde des salons: Sociabilité et mondanité à Paris au XVIIIe siècle* (Paris, 2005).

17. François La Rochefoucauld, "De la conversation," in *Oeuvres complètes*, ed. Robert Kanters, Jean Marchand, and L. Martin-Chauffier (Paris, 1964), 509–10; Goldsmith, *Exclusive Conversations*, esp. 5–13.

18. La Rochefoucauld, *Oeuvres complètes*, 506.

19. Dominique Bouhours, "Le je ne sais quoi," in *Les entretiens d'Ariste et d'Eugène* (1671; Paris, 1920), 284.

20. Scholar, *The* je-ne-sais-quoi, esp. 182–211.

21. Joan DeJean, *Tender Geographies: Women and the Origin of the Novel in France* (New York, 1991), 182.

22. Joan DeJean, *Ancients Against Moderns: Culture Wars and the Making of a Fin de Siècle* (Chicago, 1997), esp. 31–64.

23. Carolyn C. Lougee, *Le Paradis des Femmes: Women, Salons, and Social Stratification in Seventeenth-Century France* (Princeton, 1976), esp. 41–55; Gordon, *Citizens Without Sovereignty*.

24. Charly Coleman, *The Virtues of Abandon: An Anti-Individualist History of the French Enlightenment* (Stanford, 2014), esp. 22–31.

25. Georg Simmel, "Soziologie der Geselligkeit," in Simmel, *Aufsätze und Abhandlungen 1909–1918*, ed. Rüdiger Kramme and Angela Rammstedt (Frankfurt am Main, 2001), 177–93. Further references in parentheses in the text. I am indebted to Elizabeth Goldsmith for making me aware of this text with her skillful use of it *Exclusive Conversations*.

26. Margaret Susman, quoted in David Frisby, *Georg Simmel*, rev. ed. (London, 2002), 35–36. Frisby's book is a valuable reevaluation of Simmel's thought.

27. I rely heavily here on William H. Sewell, Jr., *Logics of History: Social Theory and Social Transformation* (Chicago, 2005), esp. 124–96.

28. Pierre Bourdieu, *Distinction: A Social Critique of the Judgement of Taste*, trans. Richard Nice (Cambridge, 1984), 169–72.

29. Bourdieu, *Distinction*, 6, 54.

30. See the critique of Bourdieu in Sewell, *Logics of History*, 137–43.

31. Ibid., 166.

32. Antoine Gombaud, chevalier de Méré, "De la conversation," in *Oeuvres complètes du chevalier de Méré*, ed. Charles-Henri Boudhors, 3 vols. (Paris, 1930), 2:121. On Méré, see Jean-Pierre Dens, "Le chevalier de Méré et la critique mondaine," *XVIIe Siècle* 101 (1973): 41–50; Dens, " 'Les agréments qui ne lassent point': Le chevalier de Méré et l'art de plaire," *L'Esprit Créateur* 15 (1975): 221–27; Gordon, *Citizens Without Sovereignty*, 101–5. The natural "style of interaction" is well described in Russo, *Styles of Enlightenment*, 37–38.

33. For a discussion of the complex status distinctions between manual and intellectual labor in the old-regime corporate hierarchy, see William H. Sewell, Jr., *Work and Revolution in France: The*

Language of Labor from the Old Regime to 1848 (Cambridge, 1980), 19–25. On the centrality of leisure to the culture of *honnêteté*, see Fumaroli, "L'empire des femmes"; Alain Montandon, "L'honnête homme," *L'honnête homme et le dandy* (Tübingen, 1993), 240; Stanton, *The Aristocrat as Art*, 94–99; Strosetzki, *Rhétorique de la conversation*, 124, 146.

34. Méré, "De la conversation," 100, 109, and "De l'éloquence," in *Oeuvres complètes*, 3:103–5.

35. Scudéry, "De la conversation," in *"De l'air galant"*, 73. See also Méré, "De la conversation," 119.

36. Stanton, *The Aristocrat as Art*, 192–98.

37. La Bruyère, *Caractères*, 289–90.

38. Méré, "De l'éloquence," 115–19.

39. Jerrold Seigel, *The Idea of the Self: Thought and Experience in Western Europe Since the Seventeenth Century* (Cambridge, 2005), 5.

40. Jacques du Bosc, *L'honneste femme* (Paris, 1658), 48, 255–57. Originally published in three parts from 1632 to 1636.

41. Coleman, *The Virtues of Abandon*, esp. 53–87; Daniela Kostroun, *Feminism, Absolutism, and Jansenism: Louis XIV and the Port-Royal Nuns* (New York, 2011).

42. Seigel, *The Idea of the Self*, 6.

43. Rebecca M. Wilkin, *Women, Imagination and the Search for Truth in Early Modern France* (Aldershot, 2008), esp. 124–26, 137–39.

44. Balzac, "Suite d'un entretien," 85.

45. Charles de Saint-Évremond, "Sur les plaisirs," in *Oeuvres en prose*, ed. René Ternois, 4 vols. (Paris, 1962–69), 4:348–59, 4:12.

46. Fumaroli, "De l'âge de l'éloquence," 28.

47. Michel de Montaigne, "Of Pedantry," in *The Complete Essays of Montaigne*, trans. Donald M. Frame (Stanford, 1965), 99–106.

48. Montaigne, "Of the Art of Discussion," in ibid., 704–5.

49. The various dimensions of the seventeenth-century figure of the "pedant" are well documented in Klaus Breiding, *Untersuchungen zum Typus des Pedanten in der französischen Literatur des 17. Jahrhunderts* (Frankfurt am Main, 1970). Important discussions of the meaning of the stereotype are Noémi Hepp, "La belle et la bête, ou la femme et le pédant dans l'univers romanesque du XVIIe siècle," *Revue d'Histoire Littéraire de la France* 77, 3/4 (May–August 1977): 564–77; Françoise Waquet, *Latin or the Empire of the Sign*, trans. John Howe (London, 2001), 208–10.

50. Jean-Baptiste Morvan de Bellegarde, *Réflexions sur le ridicule* (Paris, 1696), 333, quoted in Breiding, *Untersuchungen*, 88.

51. Waquet, *Latin*, 210–11. La Bruyère portrays such a figure in *Caractères*, 189.

52. Dominique Bouhours, *Les entretiens d'Ariste et d'Eugène* (1671; Paris, 1920).

53. Ibid., 239.

54. Ibid., 152.

55. Ibid., 170.

56. Ibid., 170–74.

57. Ibid., 242.

58. Pierre-Daniel Huet, *Traité de l'origine des romans*, 2 vols. (1670; Stuttgart, 1966).

59. DeJean, *Ancients Against Moderns*, 169–76. April Shelford, *Transforming the Republic of Letters: Pierre-Daniel Huet and European Intellectual Life* (Rochester, 2007), 98–113, is a nuanced and convincing corrective to DeJean's reading of Huet, mapping his ultimately unsuccessful efforts to bridge the worlds of learning and the worldly "empire of women."

60. Huet, *Traité*, 2:97. See also Huet's praise for Scudéry's talents in Pierre-Daniel Huet, *Memoirs of the Life of Peter Daniel Huet*, trans. John Aikin (London, 1810), 18–19.

61. Du Bosc, *L'honneste femme*, 18–20.

62. Huet, *Traité*, 80–89.

63. Ibid., 93. See also Huet's recollection of the ten years of almost superhuman labor he devoted to a scholarly defense of Christianity, despite his courtly duties as tutor to the Dauphin, in *Memoirs* 2, 157–59.

64. Shelford, *Transforming the Republic of Letters*, 98.

65. Bouhours, *Entretiens d'Ariste et d'Eugène*, 190–91.

66. Ian Maclean, *The Renaissance Notion of Woman* (Cambridge, 1980), 8–10; Londa Schiebinger, *The Mind Has No Sex? Women in the Origins of Modern Science* (Cambridge, 1989), 160–65. This logic underlay La Bruyère's view that women's natural defects prevented them from being *savants*. *Caractères*, 76–77.

67. See also La Bruyère, *Caractères*, 76–77.

68. For detailed background on the *querelle des femmes*, see esp. Maclean, *Woman Triumphant*; Linda Timmermans, *L'accès des femmes à la culture (1598–1715): Un débat d'idées de Saint François de Sales à la marquise de Lambert* (Paris, 1993).

69. Waquet, *Latin*, esp. 190–91.

70. Dufour-Maître, *Les précieuses*, 598–600; Katharine J. Hamerton, "Malebranche, Taste, and Sensibility: The Origins of Sensitive Taste and a Reconsideration of Cartesianism's Feminist Potential," *Journal of the History of Ideas* 69, 4 (October 2008): 542.

71. Dena Goodman, "*L'ortografe des dames*: Gender and Language in the Old Regime," in Knott and Taylor, *Women, Gender and Enlightenment*, 195–223.

72. Quentin Skinner, "Retrospect: Studying Rhetoric and Conceptual Change," in *Visions of Politics*, vol. 1, *Regarding Method* (Cambridge, 2002), 182–83.

73. Hamerton, "Malebranche, Taste, and Sensibility," 536.

74. Du Bosc, *L'honneste femme*, 3–4, 35–54, 135–38.

75. Stanton, *The Aristocrat as Art*, 120–22.

76. Bernard Le Bovier de Fontenelle, *Conversations on the Plurality of Worlds*, trans. H. A. Hargreaves, intro. Nina Rattner Gelbart (Berkeley, 1990), 72.

77. J. B. Shank, "Neither Natural Philosophy, nor Science, nor Literature: Gender, Writing and the Pursuit of Nature in Fontenelle's *Entretiens sur la pluralité des mondes habités*," in *Women, Men, and the Birthing of Modern Science*, ed. Judith P. Zinsser (DeKalb, 2005), 85–86.

78. Ibid., 88–93.

79. Fontenelle, *Conversations*, 11.

80. Shank, "Neither Natural Philosophy, nor Science, nor Literature," 103.

81. Ibid., 97.

82. Fontenelle, *Conversations*, 3–5.

83. Ibid., 18.

84. Ibid., 7.

85. Scudéry, "De parler trop ou trop peu, et comment it faut parler" in Scudéry, *"De l'air galant,"* 93–94.

Chapter 2. Poullain de la Barre: Feminism, Radical and Polite

1. François Poullain de la Barre, *De l'égalité des deux sexes* (1673; Fayard, 1984); *De l'éducation des dames pour la conduite de l'esprit dans les sciences et dans les moeurs: Entretiens* (1679; ed. Bernard Magné, Université de Toulouse Le Marail, 1980); *De l'excellence des hommes, contre l'égalité des sexes* (Paris, 1675). My translations are from these texts. All three texts have been translated in François Poullain de la Barre, *Three Cartesian Feminist Treatises*, intro. Marcelle Maistre Welch, trans. Vivien Bosley (Chicago, 2002). There is now a concise history of the reception of Poullain's writings in Siep Stuurman, *François Poulain de la Barre and the Invention of Modern Equality* (Cambridge, 2004), 277–83.

2. Lorraine Daston, "The Naturalized Female Intellect," *Science in Context* 5, 2 (1992): 228; Stuurman, *François Poulain de la Barre*, 296; Lieselotte Steinbrügge, *The Moral Sex: Woman's Nature in the French Enlightenment*, trans. Pamela E. Selwyn (New York, 1995), 11–12.

3. Madeleine Alcover, *Poullain de la Barre: Une aventure philosophique* (Paris, 1981). The extant biographical information is now available in Stuurman, *François Poulain de la Barre*, which supersedes all previous work on Poullain.

4. François Poullain de la Barre, *Essai des remarques particulières sur la langue françoise pour la ville de Genève* (Geneva, 1691); Poullain de la Barre, *La doctrine des protestans sur la liberté de lire l'Écriture*

Sainte, le service divin en langue entendue, l'invocation des saints, le sacrement de l'eucharistie (Geneva, 1720).

5. An interesting exception is Marcelle Maistre Welch, "*De l'éducation des dames pour la conduite de l'esprit dans les sciences et les moeurs* (1674) ou le rêve cartésien de Poullain de la Barre," in *L'éducation des femmes en Europe et en Amérique du Nord de la Renaissance à 1848*, ed. Guyonne Leduc (Paris, 1997), 135–43.

6. Cf., in addition to Stuurman's book, Florence Lotterie, *Le genre des Lumières: Femme et philosophie au XVIIIe siècle* (Paris, 2013), 62–68.

7. Though the need to relate gender to status as well as class is often acknowledged in historical scholarship, the triad is seldom given in-depth contextual analysis. Notable exceptions are Mary Terrall, "Émilie du Châtelet and the Gendering of Science," *History of Science* 33 (1995): 282–310; Paula Findlen, "Women in the Verge of Science: Aristocratic Women and Knowledge in Early Eighteenth-Century Italy," in *Women, Gender and Enlightenment*, ed. Sarah Knott and Barbara Taylor (Houndsmill, 2005), 265–87; Norma Clarke, "Bluestocking Fictions: Devotional Writings, Didactic Literature, and the Imperative of Female Improvement," in ibid., 460–73.

8. Poullain, *De l'éducation*, 332–36. Subsequent page references in parentheses in the text.

9. Poullain, *De l'égalité*, 9–12.

10. Linda Timmermans, *L'accès des femmes à la culture (1598–1715): Un débat d'idées de Saint François de Sales à la marquise de Lambert* (Paris, 1993), esp. 378–85; Erica Harth, *Cartesian Women: Versions and Subversions of Rational Discourse in the Old Regime* (Ithaca, 1992).

11. Stuurman notes the relevance of salon culture to Poullain's thought, but does not develop the theme. See his *François Poulain de la Barre*, 27–28, 62–63. See also Ian Maclean, *Woman Triumphant: Feminism in French Literature, 1610–1652* (Oxford, 1977), esp. 143–54.

12. Poullain, *De l'égalité*, 29.

13. Poullain, *De l'éducation*, 24.

14. On the "egalitarian "implications of Descartes's thought, and on Poullain's appropriation of it, the most important discussion is now Stuurman, *François Poulain de la Barre*, esp. 87–123.

15. Poullain, *De l'égalité*, 85–86.

16. Matthew L. Jones, "Descartes's Geometry as Spiritual Exercise," *Critical Inquiry* 28 (August 2001): 46–50.

17. Poullain, *De l'éducation*, "Avertissement."

18. Ibid., 351–52.

19. In his insightful "Descartes's Geometry," Jones sees Descartes's philosophy contributing to a "vision of *honnêteté*" in which "a genteel specialization, proper manners, and truth making outside of formal institutions were intertwined with elements of taste broadly conceived," but he also characterizes Descartes's "scheme for self-cultivation" as a "spiritual exercise" requiring "methodic practice" (42, 48, 70). On the philosophical tradition of askesis, see Pierre Hadot, *Philosophy as a Way of Life: Spiritual Exercises from Socrates to Foucault*, ed. Arnold I. Davidson, trans. Michael Chase (Malden, 1995).

20. René Descartes, "The Search for Truth by Means of the Natural Light," in *The Philosophical Writings of Descartes*, ed. John Cottingham, Robert Stoothoff, and Dugald Murdoch, vol. 2 (Cambridge, 1984), 400–420.

21. René Descartes, *A Discourse on Method: Meditations and Principles*, trans. John Veitch (London, 1994), 23–24.

22. Poullain, *De l'éducation*, 52–84.

23. Ibid., 121–22, 129, 139–40.

24. Ibid., 141–69.

25. Ibid., 342–48.

26. Madeleine de Scudéry, "De la politesse," in *"De l'air galant" et autres conversations (1653–1684): Pour une étude de l'archive galante*, ed. Delphine Denis (Paris, 1998), 134–35.

27. Harth, *Cartesian Women*.

28. Poullain, *De l'éducation*, 147–48.

29. Ibid., 226.

30. Stuurman makes a similar point in *François Poulain de la Barre*, 118–19.

31. Poullain, *De l'éducation*, 185–89.

32. Ibid., 246–48.

33. On Descartes's contribution to the development of a French culture of "self-ownership," see Charly Coleman, *The Virtues of Abandon: An Anti-Individualist History of the French Enlightenment* (Stanford, 2014), 39–43.

34. Poullain, *De l'éducation*, 246–48.

35. Ibid., 250–51.

36. Poullain, *Essai des remarques particulières sur la langue françoise pour la ville de Genève*, 2–3.

37. Stuurman, *François Poulain de la Barre*, 294–96.

Chapter 3. Malebranche and the *Bel Esprit*

1. Nicolas Malebranche, *The Search After Truth*, trans. and ed. Thomas M. Lennon and Paul J. Olscamp (Cambridge, 1997), 1. (Subsequent references in parentheses in the text.)

2. Katharine J. Hamerton, "Malebranche, Taste, and Sensibility: The Origins of Sensitive Taste and a Reconsideration of Cartesianism's Feminist Potential," *Journal of the History of Ideas* 69, 4 (October 2008): 554.

3. Antony McKenna, *De Pascale à Voltaire* (Oxford, 1990), 256–63.

4. Nicolas Malebranche, *Oeuvres complètes*, vol. 20, *Malebanche vivant: Biographie, bibliographie* (Paris, 1967), 25. The *Oeuvres complètes* are cited hereafter as OC.

5. The best introduction to Malebranche's biography is still Henri Gouhier, *La vocation de Malebranche* (Paris, 1936). Neither the history of philosophy nor intellectual history has produced a much-needed new biography.

6. This limitation is stressed in Gouhier, *Vocation*, 1–8.

7. Claude Clerselier, ed., *L'homme de Rene' Descartes et un traité de la formation du fetus du mesme autheur avec les remarques de Louys de La Forge* (Paris, 1664).

8. OC, 20:57–63.

9. Ibid., 999.

10. Ibid., 15.

11. Ibid., 32–34.

12. Ibid., 264.

13. Ibid., 231–83.

14. Gouhier, *Vocation*, 49–63.

15. OC, 20:13–17.

16. Mark Hatfield, "Descartes' Physiology and Its Relation to His Psychology," in *The Cambridge Companion to Descartes*, ed. John Cottingham (Cambridge, 1992), 335–70, is a clear explanation of the differences between Cartesian mechanism and Aristotelianism.

17. OC, 20:21.

18. Henri Gouhier, *La philosophie de Malebranche et son expérience religieuse* (Paris, 1948), 281. Martin's compendium was titled *Philosophia Christiana*, and was published under the pseudonym Ambrosius Victor. Gouhier, *Vocation*, 77–78.

19. See esp. Michael Hanby, *Augustine and Modernity* (London, 2003); Charles Taylor, *Sources of the Self: The Making of the Modern Identity* (Cambridge, 1989), 127–58. For an important historical alternative to Taylor on Augustine and Descartes, see Jerrold Seigel, *The Idea of the Self: Thought and Experience in Western Europe Since the Seventeenth Century* (Cambridge, 2005), 57–74.

20. Perhaps Malebranche's clearest introduction to his metaphysical, moral, and social thought is Nicolas Malebranche, *Dialogues on Metaphysics and on Religion*, ed. Nicholas Jolley and David Scott (1668; Cambridge, 1997). Indispensable for my analysis were Michael Moriarty, *Early Modern French Thought: The Age of Suspicion* (Oxford, 2003); and Hamerton, "Malebranche, Taste, and Sensibility."

21. Jean-François Senault, *L'homme criminel, ou la corruption de la nature par le péché selon les sentimens de Saint Augustin* (Paris, 1656).

22. John Cottingham, "Descartes as Sage: Spiritual *askesis* in Cartesian Philosophy," in *The Philosopher in Early Modern Europe: The Nature of a Contested Identity*, ed. Conal Condren, Stephen Gaulroger, and Ian Hunter (Cambridge 2006), 182–201.

23. See also *Entretien 1* of *Conversations chrétiennes*, in Nicolas Malebranche, *Oeuvres*, ed. Geneviève Rodis-Lewis and Germain Malbreil, 2 vols. (Paris, 1979), 1:1132 (cited hereafter as MO).

24. *Entretien 4* of *Conversations chrétiennes*, in MO, 1:1207–8.

25. Ibid., 1212–16.

26. OC, 20:26–28.

27. Ibid., 29.

28. Benedetta Craveri, *The Age of Conversation*, trans. Teresa Waugh (New York, 2005), 105–23; John J. Conley S.J., *The Suspicion of Virtue: Women Philosophers in Neoclassical France* (Ithaca, 2002), 20–44.

29. Quoted in Conley, *The Suspicion of Virtue*, 81; Craveri, *Age of Conversation*, 216. One of the volumes in Sablière's library was Malebranche's *The Search After Truth*. On her life see Craveri, *Age of Conversation*, 209–17.

30. OC, 20:176–87.

31. Quoted in Craveri, *Age of Conversation*, 91.

32. Ibid., 96.

33. For brief portraits of Rancé see ibid., 89–96; A. J. Krailsheimer, *Rancé and the Trappist Legacy* (Kalamazoo, 1985).

34. Armand-Jean de Rancé, *The Letters of Armand-Jean de Rancé, Abbot and Reformer of La Trappe*, ed. A. J. Krailsheimer, 2 vols. (Kalamazoo, 1984), 1:57–58.

35. Armand Jean de Rancé, *De la sainteté et des devoirs de la vie monastique*, pt. 2 (Paris, 1683), 370. See also Blandine Barret-Kriegel, *La querelle Mabillon-Rancé* (Paris, 1992), 10.

36. Abbé de Marsollier, *La vie de Dom Armand-Jean Le Bouthillier de Rancé, abbé régulier et réformateur du monastère de La Trappe, de l'étroite observance de Cisteaux* (Paris, 1703), liij, lxxiv.

37. Malebranche, *Dialogues*, 87.

38. Pierre Nicole, "Discours où l'on fait voir combien les entretiens des hommes sont dangereux," in Nicole, *Essais de morale*, vol. 2 (Paris, new ed., 1682), esp. 252–61.

39. Hamerton, "Malebranche, Taste, and Sensibility," 551–52.

40. Malebranche, *Traité de morale*, in MO, 2.

41. Yves Marie André, *La vie du R. P. Malebranche, prêtre de l'Oratoire* (1886; Geneva, 1970), 423.

42. Alain Niderst, *Fontenelle à la recherche de lui-même (1657–1702)* (Paris, 1972), 306–21.

43. Bernard Le Bovier de Fontenelle, *Choix d'éloges de savants* (Paris, 1981), 99–104, 115.

44. Ibid., 91–92.

45. Quoted in Michel Le Guern, "Sur la place de la question des styles dans les traités de rhétorique de l'âge classique," in *Qu'est-ce que le style: Actes du colloque international*, ed. Georges Molinié and Pierre Cahné (Paris, 1994), 176.

46. On the idea of a "rhetorical community," see esp. Susan Manning, *Poetics of Character: Transatlantic Encounters 1700–1900* (Cambridge, 2013).

47. See, e.g., OC, 2: 526–27.

48. Quoted in Véronique Wiel, *Écriture et philosophie chez Malebranche* (Paris, 2004), 29, 34.

49. Ibid.

50. Malebranche, *Dialogues*, 36–37.

51. Ibid., 84–85.

52. Wiel, *Écriture et philosophie*.

53. *Entretiens sur la métaphysique, sur la religion, et sur la mort*, in MO, 2:651–1040.

54. See especially Michael Prince, *Philosophical Dialogue in the British Enlightenment: Theology, Aesthetics, and the Novel* (Cambridge, 1996).

55. MO, 1:1133–34.

56. Ibid., 1140.

57. Ibid., 1307–17.

58. "Méditations chrétiennes et métaphysiques," in MO, 2:195–419.

59. Ibid., 205–12.

60. Ibid., 194.

61. MO, 2:669–71.

62. Ibid., 670.

63. Ibid., 773.

64. Fontenelle, *Choix d'éloges*, 101–2.

Chapter 4. Love, Gallantry, and Friendship

1. An excellent discussion of friendship, love, and marriage in the seventeenth-century aristocracy is Jonathan Dewald, *Aristocratic Experience and the Origins of Modern Culture: France, 1650–1715* (Berkeley, 1993), 104–45.

2. Jean de La Bruyère, *Les caractères de La Bruyère* (Paris, 1843; repr. 2006), 85.

3. Madeleine de Scudéry, "De la politesse," in de Scudéry, *"De l'air galant" et autres conversations: Pour une étude de l'archive galante*, ed. Delphine Denis (Paris, 1998), 130–32.

4. Marcus Tullius Cicero, *De senectute, De amicitia, De divinatione*, trans. William Armistead Falconer (Cambridge, 1992), esp. 139, 185.

5. Peter N. Miller, *Peiresc's Europe: Learning and Virtue in the Seventeenth Century* (New Haven, 2000), 49–75. On social interaction in the Republic of Letters, with considerable attention to frequent violation of its norms, see Anne Goldgar, *Impolite Learning: Conduct and Community in the Republic of Letters 1680–1750* (New Haven, 1995).

6. April Shelford, *Transforming the Republic of Letters: Pierre-Daniel Huet and European Intellectual Life* (Rochester, 2007), 38–44. See also Myriam Dufour-Maître, *Les précieuses: Naissance des femmes de lettres en France au XVIIe siècle* (Paris, 1999), 232–35.

7. Alain Viala, *La France galante: Essai historique sur une catégorie culturelle, de ses origines jusqu'à la Révolution* (Paris, 2008), 155.

8. There has been extended debate over whether the *précieuses* actually existed, who they were, and how they dealt with marriage. Dufour-Maître, *Les précieuses*, 575–87, is a judicious treatment of this subject.

9. Dewald, *Aristocratic Experience*, 104–45; Viala, *La France galante*, esp. 150–59.

10. Scudéry, "De l'air galant," in *"De l'air galant,"* 53–55.

11. Ibid., 51–52, 55.

12. Ibid., 57.

13. Viala, *La France galante*, esp. 40–65.

14. Scudéry, "De l'air galant," 51.

15. Quentin Hope, *Saint-Evremond and His Friends* (Geneva, 1999), has not received the attention it deserves in scholarship on seventeenth-century French literature. See also D. Bensoussan, "L'honnêteté chez Saint-Évremond: Élégance et commodité," in *L'honnête homme et le dandy*, ed. Alan Montandon (Tübingen, 1993), 76–106.

16. Quentin Hope, *Saint-Evremond: The honnête homme as Critic* (Bloomington, 1962).

17. Charles de Saint-Évremond, "Sur les anciens," in Saint-Évremond, *Oeuvres en prose*, ed. René Ternois, 4 vols. (Paris, 1962–69), 4:348–59 (cited hereafter as SEO); "Saint-Évremond to the Duchess Mazarin," 1677 or 1678, in *Lettres: Textes publiés avec introduction, notices et notes par René Ternois*, 2 vols. (Paris, 1967–1968), 1:44 (cited hereafter as SEL).

18. "Lettre écrit à la Comtesse d'Olonne en luy en envoyant son Caractère," SEO, 1:19–24.

19. "L'idée de la femme qui ne se trouve point et qui ne se trouvera jamais," SEO, 2:46–53. This is the 1669 edition.

20. Ibid., 46.

21. Ibid., 48–49.

22. Ibid., 50.

23. Ibid., 53.

24. Cf. Hope, *Saint-Evremond and His Friends*, 46–49, for a slightly more skeptical reading of this essay.

25. Joan Wallach Scott, *The Fantasy of Feminist History* (Durham, 2011), 19.

26. Cf. Hope, *Saint-Evremond and His Friends*, 146–49.

27. Ibid.; Hope, *Saint-Evremond*, 101–18; Benedetta Craveri, *The Age of Conversation*, trans. Teresa Waugh (New York, 2005), 219–30.

28. Craveri, *The Age of Conversation*, 228.

29. SEL, 2:237.

30. Hope, *Saint-Evremond and His Friends*, 107–18.

31. "Sur les plaisirs: À Monsieur le Comte D'Olonne," SEO, 4:17–18.

32. Ibid., 53.

33. "Sur l'amitié," SEO, 3: 310; see also Dewald, *Aristocratic Experience*, 116–17.

34. "Sur l'amitié," 315–17.

35. This account is based on Hope, *Saint-Evremond and His Friends*, 383–413; and Elizabeth C. Goldsmith, *The Kings' Mistresses: The Liberated Lives of Marie Mancini, Princess Colonna, and Her Sister Hortense, Duchess Mazarin* (New York, 2012). See also the essays in Susan Shifrin, ed., "*The Wandering Life I Led*": *Essays on Hortense Mancini, Duchess Mazarin and Early Modern Women's Border Crossings*, ed. Susan Shifrin (Newcastle upon Tyne, 2009).

36. Goldsmith, *The Kings' Mistresses*, 2–6.

37. SEO, 4: 222–25; Goldsmith, *The Kings' Mistresses*, 32–33.

38. Goldsmith, *The Kings' Mistresses*, 118–27.

39. Ibid., 123–25.

40. *Hortense Mancini and Marie Manzini. Memoirs*, ed. and trans. Sarah Nelson (Chicago and London, 2008), 27. The memoir was originally published under the semi-anonymous title *Mémoires D.M.L.D.M*, but some copies were titled *Mémoires de Mme la Duchesse de Mazarin*. It was translated into English in 1676 and Italian in 1678 (9).

41. Ibid., 31; Goldsmith, *The Kings' Mistresses*, 120.

42. Goldsmith, *The Kings' Mistresses*, 141–42.

43. Ibid., 154–56.

44. SEO, 4:203–7.

45. SEL, 1:349.

46. SEL, 2:4–5, 13, 41–45.

47. Saint-Évremond, "Sur l'amitié," SEO, 3:321.

48. SEL, 2:284.

49. Goldsmith, *The Kings' Mistresses*, 210–13. See also Denys Potts, "The Duchess Mazarin and Saint-Évremond: The Final Journey," in Shifrin, ed., "*The Wandering Life I Led*," 157–92, an informative and sensitive account of the troubled but persevering friendship and the friends' devotion to each other in the duchess's final years.

50. SEL, 2:281.

51. SEL, 2:258.

52. Mme de Lambert, "Réflexions nouvelles sur les femmes," in Mme de Lambert, *Oeuvres*, ed. Robert Granderoute (Paris, 1990), 214–37. A good translation is Mme de Lambert, *New Reflections on Women by the Marchioness de Lambert* (1727), trans. and intro. Ellen McNiven Hine (New York, 1995).

53. Lambert, "Réflexions," 214–15. In "Avis d'une mère à sa fille," in *Oeuvres*, 112, Lambert nonetheless warned young women not to do too much novel reading, which was "dangerous" in the way it stirred the imagination, weakened modesty, and caused emotional disorder.

54. Lambert, "Réflexions," 217.

55. Indispensable is Roger Marchal, *Madame de Lambert et son milieu* (Oxford, 1991), esp. 483–525.

56. Katharine J. Hamerton, "A Feminist Voice in the Enlightenment Salon: Madame de Lambert on Taste, Sensibility, and the Feminine Mind," *Modern Intellectual History* 7, 2 (August 2010): 209–38.

57. Lambert, "Réflexions," 220–21.

58. Ibid., 215.

59. Ibid., 220.

60. Ibid., 214.

61. Ibid., 223.

62. Ibid., 217.

63. Ibid., 221–22. See also Lieselotte Steinbrügge, *The Moral Sex: Woman's Nature in the French Enlightenment*, trans. Pamela E. Selwyn (New York, 1995), 19; and Mary Terrall, "Émilie du Châtelet and the Gendering of Science," *History of Science* 33 (1995): 299.

64. Louis-Silvestre de Sacy, *An essay upon friendship, from the ingenious Monsieur de Sacy's, lately publish'd. In three parts* (London, 1704).

65. Lambert, "Traité de l'amitié," in *Oeuvres*, 168.

66. Ibid., 169–70.

67. Lambert, "Réflexions," 226.

68. Ibid., 226, 235–36.

Chapter 5. Shaftesbury's Quest for Fraternity

1. K. H. D. Haley, *The First Earl of Shaftesbury* (Oxford, 1968), covers both the family life and the political career of the first earl in great detail. On the first earl's personality, see also *Anthony Ashley Cooper, Third Earl of Shaftesbury: Complete Works, Standard Edition*, ed. with German translation (Stuttgart, 2011), 2, 6:65 (cited hereafter as SSE).

2. These and many other details of Shaftesbury's biography are from Robert Voitle, *The Third Earl of Shaftesbury, 1671–1713* (Baton Rouge, 1984), which remains indispensable to Shaftesbury studies. See also Roger Woolhouse, *Locke: A Biography* (Cambridge, 2007), esp. 71–72, 77–80; Maurice Cranston, *John Locke: A Biography* (New York, 1957), 93–95, 105–16.

3. Quoted in Voitle, *Shaftesbury*, 178.

4. SSE, 2, 6. Further references in parentheses in the text.

5. For a clear synopsis of early modern neo-Stoicism, see Dorinda Outram, *The Body and the French Revolution: Sex, Class, and Political Culture* (New Haven, 1989), esp. 68–72.

6. Lawrence E. Klein, *Shaftesbury and the Culture of Politeness: Moral Discourse and Cultural Politics in Early Eighteenth-Century England* (Cambridge, 1994), includes two excellent chapters on the notebooks. See also the introduction and the editorial notes in the French edition of the *Askêmata*: Shaftesbury, *Exercices [Askêmata]*, trans. and ed. Laurent Jaffro (Paris, 1993). Still useful is Stanley Grean, *Shaftesbury's Philosophy of Religion and Ethics: A Study in Enthusiasm* (Athens, Ohio, 1967). For my purposes the indispensable work on Stoicism is Pierre Hadot, *The Inner Citadel: The Meditations of Marcus Aurelius*, trans. Michael Chase (Cambridge, 2001). I disagree with Christopher Brooke, *Philosophical Pride: Stoicism and Political Thought from Lipsius to Rousseau* (Princeton, 2012), 122–23, which argues for a reading of many reflections in the *Askêmata* not as a "report of inner mental states," but, as he reads Hadot, "a set of technical philosophical exercises."

7. Anthony Ashley Cooper, Earl of Shaftesbury, *Characteristics of Men, Manners, Opinions, Times*, ed. Lawrence E. Klein (Cambridge, 1999) (cited hereafter as SC).

8. Quoted in Klein, *Shaftesbury*, 60.

9. Great Britain, Public Record Office (cited hereafter as PRO), 30/24/22/2. The Shaftesbury papers are now in the National Archives, Kew, under PRO.

10. The letter, dated June 3, 1709, was to Michael Ainsworth, a young man whose education for the Anglican clergy Shaftesbury was helping to support. Klein, *Shaftesbury*, 65.

11. Quoted in Klein, *Shaftesbury*, 27.

12. Jerrold Seigel, *The Idea of the Self: Thought and Experience in Western Europe Since the Seventeenth Century* (Cambridge, 2005), 87–110.

13. Voitle, *Shaftesbury*, 39.

14. Quoted in Voitle, *Shaftesbury*, 43–44.

15. Ibid., 45–47.

16. Ibid., 78–83.

17. See esp. Hadot, *The Inner Citadel*, esp. 101–79.

18. James L. Axtell, ed., *The Educational Writings of John Locke* (Cambridge, 1968), esp. 114–27, 221–25.

19. PRO, 30/24/22/4; Voitle, *Shaftesbury*, 77.

20. Voitle, *Shaftesbury*, 78.

21. Shaftesbury, *Second Characters; or, the Language of Forms*, ed. Benjamin Rand (Bristol, 1914), 22–23. "A Letter concerning the Art or Science of Design" is also available in Shaftesbury, *Characteristicks of Men, Manners, Opinions, Times*, 3 vols., ed. Douglas Den Uyl (Indianapolis, 2001), 3:243–51.

22. Shaftesbury, *Second Characters*, passim.

23. See esp. Michael Meehan, *Liberty and Poetics in Eighteenth-Century England* (London, 1986), 25–41; Klein, *Shaftesbury*; Iain Hampsher-Monk, "From Virtue to Politeness," in *Republicanism: A Shared European Heritage*, ed. Martin van Gelderen and Quentin Skinner, vol. 2, *The Values of Republicanism in Early Modern Europe* (Cambridge, 2002), esp. 88–94.

24. Christopher J. Berry, *The Idea of Luxury: A Conceptual and Historical Investigation* (Cambridge, 1994), esp. 3–86. On English civic humanism and republican discourse, see Caroline Robbins, *The Eighteenth Century Commonwealthman* (Cambridge, 1959), which includes an informative discussion of Shaftesbury and his friend Robert Molesworth (88–133); Markku Peltonen, *Classical Humanism and Republicanism in English Political Thought, 1570–1640* (Cambridge, 1995); Quentin Skinner, "Classical Liberty and the Coming of the English Civil War," in *Republicanism*, ed. Van Gelderen and Skinner, 2:9–28.

25. PRO, 30/24/22/4. The letter has been printed in Horst Meyer, *Limae labor: Untersuchungen zur Textgenese und Druckgeschichte von Shaftesburys "The Moralist,"* 2 vols. (Frankfurt am Main, 1978), 2:711–16. A new edition of "The Sociable Enthusiast" is in SSE, 2.1, *Moral and Political Philosophy*, ed. Wolfram Benda, Gerd Hemmerich, and Ulrich Schödlbauer (Stuttgart, 1987).

26. PRO, 30/24/22/4.

27. Steven Pincus, "The English Debate over Universal Monarchy," in *A Union for Empire: Political Thought and the British Union of 1707*, ed. John Robertson (Cambridge, 1995), esp. 43–50; Pincus, "From Butterboxes to Wooden Shoes: The Shift in English Popular Sentiment from Anti-Dutch to Anti-French in the 1670s," *Historical Journal* 38, 2 (1995), esp. 346–59.

28. See esp. David M. Posner, *The Performance of Nobility in Early Modern European Literature* (Cambridge, 1999), 181–210.

29. PRO, 30/24/21, pt. 1; PRO, 30/2/22/4.

30. J. B. Schneewind posits a similar shift from civic humanism to Shaftesbury's thought, without reference to the culture of politeness, in *The Invention of Autonomy: A History of Modern Moral Philosophy* (Cambridge, 1998), 285–309.

31. See esp. Klein, *Shaftesbury*, 49–51. Klein aptly describes the "Inquiry" as a defense of human sociability that was "somehow unsociable."

32. SC, 342.

33. Ibid., 396.

34. PRO, 30/24/22/4.

35. See Chapter 1.

36. PRO, 30/24/110. Parts of the letter are printed in Voitle, *Shaftesbury*, 244.

37. PRO, 30/24/27/14.

38. See esp. Brian Cowan, "Reasonable Ecstasies: Shaftesbury and the Languages of Libertinism," *Journal of British Studies* 37, 2 (April 1998): 111–38.

39. PRO, 30/24/20/11.

40. Elena Russo, *Styles of Enlightenment: Taste, Politics, and Authorship in Eighteenth-Century France* (Baltimore, 2007), esp. 8–15, 41–140.

41. SSE, 2, 5, *Chartae Socraticae: Design of a Socratick History*; see 23–25 for the editors' dating of this manuscript.

42. The encounter with Theodote is in Xenophon, *Memorabilia*, trans. and ed. Amy L. Bonnette (Ithaca, 1994), 101–5.

43. In *Some Thoughts Concerning Education* Locke warned that "those who would secure themselves from provoking others, especially all Young People, should carefully abstain from *Raillery*." "The right management of so nice and tickle a business" was very difficult. Axtell, *Educational Writings*, 248.

44. Shaftesbury, "Sensus communis, an essay on the freedom of wit and humour in a letter to a friend," in SC, 29–69. Further references in parentheses in the text.

45. On the development of literary criticism, see *The Cambridge History of Literary Criticism*, vol. 4, *The Eighteenth Century*, ed. H. B. Nisbet and Claude Rawson (Cambridge, 1997). Particularly important for my purposes is David Marshall, "Shaftesbury and Addison: Criticism and Public Taste," *Cambridge History of Literary Criticism* 4:633–57.

46. Shaftesbury, "Soliloquy," in SC, 70–71. Further references in parentheses in the text.

47. Grean, *Shaftesbury's Philosophy*, 246–57.

48. SC, Miscellany 5, 454.

49. Catherine Ingrassia, *Authorship, Commerce, and Gender in Early Eighteenth-Century England: A Culture of Paper Credit* (Cambridge, 1998), 1–76; E. J. Clery, *The Feminization Debate in Eighteenth-Century England: Literature, Commerce, and Luxury* (Houndmills, 2004), 1–12, 51–73.

50. SC, 409.

51. See esp. Jean-Christophe Agnew, *Worlds Apart: The Market and the Theater in Anglo-American Thought, 1550–1750* (Cambridge, 1986), 162–69.

52. This dilemma is explored, from a somewhat different angle, in David Marshall, *The Figure of Theater: Shaftesbury, Defoe, Adam Smith, and George Eliot* (New York, 1986), 9–70.

53. SC, 408.

54. PRO, 30/24/27/14; Klein, *Shaftesbury*, 107–11.

55. See the reading of Shaftesbury's letter on Horace to Pierre Coste, November 15, 1706, in Klein, *Shaftesbury*, 176–77.

56. SC, 458–60.

57. Especially important on the relationship between dialogic form and content in "The Moralists" is Michael Prince, *Philosophical Dialogue in the British Enlightenment: Theology, Aesthetics, and the Novel* (Cambridge, 1996), 23–73.

58. PRO, 30/24/22/4.

59. SC, 231–33, 236–37.

60. Ibid., 231–36.

61. Ibid., 460.

62. Prince, *Philosophical Dialogue*, 60–62.

63. Ibid., 49–55.

64. On the uses of "enthusiasm" see Lawrence E. Klein and Anthony J. La Vopa, eds., *Enthusiasm and Enlightenment in Europe, 1650–1850* (San Marino, 1998).

65. SSE, 2, 1, juxtaposes "The Moralists" and "The Sociable Enthusiast." The relevant passage is on 76.

66. Cowan, "Reasonable Ecstasies," esp. 124, 130.

67. Adam Smith, *Lectures on Rhetoric and Belles Lettres*, ed. J. C. Bryce (Indianapolis, 1985), 55.

68. Ibid., 55–61.

69. Ibid., 52–54.

70. Cf. Jonathan Israel, *Enlightenment Contested: Philosophy, Modernity, and the Emancipation of Man, 1670–1752* (Oxford, 2006), 348–49. See also Anthony J. La Vopa, "A New Intellectual History? Jonathan Israel's Enlightenment," *Historical Journal* 52, 3 (September 2009): 717–38.

Chapter 6. The Labors of David Hume

1. David Hume, *Essays Moral, Political, and Literary*, ed. Eugene F. Miller (Indianapolis, 1985), xxxiv; further references to this volume in parentheses in the text. The major exceptions to the neglect of the essay are Donald W. Livingston, *Philosophical Melancholy and Delirium: Hume's Pathology of*

Philosophy (Chicago, 1998), 130–35; James A. Harris, *Hume: An Intellectual Biography* (New York, 2015), 154–56. All other efforts to understand the many dimensions of Hume's intellectual career have been superseded by Harris's book.

2. G. J. Barker-Benfield, *The Culture of Sensibility: Sex and Society in Eighteenth-Century Britain* (Chicago, 1992); Julie K. Ellison, *Cato's Tears and the Making of Anglo-American Emotion* (Chicago, 1999); Philip Carter, *Men and the Emergence of Polite Society, Britain 1660–1800* (Harlow, 2001), esp. 53–162.

3. On Hume's view of female "sensibility" see Barker-Benfield, *The Culture of Sensibility*, 132–36.

4. On Hume's protofeminism see esp. Annette C. Baier, "Hume: The Reflective Woman's Epistemologist?" in *Feminist Interpretations of David Hume*, ed. Anne Japp Jacobson (University Park, 1992), 19–38; Genevieve Lloyd, "Hume on the Passion for Truth," in ibid., 39–58. For opposing views see, e.g., Joyce L. Jenkins and Robert Shaver, " 'Mr. Hobbes Could Have Said No More,' " in ibid., 137–55; Christine Battersby, "An Enquiry Concerning the Humean Woman," in *David Hume: Critical Assessments*, ed. Stanley Tweyman, vol. 6 (London, 1995), 255–64.

5. James Moore, "The Eclectic Stoic, the Mitigated Skeptic," in *New Essays on David Hume*, ed. Emilio Mazza and Emanuele Ronchetti (Milan, 2007), 133–70; James A. Harris, "The Epicurean in Hume," in *Epicurus in the Enlightenment*, ed. Neven Leddy and Avi S. Lifschitz (Oxford, 2009), esp. 162–63.

6. M. A. Stewart, "Hume's Intellectual Development, 1711–1752," in *Impressions of Hume*, ed. Marina Frasca-Spada and P. J. E. Kail (Oxford, 2005), 11–58.

7. David Hume, *The Letters of David Hume*, 2 vols., ed. J. Y. T. Greig (Oxford, 1932), 1:12–18 (cited hereafter as HL).

8. HL, 1:16.

9. Ibid., 12.

10. Harris, *Hume*, 76–77.

11. The case for Arbuthnot is made in Ernest Campbell Mossner, "Hume's Epistle to Dr. Arbuthnot, 1734: The Biographical Significance," *Huntington Library Quarterly* 7, 2 (February 1944): 135–52. Cf. Helen Deutsch, "Symptomatic Correspondences: The Author's Case in Eighteenth-Century Britain," *Cultural Critique* 42 (Spring 1999): 58–59, which takes Cheyne to be the intended recipient.

12. For most of the biographical detail I have relied on Ernest Campbell Mossner, *The Life of David Hume*, 2nd ed. (Oxford, 1980). Also indispensable is Stewart, "Hume's Intellectual Development."

13. John P. Wright, *The Sceptical Realism of David Hume* (Minneapolis, 1983), 190–91. For an overview of a pluralistic medical field, see Roy Porter, *Bodies Politic: Disease, Death, and Doctors in Britain, 1650–1900* (Ithaca, 2001). On developments among the "mechanists" from Descartes onward, see George S. Rousseau, "Nerves, Spirits and Fibres: Toward the Origins of Sensibility (1975)," in Rousseau, *Nervous Acts: Essays on Literature, Culture and Sensibility* (Houndmills, 2004), 157–84.

14. Christopher Brooke, *Philosophical Pride: Stoicism and Political Thought from Lipsius to Rousseau* (Princeton, 2012), 174–80.

15. On the possible early influence of Shaftesbury on Hume, with attention to his Stoicism, see Harris, *Hume*, 15, 38–51.

16. Bernard Mandeville, *A Treatise of the Hypochondriack and Hysterick Passions* (1711; New York, 1976), 174.

17. Sylvana Tomaselli, "The Enlightenment Debate on Women," *History Workshop Journal* 20 (1985): 101–24; Mary Catherine Moran, "Between the Savage and the Civil: Dr. John Gregory's Natural History of Femininity," in *Women, Gender, and Enlightenment*, ed. Sarah Knott and Barbara Taylor (London, 2005), 8–29; Silvia Sebastiani, *The Scottish Enlightenment: Race, Gender, and the Limits of Progress* (New York, 2013), 133–62; Karen O'Brien, *Women and Enlightenment in Eighteenth-Century Britain* (Cambridge, 2009), 68–109.

18. On the changing meaning of "genius," see Darrin McMahon, *Divine Fury: A History of Genius* (New York, 2013); Patricia Fara, *Newton: The Making of Genius* (New York, 2002), 155–81.

19. Abbé Jean-Baptiste Du Bos, *Réflexions critiques sur la poésie et sur la peinture*, 2 vols. (Paris, 1719). I have used the translation, *Critical Reflections on Poetry, Painting, and Music: With an Inquiry into the Rise and Progress of the Theatrical Entertainments of the Ancients* (London, 1748), esp. vol. 2, 1–56.

20. Ernest Campbell Mossner, "Hume's Early Memoranda, 1729–1740: The Complete Text," *Journal of the History of Ideas* 9, 4 (October 1948): 500.

21. David Hume, *A Treatise of Human Nature*, ed. David Fate Norton and Mary J. Norton (Oxford, 2003), 53–55 (cited hereafter as HT). My reading of the *Treatise* relies heavily on Livingston, *Philosophical Melancholy and Delirium*, 17–52.

22. HT, 164.

23. HT, 165.

24. HT, 172–75.

25. HT, 171. Cf. John J. Richetti, *Philosophical Writing: Locke, Berkeley, and Hume* (Cambridge, 1983), esp. 226–29.

26. HT, 172–75.

27. HT, 176.

28. HT, 206–9.

29. HT, 177.

30. HT, 171–72.

31. Jacob Sider Jost, "Hume's Four Philosophers: Recasting the *Treatise of Human Nature*," *Modern Intellectual History* 6, 1 (2009): 1–25.

32. David Hume, *New Letters of David Hume*, ed. Raymond Klibansky and Ernest C. Mossner (Oxford, 1954), 5 (cited hereafter as HNL).

33. On Hume's transition from the *Treatise* to the essays see esp. M. A. Box, *The Suasive Art of David Hume* (Princeton, 1990), 53–162.

34. HT, 292.

35. HL, 1:32–34.

36. Timothy J. Engström, "Foundational Standards and the Conversational Style: The Humean Essay as an Issue of Philosophical Genre," *Philosophy and Rhetoric* 30, 2 (1997): 150–75.

37. James Fieser, ed., *Early Responses to Hume's Metaphysical and Epistemological Writings*, vol. 1, *Eighteenth-Century Responses* (Bristol, 2000), 1–40.

38. Anthony La Vopa, "The Not-So-Prodigal Son: James Boswell and the Scottish Enlightenment," in *Character, Self, and Sociability in the Scottish Enlightenment*, ed. Thomas Ahnert and Susan Manning (New York, 2011), 85–103.

39. HNL, 2.

40. On the influence of Addison see Harris, *Hume*, 143–45, 154–66.

41. Dror Wahrman, *Imagining the Middle Class: The Political Representation of Class in Britain, c. 1780–1840* (Cambridge, 1995). Wahrman focuses on country gentlemen and the commercial classes.

42. See Nicholas T. Phillipson, *The Scottish Whigs and the Reform of the Court of Session 1785–1830* (Edinburgh, 1990); Phillipson, "The Social Structure of the Faculty of Advocates in Scotland 1661–1840," in *Law-Making and Law-Makers in British History*, ed. Allan Harding (London, 1980), 146–56.

43. Nancy Armstrong, *Desire and Domestic Fiction: A Political History of the Novel* (Oxford, 1987), 75–81.

44. Barker-Benfield, *The Culture of Sensibility*, esp. 154–214. For more socially detailed and informative studies see Katharine Glover, *Elite Women and Polite Society in Eighteenth-Century Scotland* (Woodbridge, 2011); Katie Barclay and Deborah Simonton, eds., *Women in Eighteenth-Century Scotland: Intimate, Intellectual, and Public Lives* (Farnham, 2013); Jerrold Seigel, *Modernity and Bourgeois Life: Society, Politics, and Culture in England, France, and Germany Since 1750* (Cambridge, 2012), esp. 305–50.

45. For insightful remarks on women and consumerism see Jonathan Brody Kramnick, *Making the English Canon: Print Capitalism and the Cultural Past, 1700–1770* (Cambridge, 1998), esp. 39–43, 69–73

46. HL, 1:196.

47. HL, 2:252.

48. "Dalrymple to Boswell, May 30, 1763," quoted in La Vopa, "The Not-So-Prodigal Son," 93–94.

49. Richard B. Sher, *Church and University in the Scottish Enlightenment: The Moderate Literati of Edinburgh* (Princeton, 1985).

50. Nicholas Phillipson, *Adam Smith: An Enlightened Life* (London, 2010), esp. 33–38.

51. For a similar projection of "horizontal" solidarity, traceable in conduct books, see Armstrong, *Desire and Domestic Fiction*, 56–95.

52. Hugh Blair, *Sermons*, vol. 1, 19th ed. (London, 1794), 337. Thomas Ahnert, *The Moral Culture of the Scottish Enlightenment, 1690–1805* (New Haven, 2015), is an important revisionist study of the role of religious belief, including belief in Providence, in Scottish Enlightenment thought.

53. Blair, *Sermons*, 1:93–94.

54. La Vopa, "The Not-So-Prodigal Son."

55. HL, 1:36.

56. Barbara Taylor, "Feminists Versus Gallants: Sexual Manners and Morals in Enlightenment Britain," in *Women, Gender and Enlightenment*, ed. Knott and Taylor, 30–52.

57. See the discussion of Hume's views of women studying history in J. G. A. Pocock, *Barbarism and Religion*, vol. 2, *Narratives of Civil Government* (Cambridge, 1999), 177–98.

58. Ingrassia, *Authorship, Commerce, and Gender*, 17–76; Robert W. Jones, *Gender and the Formation of Taste in Eighteenth-Century Britain: The Analysis of Beauty* (Cambridge, 1998), 1–78.

59. Michèle Cohen, *Fashioning Masculinity: National Identity and Language in the Eighteenth Century* (London, 1996), esp. 26–53; Linda Colley, *Britons: Forging the Nation, 1707–1837*, 2nd ed. (New Haven, 2005), passim; John Sekora, *Luxury: The Concept in Western Thought, Eden to Smollett* (Baltimore, 1977), 63–109.

60. HL, 1:53. See also Stephen Copley, "Commerce, Conversation and Politeness in the Early Eighteenth-Century Periodical," *Journal of Eighteenth-Century Studies* 18, 1 (Spring 1995): 63–77.

61. HL, 1:20.

62. This view of the complementarity of labor and leisure contrasts with the apotheosis of male authors' nervous disorders resulting from excessive labor, as described in Deutsch, "Symptomatic Correspondences."

63. David Hume, "Of the Standard of Taste," in Hume, *Essays Moral, Political, and Literary*, 226–49. Further page references to the essay are in parentheses in the text.

64. My discussion of this text is especially indebted to Kramnick, *Canon*, 71–74, and Engström, "Foundational Standards."

65. Ernst Cassirer, *The Philosophy of the Enlightenment*, trans. Fritz C. A. Koelln and James P. Pettegrove (1932; Princeton, 1968), 307.

66. Kramnick, *Canon*, 65–71. On Burke's aesthetics see Tom Furniss, *Edmund Burke's Aesthetic Ideology: Language, Gender, and Political Economy in Revolution* (Cambridge, 1993).

67. Still indispensable is Cassirer, *The Philosophy of the Enlightenment*, 275–360. An important recent contribution is James Engell, *Forming the Critical Mind: Dryden to Coleridge* (Cambridge, 1989). See also Jones, *Gender and the Formation of Taste*, 37–78.

68. HT, 4.

69. Nicolas Boileau, *Oeuvres complètes* (Paris, 1966), 3.

70. There is an insightful discussion of Du Bos's significance in Thomas M. Kavanaugh, *Enlightened Pleasures: Eighteenth-Century France and the New Epicureanism* (New Haven, 2010), 72–102.

71. Du Bos, *Critical Reflections*, 2: esp. 237–45.

72. Bernard Mandeville, *The Fable of the Bees and Other Writings*, ed. E. J. Hundert (Indianapolis, 1997). Hundert provides an excellent introduction to the historical significance of the *Fable* (xx–xxxii).

73. Jean-Jacques Rousseau, *The First and Second Discourses Together with the Replies to Critics and Essay on the Origin of Languages*, ed. and trans. Victor Gourevitch (New York, 1986), 15–16.

74. Ibid.

75. Ibid., 11, 17–18.

76. See esp. John W. Cairns, "Rhetoric, Language, and Roman Law: Legal Education and Improvement in Eighteenth-Century Scotland," *Law and History Review* 9 (1991): 31–58; Cairns, "Legal Study in Utrecht in the Late 1740s: The Education of Sir David Dalrymple, Lord Hailes," *Fundamina* 8 (2002): 30–74.

77. Quoted in Phillipson, *Adam Smith*, 85.

78. Adam Ferguson, *The Manuscripts of Adam Ferguson*, ed. Vincenzo Merolle (London, 2006), 146. See also La Vopa, "The Not-So-Prodigal Son."

79. Henry Home, Lord Kames, *Elements of Criticism*, 2 vols., 6th ed. (Edinburgh, 1785), 1:12–19. See also Franklin E. Court, "Adam Smith and Hugh Blair: The Politics of Conduct and Taste," in *Institutionalizing English Literature: The Culture and Politics of Literary Study, 1750–1900* (Stanford, 1992), 17–38.

80. Kames, *Elements*, 1:14.

81. Alexander Gerard, *An Essay on Taste* (1759), intro. Walter J Hipple, Jr., 3rd ed. (1780; Delmar, 1978).

82. Ibid., 174, 246.

83. HL, 1:110. Hume was not always immune to passionate attachments. See E. Mazza and E. Piccoli, " 'Disguised in Scarlet': Hume and Turin in 1748," in *Hume, nuovi saggi / Hume, New Essays*, in *I castelli di Yale: Quaderni di Filosofia* 11 (2010–2011): 71–108.

84. The entire letter is available in Mossner, *Life*, 425–26. HL, 2, appendix E, 366–74, includes selections from the letters from the countess tó Hume. I have quoted from the appendix whenever possible. The originals of the countess's letters to Hume are in the Hume Papers, National Library of Scotland. Cf. Jerome Christensen, *Practicing Enlightenment: Hume and the Formation of a Literary Career* (Madison, 1987), which reads this episode in a quite different theoretical framework. Very informative is the entry on the countess in Raymond Trousson and Frédéric S. Eigeldinger, eds., *Dictionnaire de Jean-Jacques Rousseau* (Paris, 1996), 109–12. Also informative is the entry on Conti in ibid., 173–76.

85. Quoted in Mossner, *Life*, 456–57.

86. Antoine Lilti, *Le monde des salons: Sociabilité et mondanité au XVIIIe siècle* (Paris, 2005).

87. P. E. Schazmann, *La Comtesse de Boufflers* (Paris, 1933), 145.

88. HL, 1:314.

89. HL, 2:366.

90. HL, 1:345.

91. Ibid., 232.

92. Ibid., 369.

93. Ibid., 407.

94. Ibid., 418.

95. Ibid., 438.

96. Ibid., 449.

97. HL, 2:370.

98. HL, 1:451.

99. HL, 2:371.

100. HL, 1:457.

101. HL, 2:372.

102. HL, 1:458.

103. The countess's comments on *Douglas* were omitted from the edited version of the letter in HL, 2, appendix E, 369–70.

104. HL, 1:452–53.

105. HL, 1:462–63.

106. HL, 2:370–71.

107. HL, 1:476.

108. HL, 1:485–87.

109. HL, 1:469.

110. HL, 1:469–70.

111. HL, 1:521.

112. Adam Smith, *The Correspondence of Adam Smith*, ed. Ernest Campbell Mossner and Ian Simpson Ross (Oxford, 1987), 107–8.

Chapter 7. Genius and the Social: Antoine-Léonard Thomas and Suzanne Curchod Necker

1. Antoine-Léonard Thomas, "Essai sur le caractère, les moeurs et l'esprit des femmes dans les différents siècles," in *Q'est-ce qu'une femme?*, ed. Elisabeth Badinter (Paris, 1989), 51–161 (further references in parentheses in the text); Thomas, *Essai sur les éloges ou histoire de la littérature de l'éloquence appliquées à ce genre d'ouvrage*, 2 vols. (1773; Paris, 1811).

2. On genius, see Darrin M. McMahon, *Divine Fury: A History of Genius* (New York, 2011); Dorothea W. von Mücke, *The Practices of the Enlightenment: Aesthetics, Authorship, and the Public* (New York, 2015), esp. 51–62. On celebrity, Antoine Lilti, *Figures publiques: L'invention de la célébrité 1750–1850* (Paris, 2014). On Thomas's extraordinary success as a eulogist, Jean-Claude Bonnet, *Naissance du Panthéon: Essai sur le culte des grands hommes* (Paris, 1998), 67–82.

3. Etienne Micard, *Un écrivain académique au XVIIIe siècle: Antoine-Léonard Thomas (1732–1785)* (Paris, 1924), 27, 119–52.

4. Ibid., 198 (quoting a critique of the *Essay* by Daillant de la Touche).

5. "D'Épinay to Galiani, March 14, 1772," in *Qu'est-ce qu'une femme?*, ed. Badinter, 190.

6. On Denis Diderot's reaction see Chapter 8.

7. See esp. David Bell, *The Cult of the Nation in France: Inventing Nationalism, 1680–1800* (Cambridge, 2001); Bonnet, *Naissance du Panthéon*.

8. See esp. Sarah Maza, *Private Lives and Public Affairs: The Causes Célèbres of Prerevolutionary France* (Berkeley, 2003); Jay M. Smith, *Nobility Reimagined: The Patriotic Nation in Eighteenth Century France* (Ithaca, 2005).

9. Micard, *Un écrivain académique*, 120–24; Bonnet, *Naissance du Panthéon*, 61–66.

10. Elena Russo, *Styles of Enlightenment: Taste, Politics, and Authorship in Eighteenth-Century France* (Baltimore, 2007), esp. 16–35.

11. Micard, *Un écrivain académique*, 174.

12. Antoine-Léonard Thomas, *Oeuvres complètes de M. Antoine-Léonard Thomas* (Paris, 1825), 6:138.

13. Ibid., 142.

14. Ibid., 148–51.

15. Ibid., 176–79.

16. Barbara Taylor, "Feminists Versus Gallants: Sexual Manners and Morals in Enlightenment Britain," in *Women, Gender and Enlightenment*, ed. Sarah Knott and Barbara Taylor (Houndmills, 2005), 30–52.

17. Suzanne Curchod Necker, *Mélanges des manuscrits*, 3 vols. (Paris, 1798), 1:xvi (cited hereafter as M).

18. *Revue d'Histoire Littéraire de la France* 26 (1919): 147–48 (cited hereafter as RHL). We are indebted to Maurice Henriet, who found a cache of Thomas's letters to Barthe and other friends in a faubourg outside Soissons on the Western Front. He hand-copied the originals during the war, and meticulously edited them for the RHL. Apparently the letters were destroyed later in the war, perhaps in the Second Battle of the Marne.

19. RHL 25 (1918): 502.

20. Sonja Boon, *The Life of Madame Necker: Sin, Redemption and the Parisian Salon* (London, 2011), esp. 110. Thomas's illnesses may have acted out "the author's case" described in Helena Deutsch, "Symptomatic Correspondences: The Author's Case in Eighteenth-Century Britain," *Cultural Critique* 42 (Spring 1999): 35–80.

21. *Nouveaux mélanges extraits des manuscrits de Mme Necker*, 2 vols. (Paris, 1801), 1:45 (cited hereafter as NM).

22. Sabine Arnaud, *On Hysteria: The Invention of a Medical Category Between 1670 and 1820* (Chicago, 2015), 136–62.

23. Thomas, *Essai sur les éloges*, 2:237.

24. M1, 136, 183.

25. M2, 37.

26. There is a nuanced portrait of Marmontel in Peter France, *Politeness and Its Discontents: Problems in French Classical Culture* (Cambridge, 1992), 115–21. On the role of salon women as literary patrons see Michael Sonenscher, *Sans-Culottes: An Eighteenth-Century Emblem in the French Revolution* (Princeton, 2008), esp. 5–6, 59.

27. RHL 26, 1 (1919): 130.

28. Bonnet, *Naissance du Panthéon*, 72.

29. Ibid., 27–28 (quoted from *Correspondance littéraire*, September 1763).

30. Robert Darnton, "The High Enlightenment and the Low-Life of Literature," in *The Literary Underground of the Old Regime* (Cambridge, 1982), 1–40.

31. For a similar point on the world of the theater, see Gregory S. Brown, *A Field of Honor: Writers, Court Culture and Public Theater in French Literary Life from Racine to the Revolution* (New York, 2005).

32. Jean Le Rond d'Alembert, "Essai sur la société des gens de lettres et des grands: Sur la réputation, sur les mécènes, et sur les récompenses littéraires," in *Oeuvres complètes de d'Alembert*, vol. 4, pt. 1 (Paris, 1822), 355–56.

33. Antoine-Léonard Thomas, "Discours prononcé à la réception de l'archevêque de Toulouse, le 6 septembre 1770," in *Oeuvres complètes*, 4:224.

34. RHL 25 (1918): 456.

35. Jacques Delille, *Oeuvres, avec les notes de Parseval* (Paris, 1836), 50–54.

36. Jacques Delille, *La conversation* (Paris, 1812), esp. 7–8; Dena Goodman, *The Republic of Letters: A Cultural History of the French Enlightenment* (Ithaca, 1994), 133–35. Goodman uses this poem to argue that, as the philosophes often acknowledged, "the restraining force of the *salonnières*" had kept the Republic of Letters from anarchy. She ignores "Epistle to the Utility of Retreat," although it arguably gives us a more reliable indication of what young men like Delille thought of the salons in the pre-Revolutionary era. *La Conversation* may be better read as an unreliable exercise in nostalgia.

37. d'Alembert, "Essai sur la société des gens de letttres et des grands," 369–70.

38. John Lough, "Did the *Philosophes* Take Over the Académie Française?" *Studies on Voltaire and the Eighteenth Century* 336 (1996): 153–94.

39. Thomas, *Oeuvres complètes*, 6:152.

40. RHL 27 (1920): 600.

41. Bonnet, *Naissance du Panthéon*, 68.

42. Ibid., 75.

43. Ibid., 78.

44. Antoine-Léonard Thomas, "Discours prononcé à l'Académie française par M. Thomas . . . le 22 janvier 1767," in *Oeuvres complètes*, 4:191–216.

45. Micard, *Un écrivain académique*, 36–37.

46. M3, 222, 226. See also Marmontel's portrait, quoted in Micard, *Un écrivain académique*, 33.

47. Boon, *The Life of Madame Necker*, 107–9.

48. M1, iv–vii.

49. I have relied heavily on Catherine Dubeau, *La lettre et la mère: Roman familial et écriture de la passion chez Suzanne Necker et Germaine de Staël* (Quebec, 2013). Recent portraits of Necker as a *salonnière* diverge markedly. See, e.g., Goodman, *The Republic of Letters*, 79–82; Benedetta Craveri, *The Age of Conversation*, trans. Teresa Waugh (New York, 2005), 367–71. Cf. the reading of the journals in Dena Goodman, "Suzanne Necker's *Mélanges*: Gender, Writing, and Publicity," in *Going Public: Women*

and Publishing in Early Modern France, ed. Elizabeth C. Goldsmith and Dena Goodman (Ithaca, 1995), 210–23.

50. Necker to Henriette Réverdil, July 15, 1766, ms. Suppl. 717, f.11, Bibliothèque Publique de Genève, quoted in Boon, *The Life of Madame Necker,* 17.

51. M2, 2, 11, 16, 21; NM, 1:100–101.

52. Geneviève Soumoy-Thibert, "Les idées de Mme Necker," *Dix-Huitième Siècle* 21 (1989): 357–68. Soumoy-Thibert aptly describes this "hidden work" as "practically an askesis" (359).

53. NM 1: 34.

54. Jean-François Marmontel, *Mémoires,* 2 vols. (Clermont-Ferrand, 1972), 1:288.

55. M1, 184.

56. M1, 224.

57. M1, 229, 248; M2, 223; M3, 10; NM, 1:46–49.

58. M1, 124.

59. McMahon, *Divine Fury,* esp. 67–78; John Hope Mason, *The Value of Creativity: The Origins and Emergence of a Modern Belief* (Aldershot, 2003), 107–56.

60. M1, 39.

61. M1, 282.

62. M3, 223.

63. Thomas, *Oeuvres complètes,* 6: 164.

64. M2, 237.

65. RHL 25, 3 (1918): 488.

66. RHL 26, 1 (1919): 137, 147.

67. RHL 27, 1 (1920): 277–79; 27, 4 (1920): 600.

68. RHL 27, 2 (1920): 260.

69. M1, 130–33.

70. M3, 165–68.

71. M1, 133.

72. Charles Pinot Duclos, *Les considérations sur les moeurs de ce siècle,* ed. Carole Dornier (Paris, 2000). Dornier's introduction is invaluable in explaining the intellectual and social contexts of the book. My understanding of both texts differs from what I take to be Robert Darnton's misreading of their emphases in *The Literary Underground,* 12–14.

73. Duclos, *Considérations,* 199.

74. Charles Pinot Duclos, *Mémoires sur la vie de Duclos, écrits par lui-même,* ed. Mathurin François-Adolphe Lescure (Paris, 1888), 11–13.

75. Ibid., 24–33; Jacques Brengues, *Charles Duclos (1704–1772), ou l'obsession de la vertu* (Saint-Brieuc, 1971), 5–60.

76. Duclos, *Considérations,* 100–102.

77. Ibid., 192.

78. See also Jean Le Rond d'Alembert, "Discours lu à l'Académie française, le 25 août 1771, avant la distribution des prix d'éloquence et de poésie," in *Oeuvres complètes,* vol. 4, pt. 1, 309–20.

79. Ronald Grimsley, *Jean d'Alembert, 1717–83* (Oxford, 1963), 78–81.

80. d'Alembert, *"Essai sur la Société des gens de lettre et des grande,"* 337.

81. Ibid., 343–44.

82. Ibid., 370.

83. Ibid., 372.

84. Ibid., 372.

85. Ibid., 367.

86. Ibid., 368.

87. Ibid., 354.

88. Duclos, *Considérations,* 194–96.

89. Arnaud, *On Hysteria,* 148–50.

90. Quoted in John Pappas, "Condorcet, 'le seul' et 'le premier' féministe du 18e siècle?" *Dix-huitième Siècle* 23 (1991): 441–43.

91. Helena Rosenblatt, *Rousseau and Geneva: From the* First Discourse *to the* Social Contract, *1749–1762* (Cambridge, 1997), 10–17; J. G. A. Pocock, *Barbarism and Religion*, vol. 1, *The Enlightenments of Edward Gibbon, 1737–1764* (Cambridge, 1999), 50–71.

92. NM, 2:110–14.

93. Christopher Brooke, *Philosophical Pride: Stoicism and Political Thought from Lipsius to Rousseau* (Princeton, 2012), 127–48.

94. Micard, *Un écrivain académique*, 181.

95. M1, 363–70; NM, 1:19.

96. Necker's thought is in the tradition of a culture of self-ownership, analyzed in Charly Coleman, *The Virtues of Abandon: An Anti-Individualist History of the French Enlightenment* (Stanford, 2014), esp. 21–51.

97. M1, 167–68, 179.

98. M1, 66–68.

99. M1, 26–27, 370–71.

100. NM, 2:31.

101. M1, 69–70.

102. On the uses of the trope of "enthusiasm" see Lawrence E. Klein and Anthony J. La Vopa, eds., *Enthusiasm and Enlightenment in Europe, 1650–1850* (San Marino, 1998).

103. Thomas, *Essai sur les éloges*, 228–39.

104. McMahon, *Divine Fury*, 52.

105. M1, 23–26, 301.

106. "Sur un nouveau genre de Spectateur. Fragment," NM, 2:62–70.

107. Ibid., 63.

108. Ibid., 64–69.

109. "Commencement d'un éloge de Mme de Sévigné," NM, 2:382–432.

110. Catherine Montfort-Howard, *Les fortunes de Madame de Sévigné au XVIIème et au XVIIIème siècles* (Tübingen, 1982), 53–55.

111. Ibid., 60–61.

112. Ibid., 73, 77.

113. M3, 382.

114. M3, 382–85.

115. Cf. Montfort-Howard, *Les fortunes*, 83.

116. Necker may have been familiar with La Bruyère's remarks on the *femme savante*. See Jean de La Bruyère, *Les caractères de La Bruyère* (Paris, 1843), 76–77.

117. NM, 1:81.

118. M3, 397.

119. M3, 414–18.

120. M3, 428.

121. M3, 403–4, 406.

122. An important British exception to the exclusion of women from exercising cultural authority as literary critics was Anna Seward. See Norma Clarke, *The Rise and Fall of the Woman of Letters* (London, 2004), 10–52.

123. M3, 430–32.

124. Lorraine Daston, "The Naturalized Female Intellect," *Science in Context* 5, 2 (1992): 209–35. The new vitalist medical philosophy will be considered in more detail in Chapter 8.

125. Cf. Erica Harth, "The Salon Woman Goes Public . . . or Does She?" in *Going Public*, ed. Goldsmith and Goodman, 192–93.

126. M3, 161.

127. M1, 248. Necker may have been echoing Buffon here. See Georges-Louis Leclerc, Comte de Buffon, "Discours sur le style," in Buffon, *Oeuvres*, ed. Michel Delon (Paris, 2007), 419–28.

128. NM, 1:79.
129. Ibid.
130. NM, 1:76.
131. Badinter, *Qu'est-ce qu'une femme?*, 193.

Chapter 8. Minds Not Meeting: Denis Diderot and Louise d'Épinay

1. The second version of the text appeared in July 1772, and the third in April 1777, both in the *Correspondance littéraire* (cited hereafter as CL). The final, enlarged version, in manuscript, was prepared in 1780; "On Women," in Denis Diderot, *Oeuvres*, ed. Laurent Versini, 5 vols. (Paris, 1994–97), vol. 1, *Philosophie*, 945–61. The 1780 version is also in Elisabeth Badinter, ed., *Qu'est-ce qu'une femme?* (Paris, 1989), 163–85. Parenthetical page references are to this edition.

2. CL, pt. 3, vol. 2, 216–18.

3. Elena Russo, *Styles of Enlightenment: Taste, Politics, and Authorship in Eighteenth-Century France* (Baltimore, 2007), passim.

4. Joseph Royall Smiley, *Diderot's Relations with Grimm* (Urbana, 1950), 24–25.

5. Denis Diderot, "In Praise of Richardson" in Diderot, *Selected Writings on Art and Literature*, trans. and ed. Geoffrey Bremner (London, 1994), 96–97.

6. Angelica Goodden, *Diderot and the Body* (Oxford, 2001), 147–76, is a judicious attempt to make sense of Diderot's scattered thoughts on these subjects.

7. The major exception is Jenny Mander, "No Woman Is an Island: The Female Figure in French Enlightenment Anthropology," in *Women, Gender and Enlightenment*, ed. Sarah Knott and Barbara Taylor (Houndmills, 2005), 97–116, which effectively reads "On Women" in relation to Diderot's writings on colonialism.

8. Elisabeth de Fontenay, "Diderot gynéconome," *Diagraphe* 7 (1976): 29–50. See also Annie Ibrahim, *Diderot: Un matérialisme éclectique* (Paris, 2010), esp. 459–60; Michel Delon, "Le prétexte anatomique," *Dix-Huitième Siècle* 12 (1980): 38, 47–48. But cf. Goodden, *Diderot and the Body*, esp. 162, 170, and the discussion of Diderot's ambiguity in Michèle Duchet, "Du sexe des livres: *Sur les femmes* de Diderot," *Revue des Sciences Humaines* 44, 168 (October–December 1977): 525–36.

9. Lieselotte Steinbrügge, *The Moral Sex: Women's Nature in the French Enlightenment*, trans. Pamela E. Selwyn (New York, 1995), 44–47.

10. On fear of the overactive imagination in eighteenth-century France, see Jan Goldstein, *The Post-Revolutionary Self, Politics and Psyche in France, 1750–1850* (Cambridge, 2005), 21–59.

11. On the distinctive characteristics of the eighteenth-century French bourgeoisie see Jerrold Seigel, *Modernity and Bourgeois Life: Society, Politics, and Culture in England, France, and Germany Since 1750* (Cambridge, 2012), 73–113.

12. William F. Edmiston, *Diderot and the Family: A Conflict of Nature and Law* (Saratoga, 1985), 28–30. For a detailed biographical narrative see Arthur M. Wilson, *Diderot* (New York, 1972), 37–46. Still useful is Franco Venturi, *Jeunesse de Diderot (de 1713 à 1753)*, trans. Juliette Bertrand (Paris, 1939). Most of what we know of Diderot's early life in Paris comes from his later accounts to his daughter.

13. Marie-France Silver, "Mme de Puisieux ou l'ambition d'être femme des lettres," in *Femmes savantes et femmes d'esprit: Women Intellectuals of the French Eighteenth Century*, ed. Roland Bonnel and Catherine Rubinger (New York, 1994), 183–201; Alice M. Laborde, *Diderot et Madame de Puisieux* (Stanford, 1984), esp. 15–36, 58–88.

14. Edmiston, *Diderot and the Family*, 26–38.

15. Mander, "No Woman Is an Island," emphasizes Diderot's "resolutely bourgeois analysis" (102).

16. There is a solid account of Diderot's efforts and their results in Edmiston, *Diderot and the Family*, 38–43.

17. Denis Diderot, *Correspondance*, ed. Georges Roth and Jean Varloot, 16 vols. (Paris, 1955–70), 12:127.

18. Ibid., 123, 125.

19. Ibid., 123.

20. Ibid., 125–26.

21. Diderot, *Correspondance*, 11:137–44.

22. Diderot, *Correspondance*, 12:178–81.

23. Quoted in Jerrold Seigel, *The Idea of the Self: Thought and Experience in Western Europe Since the Seventeenth Century* (Cambridge, 2005), 197.

24. Ibid., 203–6.

25. Edmiston, *Diderot and the Family*, 89–98.

26. I disagree with the reading of Diderot's radical materialism in Jonathan Israel, *Enlightenment Contested: Philosophy, Modernity and the Emancipation of Man* (Oxford, 2006), 781–839. See also Anthony J. La Vopa, "A New Intellectual History? Jonathan Israel's Enlightenment," *Historical Journal* 52, 3 (August 2009): 717–38.

27. See esp. Aram Vartanian, "La Mettrie, Diderot, and Sexology in the Enlightenment," in *Essays on the Age of Enlightenment in Honor of Ira O. Wade* (Geneva, 1977), 347–67.

28. Edmiston, *Diderot and the Family*, 95–96.

29. On the evolution of Diderot's thought see esp. Carol Blum, *Diderot: The Virtue of a Philosopher* (New York, 1974); and Seigel, *The Idea of the Self*, 187–209.

30. Claude-Adrien Helvétius, *De l'homme, de ses facultés intellectuelles, et de son éducation*, 2 vols. (Fayard, 1989), 2:948. The discussion of Locke is part of Helvétius's "Recapitulation" of his ideas in vol. 2, 929–61.

31. Denis Diderot, *Réfutation suivie de l'ouvrage d'Helvétius intitulé L'HOMME*," quoted in Jean Starobinski, "Le ramage et le cri," in *Diderot, un diable de ramage* (Paris, 2012), 12–13. The full text is in Diderot, *Oeuvres*, 1:773–923.

32. Still indispensable is Herbert Dieckmann, "Diderot's Conception of Genius," *Journal of the History of Ideas* 2, 2 (April 1941): 151–82. See also Darrin McMahon, *Divine Fury: A History of Genius* (New York, 2013), 67–103.

33. Cf. the insightful discussion of the dialectic between self-ownership and self-dispossession in Diderot's thought in Charly Coleman, *The Virtues of Abandon: An Anti-Individualist History of the French Enlightenment* (Stanford, 2014), 159–201.

34. Denis Diderot, "Génie," in *Oeuvres esthétiques*, ed. Paul Vernière (Paris, 1959), 14.

35. Ibid., 12.

36. Diderot, "In Praise of Richardson," 96–97.

37. Quoted in Starobinski, "Le ramage et le cri," 22–23.

38. This shift is emphasized in Blum, *Diderot*; and Seigel, *The Idea of the Self*, 187–209.

39. *Compact Edition, Encyclopédie ou dictionnaire raisonné des sciences, des arts et des métiers, par une societé des gens de lettres*, 5 vols. (Paris, n.d.), 3:618–19.

40. Denis Diderot, *Rameau's Nephew and d'Alembert's Dream*, trans. and intro. Leonard Tancock (Harmondsworth, 1978), 212–13.

41. Denis Diderot, *Oeuvres complètes de Diderot: Revues sur les éditions originales*, ed. Jules Assézat, 20 vols. (Paris, 1875–77), 4:26–27.

42. Quoted in Alexandre Wenger, *Le médecin et le philosophe: Théophile Bordeu selon Diderot* (Paris, 2012), 60.

43. Indispensable are Anne C. Villa, *Enlightenment and Pathology: Sensibility in the Literature and Medicine of Eighteenth-Century France* (Baltimore, 1998), esp. 43–79; Sergio Moravia, "From Homme Machine to Homme Sensible: Changing Eighteenth-Century Models of Man's Image," *Journal of the History of Ideas* 39, 1 (January–March 1978): 45–60.

44. Théophile de Bordeu, "Crise," *Compact Edition, Encyclopédie*, 2:832–87; Villa, *Enlightenment and Pathology*, 65–72, 162–66; Wenger, *Le médecin et le philosophe*, 42–48.

45. Bordeu, "Crise."

46. Diderot, "Efféminé," in *Oeuvres complètes*, 8:116.

47. Jeannette Geffriaud Rosso, *Diderot et le portrait* (Pisa, 1998), 41–50; Russo, *Styles of Enlightenment*, 44.

48. Thomas Laqueur, *Making Sex: Body and Gender from the Greeks to Freud* (Cambridge, 1992), esp. 149–63; Lorraine Daston, "The Naturalized Female Intellect," *Science in Context* 5, 2 (1992): 209–35.

49. Sabine Arnaud, *On Hysteria: The Invention of a Medical Category Between 1670 and 1820* (Chicago, 2015).

50. Lawrence E. Klein and Anthony J. La Vopa, eds., *Enthusiasm and Enlightenment in Europe* (San Marino, 1998); Arnaud, *On Hysteria*, 51–60.

51. John Millar, *The Origin of the Distinctions of Ranks; or, an Inquiry into the Circumstances Which Give Rise to Influence and Authority in the Different Members of Society*, ed. and intro. Aaron Garrett (Indianapolis, 2006). See the discussion of Millar's book in Jane Rendall, *The Origins of Modern Feminism: Women in Britain, France and the United States* (Chicago, 1985), 25–28. My discussion of the Scottish Enlightenment is especially indebted to Mary Catherine Moran, "Between the Savage and the Civil: Dr. John Gregory's Natural History of Femininity," in Sarah Knott and Barbara Taylor, eds., *Women, Gender, and Enlightenment* (London, 2005), 8–29; Silvia Sebastiani, *The Scottish Enlightenment: Race, Gender, and the Limits of Progress* (New York, 2013), esp. 133–62.

52. Thomas Ahnert, *The Moral Culture of the Scottish Enlightenment, 1690–1805* (New Haven, 2015).

53. Millar, *The Origin of the Distinctions of Ranks*, 93–96.

54. Ibid., 143–45.

55. Ibid., 150–51.

56. See esp. Sebastiani, *The Scottish Enlightenment*, 143–50.

57. Starobinski, "Le ramage et le cri," 24–25.

58. Wilson, *Diderot*, 696.

59. The letter has been reprinted in Badinter, *Qu'est-ce qu'une femme?*, 189–94. The details of d'Épinay's biography can be found in Elisabeth Badinter, *Emilie, Emilie: L'ambition féminine au XVIIIème siècle* (Paris, 1983); Ruth Plaut Weinreb, *Eagle in a Gauze Cage: Louise d'Épinay femme de lettres* (New York, 1993); Francis Steegmuller, *A Woman, a Man, and Two Kingdoms: The Story of Madame d'Épinay and the Abbé Galiani* (New York, 1991), 3–44.

60. Ferdinando Galiani and Louise d'Épinay, *Correspondance*, vol. 3, ed. Daniel Maggetti and Georges Dulac (Paris, 1994), 249–59.

61. Diderot, *Correspondance*, vol. 12 (January 1772–June 1773), ed. Georges Roth (Paris, 1965), 34.

62. On this disagreement cf. Mary Trouille, "Sexual/Textual Politics in the Enlightenment: Diderot and d'Épinay Respond to Thomas's Essay on Women," in *Women Writers in Pre-Revolutionary France: Strategies of Emancipation*, ed. Colette H. Winn and Donna Kuizenga (New York, 1997), 163–83.

63. Parts of the letter have been reprinted in Louise d'Épinay, *Lettres à mon fils: Essais sur l'éducation; et, morceaux choisis, correspondance et extraits*, ed. Ruth Plaut Weinreb (Concord, 1989), 102–4.

64. Ibid., 102.

65. Ibid., 102–3.

66. Ibid., 103–4.

67. Badinter, *Qu'est-ce qu'une femme?*, 193.

68. Ibid., 191.

69. Ibid., 194.

70. Nina Rattner Gelbart, *Feminine and Opposition Journalism in Old Regime France: Le Journal des Dames* (Berkeley, 1987), esp. 29–37, 291–303.

71. Quoted in Alyssa Goldstein Sepinwall, "Robespierre, Old Regime Feminist? Gender, the Late Eighteenth Century, and the French Revolution Revisited," *Journal of Modern History* 82 (March 2010): 6–8.

72. Cf. Gelbart, *Feminine and Opposition Journalism*, 35–36.

73. Louise d'Épinay, *Histoire de Madame de Montbrillant*, ed. Georges Roth (Tours, 1951). Badinter, *Emilie, Emilie*, tends to take this text as factually reliable autobiography, while Weinreb, *Eagle in a Gauze Cage*, reads it as literary fiction and emphasizes its value as such.

74. Steegmuller, *A Woman, a Man, and Two Kingdoms*, 21–22.

75. Weinreb, *Eagle in a Gauze Cage*, 18.

76. There is a more detailed contrast of the portraits in ibid., 21–22.

77. See, e.g., Denis Diderot, *Diderot's Letters to Sophie Volland*, trans. Peter France (London, 1972), 66, 80–83.

78. Weinreb, *Eagle in a Gauze Cage*, 99.

79. Ibid., 9.

80. Quoted in Steegmuller, *A Woman, a Man, and Two Kingdoms*, 40. See also Smiley, *Diderot's Relations with Grimm*, 28.

81. Smiley, *Diderot's Relations with Grimm*, 28–30.

82. Weinreb, *Eagle in a Gauze Cage*, 110–11.

83. Ibid., 125.

84. Diderot, *Correspondance*, 9:228–29.

85. d'Épinay, *Lettres à mon fils*, 81–82.

86. Ibid., 79–83.

87. See esp. Helena Rosenblatt, *Rousseau and Geneva: From the First Discourse to the Social Contract, 1749–1762* (Cambridge, 1997).

88. d'Épinay, *Lettres à mon fils*, 79–81.

89. Weinreb, *Eagle in a Gauze Cage*, 30–31. Weinreb gives no citation for d'Épinay's letter in response to Tronchin, and it is not to be found in the Bibliothèque de Genève, Département des Manuscrits. I have nonetheless used the quote because d'Épinay's conviction of the vital importance of friendships recurs in her writings and correspondence. In Arnaud, *On Hysteria*, 130–38, Tronchin is singled out as a physician whose correspondence won his patient's confidence with moral as well as medical counsel.

90. d'Épinay, *Lettres à mon fils*, 85–87.

91. Ibid., 110–13.

Index

academic study: criticisms of, 47; labor and, 40. *See also* scholars

Addison, Joseph, 13, 160

aesthetic intelligence, 8

aisance: as feminine characteristic, 5, 301; labor vs., 10, 30–33, 42–43, 216, 303; meaning of, ix; neo-Stoicism vs., 32–33

Alembert, Jean Le Ronde d', 217, 228, 236–41, 289, 295, 303; "Essay on the Society of Men of Letters and the Great," 225–26

ambition, 176, 184, 197, 226, 235, 238–39

ancients and moderns. *See* battle of the ancients and the moderns

André, Y. M., 68, 86

Angiviller, Comte d', 229

Arbuthnot, John, 166, 168

aristocracy: challenging of, 179–80, 183, 185, 187, 216, 227–28, 233, 237–38; and *mondanité*, 25

Aristotle, 38, 71, 90, 113, 136, 185, 222; *Nicomachean Ethics*, 23, 97–98

Arnauld, Antoine, 64, 70, 87

Ashley Cooper, Maurice, 123

askesis: criticisms of, 184; Hume's rejection of, 175; Malebranche and, 76; rigorous character of, 11, 12, 32, 59, 76, 133, 147; Shaftesbury and, 16, 117–18, 124–25, 133, 138–39; Stoic tradition of, 11, 12, 59, 76, 98

Augustine, Saint, and Augustinianism: Cartesianism and, 72–74, 76–77; in French culture, 64, 70; on the human condition, 73; Malebranche and, 3, 18, 64, 72–79, 92; on original sin, 64; on the self, 83; spiritual tradition of, 241

authorial style, 14; Diderot and, 258–59, 309; Hume and, 169–70, 171, 178, 190, 309; Malebranche and, 14, 88–89, 91–93, 96, 309; personal and social character of, 88; of Sévigné, 246; Shaftesbury and, 119, 269, 309; Thomas and, 245, 258

authority: Descartes's questioning of, 51; grounds of, 146–48; Malebranche's questioning of, 89–90; of philosophy, 186; Poullain's questioning of, 52, 55–57, 59; power disguised as, 91–92, 141, 148, 161; Shaftesbury's questioning of, 135, 141, 143, 146, 148, 154, 161; of taste, 193–96, 199–201, 299–300

authorship: female, 110–11, 139–40, 244–49; Shaftesbury and, 118–19, 142–49, 152–53, 157

autonomy: Hume and, 187, 202, 205, 213–14, 239; intellectual, 52, 59, 159, 240; of the manly mind, 224; of men of letters, 237–40; of middle station members, 186; moral, 119, 126, 145, 153–54; of reason, 172; of the self, 56–57, 59, 91, 98, 117, 126, 130, 141, 146–48, 161; as Stoic principle, 12, 117, 126, 130, 141, 145, 224, 238; of view from nowhere, 172, 174, 194, 201

Bacon, Francis, 70

Badinter, Elisabeth, 335n73

Balzac, Jean-Louis Guez de. *See* Guez de Balzac, Jean-Louis

Barthe, Nicolas, 234–35

battle of the ancients and the moderns, 101, 196

Bawble (friend of Shaftesbury), 136–37

Bayle, Pierre, 135–36, 141

beauty, 149

bel esprit: associated with effeminacy, 63; associated with masculinity, 35–36, 38–39; Bouhours on, 35–36, 38–39; criticisms of, 233, 237, 243, 258; genius distinguished from, 233–34; Malebranche on, 63, 84–86, 95

Bellegarde, Denis-Joseph Lalive de, 291

Berrand, Pierre, 80

Bérulle, Pierre de, 68, 70

biography, 17

Blair, Hugh, 183–84

Bloch, Ernst, 13

Blue Room, Paris, 2, 22–24, 80

body: Aristotelian conception of, 71; Cartesian conception of, 48, 71; mind in relation to, 47–48, 72–78; Shaftesbury's conception of, 126

Boileau, Nicolas, 195–96, 200

Bordeu, Théophile de, 270, 272–76

Bosc, Jacques du, 32, 37, 40

Boswell, James, 179, 182–83

Boufflers-Rouvera, Marie-Charlotte-Hippolyte, Comtesse de, 203–14, 304

Bouhier, Jean, 245

Bouhours, Dominique, 26, 110, 303; *The Conversations of Ariste and Eugène*, 34–36, 38–39

Bourdieu, Pierre, 12, 29–30

bourgeoisie: Diderot and, 265, 270, 281; men of letters in relation to, 236

Boyle, Robert, 70

brain: mind in relation to, 6–7; of women, 48–49, 274

Brooke, Christopher, 322n6

Buffon, Georges-Louis Leclerc, Comte de, 217, 240–41, 251

Burke, Edmund, 194

Butler, Judith, 7

Caesar, Julius, 23

Calvinism, 20, 60, 73, 184, 241

Cambridge Platonists, 149

Caroillon, Abel-François-Nicolas, 263–65

Cassirer, Ernst, 193

Catholicism: and Cartesianism, 70; English opposition to, 128; extreme behaviors associated with, 106–7; Malebranche and, 68–69

cause and effect, 172–73

celebrity, 215, 226, 246

certainty, 172–73

Cervantes, Miguel de, *Don Quixote*, 109

Champion, Anne-Toinette, 261–63

Chapelain, Jean, 22

character: decline of, 11; environment as influence on, 125–26, 132–33, 268; taste in relation to, 194, 199; vitalist materialist view of, 268. *See also* morality

Charles II, 106, 108

Cheyne, George, 166

chivalry, 13, 99, 130, 145, 252–54, 282

Choiseul-Praslin, duc de, 229

Christianity, 32. *See also* Catholicism

Cicero, 113, 136, 185, 246; *De amicitia*, 98

civic humanism, 11, 132–33, 189–90, 191, 197, 252, 254

Clairvaux, Bernard de, 80

class, 27, 302

Cleopatra, 23

Clerselier, Claude, 68, 70, 72

cognition. *See* intelligence

complaisance: criticisms of, 145, 148, 197; as inner satisfaction, 297; and the market, 146; meaning of, ix; as obstacle to truth, 55, 135, 140; role of, in polite society, 47, 86, 142, 192

concupiscence, 73, 75, 77, 83, 91

Condorcet, Marie Jean Antoine Nicolas de Caritat, marquis de, 301

constructionism, 4–5

consumerism, 180–81

contagion, 83, 90, 133, 243–44, 279

contextualism, 15, 17–18

Conti, Prince de, 203–4, 206, 208–9, 212–14

conversation: art and characteristics of, 22–23, 25–26, 28, 30–31, 35–36; friendship and, 98; masculine aspects of, 33–34; pedantry inimical to, 33–34; and the pursuit of truth, 57–60; Saint-Évremond and, 101; Shaftesbury and, 140–42; silence vs., 80, 82; of women, 24, 31, 33, 38–40. *See also* language

Correspondance littéraire (newsletter), 293–94

country ideology, in England, 127–29, 132

country perspective, in England, 115

Crébillon, Claude Prosper Jolyot de, "fils," 291

critics and criticism, 143, 145, 147–48, 198–201, 304. *See also* judgment; taste

Cropley, John, 136, 139

custom: authority of, 46, 55, 120; Hume and, 172–73, 191–92; questioning of, 50; taste and, 193–94, 199–201

Dalrymple, David, 182–83

Dauphin (son of Louis XV), 229, 244, 258

Declaration of Rights and Sentiments, 21

Deffand, Mme du, 204, 237

Defoe, Daniel, 179

De Fontenay, Elisabeth, 259

DeJean, Joan, 26–27, 37, 42

delicacy: meaning of, ix; of mind and intelligence, 39–41, 49–50, 200; pleasure and, 105; taste and, 170, 185, 189, 200–201, 211; women associated with, 39, 40, 49–50, 163, 169–70, 194, 202, 301

Delille, Jacques, 226–27

Democritus, 119

Descartes, René, and Cartesianism: Augustinianism and, 72–74, 76–77; on the body, 48, 71, 300; dualism of, 47–48, 72–74, 78; *honnêteté* and, 47–59, 62, 317n19; *On the Human Being*, 70–71; Hume and, 173; Malebranche and, 17, 64, 68, 70–79, 90; popular reception of, 58; Poullain and, 44–62; questioning of custom and authority by, 46, 50, 54–59; and selfhood, 54–58; Shaftesbury and, 122; and women's equality, 46–62

Desloges, Mme, 24

Diderot, Denis, 3, 11, 18, 215, 217, 237, 300, 301; and the bourgeoisie, 265, 270, 281; clinical voice of, 260, 267–79; criticisms of Thomas by, 229, 257–59, 274, 278–79, 284, 285; *The Dream of d'Alembert*, 267, 270; and effeminacy, 275; *Elements of Physiology*, 267; *Entretien d'un père*, 294; d'Épinay and, 290–94; and the essay form, 276; "Eulogy of Richardson," 258–59, 269–70; feminist scholarship on, 259–60; and gallantry, 283–84, 306; and gendered imagination, 14; and genius, 258, 268–71; and *goût moderne*, 19; *Jacques the Fatalist and His Master*, 160, 265; life of, 17, 260–65; and marriage, 261–66; materialism of, 241, 251, 266–79, 283; and nature, 260, 265–66, 269, 271, 274–75, 283, 308; "On Women," 17, 257–60, 265–66, 273, 275–85, 305, 309; *Paradox of the Actor*, 267; paternal voice of, 260–67, 278; and politeness, 276–77; *Rameau's Nephew*, 160; *Refutation of Helvétius*, 267–68; and religion, 267, 278–79; and rhetoric, 16; salon appearances of, 13; and Stoicism, 270, 308; and style, 258–59, 309; *Supplement to the Voyage of Bougainville*, 266; and women, 257–85

diversion, 23, 31–32

divorce, 266

domesticity, 180–81, 240, 255–56

Du Bos, Abbé Jean-Baptiste, *Critical Reflections on Poetry and Painting*, 171, 196, 201, 211

Duclos, Charles Pinot, 217, 236–37, 239, 291, 295

Dundas, Henry, 198

Dysart, Mrs., 181

Edict of Nantes, 251

Edinburgh Society for Encouraging Arts, Sciences, Manufactures, and Agriculture in Scotland, 194

effeminacy, 1, 305; *bel esprit* associated with, 63, 84–86; of culture, 1, 11, 170; Diderot and,

275; features of, 275; Malebranche on, 63–67, 72–73, 78–79, 84–86, 118; male weakness and, 78; of *le monde*, 227; Shaftesbury and, 11, 118–19, 125–27, 129–33, 137, 153, 155–56, 161, 305

Elliott, Gilbert, 213

Encyclopédie, 215, 225, 237, 246, 267, 269, 270, 275

Enlightenment: feminist conception of, 9; gender issues in, 3–4; labor and, 20; reason and, 9. *See also* Scottish Enlightenment

enthusiasm, 149, 151, 154–56, 167, 243, 279

environment, as influence on character and intelligence, 125–26, 132–33, 268

Epictetus, 117, 126, 134

Epicurus and Epicureanism, 104–5, 119–20, 122, 130, 134, 184

Épinay, Louise, d', 3, 11, 15, 17, 215, 249, 255, 285–97, 300–301, 307, 308, 309; *Conversations of Emilie*, 293, 297; *The History of Madame de Montbrillant*, 290, 335n73; *Letters to My Son*, 293, 294–97; *My Happy Moments*, 293

epistles. *See* intimate epistles

eroticism. *See* sexuality and eroticism

erudition, 198

esprit, ix, 8–9, 23. See also *bel esprit*

essays: Diderot and, 276; Hume and, 164–65, 178–79, 182, 187–88; Saint-Évremond and, 101; Shaftesbury and, 119, 134–35, 138–39, 143, 149–50, 153, 160, 305

essentialism, 172–73

eulogies. *See* patriotic eulogies

Ewer, Jane, 132

feminine mind: *aisance* as characteristic of, 5; character of, 1; Poullain on, 48; scholarly questions concerning, 2

feminism: contemporary normalization of, 5–6; and Diderot, 259–60; early modern, 303; d'Épinay and, 285–97; and *honnêteté*, 62; and Hume, 174–75, 189; intellectual history and, 11; and intelligence, 8–9; labor and, 21; Lambert's *New Reflections on Women* and, 111–12; modern literature and, 26–27; Poullain and, 2, 44, 302; universalist logic for, 286, 288–89

femmes savantes, 12, 43, 164, 205, 231–32, 253, 254, 286, 302, 303

Fenelon, François, 255

Ferguson, Adam, 198

Fontenelle, Bernard Le Bovier de, 2, 19, 69, 85, 86–88, 93, 95–96, 110, 165, 233, 246; *Conversations on the Plurality of Worlds*, 2, 41–43, 52, 58, 109, 176
fops, 11
Fouquet, Nicolas, 105
France: Hume and, 4, 165, 171–72, 191, 203–14; literary culture in, 19–20, 26–27; Shaftesbury's criticisms of, 128–33; social aesthetic of play in, 19–43; stereotypes of, 4
Francueil, Claude-Louis Dupin de, 291
freedom/liberty: English spirit of, 119, 128–29, 131; natural, 30. *See also* autonomy
French Academy, 40, 196, 215–17, 228–30, 239
Freud, Sigmund, 14
friendship, 14–15; Aristotle on, 97–98; conversation and, 98; Hume and, 185, 187, 203, 212, 214; love in relation to, 113, 222; male-female, 97, 100, 103, 113, 181, 222–23, 307; in the middle station, 185; natural, 98, 105; Shaftesbury and, 131, 135–42, 306; types of, 97–98
friendship of heroic virtue, 98, 113, 131, 136, 307
Furley, Benjamin, 135–36

galant homme, 24, 25
Galen, 38, 300
Galiani, Ferdinando, 3, 285, 292, 293, 294
Galileo Galilei, 70
gallantry: condescension characteristics of, 219; corruption of, 99–100; Diderot and, 283–84, 306; and friendship, 98–99; Hume and, 13, 170, 189–90, 192, 306; irony and, 100, 102; and male-female relations, 99; meaning of, 13–14; Saint-Évremond and, 101–10; Shaftesbury's criticism of, 129–30, 145–46, 150, 306; social effects of, 99; Thomas and, 219, 253–54
Gassendi, Pierre, 70, 104
gender: binaries in gender differentiation, 12–14, 300; complementarity of, 281; early modern perceptions of difference in, 12–14; friendship and, 97, 100, 103, 113, 181, 222–23, 307; historicizing of, 5–6, 11; Hume and, 163–64; intelligence in relation to, 6, 8–9, 38–43, 79, 174–75, 240–41, 260, 277, 286, 289, 298–99; and labor, 303; medical paradigms of, 250; and modernity, 4; naturalization/denaturalization of differences in, 11, 169, 260, 267–79, 298; Necker and, 233–34; Poullain on, 44–62; and power, 277–78, 283; as social construction, 4;

status norms in relation to, 10, 21, 302; Thomas and, 215, 233–35
genius: *bel esprit* distinguished from, 233–34; civic contributions of, 242–44; Diderot and, 258, 268–71; enthusiasm of, 243; Hume and, 171; meanings of, 234; Necker and, 243; Thomas and, 215, 242–44, 251, 258
genres: essays, 101, 119, 134–35, 138–39, 143, 149–50, 153, 160, 164–65, 178–79, 182, 187–88, 276, 305; intimate epistles, 245–48; philosophical dialogues, 92–95, 149–59
Geoffrin, Mme, 221, 237
Gerard, Alexander, 194, 199–200
Gilligan, Carol, 8–9
God: occasionalist theory of, 71, 87; theist conception of, 120, 151, 267
Goodman, Dena, 330n36
goût moderne, 19, 19–20, 233, 258
Greenblatt, Stephen, 7
Grimm, Friedrich Melchior, 215, 217, 225, 229, 257, 263, 290–94
Guez de Balzac, Jean-Louis, 2, 22–24, 33, 35, 90, 303; *Lettres*, 22–24; *Oeuvres diverses*, 22
Guyon, Mme, 32

Habermas, Jürgen, 27
habitus, 29
Helvétius, Claude-Adrien, 268
historical sociology of knowledge, 21
history, discipline of, 9–10, 15–16, 298, 300
Hobbes, Thomas, 120, 122
Holbach family, 291, 292
Holmes, Richard, 16
Home, Alexander, 181, 194
Home, John, *Douglas*, 210–11
homosexuality, 137
honnêteté: Cartesianism and, 47–59, 62, 317n19; discourse of, 25–26, 29–34, 40–41, 86, 131; features of, 31–34; feminism and, 62; Lambert and, 111–12; Malebranche and, 64–65, 84; meaning of, ix; in *le monde*, 21; Necker and, 232, 246; Poullain and, 44–45, 64; relational selfhood and, 54; Saint-Évremond and, 100–110; and selfhood, 32; Shaftesbury's criticism of, 133; women and, 32, 40–41, 47–51, 66–67, 86. *See* also politeness
honor, 10, 28, 302–3. *See also* status
Horace, 134, 148
Huet, Pierre Daniel, 36–38, 303
human condition: Augustinian conception of, 73; Malebranche's conception of, 73–79, 83

Hume, David, 3, 11, 15, 162–214, 226, 280, 301; and Comtesse de Boufflers-Rouvera, 203–14; criticisms of, 178–79; and custom, 172–73, 191–92; *Enquiries*, 187, 207; and the essay form, 101, 164–65, 178–79, 182, 187–88; *Essays, Moral and Political*, 177–78; feminism and, 174–75, 189; and French culture, 4, 165, 171–72, 191, 203–14; and friendship, 185, 187, 203, 212, 214; and gallantry, 13, 170, 189–90, 192, 306; and gender, 163–64; health of, 165–72; *The History of England*, 181, 187, 203, 207; independence valued by, 187, 202, 205, 213–14, 239; and labor, 183–87, 191–93, 295; life of, 17, 165–72, 179, 181–82, 187, 202–14; and masculinity, 189; "My Own Life," 187, 203; and naturalness, 175–77, 183–84, 186, 191–93, 308; "Of the Delicacy of Taste and Passion," 170, 185–86, 189; "Of Essay Writing," 187–88, 190; "Of Love and Marriage," 164; "Of the Middle Station of Life," 179, 185; "Of Moral Prejudices," 162, 173; "Of Refinement in the Arts," 190–91; "Of the Rise and Progress of the Arts and Sciences," 170, 191–92; "Of the Standard of Taste," 193–94, 199–202, 211, 304; "Of the Study of History," 189; and philosophy, 162–63, 165–76, 184, 186–88, 304–5; and politeness, 192–93; religious views of, 181–82, 184, 205; and rhetoric, 16; Scottish ties of, 179–80, 187, 197–99, 205–6; and Shaftesbury, 165, 169, 190–92; "The Stoic," 184–85; and Stoicism, 162–63, 165, 167, 173, 184–86; style of, 169–70, 171, 178–79, 190, 309; and taste, 193–202, 210–11; Thomas and, 253–54; *A Treatise of Human Nature*, 162, 164–79, 184, 186–87, 272, 305; and women, 13, 14, 181–82, 188–93, 203–14
humoral theory, 38–39
Hutcheson, Francis, 178
Huygens, Christiaan, 70
hysteria, 169–70, 269, 279

identificationist fallacy, 16–17
ideology, 83–84
imagination, 64–67, 78–79, 85, 88, 91, 155, 174, 260, 272–73
imitation, 82
independence. *See* autonomy; freedom/liberty
intellectual history, 10, 11, 15–18
intelligence: autonomy and, 52, 59, 159, 240; concept of, 6; feminist conception of, 8–9; gender in relation to, 6, 8–9, 38–43, 79, 174–75, 240–41, 260, 277, 286, 289, 298–99; mind-brain relationship and, 6–7; nature and, 307–8; performance of, 7–8; social character of, 112, 174–75; of women, 38–43, 49–51, 66, 111–12, 181, 215, 240–41, 244, 249–50, 259, 274, 284, 286–87, 301–2 (see also *femmes savantes*). *See also* aesthetic intelligence; reason; relational intelligence
intimate epistles, 245–48
irony, gallant, 100, 102
Italian Renaissance, 244, 252, 253, 254

James II, 128
Jansenism, 20, 32, 64, 65, 70, 73, 77, 80, 83, 94
Jansenius, Cornelius, *Augustinus*, 64
jargon, 270
je ne sais quoi, 26, 35
Jesuit *collèges*, 34
Johnson, Samuel, 179
Jones, Matthew L., 317n19
Journal des Dames, 288
judgment: aesthetic, 193–95, 199–202; moral, 195; women's capacity for, 188–89, 201–2, 246. *See also* critics and criticism
Juvenal, 143

Kames, Henry Home, Lord, 194, 198, 199, 280
Kepler, Johannes, 70
Klein, Lawrence E., 323n31
Knox, Vicesimus, 11

labor: aesthetic, 147–49; *aisance* vs., 10, 30–33, 42–43, 216, 303; concept of, 5; equal rights to, 21; gender and, 303; Hume and, 183–87, 191–93, 295; Malebranche and, 76–77; the manly mind and, 299; of men of letters, 216, 237, 239; modern conception of, 20; Poullain and, 45, 61; in pursuit of truth, 58–59, 76–77; reason associated with, 239–43; Shaftesbury and, 149; stigmatization of, 30; study and, 40; taste as a product of, 201; Thomas and, 234–35; women and, 50, 58–59, 62
La Bruyère, Jean de, 25, 31, 97, 131, 233
Lacan, Jacques, 14
Lafayette, Mme de, 19, 27, 37, 81, 245; novels of, 26–27, 139, 254; *La princesse de Clèves*, 20; *Zaïde*, 20, 37
La Fontaine, Jean de, 80
La Harpe, Jean-François de, 294
Lambert, Anne-Thérèse de Marguenat de Courcelles, marquise de, 3, 11, 15, 17, 110–14, 294–95, 302, 306, 307, 308, 321n53; *New Reflections on Women*, 110–13

La Mettrie, Julien Offray de, 266
La Mothe Le Vayer, François de, 88
language, women's use of, 40, 49–50, 301. *See also* conversation
La Porte de La Meilleraye, Armand Charles de, 106–7
La Rochefoucauld, François de, 25–26
La Sablière, Marguerite Hessein Rambouillet de, 80, 81
Latin, 34, 40, 97, 98
La Trappe, 81–82, 89
Lauzon, Catherine de, 68
law and lawyers, 182, 198
Leibniz, Gottfried Wilhelm, 70
leisure, 22–24, 191, 193
Lelong, J., 67–70, 81
Lenclos, Anne "Ninon," 103–4, 110
Lenclos, Henri de, 103–4
Lespinasse, Mlle de, 284
letters. *See* intimate epistles
liberty. *See* freedom/liberty
Lilti, Antoine, 25
Liotard, Jean-Étienne, 292
Lipsius, Justus, 117
literary criticism, 246
literary hermeneutics, 10
literature. *See* modern literature; polite literature
Lloyd, Genevieve, 9
Locke, John, 20, 115, 116, 121–23, 125–26, 132, 159, 160, 234, 268, 269, 324n43
Louis XIV, 105–7, 118, 128, 130–31, 251, 254
love: friendship in relation to, 113, 222; Shaftesbury's aesthetics and, 156–57, 159
Lovejoy, Arthur, 15
Loyola, Ignatius, 54, 76
Lutheranism, 73
luxury: negative views of, 11, 129, 132, 141, 144, 147, 180, 190, 197, 254; positive views of, 105, 190–91

Machiavelli, Niccolò, 189
Malebranche, Nicolas, 2–3, 11, 63–96, 233, 258, 309; and Augustinianism, 3, 18, 64, 92; as author, 88–96; and authorial style, 14, 88–89, 91–93, 96, 309; on *bel esprit*, 84–86; and Cartesianism, 17, 64, 68, 70–79, 90; *Christian and Metaphysical Meditations*, 94; *Christian Conversations*, 92–94; *Conversation on Metaphysics, Religion, and Death*, 92–95; *Dialogues on Metaphysics and Religion*, 82; on effeminacy, 63–67, 72–73, 78–79, 84–86, 118; Fontenelle's eulogy of, 69, 86–88, 95–96; health and

physical condition of, 69, 71, 81; his conception of women, 78; and *honnêteté*, 64–65; on the human condition, 73–79; Hume and, 173; library of, 69–70; life of, 17, 63–64, 67–73, 79, 81–82, 87; on Montaigne, 64–67, 88–89; Necker and, 232, 241, 242; philosophical dialogues written by, 92–95; popular reception of, 63; Poullain compared to, 63–64, 67, 96–97; *The Search After Truth*, 63–65, 67, 73–79, 82, 84, 89, 215; Shaftesbury compared to, 118–19, 142, 146–47, 305–6; solitude valued by, 79–82; *Treatise of Morality*, 85; *Treatise on Nature and Grace*, 64
Mallet, David, 207
Mandeville, Bernard, 162, 166, 169–70, 196–97, 199
manly mind: autonomy of, 224; *bel esprit* and, 36; characteristics of, 6, 10–11; corruptions of, 11; disappearance of, 1; labor of, 299; and pedantry, 34; scholarly questions concerning, 2; Stoic roots of, 224
Manzini, Girolama, 106
Marchmont, third earl of, 203
Marcus Aurelius, 117, 123, 126, 134, 230, 242
Marivaux, Pierre de, 110
Marmontel, Jean-François, 217, 224–25, 229, 232, 284, 292
marriage: arranged, 99; as companionate and complementary, 180; Diderot and, 261–66; monogamous and permanent, 281
Martin, André, 72
Martin, Father, 92
masculinity. *See* men and masculinity
materialism: of Diderot, 241, 251, 266–79, 283; and gender roles, 273–78; Necker's opposition to, 241; Shaftesbury's opposition to, 123, 141, 158–59. *See also* vitalist materialism
Maupeou, René Charles Augustin de, 230
Maupertuis, Pierre Louis, 237
Mazarin, Cardinal, 106
Mazarin, Hortense Mancini, Duchess, 106–10
McGinn, Colin, 6–7
McMahon, Darrin, 15
medicine, 166–68, 250, 272–76, 300
meditation, Malebranche and, 72, 76–80, 82, 88–90, 93–94
men and masculinity: *bel esprit* associated with, 35–36, 38–39; and conversation, 33–34; and friendship, 135–42; Hume and, 189; independence valued by, 224, 226; and politeness, 304; praise for contributions of, 237–38; Shaftesbury and, 14, 15, 125–27, 129–33,

135–42, 147, 150, 161; strength/weakness of, 6, 39; taste as purview of, 299–300

men of letters: autonomy of, 237–40; bourgeoisie in relation to, 236; and labor, 216, 237, 239; status of, 217; types of, 225–26

Méré, Antoine Gombaud, chevalier de, 30, 31, 33, 85

merit, 53, 144, 182, 228–29, 233, 237, 238, 249, 295

Micklethywate, Thomas, 136

middle station, 3, 4, 179–86, 193, 198, 226, 280

Millar, John, *The Origin of the Distinction of Ranks,* 279–83

mind: body in relation to, 47–48, 72–78; brain in relation to, 6–7; Cartesian conception of, 47–48. *See also* feminine mind; intelligence; manly mind

misogyny, 78–79, 260

modernity: gender and, 4; labor and, 20; unmodern, 13, 21

modern literature, 19–20, 26–27

Molesworth, Robert, 116

Molière, *The Learned Ladies,* 47

mondanité: aristocracy and, 25; criticisms of, 35–36, 220–22, 227, 233, 243; eighteenth-century, 204, 206–7; meaning of, ix; Necker and, 220–21, 224, 230–33; social and cultural logic of, 30; Thomas and, 220–21, 224–30, 233

le monde: Diderot's criticisms of, 270; effeminacy of, 227; features of, 13; friendship in tradition of, 98–99; gender roles in, 13; Guez de Balzac and, 22–23; habitus of, 29; Hume and, 185, 207, 214; labor and, 21; modern literature associated with, 19–20; values of, 10; women in, 21

Montaigne, Michel de, 88–89, 91, 222–23, 245; *Essays,* 64–67, 109; "Of Pedantry," 33–34

Montbazon, Marie de, 81

Montesquieu, Charles-Louis de Secondat, baron de, 1, 255

morality: autonomy and, 119, 126, 145, 153–54; gender and, 8; novels and, 37; Shaftesbury on, 120, 121–22, 132–33, 195; taste in relation to, 195. *See also* character

Moreaud, Mariette, 218–20

Morellet, André, 217

Morin (gambler), 109

Moyn, Samuel, 10

Mure, William, 190

Murray, Alexander, 211

Nagel, Thomas, 172

nation, ideology of, 216–17

naturalness: in conversation, 30; in friendship, 98, 105; Hume and, 175–77, 183–84, 186, 191–93, 308; and intelligence, 307–8; Rousseau and, 197; women associated with, 39–41, 49. *See also* nature

nature: concept of, 4; Diderot's conception of, as related to individual development, 260, 265–66, 269, 271, 274–75, 283, 308; Shaftesbury and, 155–56. *See also* naturalness; vitalist materialism

Necker, Jacques, 230–31

Necker, Suzanne Curchod, 3, 11, 15, 299, 303, 304, 308; "Beginning of a Eulogy of Mme de Sévigné," 245–49, 251; Diderot and, 267; and female authorship, 14; and gender equality, 250–51; and genius, 233–34, 243; health of, 221, 230; journals of, 230–33, 244–45; life of, 230–32; and *mondanité,* 220–21, 224, 230–33; "On a New Kind of Spectator," 244; and religion, 241–42; and rhetoric, 16, 244; salon of, 13, 217, 224, 232; and selfhood, 241–42; and Stoicism, 241, 308; Thomas's friendship with, 217, 220–22, 230, 233–35, 241, 248, 251, 254, 257, 307; on women as writers, 244–49

neo-Epicureanism, 155

neo-Platonism, 143, 149, 151, 161

neo-Stoicism, 32–33, 117, 242

nerves, 169

New Historicism, 7

new science, 41, 58, 69

Newton, Isaac, 70, 300

Nicole, Pierre, 64, 70, 77, 83

novels: moral nature of, 37; women as readers of, 37–38, 321n53; women as writers of, 110–11, 139–40

observateurs, 271, 272

objectivity, 248–49

occasionalism, 71, 87

Olonne, Countess d', 102

opinion, 83, 118, 133

Oratory (clerical order), 68–70, 80

original sin, 64, 73–75, 78–79

Pascal, Blaise, 64, 65, 70, 73, 77, 83, 246

patriotic eulogies, 215, 217

pedantry, 33–34, 36, 65, 188, 198, 231–32, 297, 304

Perdriau, Mme, 60

performance: concept of, 7–8; of honor, 28; of
    intelligence, 7–8; of rhetorical personae,
    15–17
Petronius, 105
philosophes, 215, 249, 266, 267, 286
philosophical dialogues, 149–59
philosophy: authority of, 186; Hume and,
    162–63, 165–76, 184, 186–88, 304–5; and the
    middle station, 186; rhetoric in relation to, 88,
    90; Shaftesbury on modern, 119–20, 122, 130,
    149–60; social character of, 177
Plato, 113
Platonism. See neo-Platonism
Pliny, 246, 247
Plutarch, 189
polite literature, 101, 143–44
politeness: Diderot and, 276–77, 305; Hume
    and, 192–93; men and, 304; Shaftesbury and,
    129–35, 138–40, 145–47, 150. See also
    honnête; politesse
politesse, 20, 24–25. See also politeness
Pope, Alexander, 189, 195, 219; Dunciad, 144
Poullain de la Barre, François, 44–62; and Carte-
    sianism, 44–62; and cultural transformation,
    50–51; development in thought of, 45; and
    feminism, 2, 44, 302; and gender roles, 5, 14,
    45, 46, 50, 61–62; and honnêteté, 44–45, 64;
    and labor, 45, 61; life of, 17, 44, 46; Male-
    branche compared to, 63–64, 67, 96–97; On
    the Education of Ladies for the Behavior of the
    Mind in the Sciences and in Mores, 45, 47,
    51–62, 302; On the Equality of the Two Sexes, 2,
    42, 45–51, 53, 55, 61, 112, 215, 290, 300–301,
    302
power: disguised as authority, 91–92, 141, 148,
    161; gender and, 277–78, 283; in interper-
    sonal relations, 82–83; Malebranche's
    criticism of, 84; nature as concept in service of,
    4; Shaftesbury's criticism of, 141–42, 148,
    161; speech as, 96; of women, 86, 91, 118, 127,
    130, 145, 181, 277–79, 283
les précieuses, 2, 99, 231
presentism, 10, 16–17, 21, 27, 300, 303
print culture: authors' role in, 144; corruption
    attributed to, 197; English, 119, 143–49;
    market in, 143–45; women as readers in, 13,
    144
Puisieux, Madeleine d'Arsant de, 261

Quinault, Mlle, 291

raillery, 140–42, 150
Rambouillet, Catherine de Vivonne, marquise de,
    2, 22–24

Rancé, Armand Jean Le Bouthillier de, 80–82
Raynal, Guillaume-Thomas, 217, 257
reason: autonomy of, 172; Enlightenment and, 9;
    gender and, 9. See also intelligence
reductionism, 7, 15, 17
relational intelligence, 8, 41, 103, 301. See also
    friendship
relativism, 120, 193–94, 201, 304
religion: Diderot and, 267, 278–79; Hume and,
    181–82, 184, 205; Necker and, 241–42;
    women and, 278–79. See also Catholicism;
    Christianity; God
republican values, 23, 24, 96, 130, 132, 154, 295
Republic of Letters, 98, 136, 188, 217, 228, 239,
    241
rhetoric, 15–18, 308–9; Malebranche and,
    91–92; Necker and, 244; philosophy in
    relation to, 88, 90; Shaftesbury and, 147–48;
    Thomas and, 244; and truth, 91–92
rhetorical personae, 15–17
Richardson, Samuel, 258–59, 269–70, 290;
    Pamela, 163, 181
Riley, Denise, 6
Ringer, Fritz K., 16
Robespierre, Maximilian, 289
Rome, ancient, 22–23
Rousseau, Jean-Jacques, 30, 96, 197, 199, 206,
    215, 221–22, 228, 232, 237, 245, 252, 255,
    284, 290, 291, 292, 295; Julie, 293; Letter to M.
    d'Alembert on the Theater, 241
Roussel, Pierre, 274

Sablé, Madeleine de, 80
Sacy, Louis-Silvestre de, 113
Saint-Évremond, Charles de, 2, 15, 33, 85,
    100–110, 165, 246, 251, 307
Saint-Lambert, Marquis de, 292
Saint-Pierre, abbé de, 236
Saint-Réal, César Vichard de, 107
Sales, Francis de, 32
salons: Blue Room as model of, 24; of Boufflers-
    Rouvera, 204–5; class and status diversity of,
    27–28; Diderot on, 284; labor not a feature of,
    31; of Lambert, 110–11; of Necker, 217, 224,
    232; Poullain and, 45–47, 61
Savoy, Charles-Emmanuel, duke of, 107–8
Schneewind, J. B., 323n30
scholars, 34–37, 47. See also academic study
scholasticism, 23, 38, 44, 46
Scott, Joan Wallach, 6, 14–15, 103
Scottish Enlightenment, 179–80, 198, 280–82
Scriblerus Club, 166

Scudéry, Madeleine de, 2, 24, 302–3, 306; *Artamène, ou le Grand Cyrus*, 20; on conversation, 31; on Descartes, 58; and *goût moderne*, 19, 20; on male-female friendships, 97; novels of, 26–27, 37, 254; "Of the *galant* air," 99–100; and *les précieuses*, 99; salon of, 37; social role of, 27; on women's role, 43

Séguier, Antoine-Louis, 229–30

Seigel, Jerrold, 8, 32

selfhood: autonomous, 56–57, 59, 91, 98, 117, 119, 126, 130, 141, 146–48, 161; Cartesian, 54–58; corrupt/sinful, 82–83; Hume's conception of, 173; Locke's conception of, 122–23; Necker's conception of, 241–42; relational, 32, 54–58, 80; sensibility and, 247–49; Shaftesbury and, 117–27, 131–33, 138–41, 143–47, 151, 158; Stoic, 120–21; Thomas's conception of, 241–42. *See also* subjectivity

Sénault, Jean-François, 73

Seneca, 65, 91

Seneca Falls Convention, 21

sensibility: cult of, 163; Diderot's criticisms of, 270, 271, 273; and gender-intelligence relationship, 260; and the self, 247–49; of women, 111, 163, 271

sentir, 257

Sévigné, Mme de, 245–48, 251, 309

Seward, Anna, 332n122

Sewell, William H., Jr., 12, 30

sexuality and eroticism: Diderot and, 257, 266–67, 274, 276–78; friendship in relation to, 98, 103, 113; gallantry and, 99–101; Shaftesbury and, 137, 157, 159; threat represented by, 202–3, 220, 250

Shaftesbury, Anthony Ashley Cooper, second earl of, 115–16, 123–24

Shaftesbury, Anthony Ashley Cooper, third earl of, 3, 11, 115–61, 258, 307; *Askêmata*, 116–17, 138–39, 143, 147, 161, 269, 308, 322n6; and authorial style, 269, 309; and authorship, 118–19, 142–49, 152–53, 157; *Characteristics of Men, Manners, Opinions, Times*, 118, 134, 142, 149, 190, 254; and conversation, 140–42; Diderot and, 267, 269; and effeminacy, 11, 118–19, 125–27, 129–33, 137, 150, 153, 155–56, 161, 305; on English culture, 128–33; and the essay form, 119, 134–35, 138–39, 143, 149–50, 153, 160, 305; on French culture and politics, 128–33; and friendship, 131, 135–42, 306; on gallantry, 129–30, 145–46, 150, 306; health of, 116, 121, 125–27, 159; Hume and, 165, 169, 190–92; "An Inquiry Concerning Virtue," 134, 323n31; life of, 17, 115–16, 119, 121, 123–27, 132; on literature, 142–49; and Locke, 115, 116, 121–23; Malebranche compared to, 118–19, 142, 146–47, 305–6; marriage of, 132; and masculinity, 14, 15, 125–27, 129–33, 135–42, 147, 150, 161; on modern philosophy, 119–20, 122, 130, 149–60; "The Moralists," 149–61; on morality, 120, 121–22, 132–33, 195; *Paradoxes of State*, 128; and politeness, 129–35, 138–40, 145–47, 150; and politics, 116, 118–19, 127–29; and print culture, 142–49; and rhetoric, 16; and selfhood, 117–27, 131–33, 138–41, 143–47, 151, 158; "Sensus communis," 141–42; Smith's critique of, 159–61, 190, 269; and sociability, 132–33, 137–38, 147; "The Social Enthusiast," 130, 149; "Soliloquy, or advice to an author," 142–49, 160; and Stoicism, 17, 18, 117–27, 133–35, 138–39, 143, 148–49, 155, 239, 306, 308; and taste, 144, 146–49, 195; Thomas and, 253–54; on women as readers, 13

Shaftesbury, Ashley Cooper, first earl of, 115, 121, 123, 127, 129, 130

Shaftesbury, Dorothy, Lady, 124

Shank, J. B., 4

silence and solitude, 79–82, 242–43

Simmel, Georg, 28–29, 32

sin, 75. *See also* original sin

skepticism, 172–73, 176

Skinner, Quentin, 16, 312n26

Smith, Adam, 159–61, 190, 194, 205, 213–14, 269, 280, 309

sociability: reading and, 186; Shaftesbury and, 132–33, 137–38, 147; values and characteristics of, 26, 28–29

social aesthetic of play, 19–43; *aisance* and labor in, 22–38; characteristics of, 5; gender and intelligence in, 38–43; Hume and, 192–93; literature and, 101

social hierarchy, 27–28

Socrates, 122, 135, 137, 139–40, 152

solitude. *See* silence and solitude

Somers, Lord, 130, 149

The Spectator (periodical), 13, 160, 179, 245

Spinoza, Baruch, 173, 242

stadial paradigm, 253–54, 279–83

Starobinski, Jean, 284

status, 10, 21, 27–28, 302

Steele, Richard, 13

Steinbrügge, Lieselotte, 260

Stoicism, 11–12; *aisance* vs., 32–33; d'Alembert
    and, 237; autonomy as principle of, 12, 117,
    126, 130, 141, 145, 224, 238; Diderot and,
    270, 308; early modern revival of, 117;
    d'Épinay and, 296, 308; friendship in tradition
    of, 98; Hume and, 162–63, 165, 167, 173,
    184–86; Malebranche and, 76; and the manly
    mind, 224; Necker and, 241, 308; principles
    of, 120–21; and selfhood, 54; Shaftesbury and,
    17, 18, 117–27, 133–35, 138–39, 143, 148–49,
    155, 239, 306, 308; spiritual tradition of, 241;
    Thomas and, 241–42, 252, 256. *See also*
    askesis; neo-Stoicism
style. *See* authorial style
subjectivity: Montaigne and, 65–66; of women,
    20, 248–49. *See also* selfhood
sympathy, 174, 176, 185

Tahiti, 266
taste: character in relation to, 194, 199; concep-
    tions of, 194, 199–200; custom and, 193–94,
    199–201; delicacy associated with, 170, 185,
    189, 200–201, 211; in eighteenth-century
    culture, 194–98; Hume and, 193–202,
    210–11; judgments of, 193–95, 199; labor
    required for, 201; modern, 19–20; morality in
    relation to, 195; Shaftesbury and, 144,
    146–49, 195; standards of, 193–96, 199–201,
    299–300, 304; women associated with, 8,
    40–41, 66–67, 111–12, 196, 301. *See also*
    critics and criticism
The Tatler (periodical), 13
Tertullian, 65, 91
theism, 120, 151, 267
Theresa of Avila, Saint, 80
Thomas, Antoine-Léonard, 3, 15, 215–56;
    amphibian character of, 226, 230; criticisms of,
    215–16; Diderot's criticisms of, 229, 257–59,
    274, 278–79, 284, 285; d'Épinay on, 285,
    287–88; "Epistle to the People," 229; *Essay on
    Eulogies*, 215–16, 222, 249, 251–56; eulogies
    by, 225, 229, 242, 243–44; on friendship, 222;
    and gallantry, 219, 253–54; and genius, 215,
    233–35, 242–44, 251, 258; health of, 218, 221,
    235, 250; and history of women in society,
    252–54; and labor, 234–35; life of, 17, 225–26,
    229–30, 257; and *mondanité*, 220–21, 224–30,
    233; Necker's friendship with, 217, 220–22,
    230, 233–35, 241, 248, 251, 254, 257, 307; and
    patriotic eulogies, 215, 217; reputation of,
    215; and rhetoric, 244; and selfhood, 241–42;
    and Stoicism, 241–42, 252, 256; style of, 245,

258; and women, 217–24, 227–28, 244,
    249–57
Toland, John, 134
Tories, 127–28
Transcendental Naturalism, 7
Tronchin, Théodore, 296, 336n89
truth: Hume and, 177, 178; Malebranche and,
    63, 91–92; Poullain and, 55–60; rhetoric and,
    91–92; women and, 111

Universal Declaration of Human Rights, 21
unmodern modernity, 13, 21
urbanity, 23, 24
uterus, 259, 274, 277, 279
utility, 20, 28, 217, 233, 236, 281, 288, 294–95

Van Loo, Louis-Michel, 275
Viala, Alain, 99
view from nowhere, 172, 174, 194, 201
virtue. *See* character; morality
vitalist materialism, 250, 267, 268, 272–74, 279,
    283
Voiture, Vincent, 19, 24, 35–36, 85, 247, 254
Volland, Sophie, 261
Voltaire, 218, 224, 225, 226, 245, 246, 267, 295

Walpole, Robert, 190
Weber, Max, 4, 27
Weinreb, Ruth Plaut, 335n73
Wharton, Edith, *The House of Mirth*, 5
Whigs, 115–16, 127–28
wholeness, fantasies of, 14–15, 103, 105, 113
Wollstonecraft, Mary, 188
women: and *aisance*, 5, 301; brain of, 48–49, 274;
    Cartesianism and, 46–62; conversation of, 24,
    31, 33, 38–40; delicacy associated with, 39, 40,
    49–50, 163, 169–70, 194, 202, 301; Diderot
    and, 257–85; d'Épinay on, 285–90; equal
    rights of, 21; and *goût moderne*, 20; and
    honnêteté, 32, 40–41, 47–51, 66–67, 86; Hume
    and, 13, 14, 181–82, 188–93, 203–14; imagi-
    nation of, 78; intelligence of, 38–43, 49–51,
    66, 111–12, 181, 215, 240–41, 244, 249–50,
    259, 274, 284, 286–87, 301–2 (see also *femmes
    savantes*); and judgment, 188–89, 201–2, 246;
    and labor, 50, 58–59, 62; Malebranche and,
    78–79; in *le monde*, 21; Montaigne's view of,
    222–23; naturalness of, 39–41, 49; as novel
    readers, 37–38, 321n53 (*see also* as readers); as
    novel writers, 110–11, 139–40 (*see also* as
    writers); Poullain and, 44–62; power of, 86,
    91, 118, 127, 130, 145, 181, 277–79, 283; as

readers, 13, 14, 144, 181 (*see* also as novel readers); and religion, 278–79; Saint-Évremond and, 101–10; in the Scottish society, 180–81; sensibility of, 111, 163, 271; Shaftesbury's conception of, 127; stadial narrative of, 253–54, 280–83; strength/weakness of, 6, 39–41, 48–49, 127, 169–70, 222–24, 266–67; subjectivity of, 20, 248–49; subordinate role of, 24; taste associated with, 8, 40–41, 66–67, 111–12, 196, 301; Thomas and, 217–24, 227–28, 244, 249–57; and truth, 111; use of language by, 40, 49–50; as writers, 244–49 (*see also* as novel writers). *See also* effeminacy

Xenophon, 119, 135, 137, 139–40

Acknowledgments

A Research Fellowship from the Leverhulme Trust allowed me to spend the academic year 2006–2007 at the Institute for Advanced Studies in the Humanities (IASH) at the University of Edinburgh. Special thanks to Anthea Taylor, the Institute Administrator, and Donald Ferguson, the Institute Secretary, for their many kindnesses.

I am grateful to the John Simon Guggenheim Memorial Foundation for awarding me a fellowship in 2007.

In the fall of 2010 I was a Max Weber Senior Fellow at the European University Institute in Fiesole. My work with several doctoral students there was one of the richest experiences of my career. Special thanks to Bartolomé Yun Casalilla, Chair of the Department of History and Civilization, Antonella Romano, Director of Graduate Studies, and Francesca Elia for their warm hospitality and practical assistance.

I spent the spring of 2015 as a Senior Fellow at the Lichtenberg Kolleg at the University of Göttingen, a most congenial place to work. Thanks to all my colleagues there, and especially to Dominik Huenniger and the other members of the Kolleg's Enlightenment Workshop.

I am once again greatly indebted to the Triangle Intellectual History Seminar, which has been my intellectual home for the past twenty years.

Lawrence E. Klein generously shared with me notes from his Shaftesbury research, without which I could not have found my way through the Shaftesbury papers at The National Archives in London. Several years before the *Standard Edition*'s volume of the *Askêmata* appeared in 2011, the editors of the project provided me with a typescript of the original manuscript. Friedrich A. Uehlein kindly sent me the citations I was unable to find in the reorganized text of the edited volume.

Like my previous book projects, this one would not have been possible without the competence and patience of the Interlibrary Loan Service at North Carolina State University/Raleigh.

Thanks to Jaimie Lissette Diaz for her secretarial assistance.

For reading parts of the manuscript, or for listening to me go on about it, I thank Thomas Ahnert, Hans Erich Bödeker, Melissa M. Bullard, Charles Capper,

David Gilmartin, Martin van Gelderen, Martin Gierl, Katharine Hamerton, James Harris, Gerald N. Izenberg, Catherine Jones, Mi Gyung Kim, Avi S. Lifschitz, Antoine Lilti, Phyllis Mack, Ioana Manea, Robert Mankin, Emilio Mazza, Julie Mell, Martin Miller, Karen O'Brien, Thomas Ort, Pauline Phemister, Jane Rendall, Antonella Romano, Joan Wallach Scott, Jerrold Seigel, Maria Semi, Noah Strote, Barbara Taylor, and K. Steven Vincent.

I am particularly grateful to Suzanne L. Marchand and Silvia Sebastiani, both of whom read the entire manuscript in draft and guided me through revisions chapter by chapter. It is my great good fortune that these two cherished friends were at once astute and morale-boosting.

Invaluable were my many exchanges about history and literary studies with another dear friend, Susan Manning, the Director of IASH when I was there. By the time of her death she had commented on about two-thirds of the manuscript. Her influence pervades every page.

Without the support of my beloved wife and fellow historian Gail Williams O'Brien the writing of this book would have ground to a halt at several points. The book is dedicated to her.